ONE DAMN THING
AFTER ANOTHER

ONE DAMN THING AFTER ANOTHER

Memoirs of an Attorney General

———

WILLIAM P. BARR

WILLIAM MORROW
An Imprint of HarperCollins*Publishers*

Pages 569–570 constitute an extension of this copyright page.

ONE DAMN THING AFTER ANOTHER. Copyright © 2022 by William Pelham Barr. All rights reserved. Printed in the United States of America. No part of this book may be used or reproduced in any manner whatsoever without written permission except in the case of brief quotations embodied in critical articles and reviews. For information, address HarperCollins Publishers, 195 Broadway, New York, NY 10007.

HarperCollins books may be purchased for educational, business, or sales promotional use. For information, please e-mail the Special Markets Department at SPsales@harpercollins.com.

A hardcover edition of this book was published in 2022 by William Morrow, an imprint of HarperCollins Publishers.

FIRST WILLIAM MORROW PAPERBACK EDITION PUBLISHED 2023.

Library of Congress Cataloging-in-Publication Data has been applied for.

ISBN 978-0-06-315861-0

23 24 25 26 27 LBC 5 4 3 2 1

To my wife, Christine

CONTENTS

For forty years, successive Attorneys General have heard the story. After President Ronald Reagan nominated him in late 1980 to serve as Attorney General of the United States, William French Smith, preparing for his new duties, talked to Ed Levi, who, four years earlier, had served as Attorney General under President Gerald Ford and, before that, had been Dean of the University of Chicago Law School, and then president of that university. With his pipe-smoking, bow ties, and intellectual demeanor, Levi seemed the quintessential academic. When Smith asked Levi to describe the job of Attorney General, he was expecting him to launch into a philosophical discourse about the Founding Fathers, the rule of law, and the principles of democracy. Levi, taking a leisurely puff on his pipe, paused a moment, and said: *"It's just one damn thing after another."*

Having held the post twice, I can say—and I know all my fellow former Attorneys General will agree—that description perfectly captures the essence of the job.

ONE DAMN THING
AFTER ANOTHER

PROLOGUE

The first day of December 2020, almost a month after the presidential election, was gray and rainy. That afternoon, the President, struggling to come to terms with the election result, had heard I was at the White House for another meeting and sent word that I was to come see him immediately. I knew what was coming. I soon found myself standing in the President's small dining room off of the Oval Office. The President was as angry as I had ever seen him.

More than two hours earlier, when I had left the Justice Department for the White House, I told my personal assistant, Theresa Watson, that there was a good chance the President would fire me. If he does, I said, he will probably direct me not to return to the office, so she might have to pack up for me. "Oh, POTUS always says that," Theresa responded, using the government acronym referring to the President of the United States. "But everyone ignores it, and if it happens, you just come back," she said. As I walked out the door, Theresa called after me, "But anyway, he's not going to fire you."

My chief of staff, Will Levi, was with me. "You know," Will said with a worried look, "he just might."

"I know," I said. "As the President likes to say, 'We'll see.'"

Over the preceding weeks, I had been increasingly concerned about claims by the President and the team of outside lawyers advising him that the election had been "stolen" through widespread voting "fraud." I had no doubt there was *some* fraud in the 2020 presidential elections. There's always *some* fraud in an election that large. There may have been more than usual in 2020. But the department had been looking into the claims of fraud made by the President's team, and we had yet to see evidence of it on the scale necessary to change the outcome of the election.

The data suggested to me that the Democrats had taken advantage of rule changes—especially extended voting periods and voting by mail—to marshal the turnout they needed in their strongholds in key states. I had been a vocal critic of these rule changes precisely because they would increase the opportunity for fraud and thus undercut public confidence in the election results. There was also no question that, in some areas, state rules meant to guard against fraud—for example, the requirement that voters file applications for mail-in ballots—were not followed. This also increased the opportunity for fraud.

Still, the *opportunity* for fraud isn't *evidence* of fraud.

Under our system, the states have responsibility for running elections. Claims that the election rules are not being followed fall under the state's jurisdiction, and the burden is on the complaining party to raise the matter with state officials and courts to have it addressed. This often requires pressing the states to conduct in-depth audits of relevant districts needed to resolve alleged irregularities. The Justice Department does not have the authority or the tools to perform that function. Instead, its role is to investigate specific and credible allegations of voting fraud for the purpose of criminal prosecution. A complaint just saying the rules were not followed is not enough. There must be some indication of actual fraud.

When I looked at the voting patterns, it also appeared to me that President Trump had underperformed among certain Republican and independent voters in some key suburban areas in the swing states. He ran weaker in these areas than he had in 2016. It seemed this shortfall could explain the outcome. The fact that, in many key areas, Trump ran behind Republican candidates below him on the ballot suggested this conclusion and appeared inconsistent with the fraud narrative.

As I had said in my confirmation hearing two years earlier, our country is deeply divided, but our saving grace is the ability to carry out the peaceful transfer of power through elections. If the American people lose confidence in the integrity of their elections, and the legitimacy of an elected administration, we are headed toward a very dark place. That is why I was so disgusted by efforts in 2016 to delegitimize President Trump and "resist" his duly elected administration. But now the situation was completely reversed. It is one thing to say that the rules were unfairly skewed; it is another to say that the election's outcome was the result of fraud. President Trump's legal team was feeding his supporters a steady diet of sensational fraud claims, without anything resembling substantiation. But if election results are going to be set aside on the grounds of fraud, it must be based on clear evidence, and it should be fraud of such magnitude as to be material to the outcome of the election. Proving fraud after the fact is exceptionally difficult, which makes it all the more important to have safeguards in place that prevent it from happening in the first instance.

In the weeks after the election, accusations of major fraud centered on several claims: allegations that counting machines from the Dominion Voting Systems Corporation had been rigged; that video footage from Fulton County, Georgia, showed a box of bogus ballots being insinuated into the vote count while poll watchers were absent; that massive numbers of ballots for Joe Biden had been inexplicitly dumped in the early morning hours in Detroit and Milwaukee; that thousands of votes in Nevada had been cast by nonresidents; that more absentee ballots than had been requested were cast in Pennsylvania; and that a truck driver had delivered many thousands of filled-out ballots from Bethpage, Long Island, to Pennsylvania. I had asked all the Department of Justice (DOJ) office heads around the country, working with the FBI, to look into these and a number of similar claims. Some turned out to be patently frivolous; others just were not supported by the available evidence.

I had repeatedly informed the President through his staff that the department was looking at substantial claims of fraud but so far hadn't found them to have merit. For more than a week, I had been getting calls from Republican senators and members of Congress deeply concerned about the direction of things, especially the President's expanding his challenge from the courts to the state legislatures. They were concerned that, if President Trump continued claiming he won the election, without hard evidence, the country could be headed for a constitutional crisis. They wanted to know my thoughts on the fraud claims and asked if I could do something to inject more caution into the President's rhetoric about a stolen election. It was not lost on me that, with two Georgia runoff elections for senator coming up the first week in January, Republican senators still hoped for the President's help and could ill afford picking a public fight with him. On the other hand, as Attorney General, I uniquely had the ability to counteract the speculation and misinformation by arming myself with the facts from the relevant US attorneys.

On November 29 the President, appearing on Fox News Channel's *Sunday Morning Futures* program, hosted by Maria Bartiromo, had claimed the election was rigged and stolen and attacked the Department of Justice as "missing in action." Based on my previous discussions with the President and his staff, he knew that the department was playing its proper role: when we received specific, credible allegations of substantial fraud, we investigated them. But President Trump appeared to think we were missing in action unless we worked with his legal team to reverse the results of the election.

At noon on December 1 I sat down for lunch in the Attorney General's private dining room with Mike Balsamo, the Associated Press reporter who covers the department. I was joined by Will Levi and Kerri Kupec, the head of the Office of Public Affairs. Mike asked me about the President's criticisms over the weekend. I told him that, contrary to the President's comments, we had been looking into substantial claims of fraud. "What have you been finding?" Mike asked.

My response: "To date, we have not seen fraud on a scale that could have effected a different outcome in the election."

Moments later, news was blasting out across media outlets that the Attorney General had contradicted the President by declaring that the department had yet to find evidence of widespread voter fraud sufficient to change the election's result. Will and I then left for my previously scheduled meeting in the West Wing with the President's chief of staff, Mark Meadows, and Pat Cipollone, the White House counsel.

As I had expected, once the President heard I was in Pat's office, he hailed both of us down to meet with him. While Pat headed down to the Oval, I took a few minutes to check how the media were covering my AP interview. I then proceeded to the Oval for what I knew would be an unpleasant meeting. As I walked into the outer office, the President's confidential assistant, Molly Michael, pointed to the back.

"He's all the way in the back," she said, "and he's waiting for you."

Will and I walked through the Oval and along the narrow hallway that leads to a small rectangular dining room that President Trump also used as a work area. POTUS was sitting as usual to my left at the head of the dining table. The opposing head of the table to the right was unoccupied, but looming on the wall behind it was a large-screen TV. It was tuned to the One America News (OAN) channel covering a Michigan legislative hearing on voter fraud allegations. Facing me on the far side of the table sat Meadows, Cipollone, and Deputy Counsel Pat Philbin. Standing to my right was a White House lawyer, Eric Herschmann, who had been on the first impeachment defense team before being pressed into service on the White House staff. The side of the table closest to me was empty. I walked over to the chair on my side of the table close to the President, rested my hands on the top of the backrest, and remained standing. The President, holding the remote, turned down the volume a bit but kept it audible in the background.

I looked at POTUS and greeted him. "Hello, Mr. President."

There was an awkward silence. He put down the remote control, at first not looking at me. I could tell he was enraged, struggling to keep his temper under control. He shuffled through some papers on the table, looking for something, his breathing a little heavier than usual, his nostrils flaring slightly. Finding what he wanted, he thrust a news clipping at me. "Did you say this?" he snapped.

It was the Balsamo article. "Yes, I did, Mr. President," I responded.

"Why would you say that?" he demanded, his voice rising.

"Because it is true, Mr. President," I replied. "The reporter asked me what the department had found to date, and I told him."

"But you did not have to say that!" he barked. "You could have just said, 'No comment.' This is killing me—killing me. This is pulling the rug out from under me." He stopped for a moment and then said, "You must hate Trump. You would only do this if you hate Trump."

I had no problem arguing with the President one-on-one, but I had learned that when you fight with him in front of an audience, things can get out of control very quickly. I was determined to stay calm.

"No, Mr. President, I don't hate you," I said. "You know I sacrificed a lot personally to come in to help you when I thought you were being wronged." The President nodded, almost involuntarily conceding the point. "But over the weekend, you started blaming the department for the inability of your legal team to come up with evidence of fraud. The department is not an extension of your legal team. Our mission is to investigate and prosecute actual fraud. The fact is, we have looked at the major claims your people are making, and they are bullshit." The President looked defiant. I continued, "I've told you that the fraud claims are not supported." I gestured to some others in the room. "And others have also told you this. But your legal team continues to shovel this shit out to the American people. And it is wrong."

The President motioned toward the TV. "Have you listened to any of these hearings?" he asked.

"No, I haven't, Mr. President," I said, "but I am familiar with the allegations."

The President leaned back in his chair and crossed his arms over his chest, rocking a little from side to side, staring at me, his face getting redder. He was seething, but appeared willing to let me continue. Normally, when Trump is being told something he doesn't want to hear, he filibusters—he just keeps talking, so no one else can get a word in edgewise. There was nothing he wanted to hear less than what I was telling him, but he was letting me talk.

I explained quietly that it is very difficult to challenge the results of a presidential election because there is only a five- or six-week window to make a case before the Electoral College acts. The responsibility for mounting a challenge lies with the lawyers of the campaign and each state's GOP. They have the burden of persuading the state authorities or the courts to conduct the kind of deep-dive review needed to assess the validity of the election results. The Department of Justice does not play a role in this. We don't have the legal authority or the tools to do that kind of audit-style review.

The President shook his head in disgust.

"Mr. President, when we get credible claims of fraud, we are looking into them," I said.

Pat Cipollone jumped in. "DOJ has been following up on fraud claims, Mr. President," he said supportively.

I continued, "Your legal team keeps publicly saying 'fraud,' but their arguments in courts *don't* claim fraud. They're really saying the state didn't follow the rules—like excluding Republican monitors. That might create an *opportunity* for fraud. But that is not the same as *evidence* of fraud."

"There is a mountain of evidence," Trump protested, gesturing to the hearing on TV.

"Mr. President," I said, "the reason you are in this position is that, instead of having a crackerjack legal team that had its shit together from day one, you wheeled out a clown show, and no quality lawyers who would otherwise be willing to help will get anywhere near it."

"Maybe," he said, almost pensively, "maybe." But he was not assuaged.

"Look, Mr. President, they wasted a whole month with this idiotic claim about Dominion machines," I continued. "First, there is no evidence they were compromised. Your team picked the one theory that can be easily disproven." I explained that the machines are simply tabulation machines that count the paper ballots fed into them. Because the paper ballots are retained, it is easy to verify the machine's accuracy by comparing the machine's tally with the retained stack of ballots. As far as I knew, I said, wherever this had been done, there had been no material discrepancy, and no one had yet pointed to one.

"Have you seen the thousands of Biden ballots dumped in the early morning in Detroit?" he asked. "People saw boxes of ballots being carried into the building in the early morning."

"We have looked into that also," I replied. "Detroit has over six hundred precincts, and, unlike other places, all the ballots are transported to a separate processing center for counting. It's not surprising that boxes of ballots would arrive through the night. Detroit's votes usually come in late, and this time the vote totals were comparable to previous elections," I assured him. "In Detroit, you actually did slightly better than in 2016, and Biden did slightly worse than Hillary Clinton."

The President seemed a bit taken aback that I seemed to know what I was talking about. I *had* been looking into things, but he seemed just as angry as when we'd started.

"Have you bothered to ask the people who are feeding you this shit how the votes compared to the last election?" I pressed.

The President glared at me and shifted the conversation away from the election, mentioning other areas where he felt I had failed him. The big one was the failure to bring to conclusion before the 2020 election US attorney John Durham's inquiry into the origins and conduct of the Russian collusion investigation. "I regret it's taking so long," I said, "but, as I have told you, a big part of that is Covid."

"When will it be done?" he snorted.

"I am not sure, but I'm hoping it will be done in the first part of the Biden administration," I replied.

"The first part of the Biden administration!" the President roared harshly, staring daggers at me. I could not tell if he was mad at the delay or at my explicit recognition that Joe Biden would be the president.

The President then started raking me over the coals about his longest-standing grievance against me: my August 2019 decision not to indict former FBI director James Comey for giving his lawyers memos that were later found to contain a few words of confidential information.

"I've explained a million times, Mr. President, everyone at the department agreed the evidence showed Comey lacked criminal intent. No one thought that prosecution could be justified."

"You could have gotten him. I read the report. All eighty pages," Trump shot back.

I tried to bring the conversation to conclusion. "I understand you are very frustrated with me, Mr. President, and I am willing to submit my resignation. But I have—"

Bang.

A loud sound, almost like a gunshot, cut me off and jolted us all.

"Accepted!" the President yelled. It took me a second to see that

President Trump had slammed the table with his palm. "Accepted!" he yelled again.

Bang.

He hit the table once more; his face was quivering. "Leave, and don't go back to your office. You are done right now. Go home!" he barked.

I nodded and said, "I understand, Mr. President." I gestured to Will, and we started walking out. Just recovering from the surprise themselves, Pat Cipollone and Eric Herschmann both yelled loudly at the same time, "No!"

Pat continued, "This is a big mistake, Mr. President."

As I walked with Will through the Oval toward the outer office, I heard Pat and Eric still protesting. I looked at Will, who smiled a bit sheepishly. I smiled back and gave a shrug. We had gotten only about fifty feet down the hallway leading to the stairs, when my cell phone rang.

"Don't leave!" Eric said insistently.

"I am getting the hell out," I replied before the call was dropped.

It was rainy and dark as I emerged onto "West Exec"—the drive running along the side of the West Wing. The FBI agents on my protective detail met me, and Will and I climbed into the armored black Chevy Suburban.

"Where to, boss?" the agent in charge asked.

"The department," I said, as the Suburban drifted slowly down the drive toward the exit gate.

Suddenly the thudding, heavy sound of fists pounding on the backseat windows on both sides of the vehicle made me and the FBI agents in the front seats jump. In the dark and rain, I could barely make out Pat on one side and Eric on the other. We pulled over. Will climbed back into the third-row seats, followed by Herschmann, while Pat climbed in next to me. Pat explained: "Bill, as soon as you walked out the door, the President told us not to let you leave the building. He did not mean it. He is not firing you. Come on back in."

"I hear you, Pat, but I am not going back in tonight," I said. "Talking any more about this tonight wouldn't be helpful."

"You're right," Herschmann chimed in. "But you agree there's no change in your status, right?"

"Let's let cooler heads prevail and talk more tomorrow," Cipollone advised.

"Okay," I agreed. "But I don't know where he's going with this stolen election stuff."

"So, what are you going to say about what happened tonight?" Eric asked.

"Nothing happened tonight," I said, "except I'm going home and having a stiff scotch." Pat and Eric jumped out, and we drove off.

But this was far from the end of the story.

When I am introduced as only the second person to serve as Attorney General twice—the first being John Crittenden, who served in 1841 and again from 1850 to 1853—I have quipped that I am the first person to serve twice as Attorney General in two different centuries. Though I served two vastly different presidents, George Herbert Walker Bush and Donald J. Trump, in two vastly different eras, I'd like to believe I was the same man throughout.

The journey to my first tour as Attorney General, at the age of forty-one, took many serendipitous twists and turns. How I went from being a China scholar to the government's top legal post in eighteen years still surprises me and was largely the result of chance—a sequence of coincidences. My second tour, at sixty-nine, after retiring from a successful legal career, was the result of choice—a deliberate and difficult one. I agreed to join the besieged Trump administration as it careened toward a constitutional crisis.

This is a book about the history I observed and, in some cases, had the opportunity to influence in those eras. It also is about a set of beliefs and principles that I believe are vital to the preservation of our democratic system—ideals I tried to protect and advance.

PART I

EARLY YEARS

CHAPTER 1

PLANNING AHEAD

I grew up in the Columbia University neighborhood on the Upper West Side of New York City. My parents, Donald and Mary Barr, were on the Columbia faculty, and we lived in a stately apartment building owned by the university on Riverside Drive at 116th Street. From our living room window, we looked out directly over Riverside Park, with a panoramic view across the Hudson River to the cliffs of the New Jersey Palisades on the other side.

My father grew up on the same block. His father, Pelham Barr, had been born in London and immigrated to the United States with his mother and father at the age of fifteen. His parents were shopkeepers—Ashkenazi Jews who fled Ukraine to settle first in England and eventually in America. Pelham graduated from Columbia University in 1916 and worked as an economic consultant in New York City. In his last year at Columbia, he married a mailman's daughter, Estelle De Young, a Barnard College graduate who went on to practice as a psychologist. Estelle's parents were both from Dutch Jewish families. Pelham and Estelle had two children. Their daughter died of leukemia in her twenties. Donald, my father, was born in 1921 and graduated from Columbia University in 1941. Soon afterward, he was drafted into the army.

My mother was Irish Catholic. Her father, William Ahern, was born into a struggling farming family in County Cork, Ireland. His parents were native Gaelic speakers and could not read or write. He immigrated as a young man, and settled in Hartford, Connecticut, working for the Colt gun factory as a drop press operator. In 1917 he married Catherine ("Katie") Flynn, from County Clare, the oldest of eleven children in a farming family. She had immigrated as a young woman and found work as a nurse's aide in Hartford. William and Katie had their first child the following year, 1918: my mother, Mary Margaret Ahern. She graduated in 1939 from St. Joseph College, at that time the Catholic all-women's college in West Hartford, and then—uncommon for a woman in those days—went on to Yale University to receive a master of arts degree in English literature.

Like many in my generation, World War II brought my parents together. In 1942, before the Allied invasion of Italy, the army had sent my father to learn Italian at the University of Missouri, in Columbia. One day he was walking through a classroom building and spotted a beautiful young woman teaching an undergraduate class on Shakespeare. This was Mary Ahern in her first teaching job since leaving Yale. Transfixed, my father hung by the classroom door watching her teach. After class, he walked her home. He tried for months to get her to go on a date with him. She refused.

In later years, my brothers and I teasingly pressed our mother on why she put off Pop for so long. When she said she was worried "he was a New York wolf," we all erupted in laughter—including my mother.

Pop was manifestly far from a "wolf." Flesh-toned, horn-rim glasses; benign, boyish face; gentle temperament—he was the bookish, intellectual type. The real reason for my mother's resistance was that, as a committed Catholic, she found it hard to imagine marrying a secular Jew raised without any religion. But my father was persistent, wrote her poetry, and impressed her with his broad erudition. She saw he had a genuine respect for Catholicism, and he pledged that, if they ended up together, he would raise their children as Catholics. She relented, and, before long, they were engaged. My father, meanwhile, had transferred to the recently established US Office of Strategic Services (OSS), the precursor of the Central Intelligence Agency (CIA). When he returned from Europe at the end of the war, he and Mary Ahern were married in New York City. They remained devoted to each other for fifty-five years, parted only by death.

For the first fifteen of those years, they struggled. Four sons arrived in close succession: Christopher in 1947, me in 1950, Hilary in 1952, and Stephen in 1953. My mother worked as an editor for a variety of women's magazines, which allowed her often to work from home. My father taught English at Columbia while studying for his doctorate. He got his master's degree the year I was born, but the demands of his growing family derailed his plans for a PhD. To make ends meet, he expanded his teaching assignments at Columbia and supplemented his income by teaching night courses at Pace College and City College of New York (CCNY)—teaching at all three colleges during the same school year. Our apartment was crammed with stacks of "blue books" from the three institutions. I remember my father telling me that all his income together amounted to "less than the pay of a New York City garbageman." It wasn't hyperbole.

We had the largest family but smallest apartment in the building. It had only two bedrooms. My older brother, Christopher, and I slept in one, and my parents briefly rented the other to a foreign grad student to generate a little extra income. They converted the dining room into their bedroom—an odd arrangement, but it worked. When Hilary and Stephen came along, the foreign student had to leave. Because the dining room was otherwise occupied, our family usually ate dinner together in the kitchen, but we also used a section of our large living room when needed for formal dining.

Our apartment had a solitary bathroom for all six of us—a fact that effectively enforced the Golden Rule. When one of us boys urgently needed access, we had to rely on the goodwill of the other to relinquish possession. Fights and ill will among brothers could not be carried too far, since each knew that, before long, he'd be shifting from foot to foot outside the bathroom door pleading with his antagonist to "please hurry!" The principle of "mutually assured destruction" moderated sibling conflict in the Barr household.

At five years old, I was a scrawny, pale child and collapsed one day on the street while walking to kindergarten. When tests showed I was anemic, I was admitted to nearby St. Luke's Hospital for evaluation. Some doctors thought the X-rays showed a growth on my heart and wanted to conduct exploratory surgery; others thought it was just a shadow. I was going into my second week of tests, when my Irish-born grandmother arrived from Hartford, as did a priest, also from Ireland, who was close to my mother's family. Quickly pooh-poohing any idea of an operation, they instead prescribed at least eight ounces of Guinness stout a day. I was discharged from the hospital, and, until I was twelve years old, I drank a glass of stout every day—much to my brothers' envy. Treatment was discontinued when it became apparent that I had become anything but scrawny.

My mother was a good match for my father intellectually, but she was more practical. When any problem emerged, her approach was to grab the bull by the horns and wrestle it to the ground as quickly as possible. She ran the household with a hawk eye and a firm hand—a necessity with four rambunctious boys. Fortunately, she had charge of the finances, and I remember her sitting at the kitchen table every evening reconciling her budget journal, keeping track of every penny that came in and went out. I still have some of those journals. They show how she juggled bills and looked for every opportunity to cut costs just to get through each month.

My mother was gregarious, with a great sense of humor and a ready laugh. But as a child of the Great Depression, she was always anxious that the bottom was about to fall out and always thinking about how she could make provision against things going wrong. She called it her "Celtic gloom" and told me I'd inherited it. To a degree, she was right. That little voice in my head always warning me of what could go wrong and how I needed to protect against it is my mother's voice. For a lawyer, it is a great trait, since that is what good lawyers do: anticipate what could go wrong.

The difference between my father and my mother showed itself whenever any of us would ask for help on homework—usually a math question. My mother would get right to the question at hand and explain quickly whatever we needed to know to solve the precise problem. My father would put down the book he was reading, grab a yellow pad, draw a line across the page, and say: "Now, let's start with the number line." An hour later, he'd be just getting into the mysteries of long division, and we'd be ready for bed. My brothers and I referred to this as getting the "number line" treatment.

My efforts to learn about the birds and the bees ran afoul of this treatment. I was about ten and had already picked up a few tantalizing shreds of information from neighborhood buddies. I was having my hair cut by my mother in the kitchen and started to pump her for more information. Things reached an impasse when I asked, "Exactly how does a man 'fertilize' a woman?"

"You have to ask Pop about that."

As usual, my father pulled out a yellow pad and started drawing pictures of . . . cells. He started talking about protozoa. Uh-oh, I thought, this is going to be a long night. He worked his way through the division of cells and had gotten to DNA and chromosomes, when I tried to move things along.

"When are you going to get to, um, sticking it in?" I asked.

"Oh!" he said, surprised that I would want to miss hearing the good stuff about haploid gametes. At that point, he rushed through a thirty-second explanation of intercourse heavy on ten-cent words I did not understand, like tumescence. It was disappointing. It was back to the gutter for me, where at least I could get a straight answer.

For my parents, education was a priority, and they sacrificed happily to give us the best education they could. But for them, the primary educational arena was the home. Both my parents were natural teachers who loved explaining things and answering our questions—on history, or current events, or religion. Reading to us each evening was a routine. When we were little, my mother took the laboring oar, but as we got older, my father would give bravura readings of Treasure Island, Kidnapped, and other great novels, performing all the parts in different voices and dialects to great dramatic effect.

The main forum for education, however, was the dinner table. And the Barr family dinner table was a loud free-for-all. There was little small talk. We liked discussing the issues of the day, and, as we grew older, debate got more robust. In debates, our father's word on a topic was dispositive. As his number-line approach revealed, he loved expounding on matters, and, given his broad erudition, we considered him the font of wisdom on almost everything. While our arguments could get heated sometimes, more often our dinners were marked by hearty laughter. Everyone in the family had a good sense of humor. My father had an interesting style when he expounded on a subject. He would use an elevated, scholarly, and refined delivery, but then punctuate it with earthy and rougher language to drive home his point. The contrast was quite effective. He was far from a prig, and as we all got older, he was willing to use more off-color language, which my mother always felt obliged to respond to with mock horror.

When it came to parenting, my parents were old-school. They were not our chums—they held the offices of father and mother, and there was never doubt as to who was in charge. They believed that a child-centered home led to a self-centered child. We knew they would sacrifice unstintingly for our good, but they also understood that saying no can be as much an expression of love as saying yes. They believed that, if a child was to develop self-control, it was essential that parents set clear limits and enforce them dependably. They never made idle threats. When they mandated something under penalty of punishment, you were guaranteed to meet with the promised penalty if you defied them. Close in age, and living at close quarters, the four of us boys could be boisterous, and physical fights were not uncommon. Keeping order sometimes required a good spanking, but more often a credible threat of force was enough to bring peace. My father would calmly enter the room where offenses were under way and hang his army belt on the doorknob, look at us severely, and then walk out. We all knew what that meant.

For elementary school, we all went to the Catholic parochial school at Corpus Christi Church, the parish for the Columbia University neighborhood. Then under the pastorship of the great liberal champion Father George Barry Ford, the parish was renowned for three things: the beauty of the church, the magnificence of its liturgical music, and the excellence of its school. Over the years, I have come to realize that, apart from the role of my parents, my time at Corpus Christi had the most profound formative influence on my life.

Tucked away on West 121st Street just off Broadway, Corpus Christi's neo-Georgian building housed the church, the school, and a convent for the nuns who taught there. All the Barr children were altar boys. With three Masses a day on weekdays and four on Sunday, it was a rare day that one or more of us was not on duty, frequently paired together. These were still the days of the old Tridentine Mass—said entirely in Latin, with the priest's back to the congregation. The parish's liturgical prowess was most on display in its majestic High Masses, where the school choir was joined by a strong professional choir singing Gregorian chant, Renaissance polyphony, or Baroque choral music. Except for memories of family life, my most vivid childhood memories are of participating in these ceremonies. I think what fastened me to my faith in those early years was not just the appeal of its teachings to mind and heart, but also the splendor of its worship. The flowing chants in a strange language, the smell of incense, the solemn silences, and the angelic voices weaving a sumptuous tapestry of sound—all this made a profound impression on me. It wasn't just the external aesthetics; it was that sense of transcendence and mystery stirred within me. These rituals spoke truth to me.

The school was ethnically diverse, drawing heavily from neighborhoods bordering on West Harlem. The students were mainly Hispanic and working- and middle-class Irish American. Not many Columbia faculty sent their children to Corpus Christi. In my class of thirty-two, there were only four students from Columbia households or more affluent families. Yet despite the differences, there was no ethnic tension and an easygoing affinity among the students.

The Dominican nuns who taught at Corpus Christi provided a superb education. The famous comedian George Carlin went to the school before me. He rejected the faith and was a scathing critic about almost every aspect of the Church, but he always extolled the virtues of the school and the nuns who taught there, saying that they gave him the independence and tools to think for himself. That was my experience, too. One teacher I adored was Sister Lucinda, whom I had for both fourth and fifth grades. After I left the school, she had been assigned elsewhere. Over the years, I wondered where she had ended up and thought about trying to reconnect with her but did not know how to go about finding her.

One day in 2009 I was having lunch with Edward Cardinal Egan, who had just retired as archbishop of New York. Knowing that my parish had been Corpus Christi, he said in passing, "I was taught by the Sinsinawa Dominicans also." I interrupted him. "The Sinsin—what?" It turned out the cardinal knew all about the order that had taught at my school and that their motherhouse was in Sinsinawa, Wisconsin. I later went on the Internet, found their website, and sent an e-mail to the order's archivist, inquiring about a Sister Lucinda. It turned out she was still alive at ninety-three and living at the motherhouse.

I wrote her a long letter. "Over the years," I told her, "I have realized that, of all the teachers in my life, you have had the greatest impact, and I owe the most to you." I went on: "You always gave me kind and gentle encouragement. You instilled a love of learning and gave me confidence in my abilities. You taught me not to shrink from upholding what I thought to be right and not to hesitate to lead. Your example of faith and charity helped give me a strong religious foundation, which has been the greatest gift of all."

I went to visit my old teacher in 2010, and it was a joyous reunion for both of us. Surprisingly, Sister Lucinda remembered me well and could recount details about my parents and siblings. After lunch with her and other members of the community, we spent a long time talking. I established a computer lab at Corpus Christi dedicated to her and sent her a photograph of the plaque in the lab honoring her. I visited her again two years later. She died not long after. I was grateful I had the chance to thank her.

My father did not formally convert to Catholicism until his late seventies. He struggled with moderate skepticism. Nonetheless, he seemed to know more about the faith than most theologians. Whenever I or any of my brothers went to him for guidance, he could effort-lessly cite the precise teachings of various Church councils or doctors of the church. In discussing current religious controversies, he would always espouse the orthodox position. He admired the Church deeply and did all he could to encourage our faith. Because he was a master Catholic apologist, my brothers and I were long puzzled why he had not yet been baptized. My mother never pushed him and told us to leave him alone. After we were grown, my father became a little more open with us about his own thoughts. If there is a God, he told me, he had no doubts that Jesus is the Son of God and that Catholic doctrine is the truth. The question for him was God's existence. This required, he said, a measure of faith, and he prayed daily for that faith.

At the beginning of 2000, he called me to confirm that I would be driving my daughter Patricia back up to her college in Massachusetts that weekend. He asked us to stop in Connecticut, where he and my mother were living, so that Patricia could serve as his godmother for his baptismal ceremony. That weekend, at the age of seventy-eight, he was ready to be baptized.

Our family held strong views on politics. My father, who had been a Socialist in high school, was a conservative Republican by the time he graduated from Columbia. He was the Republican leader in our Morningside Heights neighborhood, one of the most liberal areas in New York. In 1956 each class at Corpus held an election debate, and my earliest political memory—I was six years old—is of a short speech I delivered in support of President Dwight Eisenhower, who was run-ning for reelection against his same opponent from four years earlier, Democrat Adlai Stevenson. My father had worked with me on it.

In 1960 we were in an awkward position at Corpus because we were supporting Vice President Richard Nixon over the Catholic can-didate, Senator John F. Kennedy, a Democrat from Massachusetts. While Sister Lucinda took it in stride, one of my brother's teachers told my brother she would pray for him. Every two years around election time, my brothers and I always helped our father distribute campaign literature throughout the neighborhood. Having slipped Barry Goldwater brochures under apartment doors throughout much of the Upper West Side in 1964, I am no stranger to lost causes.

I didn't appreciate it at the time, but famous scholars and intellectuals were everywhere in my early years. In our academic community—clustered around 116th Street, running from Riverside Drive, past Claremont Avenue, and up to the Columbia campus—everyone knew one another. All the mothers would congregate on benches surrounding a sandbox on the upper level of Riverside Park at 116th Street, watching their children. Most of the twenty-four apartments in our building were occupied by famous professors, including the likes of Richard Neustadt, an adviser to Presidents Kennedy and Harry S. Truman, and David B. Truman, vice president of the university. We were on friendly terms with luminaries such as the great Anglo-French polymath Jacques Barzun and the American historian Richard Hofstadter. The great literary critic Lionel Trilling was a guest in our home, and his son, James, an occasional playmate. My father was friends with journalist Irving Kristol, frequently referred to as the godfather of neoconservatism, and I attended birthday parties at the home of power couple Norman Podhoretz, editor in chief of *Commentary* magazine, and Midge Decter, a prominent journalist and author. To me, of course, they all seemed like a lot of friendly and ordinary people. I had no idea they were famous and wouldn't have cared anyway. But I like to think that I and my brothers picked up something from our casual presence among these remarkable minds—even if just by playing in the sandbox with their children.

My brothers and I had a great group of pals in the neighborhood. The crew was inseparable until we all started going away to different colleges. It was a rare day when we didn't spend time together either playing sports or just hanging out. Our main outlet was playing touch football or baseball in Riverside Park. An essential item for any group of city boys in those days was the mighty "Spal-*deen*"—with a heavy accent on the second syllable. This was the pink high-bounce rubber ball about two and a half inches in diameter manufactured by Spalding. Two or three of us could spend a day playing Chinese handball with our Spaldeen up against the marble walls of the nearby nineteen-story Interchurch Center building, or playing stickball on Claremont Avenue, which had virtually no traffic.

One of my neighborhood friends and I have been together since infancy. Fred, now a retired lawyer, lived up the block. His father was a prominent Columbia professor, and our mothers walked us in carriages side by side in Riverside Park. He became like a member of our family. We went to nursery school, high school, and college together, and see each other regularly to this day.

Crime was an ever-present reality. New York has alternate side of the street parking, and my mother was held up numerous times at knifepoint when she went out to move the car. At least once a year, our group would be accosted by a gang of toughs in Riverside Park, and we would be relieved of our baseball gloves and other valuables, sometimes at knifepoint.

My mother added a dramatic page to neighborhood lore one winter. My older brother and I, ages ten and seven, were headed out of our building to walk together to school early one morning. Just as we were exiting the outer lobby, a group of a half dozen toughs surged into the building, and started stealing our gloves and hats, and searching our pockets. They were probably only fourteen or fifteen years old, but they seemed much older to me at the time. As soon as they left, I pushed the lobby intercom button and told my mother what had happened. A moment later, the elevator door opened, and my mother bolted out, still wearing her full apron. She tore out of the building, asking which way the thieves had headed. As she marched along Riverside Drive, bristling with anger, while we trotted behind her, everyone stopped to stare at this virago with no coat, only an apron, obviously out for blood.

In a few blocks, I saw the gang stopped on the street, splitting up their haul. As my mother lit after them, they froze for a moment, startled by her unconventional appearance. As they ran every which way, she caught the slowest-moving one by the scruff of his neck. She manhandled him for more than a block to the policeman always posted by our school, who took the kid into custody.

The episode has remained vividly in my mind for more than sixty years. For me, the image of my mother storming into the street captures much of what was right and beautiful about midcentury America. The indispensability of strong family life in the preservation of justice. The lack of nihilistic savagery even in criminal gangs—the boys scattered at the sight of an aproned woman! And, of course, the nearby and reliable presence of a beat cop.

In 1957 my father purchased a record album, *The Regimental Band and the Massed Pipers of the Scots Guards*. This seemingly small event ended up greatly enriching my life. From the moment the needle first touched the vinyl, and the first skirl of the bagpipes sounded, I was hooked. I could not get enough. Later that year, my parents—who believed every child should have the chance to learn a musical instrument—asked me what instrument I'd like to take up. Piano? Violin? Cello? they asked hopefully.

My unwavering answer: bagpipes.

My father, a good sport, took up the challenge of figuring out how to get me bagpipe lessons. Not unreasonably, he called the Juilliard School and several other top music schools in the city. He was met with snickers. No, he was told, this is a *music* school. We don't teach the bagpipes. My hopes were fading with each dead end. Taking a last shot, my father called a Scottish imports store in Manhattan to see if anyone there had any leads. Sure enough, he reached an old gentleman with a soft brogue who happily gave him a short list of piping teachers in the New York area. My father and I studied the list intently, having no clue how to rate their relative merits. But clearly the most impressive-sounding name was the first one on the list: Pipe Major John C. MacKenzie, Sixth Battalion, Highland Light Infantry, Retired.

"This guy sounds official, Pop. Let's try him."

I never knew either of my grandfathers. John MacKenzie became my grandfather. He was raised in Glasgow in a Highland family. He was taught piping by the legendary piper John MacDougall Gillies. MacKenzie was a brickmason by trade and also served in one of Glasgow's Territorial battalions—the equivalent of our National

Guard. In 1915 his unit was deployed to fight in Gallipoli, and he was made pipe major of the battalion, the youngest pipe major of a Scottish unit at the time. After Gallipoli, MacKenzie fought through the rest of the Great War, first in Palestine and then in northern France. Returning to Scotland after the war, he was a successful competitive piper. In the 1930s he came to New York, where he was a central figure in teaching bagpipe and leading pipe bands.

I was almost eight years old when, every Tuesday night, my father started taking me by subway up to the one-room apartment near Broadway and 168th Street where John MacKenzie, then sixty-four, lived with his wife. Bagpipe lessons and practice are done on a small wind instrument called a chanter, which is like a recorder but uses a reed and sounds like a soft bagpipe. I'd sit with Mr. MacKenzie at his small dining table, playing exercises and learning tunes under his careful eye and ear. He was a charming and delightful man, but piping, for him, wasn't some endearing hobby—it was life and honor. He was deadly serious about technique.

Whenever we took a brief break for me to catch my breath, my father and I would prompt MacKenzie to tell us about himself and his experiences in the Great War. These were magical times for me.

I think back on the sacrifice my father made so I could play the pipes—not the $2 an hour MacKenzie charged but giving up every Tuesday night to take me up to 168th Street and sit there for more than an hour—a man who, at times, was holding down three teaching jobs.

But at least he also loved bagpipes, and MacKenzie's stories too. The old pipe major would tell us about jumping up on the trench's parapet to pipe his battalion "over the top" in its first battle at Gallipoli; the bayonet charges against Turkish lines; the fighting in Palestine and the taking of Jerusalem; and the grim trench warfare in France. As a wee lad of eight, I was in seventh heaven.

After three years, I progressed enough to join the Thistle Guildry Pipe Band, which MacKenzie was overseeing. I still made the Tuesday trip—now by myself—up to his apartment for private lessons, and then I went to band practice every Friday night in the basement of the Presbyterian church on Ninety-Sixth and Central Park West. All the pipers in the band were men; except for one teenager, I was the only boy. My brother Hil became a snare drummer with the band, so we would go to practice together. During the summers, I would compete in solo contests, and my band would compete against other US and Canadian bands at various Highland Games throughout the East Coast. At sixteen, I was playing at my peak and doing well in solo competitions, and the band was making good progress.

That all came to an end in the winter of 1967. I was playing touch football after school in Riverside Park, when my father walked across the street and called me over. "I'm sorry, Billy," he began. "Mr. Mac-Kenzie died last night."

It was a heart attack. I was crushed. I played for another year or so, and then took a break from piping.

I left Corpus Christi after sixth grade, as did all my brothers, to attend Horace Mann School, a college preparatory school long considered one of the top in the country. Horace Mann's eighteen-acre campus is on a hilltop near 246th Street and Broadway in the Riverdale section of the Bronx. In those days, the school was all-boys and ran from seventh to twelfth grades. For six years, I followed the same regimen: I would take the IRT subway line from 116th and Broadway to 242nd and Broadway and then schlep four blocks up a steep hill, lugging my maroon-and-white vinyl "HM" bookbag, crammed with books.

Horace Mann was quite a cultural shock for me. The student body was overwhelmingly Jewish, and I had no previous exposure to that culture. Everyone had been to the same "temple dances" and bar mitzvahs, and in their banter would use lingo—Yiddish slang—that was unfamiliar to me. Even more alien at first was the all-male atmosphere. All the teachers were men. I vividly remember my first class—it was math taught by Mr. Athans, a burly, former University of Michigan football player with a baritone voice. When I raised my hand to answer a question and started calling out "Sister! Sister!" my classmates' heads snapped around, startled and perplexed.

The school sought to instill the intellectual virtues: the qualities of mind and character that promote intellectual growth, disciplined thinking, and the courage to pursue and uphold the truth. Although Horace Mann was an extremely demanding and competitive place, I soon became comfortable there. My classmates were generally an honorable and amiable group, and there was a degree of solidarity based on a shared commitment to academic excellence.

My family's financial fortunes had improved. The Russians' successful launch of the first unmanned satellite, *Sputnik 1*, in 1957 had galvanized the country to develop more scientists and engineers. My father, who by this time had become an associate dean at Columbia University's School of Engineering, had earned some notoriety developing Columbia's Science Honors Program, which identified talented science students in high school and provided them advanced studies and nurtured their careers. Columbia loaned him to the independent federal agency the National Science Foundation for a year to promote similar programs around the country. This attention led to his becoming the headmaster of the Dalton School in New York—at the time an all-girls school, which he was to make coed.

By the time of my junior year at HM, I had a clear sense of direction in my life. The school college guidance counselor met one-on-one with each junior to start working on a college admission strategy. My meeting started by him asking me, in a rote sort of way, if I had given any thought to what I wanted to do in life and where I might apply. I told him that my career goal was to become the director of the CIA. He looked a little startled and straightened up in his chair, studying me more closely. "Well, *that* is a very precise goal," he said. He seemed surprised at my specificity and the nature of my planned occupation—unusual at a school where almost everyone wanted to be a lawyer, doctor, or businessman. But I had put a lot of thought into it.

"I want a career in intelligence," I explained. "My strategy is to make myself an attractive candidate by becoming an expert on China."

"And do you know where you want to attend college?"

"Columbia," I said. "It has one of the best China studies programs in the country."

It was a short meeting.

I had definite aims, but at Horace Mann, I was an average student. My parents had always been relaxed about our grades. They would exhort us to do our best but never put pressure on us. At the beginning of my junior year, however, my father came into my room and got serious about grades—for the only time I can remember. "If you want to go to Columbia, Billy, you better get your ass in gear *this year*," he said. I did.

In addition to working harder in my junior year, I also gave vent to my entrepreneurial side. Hormones also had something to do with it. I was relatively shy with girls and, attending an all-boys school, rarely met them. After much thought, I decided to run a "match" between a hundred HM boys and a hundred girls from Riverdale Country School for Girls and the Dalton School. I called it "Calcu-date" and said computers would be used to help make the match—a claim everyone knew to be a joke. A couple of friends and I composed a questionnaire, and each participant submitted his or her questionnaire along with $1. The "computers" went to work. My friends and I, along with a couple of students from the girls' schools, did the matching.

I kept the $200 and ended up dating a very nice girl. However, my father caught wind of this and was angry that I had included students from Dalton. He gave me a firm, and memorable, warning: if I touched a girl while she was enrolled in his school, he would castrate me "with rusty nail clippers." That was the end of my Calcu-date career. But I was well ahead of my time and, had I stuck with it, may well have pre-empted Mark Zuckerberg.

In addition to my family's connection with Columbia University, there was also a practical reason why I aimed for that college. Because of an agreement between Dalton School and the university, I would receive a substantial tuition benefit if I went there. But it was true that Columbia had a top-notch China study program and was a perfect fit for my career plans. My focus on China was, again, largely pragmatic. I had no deep-seated attraction to China as an object of academic study. But I reasoned that, because Russia had long been the United States' main adversary, Russian experts were plentiful, whereas China was the threat of the future, and so the field was still comparatively uncrowded.

I was admitted to Columbia and started there in the fall of 1967. I lived at home through my sophomore year until my older brother returned from Vietnam, where he had served on the cruiser USS *Boston*, bombarding North Vietnam. We lived together off-campus. My most demanding course was Mandarin Chinese, which I studied throughout college, pulling countless all-nighters learning the ideographs. My major was government, and in addition to the required courses, I took as many electives as I could schedule relating to China: Chinese history, culture, and politics. The courses that ended up exciting me the most, however, were the college's "Core Curriculum"—a series of Great Books courses, as well as music and art courses, designed to give every student broad familiarity with Western civilization and the humanities. It was here that I first fell under the lasting spell of—among others—Saint Augustine, the eighteenth-century British statesman Edmund Burke, and the Founding Fathers.

The cultural revolution of the 1960s was gaining ground at Columbia. Although the majority of students were middle of the road, the militant Left was becoming more activist and vocal among students and younger faculty. My beliefs were frequently under pressure, and, more than ever before, I was forced to think through my positions and defend them. In English composition, the young instructor announced in the first class that his purpose was to lead us all to the conclusion that organized religion was humbug.

"How many here still believe in an organized religion?" he asked the class of a hundred. Two of us raised our hands—me and a Greek Orthodox student. I glanced at the back row, where athletes, mostly recruited from Catholic high schools in Ohio and Pennsylvania, liked to sit. They looked bored, not caring to engage. Our last paper for the term, counting for most of our grade, was supposed to address the worthlessness of organized religion. Drawing on the Core Curriculum I was studying at the time, I wrote a paper defending religion, presented in the tone and format of Saint Thomas Aquinas's thirteenth-century philosophical work, the *Summa Theologica*, divided into Questions and Articles. The instructor gave me an A. "I disagree with you!" he commented on the paper. "But you have ably presented your arguments with all the vigor and certitude of 2,000 years."

My social life revolved mainly around my fraternity, Sigma Nu, housed near campus in a brownstone on West 113th Street. The fraternity, at more than forty brothers, had a large contingent of Pittsburghers, originally recruited to play football, who dropped the sport after freshman year, as well as a sizable number of brothers who were in the Naval Reserve Officers Training Corps (NROTC). I became social chairman of the house and was kept very busy arranging Friday-night mixers and postgame Saturday parties.

In the spring of 1968 student riots erupted on the Columbia campus against the backdrop of expanding US involvement in Vietnam and increased racial tensions. On January 30 the Viet Cong launched its Tet Offensive, a coordinated assault on more than a hundred cities and towns in South Vietnam. Although US troops crushed the Viet Cong, America's news media portrayed the surprise attack as a major setback for the United States. At the same time, the murder of civil rights leader Dr. Martin Luther King Jr. on April 4 inflamed racial tensions, touching off days of rioting in many US cities.

The upheavals on Columbia's campus broke out on April 23, when the radical group Students for a Democratic Society, or SDS, and the Society of Afro-American Students, or SAS, occupied Hamilton Hall, the undergraduate college's principal classroom building. The immediate casus belli were the university's relationship with a think tank that did work for the Pentagon and the university's plans to build a new gymnasium in Morningside Park, which sits between the Columbia campus and Harlem. Many Harlem residents and the SAS objected to the university's encroachment on the park, as well as its plan to collocate a community center in the lower level of the building.

The next morning, the SAS kicked the larger SDS contingent out of Hamilton Hall. The Black students wanted to keep the focus on the gym and Columbia's relationship to Harlem and, from that point on, conducted a completely separate effort from SDS. The latter group, in contrast, seemed mainly interested in mobilizing opposition to the Vietnam War and pursuing a hazy "revolutionary" agenda by forcing violent confrontations with police. These demonstrators were white and predominantly from affluent families. A majority of them were not Columbia students but students from other campuses or career left-wing activists drawn to the latest "revolutionary" hotspot. Ousted from Hamilton Hall, SDS protestors went to Low Library, at the center of the campus, and seized part of the building housing the university president's office. By the twenty-fifth, protestors occupied two other classroom buildings.

The vast majority of students at the time opposed the SDS. Even those who were sympathetic to some of its goals strongly disapproved of its takeover of buildings and use of force. I was repulsed by the student radicals and their bullying tactics. I regarded them, especially the violent ones, as pampered brats. I was disgusted by their ingratitude. Here they were blessed to live in the greatest country in the world, and they responded with ignorant whining and violence. "Let it all hang out," one of their catchphrases had it. My attitude, to borrow the phrase of the great sociologist and theologian Peter L. Berger, was "Tuck it all back in."

Over the ensuing days, many students in this larger group—including me—coalesced into an ad hoc group we called the Majority Coalition. We were fine with protests on just about any issue—as long as they were not violent and did not interfere with the rights and activities of other students. The dean of the college, Henry Coleman, met with the Majority Coalition in the university gym and promised he had "no intention of letting twenty-five hundred students down because of the actions of two hundred of them."

Soon afterward, the Majority Coalition decided to force the administration's hand. We blockaded the occupied part of Low Library by setting up a chain of students around the west side of the building to prevent any food from getting in to the occupiers. Starting on April 28, fraternities, sports teams, and clubs, as well as the hundreds of individual students who were part of the Majority Coalition, manned a fifty-yard cordon around the clock.

On the afternoon of April 29 a group of about seventy-five riot-ers, supported by scores more, tried to breach the Majority Coalition line. They marched twice around the Low Library, chanting the usual inanities, and then on the third circuit formed a phalanx. They charged into our line, throwing ammonia as they came. A violent melee broke out. It lasted about four minutes. The rioters retreated. There were cuts and bruises on both sides, some bleeding profusely. One of my friends went to the hospital with a badly lacerated ear, and the proctor told us later that up to a dozen people received medical treatment, mainly for stitches, head bruises, and loose teeth. I joined the fight, but I was situated to the rear of a big football player who performed with such amazing proficiency that I never had to do anything but shove people.

A few left-wing "historians" of the 1968 riots have scoffed that this fight was the sum total of the Majority Coalition's role, and without consequence. This is false. That very week, I spoke to the university's vice president, David B. Truman, in the lobby of my par-ents' building—he was their next-door neighbor. Truman told me that once students started fighting students, the university had no choice but to take action. News of the brawl at Low Library prompted the administration to authorize New York police officers to come onto the campus in force. It started in the late afternoon after the melee, when thirty-five motorcycle police arrived and took up positions in front of the Majority Coalition to ensure no further fighting. That evening, we received word from the administration that the campus was going to be cleared that night, and anyone not wanting to be ar-rested should leave campus or go to his or her room. The motorcycle cops seconded the message. "We got it from here, guys," I remember one of them saying. "Make sure you're not out on campus tonight."

That night, the NYPD came on campus and cleared out the occu-pied buildings.

The 1968 riots set the pattern for my remaining time at Columbia. The student body slowly drifted to the Left, mainly as a response to the Vietnam War. Every spring the campus degenerated into chaos. Many departments canceled classes—but usually not the East Asian Studies Department. At the end of my junior year, the whole college was effectively shut down after US troops moved into Cambodia. In my senior year, there were planned demonstrations around graduation, and I decided not to attend.

It was at a Sigma Nu party in September of my senior year that I met Christine Moynihan. As social chairman, I was responsible for getting a big turnout of young ladies for our Friday-night mixers. One of my friends from the Corpus Christi days was a sophomore at the College of Mount Saint Vincent, an all-girls Catholic college on the Hudson River in Riverdale. I asked her to promote one of our parties at the school, and, on party night, she showed up with a busload of young women. It was a successful event. During the night, I went out on the stoop to catch some fresh air and there encountered Christine. We talked the rest of the night. She was beautiful, smart, sensible, and very centered. She had an open and kind disposition, but also, I could see, an inner strength and resilience. Her family had lived in the Washington Heights neighborhood of Manhattan but joined many of the families of Irish and Italian heritage that moved up to Rockland County, just north of the city, in the 1950s. Christine read everything. She wanted to become a librarian. An added attraction: she and her family were strong Republicans, which in those days was still a bit unusual for Irish American families out of the city. We started dating.

In the middle of my junior year, December 1969, most males in my generation were tuned in to the first draft lottery, which would determine our likelihood of being drafted. My number came out as 319, which meant I would not be drafted. Up until that point, my plan had been to apply to a US Navy program for a commission as an intelligence officer and, after that service, apply for the Central Intelligence Agency. But at the beginning of my senior year, a CIA recruiter suggested that since I wasn't going to be drafted, my quickest route to the agency would be to apply for a CIA internship. This program permits graduate students to work during the summers within agency components while completing their degrees. Interns typically get offers of permanent employment upon graduation.

That was the course I went after. I was admitted into the CIA intern program and planned to pursue a master's degree for the next two years at Columbia in the Government Department. I would concentrate on Chinese area studies. In June 1971, as soon as I was awarded my AB, I headed down to Langley, Virginia, to work at agency headquarters that summer.

My summers at the agency were some of the best times in my life. The people I met at Langley were professionals who took their duties seriously. Unlike some of the affluent white radicals at Columbia, they were grateful to be there. They welcomed inquiry and debate. An officemate I met my first day on the job, Dennis Bartlett, an erudite former Jesuit seminarian, became a lifelong friend. He and his wife had me over regularly during the week for dinner. We enjoyed long conversations on all manner of topics.

One day back at my parents' apartment, I was heading down in the elevator when I happened upon Professor Joseph Rothschild, our neighbor and a political historian at the university. He asked me what I thought so far of the agency. I said. "There's more academic freedom at the CIA than at Columbia University." Rothschild, a serious scholar concerned over the growing intolerance toward diverse viewpoints in academia, liked my answer. Later that week, he quoted me approvingly at a faculty meeting. Several times after that, I was stopped on campus by some of the old-school professors I knew who said they'd heard what I had said and, sadly, agreed.

After my second summer at the CIA, with two semesters to go on my MA degree, Christine and I became engaged. I expected to be offered a permanent job at the agency starting in June, which is when Christine would be graduating from college. We set the wedding for June 23. Christine applied to Catholic University of America's School of Library Science in Washington, DC, to pursue a master's degree.

As we plowed ahead with our plans, I received conflicting signals from my parents. My mother, always looking at the downside risk, didn't have a lot of confidence in a Chinese studies degree and a career in intelligence and wanted me to have a backup plan. Go to law school, was her advice. My father thought my plan was good. "Do what you like doing because that's what you'll do best," was his counsel.

I was still drawn to intelligence. But my studies had kindled a deep interest in the law as well, especially constitutional law. I had also seen during my summers at the agency that analysts can become so specialized that they have few outside options. I made the decision to go to law school at night while I worked at the CIA. I opted for George Washington University Law School, which had a great night program and was more accessible from Langley headquarters. I was in good company. Many CIA veterans, including Allen Dulles, the first civilian director, had gone to GW night law school.

It was the best choice I could have made. But it didn't make the next few years any easier. What might have been years of early marital bliss was instead a period of round-the-clock work and constant physical and mental exhaustion.

CHAPTER 2

A SHIFT IN PLANS

On June 23, 1973, Christine and I were married in her college's beautiful chapel overlooking the Hudson River. The next morning, a Sunday, we drove down to Northern Virginia, and I started work at the CIA the next day. We would have to wait ten years to take our honeymoon. We lived in an apartment in a complex known in those days as Arlington Towers, across from the Iwo Jima Memorial in Arlington. For the first year and a half of my time at CIA, my office was two blocks from our apartment. I started night law school in August.

For the first couple of years of married life, Chris and I hardly ever saw each other awake. I would get up at four thirty in the morning and walk to the office to read the overnight cable traffic. Later in the morning, Chris would head out to attend library school at Catholic University. After work, I would go into DC for night law school, and Chris would go to her night-shift job on the reference desk at Georgetown University's Lauinger Library. By the time my wife got home at night, I was already in bed. We kept this schedule for two years, until Chris got her master's degree and started full-time at Lauinger.

I thrived in law school. At the end of the first year, I was top in my class. Although the schedule was grinding, going to night school had its advantages. Most of those in my class had significant professional experience, holding responsible positions on Capitol Hill, in executive agencies, or in business. It was tight-knit group. On my first day, I met

Jay Ferron, who was to become my close friend. As we chatted before civil procedure class, I learned that he had just been discharged from the air force in time to start law school. Months earlier, he had been flying B-52 airstrikes over North Vietnam. We set up a study group that stayed together through our four years.

In 1975, after a series of revelations about potential abuses by the CIA, including allegations of attempted assassinations of foreign adversaries and illegal surveillance programs, Congress launched a series of investigations of the agency. At one time, there were seven different entities investigating the CIA: the House Permanent Select Committee on Intelligence, called the Pike Committee after its chairman, Otis Pike of New York; the Senate Select Committee on Intelligence, chaired by Idaho's Frank Church and commonly known as the Church Committee; four other congressional committees; and a commission chaired by Vice President Nelson Rockefeller.

In those days, there were only a few lawyers in the CIA. Since it took many months to get through the hiring process, the agency was caught short on staff able to deal with the investigations. I was already an employee and in law school, so the agency's Office of Legislative Counsel brought me over temporarily to help work on the investigations. The head of the office was George L. Cary, a calm and wise CIA veteran who did a masterful job of steering the agency through multiple inquiries. Cary became a mentor to me. He gave me increasing responsibilities and offered me a permanent position in the office. At twenty-five years old, I found myself in the thick of an often intense conflict between the agency and Congress, negotiating with hostile members of the House and the Senate over access to CIA documents and witnesses.

On one occasion, I was sent up to explain to the cantankerous chairman of the House Government Operations Committee, Jack Brooks of Texas, that we would not accede to his demands. Chewing on a cigar stub, he blistered me for a half hour with a stream of imaginative obscenities, cursing the entity he kept calling the "C, I, and A," as if it were a railroad line. I held my ground, and, as I was leaving his office, Brooks took out of his desk drawer a big Texas belt buckle emblazoned with his signature and flipped it to me. "Take this," he growled. "No hard feelings."

The Office of Legislative Counsel was on the seventh floor of the CIA's headquarters building, across from the director of Central Intelligence's office. In January 1976 President Gerald Ford replaced Director Bill Colby with George H. W. Bush, who had been serving as our ambassador to the People's Republic of China. Bush took the reins at the most challenging time in the agency's history. Previously shrouded in secrecy, it was now in the public glare, the target of bruising attacks and unprecedented scrutiny. In the wake of the Vietnam War and Watergate, Ford had minimal political capital, and while the White House tried to help where it could, the agency was largely left to fend for itself. Bush had to spend much of his tenure rectifying past missteps, defending the agency against unjustified attacks, and ensuring that its capabilities were not permanently damaged.

I first met Bush shortly after he took over at CIA. I was handling an upcoming House committee hearing related to a past CIA program. Bush, scheduled to testify, wanted to meet to discuss the testimony. He was relaxed and low-key, putting me at ease. He was interested to hear that I had a background in Chinese studies, and the former ambassador to China and I spoke a few phrases back and forth in Mandarin.

As the resident expert on the program, I accompanied the director to Capitol Hill. The hearing went mostly well, but a few members' questioning became aggressive. At one point, during a particularly heated exchange, Bush leaned back in his chair and whispered out of the side of his mouth, "How the hell do I deal with this one?"

I leaned in and whispered a possible answer.

He turned back toward his questioner and related the answer more or less as I had suggested.

I thought to myself, *Here I am, twenty-six and advising the director of the CIA on his testimony before Congress.* The only thing more surprising to me was that he took the advice.

Bush served as director for only one year, but I accompanied him to the Hill several more times. Despite his brief tenure, he had an outsize impact on the agency, reflected by the fact that the agency's Langley campus is named after him. That legacy came from his steady leadership while the agency was under siege. Unlike his successor, Admiral Stansfield Turner, Bush did not treat the agency as a pariah. He embraced it and stood up for it. He arrived with only one assistant. He did not insulate himself behind a wall of longtime aides. He was easily accessible, and he trusted CIA professionals unless they gave him a reason not to. I learned a lot watching him lift up a dispirited organization.

It was during Bush's time guiding the agency that I first met Antonin Scalia. The future Supreme Court justice was then at the Department of Justice as Assistant Attorney General for the Office of Legal Counsel (OLC), responsible for providing legal advice throughout the executive branch. We needed a lot of help at CIA, as bills were circulating on the Hill that would have crippled the agency. I visited his office several times to get his help in opposing them. Scalia was stalwart, always ready to help the agency beat back this ill-considered legislation. Nino, as his friends call him, had a brilliant mind; whatever the issue, his command of the statute and court precedents was total. He was also, as many people know, wickedly funny.

In the early fall of 1976 I was entering my fourth and final year of night law school, and I was still at the top of my class. I knew little about the legal profession, though, and did not understand the cachet that comes from clerking for a judge after graduation. My career plan was to stay on as a CIA lawyer after graduating, and I had not applied for a clerkship. One of my classmates told me I'd be crazy not to try for one, although, it being so late, most judges had already made their hiring decisions. Judges in those days usually extended offers a year before the clerkship was to start. I applied to only three judges: the conservative Republican-appointed judges on the US Court of Appeals for the DC Circuit, which was considered a prestigious court to clerk on. I immediately got a call from the only one who had not already filled his two clerk spots: Judge Malcolm Richard Wilkey. He wanted to know if I could come to interview the next day.

Judge Wilkey had a distinguished career. Under President Eisenhower, he had served at senior levels of the Department of Justice, first as US attorney in Houston, then as Assistant Attorney General for the Office of Legal Counsel, and, finally, as head of the Criminal Division. Later, after seven years as general counsel at Kennecott Copper Corporation, he was appointed to the US Court of Appeals by President Richard Nixon.

Judge Wilkey had a formal manner. I was nervous as I sat down in front of his desk for the interview. I noticed a picture of General George S. Patton on the wall behind him, next to the judge's officer's commission. I asked, "So you were in Patton's army, Your Honor?"

"Why, yes," he responded, apparently pleased I had inquired. He was commissioned as an artillery officer, he told me, but was actually a major in Patton's intelligence corps. "So," he said, "I like your intelligence background."

"Were you with Patton before the Normandy Breakout?" I asked, referring to the fact that Patton commanded troops in North Africa and Sicily before eventually leading the US Third Army in its breakout from the Normandy beachhead after D-Day and its sweep across Europe toward Nazi Germany

"Ahhh!" he exclaimed. "So you know something about Patton's campaigns?"

"A little, yes." In fact, since boyhood, I had been a World War II history buff and had read nearly every significant book about it. It's hard to hold a natural conversation in a job interview, but this broke the ice, and we talked easily about the campaigns for a half hour or more. I was able at least to show him that my appreciation for Patton went far beyond the movie. We went on to talk about intelligence, Vietnam, and Watergate, and it became increasingly clear that we were kindred spirits with similar views about protecting executive power from the erosion it had undergone in recent years. The judge asked me what my plans were after my clerkship, and I said I thought I would stay in the intelligence community. The interview lasted well over an hour, and Wilkey called me later that day to offer me the position, which I accepted. During the interim, he had called Bush.

It turned out—happy coincidence—they had been friends from the judge's days as US attorney in Houston. Bush gave Wilkey a strong recommendation.

Wilkey had moved quickly to hire me because my resume landed on his desk just as his best friend on the court, Judge Edward Tamm, beat out Wilkey for another applicant he had wanted to hire: Bob Kimmitt. A West Pointer, Kimmitt was a decorated Vietnam War veteran who had just finished Georgetown Law while working on the National Security Council at the White House. When Wilkey offered me the clerkship, he told me about his abortive effort to hire Kimmitt.

"I think you two will be friends," the judge predicted. He was right, and my life would be altered as a consequence.

My clerkship would not start until July 1977, and, in the meanwhile, I continued working in the CIA's Office of Legislative Counsel. My plans for a career in the intelligence community changed abruptly, however, after President Ford lost reelection in November, Bush stepped down in January 1977, and President Jimmy Carter appointed a new director: Admiral Stansfield Turner. The admiral was a disaster. He arrived with a retinue of naval officers who served as an impregnable palace guard. CIA officials had to conduct business in writing through these naval officers. Turner treated agency professionals with distrust and disdain. Worst of all, he decimated the clandestine service. Turner, like many political appointees since, bought into the delusional belief that intelligence work can be conducted wholly by satellites and gizmos that don't require anyone's hands getting dirty. Agency morale plummeted. I was ready to leave in July when my clerkship started.

The law clerks to the other eight judges on the court were mostly top students from the top law schools. Although my work at the CIA gave me more real-world experience than most of them, except for Bob Kimmitt, I still wondered, as a night student from George Washington, how I would fare among this crowd. I found quickly that I could hold my own. Kimmitt and I became close friends, had parallel careers and family lives, and helped each other at critical junctures along the way.

Wilkey introduced me to a man who would have a big effect on my life. Mike Uhlmann had served under President Ford as Assistant Attorney General for Legislative Affairs in the Department of Justice. In addition to being a lawyer, Mike held a PhD in political science from Claremont Graduate University. With a deep understanding of the Constitution and a principled conservative philosophy, Mike was astute, kind, and a natural teacher. He took an interest in me, and we were to have many stimulating discussions over lunch. Spending time with him was like getting a graduate education in political philosophy.

When I started my clerkship, Chris was pregnant with our first child. In December 1977 our daughter Mary was born. We went into her first pediatric appointment days after her birth, beaming with pride. The pediatrician started moving his stethoscope around her chest. He frowned. My heart jumped. Chris looked nervously at him, and then me. He called his partner to come in. His partner listened to Mary's heart and then started talking medicalese to our pediatrician.

"Yes, I think they had better get her right up to Frank," said the partner.

The pediatrician turned to us, "Don't be alarmed, but you should get Mary up to Children's Hospital. You will be going to see Dr. Frank Galioto. I will call ahead to make sure he'll see you right away."

"You mean now? What's going on?" I asked.

"She may have a congenital heart defect. The sooner we have it assessed, the better."

I drove like a maniac up to National Children's Hospital in Northwest DC, cutting down one-way streets in the wrong direction to save time. That was totally unnecessary, but I did not know that at the time. Arriving at Children's, we were quickly seen by Dr. Galioto, a kind and caring pediatric cardiologist, who ordered a battery of tests. It turned out Mary had two problems: one, a hole between her atria, which is not that uncommon, and the other, the misrouting of the major artery into the wrong part of her heart. The net effect was that only a portion of her blood was being properly oxygenated. Dr. Galioto said she would require surgery, but optimally he would wait until she was five and monitor her in the meantime. Mary's arrival, and future health care needs, got me focusing on employment after my clerkship.

During my clerkship I decided that I would not go back to the CIA. I was departing from my original plan of a career in intelligence. This was partly due to my lack of respect for Admiral Turner's leadership, but I also was becoming more enthralled by the law. I enjoyed the discipline involved in thinking about legal issues, researching them, and engaging in the give-and-take of legal argument. Law can be consuming. The old saying among lawyers is that "Law is a jealous mistress." The mistress had snared me.

Although I had decided not to return to the CIA, I really had no idea about the world of private practice. Unlike full-time law students, who spend summers working in law firms, I had never set foot in one. Judge Wilkey advised me on applying to DC law firms, recommending all the big and established names. But he also wanted to introduce me to a friend and one of his Harvard Law School classmates, whom he referred to as General Ramsay Potts, a founder of a large firm that was still very much on the rise: Shaw, Pittman, Potts & Trowbridge. I ended up applying to ten firms, including Potts's.

When I went to my first interview—at a prestigious boutique litigation firm—I knew nothing about law firms or their ethos. Lawyers generally like talking about their cases, and, as I was to learn later, the best way to ingratiate yourself with an interviewer was to show deep interest in his or her cases. My first interviewer, a litigator, spent most of the time talking about his cases and accomplishments, then paused and asked, "Well, let me see if you have any questions. What would you like to know?" This is where I was supposed to show how impressed I was with his work.

"What kind of health care benefits do you get as an associate here?" I asked. For a split second, the interviewer looked stunned and a little disdainful, as if I had just belched without excusing myself. "*That* is something you will have to ask the admin people," he said with a sniff. I did not appreciate at the time how utterly plebeian it was to make this kind of inquiry in a law firm interview. But I had exposed my shallowness. In my defense, my concerns over health care coverage were natural for a father whose new baby would be needing open-heart surgery. Of all the firms I applied to, this was the only one that did not offer me a position.

I had lunch with Judge Wilkey's friend Ramsay Potts. A fascinating man—brilliant, self-assured but not arrogant, a natural leader. One of the most highly decorated bomber pilots in World War II, Potts was a full colonel by age twenty-seven, and head of operations for the Eighth Air Force by the war's end. After law school, and a stint as aide to the first secretary of the air force, Potts and his partners had built up a highly successful DC law firm. Potts persuaded me that, although his firm was not yet as big as the older firms, it was growing fast, and I would have more opportunity there than at a more established firm. I was attracted to the idea of working with a man of Potts's character. I started as an associate at Shaw, Pittman, Potts & Trowbridge in the fall of 1978. The firm was collegial, with quality people I enjoyed being around, and I was pleased with my mix of work. I felt I had made a good choice and never regretted it.

In the summer of 1980 Christine and I had to make a decision about Mary's treatment. The skilled surgeon at Children's Hospital recommended we not wait five years but opt to have the surgery done right away. Although the risk of working on the smaller heart was theoretically a bit higher, he was confident he could be just as successful with a two-and-a-half-year-old as with a five-year-old. What's more, there was a trade-off: the longer we waited, the higher the risk the current strain on Mary's heart would have some lasting effect. Dr. Galioto was comfortable with moving ahead, and so we decided on that course. It was a stressful time: a little girl who'd been operated on just before Mary died on the operating table. This hit us especially hard because we had gotten to know the child's mother. We were with her in the waiting room. The surgeon met with Chris and me to explain that Mary's case was not as risky, but that didn't diminish our anxiety.

It was a long and elaborate operation. And it succeeded. We were profoundly grateful.

After Ronald Reagan won the 1980 presidential election, Mike

Uhlmann was asked to handle regulatory and legal policy issues on the incoming administration's transition team. He invited me to join him for this two-month assignment. I had a window of time that permitted this, and the law firm approved. My work on the transition brought me into contact with many of the people who would staff the Department of Justice and the White House. Toward the end of the transition, Mike accepted a job as special assistant to the President, on the Domestic Policy Council Staff at the White House under the counselor to the President, Edwin Meese. Mike again asked me to join him, but one of my projects at the law firm appeared to be headed for trial in the spring, and I could not abandon those responsibilities. Also, our second child, Patricia, was due right after Reagan would take office, and it wasn't the right time to make a move anyway.

But a year later, I was ready. In the spring of 1982, the case that had prevented me from leaving was resolved, and Mike renewed his offer. With the firm's blessing, I joined the White House Domestic Policy Council Staff as a "senior adviser" in May 1982. Despite the august title, my position was a junior staff position, but I welcomed the opportunity to work with key figures in the administration and see how the White House operated. I was handling a potpourri of legal and conservative social issues. As it turned out, the most fateful aspect of my brief stint in the Reagan White House was my getting to know Vice President Bush's counsel, Boyden Gray, a talented, seasoned lawyer and a joy to work with,

The White House during Reagan's first term was often presented in the media as disorganized or fractured. Come to think of it, the press presents *every* Republican White House as disorganized and fractured and every Democratic one as a well-oiled machine. But in light of all I've seen and experienced there since, the Reagan White House was the model of organization. It was run by the famous troika: James Baker, the chief of staff, making sure decision-making was reached through a coherent process and was implemented effectively; Ed Meese, the counselor to the President, in charge of developing policy; and Michael Deaver, the communications guru who orchestrated the administration's messaging. There were often tensions and infighting, of course, but still the overall process was successful at forging the different elements at the White House into an integrated effort in pursuit of the President's agenda.

But as much as I enjoyed government service, I realized I would end up spending most of my legal career in the private sector and thought it was important to make partner in the firm at the same time as my associate class. In October 1983 I returned to the firm, resumed private practice, and was elected a partner on schedule. After our third child, Margaret, was born in 1984, Chris left her library position at Georgetown and stayed at home with the girls for a time.

In the early summer of 1988 Vice President Bush, who was preparing to run for president, asked Bob Kimmitt to conduct background assessments on various vice presidential choices. Bob asked me to help him on this project, along with Fred Goldberg, former chief counsel of the Internal Revenue Service; and Jan Baran, a leading campaign finance lawyer. On a crash basis, the four of us reviewed the backgrounds of several potential running mates, including Jack Kemp, Bob Dole, Dan Quayle, and others. Our mission wasn't to make a recommendation but only to identify and assess potential controversies.

In briefing Vice President Bush about Dan Quayle, a US senator at the time, Bob went over the fact that he had joined the National Guard in 1969 after graduating from college, a move that removed him from the draft. Bob noted that Democrats and their media allies could be counted on to claim that Quayle, in effect, dodged the draft. But enlisting in the National Guard was a valid way of discharging one's military obligation, and Quayle applied to a unit that had legitimate openings. Moreover, we found no evidence of favoritism. Bush, Jim Baker, and campaign adviser Bob Teeter were aware that Quayle's National Guard service was a potential issue that would have to be addressed. I had also investigated a golfing weekend involving Quayle and several other congressmen in 1980, when a female insurance lobbyist shared the rental property used by the lawmakers. It was clear that Quayle wasn't involved in any impropriety.

Bob and all of us on his team were kept in the dark on Bush's choice until the first day of the Republican convention in New Orleans in mid-August. Once we all got to New Orleans, Bob was told to meet the Vice President's plane when it arrived and ride to the first convention event with him. Bush would be speaking from the deck of the steamboat *Natchez* to a large crowd assembled in Spanish Plaza.

Bob was with the party on the boat's deck. When he saw me, Goldberg, and Baran in the crowd, he unobtrusively traced the letter *Q* in the air with his finger. So it was Quayle. The three of us went back to the hotel to assemble all of the material we had on him.

Predictably, the press pounced on Quayle at his first press conference after his selection was announced. While the media would have hit the forty-one-year-old anyway on his alleged lack of experience—despite four years in the House and eight in the Senate—and his National Guard service, the campaign had not taken the time to prepare him for that first outing. A number of his answers gave the media an opening. There was the usual media feeding frenzy, accompanied by scurrilous rumors that Quayle had paid someone to take the bar exam for him and that he had used connections to jump over others for his National Guard position. I, along with Kimmitt and the other members of his team, spent the whole convention in our hotel rooms on the phones, running down allegations and witnesses around the country, to respond to a flood of attacks.

We used an informal network of former Reagan administration lawyers throughout the country to help us track down the facts. At the end of the convention, Jim Baker put together a team dedicated for the duration of the campaign to supporting Quayle and responding to the false allegations. That was a relief to us.

As both a congressman and a senator, Quayle boasted an impressive record of legislating. As I think about the media's attacks on Quayle for his alleged lack of experience, I have to laugh at the same media's adulatory treatment of Barack Obama, John Edwards, and Kamala Harris when they first ran for high office. *Their* lack of relevant experience made them outsiders, unsullied by Washington, above politics. Later, I would work closely with Quayle and found him highly intelligent, unaffected, and a savvy leader.

I had no formal role in the campaign, stayed at my firm, and occasionally helped out by drafting a policy paper. After Bush handily won the election against Massachusetts governor Michael Dukakis, Boyden Gray asked me to join the transition staff, working on legal and regulatory matters, and Mike Uhlmann was asked to head the transition team for the Department of Justice. I was definitely hoping to serve in the new administration.

One thing had come back into my life in these years: piping. I had put it aside in 1968, but while I worked in the Reagan White House, I had a sudden, unaccountable yearning to take it up again. I knew of a superb pipe band in the Washington area that had grown out of the old US Air Force Pipe Band, which had performed at President John F. Kennedy's funeral. It was now a civilian outfit known as Denny & Dunipace Pipe Band (not to be confused with the Scottish band of the same name). Soon after I joined, the band became the Scottish & Irish Imports Pipe Band and, later still, the City of Washington Pipe Band. I was welcomed into the fold, started attending weekly practice, and competed with the band beginning in 1982 in the United States and Canada. We made several trips to Scotland between 1984 and 1990 to compete in Scottish contests, including the World Pipe Band Championships—where the band did very well.

Piping quickly became a source of cheer and solace for me. In the frenetic years to come, I would need it.

PART II

BUSH YEARS

CHAPTER 3

TOP EGGHEAD

During the transition, Boyden Gray and Mike Uhlmann had decided that I would make a good Assistant Attorney General for the Office of Legal Counsel. This was not an office I'd had my eye on. I thought it might be a little too "ivory tower" for me—too academic. I'd often heard the OLC staff referred to as the Department of Justice's "eggheads." Those who previously held the position often went on to judgeships: Judge Wilkey, Justice Scalia, and Chief Justice William Rehnquist. I was not interested in being a judge.

Boyden told me that President Bush felt strongly that the powers of the presidency had been eroded steadily since Vietnam and Watergate, and one of his highest priorities was to gradually restore the office's authority. Both the President and Boyden wanted someone at OLC who shared that view, and they knew I did. Boyden, who was slated to serve as White House counsel, told me that, after the President picked all the cabinet heads and their deputies, I would be the first sub-cabinet-level appointment. I agreed to the job. Boyden sent me over to interview with Dick Thornburgh, who was staying on from the Reagan administration as Bush's AG.

When the office of Attorney General was established by the Judiciary Act of 1789, it was a part-time, one-person office. The AG originally had two functions: (1) to litigate on behalf of the United States in the Supreme Court; and (2) to provide his "advice and opinion upon questions of law when required by the President of the United States, or when requested by the heads of any of the departments, touching any matters that may concern their departments." The Department of Justice wasn't created until 1870, and, at that time, the AG was given authority over all federal prosecutions and most of the government's civil litigation functions. Two senior department officials are responsible for assisting the AG in carrying out that office's two original responsibilities. The Solicitor General is in charge of litigating in the Supreme Court. The Assistant Attorney General for the Office of Legal Counsel is responsible for providing advice and formal legal opinions to the President and executive branch departments and agencies.

The department's headquarters, built in 1935, is an imposing building with Art Deco features, located on Constitution Avenue between Ninth and Tenth Streets, NW. It's generally referred to in the department as Main Justice. The AG and his staff are situated in a large suite of offices on the fifth floor. Those offices are flanked by the offices of the two officials who help the AG carry out his two original duties. On one side of the AG's suite are the offices of the Solicitor General and his lawyers; on the other side, the offices of the Assistant AG for OLC. Composed of about twenty to twenty-five lawyers, OLC is supposed to be, short of the AG personally, the final arbiter of legal issues within the executive branch. Its principal customer is the White House, and therefore the office works closely with the White House counsel. But it also advises all internal DOJ components, as well as all executive departments and agencies outside the department, when any of them requires guidance on a difficult legal issue. OLC's opinions are binding within the executive branch.

I had admired Dick Thornburgh from afar but had never met him. Before succeeding Ed Meese as Attorney General at the end of the Reagan administration, he'd had a distinguished career as US attorney in Pittsburgh, the head of DOJ's Criminal Division, and governor of Pennsylvania. I was a little anxious at the prospect of being legal adviser to such an accomplished lawyer. But we had an easygoing interview, and he offered me the position. As Dick told me, he really needed help. The Deputy Attorney General's job was vacant, and he did not plan on filling the Associate AG job, the department's number three slot. Once confirmed, I would be the first Bush appointee in the building.

Confirmation went quickly and without opposition. I took office officially in April 1989. During confirmation, I established a decent relationship with the Judiciary chairman, Democratic senator Joe Biden of Delaware. In those days, he was a centrist whose views on law enforcement could almost be termed conservative.

Once I heard I'd be the nominee, I called Mike Luttig to ask if he'd consider being my principal deputy. Mike was an outstanding lawyer at the Davis Polk firm. He had clerked for Judge Scalia before Scalia had been nominated to the Supreme Court. Mike and I had both worked in the Reagan White House, and I admired his work and character immensely. I knew it was presumptuous of me to ask him to work as my deputy because Mike was as qualified as I was to head the OLC. I've always been grateful that he agreed to take the job.

Thornburgh's immediate staff was composed largely of aides who had been with him when he was governor. One of the raps against Dick was that he was insulated by this group of Pennsylvanians. While they were protective of the AG, neither I nor Luttig had much trouble working with them. It helped that we were the only Bush-appointed officials in the building for a while, and there was a constant need to consult us for legal advice.

Thornburgh's first choice to be Deputy Attorney General, or DAG, was Robert Fiske, the former US attorney in New York. He ran into opposition from some key conservative Republicans, and the nomination bogged down and was eventually withdrawn. The Deputy and Associate AG jobs remained unfilled. As a practical matter, for the first eight months of my time at the department, until December 1989, I helped Thornburgh fill that void. Ken Starr stepped down from his judgeship and joined the DOJ in May as the Solicitor General, bringing along as his principal deputy John Roberts, a top-flight lawyer from the DC firm of Hogan & Hartson. I already knew both Starr and Roberts from my time in the Reagan administration.

One key move by Thornburgh was to have a lasting effect on my career. The Attorney General usually participated on the National

Security Council (NSC) at the White House. General Brent Scowcroft was the President's national security adviser, and Robert Gates, a former senior intelligence official, was Scowcroft's deputy. Gates chaired a body called the "deputies committee," which reported to the NSC and was responsible for developing policy options and helping the council manage national security issues. Thornburgh said he wanted me to represent him on the deputies committee because I had some national security experience and because they usually wanted DOJ to provide legal advice, and that was my role. The other members of the committee were Bob Kimmitt, undersecretary of state; Paul Wolfowitz from the Defense Department; Admiral Dave Jeremiah, vice chairman of the Joint Chiefs of Staff (JCS); and Richard Kerr, deputy director of the CIA. Under Gates's superb leadership, this committee became a close-knit and smooth-working operation. It was the most effective and competent group in government I have been associated with. I believe my work with Scowcroft, Gates, and the rest of President Bush's national security team played a big role in the President's decision to appoint me Attorney General in 1991.

An issue came up early in my tenure at OLC in which the President was deeply interested. Fiscal responsibility was a dominant political matter at the time. The 1988 Republican Party platform promised to use every available tool to control spending, including consideration of the so-called inherent line-item veto power of the President. Congress frequently passes legislation that couples together in one bill separate spending provisions as part of a compromise. Some were arguing that the Constitution does not define what a "bill" is, and therefore the President can treat the two provisions as separate bills and veto one provision in the legislation presented to him, while signing the other. President Bush had said publicly that he was considering doing this, and he asked me to determine whether claiming this inherent line-item veto authority could be squared with the Constitution. One of President Reagan's heads of OLC, Chuck Cooper, had concluded that there was no such power. I had asked my OLC team to look back throughout all British history, and early Colonial and American experience, to see if it could find any supporting precedent.

One day, after an event in the East Room of the White House, the President waved me and Boyden Gray over to talk to him. "I'm getting a lot of pressure to assert line-item veto authority and take the case to the Supreme Court," he said. "You fellows have a view yet?"

"It's not looking good, Mr. President," I said. "We've gone back to the earliest precedents and can't find anything that really helps. If you asserted it, I think we'll probably lose in the Supreme Court."

Boyden agreed with me.

"Fellows," the President said in his characteristically relaxed tone, "I want to restore presidential authority. But the worst thing we could do is to reach too far and get slapped down early. We'll just end up weakening the presidency even further. There are plenty of areas where Congress is clearly out of bounds, and we can fight there first."

This was a sound judgment, in my view. As it turned out, President Bush was eventually successful in recovering a significant portion of presidential authority, particularly in the realm of war powers and foreign affairs.

I found the work at the Office of Legal Counsel rewarding. I enjoyed analyzing, researching, and drafting opinions on the toughest legal issues facing the government. Of all the positions I held in government, this was the one in which I was happiest. I had not expected that. The lawyers at OLC were all exceptionally intelligent and knowledgeable, and I liked nothing more than sitting around our conference room with them discussing thorny legal issues. Issuing formal opinions was the office's bread and butter. Two of the many opinions I authored leaked out publicly and became controversial at the time—although they shouldn't have been.

One of my controversial opinions addressed the so-called Posse Comitatus statute, which prohibits using the military "as a *posse comitatus* or otherwise to execute the laws." *Posse comitatus*—literally, "power of the county"—refers to the ancient power of the local sheriff to call out the male citizens of the county to help him enforce the law. This is the source of the word *posse* you sometimes hear in Western movies. The statutory restriction on using the military for law enforcement purposes was enacted in 1878 to pacify southern Democrats who resented the use of federal military power to police the South during Reconstruction. The question presented to me was whether this restriction applied *outside* the United States.

Actually, this inquiry popped up a couple of times during my first months in office. The first time, after only a week or so on the job, I got a call from the DOD Deputy General Counsel. Army Special Forces were apparently staging for an operation to arrest a major foreign drug kingpin on the coast of another country. He needed a verbal answer right away, with a written opinion to follow. The question was whether the soldiers' apprehension of the kingpin outside the United States would violate the Posse Comitatus statute. I have told the story—partly true—that after advising the DOD lawyer that *posse comitatus* did not apply and that they could proceed, I got off the phone and called the career deputy in the office, John McGinnis, a brilliant attorney with an encyclopedic knowledge of the law.

"John," I asked, "what is the Posse Comitatus statute?"

I say the story is only partly true because I did, in fact, have an idea of what the statute was about, and I assumed its rationale was to avoid putting the nation's military into direct conflict with American citizens. Therefore, my instinct was that it was not meant to apply outside the United States. Fortunately, McGinnis told me he thought I was right. Unfortunately, the capture operation was aborted.

A short time later, Brent Scowcroft asked for a formal opinion on the question. More and more, we were considering counterterrorism or counter-narcotics operations outside the United States that were, at least partly, law enforcement in nature and would require military forces. In November 1989 I sent Scowcroft an extensive formal opinion advising that the restriction on law enforcement use of the military does not apply to operations outside the United States. Observing that neither the language, history, nor legislative history of the act suggests that Congress intended for it to apply extraterritorially, I concluded that the normal rules of statutory interpretation require construing the restriction as having only a domestic effect. Although the liberal press criticized me, successive administrations, Democrat and Republican, have adhered to this view.

My second opinion that raised a fuss related to "informal rendition"—the practice of arresting and abducting a fugitive inside a foreign country without that country's approval. The opinion was infelicitously referred to as the "Snatch" opinion. The United States faced repeated threats involving terrorism and narcotics trafficking from criminals operating in foreign sanctuaries. The governments creating those sanctuaries either couldn't or wouldn't take action against criminal activity; they were therefore complicit in it. Almost as soon as I arrived at the Department of Justice, the FBI asked me to reassess a Carter-era OLC opinion holding that, because arresting someone in another country without that country's approval violates customary international law, the FBI's statutory arrest powers cannot be interpreted to authorize such an arrest.

That opinion was wrong. Customary international law is just what it says: behavioral norms, arising from prevailing practice, that have never been formally agreed to in a treaty and made part of US law. Because it is not part of our domestic law, violations of customary law do not create legal rights for individuals. They simply give rise to a "political" dispute between the United States and the country whose sovereignty has been infringed. My opinion ruled that the FBI and other US agencies have the power, under the President's direction, to carry out law enforcement operations in other countries even if they impinge on another country's sovereignty. As I made clear, I was not offering advice on the wisdom of conducting these operations, merely on whether we had the power to conduct them. While the commentariat criticized the opinion at the time, subsequent administrations have adhered to it.

Although OLC is often seen as an ivory tower, one of the ironies of my tenure was the office's heavy involvement in the administration's first two military and law enforcement operations. In September 1989 one of the most destructive hurricanes recorded by the National Weather Service up till that time swept through the Caribbean. Packing winds of 140 to 160 miles per hour, Hurricane Hugo struck Saint Croix in the US Virgin Islands—home to fifty thousand residents—on the evening of September 17. The storm didn't let up until the next morning. Hugo destroyed 70 percent of structures on the island. Communications were completely shut down. At two in the morning on September 19, I was awakened by a call from DOJ's Command Center. AG Thornburgh was not available, and because there still was no Deputy AG, I was next in line. The Command Center operator said a Coast Guard commander needed to talk to me about an emergency.

"Put him through," I said, shaking off my grogginess.

The connection was staticky, but I could make out what he was saying:

"Sir, we have picked up a ham radio operator on Saint Croix. Says he's a deputy US marshal, that there's a total breakdown of law and order, and things are very dangerous. Maybe five hundred or six hundred prisoners released. Armed gangs roaming the streets. Some of the National Guard is involved in the looting. Total anarchy."

"Where are you?" I asked.

"I'm heading there, full speed," he replied. "Should get there by daybreak, and I can put a small landing party ashore. Other cutters are en route. But we'll need help. The marshal wanted to make sure you know he'll try to keep your people safe, but it's dicey."

"I'll get on it," I said and signed off. The department had a US attorney's office in the Virgin Islands, and a number of lawyers, support personnel, and a couple of deputy US marshals were on Saint Croix.

I thought, *Now what? I'm the department's resident egghead, and I have this dropped in my lap.* I immediately called Floyd Clarke, the deputy FBI director. The bureau had no one on Saint Croix, and all communications with the island were out. Floyd said he would have an FBI team fly in from Puerto Rico right away on a small plane just to assess the situation. We agreed, pending more intelligence, that it might be good to start the process of getting an Air National Guard transport to position at Andrews Air Force Base, right outside DC, in case we needed to get some federal agents down there. Saint Croix is a US territory, and I had to figure out what was needed and what we had to do to supply it. I contacted the US Marshals Service (USMS) and told it to move its Special Operations Group (SOG) of more than fifty deputy marshals (based primarily in Louisiana) up to DC right away. I knew the FBI's elite Hostage Rescue Team (HRT) of more than fifty operators at the time, based in Quantico, Virginia, was always ready to go. Mike Luttig started working on all the legal issues.

By midday, I was able to give the Attorney General a good picture of the situation. The two FBI agents had flown in and come back out to report. The scene was apocalyptic: armed gangs running wild; violent prisoners on the loose; nearly everything of value looted; food and water running out; no law enforcement authority in sight. The Coast Guard reported that people were fleeing by swimming out to their cutters. A landing party had set up a small perimeter by one dock area; the refugees were telling the Coast Guard that many residents had congregated for security at the homes of households that had firearms. The local National Guard and police officers were involved in the looting. A big problem was the governor, Alexander Farrelly, who was on Saint Thomas, not Saint Croix, and kept issuing statements that there was no emergency, and he did not need any law enforcement help.

Luttig and I laid out the options for the Attorney General. There were only two choices to get law enforcement down there: either federal law enforcement officers or regular military forces. Because of the Posse Comitatus statute, the regular military ordinarily can't be used for law enforcement purposes on US territory. An exception is provided by the Insurrection Act of 1807, which allows the President to proclaim an emergency and use military force to suppress violent rioting. The last time it was employed had been more than twenty years before to deal with rioting in DC after Martin Luther King's assassination. We expected that Governor Farrelly would squawk about our sending down federal forces, but if it had to be done, his objection made no difference.

I proposed to the Attorney General that I would work on two parallel tracks that were not mutually exclusive. First, I would prepare an all-DOJ response that would allow us to act alone. We would prepare to fly down around 120 FBI and deputy US marshals to "protect federal employees, federal facilities, and the federal function" in Saint Croix. We could send in more agents if needed. We would ask the governor to delegate all local law enforcement powers to the federal agents—but we weren't counting on a friendly response.

On a second parallel track, I would alert Bob Gates at the White House what we were up to and suggest that the President might consider using the military. From all reports, the island was a humanitarian disaster area and would need a significant federal presence for a while. DOJ could provide some immediate public safety, but a longer-term solution would probably require troops.

Thornburgh liked the plan. I called Gates, filled him in, and explained what would be entailed if the President wanted to use the military. I told him we felt our DOJ people on the island were in danger, and we wanted to move as quickly as possible and would like to fly our team down as early as that evening. He asked me not to do that until we talked further. Later that afternoon, Gates called to say he was hoping not to hold us up too much, but the President was considering sending troops. He asked me to come over to the White House to meet with the chairman of the Joint Chiefs, Admiral William Crowe. When I met with Crowe in the Situation Room, he unrolled a commercial Saint Croix street map on the table. *Oh boy*, I thought. *This is gonna be back of the envelope.*

Crowe was trying to figure out what force level might be needed and how the military could sync up with agents so that law enforcement decisions would be made by our agents rather than by the soldiers. This hadn't been done in twenty years, and the military wanted to ensure that its soldiers were not dragged into legal problems they were unfamiliar with. I had already discussed this with Floyd Clarke, and I explained to the admiral that we were proposing to break into small patrol teams of federal agents buddied up with military police. Crowe liked this idea. DOJ held off conducting our own solo operation that night, hoping the military would get its act together soon.

At about seven thirty the next morning, September 20, I walked into my office to find sitting in my reception area an army lawyer, Major Bruce Kasold, with an immense binder under his arm. He had come to help OLC assemble all the legal documentation needed for deploying the army under the Insurrection Act. The binder's title was something like "Procedures for Deploying Military Forces for Domestic Emergencies." I thought: *What a gift! God bless the US Army*. It contained everything needed, including flow charts of the steps that were required and even forms for the necessary presidential proclamation and related orders. Major Kasold, a West Pointer, was a terrific lawyer, and we worked closely over the next several days, becoming friends in the process. (Later, President George W. Bush appointed Kasold as a judge on the US Court of Appeals for Veteran Claims.)

We got all the paperwork over to the White House, and . . . waited. And waited. Meanwhile, some refugees from Saint Croix had made it off the island with horror tales, and notes were being carried out by small planes. Congressmen were hearing from constituents with relatives trapped on the island, and I was getting bombarded by calls from Capitol Hill. One note carried out from a young man to his parents, written in pencil, read: "Mom and Dad, still alive. Take the worst you've heard and double it. Please send 9mm/.45 automatic. This is not a joke."

One woman who made it out said, "Everyone was looting: National Guardsmen in uniform, policemen. There's no law and order. They're holding up gas stations. They're holding up everything."

Gates got back to me. The President was signing all the papers, and well over a thousand military police would be flying down starting late that night. I was cleared to send our FBI and USMS team aboard a C-130 military transport plane that evening. The Virgin Islands governor was still saying there was no problem, and he did not need help. That afternoon, Luttig and I drafted a letter for Farrelly's signature, requesting assistance and thanking the President for sending federal law enforcement and the military. We also prepared a directive for the governor, deputizing the federal agents with all local law enforcement powers.

"I don't think he is going to sign this stuff," Mike said.

"Oh, I think he will, Mike," I said. He looked at me quizzically. "Because you're going to persuade him to."

"You want me to go down with our team?" he said. "Why me?"

"Because I am indispensable, and you are not," I deadpanned. Mike gave his usual uproarious laugh. "You tell the governor that he has a choice. He can sign these documents, and we'll all smile and present a united front, or we'll explain publicly how he's endangering the lives of his citizens and grossly neglecting his duty."

In the early evening, I got a call from Mike. He was with the transport plane at Andrews, waiting to take off. "Bill, visualize this scene," he said in a stage whisper. "The interior of the plane. Sitting rigidly on each side are rows of guys facing each other in camo, combat boots, grasping their M-16s, and looking tough. Then suddenly me—in chinos, an Izod shirt, and Hush Puppies, clutching my little portfolio of papers."

I joined in with Mike's roaring laugh.

Things went smoothly. The FBI's HRT and the US Marshals' SOG landed in Saint Croix that night and started making arrangements for the joint patrol teams that would be deployed around the island as soon as the sixteen military transport planes carrying more than 1,100 military police and equipment arrived in the hours ahead. Mike had his tête-à-tête with Governor Farrelly, who suddenly perceived the need for assistance and delegated local law enforcement authority to the federal agents. Order was restored quickly. The military was required to stay on for some weeks to help with disaster relief. Mike Luttig came home in glory, and I awarded him the OLC's first Distinguished Service Ribbon for Gallantry in the performance of legal duties. Thornburgh thanked me for my leadership in the affair and told me the President had been impressed with DOJ's quick and effective response.

For a long time, though, I would answer late-night phone calls from the Justice Command Center with a little trepidation.

Throughout 1989, the deputies committee was focused intently on General Manuel Noriega's dictatorial regime in Panama. In the last years of the Reagan administration, relations between the United States and Noriega deteriorated as he moved closer to Cuba, Nicaragua, and Libya. In February 1988 Noriega was indicted by federal grand juries in Miami and Tampa on charges of racketeering, drug smuggling, and money laundering arising from his involvement with Colombia's Medellin cocaine cartel. Following his indictment, Noriega, propped up by his fourteen-thousand-strong Panamanian Defense Force, or PDF, embarked on a campaign of harassing US military personnel and their families based in Panama. That, in addition to threatening American citizens, flagrantly violated American treaty rights. Between February 1988 and May 1989, more than six hundred incidents were reported, including beatings, sexual harassment of American females, strip searches, and prolonged detentions. Panama and the Panama Canal were strategically important to the United States. That they were run by a hostile and corrupt dictator was not acceptable.

We had hoped for an internal political solution. But in May 1989 Noriega declared null and void the results of Panama's presidential elections, in which a pro-democracy coalition led by Guillermo Endara had scored a substantial victory. Noriega's paramilitary street thugs, known, perversely enough, as "Dignity Battalions," assaulted Endara and his vice presidential running mate, Guillermo "Billy" Ford, on the streets, beating and bloodying Ford with a steel pipe and executing his bodyguard. At that point, the deputies committee started considering in earnest an array of options to protect Americans and our treaty rights in Panama. Over the summer, the United States gradually increased the number of combat troops at our bases in Panama and started drawing down American dependents in the country.

In October 1989 a Panamanian Defense Force major launched a coup attempt, planning to capture Noriega and persuade him to retire. The coup leader asked for limited US support: essentially, blocking certain roads to prevent the arrival of pro-Noriega PDF elements. We were cautious because we thought this could be a Noriega ruse to discredit America, and we also thought the plan to let Noriega retire, instead of turning him over to the United States for prosecution, was unrealistic. In any event, once the coup was launched, PDF reinforcements arrived by air, not the roads, and Noriega crushed it ruthlessly, summarily executing the PDF members who had been involved.

After the coup's failure, there was a strong consensus on the deputies committee, and among our principals, that we had to be ready to take decisive action to remove Noriega if and when events warranted. A number of options were prepared, including a military plan called Operation Blue Spoon, for taking swift control of Panama, arresting Noriega, dismantling the PDF, and supporting a pro-democracy interim government.

In December 1989 Noriega proclaimed himself "Maximum Leader." The Panamanian National Assembly met on December 15 and, led by Noriega, wielding a machete menacingly, declared that a state of war existed between the Republic of Panama and the United States. The next evening, PDF forces shot three American officers, killing one. They took a navy officer and his wife into custody, assaulted the officer and threatened to rape his wife. Although I was not aware of it at the time, President Bush reviewed Blue Spoon plans on December 17 and made the decision to proceed. The operation called for a thunderclap invasion by the approximately thirteen thousand troops stationed at US bases in Panama, reinforced by an additional thirteen thousand troops coming in from the States.

On the afternoon of Tuesday, December 19, Thornburgh was holding his Christmas Party, and the AG suite was crowded with more than 250 guests and DOJ officials. At his request, I had agreed to play my bagpipes as the entertainment. I had just finished playing, when Thornburgh came up behind me and whispered, "You need to get down to the White House right away; you are in for a long night."

I whispered back: "South of the border?"

He nodded.

There I was in kilts and full Highland regalia. The thought occurred to me that I should go directly to the Situation Room. But conventionality prevailed, and I rushed home to change clothes.

I spent the night in the Situation Room drafting the legal justifications for the operation and preparing presidential orders directing the military to arrest Noriega and other persons under indictment for drug offenses. DOJ was sending the Marshals' SOG as well as agents from the US Drug Enforcement Administration (DEA) to help make the arrest of Noriega and a limited number of Panamanian Defense

Force officers believed to have been potentially involved in his illegal activities.

The invasion of Panama, called Operation Just Cause, was justified under the United Nations Charter to protect American lives and our rights under the Panama Canal treaties. We had four objectives: one, to safeguard American lives; two, to defend the democratic election process in Panama; three, to protect US rights under the Panama Canal treaties; and four, to apprehend Noriega and return him to the United States for trial on the drug trafficking and money laundering charges. OLC and lawyers from the US State Department had helped choreograph one of the initial actions taken as part of Just Cause. That night, pro-democracy leaders were taken onto an American base, and Guillermo Endara was sworn in as the new interim president of Panama. President Bush immediately recognized him as the legitimate president, and Endara requested the United States to intervene to support him. Under US law, the President's recognition of a foreign government as the rightful government is definitive.

As initial military objectives were achieved, the law enforcement mission kicked into gear. Military units, joined by a small number of DEA agents and deputy US marshals, went in search of Noriega and PDF members on our arrest list. The plan was to apprehend Noriega and bring him to the United States as quickly as possible. We would decide later how to handle any PDF officers we took into custody. Although Noriega was at first able to evade capture, our forces quickly began cornering PDF targets. Scowcroft wanted to be sure that the law enforcement operation on the ground in Panama was strictly controlled, and he and I had previously agreed that all arrests of Panamanians would have to be cleared in advance by both of us personally. The logistics for this were a bit clunky. I already had a secure telephone—an STU-III—installed at my home; now I had a second one put in. One allowed me to communicate directly with military unit commanders and DEA agents in the field; the other directly with Scowcroft at the White House.

My parents were visiting us for Christmas and, throughout the holiday season, watched in amused fascination as Scowcroft and I co-ordinated arrests more than four thousand miles away. They would see me in my living room with a clunky telephone handset held up to each ear. On one phone would be a military commander whose unit had just captured a pocket of PDF members and needed approval to arrest one he believed to be on the list. On the other phone, I would have the White House. Once I had confirmed the captive's identity, I would get Scowcroft's approval over the phone and then immediately convey this approval to the field commander or embedded DEA agent.

On December 24, the fifth day of operations, Noriega was still at large. It was becoming an embarrassment. My daughters were singing at the National Shrine of the Immaculate Conception in Washington, DC, for the five o'clock Christmas Eve Mass. My wife and I had just arrived at the shrine early to watch rehearsal, when I received an emergency communication that the White House was sending a car to retrieve me and take me to the Situation Room. When I got there, I understood the rush.

We'd found him. Manuel Noriega had just entered the Papal Nunciature—the Vatican embassy—in Panama, seeking refuge. The army officer in charge at the scene was patched into the Situation Room on a speakerphone. He was asking advice: "Sir, we are worried that the nunciature will put Noriega in one of their diplomatic vehicles and drive him out of the compound and through our cordon. What do we do if a car comes down the drive with him in it?"

I thought for a moment, then said: "Take him out."

There was a long silence.

"Take him out, sir?"

"Remove him physically from the vehicle," I instructed, realizing suddenly the need for great precision of language. I was not going to allow Noriega to escape and lead us on another chase.

Ultimately, the nunciature pressured Noriega to surrender, which he did on January 3, 1990. He was immediately taken into custody by DEA agents and US marshals, rushed to a waiting C-130, and flown to Miami. That commenced a long and hard-fought prosecution. This was the first time in history that a foreign head of state had been brought to the United States to stand trial for offenses committed outside the country. Noriega presented a withering array of legal challenges to his arrest and prosecution, raising many of the novel issues upon which I had earlier given opinions.

Later, in the fall of 1991, when I was Acting Attorney General, I joined President Bush at a law enforcement event on the National Mall. Afterward, he asked me to ride back with him in his car. As we headed back, he observed that Noriega's trial was finally about to start.

"How confident are you we'll win a conviction?" he asked.

"We will win, Mr. President," I replied.

"Well," he continued, "I invaded Panama—sent twenty-six thousand troops to arrest him—and it would be bad form at this stage to lose the case." He smiled. "No pressure."

While he was asking gently, I knew the concern was real. The President was moving into an election year, and if we failed to convict Noriega, it would be a big black eye. I reassured him: "Don't worry, Mr. President. We have our best people on this, and I guarantee we will win."

As soon as I got back to the department, I called down to the head of the Criminal Division, Bob Mueller. More than a year and half earlier, when Noriega was arrested, Attorney General Thornburgh had bypassed the Miami US attorney and put Mueller in charge of assembling the prosecution team. He had put together a top-notch team of our best prosecutors from Florida, augmented with talent from elsewhere in the DOJ.

"Bob," I said, "I just want you to know that I guaranteed the President we would win the Noriega trial."

He laughed and said, "We will."

Bob Mueller had arrived at Main Justice shortly after I did. He had been a federal prosecutor in Boston and was initially brought in to serve on Thornburgh's staff as a counselor. He had been a classmate of Thornburgh's chief of staff, Robin Ross, first at St. Paul's prep school in New Hampshire and then at Princeton University. I admired Bob. After Princeton, he served as a US Marine officer in Vietnam and was highly decorated. We became friends, as did our wives. Bob was a hard-nosed prosecutor. I would say about Bob in those days that he was true marine: if you told him to take a hill, he would take it, no matter what the cost.

We were fortunate to have as the trial judge one of the great jurists in the country, William M. Hoeveler. He presided over a complex trial with novel issues, repeatedly made sound rulings, and brought the trial to successful conclusion. One day in April 1992, when I was Attorney General, I heard someone bellow "Hoo-rah!" from just outside my office door. Bob walked into my office, beaming. As he raised his hand to give me a high five, he boomed, "We got him—guilty!"

Noriega was sentenced to forty years in federal prison. His sentence was later reduced, and in 2010 the United States extradited him to France, where he was convicted of money laundering. A year later, France extradited Noriega to Panama to serve sentences for which he had been convicted in absentia. He died in 2017.

Not long after our successful invasion of Panama, while I was still head of OLC, a young lawyer from Jones Day somehow got himself onto my calendar for a meeting. "What is this meeting about?" I asked him as he made himself comfortable in a big red leather chair in front of my desk.

"I am here to explain to you why you should hire me," he said.

His name was Paul Cappuccio. He handed me his resume, and I perused it. Paul grew up in a working-class family in Peabody, Massachusetts, and then excelled at Georgetown University and later at Harvard Law School. He had been law clerk to both Justices Anthony Kennedy and Antonin Scalia.

"You are right," I said after a few minutes of talking to him. "I should hire you, and you are hired."

"I can't do it right away, but in a few months," he explained. "I just want to make sure you save room for me."

This was the beginning of a long friendship and collaboration both in government and later in the private sector. "Pooch," as his friends call him, is the clearest and most insightful thinker I have encountered in the law. He also retained from his upbringing a direct, no-nonsense mode of expression, as well as practical common sense.

Above all else, like his mentor Scalia, he was engaging, with a keen, sometimes wicked sense of humor.

My year and a half as head of the Office of Legal Counsel turned out to be nothing like what I had anticipated. It did involve some research into dense and arcane parts of American law, but it was far from the ivory tower experience I had feared. It helped prepare me for the more intense crises that lay ahead.

CHAPTER 4

SECOND IN COMMAND

I had just started to get used to my role at the Office of Legal Counsel when the number two spot at Justice became an unsought-for possibility.

Without a Deputy AG in place, many in the department resented the role played by Dick Thornburgh's personal staff, especially Chief of Staff Robin Ross. Feeling under pressure to name a Deputy after his original choice, Bob Fiske, had withdrawn, Thornburgh settled on Don Ayer. He had been US attorney in Sacramento, California, during the first part of the Reagan administration and later Deputy Solicitor General at Main Justice. In Thornburgh's 2003 autobiography, *Where the Evidence Leads*, he describes Ayer as having a "quirky personality." Thornburgh said he'd been warned against appointing Ayer by others in the administration, but "foolishly charged ahead." Ayer was confirmed in November 1989. By February, Thornburgh had decided the choice had been a "mistake."

Ayer had "exaggerated notions of his responsibilities," Thornburgh recollects, and resented the role played by the Attorney General's principal aides. Thornburgh became upset when Ayer made a major policy decision on sentencing in white-collar cases without running it by the AG first, and Thornburgh insisted Ayer retract his decision publicly. It was clear that Ayer could not adjust to Thornburgh's management style. Personally, I thought Ayer behaved oddly. He would stay closeted in his office with his top aide for much of the day, emerging every so often to march up to the Attorney General's office. Clutching the *Code of Federal Regulations* and citing its provisions, he would argue that he should be in charge of various department activities. I thought it would have been more sensible of him to demonstrate his competence as a manager to Thornburgh, and win his trust, than to go charging into the AG's office demanding new turf.

While tension was mounting between Thornburgh and his new Deputy, the AG was dealing with a crisis involving his own staff. Earlier in 1989, the FBI had questioned Democratic congressman Bill Gray of Philadelphia in connection with an investigation, a fact that was leaked to a CBS News reporter. Furious, Thornburgh directed the Criminal Division to conduct a leak investigation, using polygraphs as necessary. Toward the end of 1989, the division completed its report. According to Thornburgh, the report indicated that the leak likely came from Gray's own staff, but there was also some evidence that someone at the department had confirmed it. The polygraphs produced "vague and ambiguous" responses from Thornburgh aide Robin Ross and press secretary Dave Runkel.

Thornburgh was under huge pressure both from within the department and from the media and the Hill to permit further investigation of his aides by the DOJ's Office of Professional Responsibility. By early May 1990, the Attorney General was taking a big hit politically, and Luttig and I decided we owed him our best advice, as tough as it was. We were in the office working on a Saturday. I called Thornburgh at home, and he came in to talk to us. We told him that we felt his effectiveness was being seriously undermined, and it was time to "lance the boil" by moving Ross and Runkel aside. This was very hard for us to tell him—we liked both men, and they had served Thornburgh loyally for many years. But the controversy over them was killing Thornburgh—he was in a quagmire and had to get past it. He realized that, and nodded his head slowly in resignation. "Okay," he said, "what do you suggest?"

I suggested moving them out of the AG's office and putting them in lesser jobs elsewhere on ninety-day assignments. Then, I reasoned, he could decide later if they should stay in the department.

"Okay," he said at last. Then he asked: "Would you talk to them and take care of this?"

I was a little surprised he wanted me to do it but also understood this was tough for him. I said I'd do it.

On Monday, I talked to Ross and Runkel separately and told them both of the decision. Later that day, Thornburgh called me in to tell me that he was going to make changes. He had already talked to Boyden Gray and the President and had gotten their approval to ask Ayer to leave and have me nominated as Deputy Attorney General. He explained, chuckling, that he already had whiffed at the Deputy ball twice, and he knew this was his last swing. He trusted me, but, more important, he knew the President and Boyden would support me, which they did. Pending my confirmation, he wanted me to serve as "acting" Deputy AG as soon as Ayer was out the door. Mike Luttig would be nominated to replace me as Assistant AG for OLC. All of this was announced on May 11, 1990. Thornburgh was at first reluctant to bring in a new chief of staff, but Mike and I persuaded him he needed someone to run his personal staff. The AG asked Mike to serve concurrently as head of OLC and his chief counselor, which was effectively chief of staff. I was quickly and unanimously confirmed by the Senate as Deputy.

On paper, the DAG functions essentially as the DOJ's chief operating officer, running the day-to-day activities across the whole department. Because the number three position remained unfilled, all Justice Department components, both civil and criminal, were reporting through the Deputy's office. This included all ninety-three US attorneys' offices, as well as the litigating divisions at Main Justice: Criminal, Civil, Tax, Civil Rights, Environment and Natural Resources, and Antitrust. It also included all the department's law enforcement components, which at that time consisted of the FBI, DEA, USMS, the Bureau of Prisons (BOP), and the Immigration and Naturalization Service (INS).

While AGs have defined their Deputies' jobs in different ways over the years, Thornburgh asked me to perform the DAG's traditional role of managing the day-to-day work of the department, keeping him apprised of major developments, while he focused more on the international arena, fashioning a network of cooperative agreements with other countries. His international efforts ultimately provided our country with the critical framework for attacking the growing global problems of drug trafficking and foreign terrorism. Since I hadn't been out in the field as a prosecutor, I asked three highly regarded US attorneys to come to Washington, initially on ninety-day stints, and serve as my top associate Deputies. The three were Jim Richmond from the Northern District of Indiana, George Terwilliger from Vermont, and John Smietanka from the Western District of Michigan. They would continue as US attorneys in their districts. As far as we could tell, this had not been done before, but it proved an effective way to integrate the US attorneys into the overall management of the department, reducing the usual friction between the field and headquarters.

As Deputy AG, I continued my role in the national security arena as a member of the deputies committee. Over the preceding year, I had worked closely with Dan Levin, a lawyer on the NSC staff at the White House. Dan possessed a powerful intellect and good common sense—a rare combination. I asked him to come over to Justice to serve as my Associate Deputy responsible for national security matters. One of my new roles was fighting for more money for the department during the appropriations process on the Hill. To help me on this front, I recruited Tim Shea, a skillful and knowledgeable aide to Republican congressman Silvio Conte.

During my time as Deputy, three matters loomed especially large: one, the collapse of the savings and loan industry and marshaling a massive DOJ effort to prosecute the widespread fraud that had contributed to the collapse; two, advising on matters relating to the first Gulf War and coordinating US efforts to protect the homeland from Iraqi terrorist attacks; and three, reorienting the department to give greater priority to tackling the nation's high violent crime rates.

In the late 1980s and early 1990s, about one-third of the approximately 3,200 savings and loan institutions in the country failed. Because depositors' accounts were insured by the federal government, this collapse ended up costing American taxpayers between $150 billion and $175 billion. Soaring interest rates between 1979 and 1982 had caused many S&Ls to experience massive operating losses, and many went bankrupt. By 1982, hundreds were insolvent, and regulators estimated that the cost of closing them and paying off depositors would have been $25 billion. Regulators allowed them to remain in operation, hoping they would make up their losses, but instead, the losses mounted. Things got worse when, under deregulation in the early 1980s, S&Ls received less federal supervision and more power to invest in riskier assets—but still enjoyed federal insurance of their depositors' accounts.

A commission set up later by Congress to examine the S&L debacle reported on the role played by fraud. Noting that most institutions resisted temptation and continued operating safely, the commission concluded:

> While not the cause of the S&L debacle, unprecedented fraud emerged in the S&L industry. Dishonest operators flocked to S&Ls, attracted by governmental policies that unwittingly provided the means and opportunity for fraud. It was no accident so many crooks surfaced in the S&L industry. They went where the money was. In these years, the dishonest profit potential was so high—with little or no risk of financial loss—and chances of getting caught were so low that it is a wonder that fraud was not more widespread.

By the time I became Deputy, the S&L crisis had snowballed into a major political controversy, with each party trying to cast blame on the other. The magnitude of the enforcement task posed a huge managerial challenge. The Democrats were poised to lay blame on the administration for not moving quickly to clean up the mess. A number of high-profile S&L failures had already occurred, and the pipeline of fraud investigations was rapidly growing to several thousand. Lincoln Savings and Loan, a chain of banks headquartered in Irvine, California, had been seized by federal regulators, and a bipartisan group of seven senators were enmeshed in claims they had helped the S&L's owner, Charles Keating, keep federal regulators at bay before its collapse. Five senators who had received sizable contributions from Keating gained notoriety as the "Keating Five."

In a June 1990 address to US attorneys at DOJ, President Bush stressed the importance of an all-out push to investigate fraud in the S&L industry. Thornburgh announced he was appointing US attorney Jim Richmond, on my staff, to serve as Special Counsel, coordinating the thousands of investigations conducted by the twenty-six task forces Thornburgh had set up around the country. As S&Ls continued to fail, and some infamous instances of fraud were uncovered, Congress—under heavy pressure to respond—enacted the Financial Institution Reform, Recovery, and Enforcement Act in August 1990. That law imposed new regulatory standards on S&Ls and created a new watchdog agency, the Office of Thrift Supervision, to oversee them.

I asked Congress for a new bill providing the Justice Department more resources and legal authority, and spent a whole day—it lasted till two in the morning—sitting in a large room in the Capitol negotiating different provisions with an endless stream of senators. In November Congress passed the Crime Control Act of 1990, which gave DOJ additional resources to handle the flood of criminal referrals and made the Special Counsel for Financial Institution Fraud a presidentially appointed, Senate-confirmed position situated in the office of the Deputy Attorney General. Jim Richmond had done an excellent job getting the function up and running, but he was returning to private practice and recommended the acting US attorney in Chicago, Ira Raphaelson, as the new Special Counsel. Ira, a longtime career prosecutor, was confirmed without difficulty and spent the next two years driving a monumental department effort to prosecute fraud in the S&L industry.

With many thousands of referrals pouring in, potentially involving more than a thousand institutions, one of the challenges was prioritizing cases. Working closely with the FBI and regulators, Raphaelson identified certain cases as "major" and labored tirelessly with the bureau to ensure that the necessary resources—agents and prosecutors—were assigned where they were needed most. The DOJ had a 90 percent conviction rate on its highest-priority cases. By the end of the administration, more than a thousand S&L officials were found guilty, and approximately two thousand other persons were convicted for involvement in S&L fraud.

I gauged the success of this effort by the fact that, once we got rolling, there was little criticism of the department's performance from the Hill, and DOJ's response did not become an issue during the 1992 presidential campaign. Even the Clinton administration in 1995 hailed the Justice Department's "tremendous success in bringing to justice those who looted our nation's financial institutions during the 1980s." Following the larger financial collapse in 2008, the impressive track record of convictions secured after the S&L debacle was often contrasted favorably with the absence of any meaningful convictions arising from the later meltdown.

I had been Deputy for about two months when, on August 2, 1990, Iraq invaded Kuwait, a country friendly to the United States. President Bush stated that Iraqi dictator Saddam Hussein's aggression "will not stand." Saddam had amassed a large force in Kuwait within easy striking distance of Saudi Arabia's oil fields. Within days, the President started moving American forces into Saudi Arabia to protect this important ally, starting with the US Army's Eighty-Second Airborne Division, as well as substantial air and naval power. This defensive operation was called Desert Shield.

The United Nations passed a series of resolutions condemning Iraq's invasion and imposing economic sanctions and an embargo on the Middle Eastern nation. President Bush, working closely with Prime Minister Margaret Thatcher of Great Britain, built up a formidable international coalition of thirty-five countries willing to contribute military resources to Desert Shield, including Muslim countries. Over the ensuing months, the President, Secretary of Defense Dick Cheney, and Chairman of the Joint Chiefs Colin Powell steadily increased US combat strength in the region to almost six hundred thousand. Combined US and coalition forces peaked at approximately a million.

My first role relating to the Gulf crisis involved counterterrorism.

As diplomatic attempts to dislodge Saddam from Kuwait remained at an impasse, it become clear during the fall that war was likely. The deputies committee became concerned that if the United States initiated military operations, the Iraqis would try to expand the war by conducting terrorist attacks against American targets both at home and around the world. We had good reason to be concerned about attacks from Iraqi operatives, as well as attacks by sympathetic Islamic extremists. Iraq had an active biological and chemical warfare program, and the doomsday scenario was a successful biological attack on the homeland. We could not wait for hostilities to start preparing our defenses. I was asked to convene an interagency group and coordinate counterterrorism efforts to protect against attacks inside the United States.

In those days, our ability to defend the homeland from terrorism was primitive compared to what it would eventually become. This was an era when there was no screening of air passengers. There was no Department of Homeland Security, and no single agency had authority to oversee all the facets of domestic security. The main responsibility lay with the DOJ, and specifically with the FBI and the US Immigration and Naturalization Service. I convened a senior-level group consisting of DOJ components (FBI, INS, USMS), Treasury Department components (Bureau of Alcohol, Tobacco, and Firearms, or ATF; US Customs Service; and US Secret Service), the US Postal Service, and a few other elements. The array of challenges was sobering. The problems ranged from tightening up on the scrutiny of people and packages coming into the country to protecting large public events—especially NFL football games scheduled for the fall and winter.

Normally, this sort of overarching initiative from the President would result in defensiveness and complaints about turf. There was none of that in this case. The threat of war and terrorist reprisals brought out a spirit of solidarity that one rarely sees in government.

We jury-rigged solutions to deal with the many holes in our defenses. I leaned heavily on FBI deputy director Floyd Clarke and his team at the bureau. The FBI worked its contacts in the Islamic community by asking that they be on the lookout for two things: hate crimes against Muslims, and anything that might suggest terrorist attacks on behalf of the Iraqis.

Part of our strategy was to convey to the Iraqis that the US homeland would be a tough nut to crack. To this end, we put uniformed agents, including Border Patrol agents, in airports and targeted certain flights for meticulous screening of passengers before allowing entry. The FBI took the laboring oar, working with local law enforcement to step up security at major public events. What we were able to get in place was a pale comparison to what we have today, but we did our best with what we had.

As our troop buildup continued in the Gulf, it was clear to me that, unless Saddam withdrew from Kuwait, the President had every intention of using those forces. He had not deployed a massive military force for show. He meant business. But many Democrats were skittish and saying they wanted to approve any use of force. I suggested to Mike Luttig that he start OLC thinking about the legal and constitutional issues that would come up about the President's authority to use those forces.

Secretary of State Jim Baker appeared before both the House and Senate foreign affairs committees in mid-October. Some Democratic members insisted he promise that Congress would have the opportunity to consider the use of force before it was used. Secretary Baker flatly told the committees that, in the current situation, the power to authorize military force had to remain in the hands of the President. He refused to pledge that Congress would have the chance to approve use of force in advance.

On November 29, 1990, the UN Security Council passed Resolution 678, which gave Iraq until January 15, 1991, to withdraw from Kuwait, and empowered member countries to use "all necessary means" to force Iraq out of Kuwait after the deadline. This started the clock running, at least for the commander in chief. President Bush said he would give Saddam one last chance to resolve the matter peacefully and sent Secretary Baker to meet with Iraq's foreign minister, Tariq Aziz. On January 9, the world held its breath as Baker and Aziz sat down together in Geneva, Switzerland, for seven hours.

Baker emerged from the meeting. After a brief opening statement, he said: "Regrettably, I heard nothing today that suggested to me any Iraqi flexibility." The die was cast.

A debate took place within the President's national security circle. The question was whether Bush should try to get a vote from Congress formally approving operations before launching an offensive. My own view was that, under the circumstances, the President could use force against the Iraqi military in Kuwait without express congressional approval. But I also thought that, if the President worked Congress hard to obtain approval, he would get it. On the other hand, I thought, if he did not press for approval, the Democrats would continue to delay. This would allow them to have their cake and eat it too: if the President acted unilaterally, they could snipe at him, especially if the operation proved costly; and if it was a smashing success, they could claim they were always for it even as they criticized President Bush for going to war unilaterally.

On January 8, 1991, I was called, in Thornburgh's absence, to an expanded National Security Council meeting in the Cabinet Room, the purpose of which was to resolve whether the President should try to get Congress to approve offensive operations. As I was putting on my jacket to leave my office for the White House, I glanced at the TV and saw a senator say that any lawyer who advises the President he can act without congressional approval would be impeached. I was not worried about this, but the comment showed the mounting tensions at the time. In the Cabinet Room, I was seated in the Attorney General's usual position, on the Vice President's left, right across from the President.

George Bush looked serious and determined as he chewed gently on the earpiece of his glasses. He glanced around the table, taking stock of those present: Cheney on the President's left; Deputy Secretary of State Larry Eagleburger, sitting in for Jim Baker, on his right; Scowcroft; Boyden Gray; and the President's chief of staff, John Sununu. Most of the NSC members had also brought their lawyers with them.

"Bill," the President began, "I've been reading all these editorials saying I don't have the power to launch this operation without congressional approval. What is the department's position?"

I wished someone had previewed this question with me. I felt almost like I was having an out-of-body experience. This is probably the ultimate question to ask a constitutional lawyer, and it falls into a gray zone.

I had consulted with Mike Luttig before heading to the meeting. Although the Office of Legal Counsel had not drafted an opinion, it had conducted extensive research, and we were both of the opinion that, under the circumstances, the President could act without explicit congressional approval. I told President Bush I thought there were two reasons he could act unilaterally. First, as commander in chief, the President can use military force to protect our allies and vital US interests. Throughout our history, there have been only five wars declared, yet the President has used military force to protect American interests close to two hundred times—the Korean War being the situation most like what we were facing in Kuwait. Here the United Nations had effectively approved the use of force, and Congress, through a series of acts, had approved and facilitated the deployment of a massive force to deal with Iraq's invasion of Kuwait. The question of how those troops were to be used was a matter for the commander in chief.

I felt there was a second reason the President could unilaterally initiate operations. We were in a situation where almost 600,000 US troops were sitting nose-to-nose with more than 650,000 Iraqi troops in Kuwait alone. After the UN resolution authorizing use of force after January 15, things were on a hair trigger—and even more so now that our diplomatic ultimatum had been rejected. The Iraqis had chemical and biological capabilities, and there was a real prospect they might—if they believed our attack was inevitable—try to hit us first with a preemptive attack that could disrupt our plans. This was a volatile situation and not something Congress could safely manage. As commander in chief, the President had to err on the side of protecting his forces. I advised that, whenever President Bush felt our forces were facing an unacceptable risk of a preemptive attack from the Iraqis, he could clearly act without the approval of Congress.

Nonetheless, I completed my advice by saying that this is a gray zone of law, and that, while not necessary, the President would clearly be in the strongest position if he obtained congressional support for use of force. I added my two cents that I thought a full-court press on the Hill would succeed in getting a resolution passed. Dick Cheney seemed opposed to seeking congressional permission. He asked me if this was legal advice or political advice.

"Both," I answered. "But I am not saying he needs approval."

"Suppose we ask Congress and don't get a resolution?" Cheney challenged. "What would be your advice then?"

"The same. The President could still decide to use force."

"Then he will be in a hole," Cheney said.

His argument was a good one. I agreed that the President would take more of a hit, "but," I said, "I think the chances of getting approval are good, and there's no better way of going to war than with everybody on board." Still, I insisted, what really mattered was how successful the operation would be. If it was a success, everybody would be united. If it turned into a disaster, the White House would be in a lot of trouble.

President Bush went around the table, asking each principal's views. The lawyers present agreed with me, and most of the principals recommended the President go all out to get congressional approval. That day, Bush sent to the Hill a letter crafted to avoid any suggestion that he was constitutionally required to obtain congressional approval. He described the issue as sending Saddam a strong signal of our resolve. "I therefore request that the House of Representatives and the Senate adopt a Resolution stating that Congress supports the use of all necessary means to implement UN Security Council Resolution 678," the President wrote. "Such action would send the clearest possible message to Saddam Hussein that he must withdraw without condition or delay from Kuwait. Anything less would only encourage Iraqi intransigence; anything else would risk detracting from the international coalition arrayed against Iraq's aggression."

The administration worked hard to get the resolutions passed. I had the TV in my office tuned in to the debate and watched for what felt like an eternity. On January 12 Congress gave the President what he had sought, voting to authorize the use of force unless Iraq withdrew from Kuwait. The Senate voted 52 to 47 for the Authorization for Use of Military Force Against Iraq Resolution, as ten Democrats joined with virtually unanimous Republicans in support of the resolution. A short time later, the House approved identical legislation by a vote of 250 to 183.

Once the UN deadline of January 15 passed, the President acted with lightning speed. Thornburgh and I were given advanced notice that the US bombing campaign would begin on the evening of January 16 Eastern Standard Time, so we could ensure our counterterrorism measures were at optimal readiness. That night, I turned on the TV just before our first strikes were scheduled to occur. Right on schedule, American reporters broke into the evening news programs to report that the skies over the Iraqi capital of Baghdad were lit up. This relentless bombing campaign was to continue for five weeks. The offensive to drive the Iraqis out of Kuwait was named Operation Desert Storm.

Before hostilities commenced in the Gulf, the Deputy Attorney General was not assigned any personal security. But once Bush launched Desert Storm, that changed. The FBI started providing an armored vehicle and at least one agent to protect me. The head of AG Thornburgh's detail, Supervisory Agent Jim Kramarsic, assigned one of the AG's agents, Jeff Favitta, to start covering me. I still remember the sobering feeling when I first climbed into the armored limo with Favitta sitting in the front passenger's seat. As the car rolled out of my driveway, I heard the metallic clank as Favitta pulled back the cocking lever on his MP5 submachine gun.

The day after our bombing campaign started, a deadly bomb was found at the residence of our ambassador to Indonesia, hidden in a planter "next to where the ambassador eats breakfast." The battery for the bomb's timer had run down. The attempt was believed to have been carried out by the Iraqis. The next day, a powerful bomb exploded prematurely in Manila, Philippines, as it was being carried by two Iraqi operatives on the way to attack an American target. The evidence was overwhelming that the Iraqi operatives—one of whom survived the blast—were being handled by the Iraqi embassy in Manila. The Philippines expelled a number of Iraqi embassy personnel. The *Los Angeles Times* quoted a senior diplomat as warning, "There's no question in our minds these two were Iraqi terrorists, and they were part of a group dispatched in teams to various parts of the world to carry out terrorist acts in what they call 'deep in the enemy rear.' These guys have been posted all over." Our allies around the world expelled Iraqi diplomats to preempt any terrorist activities. We continued to buttress our domestic defenses as best we could. Especially heightened security was deployed at the Super Bowl and similar high-profile events during the crisis. By the spring, there had been no attacks in the United States, and everyone on the interagency group started breathing easier.

After the five-week bombing campaign, President Bush gave Saddam one last chance to withdraw from Kuwait. Once again he rejected the offer. The next day, February 24, coalition forces launched a massive ground assault that quickly overwhelmed the Iraqis. Coalition forces suffered 147 killed in action, as compared with an estimated 20,000 to 50,000 Iraqis killed. Although the United States and our allies had destroyed the Iraqi military, and some were urging the President to continue on "to Baghdad" to oust Saddam, President Bush ceased our offensive operations once we had liberated Kuwait and achieved our strategic objectives.

Following the failure of our military efforts in the sixties and early seventies in Southeast Asia, President Reagan had described the American people as suffering from "Vietnam syndrome"—an aversion to using military force to defend vital US interests abroad. President Bush's strong leadership during the Gulf crisis, which included methodically building a broad international coalition, and the stunningly effective, clockwork execution of military operations, went a long way to eliminating the Vietnam syndrome—for a time. He showed that the United States was capable of using its military might effectively to defeat aggressors by setting a defined, attainable objective; applying ample military force to achieve victory in the shortest time possible; and then refraining from getting drawn into murkier, open-ended agendas.

Americans watched with pride as the commander of Desert Storm, General Norman Schwarzkopf, led a victory parade down Constitution Avenue. It was the last time the United States would achieve total and indisputable victory in a major military conflict. Our success in that war was in no small measure the result of the careful, competent, and decisive leadership of George H. W. Bush. I only regret that such an achievement was so soon forgotten.

In July 1990 Justice William Brennan, one of the most liberal members of the Supreme Court, had announced his retirement. Since the inception of the administration, OLC had kept a large notebook, assessing about a dozen jurists and distinguished lawyers as potential candidates for Supreme Court appointment in the event of a vacancy. Mike Luttig and I provided support to Attorney General Thornburgh, as he discussed possible candidates with the President, Boyden Gray, and John Sununu. Out of these discussions, initially three principal candidates emerged. Two had always been on the OLC list: our Solicitor General, Ken Starr, and Judge Edith Jones, a federal appellate judge in Texas.

Ken's long tenure in conservative circles in Washington ended up working against him. Over time he had the occasion to disappoint some conservatives on one issue or another and so wasn't thought sufficiently solid. I also sensed that Thornburgh had the feeling that Ken's support on various issues that arose within the department was not as strong as it could have been. The White House started coalescing around two candidates: Jones, a strong and unambiguously conservative candidate, and Judge David Souter, a federal appellate judge in New Hampshire—a dark horse who had not been on the OLC list.

I had interviewed Souter when I was at the Office of Legal Counsel and he was being considered for the First Circuit Court of Appeals, which included New Hampshire. I had not been particularly impressed—his judicial philosophy seemed inchoate. He ended up getting that appeals court slot because he was vigorously supported by his old friends John Sununu (a former governor of New Hampshire) and Senator Warren Rudman of that state. Rudman, one of the President's chief backers on Capitol Hill, was now pushing Souter hard for the Supreme Court, and his support carried weight. Sununu favored considering Souter but wasn't yet committed to him.

The theory for Souter was that he was really a conservative but with no track record, and so he could be a "stealth" candidate. This option held some attraction for the President, who did not want to burn up capital in a fierce ideological battle in the Senate if he could help it. Before heading over to the Oval Office to help the President make his choice, Thornburgh polled Luttig and me for our recommendations. We both recommended Jones. Sununu and Vice President Quayle also recommended Jones. Thornburgh and Gray recommended Souter.

The President chose Souter, who turned out to be one of the court's most liberal members. A colossal mistake.

While the administration had been gaining foreign policy successes, at home the problem of violent crime had become a pressing issue. Before 1960, violent crime had remained stable and at modest levels. Starting in 1960, however, it nearly quintupled in three decades. Most of the increase had occurred during the permissive 1960s and 1970s under the prevailing liberal dogma that criminals were society's victims rather than its victimizers. During this time, as violent crime soared, the incarceration rate dropped. In the 1980s, however, the federal government and a few major states adopted tougher anticrime policies, and, as a result, the trajectory of violent crime's increase had flattened.

By 1991, although crime's rate of increase had slowed, violent crime was at an all-time high and was still escalating. No one was hurt more than those living in the inner cities. I will never forget a meeting I had in a neighborhood barbershop in Trenton, New Jersey. A group of seniors—all African Americans—expressed desperation about crime levels in their neighborhood. "Mr. Barr, we are in our golden years," one silver-haired gentleman said. "After a lifetime of hard work, we should be able to live in peace. Look down the street. See the bars on all the windows? We are the ones behind those bars. We live behind bars while these punks use our streets as a shooting gallery. We are the prisoners—afraid to go out. Please, can the federal government help us?" This was just one of many such encounters I had in cities around the country.

This surge in violent crime posed as serious a problem as we have faced as a nation. I started thinking about how the federal government could help address the crisis. Previously, the federal government's role in battling violent crime had been very limited. But although 95 percent of violent crime falls under state and local jurisdiction, I thought there were ways we at the federal level could bring tough laws to bear, working collaboratively with the state and local law enforcement. I commissioned a series of studies of the violent crime problem and started consulting broadly with state and local law enforcement officials on a bipartisan basis.

Based on my analysis, I concluded that the problem of predatory violent crime was the problem of the chronic violent offender. Numerous studies showed that a tiny fraction of the population were habitual violent offenders who committed most of the predatory violence in our society. These chronic violent criminals committed a staggering number of crimes when they were out on the streets. For example, a 1982 study of 240 criminals found that this small group was responsible for a half million crimes over an eleven-year period—an average of 190 crimes a year. Another study of various state prisoners found that 25 percent of them committed 135 crimes a year, while 10 percent committed 600 crimes a year. A California study of convicted males found that just 3.5 percent of those males committed 60 percent of the crimes committed by the whole group. Numerous other studies came to the same conclusion: a tiny cohort of chronic offenders is disproportionately responsible for the vast amount of predatory violence. This is the crime that is predictable and can be most effectively prevented by the intervention of our criminal justice system.

The identity of these career offenders was not a mystery. They started committing crimes as juveniles—for which they are never held accountable—and kept on committing crimes as adults. They continued committing crimes whenever they were let out of prison on bail, parole, and probation. As a general rule, the recidivism rate of this hard-core element remained stubbornly high and started dropping appreciably only after they reached forty years old.

I concluded that the primary goal of the criminal justice system must be to identify, target, and incapacitate this hard-core group of offenders by making them serve adequate sentences dictated by the imperative of public safety rather than artificial constraints such as prison space. I felt that, if we wanted to reduce violent crime in our children's lifetime, this policy of incapacitating repeat violent offenders was the only approach that had any prospects for success. The government's highest duty, I believed, is to protect its citizens from the predations of violent aggressors. That is the primary justification for setting up governments in the first place. A government that can't or won't spend sufficient resources to prevent habitual violent criminals from continuously preying on peaceful citizens breaches its most fundamental obligation.

As I reviewed the data, it was plain that the main challenge we faced in reducing violent crime was the increasing dysfunctionality of many of the states' criminal justice systems and their failure to incapacitate habitual violent criminals. Many states had relapsed to the kind of revolving-door justice that predominated during the 1960s and 1970s. This was a consequence of state budget pressures and the reemergence of liberal policies that excused criminality and undervalued individual responsibility. Nationwide, on average, prisoners were serving only 37 percent of their sentences before being released early. The average sentence for murder was fifteen years, but the average served was only five and a half years; similarly, the average sentence for rape was eight years, but the average time served was only three years—and rapists are among the violent criminals most likely to repeat. In some heavily populated states, such as Texas and Florida, prisoners were serving only about 15 percent of their sentences. Thirty percent of murders in the country were committed by persons *while* they were on bail, probation, or parole. Assuming that roughly half of murders are crimes of passion, this would suggest that up to 60 percent of predatory murders were being committed when the murderer was under "supervision" by the criminal justice system. Unsurprisingly, the states with the fastest revolving doors were experiencing the largest increases in violent crime.

I recommended to Attorney General Thornburgh that the Justice Department engage in a significant shift in our priorities and identify combating violent crime as our primary goal. I suggested that we embark on a three-prong strategy, working in partnership with state and local law enforcement. The first step was to vastly expand joint federal-state-local task forces that would target career criminals and use tough federal laws on guns, gangs, and drug trafficking to incapacitate these criminals with substantial prison sentences. These task forces, led by a few federal agents, would be composed of many more local and state police officers, deputized as federal officers.

The second was to establish a neighborhood-based anticrime program that brought together all levels of law enforcement, social and economic programs, and community leadership in a concerted and holistic effort to reclaim neighborhoods from crime.

The strategy's third prong was to spearhead a national movement for the states to reform their justice systems and fund them adequately so that they could deal effectively with repeat violent criminals and stop the revolving doors. Thornburgh approved and charged me with developing these initiatives.

I still remember his remark to me at the time: "Before we can be kinder and gentler, we need to be rougher and tougher on crime"—an allusion to the President's 1988 nomination acceptance speech, in which he said he wanted a "kinder and gentler nation." George Terwilliger, the Vermont US attorney who was serving as my associate deputy, took the lead in helping me to develop these initiatives.

One of the principal drivers of urban violence was the growing prominence of violent street gangs. Some were adjuncts to national gangs, such as the Crips and the Bloods. Others were local or regional groups. Crack cocaine fueled much of the gang violence of the 1980s and early 1990s, as did the growing number of families with absent fathers. We started a pilot program in Philadelphia to test the concept of establishing federal-state-local antigang task forces that would target violent street gangs, using the federal Racketeer Influenced and Corrupt Organization (RICO) Act. The advantage of RICO, a statute originally designed for use against the Mafia, was that it enabled law enforcement to take down a gang in one fell swoop and prosecute all its members for their participation in the criminal organization.

In Philadelphia, we had strong allies in the newly elected Democratic mayor, Ed Rendell, who had been the district attorney, as well as District Attorney Lynne Abraham and the chief of police. From the start, our Violent Traffickers Project had phenomenal success. The pilot project continued for more than two years, ending shortly after I became Attorney General. During that time, using primarily RICO and other strong federal laws, we ultimately dismantled thirty-eight gangs and convicted more than six hundred gang members. These criminals were held in federal pretrial detention and, after conviction, were given tough federal sentences without the prospect of parole. They left the streets the day they were arrested and did not return until they'd finished their sentences. When citizens found out that arrested gang members wouldn't be back any time soon, fear in the neighborhoods dissipated, and people started providing more information to the task force about gangs. As more tips came in, the crackdown on gangs snowballed.

One scene has stuck with me. During the takedown of one gang—with scores of arrests made in one neighborhood—the citizens came out onto their stoops and applauded the police and agents. The gang members, all in handcuffs, laughed contemptuously. They thought they were headed for the usual revolving door and would be back out on the street later that same day. When they turned the corner and saw federal vehicles and agents waiting to take them for booking, several started crying. One of them just stood next to the federal van, banging his head against it.

It struck me that so many state criminal justice systems had become so dysfunctional that they evoked derisive laughter from criminals, even during arrests. But there was one system that made criminals cry: the federal system. If all fifty states made their systems as strong as the federal system, we would not have a violent crime problem in our country.

After two years, Philadelphia was the only city in the United States to experience an appreciable decrease in its homicide rate. Drug-related homicides there dropped by almost 40 percent, and there was a substantial decrease in the homicide rate relative to all the other cities in the country. Local leaders believed that our joint antigang initiative played a major role in bringing that about.

A second initiative we developed was a program we called Operation Triggerlock. The idea was to work with our local counterparts to identify the worst violent offenders who were eligible to be prosecuted under federal gun laws and then route their cases into the federal system for prosecution. In this way, we could take the worst violent criminals off the streets, hold them federally on pretrial detention, and ultimately secure a heavy federal sentence. Local police and district attorneys embraced this program warmly because, without the federal option, these criminals would frequently get out immediately on bail and eventually receive only de minimis sentences in the state system. In April 1991 we started rolling out Triggerlock in selected cities and soon saw that it would be wildly popular and successful.

We also started laying the groundwork for a neighborhood-based initiative. The philosophy behind it was that law enforcement efforts and social programs to revitalize neighborhoods must go hand in hand. The working name we gave this project was "Weed & Seed": first, make the community safe by weeding out the crime, and then seed it with educational and social opportunities, small business programs, and the like, to improve the quality of life and foster economic opportunity. We planned ultimately to make these communities enterprise zones. Neighborhood buy-in was essential. This was not something that would be done *to* communities but *with* them. The concept was that the local US attorney would chair a steering committee composed of neighborhood leaders, local law enforcement, and representatives of federal and state social service agencies such as the US Department of Housing and Urban Development (HUD) and the Department of Education. HUD secretary Jack Kemp became a champion of this approach, which dovetailed well with his signature idea of enterprise zones. George Terwilliger and his team did a lot of preparatory work, exploring what resources other key federal agencies were willing to bring to the table and pressing for augmenting our budget to support the effort.

We also started working with all the key national law enforcement and victims' groups to set the stage for the third prong of a comprehensive attack on violent crime: a national push for criminal justice reform on the state level. This was accomplished on a broad, nonpartisan basis. The basic theme of this drive was that, to make real progress in combating violent crime, the states had to follow the federal model and reform their systems to make them just as tough on crime. We found strong allies in the National District Attorneys Association, the International Association of Chiefs of Police, the National Sheriffs' Association, the Violent Crime Committee of State Attorneys General, and major national victims' rights organizations. With these organizations and our own research arms at the Department of Justice, we performed a comprehensive analysis of state criminal justice systems and assessed the tools needed for these systems to be more effective.

There was also some unfinished business at the federal level. Crime legislation under President Reagan had gone far to strengthen the federal system by enhancing the ability to detain dangerous defendants before trial, abolishing parole and establishing determinate sentencing, and obtaining mandatory minimum sentences for certain serious crimes. But President Bush had proposed a comprehensive new crime bill seeking four key reforms: one, remedying legal defects identified by the Supreme Court in the federal death penalty law; two, reforming federal habeas corpus litigation to stop defendants from bringing endless challenges to their convictions; three, recognizing a good-faith exception to the so-called exclusionary rule, so that evidence doesn't have to be suppressed for a violation of the Fourth Amendment simply because the police officer made an unintentional procedural mistake; and four, new mandatory minimums for violent criminals who use firearms.

During my tenure as Deputy, I spent substantial time negotiating a resolution on this major crime legislation. Most of these discussions were with Delaware senator Joe Biden, chairman of the Judiciary Committee, and New York's Chuck Schumer, chairman of the House Judiciary Committee's Subcommittee on Crime. But things remained at an impasse. The Democrats were never willing to go as far as we felt necessary on habeas corpus and were opposed to an exception to the exclusionary rule. One issue was proposed legislation titled the Brady Handgun Violence Prevention Act, commonly called the "Brady Bill," which called for a waiting period before the purchase of a firearm, during which a background investigation could be performed. We had no problem with background checks but pointed out that for any check to be useful, we needed funding to get the states to put their records into a central database. Once a database was set up, no waiting period was necessary because a check could be run at the time of sale that would be as effective as one run two weeks later. At the President's instruction, I indicated that we were willing to consider an adequately funded background check bill if the Democrats would agree to some of our anticrime measures. But this did not break the logjam.

On April 4, 1991, I was scheduled to brief AG Thornburgh on a sensitive case. He was on the phone when I walked into his office, and I could tell something was wrong. He sat motionless, erect behind his desk, his face ashen, the receiver pressed to his ear. For an uncomfortably long time, he sat still and silent, listening to a voice on the other end of the line. Hanging up slowly, he shook his head.

"John Heinz," he said—he was talking about the Republican US senator from Pennsylvania—"was just killed in a plane crash outside Philly."

The Attorney General's face was starting to flush. Thornburgh had been a popular two-term governor of Pennsylvania. We looked at each other quietly as the news sank in. I think we both knew at that moment that this tragedy would change both our lives.

CHAPTER 5

LEADING THE DEPARTMENT

I had been serving as Thornburgh's deputy for just under one year when the senior senator from Pennsylvania, John Heinz, heir to the H. J. Heinz Company, met his untimely death. Thornburgh and I had become an effective team, but it was now clear that our days together were numbered. Heinz's vacant Senate seat would be filled by way of a special election in November. It was a must-win race for the Republicans, and Thornburgh, as the distinguished former governor of Pennsylvania, would naturally be seen as the candidate best able to hold the seat. I realized that the party would do all it could to dragoon Dick into the race, and while I knew he would hate leaving the department, I also knew that he would ultimately agree to serve the greater good.

And so it was. Thornburgh agreed to run for Senate and made plans to leave the Justice Department. There was one more major matter for him to deal with, however. In late June, the White House got word that Justice Thurgood Marshall, the first and only African American ever to serve on the court, was about to retire. The President's decision on a nominee to replace him didn't take long. He had long considered Judge Clarence Thomas, also an African American, a prime candidate for the Court. Bush had appointed Thomas to the Court of Appeals for the DC Circuit two years earlier. I had known Thomas since I worked in the Reagan White House. He was serving at the time as the chairman of the Equal Employment Opportunity Commission

(EEOC) and frequently came over to visit his friend, and my boss, Mike Uhlmann. Mike considered him a real talent, and I was impressed with his intellect and liked his hearty sense of humor. Mike Luttig also knew Thomas. Both of us interviewed him; neither had to be sold. The President also wanted us to talk to Judge Emilio Garza on the Fifth Circuit Court of Appeals. He was also impressive, but we thought he could use a little more time as a federal appellate judge before moving up to the Supreme Court. There was general consensus that Thomas should be the choice, and the President nominated him on July 1, 1991.

On August 15, 1991, Dick Thornburgh and I said our farewells, as he left the department to run for the Senate.

The President appointed me Acting Attorney General, with clear marching orders: keep things calm and on track, while the White House focused on getting Judge Thomas through confirmation in the fall. After that, Bush would decide on a nominee to permanently replace Thornburgh. On Monday morning, as I settled into my new responsibilities, I felt lucky it was August—dog days in Washington. During the run-up to Labor Day, with Congress out of session and much of the city's workforce on vacation, the capital is at its sleepiest. A good time to ease into the job, I thought.

Upon assuming the duties of Attorney General, I asked Dan Levin to serve as chief of staff. and Jeff Favitta, the lone FBI agent who had been protecting me, suddenly got company. The nine agents on the AG's security detail, headed by Jim Kramarsic, started giving me 24/7 protection. The agents, whom I got to know well, became very close to me and my family.

Ten days after becoming Acting AG, on the afternoon of Wednesday, August 21, I received an urgent message that the director of the Federal Bureau of Prisons (BOP), Mike Quinlan, needed to see me about an emergency. Moments later, Quinlan appeared in my office and crisply briefed me on a crisis at the federal prison facility in Talladega, Alabama.

Pending their imminent deportation to Cuba, 120 of the most dangerous, sociopathic Cuban criminals who'd entered the United States during the 1980 Mariel boatlift had been housed together in the prison's Alpha unit—one of several free-standing buildings containing cell block units at the facility. That morning, they had somehow overpowered the staff, taken over the unit, and were holding eleven staff as hostages: eight BOP employees and three from the US Immigration and Naturalization Service (INS). The Cuban inmates were desperate. Convinced that a return to Cuba would mean certain death, they much preferred to be incarcerated for life in the United States. They threatened to slit the hostages' throats if we attempted a rescue or failed to rescind their deportation.

The Cuban inmates, as they saw it, had nothing to lose. There was nothing to deter them from harming the hostages. We knew the inmates were armed, at a minimum, with knives and spears. As Quinlan unrolled a map of the facility, it was clear that the obstacles to a successful hostage rescue were daunting. The Alpha unit was essentially a large concrete fortress into which there was effectively no visibility. The entrance was secured by heavy steel doors. The only route for rescuers would lead into a large, atrium-like common area opening up onto two tiers of cells, with a number of separate functional rooms in different locations around the unit. We had no idea where the hostages were located within the structure—whether they were being held apart in separate cells or congregated together in one place; whether they were being held stationary or moved around regularly.

After a brief break, while Quinlan gathered more information and made sure the situation had been stabilized, we reconvened in my conference room, joined by two key FBI leaders I had asked to come over: Deputy Director Floyd Clarke and Assistant Director Bill Baker, the latter of whom was in charge of the bureau's Criminal Division. I had worked closely with these men for the past two years and had supreme confidence in them. Quinlan started by outlining his plan to retake the prison, which he wanted to launch right away. Because the Bureau of Prisons had lost the facility, he argued, it was their responsibility to get it back. He proposed that his Special Operations Response Teams (SORT) would use bolt cutters and power saws to gain access and flood in to locate and secure the hostages.

I asked, "How long do you estimate from the time you begin entry to the time you find and reach the hostages?"

"Twenty to thirty minutes," Quinlan answered. At least he was honest.

"I don't like this plan, Mike," I said.

Although I understood BOP's desire to deal with its own mess, this kind of operation really required the expertise and capabilities of the FBI. Indeed, the bureau had stood up a unit precisely to resolve hostage situations. The FBI's Hostage Rescue Team, or HRT, was an elite tactical unit established after the massacre of Israeli hostages at the Munich Olympic Games in 1972, with the specific mission of conducting hostage rescues. With a strength at that time of more than fifty special operators, the unit was like a super full-time SWAT team. Based at the bureau's facility at Quantico, HRT operators spent all their time training for their mission. As Deputy AG, I had visited the team at Quantico several times and was deeply impressed by its professionalism.

After Quinlan updated us all on the latest situation report, I conveyed my decisions to the group. Because we could never agree to the inmates' terms, I instructed that the FBI would have direct command authority over resolving the situation in Alpha unit, and the chain of command would come up through the FBI to me personally. I explained that, given the inmates' demands, this would likely end with a hostage rescue, and I wanted the FBI to start planning and practicing an operation. Quinlan would provide HRT a Bureau of Prisons unit identical to the one held by the Cubans, so that they could start practicing their plan. FBI director William Sessions was away on vacation, but I did not have confidence in Sessions's abilities, and I was happy to be dealing with Floyd Clarke. Floyd told me he was sending three of his best special agents in charge (SACs)—the senior FBI agents heading the FBI field offices around the country—down to help the local SAC in Alabama. I knew the three SACs in question, and they were top-notch. There was little food inside the block unit, and I knew it would only be a matter of time before the inmates became desperately hungry. I made clear that I would have to personally approve any provision of food and directed that the media be kept off the prison's campus, so the inmates would have no contact with the press.

A phone line was open to the inmates, and FBI hostage negotiators started to engage with their leaders. One of the eleven hostages, who had been injured in the takeover, was released early on. But from the beginning, negotiations were not promising. We could never meet the inmates' only goal: avoiding repatriation to Cuba. Among other reasons, to do so would endanger in the future all BOP employees who work inside our prisons. By the sixth and seventh days, the position of the inmates appeared to be hardening. There were indications that a more aggressive group was emerging to supplant the original leaders. They vowed to kill the hostages if we stormed the unit.

Clarke and Baker came over to my office at least twice a day to review developments and potential rescue plans. We faced a major challenge: Where exactly were the hostages being held? The nightmare scenario was that the inmates were moving them around or spreading them out among the facility's more than one hundred cells. In that case, once the Hostage Rescue Team entered the unit, they would not be able to find the hostages within a reasonable amount of time.

Our first break came from an unexpected source. There were eighteen American prisoners in Alpha unit—not American hostages or Cuban hostage takers but inmates. The Cubans had returned these men to their cells. One of the FBI agents outside the unit—manning the cordon around it—noticed a prisoner standing by his window and repeatedly tapping on his head. The American inmate appeared to be communicating a message. But what was it? The agent spent a long time watching and trying to figure out what he was attempting to say. At last, he caught on. It was a rudimentary code—one tap was *A*; two taps, *B*; three taps, *C*; and so on. It looked like he was tapping out the letters *INS*: One of the larger meeting rooms inside the unit was reserved for INS personnel to conduct interviews, and prison staff referred to it as the "INS room." We thought this prisoner was saying the hostages were being held in the INS room.

The next day, August 28, the inmates informed us that one of the hostages, a prison secretary, Kitty Suddeth, appeared to be very ill. I knew the inmate leaders desperately wanted to speak to journalist Cynthia Corzo at the Spanish-language edition of the *Miami Herald*, to get out their message. I agreed that, if they gave us Suddeth, we would allow them to meet with Corzo and a photographer, but the conversation would be held through the bars at the entrance to the unit. Suddeth was released, and she gave us critical information. At that time, the hostages were being held all together in the INS room. Several inmates carrying knives were standing guard immediately outside the room, with instructions to kill the hostages if there was any rescue attempt. According to Suddeth, the hostages had formulated their own plan: as soon as they heard a rescue attempt had started, they would use their mattresses to block the door, holding the inmates at bay as long as they could. We also learned the inmates were running low on food and were now starting to eat ketchup mixed with hot water.

The following day, August 29, the inmates told us that they were going to start killing the hostages one by one, drawing their names from a pillow case until their demands were met. By means of some limited audio surveillance capability, we heard the inmates collecting the hostages' name tags. I met with Clarke, Baker, and Quinlan, and they agreed we had to move soon. The FBI leaders told me that the optimal time for a rescue attempt would be around four o'clock in the morning. We tentatively set the rescue operation for the very next morning.

I suggested that we propose a deal. We would send in food for them—the first time in eight days—on the condition that they allowed our agent medics to meet all of the hostages through the bars at the unit entrance and feed them directly so that we could ensure they'd been fed adequately. This move could help us in several ways: First, the inmates would view this as a major victory, and it could distract them from their Russian roulette plan. Also, feeding the inmates a big meal after they'd had little to eat for many days would make them much more lethargic when the operation started. And our getting to interact with the hostages, even if only briefly and under supervision, would give us an opportunity to glean a little more intelligence. The inmates quickly accepted our proposal, and we picked up audio of them celebrating their victory.

I contacted Mike Moore, the head of the US Marshals Service, and asked him to have its Boeing 727 aircraft pre-positioned in Talladega and ready to fly the Cubans to Cuba as soon as we freed the hostages.

In the meantime, I called the President's chief of staff, Governor Sununu, who was with the President at the Bush family's summer retreat in Kennebunkport, Maine. "I'm not asking for permission. I'm just telling you what I am doing," I started. "We're going to mount a rescue attempt at four tomorrow morning. If it's a mess, it's on me."

Sununu understood immediately what I was doing: giving him a heads-up but not asking for approval, so that the President would have a modicum of insulation if things went badly.

"Bill, I hear you," he said. "Some friendly advice: if you have not already done so, poll each of the hostage negotiators and get them on record. That is all I'm saying. Good luck, and call me as soon as you have news."

It was good advice. Clarke set up a conference call with the whole FBI leadership team down at Talladega and all the hostage negotiators. In the meantime, we got reports back from the FBI agents who had met with the hostages to feed them through the bars at the unit entrance. The Cubans required the hostages to be fed only one at a time, and the agents' interactions with the hostages were watched closely by the inmates, so the ability to have any conversation was very limited. Nevertheless, we derived some information: after being served their food, each of the hostages seemed to start back in the general direction of the INS room. This was not dispositive by any means, but it correlated with the other information we had. But then we got a real curveball. One of the hostages said softly in Spanish to the FBI agent that she was being held in a "cell." She used the Spanish word *celda*. Did this mean that the inmates had moved the hostages into separate cells, and they were no longer all together in the INS room? If so, the operation would end up in disaster. The agent in question was contacted immediately, and every aspect of his interaction with the hostage was parsed.

I asked about our "tapper"—the American prisoner who could be seen at his cell window, trying to communicate silently with an FBI agent. "When was the last we heard from the tapper?" It had been awhile before we fed the hostages, but he had still been tapping *INS*.

I went to the FBI's operations center in its headquarters building. The core team of me, Floyd Clarke, Bill Baker, and my Deputy, George Terwilliger, sat together at a small, round table. (FBI director Sessions had just returned from Hilton Head, South Carolina, but had the good sense to let Clarke and Baker continue running things.) The first item of business was the conference call with the hostage negotiators and the FBI special agents in charge at Talladega. The conversation was piped in to the op center over a speaker. Each of the hostage negotiators spoke separately. All said the same: that all options had been exhausted, there was no realistic prospect of a negotiated resolution, the hostages were in danger, and the best option was to attempt a rescue.

After the call, Clarke, Baker, Terwilliger, and I wrestled with the discordant information suggesting that the hostages might have been moved to cells. I decided that the hostage's use of the term was contrary to the weight of the evidence, and she seemed to be talking casually. The hardest information was from Suddeth, and we had not picked up any audio suggesting a move of the hostages from the INS room. It was about three in the morning when we called the head of the HRT, Dick Rogers, and gave him the green light.

We now had to wait. Up to then, it would be the longest wait of my life. Although the Hostage Rescue Team had been founded in the early seventies, this was to be its first actual rescue attempt. It also involved one of the most difficult breaches any rescue has attempted: blowing through massive steel doors embedded in heavy concrete. Bill Baker helped break the tension with some very humorous jokes.

Suddenly a voice came over the speaker. It was the SAC who would give us the real-time report on the operation as it unfolded. He talked in the quasi-whisper used by golf announcers on TV. Before we got started, he told us they had picked up audio an hour before of one of the Cuban leaders boasting that they had won, encouraging everyone to get some sleep, and saying that they would be eating cake in the morning.

An FBI official standing nearby quipped grimly, "The only thing you'll be eating in the morning is concrete, buddy."

At the prison, the FBI had established a cordon around Alpha unit, with huge floodlights pointed at every aperture of the structure. This meant that the inmates, even if they had lookouts, couldn't see anything beyond the lights. The plan called for HRT to pack into and onto several Suburban vans—with most hanging off the sides and mounted on the roofs for quick dismount—which would then race through the cordon and up to the unit's front entrance. HRT would quickly place their charges, blow through, and flood into the unit. The rescue team's main objective was to reach the INS room before the inmates could push their way in and kill the hostages. Meanwhile, more than two hundred Prison Bureau SORT team officers would dash up to the unit and enter after the HRT to handcuff and remove the Cubans.

As the SAC started giving his blow-by-blow account in his golf-announcer whisper, my heart began to pound.

HRT is boarding the vans . . . They are mounted . . . They are on the way . . . Picking up speed . . . Picking up speed . . . They are past the lights. Past the lights . . . Dismounting . . . Breachers are placing the charges.

Suddenly a huge explosion thundered over the speaker. I wasn't expecting the loud volume and literally jumped. "Holy shit!" the SAC doing the play-by-play shouted at the top of his lungs.

It sounded like the whole building could have collapsed. There was silence for a second, then it sounded like rapid gunfire. "What is going on?" I asked.

"A hell of a breach, but they're in," the SAC responded.

As the rapid pops sounded, I looked nervously at Clarke and Baker. "Sounds like a slaughter."

"Those are flashbangs, not gunfire," they said confidently. Flashbangs are nonlethal explosive devices like small grenades that make a huge bang and bright flash to stun, disorient, and distract the targets.

The speaker crackled again. "We have them: all nine hostages," the special agent announced with relief.

"Confirm the count and then let me know," I asked.

As soon as the nose count of hostages was confirmed, I called Sununu. "It worked, John. And no one killed or seriously injured on either side."

"Good work, Bill," Sununu said. "Congratulate the bureau. I'll tell the boss when he's up."

From the time of the breach, the HRT had reached the hostages in less than a minute. But there was no time to spare. The agents got there just as the inmates guarding the INS room had the door partially opened and were pushing to get inside to the hostages.

The four of us in the op center were still very pumped up. We went down to the FBI's executive dining room for a big breakfast. As we sat down, Terwilliger said, "You know, this would make a good movie."

I looked over at Clarke and Baker, both the quintessential handsome G-men. "You guys can fight over which of you is played by Clint Eastwood."

"Who is going to play you?" Terwilliger asked me.

"John Candy, of course."

After breakfast, we all flew down on the FBI director's plane to Talladega, still getting there before nine o'clock. All the inmates had been methodically searched, X-rayed for hidden weapons, and taken to the Marshals' plane. By the time the country heard about the successful operation that morning, the Cubans were already in the air heading to Cuba.

The hostages and their families had asked to meet with me privately. We had a joyful and tearful time together. Weeks later, they presented me a beautiful plaque signed by all the hostages. I still treasure it. When people ask me to name my most significant accomplishment as Attorney General, it was Talladega. Lives were directly at stake.

President Bush called me later in the day to congratulate me and the FBI on the successful hostage rescue. An important endnote: I found out who the tapper was. He was a Native American convict with a very long time left on a long sentence. I took the necessary steps to have him released.

There had been speculation about whom Bush would nominate to succeed Thornburgh as the next Attorney General. The media were focusing on several prominent Republican politicians, such as former California governor George Deukmejian and Governor John Ashcroft of Missouri. I was considered, if at all, a very dark horse. Thornburgh told me he had recommended me to the President, but I did not think I had much of a chance given my age (forty-one) and low profile. It would be great to get the job, I thought, but I was not panting for it. However, I had learned over the past couple of weeks that I had more backing inside the administration than I imagined. I was told that Sununu and Gray were positive about me, as were Brent Scowcroft and Bob Gates.

As we all expected, Clarence Thomas's confirmation was bound to be a fight—we just did not know how much of one. As was the usual practice, Mike Luttig and OLC were providing support to the Supreme Court nominee, helping him review his past writings and analyze topical areas of constitutional law. During the first week of October 1991, Thomas's hearings had been completed, and his confirmation was being debated on the Senate floor.

On Sunday, October 6, Thomas's confirmation was expected within days. It was the day before the new term of the Supreme Court started. The traditional Red Mass, which is held annually in the Catholic Church to honor the judiciary, government legal officials, and the legal profession—a practice that dates back to the Middle Ages—was being held in the Cathedral of St. Matthew the Apostle, in Washington. Intended for people of all faiths, justices of the Supreme Court as well as senior DOJ officials and other government officials usually attend. At the end of the Mass, as I was heading out, Sununu drew up alongside me in the main aisle.

"Things are looking good," he whispered, and winked. "Hang in there. It will be soon." This meant that Sununu thought the President was leaning toward selecting me as Attorney General.

That very day, a news story broke, based on a leak of information supplied to the Senate Judiciary Committee. One of Thomas's former colleagues, Anita Hill, had accused him of making sexual comments to her when they worked together at the Education Department and the Equal Employment Opportunity Commission. Senator Biden, then committee chairman, was under pressure to reopen confirmation hearings to explore Ms. Hill's allegations.

I got a call from Duke Short, chief aide to the ranking Republican member on the committee, Senator Strom Thurmond. "Bill, there should be a courier arriving in the next few minutes," he said ominously. "Read what's enclosed and then call me."

The document that was delivered was an affidavit from Anita Hill, describing her allegations in detail. I immediately called Luttig, who was vacationing in Hawaii. He had helped Thomas get through his first hearing—successfully, we had thought—and was resting before leaving the department to serve as a federal appellate judge. I read the affidavit to him, focusing on the more salacious parts. "Do you think we have a problem, Mike?" I asked.

"Yah. I'd say we have a problem," he said.

"Well, get your ass back here. It looks like we're going once more into the breach," I said. "I am sorry, Mike."

"I'm on my way," he said resignedly.

Chairman Biden reopened his committee hearings on the nomination. The dramatic hearings, during which both Anita Hill and Clarence Thomas testified, unfolded over three days in mid-October.

Chairman Biden would try to have it both ways. According to a memoir by his Judiciary colleague Arlen Specter, the Republican senator from Pennsylvania, Biden told him, "It was clear to me from the way she was answering the questions, she was lying." But when he sought the Democratic presidential nomination in 2020, he claimed he had believed her story.

Thomas testified convincingly, while Hill's account did not add up and was significantly undermined by other evidence. I, along with a clear majority of Americans at the time, believed Thomas. I viewed the whole spectacle as an attempt to destroy him for the crime of holding conservative views. This episode—more than even the 1987 confirmation hearings for Reagan nominee Judge Robert Bork, which for all their nastiness had mainly to do with the nominee's opinions, not his personal conduct—legitimized the now-conventional Democratic strategy of maligning the character of any Supreme Court nominee named by a Republican. Thomas was justified in calling it a "high-tech lynching." It did not work. After the hearings, the full Senate resumed its deliberations and, on October 15, 1991, confirmed Thomas by a 52-to-48 vote.

The day after Judge Thomas was confirmed, I was on Capitol Hill briefing the House Republican caucus on administration legislative positions when I got a message from Sununu. He asked me to head down to the White House to see if I could catch the President just before our scheduled cabinet meeting. "This is it," the message said. I knew Sununu had been rooting for me to get the Attorney General job, and the message meant the President was going to select me.

I did not arrive at the White House in time to meet with President Bush prior to the cabinet meeting, but Sununu said he would grab me right afterward. When the meeting concluded, the President stood and waved at me to come back to the Oval. As I walked toward the Oval, Sununu paused with me. "Here's the deal," he said. "The President wants you as Attorney General, but you don't have the profile to give us any political benefit. So, we will name your Deputy. Is that okay?"

"That could be a problem, Governor," I said. "At the department, it's essential to have a Deputy you know and trust."

Sununu looked a little surprised. "Okay, just talk it through with the President," he said, as he took my arm and guided me into the Oval Office.

President Bush was settling into his desk chair and swiveled in my direction. "Well, Bill, I am real happy about this. I'd be proud to have you as my Attorney General."

"Thank you, Mr. President. It is great honor for me," I said. "I know I don't get you much on the political front."

"Well, the *best* politics at the Department of Justice is *no* politics," he responded.

What a great aphorism, I thought to myself. I wondered if he had just made it up.

"You have been doing a terrific job running the department," the President went on. "And I know you did a great job for Dick. Steady on course. That is the best politics." He gestured toward Sununu. "I guess John has already talked to you about the other thing?"

"Yes, Mr. President," I said, getting nervous that I was about to blow the deal.

"Is it all right?" he asked.

"Well, here's my problem, Mr. President," I said. "I've watched how things work at the department for many years, and I think it's critical for me to really know my Deputy and have complete trust in him." The President nodded, inviting me to continue. "To be plain, Mr. President, the Attorney General's balls are in the Deputy's pocket, and I ain't putting my balls into someone's pocket who I do not know."

Coarse, perhaps, but it made the point. A look of understanding came over his face. "Okay, I see," he said.

"Whenever there is daylight between the AG and the Deputy, the department gets tied in knots," I explained. "Think of Meese and Arnie Burns, and the trouble there. And Thornburgh's trouble with Don Ayer."

The President nodded. "Do you have anyone in mind?" he asked.

"Well, my principal assistant right now is George Terwilliger. He is the US attorney in Vermont, so he doesn't get you anything politically, but he would be my choice," I said. "We have a detailed game plan to execute this coming year on violent crime, and he helped put it together, so he'd be perfect to help me execute on it."

"I tell you what, Bill. If we come up with a candidate, just talk to him. But if you still want your guy, that is fine," Bush said.

"There is another thing, Mr. President," I continued. "The number three position—the Associate Attorney General—has been vacant all this time. I have a good candidate you might want to consider: Wayne Budd, the US attorney in Massachusetts. Great guy. He is an African American. His father was the police chief in Springfield. A real class act. He'd be a home run."

The President looked over at Sununu. "That sounds interesting. John, follow up with Bill on that. But let's get Bill announced now."

"Now, Mr. President?" I asked.

"We have a Rose Garden ceremony for Justice award recipients in less than an hour, right?" the President asked, looking at his watch. "Let's just go out and do it then."

The President suggested I try to reach my wife. I called Christine to see if she could make it down to the White House but couldn't reach her. (No cell phone in those days.) She was later to hear the news on her car radio that the President had just announced me as his choice for Attorney General during a Rose Garden ceremony.

The President's spokesman, Marlin Fitzwater, told reporters that I had been the leading choice from the beginning—which was news to me. Beyond our connection going back to the CIA, Bush had been impressed with my management of the department under Thornburgh. He also appreciated the way I handled Talladega—"professional and without fanfare," as he put it. Even the media coverage was relatively benign, owing mainly to the fact that I was not a politician. Most stories noted that I had generally received "high marks" for my running of the department. A *Washington Post* article marveled that, only fourteen years earlier, I had been a night law student. "Barr is known as a cool-headed manager without political ambitions," it said. "In 18 months as deputy attorney general, Barr was considered a conciliator at a Justice Department in turmoil during most of Attorney General Dick Thornburgh's tenure. Department officials say Barr tempered candor with discretion, a strong will with a tolerance for the personalities and views of others."

Once I was confirmed, and we entered an election year, the mainstream media had little use for me.

Three years before, on the evening of December 21, 1988, Pan Am Flight 103 took off from London's Heathrow Airport bound for New York City. As it flew thirty-one thousand feet above Lockerbie, Scotland, at 7:03 p.m. local time, the massive Boeing 747 plane, known as the *Clipper Maid of the Seas,* blew apart. The plane and its passengers plunged to the ground for thirty-six seconds. Those who weren't killed immediately by the blast likely lost consciousness due to the lack of oxygen. Some, however, may have revived at fifteen thousand feet so they could witness the final moments of their fall.

It appeared, based on some of the bodies recovered, that some victims had prepared for their deaths by clutching crucifixes. One woman had held her baby tight. The explosion killed all 259 people on board—243 passengers and 16 crew members, including 190 Americans, many of whom were students heading home for the holidays.

Countless pieces were scattered across 840 square miles, nearly the entire width of Scotland. Falling debris claimed the lives of eleven Lockerbie residents on the ground. The Lockerbie bombing remains the deadliest single terrorist attack in the history of the United Kingdom. It was, until 9/11, also the deadliest terrorist attack on the United States.

The bombing of Pan Am 103 set off one of the most complex international terrorism investigations in history, led by Scotland and the United States. Bob Mueller, who, as Assistant AG for the Criminal Division, oversaw the investigation on the American side, described how "Scottish police searched every blade of grass to pick up every conceivable fragment that could be found." Investigators fanned out across the globe, eventually interviewing more than ten thousand people. When I arrived at the Justice Department a month after the attack, the FBI was sparing no effort to find the perpetrators.

For almost three years, the investigation moved relentlessly forward. I had some early involvement in it during my tenure as head of the Office of Legal Counsel. In the hallway outside the OLC offices hung a plaque commemorating that from July 2 to August 1, 1942, a secret trial was held in the offices before a military tribunal of eight Nazi saboteurs who had been caught after landing from submarines in the United States in June 1942. This got me thinking about the role of military tribunals in dealing with foreign enemies who violate the rules of war—in this case, German soldiers captured in civilian clothes attempting to carry out sabotage on American soil. I started to think that military commissions were the right way to approach acts of foreign terrorism like Pan Am 103.

I pulled information about this case and studied it. All eight Germans had lived in the United States—two were naturalized citizens—and had gone back to Germany before 1941 to fight for the Nazis. After landing in June 1942, two of the saboteurs—including one of the Americans—turned themselves in, which allowed the FBI to roll up the whole group. On July 2 President Franklin D. Roosevelt issued an executive proclamation establishing a seven-member military commission to try the Germans for violating the laws of war and spying. A month later, August 1, the trial was over. The defense counsel had argued that the Germans should be tried in our civilian courts. But the Department of Justice contended that foreign enemies accused of violating the laws of war should be tried by military commissions. The Supreme Court, on summer recess, returned to Washington for a secret hearing on the case and, on July 29, issued a confidential ruling—and months later a public opinion (*Ex parte Quirin*)—that, under the Constitution, the President is authorized to try enemies for violations of the laws of war in military commissions.

On August 3 all eight were convicted and sentenced to death. President Roosevelt commuted the sentences of the two Germans who had turned themselves in. On August 8 the six others were executed. Thus, in less than two months, the saboteurs were caught, tried, and executed. That generation did not dither around when it came to defending the country.

This episode got me thinking about military commissions—not only as the proper place to try foreign terrorists but also as a vehicle that could solve a brewing problem: which country was going to try whoever was responsible for the bombing. The Scots, whose justice system is distinct from England's, were intent on trying the case. They had a decent claim, since the crime was committed over their territory, and they lost citizens. As a practical matter, they also controlled a lot of the evidence. It would be hard to oust the Scots from trying the case, but I was concerned that, if we provided substantial assistance to the Scots in their trial—which was essential—the United States could be precluded from trying the same defendants for the same terrorist acts. There was also a serious risk that the Scots, who had abolished the death penalty, would not surrender the defendants to America unless we agreed to forgo the death penalty. Beyond that, Scottish sentences tended to be extremely lenient. So, although we had no choice, I was never happy about ceding trial of the case to the Scots. To me, it would ensure that the perpetrators would get off easy—by US standards.

Although I got the idea of a military commission while at OLC, I did not broach it with the Scots until I was Acting Attorney General in the fall of 1991. I gently and informally raised the possibility of forming a joint military commission, for which there was precedent in World War II. This would allow both countries to participate in the trial, thus giving due recognition to the realities that Pan Am was an American carrier, that most victims were Americans, and that the attack was obviously meant as an attack on the United States. It could also permit imposition of the death penalty on those found guilty. My Scottish counterparts quickly brushed aside the idea as unworkable.

When I'd moved up to the Deputy spot in May 1990, I had started receiving regular briefings on the investigation's progress. Theories abounded, with claims that Iraq, Iran, Syria, or a Palestinian group had been involved in the attack. But by the time I became Acting Attorney General in August 1991, the evidence showed that the Libyans were responsible. By the fall, the evidence proved beyond a reasonable doubt that the bombing was conducted by two members of the Libyan intelligence service, the Jamahiriya Security Organization, or JSO—Abdel Baset Ali al-Megrahi and Lamen Khalifa Fhimah—acting with other conspirators. The department and Scottish authorities were prepared to file charges against these individuals simultaneously in our respective countries. I alerted the President, and he asked that I brief the full National Security Council.

As I laid out the evidence showing Libyan guilt, the President and the NSC members sat in the Cabinet Room transfixed. From among the many thousands of bits of evidence collected from the Scottish countryside, and using forensic testing, investigators were able to associate charred pieces of a suitcase; shreds of charred clothing; and a tiny fragment of a circuit board, no larger than a fingernail, from a Toshiba radio. From this they established that a Semtex plastic explosive bomb had been placed inside the radio, wrapped in certain items of clothing, and packed in a Samsonite suitcase. One of the items of clothing tied to the suitcase was a brand of trousers manufactured in either Ireland or Malta. Shreds of a "Made in Malta" label were found in pieces of clothing from the suitcase. At the clothing brand's Malta outlet, the manager remembered selling the items of clothing used to wrap the radio to a man of Arabic appearance who spoke in a Libyan accent—a man he was later able to identify as al-Megrahi. It was determined that the clothing was purchased on December 7, 1988, at an outlet just three hundred yards from the hotel where al-Megrahi was staying at the time. The United States had identified al-Megrahi as a Libyan intelligence agent. Tiny fragments found embedded in a charred shirt were identified as pieces of a timer device made by a Swiss firm, MEBO. The cofounder of the firm confirmed that MEBO had sold as many as twenty timers to the Libyans in 1985 and was able to identify al-Megrahi as a business contact.

Records indicated that, on the morning of December 21, an unaccompanied suitcase had been routed on an Air Malta flight from Malta to Frankfurt, Germany, where it had been loaded onto Pan Am 103A, the feeder flight to London. If the tag on that suitcase had so directed, the unaccompanied suitcase would have been loaded onto Pan Am 103 in London. Al-Megrahi's associate, Fhimah, had written an entry in his diary on December 15 that al-Megrahi "is coming from Zurich" and "take taggs [sic] from Air Malta." Al-Megrahi arrived in Malta under a false passport shortly before the suitcase was placed on the Air Malta flight.

Ending my presentation, I stated that all of this evidence, in addition to other evidence, gave us confidence that the attack was carried out by the Libyans. No one doubted this conclusion. But I was disheartened when my colleagues started talking about adopting a package of measures—additional sanctions and diplomatic measures—that might pressure Libyan dictator Mu'ammar Muḥammad al-Gadhafi to surrender the two Libyan intelligence officers to stand trial. This was, after all, not Gadhafi's first offense. He had previously financed overseas attacks on American soldiers and civilians, and in 1986 Ronald Reagan ordered airstrikes against Libya in retaliation for recent Libyan terrorist attacks in Rome, Vienna, and West Berlin.

I interjected. "These JSO mopes were not acting by themselves. Is there any doubt that this was an officially sanctioned terrorist act by Gadhafi himself!"

Larry Eagleburger, representing the State Department, asked, "So what are you saying, Bill?"

I answered, "Does anyone really think that putting these two guys on trial should be our end game?" I responded. "That this would be an adequate response to the most deadly terrorist act ever committed against the United States?"

I turned to the President, who was to my right. George Herbert Walker Bush was listening to the conversation intently.

"Mr. President, if I had come to you the day after Pan Am 103 went down, while the bodies were still being recovered, and I gave you this proof that it was clearly the Libyans who had committed this atrocity, what would you have done? Would you have thought it sufficient to impose oil sanctions to force surrender of the particular agents who carried out Gadhafi's orders?"

The President, sitting back in his chair and taking it all in, looked pensive and a little pained.

"Because we are a civilized country, we have taken three years to gather sufficient evidence to prove beyond a reasonable doubt that it was Gadhafi," I continued. "That is the highest standard of proof we have. And just because we took that time, and the blood has cooled, does that mean we now just walk away from the biggest terrorist attack we've been hit with?"

Admiral David Jeremiah of the Joint Chiefs of Staff, guessing where I was headed, jumped in: "So what are you proposing?"

"I think at a minimum we should reduce the JSO headquarters to smoking rubble; beyond that, we should think about strikes on military targets, if not Gadhafi himself. I think that we should establish a firm principle that any government that launches a terrorist attack killing Americans like this is signing its own death warrant."

Jeremiah quipped, "I thought *I* was Defense, and *you* are *Justice*."

"That is exactly what I am talking about, Dave: *justice*. Are the demands of justice satisfied here," I asked, "if we spend years trying to get our hands on these two errand boys, and, if we get them, putting them on trial?" I pointed out that I was the one working directly with the victims' families, and, in my view, the measures being discussed were just too weak in relation to the scale of human suffering caused by the attack.

As the discussion continued, it was clear that several of my colleagues agreed with me in principle but were concerned that a military strike could disrupt our efforts to mobilize international support for strengthening sanctions against Libya and further isolating Gadhafi. This was a valid consideration. So soon after the Gulf War, we had to consider the diplomatic ramifications of a retaliatory strike on another Muslim country of the Middle East.

Personally, I did not think these arguments outweighed the moral and long-term geopolitical costs of failing to destroy the organizations and men who murdered 190 Americans as a means of humiliating the United States.

As for Bush, I could tell he was torn. He adjourned the meeting without making a formal decision, but I knew from previous experience that he would make up his mind only after further private discussions in the Oval Office with his core national security team: Secretary of Defense Dick Cheney, Secretary of State Jim Baker, and National Security Adviser Brent Scowcroft. This was their turf, after all, and they had a better sense of all the relevant considerations. Knowing them as well as I did, I expected we would end up going the sanctions route. But at least I had tried.

On November 14, the day after my confirmation hearings concluded, I announced our indictment of the two Libyan JSO officers. We reluctantly agreed with Scotland that, if we gained custody of the defendants, it would try them first. In 1999, after mounting pressure from UN sanctions, Gadhafi handed over the two men for trial by the Scots in a specially convened court in the Netherlands. In January 2001 al-Megrahi was convicted on all charges and sentenced to life, but Fhimah was acquitted. In strange twist, I was on vacation in Scotland in August 2009, when the Scots announced they were releasing al-Megrahi for compassionate reasons after he was diagnosed with prostate cancer. They claimed he had only months to live. He returned to Libya and died in May 2012.

Years later, after the 9/11 attacks, a mutual friend told me that President Bush had mused to him that, in retrospect, the United States perhaps should have taken a stronger response to the Pan Am 103 bombing. But things are always clearer in retrospect, and, at the end of the day, Gadhafi got what he deserved. As fate would have it, the Pan Am 103 saga was not over for me. It was to arise again during my next tour as Attorney General almost thirty years in the future.

I was confirmed as the seventy-seventh Attorney General of the United States without opposition by the Senate and was sworn in on November 26, 1991. President Bush came over to Main Justice for the ceremony in the department's Great Hall. Dan Levin continued as chief of staff and calmly kept order throughout my tenure.

I made it clear from the start that my highest priority remained addressing the intolerable levels of violent crime around the country.

One of my first actions was to direct the FBI to transfer three hundred agents from its counterintelligence program—where they focused on Soviet espionage during the Cold War—to a new national antigang program modeled after our experience in Philadelphia. This was, up till that time, the largest reprogramming in bureau history.

FBI agents were to provide the nucleus of joint federal-state-local antigang task forces in every major city suffering significant levels of gang violence.

This initiative was the beginning of the FBI's signature violent crime program—Violent Gangs Safe Streets Task Forces—which today numbers 160 task forces.

I also expanded Project Triggerlock, which we had started to roll out the previous April. This initiative, which targeted chronic violent offenders for prosecution under federal gun laws, was now implemented in all US attorneys' offices around the country. By April 1992, after its first year in operation, Triggerlock had doubled federal firearms prosecutions and charged more than 6,400 defendants with gun crimes. The program was achieving a conviction rate of more than 90 percent. After I became Attorney General, Triggerlock prosecutions continued to ramp up, and by the time I left office, we were charging a thousand cases a month.

As our crackdown on violent criminals pushed forward, the predictable naysayers became louder. Critics argued that "locking people up" does not solve violent crime, but rather we should spend more on social programs to address the "root causes" of crime. They would say: "We don't need more prisons, we need more schools!" Or, "We don't need more police, we need more social workers!" Proponents of addressing the root causes of crime through social programs always presented their approach as an *alternative* to strong law enforcement.

In my view, this was a false dichotomy. To meet this criticism, I argued that, even assuming we are capable of framing social programs that can ameliorate conditions contributing to crime, these social programs cannot substitute for strong law enforcement. These programs can complement law enforcement measures, but they cannot replace them. On the contrary, while strong law enforcement may not be sufficient on its own to solve all of society's problems, it is the necessary prerequisite for any social progress. Law enforcement—safe neighborhoods— must be the foundation upon which all else is built. Providing public safety must be paramount.

In the first place, violent crime was at record-high levels, and the carnage on our streets was intolerable. It is all very well to look ahead and hope that social intervention will lead to a more peaceful community in the distant future. But citizens need and deserve protection in the present. Even if social programs proved effective, they would not bear tangible fruit for many years. How do we stop the slaughter in the here and now? Schools and social workers are not an adequate answer to that question.

More fundamentally, in a pervasive atmosphere of violence and fear, even the best-designed social programs cannot take root. The truth was that, as we spent more and more on social programs, our efforts at revitalizing urban communities had been strangled by crime. It was increasingly clear that suppressing crime was a precondition for social programs to be successful. I had seen all the high hopes for the social programs that had been focused on the Cabrini-Green housing project in Chicago, for example. But the number one concern for parents in that project was the bullets from gang warfare that started flying around on Thursday nights and continued through the weekend. It was so bad that parents put their children to sleep in the metal bathtubs. We had come to the age of "armored cribs." That was not the kind of environment in which social programs had any hope of success. Any effort at attacking the root causes of crime would be smothered unless we had law enforcement making communities safe.

It was once a shibboleth that "poverty causes crime," but I argued the opposite was true: "crime causes poverty." Businesses were being driven from crime-ridden neighborhoods, taking jobs and opportunities with them. The fact is that no urban development program can arrest the decline of our inner cities—and no antipoverty social programs can take hold—unless they are combined with tough law enforcement measures to reduce crime.

I also pointed out that merely spending more money on social programs was not the solution. Starting with President Lyndon Johnson's Great Society domestic program in the mid-1960s, the country had been spending trillions of dollars on social programs. And yet all this spending failed. There was much more crime. In fact, it seemed the more we spent on social programs, the higher the crime rate soared.

The truth is that the correlation between poverty and crime is a weak one. Far and away, the most important factor in predicting crime is the presence or absence of a father in the family. And, here, there was a strong case—made persuasively by Stanford University economist Thomas Sowell, among others—that some of the country's social programs had contributed to the breakdown of families.

The problem with our social spending was not the scale of the programs, but their structure. What I argued for was a neighborhood-based, holistic approach in which community leaders had a seat at the table and in which law enforcement efforts were closely integrated with social programs. The problem in the past was that federal resources were spewed out by a host of different agencies—the Department of Health and Human Services, the Department of Housing and Urban Development, the Education Department, the Small Business Administration, and so forth—without any coordination among themselves or with private philanthropic efforts. Similarly, law enforcement efforts in particular neighborhoods were not coordinated with various social programs that could complement policing activities. I argued that all these initiatives should be fused in a focused and sustained effort based on neighborhoods and responsive to the needs of neighborhood families.

I worked hard to provide a tangible example of the approach I was advocating in our Weed & Seed project. No one ever came up with a better name, and the moniker caught on. When I became Attorney General, this was a fledgling concept that we were trying in a few select cities, like Richmond, Virginia. I did not have much new money to spend on the initiative, although President Bush agreed to add $500 million for it in the next year's budget. But Weed & Seed really did not require new money as much as more coordination. The key ingredient was finding communities whose natural leaders were interested in helping to run the effort. The idea became very popular, and I was inundated by calls and visits from congressmen and state leaders seeking a Weed & Seed program in their cities. Before I left office, we had inaugurated Weed & Seed designated neighborhoods in twenty cities.

The final part of my agenda on violent crime was to encourage a movement to reform the state criminal justice systems. On July 28, 1992, I held an event at the Department of Justice, attended by most of the national law enforcement groups and victims' organizations, where I released a report assessing state criminal justice systems and making twenty-four recommendations on how they could be reformed to make them more effective in reducing violent crime. The report, *Combating Violent Crime: 24 Recommendations to Strengthen Criminal Justice*, was widely endorsed by law enforcement organizations nationwide—and on a bipartisan basis. This permitted citizens to rate the effectiveness of their own state's system. The report became the launching pad for a broad campaign, involving victims' and law enforcement groups, to stop revolving-door justice and to keep chronic violent offenders off the streets.

In October 1992 I issued as a report what had been an internal working paper, *The Case for More Incarceration*, analyzing the high costs imposed on society by prematurely releasing repeat violent offenders back onto the streets so they can commit more crimes. This report argued that it was far more costly for society to free chronic offenders early than to keep them in prison for the full sentences they deserved.

I gave more than forty speeches around the country, hammering home three basic themes: First, the only way to reduce violent crime in our society is to incapacitate chronic violent offenders through a tough policy of incarceration. Second, while the federal government can help in the war on violent crime in limited ways, ultimately the answer is for the states to toughen their own criminal justice systems. And third, although law enforcement cannot do the job alone, social programs can't take the place of tough law enforcement policies. We must be smarter about the way we pursue social programs in high-crime areas and integrate them with the law enforcement activity. Those programs shouldn't foster dependency but stimulate the communities' own resourcefulness.

Our time to pursue these policies was cut short by the 1992 election, but subsequent events proved the correctness of our position. The Clinton administration saw two fairly tough anticrime bills through Congress in 1994 and 1996, the latter enacted in the wake of the 1993

Twin Tower bombing and the 1995 Oklahoma City bombing. Many of the ideas in these bills had been proposed in President Bush's crime bill, and Senator Biden had become a major advocate for them. Moreover, in the 1990s many states reformed their criminal justice systems and adopted key recommendations I had been pushing.

I believe our expansion of the federal role in fighting violent crime and our pushing for state reforms that allowed states to keep career criminals locked up had a dramatic impact. Starting in 1991–92, the sharpest shift in the direction of violent crime in our history occurred. As the federal and state governments sent more chronic violent offenders to prison—the prison population doubled during these next two decades—crime rates plummeted. For the next twenty-two years, violent crime fell every year. By 2014, it had been cut in half from its high point in 1991–92. Homicides were more than halved, dropping from 9.7 per 100,000 population in 1991 to 4.4 per 100,000 in 2014. This represents tens of thousands of lives saved during these decades. Hundreds of thousands of people in low-income neighborhoods—people who would otherwise have been victimized and preyed upon by criminals—were permitted to live and work in peace and a measure of stability.

Of course, in the last year of the H. W. Bush administration, the troubles of America's inner cities and the reality of urban violence dominated the country's consciousness. Not because of anything the administration did, but because of what happened on the night of April 29, 1992.

CHAPTER 6

A WHIRLWIND YEAR

In early 1992, CBS reporter Bob Schieffer devoted one of his Washington Notebook segments to the steady stream of law enforcement initiatives coming out of the Department of Justice. He started by saying that, since I had taken the reins, the department had "become anything but a quiet corner of the government." He titled the segment "The New Whirlwind at Justice." Indeed, it felt like a whirlwind; we were very busy. I had stressed to my staff that, in an election year, we could not allow ourselves to be distracted by the political fray and that it was vital we poured our energies into executing our affirmative agenda. But outside events were not about to make this easy.

On March 3, 1991, a twenty-six-year-old Black man named Rodney King led police on an eight-mile high-speed chase through Los Angeles. He was pulled over and, along with two passengers, arrested by officers of the California Highway Patrol and the Los Angeles Police Department. King was on parole for robbery and said later that he didn't stop for police because he was intoxicated, which violated the rules of his parole.

When King was slow in complying with the officers' order to lie down flat, a group of LAPD officers tried to force him down. They used a taser on him twice. A video taken from a nearby apartment complex shows four LAPD officers relentlessly beating King with powerful baton strokes, punches, and kicks for almost a minute and a half before he was handcuffed. When the LAPD chief of police, Daryl Gates, watched the videotape, he was aghast at the violence.

When parts of the videotapes went public later in March, President Bush condemned King's mistreatment immediately: "Those terrible scenes stir us all to demand an end to gratuitous violence and brutality. Law enforcement officials cannot place themselves above the law that they are sworn to defend. . . . It was sickening to see the beating that was rendered, and there's no way—no way, in my view—to explain that away. It was outrageous." Dick Thornburgh announced a review of all police brutality complaints to the federal government over the past six years, and the President directed him to determine whether any of those cases involved violations of federal law.

When police officers use excessive force, they can be found criminally liable both under state law, for assault and excessive force, and also under federal law, for intentional violation of civil rights. Generally, the federal government lets the state finish its case first before deciding how to proceed. Under the Department of Justice's Petite policy, so named for the 1960 Supreme Court decision *Petite v. United States*, the DOJ will usually not try defendants on federal charges for the same event if a state conviction vindicates the federal government's interests sufficiently. Only when the state result is inadequate will the federal government step in.

In the case of Rodney King, the Los Angeles district attorney moved promptly to charge four LAPD officers with assault and excessive force. DOJ waited to pursue charges against them until after the state trial. By the time the case went to trial, I had become Attorney General. Because of pretrial publicity, a state judge had moved the venue of the officers' trial from Los Angeles to neighboring Ventura County. On Wednesday, April 29, a little more than a year after King's beating, the state jury found three of the officers not guilty and deadlocked on the fourth.

The jury verdicts were announced in the evening at six forty-five Eastern Standard Time. That night, all hell broke loose in parts of Los Angeles, especially in the area of Florence and Normandie Avenues.

TV reports showed several truck drivers being pulled from their vehicles and beaten.

The next morning, I talked to the President, who expressed disbelief and chagrin at the verdicts. California governor Pete Wilson had activated the National Guard, and it was unclear at that stage whether the rioting would continue unabated. I told President Bush I would be holding a press conference at noon, California time, to explain that DOJ was moving into high gear on its federal civil rights investigation.

At my press conference, I explained that the state's case was "not the end of this process." As soon as the acquittals came down, I told reporters, I had directed that the federal investigation go forward as quickly as possible. I announced that the investigation would be overseen by the number three official in the department, Associate Attorney General Wayne Budd, who was Black, and that I had asked Wayne to go to Los Angeles immediately to take charge of the investigation, which was being handled by the FBI, the DOJ Civil Rights Division, and the Los Angeles US Attorney's Office. I promised that the case would be pursued aggressively and called for an end to the violence, echoing the President's similar message that day.

As rioting, arson, and killings mounted on Thursday, we got word that the National Guard would be delayed getting out on the streets and that Governor Wilson might ask for federal assistance. I was notified that I was to attend a meeting with President Bush and the chairman of the Joint Chiefs, Colin Powell, in the Oval Office at five in the morning to discuss how we could help the governor.

I did not want to use regular troops if there was an effective alternative. I asked George Terwilliger, the Deputy Attorney General, to work with FBI deputy director Floyd Clarke and all other components the rest of the afternoon, and all night, if necessary, to develop an alternative to using regular military forces. Terwilliger and his team got to work in the DOJ Command Center. My goal was to be able to deliver roughly two thousand federal law enforcement officers to Los Angeles by late afternoon the next day, Friday, May 1.

By midnight, when I visited Terwilliger in the Command Center, he had the makings of an excellent plan. First, we had identified every tactical unit that we could find in the federal government that was not needed otherwise. These included units from DOJ agencies—US Marshals, FBI SWAT teams and HRT, Border Patrol units, Bureau of Prisons Special Operations Response Teams—as well as units from elsewhere in the government, including the US Park Police and the Bureau of Alcohol, Tobacco, and Firearms. Those within driving distance of LA were to move out as soon as possible, while those farther away were to go to a designated airport. Air transport would be provided by a series of military transport aircraft, starting on the East Coast and hopscotching from airport to airport across the country. There would be northern, central, and southern routes for the planes to fly as they swept up all the teams waiting at the designated airports. Everything on the law enforcement side was already in motion. All that was necessary was Defense Department approval of the air transport.

A brief historical note: in 2020 some of the press coverage surrounding the rioting after George Floyd's killing suggested that I had pushed for the use of the military in responding to the LA riots in 1992. This was false. When I arrived at the White House early Friday morning, my purpose was to give President Bush an option *other than* using the military.

As we gathered in the Oval Office, the rioting had continued unabated—there had already been more than a thousand fires and at least twenty-five people killed. The President talked to LA mayor Tom Bradley and Governor Wilson, with me and Powell on the line. Equipment delays and other factors were slowing the deployment of the National Guard, and Wilson thought it would be necessary to have more federal support.

After our calls, the President sat in his usual spot—an armchair across the room from his desk, with his back to the fireplace—with everyone else arrayed on the twin couches facing each other on either side: the Vice President; me; Boyden Gray; Colin Powell; Deputy Secretary of Defense Don Atwood; and FBI director Bill Sessions. The President asked me what the options were for providing assistance to Governor Wilson.

Sessions jumped in—uninvited. "We can send the FBI's Hostage Rescue Team, Mr. President."

I had already told President Bush that I thought Sessions should be asked to leave the bureau if there was a second term. He glanced at me with a knowing look. "How many is that, Judge?" (Sessions had been a federal judge before he'd been appointed by Reagan to lead the FBI.)

"Close to seventy, Mr. President," Sessions said with a military snap.

"Well," Bush said with a wry smile, "I think we'll need a few more than that."

I explained one option was to use civilian law enforcement. I said, looking at General Powell, "If the chairman can facilitate air transport across country—and we are talking quite a few planes making a lot of stops along the way—I can provide over a thousand agents by late afternoon, followed by another thousand in fairly short order."

Powell smiled. I knew he was loath to put regular troops out in the streets, as most military men would be. He quickly gave me the name of a general to call at the Pentagon to expedite the transport. "I'll alert him now," said Powell. "We're glad to help."

"Pete [Wilson] mentioned regular military," the President said. "He is an old marine, and he knows we have a lot of marines nearby. I guess we can get them there the fastest. But I suppose we have to do that proclamation we did in Saint Croix?"

"That's right, Mr. President," I said. "You have two options. You can invoke the Insurrection Act and just take control of the National Guard; or you can invoke the act and use regular military. Or both, for that matter."

The President looked at Powell. The general rattled off all the military units in the immediate vicinity, including the marines at Camp Pendleton, seventy miles from Los Angeles. He also reminded President Bush that it is never optimal to put military forces, unaccustomed to performing a law enforcement role, onto the streets to face volatile situations.

"I have a suggestion, Mr. President," I interjected. "Let's move forward on both tracks, but don't make the call on the military until you have to. Whether or not you opt for the military, we should get the law enforcement folks out there ASAP. Meanwhile, we can get all the paperwork done so you can move the military if you later decide they are needed. DOD can get the troops into position to move fast if called on. But hopefully you won't need them." The President agreed, and the meeting broke up.

As Sessions and I walked out to our cars, I told him I wanted him to send the special agent in charge from Dallas, Buck Revell, out to LA. I wanted strong DOJ leaders in the city because they would be dealing with a complex situation involving the military and state and city officials. I also informed the FBI director that I was sending out Bob Mueller, head of the Criminal Division. Along with Revell, that gave me two very forceful leaders on the ground. Sessions opposed sending Revell, but I overruled him.

Friday was a busy day. Terwilliger and his team worked up in the Command Center, making sure all the law enforcement got to where they had to be. I was impressed with the results. The military planes flew as we asked; by midafternoon on the West Coast, law enforcement units started landing at an air base near Los Angeles, where busses were waiting to take them into the city. That flow kept up all the rest of the afternoon and all night. Meanwhile, Wayne Budd arrived in downtown LA and gave a press conference to reassure people that the federal civil rights case was "of the highest priority and will be vigorously pursued." On the same theme, I told the press in Washington that "federal grand jury activity is under way today in Los Angeles. Subpoenas have been served. Evidence is being reviewed." I added that the "federal civil rights investigation was put into high gear within an hour of the verdicts and is being aggressively pursued."

That evening, President Bush went on television. He said there were two issues. One was addressing the issue of excessive force, and the federal process was moving forward aggressively. The other was stopping the violent rioting, and he pledged to use whatever force was necessary to deal with the lawlessness. But I was surprised that night because the President invoked the Insurrection Act and cleared the way for using the regular military. When our meeting had broken up that morning at the White House, I thought there was still a chance we could rely solely on federal law enforcement and state-controlled National Guard. But the destruction had been horrendous on Friday. By evening, the overall death toll had increased to forty and more than 4,500 fires had been set.

In the end, regular military forces were deployed, but not many. The large number of federal law enforcement officers—about two thousand at their peak—and the arrival of the National Guardsmen on the streets, albeit late, limited the need for regular military forces.

One of the main uses for federal law enforcement SWAT teams was to accompany the LA Fire Department on its calls. Fires were a major challenge. By Saturday, more than 5,500 had been set. On several occasions, snipers had fired on firefighters.

I traveled out to Los Angeles a couple of times after the riots. While Associate AG Wayne Budd was supervising the civil rights case related to King's beating, a federal task force was working with state and local law enforcement investigating the rioting. On my first visit, I focused on the investigation of the rioters and visited the case rooms where the task force was investigating particular gangs and their instigation of violence. I received detailed briefings on how and where the violence unfolded, and how it correlated to gang activity. It was impressive work based on voluminous video and photos, as well as witnesses. There was no question that gangs played a large role in propelling the violence and arson in the city. ATF estimated that between four thousand and six thousand guns were stolen from stores during the rioting and believed that this was carried out by gangs.

In July I made another trip to LA. In addition to reviewing the evidence against gang members for their violent participation in the rioting, I spent time with Associate AG Budd, reviewing the evidence on the four police officers who been involved in Rodney King's beating. We sat together by ourselves in a darkened conference room watching and re-watching an enhanced version of the video showing King's beating. We also reviewed the other evidence. Under the federal civil rights statute, the government must show that the officers deprived King of his civil rights by willfully using unreasonable force. The willfulness standard is a high one, and I wanted our decisions on the four officers to be determined solely by the evidence—not by the political environment or the likelihood of future rioting if the cops went free. Wayne and I analyzed the case carefully. He believed strongly that we should proceed with a federal indictment of three of the officers for beating King, and one of the officers, the supervisor, for failing to intervene. I agreed, and the indictments were returned on August 4.

The federal trial did not take place until February and March 1993, after the Bush administration had ended. The jury ended up acquitting two of the officers, and the supervisor and one officer were found guilty, and the trial judge sentenced them each to thirty months, less than the six to seven years the department and federal sentencing guidelines recommended. The department appealed the lower sentence, but it was eventually upheld by the US Supreme Court.

The final toll of five days of rioting in LA were sixty-five killed, more than twelve thousand arrests, more than seven thousand fires, and in excess of $1 billion in losses.

Unfortunately, much of the work done by our federal task force to bring violent gang members to justice for their role in the rioting went for naught. The Clinton administration and local authorities showed little interest in pursuing cases against all but a few rioters and a number of arsonists.

In the wake of the Gulf War, the President stood at record levels of popularity. His approval rating was an astounding 89 percent. With a little more than eighteen months to go before the 1992 election, this posed a formidable problem for the Democrats. But the Democratic Party had a strong ally in the media—one that had become more aggressively partisan since the 1970s. Over that ensuing year and a half, Bush was exposed to a savage and unrelenting carpet bombing by the press—a campaign based on gross distortions and outright lies.

The first part of the media's sustained assault on the President was its distorted coverage of the economy. For eight months, beginning the previous summer, the economy had dipped into a short-lived recession. This kind of cyclical pause is normal and helps maintain long-term growth by allowing the efficient reallocation of resources needed to attain higher productivity and future economic expansion. Business-cycle recessions prepare the economy for the next period of sustained growth. But the media took one of the mildest and shortest business-cycle recessions in modern times and presented it as something akin to the Great Depression.

Ironically, when the media turned their attention from the Gulf War to the economy in March 1991, the recession had already ended. From then till the election, the economy was recovering, with nineteen months of consecutive growth. And yet—not for the last time desperate for bad news during a Republican administration—each day the media produced dozens of stories portraying the country as in the depths of a catastrophe. More than 90 percent of the economic news in newspapers and on networks was negative. As Harvard Kennedy School professor of government and the press Thomas Patterson put it, *"The networks' portrayal of the economy got worse as the economy improved"* (emphasis in original). As soon as Bill Clinton was elected, the news coverage of the economy reversed on a dime: in November 1992 only 14 percent of the economic news was negative.

The media also collectively hammered away on a theme first introduced by a *New York Times* story portraying Bush as "out of touch." The centerpiece of the story was the claim that Bush had never seen a checkout scanner before—that he had been "amazed" when he saw one at a grocers' convention. The sneering front-page story by *Times* reporter Andrew Rosenthal carried the headline BUSH ENCOUNTERS THE SUPERMARKET, AMAZED.

The story established the narrative in the first paragraph:

> As President Bush travels the country in search of reelection, he seems unable to escape a central problem: This career politician, who has lived the cloistered life of a top Washington bureaucrat for decades, is having trouble presenting himself to the electorate as a man in touch with middle-class life.

Then, describing an interaction at an exhibition of a National Grocers Association convention, the reporter explained that Bush had "grabbed a quart of milk, a lightbulb, and a bag of candy and ran them over an electronic scanner. The look of wonder flickered across his face again as he saw the item and price registered on the cash register screen. 'This is for checking out?' asked Mr. Bush. 'I just took a tour through the exhibits here,' he told the grocers later. 'Amazed by some of the technology.'"

The story was meant to suggest that Bush had never encountered an ordinary supermarket scanner. It was a lie. Despite video of the episode showing its falsity, as well as an Associated Press story reciting the facts, this fabrication was repeated and amplified in media coverage throughout the election and is still repeated today.

The demonstration was prearranged by NCR Corporation to show the President how its latest generation of scanner was capable of reading torn and damaged product codes. As the video shows and the AP story recounts, Bush approached the demonstration and asked if the scanner was the "newest" one and agreed it looked like a typical scanner. The NCR exhibitor then showed him some features, including a new feature the exhibitor said was "really quite amazing." He gave Bush a ripped-up product code card and had him run the card through the machine. The scanner read it accurately and reported the correct sale. "Isn't that something!" the President remarked.

When interviewed later, the NCR exhibitor said, "The whole thing is ludicrous. What he was amazed about was the ability of the scanner to take that torn label and reassemble it." But the truth never caught up to the false narrative, which the media continued to fan until the President was defeated. The story that Bush had never seen a supermarket scanner is still repeated as fact.

While the propaganda campaign on the economy damaged Bush, the media's abuses perpetrating the Big Lie of "Iraqgate" were unequaled until the "Russiagate" lies used against President Trump. In March 1991, at the end of the Gulf War, the mainstream media, almost acting as one, collectively took up and propagandized the totally baseless allegation that, before the war, Bush had secretly and illegally engaged in a program to build up Saddam Hussein's armed forces. This was accompanied by the further lie that Bush covered up the program by having his Attorneys General, Thornburgh and me, "obstruct" the Justice Department's investigation of illegal loans made to Iraq by the Atlanta branch of an Italian bank, Banca Nazionale del Lavoro, or BNL.

I was required to spend much of my time in 1992 dealing with Iraqgate, declining repeated demands from Democrats that an independent counsel be appointed. It was clear to me that the claims were absurd. The first part of the allegation was that, after the end of the eight-year war between Iraq and Iran in 1988, Bush funded Iraq's military buildup by secretly allowing it to divert $1 billion in "loans" or "loan guarantees" intended for agricultural commodities to buy military equipment instead, and also approved the sale of $1.5 billion in "dual use" equipment—trucks, industrial tools, computers— that Saddam Hussein used for his military. Both sets of allegations were lies.

The media coverage tried to create the impression that the Bush administration had secretly funneled $1 billion in cash into Hussein's hands either through direct US loans or bank loans guaranteed by the United States, and that the cash was diverted to buy arms. The media didn't even try to understand the program. Besides the fact that there was nothing secret about the agricultural program—it was completely in the open and had been going on for many years—it involved agricultural *credits*, not loans. All the Iraqis got was grain—and it was $392 million worth of grain in fiscal year 1990, the only year in which the Bush administration approved the credits to Iraq. Banks paid the American farmers and extended Iraq credit. Iraq was required to pay back the banks on a three-year schedule. There was never a scintilla of evidence that these grain shipments contributed in any way to Hussein's arms procurement.

Once the media's false idea that the program involved loans was exposed, some fell back on the argument that providing grain freed up Iraq from having to buy grain with its own hard currency and therefore allowed Iraq to use that currency for arms instead. Dead wrong, again. In 1990 Iraq owed banks $847 million for past grain shipments. Hussein had threatened to default on these payments if the Bush administration discontinued the program. Thus, extension of the credits by the Bush administration had the effect of requiring Hussein to deplete his hard currency by $847 billion needed to pay off the amount owed the banks.

The media's claims that Bush had helped rearm Iraq through $1.5 billion in dual-use equipment was also a gross distortion. Lots of commercial items can be used for military purposes. Sales of such dual-use equipment are scrutinized to assess the potential impact of diversion to military use and can be rejected if they pose too much of a risk. During the Iran-Iraq War, there was broad bipartisan support for US policy of "tilting" to Iraq and allowing certain dual-use sales. Of the $1.5 billion figure cited, most of this refers to sales during the Iran-Iraq War, and $1 billion of this amount was never sent because Hussein canceled a large order for trucks.

The only shipments of dual-use equipment made under the Bush administration amounted to $75 million. Even assuming all of this was diverted for military use, the amount was de minimis in relation to the many billions Hussein was spending on his military. The reality is that the United States under the Bush administration maintained the most severe restrictions on exports to Iraq of any Western country. On the eve of Saddam's invasion of Kuwait, the dictator complained to the US ambassador to Baghdad, April Glaspie, that all he could get from America was wheat. "Because every time we want to buy something, they say it is forbidden."

In a 1994 *American Lawyer* article, "Mediagate: The Anatomy of a Feeding Frenzy," Stuart Taylor Jr., a journalist who still cares about the truth, provided a detailed postmortem of the breathtaking mendacity involved in the phony Iraqgate scandal. What Taylor calls "the biggest lie of all" was the claim that Thornburgh and I attempted to conceal this "secret program" by "obstructing" a DOJ investigation into the Atlanta branch of BNL. That investigation, handled by career prosecutors in the Atlanta US Attorney's Office, started in August 1989 based on tips from two branch employees. The investigation found that the branch manager, Christopher Drogoul, with the help of subordinates and using elaborate schemes to hide the transactions from his superiors in Rome, had made $4 billion in loans to Iraq, skirting US bank regulations and BNL restrictions. The key question all along was whether Drogoul acted alone in return for kickbacks, or whether he had the approval of Banca Nazionale del Lavoro headquarters in Rome. Democratic conspiracy theorists in Congress and the media claimed that Drogoul's actions were approved by BNL as part of an alleged secret plan by the United States and Italy to rearm Hussein—a theory unsupported by any shred of evidence. The career prosecutors in Atlanta believed that Drogoul had acted without authority and that BNL was the victim. DOJ lawyers in Washington were initially skeptical of the lone-wolf theory and pushed the Atlanta team for more than a year to exhaust the possibility of Rome's complicity. By February 1991, the career lawyers in both Atlanta and Washington agreed that BNL had not authorized the loans, although Drogoul might have had some accomplices in Rome, and the branch manager was indicted.

Drogoul, repeatedly confirming that he had acted without authority, agreed to plead guilty. At a June 2, 1992, hearing on the plea deal, the federal district judge, Marvin Shoob, a Democratic appointee who repeatedly showed woeful ignorance of the facts and alarming partisanship, said he did not believe that Drogoul's actions were taken alone and suggested the Justice Department was muzzling him in order to make him give a "sanitized" account. Shockingly, the judge threatened Drogoul that unless he changed his story by the time he came back for sentencing, "he is never going to get out of jail." At a later conference, Shoob said he was going to make sure to schedule the sentencing before the presidential election. These developments helped give impetus to demands from Democrats on the House Judiciary Committee that I allow a special prosecutor to be appointed under the independent counsel statute to investigate Iraqgate. On August 10, on the advice of the career prosecutors in the department's Public Integrity Section—advice communicated in a ninety-seven-page memorandum—I rejected the House Committee's demand. I was widely attacked in the press as "lawless" and the leader of a "cover-up."

The circus continued at the sentencing hearing, scheduled to start on September 14. Unsurprisingly, given Judge Shoob's threat that he needed to change his story, Drogoul replaced his defense attorney with a longtime friend of the judge and a big Democratic donor. On September 2 a fellow inmate of Drogoul at the federal penitentiary wrote the prosecutor that Drogoul had told him that the defense didn't want Bush reelected and that its "ploy" was to stretch out sentencing so that it lasted through the election. The sentencing hearing dragged out until October 1, with Drogoul now claiming—contrary to more than a dozen statements made over the preceding three years—he was authorized to make the loans. His lawyer pronounced the case "the mother of all cover-ups," and the judge played his role, suggesting darkly that the government was not coming clean.

With the continuing attacks on Drogoul's guilty plea as part of a cover-up, on October 2 the department threw down the gauntlet, announcing we were willing for Drogoul to abandon his guilty plea and were prepared to go to trial. The DOJ also moved for Judge Shoob to recuse himself from the case, which he did. The judicial proceedings were effectively on hold until after the election.

Another twist came on the House floor on September 14 when Henry Gonzales, a longtime Democratic congressman from Texas, alleged that the CIA had evidence showing that Banca Nazionale del Lavoro's Rome headquarters was complicit in the loans. The claim was that the Department of Justice had suppressed this information. The DOJ lawyers working with the bank had not *seen* this supposed evidence, and finger-pointing between the department and the CIA helped embolden the ignoramuses alleging a conspiracy. But it turned out the "evidence" amounted to an informant's speculation and had little or no evidentiary value. It had never made it to DOJ, for innocent reasons. A few months later, a staff report by the Democratic-controlled Senate Intelligence Committee found that the CIA-DOJ episode stemmed from mistakes, not a cover-up conspiracy. Even before that, however, I had appointed a highly regarded former federal judge from New Jersey, Fred Lacey, to come to the department on a ninety-day assignment to review its handling of the BNL case.

The fact that Iraqgate's allegations were utterly baseless was confirmed by multiple investigations after the 1992 election. Judge Lacey's report, released in December 1992; Stuart Taylor's "Mediagate: Anatomy of a Feeding Frenzy," published in the journal *American Lawyer* in 1994; Kenneth Juster's "The Myth of Iraqgate," published in *Foreign Policy* magazine the same year—each demolished the entire faux scandal and revealed the dishonesty of its chief proponents, including reporters at the *Washington Post* and the *Los Angeles Times*, the *New York Times* editorial board, William Safire of the same newspaper, and Mike Wallace of CBS News's *60 Minutes*.

But the most important postmortem was conducted by Bill Clinton's Department of Justice. In June 1993 Attorney General Janet Reno tasked her longtime aide John Hogan to conduct a comprehensive review of Iraqgate allegations. Using nearly twenty prosecutors and investigators, Hogan's investigation went on for fifteen months and concluded with a 119-page report. "Neither I nor the Justice Department have any stake in protecting earlier administrations from embarrassment," Hogan stated. But he concluded: "We did not find evidence that US agencies or officials illegally armed Iraq. . . . We also considered whether the Justice Department's earlier work . . . was subverted for political purposes, and found that it was not. . . . I found no evidence of corruption or incompetence. . . . On the contrary, the work of the department and other agencies has by and large been thorough, persistent, and careful."

The truth never made a difference to the partisan media. Their bogus narrative was an unmitigated success. In less than two years under unremitting pounding by the media, President George Bush's great success in the Gulf War—a performance that won him unprecedentedly high approval ratings—had been converted into a liability. Days before the election, ABC News reported that a "Wall Street Journal/ NBC poll showed that 68 percent of the American public has major doubts about George Bush's explanations of his administration's role in providing aid to Saddam Hussein before the Persian Gulf War." The Democrats and their chums in the press had sold the narrative. As the Democratic candidate for Vice President, Al Gore, said in a preelection speech: "George Bush wants the American people to see him as the hero who put out a raging fire. But new evidence now shows that he is the one who set the fire."

The media's bias was blatant. Even their members—only 7 percent of whom voted for Bush—saw that. A Pew Research Center poll found that 55 percent of American journalists believed that George Bush's candidacy was damaged by the way the press covered him. A pro-Bush bumper sticker put it well: "Annoy the Media, Reelect Bush."

Stuart Taylor explained why he had taken the time to dissect the media's behavior two years after the fact:

> Because the falsehoods and distortions that pervaded reporting and commentary about Iraqgate in 1992 were truly outrageous. Because compelling evidence of their falsity has been piling up, virtually ignored by the media. Because phony scandals like this one . . . are a recurring phenomenon. Because the costs—which include the smearing of innocent officials of all ranks and the spread of cynicism about government, the media, and public affairs—are heavy.
>
> And because all this suggests that the media are badly botching their fundamental job of telling the truth about major public issues, due to political bias, sloppiness with facts, and old-fashioned sensationalism.

Things have only gotten worse.

But that wasn't the only faux scandal hawked by the media during that election year. By then, an independent counsel, Lawrence Walsh, had been investigating the so-called Iran-Contra affair for almost six years. That matter had arisen during the Reagan administration, and Walsh had been appointed to investigate it under the independent counsel statute, first enacted in 1974 and reauthorized ten years later. The statute, which would expire in December 1992, provided that if there were reasonable grounds to investigate potential criminality by certain designated officials—including the President, cabinet officials, and senior White House staff—a three-judge court must appoint an independent prosecutor to conduct the investigation and any resulting prosecutions. Prosecutors appointed under the statute can be removed only "for good cause," and thus, as a practical matter, operate independently from the department, although they were supposed to adhere to Justice Department policies.

The Iran-Contra matter involved two different operations. First, in 1985 President Reagan authorized the secret sale of antitank and antiaircraft weaponry to Iran both to facilitate the release of hostages being held by the terrorist organization Hezbollah in Lebanon and also to build bridges to perceived moderate elements in Iran. These arms transfers were intricate transactions and were conducted in 1985 and 1986. The DOJ position was that the sales were legal and there was never any question about the fact that the National Security Council principals—including the President, Vice President Bush, Secretary of Defense Caspar Weinberger, and Secretary of State George Shultz—were aware of the basic facts. It was always acknowledged that Bush knew about the program.

And Walsh, whose investigation started at the end of 1986, never concluded that the arms sales were illegal. Nor did he find that the principals' knowledge of the arms sales program was illegal.

His claims of illegality focused instead on a second secret operation carried out by NSC staff members. This involved the diversion of some of the proceeds from the arms sales to support the Contras—a CIA-backed anti-Communist force fighting the Sandinistas in Nicaragua. Walsh believed the diversion constituted a conspiracy to violate the so-called Boland Amendment, which barred use of intelligence funds to support the Contras. The independent counsel never claimed that the principals, including the President and Vice President, were aware of the diversion. Indeed, he specifically found "no evidence that Bush was aware of the diversion."

Walsh's investigation went on for six years. He initially focused on the people from NSC staff involved in the diversion, but his convictions of NSC officials—Oliver North and John Poindexter—were overturned. In the last couple of years of his investigation, he fixed his attention on people who had, Walsh alleged, misled Congress about the programs. Both administrations had treated Walsh with respect, but he developed what appeared to be an intense dislike for President Bush.

By the time of the 1992 election, three people had pleaded guilty to misdemeanors and been given probation: Robert McFarlane of the NSC, Elliott Abrams of the State Department, and Alan Fiers of the CIA. A fourth, Clair George, formerly head of Operations for the CIA, had been convicted of false statements to Congress and was awaiting sentencing. Two more, Weinberger and CIA operations officer Dewey Clarridge, had been charged with making false statements to Congress and were awaiting trial.

On Friday, October 30, 1992—four days before the election—polls showed Bush closing the gap with Clinton. According to the Gallup poll, the Arkansas governor held only a 1-point lead, 41 percent to 40 percent, while Bush's own tracking polls had the race tied at 39 percent. There was no question that the incumbent was picking up steam heading into the last weekend.

But on Friday, Walsh filed a reindictment of Caspar Weinberger. It focused on the fact that, in producing documents to the prosecutor, the former defense secretary had not turned over a diary. Walsh also violated department policy by gratuitously including a reference to a passage in Weinberger's diary indicating that the Vice President had been at a meeting in which the Iranian arm sales had been discussed and had favored the arms transfer. There was no justification for filing the new indictment four days before the election or for mentioning Bush, and a number of lawyers on Walsh's team complained to him about including the reference to Bush. It was not news, as Walsh admitted later. Bush's knowledge of the arms sale was never disputed. There was no other explanation for its inclusion than that, four days before the election, it gave the press a reason to imply that Bush had lied or done something wrong. It worked. Bush was battered by front-page stories Saturday and through the weekend, suggesting that

Weinberger's diary somehow implicated the President. His polling gains collapsed. He lost the election.

Walsh's personal animus against the President was apparent. Everyone in the administration felt what he had done had been grossly partisan, wildly irresponsible, and deliberate. Bush flew back to Washington from Houston the day after the election. A large crowd of his political appointees had gathered at the White House to welcome him and his wife, Barbara, as they got off Marine One. Bush felt that Walsh and his team had deliberately sabotaged his reelection, and he was furious. As the President made his way to the White House, he saw me in the crowd and gestured for me to follow him. Once we arrived at the Oval, the President unleashed on Walsh in a sharp tone filled with anger, but still under control.

"That son of a bitch Walsh," he said. "What he did was despicable. Is there any justification for what he did? It was political—cost me the election."

I told him I agreed it was politically motivated and an egregious abuse of power. "The department would never have dropped an indictment like that on the eve of the election—or on the eve of any election. There was no reason for it, and certainly no reason to mention you in it. Some of the old-line career lawyers at the department are mortified."

The President shook his head in disgust. "It cost me the goddamn election—I had the momentum, and he pulled the rug out from under me."

"I'd like to have fired him before this," I said. "He's been milking this case for all it's worth for six years, running up huge expenses and living like a king on the taxpayers' backs. And we're still looking at whether he lied about mishandling of classified documents."

"This was a *flagrant* abuse," the President kept saying.

"You know he's protected under the statute," I said, "and we all thought trying to fire him would just guarantee a firestorm. Anyway, the court would just appoint another—probably one of his lieutenants. But this outrage justifies firing the prick."

The President asked me to follow up with Boyden Gray, and I left the Oval. I felt miserable about what had happened. Here was a man who had nobly and repeatedly served the country, starting when he enlisted in the navy after high school to fight in World War II. He had conducted American foreign policy with amazing deftness—helping to deliver the end of the Cold War, the collapse of the Soviet Union, the peaceful liberation of Eastern Europe, and the broad, powerful international coalition that defeated aggression in the Mideast. And by rejecting calls for quick fixes that would hurt the economy over the long term, he stayed the course through the 1990–91 recession. After one of the shortest and least consequential recessions of the modern era, the US economy was rebounding. Yet the American people rejected him in favor of Bill Clinton. For all of us in the Bush administration, it was no secret why this happened: it was the relentless, savage attacks of the media.

In December 1992, in the last days of the administration, I was asked to come over to the Oval Office to talk with the President about possible pardons for Weinberger and others. I knew Bush thought Weinberger deserved a pardon. He said Cap Weinberger had been a principal architect of the nation's Cold War victory, and he had a long and distinguished career of service to the country. Weinberger was seventy-five and ill, and his wife had cancer. Bush believed he deserved honor, not the torment of an arduous legal proceeding. Indeed, while there was nothing illegal about the arms transfers, he had been the one who most opposed them. I agreed strongly that Weinberger should be pardoned, as did everyone else I can recall speaking with.

We knew that the President's critics would claim he was pardoning Weinberger to protect himself from criminal exposure. This was preposterous. Neither Weinberger nor any of the other five individuals pardoned had any information that would implicate Bush in any crime. Walsh had never claimed that Bush knew about the diversion—the only component of Iran-Contra that came close to a criminal offense. In his final report, the independent counsel acknowledges specifically that there was no evidence Bush knew about the diversion. Nor does he suggest that Weinberger's diary or anything else indicated otherwise. The diary stunt was Lawrence Walsh's October surprise.

There was some talk, however, that the President should limit the pardons to two or three. I took the position that President Bush should pardon all six men. I was particularly concerned that it would not be fair to pardon only the political-level officials while leaving out the CIA officers. All three—Clair and Clarridge in particular—were legends within the agency and had long and distinguished careers fighting the Cold War. I thought leaving them out after their courageous service would not go over well at the agency. My view, as I said at the time, was "In for a penny, in for a pound."

President Bush issued an eloquent proclamation explaining why he believed those pardons were required by "honor, decency, and fairness." He noted four considerations: they acted out of patriotism, they did not seek or obtain any profit, each had a long record of distinguished service, and they had already paid a price grossly disproportionate to any misdeeds.

The pardons were the right thing to do. I supported them at the time and still do.

Despite how the election had ended, I left the Department of Justice satisfied that I had served an honest and capable President and done so with honor. Stunts like Walsh's, the media's savage partisanship, the Democrats' constant invention of new allegations—these have become the lot of any Republican administration. But we had advanced the interests of the country for four years, and that was the most an administration could do.

Still, I was ready for a long vacation.

As I left the Department of Justice for the last time, I assumed I wouldn't be back.

PART III

INTERLUDE

—————

CHAPTER 7

RETURN TO CIVILIAN LIFE

After leaving the government in January 1993, I was to spend the next twenty-six years in the private sector, with no intention of going into public service again. Initially, I returned to my old law firm, Shaw, Pittman, but soon a number of corporations approached me about serving as general counsel—the top legal position in a corporation.

In July 1994 I decided to join GTE Corp., based in Stamford, Connecticut, as general counsel and head of regulatory affairs. At the time, GTE was the largest independent telephone company in the United States outside the Bell system and the third-largest publicly owned telecommunications company in the world. I opted for GTE because the telecommunications industry was going through revolutionary changes—with the wireless sector taking off and the consumer Internet just starting to emerge. This transformation required a major reform of the regulatory structure of the industry, and there were already major battles under way over the direction those changes should take. This meant that, in a telecom company, the legal and regulatory functions were not merely a support service within the business, but played a central role.

When I was interviewing with GTE, I told its chief executive officer, Chuck Lee, that I knew nothing about the telecom industry except that phones ring. Chuck said that he considered that an advantage. The phone business had been set in its ways for many decades, he explained, but things were changing radically, and he wanted someone with broad experience who was not weighed down by past thinking and could look at everything afresh. GTE was headed into a regulatory free-for-all, he said, and he wanted someone who would be imaginative and aggressive in pursuing its interests. I was attracted by Chuck's attitude. One of the problems with regulated companies is that they kowtow too often to the regulators and shy away from standing up for themselves because they are afraid the regulators will retaliate. Some act like hostages suffering from Stockholm syndrome. Chuck made it clear this was not his approach. He wanted me to fight hard and would back me up.

The revolution in the telecom industry had gotten under way in 1984, with the breakup of the old Bell System monopoly, led by AT&T. As the result of a Department of Justice antitrust suit, AT&T was confined to the long-distance business, while Bell System's local phone business was divided among seven separate public companies known as Regional Bell Operating Companies, or "Baby Bells," each responsible for a separate region of the country. GTE's local phone business consisted of more than twenty million lines in forty states, serving mostly secondary markets that had not been part of the Bell System. The corporation was also the second-largest provider of cellular telephone services at the time.

Because my daughters were attached to the all-girls school they were attending, they were reluctant to move to Connecticut, and so I decided to commute up to Stamford weekly from our home in Northern Virginia. This made sense because, in addition to serving as general counsel, I was also in charge of the company's governmental affairs and regulatory office in Washington, DC. With all the regulatory activity under way, I ended up splitting my time between Stamford and Washington.

Going in-house as a corporation's general counsel was the best professional decision I made. As pleasant as Shaw, Pittman was, when you have only one client—your company—and your whole in-house legal team is dedicated to representing that company, there is more of a sense of mission and a stronger feeling of collegiality. I was fortunate to find at GTE an exceptionally able personal assistant, Diane, who was to help me immeasurably throughout the next nearly fifteen years.

Once ensconced at GTE, my wife and I decided to splurge on a series of family trips. We had not had much quality family time when I was at DOJ. Over three years, we visited Rome, the highlight of which was a private audience with Pope John Paul II in his library; London, where the girls had a private tour of Number 10 Downing Street, the official residence of the British prime minister; and Ireland, where we took the girls to see the tiny cottages on the west coast in County Mayo and County Clare, where Chris's grandparents and my grandmother grew up, respectively.

Even in the private sector, I was able to address crime policy. In 1994, the new governor of Virginia, George Allen, asked me to co-chair—along with my friend Richard Cullen, the former US Attorney in Richmond—Virginia's commission to abolish parole. Our proposals were adopted and greatly strengthened the state's justice system.

Meanwhile, my work at GTE was all I had hoped for. When I arrived at the company, Congress was in the midst of considering the first major overhaul of the telecommunications laws in more than sixty years. Partly due to the excellent work of our legislative office, and partly because we were not as dominant as the Baby Bells in our states, we managed to get GTE exempted from many of the more onerous provisions in the proposed legislation. But once Congress enacted the statute—the Telecommunications Act of 1996—the Federal Communications Commission went about implementing it in the most lamebrain way imaginable. It issued elaborate rules in a series of three tranches, or what the FCC called its "trilogy." After the FCC chairman released the first part of his trilogy with great fanfare, the press asked me what I thought. I said that, after seeing Moe, I wasn't holding my breath for Larry and Curly.

The fundamental problem with the FCC rules was that, instead of promoting the *real* competition that was now possible with new technologies, they actually throttled genuine competition. The rules came at a time when technology—like Internet protocol, mobile and fixed wireless, and satellite—was providing new ways to bypass the phone companies' copper wire into the home. For example, by using Internet protocol (IP), cable systems could be converted from one-way broadcast systems into two-way communications networks—as they have been today. But instead of stimulating innovation and the development of alternative facilities, the FCC rules required the Baby Bells and GTE to offer their entire networks at deeply discounted wholesale prices to companies that would do nothing but resell this local service under their own brand name. The artificially low wholesale prices not only failed to compensate the local companies for their actual costs but also enabled resellers to set such low retail prices that neither the incumbent nor an entrant could justify investing in new facilities. Thus, under the Federal Communications Commission's vision, competition for local phone service would end up as an illusion: resellers, such as long-distance companies AT&T, MCI, and Sprint, were simply slapping their own labels on the underlying local service provided by the single incumbent local company.

Not only did the FCC rules snuff out investment in alternative facilities by would-be competitors, but also the rules came at a time when the phone companies needed to upgrade their lines from copper to glass fiber in order to bring robust broadband to the home. These upgrades would cost tens of billions of dollars of new investment by the local phone companies. But the FCC rules froze this deployment by leaving unresolved how the wholesale obligations and discounts would apply to these new networks.

I believed that the FCC's wholesale rules went beyond its statutory authority, and GTE's objective was to scuttle them. The Baby Bells generally agreed, and we joined together in a series of legal challenges. My key outside adviser was Paul Cappuccio, my old aide from DOJ, who had joined the Kirkland & Ellis law firm. We pursued two lines of attack. The first was that the Federal Communications Commission had been too sweeping in defining the parts of the incumbents' networks that had to be "unbundled" and provided to competitors at wholesale rates. The statute required that competitors get access only to those parts of the incumbent's network where that access was "necessary" for them to compete and where failure to provide access to a proprietary part would "impair" their ability to compete. Instead of going through that analysis, the FCC rules simply declared ipse dixit that competitors must be given access to the entire local company's network from stem to stern—as if it were one element.

The second line of attack was on the wholesale prices dictated by the FCC. We claimed that the wholesale rates did not adequately compensate the incumbents for the actual costs of supplying the network. These two separate claims were pursued through two different sets of court challenges, involving numerous appellate cases around the country and two Supreme Court cases. I ended up arguing many of the cases on behalf of the local phone companies, including the cases before the Supreme Court.

Ultimately, we succeeded in knocking out the FCC rules by winning the first argument. In late 1998 I argued before the Supreme Court that, in defining the parts of the incumbents' networks to which competitors had to be given access, the FCC failed to apply the statutory standards of "necessary" to compete and "impairment" of competition. The court agreed and struck down this section of the rules. This effectively froze the entire wholesale regime until the FCC could come up with an acceptable new rule. But the Federal Communications Commission could never get a new rule off the ground. Its first effort to cure the defect was struck down again in 2002 by the DC Circuit Court of Appeals for much the same reason as the Supreme Court had struck down the original rule. Finally, in 2004, the same court considered the FCC's third and last effort to define the network parts that incumbents had to provide. Once again the rule was struck down on multiple grounds. Realizing how the FCC's misbegotten rulemaking was delaying the deployment of broadband, President George W. Bush's administration refused to authorize an appeal, and the FCC finally gave up.

As markets and technology evolved, the telecom industry was ripe for consolidation, and the process began a couple of years after I arrived at GTE, starting with combinations of Baby Bells. The first wave came in April 1996, when NYNEX Corporation, which operated in

New England and New York, and Bell Atlantic, which served the Mid-Atlantic states, announced a merger of equals, with the surviving company to be called Bell Atlantic. That same month, the Baby Bell, Southwestern Bell, which operated from Missouri down through Texas—soon after changing its name to SBC Communications (SBC)—announced the acquisition of Pacific Telesis Group (commonly called PacTel), which operated in California and Nevada.

The next wave came two years later in 1998, when SBC announced its acquisition of Ameritech, which operated in the upper Midwest. As that deal was unfolding, GTE was negotiating a merger of equals with Bell Atlantic. This deal was immensely complicated from a regulatory standpoint because GTE held assets involving long-distance traffic that Bell Atlantic was foreclosed from owning until it satisfied certain regulatory benchmarks. Nonetheless, we were able to hammer out an agreement, which was announced in July 1998.

In 1997, a year before the Bell Atlantic–GTE deal was inked, WorldCom, a long-distance company, reached an agreement to acquire MCI. Both companies carried major shares of Internet traffic, and together they would control more than half of all Internet traffic. I was concerned that the combination would have "network effects"—a phenomenon I will discuss in a later chapter about Big Tech today. Basically, once a network captures a large share of users relative to other players, its lead reaches a tipping point in some markets and will snowball, inexorably achieving market dominance. GTE was just getting into the business of transporting Internet traffic, and I decided to do something that had not been done before in our industry. I challenged the WorldCom-MCI transaction in the European Union and went over to Brussels, Belgium, to argue the case personally before the EU's competition directorate. I hired some excellent French economists, who did groundbreaking analysis supporting our network effects argument.

The format of the proceeding itself was new to me. It took place in a large amphitheater, with the parties and advisers seated around a huge table, roughly fifty by fifteen feet. At one end of the table, the commission's case-team panel, responsible for investigating the proposed merger, sat on a dais. Around the walls were commission staff, observers, and glass-enclosed translators' booths. The lawyer for WorldCom was a British barrister, who spoke first and, while seated, read his entire presentation in a monotone from a large binder. He droned on and on, reading every word. I had not been aware this was the way the panel expected arguments to be given, but I was not going to change what I had in mind.

I got up and talked animatedly as I walked around the table, using a laser pointer to illustrate exhibits on a large screen. I had steeped myself in the material and economic arguments, so I spoke without notes, often with some pungency. At one point, I caught movement out of the corner of my eye, and, looking up, I saw the French translator inside her booth getting into the spirit of my presentation and waving her arms around. After I spoke, there was a break, and numerous European staff and panel members came up to tell me that they "had never seen anything like it," loved it, and would like to see more of this kind of advocacy.

We won. The commission agreed with our "network effects" argument and ordered, as a condition of approving the merger, that World-Com and MCI not only divest some of their Internet facilities but also that MCI sell off contracts for thousands of its business and residential Internet customers.

Meanwhile, as it turned out, the GTE–Bell Atlantic merger agreement was one of the longest pending deals on record. It took almost two years—until June 2000—to get it approved by the FCC and the DOJ, as well as numerous state regulators. Once we consummated the merger, the resulting combined company was rebranded Verizon. I was asked to stay on as general counsel of the new combined company. GTE's leader, Chuck Lee, served as chairman, and his counterpart at Bell Atlantic, Ivan Seidenberg, became CEO of the new company. I started splitting my time between our new headquarters in New York City and our governmental affairs and regulatory offices in Washington.

On September 11, 2001, I was home in Virginia, preparing to leave for downtown when the planes struck the World Trade Center towers.

Watching the initial news coverage, I realized it was a terrorist attack. I left home for the DC office and was on the George Washington Memorial Parkway, which runs along the Virginia side of the Potomac, when the radio reported that other planes were at large and further attacks were possible. I had a view of the Pentagon and suddenly saw a huge plume of billowing smoke. Little did I know at the time that one of our friends was on the plane that hit the Pentagon: Barbara Olson, the wife of the Solicitor General, Ted Olson. Within days, I drove up to New York. We could clearly see from our office windows the smoke still rising over Lower Manhattan.

Over the next couple of days, I heard a number of officials refer to the World Trade Center as a "crime scene." I became concerned that we would treat Al Qaeda's attacks as a matter to be handled through the criminal justice system rather than as a national security matter. On September 13 I called the deputy counsel to President George W. Bush, Tim Flanagan, who had served as head of the Office of Legal Counsel during the last few months of my tenure as Attorney General. I made the case to Tim that these terrorist attacks were acts of armed foreign aggression in violation of the laws of war. As such, if there was to be any trial, those proceedings should be before military commissions, not our domestic civilian courts. I reminded him of some of the legal research we had done at OLC almost a decade earlier relating to the Pan Am 103 bombing. It turned out that Vice President Dick Cheney had the same view, and President Bush issued an executive order establishing military tribunals.

Over the next few years, I was asked to testify before various congressional committees in support of the Bush administration's handling of the war on terror. I explained the difference under our Constitution between actions taken to enforce our domestic laws against errant individuals and actions taken to defend the country from foreign adversaries who attack the country. Unfortunately, a series of ill-considered Supreme Court cases have utterly confused these two distinct spheres and have thus succeeded in tying the country's antiterrorism efforts in knots. That the five coconspirators charged with planning the 9/11 attacks have yet to face justice twenty years after the fact is a national disgrace.

In 2003 Chuck Lee took a well-earned bow and stepped down as chairman at Verizon. Ivan Seidenberg assumed both the role of chairman and CEO. Ivan—always referred to as just "Ivan" at all levels of the company—was a phenomenal leader. Growing up in the Bronx, he first worked for New York Bell as a cable splicer. After serving in combat in Vietnam, Ivan returned to the phone company and worked his way through college and business school at night, eventually becoming CEO of NYNEX. Seidenberg was a master strategist and, through a series of deft deals—mergers with Bell Atlantic and then GTE, and multiple wireless deals—he built up Verizon into one of the two main telecom companies in the United States. After Chuck left, Ivan grew the business more by acquiring MCI in 2005 and the wireless company Alltel in 2008. Although Verizon was a huge and complex corporation, Ivan had mastery over all aspects of the business and ran it with a sure hand. I learned a lot about management and leadership from him.

My nearly fifteen years in the telecom business coincided with the most exciting era in the industry. The legal and regulatory issues I got to handle were, in Judge Robert Bork's phrase, "an intellectual feast." My daily fare involved novel regulatory issues, hard-fought legal battles in the antitrust and intellectual property arenas, and major transactions. One of the ironies is that, when I started in 1994, the conventional wisdom among most analysts was that the long-distance companies—AT&T and MCI/WorldCom—would own the future and that the stodgy local phone companies such as the Baby Bells and GTE would end up as roadkill. Exactly the opposite happened. The local companies assembled into two clusters: NYNEX, Bell Atlantic, and GTE, on the one hand, and SBC, PacTel, Ameritech, and Bell South, on the other. Then each entity acquired a long-distance company: the former entity, Verizon, bought MCI; and the latter entity, SBC, purchased AT&T (and decided to use the AT&T name).

As much as I enjoyed working with Ivan Seidenberg, I decided to retire from Verizon at the end of 2008. There were three reasons for my decision. First, by my standards, I had already made ample money—enough for Chris and me to have a decent retirement. Second, I felt I had been running full tilt for thirty-five years in a succession of stressful positions without respite, and, having spent almost fifteen years in essentially the same general counsel job, I was ready for a change of pace. The commute was becoming tiresome. Finally, I wanted to reduce my workload and have more control over my schedule. This last feeling became especially strong after my parents died within a few years of each other, and I spent a lot of time in 2005–06 alone in their home in northwestern Connecticut, going through their possessions and settling their affairs. What affected me the most as I sat in the empty house—eerily silent except for the echoes of the ticking clock—was coming across their many unfinished projects all in a state of suspended animation. It hit me hard, reminding me starkly of the shortness of life.

Throughout our marriage, an ongoing joke between Chris and me was my succession of pledges to her each time I took on a new, challenging job. I would promise that, if she would let me get through just this next one, we would finally slow down and take time for ourselves. This started while I was working and going to night law school. I promised her, "Just wait till I get law school under my belt." But after that, it was, "Just wait for me to finish this clerkship." And then, "Just wait for me to make partner at the law firm." When President George H. W. Bush came to the Department of Justice in 1991 for my swearing-in as Attorney General, I gave remarks in which I went through the whole litany, and ended with, "So Chris, I promise: once I get this Attorney Generalship under my belt, we will take time to smell the flowers." Everyone laughed. But I did not keep my word. Instead, I had accepted a demanding corporate job that had me commuting every week for nearly fifteen years to the New York area, while she bore the main burden of raising our three daughters. It was time for me to come through.

And so I retired from Verizon at the beginning of 2009. I could not have been happier how this turned out. Over the next ten years, I took on a limited number of legal matters either as "of counsel" (a senior adviser, but not a partner) to the law firm of Kirkland & Ellis or as a solo consultant. These matters for corporate clients were intellectually stimulating but not all-consuming. In addition to this legal work, I was invited to join a number of boards of directors, including the boards of two large public companies, Dominion Energy, headquartered in Richmond, and Time Warner in New York. I was fortunate to serve on these boards because it gave me the opportunity to work very closely with two superb chief executives: Tom Farrell at Dominion and Jeff Bewkes at Time Warner. Both were brilliant strategists who skillfully guided their companies through sectors undergoing rapid change: the energy and media content sectors.

As I had hoped, my retiring from Verizon gave Chris and me the chance to spend much more relaxing time together. Over the next three years, we traveled more than we ever had before—sometimes just the two of us, sometimes with the children, and other times with longtime family friends. While we especially enjoyed Italy and France, we still managed to spend time in our favorite places: Scotland, England, and Ireland. Our daughters Mary and Patricia were married by this time, and in 2010 grandchildren started arriving.

With more leisure time, I was also able to indulge my old event-planning habits from my days as social chairman at my fraternity. Starting in 2009, we held the first Barr Family Annual Ceilidh. The Gaelic word *ceilidh* in Scottish (or *ceili* in Irish), pronounced "kay-lee," means a social get-together with traditional music and dancing. I started holding these events for more than 120 guests in hotel ballrooms. It was essentially like having a large wedding reception every year. In addition to food and drink, we'd have bagpiping, of course, and I'd also book a traditional Celtic dance band and a "caller" to guide people through traditional Irish and Scottish dances—which are analogous to American square dancing. In the Baltimore area, we have some of the best traditional musicians in the world, and I would always have them play for the dancing. The pipers from my old band would provide the piping music. I then started getting more ambitious, expanding the events to feature—in addition to the local musicians—

major artists from Scotland or Ireland, who I would book while they were on tour in the United States.

I asked my daughters to invite half the guests. This large group of younger people helped keep the dancing energetic. The first big ceilidh we held was at the old Washington Club on Dupont Circle. Although the turnout was huge, I worried that no one would participate in the traditional dancing. But when the caller announced the first dance, *everyone* got up to dance. The events have been that way ever since. Quite a few prominent Washingtonians came to enjoy these parties, and I soon started getting many requests for invitations.

In January 2012 our world was turned upside down. Our daughter Meg, then twenty-seven, was diagnosed with Hodgkin's lymphoma. Meg had just completed a judicial clerkship and was two weeks into her new job as an assistant US attorney in the District of Columbia. I will always be grateful to the US attorney there, Ron Machin, and his management team for their kindness and willingness to accommodate Meg while she was ill. She was assigned to appellate work so that she could work on briefs while being treated.

Ordinarily, Hodgkin's is an eminently curable form of cancer, and, based on her initial response to chemotherapy, which was administered by a DC oncologist, it was thought her chances of being cured were close to 95 percent. Unfortunately, the disease proved to be refractory and surged back in July 2012 during her chemotherapy treatments. This dropped Meg's odds appreciably. We had already visited a wonderful oncologist at the Dana-Farber Cancer Institute in Boston and established a relationship with her just in case Meg's case became complicated. As Meg, Chris, and I sat crushed and distraught after getting the bad news, I e-mailed the Dana-Farber oncologist. She got back to us immediately even though she was on vacation, and, within days, we were heading up to Boston. I withdrew from a legal project I was working on, and Chris and I got an apartment in Boston so we could stay with Meg during her treatment. We were there for six months.

Once in Boston, Meg started a second line of chemo to prepare her for a stem cell transplant. But in another distressing setback, her disease resisted this particular drug. By this time, Meg, like me, had become a voracious consumer of medical studies and literature. We both saw charts showing that her chances for successful treatment at this stage had dropped to 17 percent. Even though Meg's oncologist told us to ignore these numbers, it was hard not to get down. The oncologist remained upbeat, however, and moved immediately to plan B: using radiation to drive down the disease, followed by high-dose chemo and the stem cell transplant. Meg's transplant was completed in late November, but the hospital wanted us to stay in the area for an additional ninety days, if possible, which we did. A PET scan to see if the disease was still detectable would not be done for six months.

We were fortunate to have a lot of support while in Boston. One of Meg's college friends from the University of Notre Dame was living there, and she visited Meg regularly, and many other high school and college friends were constantly rotating through as well. My old friend Bob Kimmitt had introduced me to a priest friend of his, Monsignor John McLaughlin, then living in Boston, who had been the head of vocations for the Catholic military chaplains. He became very close to us, and we relied heavily on his spiritual support. To my surprise, we adored the social worker assigned to us at Dana-Farber. When first offered her services, I said we did not really need a social worker, but she quickly became indispensable and made life much easier for us. While I found Dana-Farber extremely patient-friendly, the social worker helped things go more smoothly and reduced the stress.

After Meg's transplant, we were all emotionally drained and still had more anxious times ahead. With Christmas approaching, I decided to try to rent a place outside the noisy city, possibly by the shore. I called a real estate agent at random. It turned out she had worked in the Reagan White House and knew who I was. Once she learned the circumstances, she said she had an idea and would get back to me. She soon called back with the news that a former telecom executive had a large home on the shore in Scituate, Massachusetts, near Boston, which was empty for several months, and he would be delighted to let us use his house, paying just the utilities. This proved a blessing. Chris, Meg, and I spent three months cocooned in this beautiful home, taking walks together on the beach and enjoying the lovely setting. As my daughter said, it was the worst of times and the best of times.

At the time we left the Boston area at the end of February 2013, a new monoclonal antibody was showing promise as a post-transplant "consolidation" treatment, designed to knock out any lingering cancer cells. The FDA had not approved it for this use yet, although it had been approved for other uses. Meg wanted to try it. One of the great things about the American health care system is that doctors have the freedom to make off-label use of drugs if they believe it would benefit their patient. I talked to a physician at the US Food and Drug Administration who said that, if he were in my shoes, he would get the monoclonal antibody treatment for his child. Dana-Farber could not administer it, but a proponent of the treatment at Columbia University Medical Center was willing to treat Meg with it. She completed this course of immunotherapy at the end of 2013. Shortly afterward, the antibody was approved by the FDA for post-transplant consolidation in cases of Hodgkin's lymphoma.

During the three years following the transplant, we would travel up to Dana-Farber every six months for Meg to undergo a PET scan. As everyone touched by cancer knows, the anxiety around these regular imaging procedures is profound. After three years, the scans were reduced to once a year. Our daughter's last scan was at the end of 2017 and continued to show no evidence of disease.

We took nothing for granted, but as time passed, we all started to breathe a little easier. Meg continued in the US attorney's office, now able to work on trials. Meanwhile, in 2016 I learned I had prostate cancer, and my surgery for that was successful. Once that was out of the way, I took on a major matter for a corporate client and returned to Kirkland & Ellis as "of counsel" to get the support I needed to handle the matter.

PART IV

TRUMP YEARS

INTRODUCTION

I had long planned on supporting Jeb Bush for the Republican presidential nomination in 2016.

We had become friends during his father's administration many years earlier, and I campaigned for him when he ran for governor in Florida. He was down-to-earth, thoughtful, and soundly conservative, with an effective record as governor. I knew he stood for a strong national defense and was tough on crime. He understood how America's newly discovered energy abundance could allow us to become once again the world's mecca for clean and efficient manufacturing. He was also passionate about the issue I considered paramount if we are going to put our country back on the road to sanity—school choice—giving parents more control over their children's education and providing more diverse and rich educational options. I made substantial contributions to his campaign and was pulling hard for him.

On June 16, 2015, I watched on television with trepidation as Donald Trump descended the escalator to the lobby of Trump Tower to announce his presidential run. I did not know Trump and had never met him. Most of my business friends in New York who knew him did not have a favorable opinion, considering him grossly self-centered and needlessly contentious. I suspected, based on his meandering positions over the years, that Trump was a political opportunist who had no real political convictions and for whom policy positions were a matter of political expedience. I thought he was probably a typical New York businessman who didn't care much about social issues but tilted right of center on fiscal and national security issues. One of the main reservations I had about Trump was that, with his love of deal making and lack of philosophical moorings, he would cut foolish deals with the Democrats simply in order to "accomplish" something and take a victory lap.

The idea of putting the fate of the conservative movement and the Republican Party in the hands of Donald Trump was unsettling. I did not see him as our best standard-bearer, and I was worried that, if he failed to win the nomination—which I initially thought was likely—he would be a sore loser and end up dividing the party.

The stakes in the 2016 presidential contest, I felt, were the highest of any election in my lifetime. In my view, the Obama administration had pushed America onto the path of decline. His policies had throttled the economy, degraded the culture, and frittered away US strength and credibility in foreign affairs. I also believed that, for all his urbane affect, Obama was still the left-wing agitator who had patiently steered the Democratic Party toward an illiberal, identity-obsessed progressivism. He was primarily responsible, as I saw it, for the party's sharp shift to the Left. By the end of his term, this radical form of progressivism was becoming the Democrats' center of gravity, threatening our freedoms, prosperity, and what was left of our national cohesion. Four more years of Democratic rule, I feared, could take us to the point where the damage to the country could be irreversible.

For eight years, Obama's policies had squeezed the life out of the American economy. As he busily piled tax and regulatory burdens on US businesses, especially small business, the economy experienced the slowest recovery since World War II. To justify this economic torpor, the administration and its allies theorized that anemic growth must be the new normal; the days of robust economic expansion and wage growth, they argued, were over.

One of the Obama administration's saddest legacies was the increase in welfare dependency. President Obama claimed his expansions of Medicaid and other forms of social welfare would promote "equality." The opposite happened. Inequality increased under Obama, and Black Americans especially fell further behind.

On national security, Obama's policies had taken the country from our post–Cold War perch as unrivaled superpower to a position of vacillating weakness and peril. While our main adversaries—China and Russia—were building up their military forces, the United States was busy hollowing out its military. Senator John McCain lamented that Obama was leaving the country with a "military that is under-funded, undersized, and unready to meet the diverse and complex ar-ray of threats confronting our nation." Under Obama's feckless foreign policy, the array of those threats proliferated. He left unchallenged China's drive to regional hegemony and global power. His deal with Iran did nothing to stop that country from obtaining nuclear weap-ons but gave the regime billions of dollars with which to fund war and terrorism around the Mideast. Obama's incompetent pullout from Iraq led to the emergence of the Islamic State (ISIS), and his policy of placating Tehran led him to spurn our allies, especially Israel and Saudi Arabia. He allowed North Korea's nuclear capabilities to reach a dangerous level that left the United States with no good options.

I was particularly concerned that the Obama administration had lost ground in the fight against violent crime and the drug cartels. Bi-partisan, tough-on-crime policies pursued since 1992 had cut violent crime levels by half, but, under Obama, the violent crime rate started climbing again in 2014, the first time in twenty-two years. Large metro areas across the nation were hit with crime waves in 2015 and 2016. The President embraced the narrative that the troubles of the Black community had primarily to do with the racism of police. Feeling that the Obama administration was waging a "war on cops," many police agencies were pulling back from proactive policing. Violent criminals filled the void. And Obama did nothing to stem the soaring death toll of the opioid epidemic. On the contrary, as a result of his failure to ad-dress the Mexican cartels' surging shipments of heroin and the deadly synthetic opioid fentanyl, the epidemic accelerated significantly.

But these and other Obama-era policy failures were symptoms of a deeper disorder. The source of the problem, as I saw it, was the growing strength in the Democratic Party of a Far Left progressive ideology that aimed to tear down and remake American society. With its relentless attacks on middle-class and liberal democratic values, and its incipient totalitarian style, this ideology was poisoning the country's political life. Ordinary middle- and working-class Americans, meanwhile, increasingly disgusted with the Left's aggressions, wanted to push back. Donald Trump emerged as a viable candidate in 2016 as a reaction against the Obama era's increasingly strident progressivism. Trump was not the cause, but the result, of our embittered politics. And that bitterness was engendered not by Trump but by the increasing militance of the Democratic Party's progressive wing.

Few would dispute that in the decade leading up to the 2016 election, politics began to infiltrate every aspect of life: sports, entertainment, apparel, technology, religion—even our eating habits. Politics and culture had become far more rancorous than just two decades earlier. Our politics was less like a disagreement within a family and more like a blood feud between two clans. Why was this?

Some liberal and progressive commentators suggested that our polarizing politics was somehow the consequence of an upsurge in right-wing extremism, but no sentient person could take that seriously. The decisive development intensifying the political divide has been the Democratic Party's radical lurch to the Left. A left-wing journalist, Kevin Drum, known for his insightful statistical analysis—and himself "happy" about the Democratic Party's move to the Left—concluded, based on an array of survey data, including from Pew Research Center and Gallup, that Democrats had moved significantly to the left, since 2000, while Republicans had moved only slightly to the right.

"The gaps are too big and the trend too consistent," Drum observes, "to ignore the obvious conclusion that, over the past two decades, Democrats have moved left far more than Republicans have moved right." He adds, "Progressives have been bragging publicly about pushing the Democratic Party leftward since at least 2004—and they've succeeded." Drum's conclusion: "*It is not conservatives who have turned American politics into a culture war battle. It is liberals*" (emphasis in original).

This is how I saw it. But I would not call today's progressives "liberals." The leftward shift of the Democratic Party is not just an incremental step in a more "liberal" direction along the continuum of liberal democratic ideas. It is a break with the liberal democratic tradition. Radical progressivism's messianic premises; its totalizing ambitions to control all aspects of life; its need to tear down society's existing belief systems and institutions; its antagonism to free and open debate—all are alien to the values of liberal democracy.

Liberal democratic ideas—strict limits on governmental power, individual rights, press freedom, religious liberty—were framed within the great Anglo-American political tradition and are the life's blood of our republic. They were painstakingly wrought over many centuries from a rich amalgamation of different influences: classical ideas, Christian precepts, Anglo-Saxon folkways, the common law, the lessons of the seventeenth-century English Civil War and its aftermath, the political thought of the English Whigs, the moderate Enlightenment, the American Revolution, and the foundation of the American republic in 1789. The liberal order produced by these experiences has given us unprecedented human freedom and material progress. Under liberal democracy, it is not the role of the state to use its coercive power to remake man and society according to some abstract conception of perfection. The purpose of government is far more modest: maintaining the modicum of order necessary for citizens to flourish in peace as they pursue their freely chosen destiny, both as individuals and together in the free, voluntary associations that develop organically as part of private civil society.

The new radical progressivism stands in hostile opposition to these principles. Today's political conflicts don't feel like a fight within the family because they are *not*—progressive ideology has left the family. It is, at bottom, a form of Jacobinism—the same kind of revolutionary and totalitarian ideas that propelled the French Revolution, the Communists of the Russian Revolution, and the Fascists of twentieth-century Europe. Radical progressivism's core idea is that there is a preordained scheme of natural earthly perfection toward which man and society must be led inexorably by the march of history. Men and society are perfectible here on earth and can consciously accelerate progress to a state of perfection. Existing societal conventions, belief systems, and political institutions have corrupted society and impeded its progress. They must be torn down.

None of this is an extension of liberalism; it is an illiberal movement aimed at replacing liberalism. To achieve its end, it must pulverize the values of the middle and working classes, which it views as ignorant obstacles on the road to the Promised Land. Because its ambition is to remake society into a comprehensively just arrangement, the measures used must be equally comprehensive—extending control, hard or soft, over every aspect of life. Thus, unlike authoritarian regimes, whose goal is simply holding power for power's sake, while allowing people freedom so long as it does not imperil that power, progressivism's utopian ambitions give it a distinctly totalitarian temper. The conservative writer Abe Greenwald has characterized this movement, accurately in my view, as Maoist: it isn't concerned only with what you say and do; it's concerned with what you think.

Progressivism's doctrines and agenda are dictated from the top by an enlightened elite. The ideology is a conglomerate of abstruse ideas, mashing together elements of Marxism, racial and gender ideologies, radical feminism, transgender ideology, and a host of other "isms." Writers have used different names to refer to parts of this eclectic ideology: social justice politics, wokeness, cultural Marxism, and so on. American essayist Wesley Yang's term for it, the *successor ideology*, is apt. It's the successor to *modern* liberalism, seeking to supplant the liberal order itself.

The practical agenda of today's progressive movement is as eclectic as the hodgepodge of ideas undergirding it. Its proponents support racial discrimination against whites, the abolition of any male-female binary, the elimination of national borders, the active use of censorship against dissent, and the foreswearing of free speech and open debate in favor of an ideologically correct curricula of a race-fixated anti-Americanism. Its economic program, tucked under the banner of "social justice," is a version of Marxist redistributionism. The crux of it is to use the public purse to provide ever-increasing benefits to the public and so to build a permanent constituency of supporters and dependents. They want able-bodied citizens to become more dependent, subject to greater control, and sympathetic to outright dependency. The tacit goal of this project is to convert all of us into twenty-five-year-olds living in the government's basement, focusing our energies on obtaining a larger allowance rather than getting a job and moving out.

The operative goal of this eclectic ideology is destruction. Every existing foundational idea, every cultural convention and moral value, must be rooted out and replaced by something new and "equitable." And what is that new something? Like the Bolshevik movement, the successor ideology is clear about what it wants to destroy but hopelessly vague about what's to take its place.

The most impressive thing about the new ideology is the speed with which it ran through elite institutions. Political commentator Andrew Sullivan describes this "sudden, rapid, stunning shift in the belief system of the American elites" that started in the last years of the Obama administration as the "greatest radicalization of the elites since the 1960s." It began around 2013 or 2014, and, within a year or two, those institutions—universities, corporations, national professional associations—were suddenly ripping themselves apart over perceived sins of racism and other bigotries.

So how did the successor ideology overrun these institutions so easily? It certainly was not the weight of the movement itself. Nurtured originally by academics and writers, its committed vanguard was small and the substantive content of its ideas puerile. Yet, like a wrecking ball, this movement has packed a destructive force far in excess of its intrinsic heft.

The movement had leverage within the Democratic Party and the education bureaucracies, but that doesn't account adequately for the success of this ideological blitzkrieg. The essential factor, in my view, was the corruption of the mainstream news media beginning around the turn of the century. By the end of the Obama years, the problem had gone far beyond bias or even political hackery; it had become corruption. The great preponderance of media managers, editors, commentators, and reporters were simply unwilling to defend American constitutional ideals, very much including the First Amendment's guarantees of speech and press freedoms, in order to coddle a movement of progressive zealots.

Of course, media entities and individual journalists will have their own political predispositions, and, since the 1970s, those predispositions have tended overwhelmingly to the Left. That, by itself, doesn't invalidate those media organizations. The main problem with it is that the *New York Times*, the *Washington Post*, CNN, the network news organizations, and so on, don't *admit* they're liberal and pretend to be "neutral" and "objective." Even then, until recently, the mainstream media had not betrayed their mission of seeking the truth and given themselves over completely to propaganda. But starting roughly twenty years ago, journalists at venerable national news organizations began to see themselves as engaged in a higher calling than reporting facts; increasingly, they thought of themselves as agents of societal change, bearers of enlightenment, guardians of advanced wisdom. The humdrum job of relating the facts to a paying audience of news consumers was small-time stuff by comparison. In the latter years of the Obama presidency, formerly respectable news outlets simply stopped producing news and instead turned out consensus left-liberal opinion cloaked in the garb of objective "news." Well before the rise of Donald Trump, the media had become the progressive movement's propaganda arm.

You could see it happening by the increasing use of the term *narrative* to describe news reporting. The word suggests an absence of verifiable fact and objective truth; there is only a story, experienced subjectively, or constructs that may or may not correspond to reality. Everyone can have his or her own version of the facts, whatever they are. The upshot is that news journalists are free to look for stories that fit their conception of reality. For some, this means forcing the facts into preferred narratives, even if they don't admit—to themselves or anyone else—that that's what they're doing. For others, it's a justification for distorting the truth in the cause of righteousness. For still others, it's a license to lie.

Alexis de Tocqueville, the nineteenth-century French statesman and author, and the greatest chronicler of American democracy, hoped that the institution of the free press might check the natural despotic tendencies of democracy. This was not because Tocqueville believed that the American press did a good job of elevating the public's understanding and discourse; he did not. Rather, he thought the saving grace of the press was that it was highly fragmented and reflected a wide diversity of voices and localized opinion. In his view, it was precisely the wide variety of diverse voices in the press that made it hard, in a large country such as the United States, to galvanize a consolidated national faction that could impose its views on, and lord it over, the rest of the country.

It was when the press consolidated into fewer voices and presented itself as a monolith, he held, that it ceased to act as a bulwark against tyranny and instead enabled it. Once press organizations begin to "advance along the same track," wrote Tocqueville, "their influence becomes almost irresistible in the long term, and public opinion, struck always from the same side, ends by yielding under their blows."

This is what I saw happening. The corporate or mainstream press had become massively consolidated and monolithic in viewpoint at the same time that a large preponderance of journalists saw themselves less as reporters of the facts and more as agents of change. Its political uniformity has given the mainstream media an unprecedented ability to mobilize a broad segment of the public on a national scale and direct that opinion in a particular direction.

When the entire press "advances along the same track," as Tocqueville put it, the relationship between the press and its preferred faction becomes mutually reinforcing. Not only does it become easier for the press to mobilize a strong political faction, but also the mobilized faction becomes more powerful and overweening—with the press as its ally.

In addition to the media's active support for progressive ideology, I saw another phenomenon giving momentum to the political Left. This was the seeming willingness of many business and other professional elites—increasingly isolated from the lives of ordinary Americans and disdainful of their values—to lend their support to a constantly changing and radicalizing progressive agenda. These elites help to advance the progressive program not only by actively propagandizing on its behalf—for example, by allowing their businesses to be used as vehicles for indoctrination—but also by using their power to sanction people who stand up against it: for example, by boycotting states that adopt policies contrary to new leftist orthodoxy.

Some of the elites, particularly in the media, academe, and the arts, are drawn to it because it aligns with their presuppositions. But most of the elites who've fallen under the progressive banner have done so for nonphilosophical reasons. Vladimir Lenin, the Marxist revolutionary and architect of the Russian Revolution, and subsequent Soviet leaders during the Cold War, made use of Western elites who, without fully comprehending the nature of Soviet Communism, were easily manipulated to propagandize for or otherwise aid the Communist cause. These people, who craved to be seen as enlightened and progressive, were thought of contemptuously by the Communist leadership as "useful idiots."

America's gentry liberals, circa 2014 to 2016, weren't so different. Many of them, especially among the corporate and professional elites who didn't pay much attention to the content of progressivism's agenda, ended up supporting it because they wanted to be perceived as enlightened and sophisticated.

Humans have a craving for acceptance and status. They want to be part of, or approved by, the cool crowd. Many, in their teen years, are terrified of being excluded from cliques of higher status. Most move beyond this desperate need for affirmation. In short, they grow up. This often happens shortly after high school.

For others, this need for acceptance persists long after high school. In the case of the corporate, professional, and media elite I'm describing, these highly capable and successful people try to secure their elite status by striking a social and political pose they believe will win the approval of their peers. And just as in high school they feared being thought socially inept or insufficiently cool, they now fear ostracism for failing to keep up with the political program. Being called "racist" or "sexist" or "transphobic" or "nationalist" by their peers is, to them, a nightmare they would do almost anything to avoid.

Elite susceptibility to progressivism has increased as the movement has become an ersatz religion. The prevailing worldview of secularist progressivism, as many have observed, has taken on the character of a radical religious outlook that brooks no rival. In the materialist void, political progressivism is the only thing that gives life purpose and meaning. But unlike Christianity, which focuses on the importance of personal morality and the individual's duties to God and man, the new secular morality teaches a variety of macro-morality in which one's virtue isn't gauged by private conduct but by participation in political causes and group action. In this latter outlook, virtue is entirely tied up with externals: public gestures, identification with causes, righteous posturing. And because there is no reward for virtue in the hereafter, the only reward for righteous behavior is to be publicly noticed and applauded today.

This is what I saw in 2015 and 2016 as the election approached. I believed our society had become a battleground on which two fundamentally antithetical visions of man and society were waging a war that would determine the outcome of America's great experiment in republican government and political freedom. One vision, the traditional liberal democratic view that gives priority to the preservation of personal liberty, was being redefined by our political and cultural elite as an evil force; the other, a form of soft totalitarianism that aims explicitly at tearing down the liberal tradition and submerging the individual in a collectivist agenda, was on the offensive. The new antiliberal progressivism was rapidly gaining momentum—embraced by an increasing number of prominent Democrats, aided by relentless media propagandizing, and reinforced by a co-opted education system.

This is why I believed the stakes of the upcoming election were so high.

After watching the first few primary debates in 2015, I realized that, whoever won the GOP nomination, I would probably end up supporting the Republican nominee—even Trump, as off-putting as he was. The reason was simple: I thought any of the Republicans vying for the nomination was better than the alternative. None of them was so bad as to induce me to vote for Hillary Clinton or Bernie Sanders. When Trump first emerged as a serious contender, I doubted he would go the distance. But by early 2016, it was apparent that he wasn't going to fade away. Jeb, accomplished leader though he was, failed to connect this time around with Republican voters and dropped out in February. After that, I supported, in succession, the candidates I thought could edge out Trump and win the general election. Once Trump won the nomination at the Republican convention, however, I supported him and wrote a check the next day.

Trump was not my idea of a President. He was capable of charm and humor—I could see that. But I found myself, like many others, cringing at his frequently crass, bombastic, and petulant style. Especially grating to me was his ready resort to pettiness and personal name-calling. I saw some of his behavior as simply a high-octane version of the aggressive, in-your-face New York style—something I was familiar with—so I was not as repelled as some others were. But I still hoped and expected that, once he got into the general election—and certainly if he ever won the office—he would be capable of adopting a more presidential tone.

I worried about Trump's shortcomings, but I also felt he had strengths. I liked the clear and direct way he staked out a position. I appreciated his willingness to state unpleasant truths that many were thinking but were afraid to say. In an age of carefully honed evasions, his bluntness was refreshing. He was willing to confront head-on difficult issues that other politicians attempted to avoid. He seemed ready to grapple with America's most stubborn problems rather than leave them to some future generation.

A number of factors contributed to Trump's winning the nomination. The media helped by lavishing coverage on him. The crowded field, coupled with the media focus on Trump, made it hard for any competitor to break out of the pack early enough to consolidate the non-Trump vote. Part of the media's fixation on Trump was due to his unorthodox style, which made him a more interesting story than his more conventional opponents, but some in the media wanted Trump to win the Republican nomination because they considered him the easiest candidate for Hillary to beat. The Clinton campaign also believed this.

But the main reason Trump won the nomination—and later the general election—was simpler than any of that: he fit the times. Trump had explored running for president twice before, and the voters had shown little interest. This time around, he turned half the country's unease and confusion about what was happening to America into a powerful political response. In his own way, he articulated the anger that many middle- and working-class Americans felt over the excesses and condescension of the Democratic Party, the coastal elites, and especially the mainstream news media. Trump had diagnosed a decisive divide in the nation: the alienation of average Americans from the increasingly smug and isolated elites that had mismanaged the country and appeared content to preside over a declining America. They felt the old-boy system in Washington had sold them out and that it was time to disrupt the system. Many ordinary Americans were especially sick of the radical progressives' shrill disparagement of America and scornful attacks on traditional values, and they were deeply frustrated by the wildly partisan role played by the media. In short, in 2016 many voters felt like the character Howard Beale in the 1976 film *Network*: "I'm as mad as hell, and I'm not going to take this anymore!"

Trump's pugnacious style worked. These frustrated Americans found in him a fighter willing to punch back, go toe-to-toe with the press, and mount a full-throated defense of America and middle-class values. They were tired of the cooing doublespeak of professional politicians and wanted someone who would tell it like it is—straight from the shoulder—and someone willing to follow through and actually do what other politicians said they would do but never did. Trump's combativeness also enabled him to break through the distortions and smothering hostility of the partisan media and talk right past them, straight to the American people.

For many, supporting Trump was an act of defiance—a protest. The more over the top he was, the more they savored the horrified reaction of the elites, especially the media. Arguments that Trump wasn't presidential missed the point. Trump's supporters *already knew* he didn't conform to presidential norms. Their question was: Where had presidential norms gotten them? They *wanted* someone who didn't conform. The Left was taking a wrecking ball to the country. Many fed up Americans wanted to strike back with their *own* wrecking ball. I saw the logic in it. But I was also skeptical that anyone could govern effectively in constant wrecking ball mode.

In any case, once Trump became the nominee, I had no hesitancy backing him over Hillary Clinton. Substantively, he was offering policies I supported. There was no doubt in my mind that he would unleash our economy to achieve the robust growth the country needed; that he would rebuild our military power; that he would pursue a foreign policy that put the interests of Americans first; and that he would stop unfairly scapegoating police and would renew the policies that had succeeded in reducing violent crime in the past. He also promised to be strongly pro-life, defend religious liberty, and liberate inner-city children from failing schools and the racism of low expectations by empowering parents to send their children to schools of their choice. In short, he would work to make America great again. That was an agenda I could happily get behind.

I was not involved in the Trump campaign, although at one point I did offer a piece of advice. Before one presidential debate, I heard that my friend Pat Cipollone, an accomplished Washington lawyer whom I'd known since my first stint as Attorney General, was helping Trump with debate preparation. I called Pat to make a suggestion. Trump had been emphasizing the need to crack down on illegal immigration and making strong, sometimes hyperbolic comments about undesirable elements crossing the border illegally. I agreed that the federal government needed to get control of the border, but Trump's comments lent themselves easily to charges of racism and xenophobia. I thought those charges were bogus—any normal person could see that Trump didn't care about race, and the people calling him a racist use that term about anyone who gets in their way. My question to Pat was: Why give the media and the Clinton campaign the opportunity to make that accusation? I thought Trump should stress the fact that the United States has the most generous legal immigration policies in the world, that we welcome legal immigrants, and that Latin Americans who come here legally—people with a strong work ethic and family values—

contribute enormously to the country. Pat agreed with me. He gave the advice to Trump, but I didn't detect any adjustment in his rhetoric.

Of central importance to me was Trump's stated intention to appoint constitutionalist judges to the federal judiciary. When Supreme Court Justice Antonin Scalia died in February of the election year, I thought it likely, given the ages of the remaining justices, that the next President would end up appointing three new justices, thus potentially setting the Supreme Court's course for decades to come. In the following weeks, Trump would say he meant to appoint judges in the mold of Scalia, always enunciating the great man's name with emphasis: "Sca-*lee*-ah." Still, Trump was not one to discuss judicial philosophy with any precision, and I wondered if he knew why Sca-*lee*-ah was so important to conservatives. But in May 2016 he released a list of eleven potential Supreme Court picks, and in September he added ten more names. Those lists presented an impressive array of committed constitutionalists. Who did I want determining the direction of the Supreme Court for years to come: Trump or Hillary Clinton? The question was not close. On this basis alone, I would crawl over broken glass to the polls to vote for Trump.

Once Trump won the nomination, the media, after fawning over him during the primaries, suddenly discovered his character flaws, which they now suggested made him unfit for office. I did not know enough about him to make firm judgments about all aspects of his character, but I did not see anything at the time I felt disqualifying. The country should aspire to elect leaders of high moral character, to be sure. But the significance of a candidate's moral strengths and weaknesses has to be judged in relation to all the other attributes that person would bring to the office in the context of the time in which he's running—together with his policy views and leadership skills. In our age, the electorate seems to put less stock in character, as I learned sadly when it replaced George H. W. Bush with Bill Clinton. Many of our past leaders, including some idolized by the Left even today, are known to have had deep moral failings. Trump certainly had his share of them.

One important point, though, was that those failings were not as hidden as they usually are in political leaders. In Trump's case, the failings were close to the surface—mostly on full display. Trump was not as much two-faced as full-on frontal: what you saw is pretty much what you got. Many people have attributed his flaws to a deep narcissism. This would not surprise me—it is a common malady in our age, especially among celebrities, political and otherwise. But, in an election, we must make a choice between two candidates and thus must judge a candidate's attributes—including character—not in absolute but in relative terms. Whatever Trump's failings, there was one thing I was sure of: Hillary Clinton was not morally superior to Donald Trump.

The main claim against Trump was that he was an inveterate "liar." Coming from the media, Clinton, and Democratic partisans, this criticism was rich. Yet there was no question that, with his imprecise and discursive speaking style and flights of gross hyperbole, Trump often seemed to have little regard for the accuracy of his statements. I was not a fan of his madcap rhetoric, but, in my experience, the people who ended up supporting Trump were not deceived. They understood at some level that Trump was an entertainer and that many of his words were not to be taken as literal representations of his thoughts. As writer Salena Zito observed famously at the time in the *Atlantic*, when Trump makes outrageous claims, "the press takes him literally, but not seriously; his supporters take him seriously, but not literally." Ordinary thinking people could see that Trump used verbiage more or less the same way that riot police use a water cannon: not to convey accurate information but to stun his opponents and set them back on their heels. The other thing about many of Trump's verbal barrages was that often, after stripping away all the messy packaging, there was at the heart of his point an essential core of truth.

One of the other tropes about Trump was that he was an "authoritarian" who aspired to flout the Constitution and rule as a dictator. I gave no credence to this claim. There is a difference between a person who exhibits some authoritarian traits—not that uncommon in Washington—and someone who actually aspires to achieve dictatorial rule. What I saw was a man who wanted to project himself as a strongman and would occasionally display the menacing mannerisms typical of that pose. But I think he self-consciously cultivated these mannerisms as part of his schtick to project the image of strength. I did not think they signaled either the intention or willingness to wield dictatorial power in violation of the Constitution. On the contrary, I think he viewed himself as defending the constitutional order and traditional American values from the increasingly totalitarian attacks of the radical wing of the Democratic Party.

I expected that, like innumerable other bullheaded political leaders, he would chafe at the many institutional restraints built into our system. But I also thought that Trump, like most presidents most of the time, would operate within constitutional and statutory limits and would surround himself with aides and advisers prepared to ensure he did. It is an underrated virtue of our system that presidents who get elected by stirring up anger in the electorate must then find experienced and cooler-headed advisers to help them govern. That happened in Trump's presidency, even if his inability to get along with most of them seriously undermined his administration's stability and efficiency.

The system worked—until Trump's election defeat. For the preceding four years, President Trump acceded to the advice of his advisers and observed legal limits. Although his advisers had to expend an ungodly amount of energy and blood to keep him on track, the administration operated within the guardrails. The claim that he governed as an autocrat and that his administration was lawless and anti-democratic—a claim made constantly over the entire four years of his presidency—was another false narrative. During Trump's term, I would regularly ask my anti-Trump friends what they were referring to when they suggested that he was ruling as an "autocrat." I would get vacuous stares, followed by sputtering about the so-called travel ban, which temporarily restricted entry of persons traveling from several nations where terrorist groups had entrenched themselves. The fact is that the Trump administration's actions, initiatives, and proposed rules—including the travel ban—transgressed neither constitutional nor traditional norms. They were amply supported by the law and patiently litigated through the court system to vindication. Indeed, the Trump administration's use of executive prerogative looks a bit tame when you compare it to Barack Obama's aggressive use of his presidential pen. Under Obama's DACA (Deferred Action for Childhood Arrivals) program, for example—created by executive order—the administration allowed itself simply to ignore broad swathes of immigration law.

Do the events of January 6, 2021, prove that Trump really was the aspiring authoritarian dictator his enemies said he was? I'll have more to say about January 6 later in this book, but the answer is no. There is no question he changed after the election; he lost his grip—he stopped listening to his advisers, became manic and unreasonable, and went off the rails. He surrounded himself with sycophants, including many whack jobs from outside the government, who fed him a steady diet of comforting but unsupported conspiracy theories. The absurd lengths to which he took his "stolen election" claim led to the rioting on Capitol Hill. The forcible breach of the Capitol by rioters was reprehensible. As it was happening, though I had already left office, I publicly condemned it as "despicable" and called for federal law enforcement to "disperse" it immediately. But, without minimizing both the stupidity and shamefulness of what happened, at the time I did not think the republic was in genuine danger. The die was cast: the states had cast their electoral votes, and the idea that this could be circumvented by shunting the election into the House of Representatives was farcical.

But that was all in the future. As election night 2016 approached, I was cautiously optimistic that Trump was going to win. Hillary's flaws as a candidate had overshadowed her opponent's. The small segment of undecideds in the middle proved willing to give Trump a chance and, at the end, made their move to him. Late into the night, I watched the election results with my wife. I had never believed Hillary was the shoo-in the media wanted to believe she was. I am no great electoral prognosticator, but I was right. The country was in no mood for four more years of Obama-era progressivism and Clintonian mendacity.

The collective meltdown of the political and cultural elite, together with the bewildered response of the mainstream media, was something to behold. Trump's adversaries, powerful as they were, had no idea what to think. He had done it.

CHAPTER 8

FOREIGN SCHEMES AND DOMESTIC LIES

He had done it, all right. But could he govern?

That question looms over every newly elected President. It's one thing to win an election, another to run the country. The question is especially relevant to incoming presidents with limited or no political and executive experience. Whether Barack Obama could govern the nation as efficiently as he had defeated his Republican opponent was an open question, although nobody in the mainstream press was curious enough to ask it. The answer, it turned out, was that Obama conducted himself as President much as he had as a candidate—by dividing the electorate between supporters and adversaries. His tenure was really a continuation of his campaign.

What about Trump? He had managed to make a lot of money in his lifetime and to build up a global brand for himself, but he had even less governmental experience than Obama had—in fact, none at all.

I wondered, as I suspect most of his voters wondered, if he could act more "presidential" in office. Would he rise to the occasion, dial back some of the more cringe-worthy aspects of his behavior, and adopt a more dignified style appropriate to the office? I was encouraged by Trump's performance on election night. He gave a conciliatory, statesmanlike victory speech. He was gracious to Hillary Clinton, saying everyone "owed her a major debt of gratitude for her service." He called on Democrats, Republicans, and Independents to come together and work for the benefit of the American people. He pledged to be the president for all Americans and said he was "reaching out" to those who had opposed him "for your guidance and your help so that we can work together and unify our great country."

Democrats wanted no part of it. They launched what they called "the resistance": an explicit strategy to sabotage his administration and drive him from office. No tactic, no matter how abusive, was out of bounds if it helped destroy his administration. The ends truly justified any means. Talk of impeachment began the moment he won office.

This reaction was contemptible. The survival of our democratic system depends on our capacity to transfer power peacefully through elections. At a minimum, that means political leaders and the citizenry have to accept the results of elections and the legitimacy of duly elected governments. I thought this was essential in 2016, just as I later thought it was in 2020. But in 2016 the leadership of the Democratic Party, together with its progressive base and cheerleaders in the mainstream press, refused to accept the outcome of the presidential election.

The very idea of a "resistance" is beyond the pale. It is typically used to describe an insurgency against an occupying military power and connotes an illegitimate government. Use of this word was grossly irresponsible, as was the media's failure to censure it. Instead of viewing themselves as the "loyal opposition," as opposing parties have done in the past, President Trump's opponents viewed themselves essentially as guerrillas engaged in a war to cripple a duly elected government, even if it meant that the country would suffer as a result.

Those who "resisted" President Trump constantly accused his administration of "shredding" constitutional norms and trampling the rule of law. But the truth is that their scorched-earth policy of absolute obstructionism and unthinking antipathy was the supreme act of norm shredding.

A prime example is the Democrats' abuse of the Senate's advice-and-consent process, whereby presidential nominees must be confirmed by the Senate before taking office. The word *unprecedented* gets overused these days, but this strategy truly had no precedent in American history. Nearly every nominee for a senior executive branch post—agency head, deputy secretary, assistant secretary, and so forth—was either blocked or held up for as long as possible. The Senate is free to exercise its power to reject unqualified nominees, but that power was never intended to enable the Senate to prevent the President from building a functional government. From Trump's first days in office, Senate Democrats slowed the confirmation process to a snail's pace by systematically demanding thirty hours of floor debate and a cloture vote to end debate before a nominee could get a confirmation vote. By the fall of 2019, Democrats had forced cloture votes on 236 Trump nominees—each of those representing its own massive consumption of legislative time meant only to delay an inevitable confirmation. In President Obama's whole first term, cloture was invoked on his nominees just seventeen times. Facing these tactics, it would have taken the new President many years to fully staff his administration with permanent appointees. As it was, this abuse forced President Trump to leave many important positions unfilled or filled by more junior "acting" officials.

What if Trump's initial overtures had been met by a modicum of good faith on the other side? What if he had gotten just a bit of the "honeymoon" newly elected presidents have been afforded historically? We will never know, but I believe the country would have benefited and likely seen more of the constructive, problem-solving style of government that President Trump previewed on election night, and less of the combativeness that came to define his term. Obviously, clashes were inevitable in some policy areas. But there were also areas where some give-and-take was possible, and Trump at heart was a pragmatic businessman who cast himself as someone who could get things done by negotiating deals. In his victory speech, for example, he had cited a major infrastructure initiative as something both sides could get done quickly. And from the outset, he was open about his desire to negotiate a grand compromise that would strengthen immigration controls while also providing certainty and status to the DACA "Dreamers." In rebuffing Trump's opening gestures and embarking on a take-no-prisoners campaign to destroy his administration, it was the

Democrats, and their media allies, who dictated the tenor of the next four years.

The centerpiece of the resistance was the "Russian collusion" narrative—or what the media called, with an obvious note of hopefulness, Russiagate. This wasn't simply the claim that the Russians had attempted to influence the 2016 presidential election—this much was anticipated before the election and widely acknowledged after it. The collusion narrative further held that Trump's campaign had *conspired* with the Russians to defeat Hillary Clinton.

The collusion controversy was a mind-numbingly complicated episode in American political history—and a shameful one. It was in full bloom by the time I reentered the Justice Department in February 2019, so it will be necessary to explain its central details before I fully relate my own role in it.

The claim that Trump's victory came only as the result of a corrupt bargain with Russian president Vladimir Putin struck at the heart of the Trump administration's legitimacy and provided the rationale for resistance. The collusion narrative gave the President's enemies all the excuse they needed to incapacitate the country's fledgling administration—keeping Trump angry, distracted, and "on the ropes" until a case could be made to drive him from office.

Russiagate dominated the first two years of President Trump's term, looming over every aspect of the administration. I was on the outside as a private citizen during this time, and so my early reaction to the collusion claims was based on public reporting and my own informed speculation. Only in early 2019, when I joined the administration as Attorney General, did I begin to get a fuller picture of this manufactured scandal. From that time forward, it became increasingly clear to me that there were never any legitimate grounds for accusing Trump or his campaign of colluding with the Russians. This was not only my conclusion. Every investigation into the matter—including those of Special Counsel Robert Mueller and the Senate and House Intelligence Committees—also found no evidence of collusion.

I would soon make the difficult decision to go back into government in large part because I saw the way the President's adversaries had enmeshed the Department of Justice in this phony scandal and were using it to hobble his administration. Once in office, it occupied much of my time for the first six months of my tenure. It was at the heart of my most controversial decisions. Even after dealing with the Mueller report, I still had to launch US Attorney John Durham's investigation into the genesis of this bogus scandal. At the end of my first year in office, the President was impeached over a harebrained effort, involving Rudy Giuliani, to push back on the Russia collusion canard by digging up an alleged counter-scandal in Ukraine implicating the Clinton campaign or Vice President Biden and his son Hunter.

The fallout from Russiagate continued during my last year in office. My relationship with the President frayed as he became frustrated by my failure to bring charges against those who had ginned up Russiagate and the failure of Durham's investigation to produce more rapid results.

While that last year was dominated by Covid and civil unrest, there was, for me, irony in how it ended. I had started in office dealing with Russiagate, a false narrative against the President. I resigned from office opposing the President's own unsupported narrative of a "stolen election."

While I was in office, all the media wanted to talk about were politically fraught matters such as Russiagate and Ukraine, which consumed more time than I would have liked. But the saving grace of the job was that I actually got to spend most of my time doing what I enjoyed most: overseeing the department's critical work across its broad portfolio of responsibilities. Among the matters requiring my attention were stepping up our joint efforts with state and local law enforcement to help combat violent crime; strengthening our response to the opioid epidemic and the drug trafficking activities of the Mexican cartels; resuming imposition of the federal death penalty; counteracting the growing threat of espionage and technology theft by the Chinese Communist Party; applying the antitrust laws to the unprecedented concentrations of power in the online platforms of the major tech companies; implementing one of the administration's signature legislative achievements, the First Step Act, aimed at better preparing prisoners for reentry into society; and finding a solution to the challenge posed by the use of warrant-proof encryption by criminals.

I thought it likely that the Russians did try to meddle in our 2016 election. It appeared Russian military intelligence hacked into e-mail accounts related to the Clinton campaign and the Democratic National Committee in the spring of 2016 and later made public stolen e-mails through various online personas, including a major release by WikiLeaks on July 22, 2016, just before the Democratic National Convention. These disclosures were meant to embarrass Clinton. But the core question, in my mind, was never really whether the Russians could be dispositively proven to have been responsible. The heart of the matter was whether Trump, his associates, or his campaign conspired or colluded with the Russians in these activities.

As an outside spectator, I had been skeptical about the collusion claims from the beginning. The theory that the Russians and the Trump campaign had a quid pro quo struck me as implausible. Putin had good reasons of his own to embarrass Hillary Clinton and didn't need any inducement from Trump to do it. Clinton embodied everything Putin hated about American foreign policy: the schoolmarmish condescension and moralistic hectoring. He detested Clinton and believed that, when she was secretary of state from 2009 to 2013, she had personally interfered in Russian domestic politics by inciting demonstrations against him. Even before the DNC hacking was discovered, most of official Washington expected Putin to exact payback against Clinton in some way.

Nor could I see any reason the Russians would need or want to conspire with Trump or any American to carry out their plans. The "hack-and-dump" measures used by the Russians against Clinton's campaign are their stock-in-trade. The Russians are perfectly capable of executing these operations without any help from local conspirators, and generally do. Involving US political players in their actions would have greatly increased risk to Russia, with no benefit. I strongly doubted that either Putin or his intelligence services would have thought it useful or wise to involve American politicians in their plans.

The 2016 Trump campaign, moreover, was not exactly a model operation. It struck me as highly implausible that a campaign widely derided as disorganized and unprofessional could somehow pull off a secret caper with the Russians to rig a US presidential election against one of the best-funded and most experienced Democratic candidates in history. It didn't make sense.

Despite its implausibility, the collusion narrative started taking shape well before the election. By the spring of 2016, the Clinton campaign had already begun developing the general theme that Trump was Putin's stooge. As early as June 2016, Fusion GPS, a research firm working for Clinton's campaign, had hired a former British intelligence officer, Christopher Steele, to provide "opposition research" on the supposed relationship between the Russians and Trump. After the hacking of the DNC was exposed in July by publication of stolen e-mails, the Clinton campaign escalated efforts to tie these Russian activities to Trump. It is now known—though it was not public at the time—that, from at least July forward, Fusion GPS and Steele were shopping to the FBI and various news organizations Steele's infamous "dossier": a series of sensational and unverified allegations derived indirectly through a single intermediary from a hazy "network" of sources. While the dossier reports started off in June claiming that the Russians had a sex tape compromising Trump, in July the reports shifted to ever more outlandish claims that Trump and the Russians had a "well-developed conspiracy of cooperation," including a conspiracy to interfere in the election. Persons working on behalf of the Clinton campaign also conveyed to the Department of Justice and the FBI the false allegation that the Trump Organization maintained a secret computer server at Trump Tower tied directly to Moscow's Alfa-Bank, whose partners are linked to Russian president Vladimir Putin.

I always suspected that the preelection peddling of Steele's dossier and other similar collusion claims comprised an attempt to carry out a classic campaign dirty trick: first, develop scurrilous allegations about one's opponent, then get them into the hands of an investigative authority, and, finally, leak the "fact" that the allegations are being investigated. This way, unverified allegations are publicized and given instant credibility on the theory that authorities thought them worthy enough to investigate. News organizations can justify publishing dubious allegations by claiming they are really just reporting the facts of a pending investigation. Before Election Day, the Clinton campaign had a good motive for instigating the collusion narrative: besides hurting Trump, it diverted attention from her own e-mail server scandal, which seemingly came to a head in early July when FBI director Comey held a news conference sharply criticizing Clinton for her mishandling of classified e-mails.

Despite the manic efforts to hawk the Russia collusion narrative, the story got almost no traction before the election. Part of the reason for this was that, *before* the election, the media were appropriately dubious of Steele's dossier. Its allegations were not only far-fetched and unverifiable but also presented in memos so amateurish and error-laden that anyone with sense would have been skeptical. Steele did get a few nibbles, however. In September and October Yahoo! News and *Mother Jones* magazine reported vaguely on some of Steele's claims and suggested that the FBI was looking into them. Democratic Senate Minority Leader Harry Reid also tried to add kindling to the fire, first in August and then in October, alluding to Steele's information in two letters to FBI director Comey, the latter of which asserted that the FBI possessed "explosive information about close ties and coordination between Donald Trump, his top advisers, and the Russian government."

But this was all too little, too late. Trump won anyway.

It was only after Trump's surprise victory that the collusion narrative really took off. By spring—within just a few months of Trump taking office—Russiagate was swelling into a tidal wave, threatening to inundate his administration. This was driven partly by the shift in the media from skeptics to scandalmongers. Abandoning any semblance of journalistic standards, much of the media enthusiastically embraced the collusion narrative, flogging it at every turn with a torrent of misleading reporting and speculation. Any facts inconsistent with Steele's dossier were ignored, while the slightest "tie" or "connection" with anything Russian—no matter how remote or apparently innocent—was hyped with banner headlines as if it validated the story and was a revelation on the scale of Watergate. The phony scandal was also fueled by Clinton advisers and Democratic Party apparatchiks, who, stunned by her defeat and looking to paper over their own failures, claimed quickly that Trump's victory was the result of a conspiracy with the Russians. This not only provided a ready explanation for her defeat but also provided a basis for delegitimizing Trump, as well as unifying and mobilizing opposition to his administration. Within months, progressive nonprofits and Democratic Party activists had created a network of research groups supplying the media feeding frenzy with an endless supply of chum.

But more than anything else, what propelled the Russia collusion fantasy was the disclosure that the FBI had begun an investigation of the Trump campaign before the election. The existence of that investigation—the leaks about it, and especially the FBI director's portentous characterizations of it—gave momentum to the collusion narrative. A pivotal event took place on January 6, 2017, when the intelligence agency heads met with President-elect Trump for a general briefing. Afterward, Comey stayed behind to tell Trump about the "sex tape" part of Steele's dossier. He explained that the materials had been circulating in media circles and that CNN was looking desperately for a news "hook" to run with the dossier story.

Within days, Comey's meeting with the President was leaked to CNN. The network reported on the meeting, Steele's dossier, and its allegations of ties between the Russians and Trump. The report claimed that the "FBI is investigating the credibility and accuracy of the [dossier's] allegations" and that "intelligence agencies" found Steele and his sources "credible enough" to include his information in the briefing. That night, the news-and-gossip website BuzzFeed published the whole thirty-five-page dossier.

Some suspect that the January 6 meeting was a setup so that FBI officials or others could make public Steele's allegations and the fact that the FBI was investigating them. Whether true or not, the result that Fusion GPS, Steele, and others had been seeking before the election now came to fruition after the election: the made-up allegations of collusion with a foreign power were now public, and their credibility was buttressed by the claim that they were being investigated by the FBI.

The decisive disclosure was on March 20, 2017, when Director Comey, testifying before Congress, confirmed officially that the bureau was conducting, and had been since July 2016, a counterintelligence investigation into Russian election interference efforts, including the "nature of any links between individuals associated with the Trump campaign and the Russian government and whether there was any coordination between the campaign and Russia's efforts." Three weeks later, the *Washington Post* reported that, as part of the FBI's investigation before the election, the bureau had obtained under the Foreign Intelligence Surveillance Act (FISA) a warrant to "monitor" the communications of former Trump adviser Carter Page. The article noted that "according to law enforcement and other US officials," issuance of the warrant indicated that the FBI had "probable cause" to believe "Page was acting as an agent of a foreign power, in this case, Russia."

We now know that Comey authorized launching a counterintelligence investigation, code-named Crossfire Hurricane, into the Trump campaign on July 31, 2016. Over the ensuing days, the FBI opened subsidiary investigations targeting several people associated with the Trump campaign, including Page and George Papadopoulos, both peripheral, volunteer "advisers"; retired lieutenant general Michael Flynn, a senior national security adviser; and Paul Manafort, the recently appointed campaign manager. Comey's deputy, Andrew McCabe, was closely involved in these decisions. Against the advice of the head of the bureau's counterintelligence division, McCabe handpicked the number two official in that division, Peter Strzok, to run the Crossfire Hurricane investigation. McCabe and Strzok assembled a group of agents to fill out the Crossfire Hurricane team, which reported up to McCabe.

As quickly as they had initiated the investigation, Comey and McCabe authorized use of surreptitious surveillance—that is, spying—against Trump's campaign. The Crossfire Hurricane team immediately arranged for confidential sources and undercover agents to meet with Page and Papadopoulos to secretly tape conversations with them. The team also began preparing an application for a FISA warrant to surveil Page. According to Comey and McCabe, their investigation was neither prompted by, nor initially made use of, the Steele dossier. But in August, after Justice Department lawyers found insufficient evidence to show probable cause for obtaining the FISA warrant, McCabe directed the team to the Steele dossier as potentially providing additional evidence to get over this hump. The Crossfire Hurricane team then used the dossier, still unverified, to obtain the FISA warrant, and surveillance was initiated against Page in late October, shortly before the election.

It was almost inconceivable to me that the FBI opened a counterintelligence investigation against a presidential candidate's campaign in the middle of an election. As far as I was aware, this had never been done before, and for good reason. The election process is at the very core of our First Amendment liberties. From a civil liberties standpoint, one of the greatest dangers to our free system—indeed, one of the nightmare scenarios—is that officials in an incumbent administration, entrusted with the most sensitive law enforcement and intelligence tools of government power, might abuse them to spy on their opponents and inject their own proclivities into the political process under the guise of national security. The risk is not just that they might attempt to advance their own *partisan* political preferences, but also there is a more subtle form of corruption: that officials take on a "praetorian guard" mentality—a smug self-assurance that they know what is best for the country and can justifiably use their powers to prevent the people from making mistakes. The risk is that officials like this, convinced they have a higher duty to protect the country from itself, use the government's security apparatus to undermine candidates whose fitness for office or whose policy proposals don't measure up to their standards.

The main safeguard we have against this kind of abuse is the requirement that officials must have a reasonable basis for investigating an American person or group. This is what the Department of Justice refers to as "adequate predication"—there must be factual circumstances that reasonably justify the investigative steps taken. In principle, every American is protected against arbitrary investigation. But it is especially important to insist on sufficient predication before the government may intrude into sensitive constitutional areas, such as an election contest.

A central question in the Russiagate saga is whether the FBI had a sufficient predicate for launching Crossfire Hurricane in the midst of a presidential election. What were the facts that led Comey and McCabe to take this unprecedented step? The FBI officials involved claimed that the Steele dossier played no role in opening the investigation. They point instead to a sequence of events in July 2016 as the predication for the investigation.

The explanation for the investigation started to come out at the end of 2017. I could not have imagined just how flimsy the FBI's justification for beginning the investigation was. The official version of events is that on July 28, a few days after WikiLeaks dumped the hacked DNC e-mails, the FBI received a report from an Australian diplomat based in London that he recalled a conversation in a London wine bar in May with a twenty-eight-year-old Trump campaign volunteer, George Papadopoulos. According to the diplomat, Papadopoulos "suggested the Trump team had received some kind of suggestion from Russia that it could assist . . . with the anonymous release of information during the campaign that would be damaging to Mrs. Clinton." Within three days of getting this report—before even interviewing the diplomat for clarification—the FBI leadership rushed to open a full-blown counterintelligence and criminal investigation of the Trump campaign. They assumed that Papadopoulos's vague suggestion that the Russians might have "information" likely referred to the hacked DNC e-mails that had just been released by WikiLeaks. Thus, the thinking went, Papadopoulos was exhibiting in May prior knowledge of an e-mail dump that occurred in July. The FBI brass reasoned this supposed prior knowledge could well show that the Trump campaign was in cahoots with the Russians when they hacked the DNC.

It is a travesty that an FBI investigation of a presidential campaign was premised on a low-level campaign adviser's throwaway comment in a wine bar.

This was not a reasonable decision by the FBI leadership. In the first place, the wine bar conversation, as reported, was quite opaque, and the diplomat was never able to provide better clarity. It amounted to a "suggestion" of a "suggestion"—in other words, that Papadopoulos said something that *implied* to the diplomat that the campaign had received some *implication* that the Russians had information that could hurt Clinton. Nor was there anything about the conversation that indicated that the campaign reacted positively to, or encouraged, any implied overture. Moreover, it was indefensible for the FBI to assume that a mention in May of damaging information possibly held by the Russians likely referred to the hacked DNC e-mails. The May wine bar conversation occurred during the thick of the investigation into Clinton's private e-mail server. There was rampant speculation at the time, particularly in conservative political circles, that the Russians had hacked into Clinton's private server two years earlier and that Putin was going to publicly release *those* e-mails. Indeed, the day before the Papadopoulos conversation, Fox News reported a debate going on in the Russian government as to whether or not to release the e-mails obtained from Hillary Clinton's secret server. The overwhelming likelihood—assuming there was a reference to Russian information—was that Papadopoulos was merely referencing the speculation ongoing at the time.

Even if the FBI believed the diplomat's report warranted follow-up, it was not reasonable to leap immediately to a full-blown investigation of the campaign and use surreptitious surveillance. The department's practice allows for more measured alternatives. From my experience, the normal course in a case like this would have been to approach senior, reputable persons in the Trump campaign and provide a "defensive briefing," explaining the concern that the Russians may be attempting to enlist members of the campaign in their election interference efforts. This has the benefit of quickly resolving the matter in one of three ways: it could promptly elicit reassurance that there was no impropriety under way; it could allow the responsible campaign officials to discover and stop anything improper; or, even if the senior officials *were* involved in wrongdoing themselves, paying them a visit would have "braced" them—that is, scared them into abandoning any illicit activity. The FBI could have safely approached any one of several distinguished figures serving in the campaign, including Chris Christie, the governor of New Jersey and a former US attorney, or Senator Jeff Sessions, a member of the Senate Judiciary Committee and a former US attorney.

Giving a defensive briefing to the Trump campaign was clearly the right action to take if the FBI's priority was, as it claims, to protect the integrity of the election and stop any Russian interference. Earlier in 2016, when the FBI detected foreign money being channeled illegally into the Clinton campaign, it did exactly that: gave the Clinton campaign a defensive briefing. The bureau has never provided a plausible explanation why it didn't do the same for the Trump campaign. What is particularly inexplicable is that, while refusing to give the Trump campaign a defensive briefing, the intelligence chiefs agreed to "call out" the Russians directly about their activity—the actors we *knew* were the "bad guys." In August John Brennan, director of the Central Intelligence Agency, braced the head of Russian intelligence twice, signaling that the United States knew what the Russians were doing and that they had better stop it. Then President Obama talked to President Putin in September with the same message. Any claim that the FBI could not approach the Trump campaign because of a need to protect "sources and methods" rings hollow in light of these conversations. It makes no sense that the United States would be willing to inform *the Russians* that we knew what they were up to, but that the FBI would be unwilling to give a defensive briefing to an American presidential candidate's campaign.

While the feeble predication for Crossfire Hurricane raised my suspicion, the more I learned about how the investigation was conducted, the more unjustified the whole enterprise appeared. Between July and the election, Crossfire Hurricane turned up no evidence supporting the collusion narrative. On the contrary, the evidence from the secretly taped conversations with Page and Papadopoulos was exculpatory. Not only did both deny awareness of any arrangement or collusion with the Russians, but also they exploded key allegations made in the dossier, such as the existence of a communication channel between Page and Manafort.

One would think, given the flimsy basis for initiating the investigation in the first place, that the FBI would reassess this unprecedented inquiry as exculpatory evidence flowed in. But that is not what happened. Comey, McCabe, and the Crossfire Hurricane crew seemed to have ignored the evidence, put their heads down, and never looked back. In a damning report issued after I became Attorney General, the department's Inspector General, Michael Horowitz, found that the Crossfire Hurricane team, though relying on the Steele dossier in its warrant application, failed to disclose to the FISA court evidence tending to undercut Steele's credibility, the reliability of his network of sources, and the dossier's allegations.

It is particularly disturbing that, as they pressed ahead with their investigation into the Trump campaign, senior FBI officials became aware that the Clinton campaign had embarked on a propaganda strategy of trying to dirty up Trump by making him appear to be Putin's stooge. They also learned that their investigation was using materials that were part of this Clinton campaign effort.

After the election, evidence negating the collusion narrative continued to mount, and the credibility of Steele's dossier imploded. More taped conversations provided additional exculpatory evidence about both Papadopoulos and Page. The FISA surveillance of Page had produced no evidence of collusion. As for the dossier, the FBI was aware that all of Steele's information was provided by a single "primary sub-source" who claimed to derive his information from his network of sources. Incredibly, the Crossfire Hurricane team knew that the primary sub-source, a Russian living in the United States, had previously been investigated by the FBI as a suspected Russian intelligence agent, and the investigation had never been resolved. Moreover, in a series of interviews by the bureau, the primary sub-source indicated that the information presented by Steele in his dossier mischaracterized what he had passed along to Steele. In late January, the primary sub-source told the Crossfire Hurricane team that Steele's reporting was "misstated or exaggerated," that some of the information he supplied Steele was based on "rumor and speculation," and that he "never expected Steele to put [his] statements in reports or present them as facts." He added that he'd made it clear to Steele that he had no proof to support the statements from his own sub-sources and that "it was just talk." He further characterized the information supplied Steele as "word of mouth and hearsay," "conversations that [he] had with friends over beers," and statements made in "jest."

For me, the most damning aspect of Russiagate was the postelection decision by Comey and the tight group of FBI officials in charge of Crossfire Hurricane to double down on the collusion investigation just as the "evidence" previously relied on, as vaporous as it was to begin with, was completely evanescing before their eyes. By March 2017, the unjustified inference they had drawn from Papadopoulos's alleged comment in a London wine bar had been dispelled by evidence obtained from conversations with two different confidential sources. All their other efforts had failed to produce evidence of collusion. The Steele dossier, which had earlier been called on to get over the evidentiary hurdle, had now been thoroughly discredited. Indeed, the main concern presented by the Steele dossier by this time were all the red flags suggesting it may have been used as a vehicle for Russian disinformation. By March 20, when Director Comey stated so portentously that the FBI was investigating possible collusion between Russia and the Trump campaign, what, then, was the predicate of that investigation? What reasonable basis did he and his crew have for bearing down on the new President, his associates, and campaign?

It was also after the election—in late December—that Comey took precipitous action that has never been explained adequately. He bypassed normal procedures and sent two FBI agents into the White House to interview General Michael Flynn, who had just started as President Trump's national security adviser. Ostensibly, this was done as part of a counterintelligence investigation of Flynn, but, days earlier, the FBI Crossfire Hurricane team had determined there were no grounds for investigating the general. The justification offered for the interview was that Flynn had calls with the Russian ambassador during the transition, but this was not in the least unusual. Further, the

FBI had the transcripts of those calls and knew that nothing about them—either the fact they were held or their content—was unusual or suggestive of anything improper. Since this episode came to light in the first months of the Trump administration, I had long been concerned that there was no basis for interviewing Flynn other than trying to gin up a "false statement" charge against him and that Flynn's calls with the Russian ambassador were simply used as a pretext for keeping some kind of investigation going against the incoming Trump administration.

On May 9, 2017, the President fired Jim Comey as FBI director. He announced it without warning while Comey was making a speech in California, and then ordered that he not be permitted to take the FBI plane back to Washington. Whether or not Comey deserved that treatment, it showed a pettiness unbecoming of a President. Nonetheless, terminating Comey was, in my opinion, long overdue. Several months earlier, after his nomination as Attorney General, Jeff Sessions consulted me about upcoming personnel decisions at the department. One of my main recommendations was that Comey should be let go immediately. I was far from alone. Of the numerous former Republican DOJ officials consulted by Sessions and the White House counsel's office after the election, every one of them, as far as I was aware, gave the same advice—and for the same reason. It was not related to his role in Russiagate, which was largely unknown at the time. It was because we all had come to believe that Comey's high self-regard had swelled into an acute case of megalomania.

I had known Comey for more than twenty years and—I am embarrassed to say—helped him become the US attorney in New York in 2002 by getting former senator Alfonse D'Amato, who still wielded influence over such appointments, to withdraw his opposition. There was no doubt Comey was bright, exceptionally articulate, and glib, with a quick sense of humor. I respected his ability. But over the years, he seemed increasingly convinced that he was not only the smartest man in the room but also the holiest. By the time he served as Deputy Attorney General under President George W. Bush, his sanctimony had already begun to grate on many of his colleagues. It seemed Comey felt the need to convert every circumstance he encountered, no matter how mundane, into a morality drama, casting himself as saint and anybody who disagreed with him as reprobate. There are many stations in life in which this attitude is tolerable, but the head of the FBI is not one of them. It is an attitude that results in the likes of J. Edgar Hoover and the mind-set that one is a law unto himself. Perhaps only veterans of the Justice Department can appreciate fully the hubris involved in Comey's July press conference before the election. He usurped the authority of the Attorney General and, while announcing that criminal charges against Clinton were not warranted, proceeded to criticize the presidential candidate harshly for her conduct. Comey's behavior revealed a dangerous tendency to thrust himself, in a very public way, into arenas that were not his place. In President Trump's succinct description, Comey was a "grandstander."

President Trump's nose for phonies was certainly one of the reasons Comey was fired. But from what I saw, and learned later, the President's decision to dump the FBI director was triggered by what he understandably considered Comey's outrageous duplicity. Comey was repeatedly telling the President that he was *not* under investigation, but then leaks from the FBI, and Comey's own conduct in public and behind the scenes, led President Trump to believe that Comey was doing all he could to create the impression that the President *was* in jeopardy.

Putting the President under a cloud of potential legal jeopardy emboldens our enemies and endangers the country. Doing so without warrant is reprehensible. When Trump asked Comey to help lift the cloud by telling the public the same thing he was telling the President in private, Comey refused. His reason was another example of breathtaking hubris. He said that, if he accurately described the President's status to the public, and that status were to change, he would be obliged to make that new fact public at that time. That may be true, but so what? It wasn't Comey's decision to make. The possibility of future embarrassment was the President's risk. And it was the President's call whether the mere possibility of future embarrassment should prevent dispelling a real danger to the public interest today.

Trump's opponents seized on Comey's firing as an attempt by the President to put the kibosh on the FBI's collusion investigation. This was poppycock. As Special Counsel Mueller was to discover later, when the President raised firing Comey with his staff, he was advised that this would pour gas on the fire and prolong the investigation. The President acknowledged this, but said he still felt he had to fire Comey because he was not suited to be FBI director. In any event, the idea that simply removing an agency head would obstruct investigations pending within the agency has no validity. The FBI has thousands of agents, and a large team was hard at work on the investigation. An FBI director does not directly run investigations, and, in the normal course, pending investigations continue when a director departs. That certainly was the case here, since the President initially selected Comey's deputy, McCabe, to continue as acting director, and McCabe testified later to Congress there had been no effort to stop the investigation.

Predictably, the immediate effect of firing Comey was to intensify even further the feeding frenzy surrounding Russiagate. There were calls for a Special Counsel, and Comey tried to help things along by leaking memos he had written memorializing several conversations with the President. His stated purpose was to trigger appointment of a Special Counsel, although there was nothing in the self-serving memos that would have justified that. Unfortunately, President Trump exacerbated things himself with his own clumsy miscues, notably making imprecise comments in an interview with NBC News's Lester Holt and joking around with the Russian foreign minister and ambassador the day after firing Comey.

On May 17 Deputy Attorney General Rod Rosenstein, who was the Acting Attorney General for purposes of the Crossfire Hurricane investigation, made the surprise announcement he was appointing Robert Mueller as Special Counsel to investigate Russian election interference and whether Trump, his associates, or campaign had been involved. While Mueller would still be under the Acting Attorney General's overall supervision, Rosenstein made the appointment under a DOJ regulation that gave Mueller some measure of independence. This was, and remains, a controversial move, and, at the time, I questioned whether it was appropriate under the circumstances and, if it was, whether Mueller was the right person.

The reality was, however, that Trump's opponents and their media allies had already successfully incited mass hysteria around the collusion allegations. The administration was nearly immobilized under an unrelenting media assault. While there was no evidence supporting the claim that the Trump campaign had colluded with the Russians, it was hard to see how the phony scandal could be laid to rest unless someone with sufficient stature could resolve the matter. I believe Rosenstein felt that the collusion allegations were probably baseless and that the best way for the administration to get beyond the wild scandalmongering was to appoint a prominent figure who could bring things to a conclusion quickly and credibly. Until that happened, the inquiry was in the hands of the FBI—specifically McCabe and Strzok, who had become heavily invested in the collusion narrative and had every interest in vindicating their past actions. To Rosenstein, appointing Mueller must have seemed liked the least-bad option.

One of the problems was that the Special Counsel's charter was focused on only half of the issue—the wrong half. By the time of Mueller's appointment, Crossfire Hurricane was a bust. There was no real evidence of collusion. The matter really requiring investigation was how Crossfire Hurricane got started and why Comey continued it while the asserted predication for it collapsed. Technically, Mueller's charter was broad enough to pursue these issues, but he ignored them. With his ties to the FBI and the leaders who launched Crossfire Hurricane, as well as the strong personal disdain he had for Trump, he was the wrong person to investigate it anyway.

More than that, Mueller's whole approach to the investigation was unjustified. As we learned later, by May, there was no evidence to warrant continuing the investigation of Trump's campaign. The order appointing Mueller essentially told him to take over the Crossfire Hurricane investigation. But that investigation was justified a year earlier as a counterintelligence investigation. Mueller came out of the box with a heavy-handed criminal investigation. But he never seemed to have stopped to examine whether there was an adequate basis for pursuing either a counterintelligence or criminal investigation. Instead, according to an FBI agent assigned to Mueller's team, after Mueller came in, the office quickly developed a "Get Trump" attitude and began with a preexisting conviction that there must be "something criminal." The investigation became "upside down" from what should occur. Instead of letting the evidence lead the investigation, the attitude was "the evidence is there, we just have to find it." Anything that did not agree with the investigators' preconceptions was discounted, and witnesses' testimony was given the most negative interpretation possible. Perhaps Mueller's integrity prevented this from going on longer than it did, but the way the investigation was conducted made it something not so different from a witch hunt.

It is hard to tell whether Mueller's decision to staff his investigation predominantly with partisan Democrats resulted from, or was the cause of, the "Get Trump" attitude. In either event, these staffing decisions, if not partisan, were dunderheaded and grossly unfair to Rod Rosenstein. The whole purpose of appointing Mueller was to assure the public that partisanship would not be involved in the investigation. Mueller defeated the very purpose of his appointment. His staffing decisions engendered deep distrust in half the country. Based on later information about the way the investigation was conducted, those fears were not wholly unjustified.

Mueller's mind-set appears to have resulted in another glaring omission: the failure to explore the possibility that information coming through Steele's dossier, and sponsored by the Clinton campaign, was Russian disinformation intended to sow chaos during the election and afterward. The sad fact is that, by the time Mueller was appointed, the red flags that Steele's reporting could well contain Russian disinformation were far more substantial than any evidence of collusion by the Trump campaign. The FBI had received intelligence that, shortly after Steele was hired to help the Clinton campaign, Russian intelligence became aware of his assignment. The FBI also knew that the sole conduit for information provided Steele was someone they'd previously investigated as a Russian intelligence agent, and that issue had never been resolved. After the election, the Crossfire Hurricane team received intelligence reporting that a Russian intelligence service may have targeted Steele's business intelligence company, Orbis, and additional intelligence that some of Steele's reporting "was part of a Russian disinformation campaign." Even though Mueller was supposed to investigate Russian efforts to interfere in the election, he never seemed to have explored the possibility that Steele's dossier was used as a vector for Russian disinformation.

Within a couple of days of Mueller's appointment as Special Counsel, I called him. I was a private citizen at that time. I asked Bob how he was doing. He seemed to interpret this as me asking him why he took on the Special Counsel assignment. "I am not going to let them steal our democracy," he said. I was taken aback by the theatrics.

After some small talk, I told Mueller I had some friendly advice for him. I had picked up indications that some of those at the FBI who had been involved in looking into the Trump campaign were leaking. I suggested he would be well advised to bring in a fresh FBI team to work under his aegis rather than rely on the old Crossfire Hurricane group. "I think you'd be smart to make a clean break with what went on before your appointment," I said.

"Thanks for the advice," Mueller answered. I had the strong sense that he was brushing me off.

A couple of months later, Rosenstein authorized the release of texts between Peter Strzok, the senior FBI agent on Mueller's team, and FBI lawyer Lisa Page, who had been on the FBI deputy director's staff. The e-mail showed virulent and wildly inappropriate messages about Trump. By the time the texts were made public, Strzok had left the investigation. But the release of those texts undermined the credibility of Mueller's investigation.

It was one of many emerging signs that Russiagate specifically, and the resistance generally, were mendacious and fraudulent attempts to invalidate the legitimate election of an American President. Trump may not have been my ideal of a Republican President. But he stood for good policies the country needed desperately. While his grating personality traits were often counterproductive, he did not deserve this treatment. No President does.

CHAPTER 9

INTO THE STORM

Even so, I had no desire at all to go into the Trump administration. Various officials had called me for advice or recommendations—Attorney General Sessions and a few others—but I was happy to remain on the outside.

My first official connection with the Trump administration was in the first part of 2017 at my old haunt the Central Intelligence Agency. Mike Pompeo, confirmed as CIA director at the beginning of the administration, asked my friend Bob Kimmitt to chair his external advisory board—a bipartisan group of business leaders and former senior officials who meet regularly to advise the agency on a range of matters. On Bob's recommendation, Mike, whom I had not known, invited me to join the group, an unpaid advisory post. I enjoyed reconnecting with the agency and working with my colleagues on the board and with the CIA directors—initially Pompeo and, after he went to serve as secretary of state, Gina Haspel. I found Mike and Gina immensely talented, quality people, and I became friends with both of them. I heard later that Mike was among those encouraging the President to consider me as the replacement for AG Jeff Sessions.

In March 2017 a US corporate client asked me to help on a significant legal matter. Because I needed assistance handling the project, I returned to the law firm of Kirkland & Ellis as "of counsel" to get that support. That work, plus my service on corporate boards, was keeping me as busy as I wanted to be.

I met President Trump for the first time in June 2017. Shortly after Mueller's appointment, I was contacted by David Friedman, the Trump-appointed US ambassador to Israel, who asked to meet with me. Friedman, a prominent lawyer and the President's friend, was apparently trying to identify senior lawyers with Washington experience who might be willing to augment Trump's personal defense team, then headed by Marc Kasowitz. Friedman wanted my advice, even if I was not personally available to join the team. During our meeting at DC's two-hundred-year-old Willard InterContinental hotel in June, I explained that I had just taken on a major matter for an important corporate client and was not in a position to help. I recommended others who might be available. He asked me to meet with the chief executive anyway, saying he wanted President Trump to get the perspective of someone with my breadth of experience. The flattery worked; I agreed.

Early the next morning, June 20, Friedman brought me into the Oval Office for what amounted to a brief courtesy visit. As I entered, the President said cordially, "Well, finally I get to meet Bill Barr. You have an unbelievable reputation. No one has anything bad to say about you."

"I cover my tracks pretty well, Mr. President," I said. He laughed, and we shook hands. As with almost all meetings with President Trump—as I was to find out—he did most of the talking. He spoke with passion about how outrageous the Russiagate investigation was and how unjust it was to the administration and his family. He was very interested that I had been longtime friends with Bob Mueller, and asked about him, especially whether the Special Counsel would make his decisions honestly. I told him Mueller was "a straight shooter" and that, if the evidence wasn't there, I thought he'd call it straight. If Mueller is honest, he said, the case should be over soon. The President said he was sure there could be no evidence of collusion, since there had been none. He asked me how long I thought Mueller would take for his investigation, saying that Kasowitz told him it could be over in just weeks.

"Well, it should be," I said, "but I am afraid it will drag on much longer than that."

The President then asked whether I was "considering some role" on his defense team. I responded that my personal and professional obligations were such that I was unable to help. He seemed surprised. Grabbing a notepad, he asked for my phone number and said he would call me in a day or so. Friedman ushered me out.

I did not hear from the President. Such was the impression I made.

That evening at home, my wife asked me what Trump was like in person. "He's exactly like you see him on TV. No difference," I told her.

My next interaction with the President was to be almost a year and half later, when I met with him to discuss serving as Attorney General. During the interim, I'd been an outside observer, increasingly frustrated by the media's dishonest flogging of the Russia collusion narrative.

In the early summer of 2017—around the time of my dealings with Friedman, and not long after Mueller launched his investigation—news reports started popping up suggesting that Mueller's team was beginning to focus more on potential obstruction of justice charges and less on whether there had been improper collusion in the first place. This confirmed my suspicion that there had been no appreciable evidence of collusion when Mueller first arrived on the scene, and he still hadn't found any.

I was disturbed that, instead of just confirming that there had been no collusion, Mueller appeared to be artificially dragging things out by pursuing an unprecedented and strained obstruction theory. The two acts by Trump that the Special Counsel seemed to have initially relied on in going down this path were Trump's firing Comey and his comment to Comey that he hoped the FBI director could eventually "let it go"—"it" being the Flynn investigation. The idea that either of these acts was an obstruction of justice was absurd, especially if there was no underlying crime of collusion. For these actions to constitute obstruction, Mueller would have to argue they violated a particular federal statute: Section 1512(c) of the federal criminal code, adopted as part of the 2002 Sarbanes-Oxley Act's so-called anti-shredding provisions. But that statute was meant to apply to actions that destroy or alter documents or physical items, depriving a proceeding of accurate evidence. To reach the President's conduct, the statute would have to be radically stretched far beyond its intent. I was concerned—rightly, as it turned out—that Mueller was considering arguing that the statute applied to any act that influences a proceeding if taken with a bad motive—even an act taken by a President within the scope of his official responsibilities. Reading the statute this broadly is not only legally untenable, in my view, but also would have potentially disastrous implications, not just for the presidency, but for the executive branch as a whole and for the Department of Justice in particular.

By the very nature of their jobs, countless executive branch officials—from the President to the Attorney General down to each line prosecutor—take discretionary actions every day that "influence" proceedings either indirectly or directly. Those actions range from the appointment and removal of subordinates to stopping or starting an investigation in the exercise of prosecutorial discretion. If the obstruction statute was read as broadly as I thought Mueller was considering, any executive official taking an action that influences a proceeding could become the subject of a grand jury investigation based simply on an allegation that his or her subjective motivation was improper, even if the action was, on its face, a valid exercise of discretion. This would have a massively chilling effect on the executive branch, especially the Department of Justice. Mueller was a subordinate official in the department—the equivalent of a US attorney. I wanted to make sure that, before the DOJ went down such a potentially consequential path, the full implications of the theory were considered at the appropriate level.

In short, I was concerned that a "Get Trump" attitude at the Special Counsel's office might be leading to foolish precedents that would, in time, hamstring the entire executive branch.

When Deputy Attorney General Rod Rosenstein invited me for a casual lunch in March 2018, I took the occasion to raise these concerns verbally with him. I had known Rod, though not well, for many years. I believed him to be a consummate professional with a broad and deep understanding of the department's business. Rod quite properly did not react to my concerns—he has one of the best poker faces in the business. The issues were sufficiently complicated that I thought it would be useful to prepare a written analysis of my concerns. So, I wrote up a memo for Rod, which I sent him in June and distributed to other lawyers who might also have involvement in the matter or were friends whose feedback I valued. This was the so-called nineteen-page unsolicited memo that Democrats and the media made so much of during my confirmation hearing eight months later. In addition to setting forth an extensive legal analysis, my memorandum made a fundamental point:

> *[If a] DOJ investigation is going to take down a democratically elected President, it is imperative to the health of our system and to our national cohesion that any claim of wrongdoing is solidly based on evidence of a real crime—not a debatable one. It is time to travel wellworn paths; not to veer into novel, unsettled, or contested areas of the law; and not to indulge the fancies by overly zealous prosecutors.*

In my view, Mueller greatly disserved the public interest when, early in his tenure, he indulged his team by embarking on an almost two-year investigation based on an esoteric, untenable obstruction theory. Mueller never seems to have paused to consider the sheer injustice of it all. A President under investigation after being falsely accused of collusion, and angry at having his administration turned upside down and his family mauled by prosecutors, expresses anger and frustration at the investigation. Meanwhile, the prosecutor treats each angry reaction by the President to the artificial protraction of the investigation as a new obstruction.

"But," as former senior FBI official Thomas J. Baker observed, "it was all talk, no action. Mr. Trump never did anything to interfere with either the original counterintelligence investigation or with the Special Counsel's inquiry." On the contrary, the President gave the investigation unfettered access to campaign and White House documents, directed his aides to testify, and asserted no privilege.

As the 2018 midterm elections approached, speculation was rife that Attorney General Sessions would be leaving office, either on his own or forced out by the President. A few friends with ties to the White House contacted me to ask if I would have any interest in the job. I said I was not in a position to do it and suggested some other people. On October 11 a *Wall Street Journal* article reported that I was among several candidates under consideration. I dismissed this as some White House source tossing my name into the mix as a decoy to conceal the actual candidates. The article generated a lot of calls from friends and press, but I continued to say I was not available.

One of the people who talked to me about serving as Attorney General was Pat Cipollone. Pat had come to work for me as an aide twenty-five years earlier when I first served as Attorney General, and we had been good friends since then. After we left the Bush administration, we had worked together on a number of matters in private practice. I knew President Trump was preparing to offer Pat the White House counsel position after Don McGahn left the post. Pat was a great choice. He was exceptionally bright, broadly experienced, and highly ethical, with sound judgment and the utmost discretion. It was critically important to Pat that the new Attorney General be someone with whom he could work closely. During the fall, we talked frequently about possible AG candidates. Pat made clear that he very much wanted me to consider taking the job, but, as a friend, he swore off pressuring me. He realized that, from my standpoint, it made no sense.

During October, as it became clear that Sessions would be leaving, and my name first popped up as a potential successor, my wife made clear—as she had since the start of the Trump administration—that she did not want me even to consider going back into government. "It'd be crazy, and I'd divorce you," she said several times. Though said jokingly, the divorce threat underscored the depth of her feelings.

I told her not to worry. Like her, I felt it was out of the question. Meg was just reaching the five-year mark since her last cancer treatment, and, while Christine and I weren't taking anything for granted, we were just starting to breathe a bit easier. We had deferred a lot and felt it was time to spend calm time with the family, especially with our five young grandchildren. My professional situation was all I could hope for at that stage in life: I was serving on excellent boards and doing a limited amount of high-end legal consulting, but still had time to "smell the flowers." I had no ambition for further professional positions or honors. We dared to hope that perhaps we had finally reached that stage for relaxation I had always promised Chris. Serving in the Trump administration would blow that all up.

For Chris, it wasn't just the unwanted disruption to our life. "The whole political environment is insane and vicious—much worse than last time," she observed. "The Left and the press have lost their minds over Trump. They are a howling mob who will destroy whoever they see helping Trump, and I just don't want to see you savaged the way you would be."

Chris, like many conservative Republican women, supported Trump's policies but was turned off by his obnoxious behavior, verbal diarrhea, and lack of self-control, which she felt contributed needlessly to the opposition against him. "He is his own worst enemy," she kept warning, "and he isn't going to change. Any sacrifice you make will be wasted on this man. You cannot save someone like him from himself." I agreed with her and did not need persuading on that score.

This was all academic until November 7, 2018, the day after the midterm elections, when Sessions announced his resignation. That morning, I got a call from the acting counsel to the President, Emmet Flood, who asked if he could come to see me right away at my law firm office. Emmet had an outstanding reputation as a lawyer's lawyer, but I had gotten to know him only over the past year through our mutual friendship with Pat Cipollone. His reputation was well deserved. I anticipated what was coming and led Emmet into a small, out-of-the-way Kirkland & Ellis conference room, where we met privately.

Emmet told me the President had asked him to put together a list of possible successors to Sessions, and my name was at the top of his list. I appreciated Emmet's confidence and felt I owed him an explanation as to why I did not want to be considered. I explained to Emmet that Christine and I were at a stage in life where we simply could not see taking on this challenge, and that professionally I had no aspirations for further office. For me, returning as Attorney General again had no upside, only downsides.

While it is always an honor to serve the country, I also told Emmet that the prospect of serving under President Trump was not attractive to me. A new Attorney General would be coming in to deal with a highly fraught and explosive crisis—not an auspicious circumstance. It was well known among lawyers that Trump was difficult to work with. Getting him to accept good advice was like wrestling an alligator. Whatever you did, it was never enough—his attitude was "What have you done for me lately?" From what I had seen, he did not treat his subordinates well. He took shots at them behind their backs and in public rather than deal with them man-to-man. Trump had been publicly attacking a number of honorable people who had worked hard to help his presidency, including his outgoing counsel, Don McGahn, and his chief of staff, General John Kelly. This was bush-league behavior. Serving under someone like that wasn't my idea of a professional opportunity.

Emmet understood, and I suggested some other possible candidates. Mike Mukasey had been a magnificent Attorney General during the last two years of the George W. Bush administration, and I suggested they explore whether he had any interest. I also suggested former judge Mike Luttig and former Deputy Attorneys General George Terwilliger, Larry Thompson, and Mark Filip.

In the weeks that followed, as I continued advocating for other candidates, many people—former government colleagues, some senators, people from the business world—weighed in, encouraging me to consider serving again. Their basic argument was that the country was in a potential crisis and needed experienced people to step forward.

Among the voices that had the greatest impact on me were friends inside the department itself. Sessions and McGahn had done a good job assembling a strong team at DOJ—several of them, my friends. Over the two weeks following the midterm elections, some of them, one by one, got together with me for drinks after work. The watering hole of choice was the beautiful atrium at the Trump International

Hotel, a block from the department. Over drinks, each of the officials encouraged me to consider returning to Main Justice. They felt the Justice Department was being buffeted from all sides, and the internal climate was becoming dysfunctional. After pushing out Sessions as Attorney General, the President had installed Sessions's chief of staff, Matt Whitaker, as Acting Attorney General. This departed from the normal course, which would have been to have the Deputy, Rod Rosenstein, hold the post temporarily. There was growing tension between the AG's office and the Deputy's office. The DOJ officials I talked with all believed that, without a strong AG at the top, the department was vulnerable to being pushed around by Congress and within the executive branch. They felt it imperative that a permanent Attorney General be nominated quickly and that I was in the best position to get confirmed, stabilize the department, and restore regular order.

The official I was most friendly with was blunt. After we ordered another round and the Trump Hotel's best appetizer—the maple bacon—he leaned in toward me: "Bill, a lot of good people joined the department," he said, speaking of the political appointees. "It is a great group, but with Trump feuding with Sessions and now installing Whitaker, the place has become a shitshow. It's embarrassing. Of the guys I know, everyone is hoping you do it."

"How about Rod?" I asked.

"I think Rod respects you. He is in a tough spot, and, frankly, I think he'd be relieved if it's you."

"How about Chris Christie?" I asked. I thought Christie was a strong leader and an exceptionally effective advocate. I heard him speak without notes at the 2011 National Republican Congressional Committee fund-raiser and thought it was one of the best political speeches I'd heard. His name was being bandied about as a possible Attorney General or White House chief of staff, and I thought he'd make a good AG. The former New Jersey governor knew the nuts and bolts of the department and already had a relationship with Trump.

"He'd be good," my friend agreed, "but he was also part of the Trump campaign in 2016, and I think people wonder whether he would get hung up like Sessions and be forced to recuse himself from the Mueller stuff. So we'd be back where we started. He might be forced to recuse as the price of confirmation."

In the weeks following the midterms, I also stayed in touch with Pat Cipollone, who was still in the process of disengaging from his law firm so he could start as Trump's new White House counsel. Pat and Emmet Flood were the two intermediaries I was feeding the names of other possible AG candidates for the President to consider. In mid-November I called Pat to get the lay of the land. "Pat, I want to make sure you are not pushing for me," I started.

"I promise I am not, but I think the President is intrigued by you because almost everyone he is talking to is telling him you'd be a home run," Pat said. "The senators, in particular, are supportive. I think they believe you would be the easiest to confirm. I am pretty sure he's at least going to want to talk with you."

I realized that I couldn't waste the President's time by agreeing to talk unless I had already made up my mind that I would be willing to accept the job. The time had come to make a decision.

Strong encouragement also came from an unexpected source.

On November 17 I went on a weekend retreat at a CIA training facility with my colleagues on the agency's external advisory board. In addition to briefings and meetings, we had afternoon breaks for sessions on the shooting range and on the course for high-speed evasive driving. Over the two and a half days, many of my colleagues took me aside and urged me to consider taking the AG job if asked.

One conversation that made a particular impression on me took place as we were returning to our dorms after the evasive driving course. Three of my fellow board members, one a business leader from Silicon Valley and the others successful heads of national companies, buttonholed me. In the two years that I had been working with these men, I had come to respect them immensely. These leaders, who I believe leaned Democratic or Independent, were very patriotic and not partisan when it came to the welfare of the country. They expressed the view that America was facing very serious challenges and needed the most qualified people in critical positions. They argued that I was uniquely qualified by experience and temperament to serve as Attorney General during this tumultuous period. Even though they were not Republicans, nor big fans of Trump, they thought the country would be best served—and they would certainly rest easier—if I was willing to step up.

The retreat weekend turned out to be a turning point in my thinking. On the way home, I had plenty of time alone to think. That was the first time I started, in my own mind, to entertain the idea of serving again as Attorney General if the President asked me. I realized my reasons for saying no were all based on preserving my personal comfort; broader interests weighed in favor of stepping up. Trump, whatever his personal flaws, was the duly elected President pursuing policies I generally agreed with and thought essential for the United States. He faced an implacable resistance intent on nullifying the results of the 2016 election by using every means at hand to hobble his administration.

The suspect Russian collusion narrative had drawn the Department of Justice and the FBI into the political maelstrom, and many Americans sensed—with some justification—that powerful Washington politicos were using the criminal justice system as a political weapon. I revered the DOJ, the FBI, and all the department's components, and believed that I could provide stability and leadership at this critical juncture. I believed the circumstances called for someone leading the department who was truly independent—someone who did not need or want anything after the job and therefore was free to do what he thought was right without fearing how it might affect his future economic or political prospects. Because I was entering retirement and at the end of my professional life, I felt that I had the personal independence to help steer the department back to its core mission of applying one standard of justice for everyone and enforcing the law evenhandedly.

When I got home, I gave my wife a full report on the retreat as we sat at our kitchen island. I related all the encouragement I received from my board colleagues. Since October, she had been watching me recommending other possible AG candidates, but none of my ideas seemed to be gaining traction.

"Sweetheart, I hope this does not come my way, and I will not do anything to pursue it," I assured her, "but I am starting to think that, if the President ends up wanting me, I should be open to accepting the job."

There was a brief silence. Then Chris explained quietly where she stood. "I don't like Trump's behavior," she said, "but I think the behavior of the Left and the media is much worse." She had been especially infuriated by the Left's attack on Judge Brett Kavanaugh during his confirmation hearings for the Supreme Court in October. We had known Brett since he was a newly minted lawyer, and Chris took attacks on him personally. The more she digested the episode, the more she felt the behavior of those trying to sabotage the Trump administration was sickening. And the Left's shrill new assertiveness after winning control of the House in the midterms chilled her even more. Her opposition to my serving as AG had softened.

"You know," she said, "if they're able to drive Trump from office with this Russiagate stuff, the country is finished." Her voice became a little choked. "You know how hard the job was last time; well, now it is ten times worse, and I can't bear to think how viciously they'll attack you." She walked over and hugged me. "If the President decides he wants you, and if you decide you need to do it, I will support you."

Suddenly she pulled away. "But, you know, the girls would bear some of the brunt of this—things are so vicious out there," she said.

"You're right," I agreed, "and we'll talk to them and won't do it if any of them are opposed."

All three of our daughters lived close by, and the next evening, each came over to weigh in on the issue as we sat around the family room. My oldest, Mary—a veteran narcotics prosecutor with fifteen years at the department focusing on South American drug cartels—was at that point working on the Deputy Attorney General's staff as the department's lead opioid coordinator. She would be affected most directly by my decision because she felt that, if I were to become AG, she would want to step down from that position, even if not legally required. She had earlier been against the idea because of the toll it would take on me but now felt that, if I was offered the job and was willing, I should do it.

"You are in the best position to right the ship," she said, then added: "But we should be clear eyed that we're headed into a hellish situation."

My middle daughter, Patricia, had been Republican counsel to a congressional committee for more than thirteen years. She felt I should be willing to serve, but then started tearing up. "Look, Patty," I said, "this is not something I am personally driven to do, so if you don't want me to, I won't—no problem."

"No, no," she said. "I just hate to think of all the mean things they will be saying about you."

"They will," I replied, "but that's okay."

Our youngest daughter, Meg, after finishing a five-year stint as a federal prosecutor in DC, had moved to Capitol Hill, where she also served as a Republican counsel to a congressional committee. "Someone has to impose some order on all this chaos" was her position. "I don't really want you to do it because of the hammering you'll take, but I think you have to."

I have always had the deepest respect and affection for General Brent Scowcroft, whom I served with in Bush 41's administration. He had backed me for the Attorney General appointment after Dick Thornburgh left to run for the Senate in Pennsylvania. My respect for Scowcroft was undiminished when, in 2016, he supported Hillary Clinton because he considered Trump unsuited for the presidency. It is possible to disagree with people and still respect them. But after Trump was elected, when some Republican national security experts grumbled about refusing to serve in the Trump administration, he made an emotional appeal to all Republicans and Democrats to put country first and accept posts if asked. Their duty and service is *to the country*, he said, and people should be ready to serve when the President needs them because the country needs them. That is also how I looked at it. Our country needs more people like Brent Scowcroft.

The fact that President Trump had selected Pat Cipollone to serve as White House counsel also made me more willing to consider serving at Attorney General again. The President's counsel and the Attorney

General must work closely together. In Pat, I knew I would have a partner whose judgment and integrity I could count on. This would help us both do our respective jobs much more effectively. I also knew that Cipollone was planning on bringing another friend of mine, Pat Philbin, to serve as his deputy. When I was general counsel at GTE and Verizon, Philbin—who was then at Kirkland & Ellis—worked directly with me on some of my most important cases. I knew he was not only an outstanding lawyer but also someone who, like Cipollone, had the highest ethical standards.

Several days after my CIA retreat, Emmet Flood checked back in to see if I was still a firm "no." He said that a lot of people, including senators, had volunteered my name to Trump, which made the President interested in talking with me. I told him that, if none of my alternative suggestions were making headway, I would be willing to talk to him. The next day, I heard from Emmet that I would be meeting with the President in the residence at the White House on the following Tuesday morning, November 27.

This was my first time visiting the residence. The meeting was held in the Yellow Oval Room, which is the bright, spacious formal living room on the south side of the mansion's second floor. When I walked into the room, Emmet was waiting, and I heard Fox News blaring from a TV in the adjoining President's Sitting Room. After a few minutes, the TV was turned off, and the President, wearing his trademark blue suit and long, red tie, burst into view, welcomed me heartily, and gestured for me to take a seat. He made sure I had been served coffee, and we sat down side by side in matching plush upholstered chairs. Emmet Flood sat on the sofa directly across from us.

My conversation with the President was easygoing—not in the least stilted or formal. We talked directly and comfortably with each other as if we had known each other for a long time. He did not appear to remember talking to me the year before during my brief visit with Ambassador David Friedman—at least, he never brought it up. After some initial small talk about growing up in New York City around the same time, he launched into a discourse on the injustice of the Russiagate "hoax" and how it was effectively robbing him of his opportunity to conduct his administration. He said his worst decision ever in life was agreeing to appoint Sessions as Attorney General, which he did out of loyalty because Sessions had been the first US senator to endorse him. A few minutes into the meeting, the door opened, and Melania walked in. This was the first time I had seen her in person. The President jumped up to greet her and introduce us. We stood for a moment, chatting, and she then headed off to an outside event. She was more striking in person than on TV, and I was impressed by her dignity and obvious intelligence. After she left, the President expressed deep resentment about Mueller's hyperaggressive tactics and how they had brought a lot of suffering to his family.

President Trump then asked me how I conceived the job of Attorney General. I felt he would benefit from a brief explanation of the distinct roles played by that office. I moved briskly through my usual tripartite analysis. First, as his legal adviser on his authorities as chief executive, he could count on me to advise him on what I thought the best legal answer was on any legal issue. If he decided that he wanted to take a different position, I would advance it as long as I believed it was a reasonably defensible position under the law. But I told him that I agreed with something President George H. W. Bush had said to me: the best way to weaken the presidency is to take overly aggressive positions that will not be sustained. Second, in my role as policy adviser on law enforcement matters, I would be advocating for policy positions and initiatives consistent with his priorities, especially strong, tough-on-crime policies. The third role of the Attorney General is the most sensitive, I explained, and required that we have a candid conversation and clear understanding at this stage. The President perked up and signaled for me to go ahead.

As head of the Department of Justice, I continued, the Attorney General is the top prosecutor, overseeing enforcement of the laws through the criminal justice process. It is the responsibility of the Attorney General to ensure that the department's enforcement actions are insulated from political interference and are based solely on the law, the facts, and the equal treatment of all individuals, without regard to political or personal considerations. For that reason, I said, I could not tolerate political interference in criminal cases and would take the job only based on that understanding. The President agreed and said that, if he picked me, he would not interfere and would expect me to exercise my independent judgment to make the call I thought was right.

President Trump went on to complain about what he felt was a double standard at the Justice Department. It seemed, he said, that the DOJ jumped at any pretext to launch investigations of Republicans, especially Trump supporters, but brushed aside clear evidence of potential criminality by Democrats. I told him it seemed that way to me also at times. I felt there were some career prosecutors in the department, a very distinct minority, who were partisan and applied a double standard, sometimes unconsciously and sometimes deliberately. He was pleased to hear me acknowledge this problem.

I used his concern about a double standard to segue into another important point I wanted to stress. I told him that, as Attorney General, I would view my central mission as eliminating this double standard and restoring the same standard for everybody, regardless of politics. But this meant, I stressed, that I would not engage in tit for tat. Just because the other side abuses the criminal justice process does not mean we should retaliate in kind. That would only aggravate a vicious cycle, lead to the public's deeper disenchantment with our criminal justice system, and ultimately bring about the breakdown of the rule of law. The only way out of a destructive spiral over the long term is to tenaciously uphold and insist on the correct standard for everybody. He agreed in principle, though perhaps a little begrudgingly.

The President went on to make a comment about Hillary Clinton that surprised me. He said that, despite the chants of "Lock her up!" from some of his supporters, he had felt after the 2016 election that the e-mail matter should be dropped. Even if she were guilty, he said, for the election winner to seek prosecution of the loser would make the country look like a "banana republic."

As the discussion went on, it became more discursive. He wanted to know how I had interacted with President George H. W. Bush. I told him we did not talk that often, but he gave me a lot of running room.

He asked about James Baker, whom he seemed to consider the gold standard of chiefs of staff, and about how the White House ran under Presidents Reagan and Bush. I surmised he was preparing to make changes at the White House. He asked me my opinion of various officials in government, including some of the current cast of characters at DOJ, and people on the White House staff. Our opinions did not always jibe.

Once again I was put off by the way he was belittling behind their backs a number of the officials who worked for him. This explained why the government often appeared so dysfunctional from the outside. With a boss like this, how could there be any mutual trust in the organization? He was being very charming with me, but I was under no illusion that—if I ended up as AG—he'd be sniping at me this way behind my back in a couple of months.

I had been warned that the President, for some reason, wants to hear candidates for positions state firmly that they "want" the job when he offers it. He asked me, "Do you want the job?" I responded, "If I can, I'd like to help this administration succeed, Mr. President." That seemed to do the trick. Originally scheduled for a half hour, we had already gone over an hour. Suddenly the President turned to Emmet and said, "Cancel the rest of the interviews; this is the guy I want.

"He has great support among the senators. Are there any issues that could come up in confirmation we should know about?"

"Well, there is a long memo he wrote raising questions about Mueller's pursuing obstruction theories," Emmet said. "It could stir things up, but it shouldn't be a problem." The President did not seem to know what he was talking about. Emmet explained a bit more, and President Trump agreed that it didn't sound like a big deal.

"Have you thought about anyone you want to bring in with you?" the President asked me.

"It is critical to me that I select my own Deputy, Mr. President," I responded.

"Absolutely. Do you have anyone in mind?"

"Jeff Rosen, who is currently number two at the Transportation Department," I told him.

"That is fine. Yes, I know him. That is fine."

I had assumed that Rod Rosenstein wanted to leave, and this turned out to be correct. He told me later that he had a lot riding on my confirmation, since I was his "exit strategy."

I had known Jeff Rosen for many years. He had been a colleague at Kirkland & Ellis. He was an able lawyer, and the fact he was already in a confirmed position meant he should be easy to get through the confirmation process. But the main reason I wanted Jeff was that I knew he had moral courage—when he knew he was right, he was stubborn as hell, and no one could push him around. Also, like me, he was approaching the latter stages of his legal career and would have the freedom to do what he thought was right without worrying about the impact on his career.

The President asked me about Chris Wray, whom he appointed to replace Comey as FBI director, and who had taken office just three months after Comey's firing. I said that I had met Chris only briefly when he was at DOJ during Bush 43's administration, and, while I really did not know him well, people I respected had high regard for him. He mused aloud that he wasn't sure Wray was the guy who could "clean up" the bureau. I said I would want a chance to work with him.

The President wrapped up things by assuring me that, despite his views on certain DOJ people, I would have carte blanche over retention and selection of all my subordinates, not just the Deputy; he would leave personnel decisions to me. He asked whether I had any questions, and I said no. Trump observed that he had now kept some reporters waiting in the Oval Office for almost an hour, and stood up. Offering his hand, he said, "Bill, I'm happy to have you as my Attorney General."

"I am honored to serve, Mr. President," I said as I shook his hand.

The President then said he wanted to delay making this public until the week of December 9. I agreed readily, explaining that my youngest daughter, Meg, was to be married on December 8 and that I would prefer not detracting from her big day with the hubbub that might attend the announcement.

As Emmet and I headed downstairs from the residence, I asked who the President had interviewed before me. "You are the first," he told me.

After leaving the White House, I called a young man, Brian Rabbitt, who had worked with one of my daughters and whose career I had followed for fifteen years. After graduating from law school and clerking for two distinguished judges, he had been at the DC law firm of Williams & Connolly for several years. He knew the key players in the administration because he had spent the first year of the administration helping Don McGahn at the White House counsel's office before going over to the US Securities and Exchange Commission (SEC) as a senior adviser to its chairman, Jay Clayton. Brian was an exceptional talent, combining a strong work ethic, a great intellect, and good judgment. I asked him if he would be interested in helping with my confirmation and serving as my chief of staff if I ended up as the Attorney General. He agreed.

A few days later, on the morning of Saturday, December 1, 2018, I received the sad but not wholly unexpected news that President George H. W. Bush had died overnight at the age of ninety-four. The last time I had been with him was his eighty-eighth birthday party at Kennebunkport for the screening of the HBO documentary about him, *41*. He seemed full of joy as he zipped around on his mobility scooter, warmly engaging his guests, reminiscing and laughing. But in recent years, his health had been declining, especially since losing Barbara in April.

The former President's staff kept all of his "official family" informed on the long-planned funeral arrangements, and we received our marching orders within a day of the news of his death. On Tuesday, December 4, his White House staff and cabinet, and spouses, would assemble at DC's Omni Shoreham Hotel for a brief reception. We would then go as a group to the Capitol Building, where we would receive the President's remains and keep a vigil while he lay in state in the Rotunda that evening. The next day, we would assemble again at the Omni Shoreham and then attend the funeral service at the National Cathedral, where we would sit together behind the Bush family.

I had strong emotions as "41's" old team gathered on Tuesday at the hotel. To be sure, we all experienced the shared sorrow of losing this great man who had played such an important role in all our lives. We also shared great pride in our common bond: our service on behalf of a leader whose many virtues have become more apparent as the nation's political life has darkened and become more bitter. Looking around the reception, it struck me anew what a group of capable and decent men and women President Bush had drawn together in his adminis-tration.

Not surprisingly, my former colleagues had seen news stories that I was at that very moment one of the candidates President Trump was considering for Attorney General. Starting with the first reception and over the next two days, many took me aside to ask if the reports were true. I asked their advice whether I should take the job if it was offered. I didn't tell them I had already been picked.

My appointment was not news I felt able to share with my old friends and colleagues from the Bush world. Still, I was reassured that everyone I talked with supported the idea of me serving again. Most of 41's old team seemed to size up the situation much like I did. We were frequently unhappy with the current President's demeanor, im-pulsiveness, and rhetoric, but Donald Trump was the duly elected President, the country was facing serious challenges, his policies were mostly sound and consistent with Republican principles, and efforts to delegitimize his administration were harming the country. Under these circumstances, people in sympathy with a President's policies, with both the capabilities and opportunity to help the administration succeed, should be willing to step forward. Bob Gates, whom I admire immensely and who himself had returned to government to help the George W. Bush administration in difficult times and later stayed on to serve Obama, a President of the opposite party, put it succinctly. "Look, *somebody* has got to do these jobs," he said, "and what is best for the country is that we get good people who know what the hell they are doing."

On Wednesday the bus dropped the former President's cabinet off at the cathedral well before services began. The atmosphere inside was extraordinary. Political luminaries, officeholders, foreign dignitaries, media figures—all of official Washington stretching back to the Reagan administration—mingled in the aisles, taking the opportunity to greet old friends and adversaries. This state funeral had brought at least an appearance of civility, even joviality, not seen in the capital in recent years.

Someone embraced me from behind. It was Patrick Leahy, the longtime Democratic senator from Vermont. "We really miss you these days!" he exclaimed. "If only you were Attorney General!" He lowered his voice to a confidential tone: "I just told the President a few days ago—he really needs Bill Barr."

I smiled, told the senator it was good to see him, and thought to myself, *Careful what you wish for.*

When I sat down, I saw that the old cabinet's pews were directly across the center aisle from President Trump's current cabinet, most of whom I did not know. Just before the services began, I watched President Trump and the First Lady walk solemnly to their seats in the first row across the way. As the service and tributes got under way, I could not help but think how eerie the timing of this all was for me. I felt almost suspended between two different worlds. On my side of the cathedral, sitting behind the Bush family with my old colleagues from President Bush's old cabinet, I was in a time capsule of my past experiences in the Reagan-Bush years. The familiar people around me, the tributes and stories being told from the pulpit, the casket in front of me—all evoked warm memories of my earlier public service more than thirty years ago. When I occasionally glanced over across the aisle, sentimentality gave way to the starker present reality. I was looking at my future as part of President Trump's cabinet. I wondered if the experience, principles, and leadership style I brought from the past would allow me to succeed in this administration. Trump was obviously very different from the genteel Bush. It was no secret that he could be difficult to deal with; that everyone seemed to have a limited "shelf life" with him; and that, when he turned on someone, which seemed inevitable, he did so publicly and harshly. And the Trump administration was facing a more savage political environment than the one I had navigated decades

ago. Over the next two tumultuous years, I would need every bit of my
experience to confront the grueling challenges I knew lay ahead.

As the old Bush team headed back to the hotel on our bus, my cell
phone vibrated. My future was intruding on the past: it was President
Trump calling to ask if I had time to stop by for a visit. I told him I
could, but it would be awhile. He told me to come up to the residence
whenever I got there.

Upon arriving at the White House, I was told to join the President
in his Treaty Room office up in the residence. When I entered the
office, I saw he had been meeting with Vice President Mike Pence and
Emmet Flood. After some friendly small talk among the four of us,
the President said he wanted to meet with me privately, and the Vice
President and Flood excused themselves. Emmet had been present
during my earlier conversation with the President and, while I thought
it natural that Trump would want to chat privately to get to know me
better, I still wondered what he had in mind. The President said he was
hungry and asked the steward to bring in a large cold seafood platter
for both of us. The food came quickly, and the host, gracious as always,
would not rest until I also had tried everything on the platter, periodically taking the serving tongs himself to add another shrimp or crab
leg to my plate.

With the Bush funeral fresh in mind, President Trump started the
conversation by talking about the former President. It was no surprise
to me or to anyone sentient that the reservoir of affection between
the current President and nearly all of the Bushes was wanting.

In particular, President Trump seemed interested in how the ceremonies and weeklong tributes to Bush affected his own administration and how his deceased predecessor compared with himself. He
colorfully made the point that, since Bush's death, the media had
been "disgusting hypocrites." While fawning all over Bush today, he
remarked, they'd attacked him mercilessly when he was President
and ended up destroying his administration. I agreed: in 1992 the
press had made a modest, cyclical recession seem like the greatest depression in history and, even though the economy had been growing
during the last two quarters, kept bombarding the public with the

false narrative that things were bleak and Bush was "out of touch." For the media, I said, the only good Republican is one out of office and no longer a political threat to Democrats. Although the media hated Bush at the time, they now use him to make Trump look worse by comparison, which, admittedly, was a mission with which Trump occasionally cooperated.

Next, President Trump made the point that he believed that Bush's fate was partly his own fault because he had allowed himself to be beaten up so badly by the media. The President said that Bush did not know how to fight, but that he, Trump, *did* know how to fight and, unlike Bush, punched back at his detractors. The President also observed that the press had less power over him than it had over Bush because social media allowed him to circumvent the traditional media—something Bush didn't have in 1992. President Trump continued that his administration was under siege and, above all else, he needed people around him who knew how to fight.

The President's comments and something in his demeanor suggested to me that he might be having second thoughts about having me as Attorney General. This did not surprise me. I had been told that, even when he appears to decide something, he will often reopen the issue in the next conversation as if nothing has been settled. I also suspected that he had been testing the idea of nominating me with some of his circle on the outside, and I assumed that some had suggested to him that I was too much of an "establishment" Republican.

I decided to address this head-on. "Mr. President, we don't know each other. I understand why you would be hesitant to select me. I want you to know I wouldn't be in the least offended if you have second thoughts and want to go in another direction. Some candidates who you know better than me would be excellent choices." I went through some of the alternatives and pointed to their strengths.

The President protested—not too convincingly—that he hadn't been thinking of changing his mind. Our conversation meandered, with Trump doing most of the talking. The President's monologues are colorful, with flashes of humor and insight, and frequent hyperbole. During brief pauses, you occasionally find a window for reacting to what he has said. I learned during my conversation that day that Trump operates on different levels, and much of his garrulousness is for effect. When his discourse got too blustery, he would catch himself, stop suddenly, and change his tone, saying something like: "Now, Bill, I am exaggerating, of course. What I'm saying is . . ." and then briefly shift to a more measured exposition of his point.

He returned to the theme of his being a fighter and a good counterpuncher. I used this as an opportunity to raise a final point he needed to hear. I said: "Mr. President, you and I will have differences, and there will be times when you will be frustrated with me." He looked curious and asked me to continue. "I have no problem fighting, but I do not fight with everybody all the time. I believe in picking my fights. When I do fight, I want to be in the right, and I like to do so at the time and place of my choosing. The problem with immediately counterpunching all the time is that you are letting your opponents pick the time and place of the fight."

An episode from my college days popped into mind, and I decided to clinch my point with a parable. "Let me give you an example," I said. The President's interest piqued.

I told him about a time when I was at Columbia University, and my fraternity was playing flag football against another frat in Riverside Park. I had just broken up a pass play on defense, and the disappointed receiver and I were getting up off the ground when he suddenly threw a handful of sand into my face. It filled my nose and mouth and hit my open eyes full on, causing searing pain and completely blinding me for a time.

"You motherfucker!" I bellowed, as I staggered around trying to regain my sight. Both teams converged on the spot—some tending to me; others placing themselves in a position to restrain me from retaliating. After a few minutes, when I could see again, I signaled there would be no payback, and we could resume our game. As we played on, both teams kept a close watch on me and my antagonist, to ensure we did not come to blows. By the time the game ended two hours later, the matter seemed forgotten, and both fraternities set out together on the walk back to campus. At that point, I walked over to my assailant and laid him out—stupefied on the pavement—with a bloody nose.

Trump nodded, obviously pleased with the happy ending. "But here is the thing, Mr. President," I continued. "If you had been me, you would've gone after the guy immediately, and everyone would've spent the afternoon holding you apart, so the game would've never been played, and you also never would've gotten the guy. My way, the game was finished, and justice was meted out in the end."

Trump's intense combativeness may have worked for him running his own real estate business in New York, but serving as the nation's chief executive is very different. I knew that he could be a much more effective leader if he could convey calm, pick his fights, and surprise his adversaries—of which he had many—when *he* wanted to, rather than strike out immediately at every provocation. It would make his presidency more successful and would be the only path to a second term.

My advice did not seem to be a deal breaker. Nor was it clear that he had taken anything away from it that might alter his behavior.

"Well," he said, "I hear terrific things about you. So I think you are the best choice." We shook hands again.

Two days later, Friday, the President called me in the morning at home. I had been splitting my time between filling out the onerous forms and questionnaires required of all nominees, and performing the more edifying responsibilities of a wedding planner: drafting the missalette for my daughter's nuptial Mass, and working with the church's music director to ensure that the choir, orchestra, cantor, and music selections were all set. Meg had adopted the same ploy her two older sisters had for their weddings: assigning me total authority over the liturgy and music for the Mass. My daughters knew I loved this part of weddings—and getting me absorbed in it would keep me out of their hair on everything else.

With the wedding the next day, I was scurrying around, but the leader of the Free World wanted to talk. "Hi, Bill," said Trump. "I know we talked about delaying the announcement. I know your daughter is getting married, and so it is up to you entirely. But I'm about to walk to the helicopter, and all the press is there, and I'm thinking it would be an opportunity to announce you."

He stressed again, "It is up to you."

I told him that my family had discussed it, and we were fine with whenever he wanted to make the announcement. "Whatever is best from your standpoint is good with us." A minute later, the President was on the television announcing that he was going to nominate me as Attorney General.

At the wedding reception the next day, I welcomed the guests. I told them that Meg had said to me after the announcement, "Pop, you're the only father I know who would upstage his daughter's wedding."

"Look at it this way, Meg," I said. "Just as the name 'Barr' is about to be dragged through the mud, you've gone out and *changed* your name to McGaughey!"

With the wedding behind us, I started preparing for the arduous process of Senate confirmation. Republican senator Lindsey Graham of South Carolina had just become chairman of the Judiciary Committee, which would be handling the hearings. I hadn't known him well before, but I found him a keen lawyer and a pleasure to deal with. He also had a very capable staff. Graham scheduled my hearing for January 15, 2019, the earliest possible date. Getting everything in order by that time would require a Herculean effort. Brian Rabbitt joined me working day and night out of a small office on the third floor of the Main Justice Building. We had to assemble all my writings and speeches from a forty-plus-year career and prepare to respond to any questions about my previous words and actions.

On the first morning of our hearing preparation, I had second thoughts. It was a cold, dark December morning when Brian picked me up at eight o'clock at my house in Virginia for our first day of prep work at the department. I'd been serving on a few corporate boards, but it had been some time since I'd put on a suit and tie that early in the morning. As I settled into his car, I turned to him and asked: "Brian, what the *hell* have I gotten myself into?" We both laughed.

It was a question I would ask myself more than a few times over the course of the next two years.

Deputy Rod Rosenstein welcomed me warmly to the department and made sure I had everything I needed to prepare for confirmation. Rod had in place an effective staff and operation. His right-hand man, the Principal Associate Deputy Attorney General (PADAG, in DOJ parlance), was an exceptionally able federal prosecutor originally from New York named Ed O'Callaghan. Ed had one of the biggest jobs in the building, helping the Deputy run the department's day-to-day operations. Ed was a superstar—solid as a rock and an outstanding manager.

Between them, Rod and Ed kept close tabs on whatever was going on in the department. Rod made sure that teams from all of its various components came in to brief me on the hot topics in their area that might come up at my hearings. As is always the case, the DOJ does not share sensitive information with an incoming official until after he or she is actually confirmed. I was not privy, at that stage, to information about the substance of Mueller's investigation.

During my preparation, I met two people who, like Brian Rabbitt, were to become close confidants and indispensable advisers. Will Levi had graduated from Yale Law School, clerked for Supreme Court justice Samuel Alito, and had excellent private practice experience. He had recently arrived in the Office of the Attorney General and was hoping to stay on with me. Will's father, Judge David Levi, had been a US attorney on my first go-round as Attorney General and was a friend of mine. Will, besides being a brilliant lawyer, had superb judgment and remarkable people skills. He served initially as my counselor, and then, after a year, when Brian Rabbitt went to the Criminal Division, he took over as my chief of staff.

The second person I met was the head of the Office of Public Affairs, Kerri Kupec. Kerri had recently been on loan to the White House, where she had helped Brett Kavanaugh through the confirmation process. I had worked with many excellent public affairs people during my career, and found Kerri second to none. She was not only a savvy student of the media but also a good lawyer. I liked her directness and willingness to speak her mind. When I first met her in a large group meeting, she spoke up and disagreed with a point I had made. I liked that. (And she was also right.) Shortly before the Senate voted on my confirmation, she was offered the position of chief spokesperson for the President's reelection committee. I was immensely grateful that she turned it down to stay with me. I could not have done it without her.

The head of the department's Office of Legislative Affairs (OLA), Assistant Attorney General Stephen Boyd, and his able deputy, Prim Escalona, gave me excellent advice during the confirmation process as well as once I took office. Noting that the last time I had been through this had been almost thirty years ago, Boyd stressed that the game had changed completely. "In the old days," he said, "you'd be focusing on how many Democrats you might attract. Forget about it. This will be a party line vote." He explained the strategy:

"You might lose Senator Rand Paul because of your positions on national security, but you should have no problem keeping the other fifty-two Republican senators—they like you, and they want a steady hand at the department after the last two years—so just focus on keeping the Republicans," he advised, "and don't do anything that risks Republican support in a vain effort to win over Democrats." Boyd told me that a number of Democratic senators were quietly pleased at my nomination—viewing it as about as good as they could have hoped for under the administration.

It struck me how much the country and our politics had changed. Three decades ago, I was confirmed unanimously by the Senate for three successive department posts: Assistant Attorney General, Deputy, and then Attorney General. Now I would be lucky to get just three Democrats to vote for me. I had not changed. The country had.

As my confirmation hearing drew closer, and I received more press coverage, I came under the care of the FBI security detail that is assigned full-time to protect the Attorney General. During my first tenure as AG, I became very close to the nine agents who had that duty, and several of them followed me to Verizon once they retired from the bureau. This time around, I was equally fortunate to have an outstanding group of FBI agents, men and women, serving on the detail. As before, the detail is present 24/7—at the office, at home, on the road. Since 9/11, the detail had increased in size. The head of it, Mike Munn, was a thoroughgoing professional with good judgment. He was a pleasure to be around, as were all the other agents. Each one was unique: bright, able, conscientious, with his or her own particular blend of skills. Seeing the quality of these men and women every day showed me the FBI remains a great institution. Since leaving the department, I have missed them—not the security function, but as individuals.

The usual pilgrimages to Capitol Hill, visiting any senator who wanted to see me, went as expected. All the Republican meetings went well. Senator Paul of Kentucky insisted that I supply written answers to him on certain questions before he would meet with me. I declined, and so we never met. The meetings with Democratic senators were cordial and substantive, though some were not without tension. I found West Virginia senator Joe Manchin to be particularly impressive during our initial meeting. He was a throwback to the "old Washington" of the George H. W. Bush years, when it was still possible for Republicans and Democrats to work together on certain issues. He seemed to genuinely want the best for the country and West Virginia, and I found him to be someone I could work with during my time at the department.

I did not know much about the new senator from Arizona, Kyrsten Sinema, but I was pleasantly surprised that she seemed genuinely willing to approach my nomination with an open mind. We had an in-depth discussion. Later, when I was in office, Sinema did not bash me publicly when I did something controversial but instead came over to my office to hear my side of the issue. She was balanced, and, like Senator Manchin, I thought she was someone who tried to put the country first.

Because of the government being shut down due to a budget impasse, the compressed time schedule over the Christmas holidays, and the number of senators wanting to see me, the department suggested prioritizing some meetings and scheduling others for after my

hearings. Although I doubted that Minnesota senator Amy Klobuchar was approaching my nomination with an open mind, she took
offense and tweeted out her objection to this, saying that she would
have some hot coffee waiting for me if I ever deigned to show up for a
meeting. My staff set up a meeting right away, and when I walked into
her office, I asked, "Where's my coffee?"

"Right here," she said gesturing to a silver tray on the table, "and I
have a nice traditional Slovenian pastry." We had a laugh and a good
discussion on antitrust policy and the role that technology companies
play in today's society, where we found many areas of agreement. The
discussion was lively, and the pastry was exceptional. In the end, I had
many positive meetings with Democratic senators, and several told me
privately that they felt I was the right person for the job and were glad
I was willing to take it on. However, a number of Democratic senators,
including Kamala Harris of California and Hawaii's Mazie Hirono,
refused to meet with me

I had a testy meeting with Minority Leader Chuck Schumer. We
met in his office on the west side of the Capitol, which has expansive
views over the National Mall. I had actually known Schumer going
back to his days as an assemblyman in New York. Later, when I was
Bush's Attorney General, he was the chairman of the House Subcommittee on Crime and Criminal Justice. In those days, he was a law-
and-order Democrat who supported being tough on crime. He has
changed a lot. Schumer said that I had a stellar record and reputation and that he wanted to support me but could not understand why I
would ever want to work for President Trump. "I am going to work for
the country, Chuck. We all work for the country. I don't want or need
this job, but I've been asked, and I think I can do some good. That's
why." He then questioned me about the memo I had written about
obstruction and suggested that, if I pledged to recuse myself from Special Counsel Mueller's investigation, he might be able to support me. I
told him firmly I would not pledge to do that. The meeting broke up,
and Schumer made a beeline for the Senate floor, where, minutes later,
he delivered a prewritten speech denouncing me and my nomination.

From my meetings on the Hill, it was quickly apparent that three issues would dominate my confirmation process: whether I would allow Mueller to complete his investigation without interference; whether I would fully disclose his findings to Congress and the public; and whether my memo criticizing the obstruction theory I thought Mueller might be pursuing meant that I would be a mere cypher doing the President's bidding.

On the first issue, even among Republican senators, the sentiment was clear and overwhelming that Mueller must be allowed to finish his work. I did not disagree. While I had serious concerns about the way he was conducting his investigation, I thought that the country needed an objective, authoritative verdict on Russiagate. I strongly suspected that Mueller would turn up no evidence of collusion, but unless he was allowed to complete his work and issue his findings, the matter would linger on and hamstring the administration and the country for years to come.

The second issue, whether the department would publicly release the Special Counsel's findings, was trickier. Throughout the first two years of Russiagate, the media seemed to assume that Mueller would issue a public report detailing his findings, much as Independent Counsel Ken Starr had done in 1998 at the conclusion of his investigation into President Bill Clinton. But the department's Special Counsel regulations, under which Mueller was appointed, do not provide for a public report. On the contrary, they say, "At the conclusion of the Special Counsel's work, he or she shall provide the Attorney General with a *confidential* [*italics mine*] report explaining the prosecution or declination decisions reached by the Special Counsel." These regulations were written under Attorney General Janet Reno, and there are good reasons for the confidentiality requirement.

For one, it is the department's general practice to keep silent when it declines to prosecute someone. When a person is indicted, he has the opportunity to clear his name at trial. Not so when he is not charged. For that reason, the DOJ generally does not malign uncharged people by releasing derogatory information about them. A Special Counsel's report is also likely to include a great deal of classified information that can't be released publicly. That is particularly true in an investigation such as Mueller's, which relied heavily on classified information.

The Democratic senators wanted me to commit to releasing the entire report, unedited and unredacted. They were afraid that I would suppress information to protect the President. But that was not my purpose. As a practical matter, I thought the public interest required getting out as much as I could, but I knew that there were likely to be some categories of information—such as classified information or material presented to the grand jury—that were legally required to be kept confidential. At my hearing, I said: "My goal will be to provide as much transparency as I can, consistent with the law. I can assure you that where judgments are to be made, I will make those judgments based solely on the law."

As for my memo about Mueller's potential obstruction theory, the Democrats wanted me to commit to recusing myself from the investigation, or at least guarantee that I would follow the advice of the department's ethics officials. I thought the whole issue was ridiculous. I'd been clear that my memo was based on public information and speculation. All it did was outline my views on a legal question—something lawyers do every day. In any event, Justice Department rules say that the Attorney General, not department ethics officials, is responsible for making his own decision about recusal, and I was confident that I could evaluate the situation objectively once I took office. Still, I was not yet privy to the details of Mueller's investigation, although officials in the department were. I asked them, as a precaution, to consider whether I needed to recuse based on what they knew. The preliminary advice I received from the department's senior-most career ethics official was that I was not required to recuse. At my hearing, I said that, while I would consider the advice of the department's career ethics officials, I would make up my own mind on the recusal question. I wasn't going to surrender the discretion vested by law in the office just to get the job. In the end, after I was confirmed, ethics officials advised there was no need for me or my staff to recuse ourselves.

During my hearing, there was a lot of back-and-forth about what my memo meant and its logic. Senators propounded tortuous legal hypotheticals, and a few expressed disbelief that I could compose such a long, detailed legal memo myself—"including footnotes!" At one point, Democratic senator Sheldon Whitehouse of Rhode Island asked incredulously whether I'd formatted the citations myself—eyeing the staff sitting behind me with suspicion. I explained that after forty years of law practice, amazingly, I could.

My testimony was a highly charged event, and I had not appeared before a Senate committee in a long time. Under the circumstances, I thought I was doing fairly well. But there was someone watching who was very upset with my performance. At the two-hour mark, the committee took a break, and I went back into the holding room. Just as I was being told how overwhelmingly positive the reaction had been online and otherwise, Brian Rabbitt, looking very solemn, pulled me aside. Emmet Flood had called from the White House. He said the President was apoplectic that I had said nice things about Mueller and was being too conciliatory. He was bemoaning choosing me and talking about pulling the nomination. I thought to myself, *Well, that didn't take long.* Emmet himself thought I was doing perfect and should keep it up. For the rest of the day, I plowed ahead, knowing the President was having a hissy fit about me.

Later—after my hearing and before the confirmation vote—I paid a visit to President Trump in the Oval Office, just to touch base. He was in a good mood because he felt the reaction to my appointment and performance had been a political plus for him, instead of costing him political capital. Perched as usual behind his desk, he stood up when I entered, beaming, and thrust out his hand for a hearty shake. "You were great. Our people love you!" he gushed.

"Well, Mr. President," I said, "I understand that, at the beginning of the hearing, you had a bad reaction and thought you'd made a mistake."

"Well, that's true," he replied with a hint of sheepishness. "I thought you went too easy on Mueller. I think he's bad news, and I wanted you to condemn him more."

"Let's see what he has to say in his report, Mr. President," I suggested. "There is a time and place for everything."

"You know what saved you?" the President asked playfully. "Melania. She came to your rescue. She is now your biggest fan."

"Well, I could tell she has good sense."

"We were watching the hearing together, and when I got angry, she said, 'Are you crazy? Look at him. Right out of central casting. He looks and acts like an Attorney General! Leave him alone—he is carrying himself just right, and he will be confirmed, which is what you need.'"

I had always thought Melania was smarter than the President.

The confirmation vote went exactly as predicted by the head of the Office of Legislative Affairs: all the Republicans, except Senator Paul, voted for me, as did the three Democrats: Manchin, Sinema, and Alabama senator Doug Jones. Despite our coffee and pastry together, Senator Klobuchar voted no.

On February 14—Saint Valentine's Day—as C-SPAN reported the final vote tally, I packed up my temporary work space on the department's third floor and walked up to the Attorney General's suite of offices on the fifth floor. I was ready to get to work. As my wife and a few staffers looked on, I was sworn in by Lee Lofthus, a department veteran who was the Assistant Attorney General for Administration. Except for new carpet and furniture, the office suite looked much the same as it had twenty-eight years earlier. When I sat down once again behind the AG's desk after so many years, I experienced some emotion, not all good. It was a little like that nightmare in which you find yourself back in a high school math class—only it was real.

Later in the afternoon, we had a formal swearing-in with President Trump in the Oval Office. I had asked Chief Justice John Roberts to swear me in. I'd known him since we worked together in the Reagan White House, and his wife, Jane, had been my law partner at Shaw, Pittman. My whole family and a few friends attended, and the President took time to chat with everyone.

Back in 1991, soon after I was confirmed as Attorney General, I talked to the dean of the department's press corps in those days, Ron

Ostrow of the *LA Times*. He asked what my goal was now that I was Attorney General. I said, "Survival." Next, he asked me how I felt at the start of my tenure. I said, "Like I'm about to run across a river on the backs of alligators." Later, someone showed me a cartoon of a sweating Bill Barr running across the backs of alligators. I thought of that conversation and cartoon as I settled in.

Having a strong head of administration at the department is a huge help to an Attorney General. I was spoiled by having Steve Colgate during my first stint and was very lucky that Lee Lofthus was in the position this time around. Before he swore me in, I had last seen Lee in the hospital room of the legendary David Margolis, the department's revered senior career prosecutor, who died in 2016. David and I became close, and we lunched regularly together at the Prime Rib in DC. David's family had contacted me and then-Judge Merrick Garland to tell us the end was near, and, other than his family, the two of us, along with Lofthus, were the last to say good-bye to David. Many DOJ veterans believe that had David still been at the department, the Russiagate nonsense would never have made it into 2017.

I was lucky to find an extraordinary assistant waiting for me. Theresa Watson, a veteran DOJ employee, had been serving in the Deputy Attorney General's office, where she assisted my daughter Mary, who gave her rave reviews. Recently she had been brought up to the fifth floor to fill a vacancy on the AG's staff and was temporarily serving as Acting AG Whitaker's personal assistant. Theresa and I hit it off immediately, and I asked her to stay on as my personal assistant. Theresa was exceptionally bright, a great judge of people, hardworking, and always two steps ahead. I liked that she did not hesitate to come in, close the door, and give me advice on some of the difficult issues we were working on. She was invariably right. Everyone on my staff would agree that Theresa is quite capable of running the department. She took great care of me during my almost two-year tenure.

I inherited a strong team of division and component heads. Up on the fifth floor, ensconced in the next suite down the hall, was the Solicitor General, Noel Francisco, responsible for our litigation in the Supreme Court. Noel had clerked in the early 1990s for my former sidekick at the department, Judge Mike Luttig. He later clerked for Justice Scalia and compiled a stellar legal career since then. Brilliant, savvy, principled, and with a great sense of humor, Noel had become a good friend over the years. I could not have asked for a better "SG."

The Trump administration put a huge litigation burden on the department. The Civil Division and the Office of the Solicitor General were in constant, intense legal battles to fend off the onslaught of lawsuits brought to block the President's policies. Fortunately, I found already at the department a strong group of litigators who did yeoman's service beating back these attacks. Among the stars were Jeff Wall, a former Justice Thomas clerk out of the Sullivan & Cromwell firm, who served as the Deputy Solicitor General; Hashim Mooppan, a Scalia clerk, who headed the appellate staff in the Civil Division; and James Burnham, who headed the Federal Programs Branch in the same division.

Down the hall on the other side of my suite was the Office of Legal Counsel, headed by Steve Engel. Steve had previously served as Deputy in that office under President George W. Bush and had a top-notch legal background. I knew him only by his outstanding reputation. Here again, I was lucky. Steve was a lawyer's lawyer with complete intellectual honesty. He based his opinions on his best understanding of the law and stood his ground for what he believed was right. He was indispensable.

The main structural change to the department since I had last served separated the national security functions out of the Criminal Division and moved them to a new National Security Division. Both of these important divisions were led by appointees in whom I had confidence. Heading the Criminal Division was Brian Benczkowski, a friend from Kirkland & Ellis who had held senior DOJ positions under President George W. Bush. Heading the National Security Division was John Demers, a former Scalia clerk who had been a division deputy under President George W. Bush and an official at the Boeing corporation. One of the hot seats in the department is the head of the Civil Rights Division, because a lot of the most controversial matters pass through that office. I was happy to find that division in the able hands of a seasoned lawyer, Eric Dreiband, who had been a partner at the Jones Day law firm. The Antitrust Division spot was held by Makan Delrahim, whom I had known since he worked for Senator Orrin Hatch of Utah many years before. Although we had gone nose to nose when he was trying to shoot down AT&T's acquisition of Time Warner—which, as a member of the Time Warner board, I supported—we were friends. I did not hold his opposition against him—and not just because he lost.

I found another change in the Department since my last go-round: INS and most of its immigration functions had been shifted over to the Department of Homeland Security, and the Bureau of Alcohol, Tobacco, Firearms and Explosives (ATF) had been moved from the Treasury Department to DOJ. I had long advocated for this last move. ATF is primarily a crime-fighting agency, not a revenue agency. As I argued to Treasury Secretary Nick Brady decades earlier during 41's administration: "Things that go Clink belong to you; things that go Bang should belong to me." I was delighted to have ATF in the fold.

The number three position at the department, Associate Attorney General, was not filled with a permanent appointee. I asked the President to nominate Jessie Liu, the US attorney in the District of Columbia, to the post, but she ran into opposition on the Hill. After that, no permanent appointment was made during my tenure, but the position was handled very ably, first by Jesse Panuccio and later by Claire Murray.

The backbone of the department are the ninety-three United States Attorneys and their staffs of prosecutors and civil litigators around the country. I was impressed with the quality and experience of the group of US attorneys I inherited. On Friday morning, the day after being sworn in, I had a conference call with all ninety-three. I told them that, until further notice, they were to go full speed ahead on the department's existing priorities, especially fighting violent crime and gun violence. I stressed that I did not like pursuing cases just to hit numerical targets; I preferred quality over quantity. I emphasized that the prosecution power is an awesome power that can be abused and that it was their responsibility to ensure that those under investigation are treated fairly. I told them I did not like to see resources tied up interminably in pursuing questionable cases. I observed that line prosecutors sometimes get overly invested in investigations and, even when they are dragging on for years and plainly going nowhere, resist moving on. I told the US attorneys they should encourage their line prosecutors to fish or cut bait. Finally, I stressed that I wanted offices to focus on cases involving standard criminality—"meat-and-potatoes" cases—not waste a lot of time ginning up imaginative cases based on novel, esoteric theories—that often means there was no real crime, and the lawyers are headline hunting.

The following week, I had catered an afternoon-long reception in the AG's suite for all personnel at headquarters. The various divisions and offices were invited on a staggered basis so that we could accommodate everyone over the course of the afternoon. The employees who had been at the department for more than twenty-five years made a point of telling me they remembered me from the first time. I was surprised how many there were.

But there was little time for welcoming parties, learning the players, and filling out the team. The Russiagate affair, which had been building up steam for two years, was coming to a head with Mueller's investigation and his report, and was now upon me.

CHAPTER 10

ONE THING DONE,
ANOTHER BEGUN

Within days of my taking over as Attorney General, Deputy Rod Rosenstein and PADAG Ed O'Callaghan briefed me on what they knew about Mueller's investigation and the timing of its completion. Mueller's principal lieutenants, Aaron Zebley and Jim Quarles, had been signaling to O'Callaghan for weeks that they were almost done. After several delays, it now appeared we would be seeing the final work product at some point in March 2019.

Based on his conversations with Zebley, O'Callaghan expected Mueller's report would address two issues: first, allegations that the Trump campaign had colluded with the Russians in attempting to influence the election; and, second, allegations that President Trump had attempted to obstruct Mueller's investigation. From what O'Callaghan had been told, and as I expected for a long time, Mueller had not found evidence of conspiracy or collusion with the Russians. However, the Special Counsel's finding on the question of obstruction was less clear. On a number of occasions, his staff had suggested to O'Callaghan that they would not affirmatively conclude that Trump had committed obstruction. But their comments on this issue were vague. Rod, Ed, and I all thought there was still probably debate and disagreement within Mueller's team over how to handle obstruction.

To move things along, and to get clarification, I suggested that Rod and I meet with Mueller and his key lieutenants. They were happy to meet, and on March 5 we sat down together at the department. I had two primary objectives going into the meeting. First, I wanted to make sure that Mueller was preparing the report in a way that would allow me to release as much of it as possible to Congress and the public, and, just as important, to do so quickly. Ordinarily, a report like this would be confidential and reflect matters occurring before the grand jury—so-called 6(e) material—as well as classified information or otherwise sensitive information relating to other investigations still pending at the department. Classified information obviously cannot be shared publicly, and federal law makes it a crime to disclose 6(e) material to persons other than law enforcement officials.

Before I could release the report, therefore, we would have to redact all 6(e) material, classified and confidential information, and anything that might adversely impact ongoing investigations or prosecutions. As much as I wanted to make the entire report public, we could not responsibly do that. Because Mueller and his team had conducted the investigation, only they could identify the material in the report that required redaction. Without their help, we simply had no way of knowing what had been presented to the grand jury and was therefore protected. Unless Mueller's team identified that information when it delivered the report, there would have to be a significant delay between the time I received it and the time I could legally release it.

I was deeply concerned about such a delay. Given the way Washington works, and the leaks that had spilled out about Mueller's investigation, I knew the fact that Mueller had completed his work and delivered his report to me would become public almost immediately. I also knew that if the public was not informed quickly about what the Special Counsel had found, speculation would run wild. Silence from the department would lead the press and public to conclude that the President was in serious jeopardy of being indicted for conspiring with Russia to rig a presidential election. Why else would the Justice Department be sitting on the report? A constitutional crisis could ensue.

Markets would fall. America's enemies would be emboldened to take advantage of the situation. The nation's well-being demanded that we act quickly.

My second goal for the meeting with Mueller was to get a better understanding of his conclusions and thinking on obstruction. Based on previous Office of Legal Counsel opinions, it had long been the department's position that a sitting President could not be criminally indicted, although a President could be indicted after leaving office. Given the vagueness of the descriptions O'Callaghan had received to date, I thought it was possible that Mueller may have concluded that President Trump's actions constituted obstruction, but that no indictment could presently be brought due to the OLC opinions. If Mueller concluded that he had sufficient evidence to indict the President but could not do so only because of the OLC opinions, that would be a grave matter. I needed to understand what Mueller would be saying on this score.

On March 5 we met in my conference room. Mueller had Zebley and Quarles with him. Rosenstein and I were accompanied by O'Callaghan and Rabbitt. Although we'd been friends and colleagues for a long time, I had not seen Bob in person in at least two years. We greeted each other warmly, traded a few jokes, and the atmosphere remained cordial and professional throughout the meeting. I sat at the head of the conference table, and Bob sat to my immediate left, just where he used to sit at my staff meetings in the early 1990s when he was head of the Criminal Division.

"Still bringing me trouble as always, Bob," I joked. Bob laughed and replied, "I see you haven't changed."

After some small talk, he opened a portfolio case and took out some talking points on a single sheet of paper. I noticed both of his hands were trembling as he did this, and his voice was tremulous. As he spoke, I grew concerned. I knew he wasn't nervous, and I wondered if he might have an illness. Reading from the sheet of paper— which was odd—Mueller made some initial points, but then quickly turned over the meeting to Zebley and Quarles, who would handle the substance of our discussion. I glanced at Rod, and we fleetingly caught each other's eye. He appeared just as surprised and concerned as I was by Mueller's halting manner.

Zebley explained that we would be getting two substantial volumes. Volume one, which would be roughly 200 pages, would address collusion and report that the Special Counsel had not found any conspiracy or collusion with the Russians by Trump, his associates, or his campaign. The Special Counsel's findings on this point did not seem to be complicated, and we did not discuss them for long. Everyone seemed to understand that the answer to the collusion question would be "no." I was relieved—not because of personal or political loyalty to the President, but because I would not have to tell the American people that their President was a Russian asset.

Volume two, roughly 180 pages, would deal with potential obstruction, and it quickly became apparent that this would be the more controversial—and confusing—aspect of their report. Quarles handled this part of the meeting. He explained that the Special Counsel would not be making a determination whether the President committed obstruction. Instead, the report would simply identify ten episodes that raised potential obstruction issues, set forth the facts of each episode as "dispassionately" as possible, and state the legal elements that would have to be proved to make out a crime. But the report would "not go down the road" of determining, one way or the other, whether the evidence was sufficient to establish an indictable offense. In short, the Special Counsel would reach no conclusion on whether the President committed obstruction, nor attempt to do so.

On our side of the table, my team exchanged puzzled looks. Perhaps sensing our confusion, Mueller spoke up on this point, and he and Quarles both emphasized that they were not saying that, were it not for the OLC opinion, they *would* conclude that a crime had been committed. Rather, they were not reaching a conclusion one way or the other whether obstruction was committed.

To pin this down, I asked: "So you're saying that, because you couldn't indict at this stage, you aren't even embarking on the analysis necessary to determine whether the evidence is sufficient to show an obstruction?"

"That is right," the two men replied in unison, to which Mueller added, "It was our judgment that we should not try to decide whether the President's conduct constituted a crime. But we wanted to gather the relevant evidence while recollections were still fresh, and someone later could make that decision based on the record." I asked whether the report provided a record on which someone else could decide whether a crime was committed, and Mueller and his team agreed that it did.

Like me, Rod seemed surprised at the tack the Special Counsel was planning to take and pressed again for an explanation why they were not reaching a conclusion on obstruction. The thrust of Mueller's and Quarles's position seemed to be that, because they could not indict the President as long as he was in office, it would be inappropriate to have a DOJ finding of criminality hanging over him when there was no judicial forum in which he could immediately defend himself. To avoid that, they explained, they simply were not going to go through the exercise of weighing or analyzing the evidence they had gathered.

I then turned to my priority. I explained to Mueller and his team the imperative on our side: that they specifically identify the 6(e) material and classified information when they give us the report so we could quickly make the redactions necessary for public release. I pointed out that we would have no way of knowing what material was 6(e) and, therefore, could not release the report unless and until they told us what had to be redacted. I also explained that they were in the best position to identify the classified information, as well as any information that would affect ongoing investigations and cases. I said they needed to do that work now, while they were finalizing the report. If they waited until after they delivered the report, they would be imposing a significant gap between the time DOJ received the report and the time we could make it public. That would be dangerous for the department and the country. Mueller said he understood and would do as I requested.

After the meeting broke up, Rod and I walked toward my office. We paused in the anteroom and looked at each other with concern. "Wow," I said. "Bob has lost a step."

"That is not the Bob I know," Rod said, equally surprised. "I wonder if he is ill."

In the ensuing days, Rod and I discussed the Special Counsel's decision to punt on whether the President had committed obstruction. While we did not fully understand Mueller's thinking, we agreed that it was not appropriate to release a report that left it hanging whether the President had committed a crime. Mueller had completed his investigation and said his report provided a record on which someone else could make the decision. If he was not willing to make the determination, it was ultimately the responsibility of the Attorney General to do so.

As we saw it, Mueller was appointed to carry out the investigative and prosecutorial functions of the department, and he was part of the department. The role of the Justice Department is to make a binary call: Does the conduct investigated make out a crime, or doesn't it? Mueller's investigation had used criminal process to obtain information, including grand jury subpoenas. The reason the department is given the awesome power to use a grand jury and compulsory process to collect information is precisely for the purpose of making this binary determination. We felt it would be an abuse to use the department's criminal investigatory powers just to collect and disgorge information to the public, suggesting that "maybe" a crime was committed and leaving it up to the country to react. Moreover, if we concluded, upon reviewing the report, that the evidence was not sufficient to support an indictable offense, then it would be irresponsible to issue the report without stating the department's conclusions.

On Friday, March 22, the Special Counsel had his final report carried by hand over to Ed O'Callaghan, who distributed copies to Rod, me, Brian, and OLC head Steve Engel. As predicted, rumors had gotten out, and the media started staking out the department and my home in expectation of the report's delivery. I received my copy at approximately one thirty. The five of us went off separately to digest the report as fast as we could.

Volume one seemed straightforward. The Special Counsel reported there was a two-prong Russian effort to interfere in our 2016 election: first, the report alleged that an Internet group purportedly tied to the Russian government conducted a disinformation and social media operation to sow discord among Americans; second, the report concluded that Russian military intelligence hacked into computers and stole e-mails—later leaked—from individuals affiliated with the Democratic Party and Hillary Clinton's campaign. The Special Counsel did not find a conspiracy or collusion between the Russians and Trump or his campaign.

Volume two of the report was also pretty much as Mueller's team had previewed it. The critical point was that Mueller did not conclude one way or the other whether the President had committed obstruction of justice. It described ten episodes that the Special Counsel thought could potentially raise obstruction issues; set out the evidence his team had collected for each; noted that "difficult issues would need to be resolved" before reaching ultimate conclusions; and concluded that "while this report does not conclude that the President committed a crime, it also does not exonerate him."

That sentence puzzled all of us. The department—of which Mueller and his team were a part—is not in the business of "exonerating" people. The department investigates alleged crimes and, if the relevant standards are met, prosecutes those responsible. We don't endeavor to clear people's names or exonerate them, and we don't publicly editorialize on the conduct of an individual we've chosen not to indict. That is not the function of a prosecutor like Mueller, and it effectively turns the well-known "innocent until proven guilty" standard on its head.

As I initially flipped the pages, I was surprised and disappointed to see that every page of the report bore across the top in prominent lettering the warning "May Contain Material Protected Under Fed.R.Crim.P. (6)(e)." There were no redactions that we could see, and no citations identifying information that could not be released publicly. Mueller's team had not done what I requested and what it had promised to do. There were some footnotes that cited grand jury sources along with other sources, but these did not specify what text in the body of the report was covered by (6)(e) and thus required redaction.

I realized immediately that, without the information I had asked for, it would take weeks to process the report for public release.

During the afternoon, I consulted with the DOJ team again and all agreed that we should notify the White House, Congress, and then the public that Mueller had completed his work and transmitted his final report to me. It was not something we felt that we could—or should—keep secret. We also agreed that Ed should move immediately to set up an expedited review process, in collaboration with the Special Counsel's staff, to prepare the report for public release. Rod and I identified four categories of information that had to be identified for redaction: (1) grand jury (6)(e) material, (2) classified intelligence and sources and methods, (3) information that would prejudice other ongoing DOJ matters, and (4) information that would unfairly affect the privacy interests of peripheral third parties. With Mueller's team working with us, I estimated that we could get the report released publicly in about three weeks.

I prepared a letter to the Senate and House Judiciary Committees stating: "The Special Counsel has submitted to me today a 'confidential report explaining the prosecution or declination decisions' he has reached, as required by [the department's regulations.] I am reviewing the report and anticipate that I may be in a position to advise you of the Special Counsel's principal conclusions as soon as this weekend." I further advised the committees that I was already working to identify the portions of the report I could release and "remain committed to as much transparency as possible."

I wanted to minimize contact with the White House at this stage. We intended to make decisions based solely on our independent judgment applying the department's normal standards, and we did not want communications that could be misconstrued as involving White House input into our deliberations. In conversations earlier in the week, I had agreed with Pat Cipollone and Emmet Flood that it would be best to have the President go through with his plans to spend the weekend in Palm Beach, Florida, at Mar-a-Lago. The plan was to have Cipollone and Flood stay down in Mar-a-Lago with the President to help keep things on an even keel. Just before sending my letter to the Hill, I asked Brian to read it to Emmet so that, before the news went public, the White House was aware that we had received the report and would probably be saying something more about Mueller's "principal conclusions" over the weekend. Because there had also been a good deal of commentary suggesting that the report would be accompanied by a raft of indictments, I told Brian he could advise Emmet that there were no further indictments recommended by the report.

Late Friday afternoon, within minutes of my letter getting to the Hill, it went public, and all hell broke loose. The story that Mueller had finished his investigation and had just reported the results to the Attorney General blasted through almost every media outlet. A platoon of reporters immediately staked out my house, and another appeared just outside Justice. My every movement was reported in real time. We were inundated with inquiries about whether Mueller had found either collusion or obstruction. As I'd feared, commentators were speculating—and some even predicting confidently—that Mueller had found criminal wrongdoing by the President and that indictments were imminent. Others were suggesting that any delay by the department in releasing the report would mean the worst for the President. Why else would his own Justice Department delay making the results of the investigation known?

While the media wanted the immediate gratification of seeing the whole report right away, the Department of Justice could not lawfully release it until the necessary redactions were made. At the same time, it was clear to me that I could not remain completely silent for the three weeks it would take to make those redactions. The public was in a high state of agitation. Everyone wanted to know the bottom line: Did Mueller conclude that the President committed a crime or not? Were the President and/or his associates Russian assets? Did the President obstruct justice? Mueller had studied those questions for two agonizing years, and the American people wanted to know what he'd found. Even if we could not release the full report right away, the national interest dictated that we at least inform the country quickly about Mueller's "bottom-line" conclusions. I had anticipated this, and that is why, in my initial letter to Congress, I said that I expected to advise Congress of Mueller's principal conclusions as soon as the weekend.

But before we could advise the world about Mueller's principal conclusions, we had to decide ourselves whether the evidence established an obstruction of justice, since Mueller had punted on that issue. To do this, Rod and I augmented our small DOJ team with another OLC lawyer. We all cleared the decks to work long into the night and over the weekend, studying the report. I wanted to come to a decision on obstruction by Sunday midday. Mueller had told us that he had made a "thorough factual investigation" of potential obstruction and that his report provided the basis for others, including the Attorney General, to make that ultimate determination.

As we assessed the evidence, we were governed by the "principles of federal prosecution" that apply to all the department's charging decisions. In general, those principles require the department, before charging a crime, to conclude that there is enough evidence to prove each and every element of the crime beyond a reasonable doubt. To establish obstruction, the government must prove that (1) a person acting with corrupt intent, (2) engaged in an obstructive act, (3) in connection with a pending or anticipated proceeding. This was not some academic law school exercise of assessing whether there was a technical possibility that the facts as found by Mueller could, somehow, qualify as obstruction under the relevant statute. Like all department prosecutions, we had to assess how a jury would view the evidence in the real world and whether this was a case that the department should be willing to charge and prove at trial.

Significantly, none of us was coming at these issues for the first time. As Mueller's report acknowledged, establishing an obstruction offense against the President involved many unique and difficult legal and factual issues. During the course of the investigation, many of these issues had already been aired between the Special Counsel's office and responsible officials at the department. Deputy Rosenstein, O'Callaghan, and Steve Engel had been discussing these issues for months. While I had not been involved in those discussions, I had obviously done my own ruminating on these issues in the memorandum I had sent to Rod and Steve Engel on June 8, 2018. Many of the factual scenarios cited by Mueller had been reported in the media over the preceding year.

Although we decided not to rest our decisions on these grounds, Rod and I thought that, as a matter of law, at least some of the episodes canvassed in Mueller's report would not qualify as obstruction. I thought most of the episodes were legally insufficient, while Rod thought that at least some of them were. As I had argued in my June 8 memo, the principal obstruction statute relied on by the Special Counsel applied only to actions that impaired the integrity or availability of evidence, and a number of the episodes cited in the report did not involve this kind of conduct. Beyond that, under its "clear statement rule," the department does not construe generally applicable laws, such as obstruction statutes, to extend to apparently lawful exercises of the President's authority where review of that action could impinge on the President's constitutional prerogatives.

Much of volume two consists of tortuous legal arguments attempting to slalom around the impediments to applying the obstruction laws to the President's actions. Rod and Ed observed it seemed to be written by an academic, not a prosecutor. I found the reasoning for most of these arguments strained, at best. As I'd explained in my memo, if the department was going to use the criminal process to take down a democratically elected President, it needed to be on the firmest of legal and factual footings. Relying on novel and shaky legal theories would not cut it. And in any event, at the end of the day, what the Special Counsel and his team think wasn't the final word; what counted was the Attorney General's legal judgment.

I felt that we could have dismissed several of the episodes out of hand as legally insufficient to constitute obstruction. But Rod and I were both mindful of the need to ensure that our analysis was thorough, and so we assumed the Special Counsel's legal analysis was correct, ignored the substantial legal obstacles we'd identified, and assessed each of the ten episodes on the facts using the analytical framework the Special Counsel had set forth in his report. In short, we accepted his version of the law and the facts for the sake of analysis, and proceeded to consider whether the department could indict for obstruction under the principles of federal prosecution. We spent Saturday analyzing each episode and discussing the evidentiary issues associated with each. After we broke up at the end of the day, we each continued to study the report late into the night—checking and then rechecking our analysis. We gathered again on Sunday morning to review and confirm our thinking on each episode. Everyone on the team agreed that, for each of the episodes, the evidence was insufficient on one or more of the essential elements.

As I read through volume two, I was struck by its fuzzy logic. It seemed apparent to me that Mueller and his team didn't have what they needed to prove obstruction but couldn't bring themselves to say so. Whether for political reasons or because they had invested so much time and money in a futile effort, the Special Counsel's team was unwilling to say clearly in volume two what they'd freely concluded in volume one: that when it came to proving a crime had been committed, they simply didn't have the goods.

To be sure, the evidence recounted in the report was unflattering and was exactly the opposite of how a lawyer would counsel someone to handle an investigation. But any obstruction prosecution would have to overcome the simple fact that the President never did anything to interfere with the Special Counsel's investigation. To the contrary, he directed his White House not to invoke executive privilege and made witnesses freely available to speak with the Special Counsel's team. While he refused to be interviewed, that was his right. In the end, the Special Counsel chose not to subpoena the President, and he did respond to written interrogatories.

Any obstruction prosecution would also have to grapple with the question of the President's intent. It would have been very difficult to prove to an unbiased jury that the President was acting with a corrupt intent to obstruct Mueller's investigation. Apparent in the pages of the report is the President's clear frustration with the unfairness of the entire situation. He was, as we now know, innocent of collusion and had won the election fair and square. He was angry about being investigated for allegations of collusion that proved baseless. Yet Mueller continued to investigate. As is his style, the President expressed himself strongly, shifting, in Mueller's account, from anger at the investigators to disappointment with those he felt should be doing more to protect him from an unfair investigation. He was also prone to bluster and exaggeration—something his closest aides knew and understood well. But at the end of the day, the President never actually did anything to interfere with either the original counterintelligence investigation or with the Special Counsel's inquiry. Those were all facts that would make proving obstruction to a jury extremely difficult.

On Sunday, March 24, I drafted a second letter to Congress. Its purpose was to advise them of Mueller's principal conclusions, as I said I would in my letter on Friday. The letter also explained that, because Mueller had reached no determination on obstruction, we believed the department had the obligation to make the decision and had determined that the evidence was not sufficient to establish obstruction. While I wanted to get the bottom-line conclusions out quickly, I wanted to avoid confusion. When we finished drafting, I asked Ed to check with Mueller's team to see if he wanted to review the letter before we sent it. Ed reported back that they did not. At approximately 3:20 p.m., just before we released the letter, I asked Brian to notify Emmet Flood, still with the President at Mar-a-Lago, that we would shortly be releasing a letter to Congress that states the report's principal conclusions. As Brian read the letter aloud over the phone, Flood scribbled down notes and then excused himself to inform the President. It was the first time anyone at the White House—the President included—knew with certainty what Mueller had concluded. Minutes later, the letter was delivered to Capitol Hill.

As I stated in the letter, my purpose was not to summarize the whole report but simply to advise Congress and the public as to the bottom-line conclusions—the basic information everyone wanted to know: Did Mueller find that the President committed collusion or obstruction? It was like announcing a jury's final verdict: there was no need to get into all the details of the trial or the jury's deliberations. The letter's description of Mueller's conclusions on collusion was straightforward: "The Special Counsel's investigation did not find that the Trump campaign or anyone associated with it conspired or coordinated with Russia in its efforts to influence the 2016 US presidential election."

The next portion of the letter, however, triggered heated claims that I "lied" in characterizing Mueller's handling of obstruction allegations. It read:

> The report's second part addresses a number of actions by the President—most of which have been the subject of public reporting—that the Special Counsel investigated as potentially raising obstruction-of-justice concerns. After making a "thorough factual investigation" into these matters, the Special Counsel considered whether to evaluate the conduct under Department standards governing prosecution and declination decisions but ultimately determined not to make a traditional prosecutorial judgment. The Special Counsel therefore did not draw a conclusion—one way or the other—as to whether the examined conduct constituted obstruction. Instead, for each of the relevant actions investigated, the report sets out evidence on both sides of the question and leaves unresolved what the Special Counsel views as "difficult issues" of law and fact concerning whether the President's actions and intent could be viewed as obstruction. The Special Counsel states that "while this report does not conclude that the President committed a crime, it also does not exonerate him."

This, of course, was an entirely accurate description of Mueller's decision on the issue of obstruction. It was in no way misleading. The Special Counsel declined to make a decision one way or the other. And my letter stated explicitly, quoting from the report, that "while [Mueller's] report does not conclude that the President committed a crime, it also does not exonerate him." We had struggled with and debated whether to include that passage in our letter. On the one hand, that is not the proper standard for a prosecutor like Mueller to apply, and it inverted the burden of proof, suggesting that the purpose of the investigation was to determine whether the President was innocent, not whether a provable crime had been committed. As even the most junior lawyer knows, that is not how our system works, and we all considered it inappropriate for Mueller to have included that editorial commentary in his report.

On the other hand, we did not want to be accused of misrepresenting the report, and, given the political forces at play, we felt that it was important to signal that there was more to the analysis than just our bottom-line conclusion that the President had not obstructed justice. So, in the end, we decided to include the sentence.

Later claims that my letter stating Mueller's bottom line was "misleading" are drivel. The *New York Times* headline the next morning was: MUELLER FINDS NO TRUMP-RUSSIA CONSPIRACY: PRESIDENT SEES "EXONERATION," BUT BARR SAYS INQUIRY DID NOT SETTLE OBSTRUCTION ISSUE. The *Washington Post* headline was: MUELLER FINDS NO CONSPIRACY—REPORT LEAVES OPEN OBSTRUCTION QUESTION, BUT BARR SEES NO CRIME. The *Washington Times* headline read: MUELLER FINDS NO RUSSIA COLLUSION—TRUMP STILL GETS NO EXONERATION, REPORT CAUTIONS. No one was misled.

The letter went public later that afternoon, and news that Mueller had found no collusion and declined to make a decision on obstruction touched off a furor directed at him and his team. Many of Trump's most vehement adversaries had vested a lot of hope in Mueller's investigation, and they were bitter that it failed to produce a finding of criminal wrongdoing by the President. They could not understand why Mueller had punted on obstruction. At DOJ, despite considerable discussion, we did not really understand his logic, so in drafting the letter, we did not try to explain why Mueller did what he did. From our standpoint, the Special Counsel's reason for declining to make a decision was irrelevant—and, in any event, it would eventually be explained in his own words once we were able to release Mueller's full report. The evidence assembled by Mueller and canvassed in the report, as well as Mueller's analysis, was going to be publicly issued as soon as Mueller helped us identify material that had to be redacted. What was important for the country to know, at that stage, was the basic *fact* that Mueller had declined to make the decision, and that we had stepped in to do so.

On Monday morning, March 25, Mueller's top lieutenant, Zebley, called Ed O'Callaghan to ask that we release the six-page summaries of each volume of Mueller's report that they had incorporated at the front end of the volumes themselves. While I ultimately had other concerns about using those summaries, the immediate showstopper to using them was that Mueller's team still had not redacted sensitive portions from the summaries that legally had to be removed before we could make them public. Ed told Zebley he would raise his request with me and Rod, but asked Zebley in the meantime to send copies of the summaries reflecting all the redactions necessary to release them. Significantly, we did not receive those redacted summaries until Thursday morning, March 28. But even then, we found that the redactions performed on the summaries by the Special Counsel's office were incomplete; they still contained classified material. Thus, a full week after receiving the final report, we still had not received from the Special Counsel a version of summaries suitable for release.

The incompletely redacted summaries came with a cover letter signed by Mueller, dated the day before. The letter stated that my March 24 letter to Congress "did not fully capture the context, nature, and substance of this office's work and conclusions." It said there was "public confusion about critical aspects of the results of our investigation," and that release of the summaries would alleviate this misunderstanding.

When I got the letter, I was angry. It wasn't just the snitty tone—though that was bad enough. What made me angry was that, instead of calling me to discuss his concerns, Mueller and his team were taking a public shot at me. Given the steady flow of leaks about the Special Counsel's work over the course of the investigation, I was sure that this letter would soon find its way to the pages of the *New York Times*. We had asked for a report that was ready for public release, which

Mueller had failed to provide. Now we were still considering whether we could put out summaries he had prepared, and, just three days after we had asked for them, I get this letter, along with summaries that *still* weren't ready for public release? The nerve was galling.

I immediately put in a call to Mueller and was finally able to connect with him in the late morning, after he returned from getting a haircut. Rod, Ed, and Brian were listening to our conversation over the speakerphone.

"Goddamn it, Bob," I started off, "what the hell is with this letter? You could have just picked up the phone and called me."

Mueller seemed unsteady, much as he had on March 5, but said that his team was concerned that my earlier letter had not set forth the full context for certain issues in his report. All of us in the room looked at one another with confused expressions. We did not understand what he was saying. I asked Mueller point-blank: "Are you saying that my letter was inaccurate?"

"No," Mueller responded. "What the letter says is not factually wrong. We aren't saying that. But without more context, there is a vacuum that the press is filling with misrepresentations. It is the way the press is covering it that is the problem, not what you said." The gist of Mueller's complaint seemed to be that, because I had focused only on his specific conclusion and had not summarized his tortured logic on the obstruction issue, or gotten into the details of the factual scenarios discussed in the report, the media coverage was not what he and his team had expected, and the report was not having the public impact he had wanted.

"Bob, your job was to decide whether or not there was a crime and then make a confidential report to me," I said. "The report is supposed to be *confidential*. Normally, it would not see the light of day. It is really up to me, as the Attorney General, how to handle it."

It bothered me that Mueller seemed focused on the impact the report was having. He was taking a lot of heat for having failed to make a decision on obstruction. And the President and his allies were making the most of the situation, loudly proclaiming victory with the slogan "No Collusion, No Obstruction." I thought Mueller's team might be attempting to compensate for the blowback they were facing by push-ing to get out more details about the President's conduct—conduct that might cast him in a negative light, but conduct that Mueller himself would not conclude was criminal. If true, this smacked of a political agenda and was not an appropriate consideration for either Mueller or the department. I had already made clear to Mueller and to Congress that I was trying to get the whole report out to the public— good, bad, and ugly—as soon as I could. And the reason there was a delay, as I am sure Mueller knew, was that his office had not submitted the report in the form I had requested.

Zebley then entered into the conversation. He, too, had no problem with our characterization of their conclusion on collusion. But, as to obstruction, he explained that their office felt there wasn't enough con-text to help people understand why the Special Counsel did what he did—why he did not reach a conclusion on the issue. Trying to find a path forward, I said, "Guys, let's agree to work together to get the whole report ready to release as quickly as we can. In the meantime, I wasn't trying to summarize the report, or explain everything about the report's context or all the nuances of your thinking. We only wanted to state your bottom-line conclusions."

Mueller and Zebley seemed to understand what I was saying but took the opportunity to ask again that we issue their summaries. I said I would think about it, but we had concerns with the summaries, and, in any event, thought that putting out the report piecemeal would create only more confusion for the public. Mueller thanked us for our consideration, and we agreed to stay in touch. As the call wrapped up, Rod said, "Bob, can we agree that we are all one department here, and that we are all trying to work together on this?"

"Yes," Mueller replied. "Absolutely. We are all one department."

"Bob," I said, "if you have any problems in the future, just pick up the phone. I am happy to talk things through with you at any time."

After the call, I discussed with my team the possibility of putting out Mueller's summaries. It seemed to me that any summary would, by definition, be underinclusive and invite criticism from one side or the other. Volume two's treatment of obstruction was complex, nuanced, highly detailed—and confusing. For every fact or consideration on one side, there was a fact or consideration on the other. It was clear to me that a six-page summary could not do justice to the whole report. It is one thing to state a final verdict: guilty or not guilty. It is another to put out a precis of the entire trial and invite people to draw conclusions.

These concerns were confirmed when I studied the Special Counsel's summary of the obstruction investigation. For example, while the summary described certain actions by the President presented as potentially constituting obstruction, it omitted the analytical sections of the full report. Those omitted sections included descriptions of evidence suggesting that the President lacked a corrupt intent or otherwise did not act unlawfully. In short, the summaries provided a far less balanced discussion of the evidence than the full report did. That analysis reinforced what I'd been saying since early March: the best thing to do would be to release the full report as quickly as possible. I told my office to work double time to make sure that happened.

While I disagreed with Mueller's views, I was sensitive to concerns about public confusion. The next day, Friday, March 29, I sent another letter to Congress, in part to address Mueller's concerns. I informed Congress that, working with the Special Counsel, we were already well along in making the redactions necessary to release the report, which I expected to do "by mid-April, if not sooner"—in other words, just two weeks. Noting that many media reports had mischaracterized my March 24 letter as a "summary" of Mueller's report, I stressed that the letter was intended to relate only Mueller's "bottom-line" conclusions. I pointed out that the full report sets forth in nearly four hundred pages all of the Special Counsel's findings, analysis, and reasons for his conclusions, and "[e]veryone will soon be able to read it on their own." I concluded: "I do not believe it would be in the public's interest for me to attempt to summarize the full report or to release it in serial or piecemeal fashion." I was suggesting that everyone—especially Congress, the media, and Mueller's team—needed to take a deep breath, stop scrumming, and let the process unfold properly.

I turned now to my bigger problem. I was potentially on a collision course with the President. I had gone publicly way out on a limb promising transparency during my confirmation process and in my letters to Congress. Not only did I think this was the right thing to do for the country, but also there was no practical alternative. President Trump's defense team, every Republican senator, and all his White House advisers seemed to understand this. An effort to conceal the report would ultimately fail, and its costs would far outweigh the costs of releasing it. As history had shown, someone would selectively leak the bad facts from the report, and the public would never trust our assurances about its conclusions unless they could read it for themselves.

While the President had so far acquiesced in my repeated public pledges to be as transparent as I could, he had never *explicitly* agreed to the release of the redacted report. It was a hell of a time for him to backslide into his habit of reopening issues that everyone thought were resolved. But I feared that could be happening.

In early April, as we worked to process the report for release, we got word from the White House counsel that the President, while not making any decision, was raising the question whether the report should be released at all. He was also considering whether to insist on redacting any material in the report covered by executive privilege. Up until then, we had not planned on the President either reviewing the report or asserting privilege. I thought we had an understanding with the White House that I would handle the release of the report. My view was that the only way the country could move beyond Russiagate was to issue the report, with only essential redactions, and that any redactions demanded by the President would suggest a cover-up and create a worse problem than anything revealed in the report. None of his private counsel or his White House staff had a different view, as far as I knew.

Things reached a head one evening when Emmet Flood called Brian Rabbitt on his drive home from work, telling him it was imperative that I get over to speak with the President about the need to release the report. It appeared that some outside kibitzers were getting President Trump agitated on the issue, which was frequently the case when he abruptly flirted with a disastrous idea. Brian explained my views and reminded Emmet that I'd committed to releasing the report during my confirmation hearing. Emmet said he understood the gravity of the situation and advised, "At this point, your boss needs to talk to mine about this."

On my next visit to the White House, Emmet and I slipped up to the residence, where we met with the President in the Yellow Oval Room. I told President Trump that the only way to put the Russiagate lunacy to rest was to put out the report—period. Not surprisingly, Mueller had come up empty-handed on collusion, and that really was the main issue for the American people. Most of the unflattering information laid out in the volume on obstruction had already been reported in the press the prior year—it was really old news, and nothing was to be gained by redacting any of it.

DOJ had already said that the evidence was insufficient to establish an obstruction offense; the obstruction narrative in the report was underwhelming. The surest way to turn victory into defeat, I told the President, would be to try to suppress information everyone already knew all about. I also assured him that, when I issued the report, I would remind people that the Department of Justice had found the evidence of obstruction insufficient, and I would explain why that was the case. The President agreed that I could release the report.

On April 18 I held a news conference to announce its release. After reiterating Mueller's conclusions, I went on to explain briefly the department's own decision that there was insufficient evidence to establish obstruction. I was expanding on a point made in the report itself about the unusual nature of the case and the difficulty of showing corrupt intent when there was no underlying crime being concealed. I made three points. First, despite a two-year onslaught that impaired his ability to govern, it turned out there was no collusion, as the President had steadily maintained. Second, as the report acknowledged, there was substantial evidence to show that the President was frustrated and angered. And justifiably so: he believed the investigation had undermined his presidency, had been launched by his political adversaries, and was fueled by illegal leaks. And, finally, quite apart from whether the President's actions qualified as "obstructive" in the legal sense, they did not, in fact, deprive the Special Counsel of witnesses and documents, and the President cooperated by giving the investigation unfettered access to campaign and White House documents, directing his aides to testify, and asserting no privilege. I concluded that "this evidence of non-corrupt motives weighs heavily against any allegation that the President had a corrupt intent to obstruct the investigation."

Much of the media seized on these comments to accuse me of "spinning" Mueller's report and acting like the President's lawyer. But I was not addressing *Mueller's* conclusions. I was explaining *my own* decision that no criminal offense was committed. A prosecutor does not become a defense lawyer by publicly identifying some of the factors that weighed against finding an indictable offense. It is rich that the media, after spending two years obsessively flogging the false Russian collusion narrative, would be so sensitive about the public being "spun" by my accurate description of factors I considered in assessing the President's conduct. Much of the media had invested all their hopes in the Russiagate story. They had a lot riding on their bet that Mueller was the Saint George who would slay the Trump dragon. But he did not. Distraught by the implosion of the collusion narrative, the media had melted down into a collective temper tantrum.

Once I had a good sense of how Mueller would be coming down, I started thinking seriously about how best to get to the bottom of the matter that really required investigation: How did the phony Russiagate scandal get going, and why did the FBI leadership handle the matter in such an inexplicable and heavy-handed way?

I initially thought about bringing in a high-profile Special Counsel from outside the department, like Mueller, but then decided that using an experienced professional from within the DOJ with a long track record of nonpartisanship would enhance the credibility of the effort. I did not know John Durham personally, but I knew his reputation within the department as a thoroughgoing, tenacious, and fair prosecutor with the highest personal integrity. He had been given similar special assignments by a number of previous Attorneys General over the years, both Republican and Democrat. With more than thirty-five years of experience as a federal prosecutor, Durham had been appointed by President Trump as US attorney in Connecticut at the outset of the administration. I noticed that both Democratic senators from Connecticut had strongly supported him with the highest accolades. I called John and asked him if he would consider reviewing the FBI's investigation of Trump's campaign and some of the related issues that had sprung up around the Russiagate scandal. He was open to the idea, and later, after we had the chance to talk further in Washington, we agreed he'd handle the matter.

At the same time, the Justice Department's Inspector General, Michael Horowitz, was conducting a detailed review of Crossfire Hurricane, particularly the use of the Foreign Intelligence Surveillance Act against Carter Page. The scope of this investigation was broad, since the IG had to get into issues beyond just the FBI's application for a FISA warrant. Among other things, Horowitz was looking into the initiation of Crossfire Hurricane in July 2016 and the use of confidential informants after that. The Inspector General kept me briefed as the scope of his investigation evolved. I was impressed with the level of detail his investigation was getting into. Initially, Horowitz thought the investigation could be wrapped up by the spring. But it was a vast undertaking, and it took several months beyond that to complete.

Durham's investigation was up and running by the late spring. Pending IG Horowitz's completion of his review of Crossfire Hurricane, I asked Durham to focus initially on any relevant activities by the CIA, NSA, or friendly foreign intelligence services. One of the more asinine aspects of media coverage about Durham's investigation was all the heavy breathing during the summer as news seeped out that I had contacts with foreign governments on Durham's behalf. Various journalists and commentators claimed this indicated that I was personally conducting the investigation and suggested there was something nefarious about my communicating with allied governments about Russiagate. This coverage was a good example of the kind of partisan nonsense that passes as journalism these days.

One of the questions that had to be run down was whether allied intelligence services had any role in Russiagate or had any relevant information. One question was whether US officials had asked foreign intelligence services to spy on Americans. Various theories of potential involvement by British, Australian, or Italian intelligence agencies had been raised over the preceding two years. Talking to our allies about these matters was an essential part of the investigation. It should not surprise anyone that a prosecutor cannot just show up on the doorstep of a foreign intelligence agency and start asking questions. An introduction and explanation at more senior levels is required. So— gasp!—I contacted the relevant foreign ambassadors, who in turn put me in touch with an appropriate senior official in their country with authority to deal with such matters. These officials quite naturally wanted to hear from me directly about the contours of the investigation and how their information would be protected.

In a vain attempt to breathe new life into Mueller's report, Hill Democrats insisted that he come up to testify in person. Mueller did not want to go and made clear he would not say anything beyond the four corners of what he had written in his report. They decided to haul him up nonetheless. The President was not thrilled with Mueller testifying, simply because it dragged things out more. I explained to him that the worst thing I could do would be to direct Mueller not to testify and added that I was very sanguine that his appearance would end up helping the President.

As Mueller's team was preparing him for his testimony, we received an indication that they would be happy if a way could be found to avoid his appearance. I decided to try giving him an exit ramp. While visiting a federal prison in South Carolina, I told a group of reporters that, since Mueller said explicitly he would not say anything beyond what was in his report, dragging him up to the Hill was just a public spectacle. I said that, if the Special Counsel did not want to be part of that, I would support him completely. A little later, Mueller's team inquired what I meant—specifically, would I be willing to direct Mueller not to appear? I responded that I would be willing to make a joint decision with Bob that he not testify, but I would not unilaterally direct him not to appear. Apparently, Mueller decided not to take the off-ramp.

On July 24 he appeared before two House committees. It was an epiphany for the public, but not the one the Democrats had hoped for. His testimony marked the end of the Russiagate nonsense.

That evening Brian, Kerri, and others on my staff gathered in my office. We felt we had finally put Russiagate behind us—and behind the President. I brought out my tray of single malts, and soon the sound of hearty laughter and clinking glasses filled the suite. It felt like a great weight had been taken off our shoulders. We were now freed up to focus our energies on the department's normal crime-fighting responsibilities, and President Trump could focus on his positive agenda. It was a great feeling. Little did we realize how short lived it would be.

The very next day—July 25, 2019—the President had his fateful phone call with the recently elected president of Ukraine, Volodymyr Zelensky. As Attorney General, I was not normally informed about the President's calls with foreign leaders, and I did not know about this one until later in August. However, it was this conversation that triggered the President's impeachment by the House of Representatives two months later.

It was on to the next damn thing.

CHAPTER 11

EATING GRENADES

Running the Justice Department involves a constant stream of events to deal with, problems to solve, cases to handle, and controversies to negotiate—one after another; often, indeed, with several usually happening at the same time.

I often remarked that one of the biggest changes I found at the Department of Justice after more than twenty-five years was that events outside the DOJ moved much faster, while the process inside the department moved much slower. It was not a good combination.

During my first tour as AG, the only cell phone on hand was carried by my security detail and was as big as a World War II walkie-talkie. E-mail was still in a nascent state—Lotus Notes e-mail came out in 1989. The Internet was primitive—the World Wide Web had been developed the same year. There was no social media. Although CNN had been operational for a while, cable news was still in its early stages, and there was no twenty-four-hour news cycle that had to be filled constantly by pundits and talking heads. News stories took days to develop, and the department would usually get several days' notice before a story went public. The world moved more slowly and more rhythmically.

By the time I returned to the department, the world seemed to move at a breakneck pace, with urgent information coming in all day long and into the night. Even with systems in place to rationalize the flow of information, I was the target of a never-ending barrage of problems and issues—"staccato signals of constant information," as Paul Simon sang in "The Boy in the Bubble." There was rarely any respite from having to respond to and deal with all the incoming requests, queries, and small crises.

Yet the processes inside the DOJ seemed to move slower than before. Last time around, I was always amazed at how quickly matters could get from the depths of the department up to my desk. Now when I asked for information or analysis, I was surprised at how long it took to get it. I did not feel this was anyone's fault, but attributed it to institutional factors: analysis required more time because the law had become more complicated; there was more bureaucracy and more levels of review; the intensified media and congressional scrutiny made managers more risk averse; and supervisors took too much time dealing with internal disputes rather than taking disagreements up the chain quickly for resolution. I tried to deal with this by setting deadlines and encouraging managers to elevate internal disagreements quickly to me for decision.

Based on my experience, there are two kinds of cabinet secretaries. There are agency heads who are run by their agency. They do little else but respond to their in-boxes and thus are almost entirely reactive, spending their time hopping to other people's priorities and putting out fires. Then there are executives who run the agency. This requires, in addition to responding to events, clearly identifying a core set of priorities, taking direct charge of them, and applying the energy necessary to overcome institutional inertia and bring them to fruition.

By nature, a big part of the Attorney General's job is inherently reactive. Any component can raise an issue up to the AG for guidance or decision, and, for that reason, the most difficult and controversial matters frequently land on the Attorney General's desk. These issues must be dealt with, but unless an Attorney General makes a special effort, that is all he will do. Just as I had in my first tenure, I was determined to be proactive, and I identified a number of initiatives I wanted to take charge of directly as part of my affirmative agenda, including, for example, our crackdown on violent crime; our counter-narcotic efforts against the Mexican cartels and addressing the opioid crisis; and the antitrust review of the large tech companies. On other issues, I was content to let our strong team at the department take the lead.

One of the first changes I made after arriving was to streamline the regular operating procedures in the Office of the Attorney General. Frequent large staff meetings at the AG's level are a waste of time for everybody—I've always felt that. Everyone wants to talk just to say something, but very little of substance ever gets said, and those forced to listen rarely have a real interest in the subject matter. I told top department officials that my overarching management principle was that my door was always open, and that they had the obligation to tell me or my chief of staff whatever I should know, whenever I had to know it. Other than that, they were to keep the Deputy AG informed through his staff meetings.

I started each day with a staff meeting including only my chief of staff, the Deputy AG, and the Deputy's chief aide, the PADAG. Here I was briefed on any significant matters and reviewed the agenda for the day. After our initial meeting, this core group would often be joined by the head of Legislative Affairs and the head of Public Affairs to discuss any pressing congressional or media issues.

I was surprised to learn that most of the department's senior officials had not been to lunch in the Attorney General's private dining room, which is part of the AG's suite. I quickly resumed my practice from yesteryear of hosting a standing brown-bag luncheon once a week in the AG's dining room, which any component head could attend at his or her option. This provided an opportunity for anyone to raise topics of interest.

When I first took office, my regular briefings with FBI leadership were cumbersome. Every Monday, Wednesday, and Friday, long meetings were scheduled right after my own staff meeting with the FBI director, the deputy director, and a big cast of bureau and DOJ officials, usually around fifteen or more people. These meetings ate up the lion's share of three mornings a week for a whole group of senior officials. A lot of time was spent reviewing intelligence in the *President's Daily*

Brief (*PDB*), a report the intelligence community publishes every day for senior officials. Even worse, the meetings were so formulaic and crowded that no real discussion was feasible. After a few weeks, I pulled Chris Wray aside and asked him about the format of the meeting, pointing out that I could just read the *PDB* for myself.

He lit up. "That is exactly what we all think. It's a waste of time for everybody."

"So why are we holding these meetings three times a week?" I asked.

"Because that is the way it's always been done, apparently, and that's what we thought DOJ wanted," he said. "You will be a hero if you fix this."

I cut back the meetings to Monday and Wednesday, limited attendance to the key senior FBI and DOJ officials (including me and the FBI director), omitted the general intelligence briefing, and focused on discussing key matters being handled by the bureau that required attention. Wray and I then scheduled a brown-bag lunch every Friday for just the two of us and our chiefs of staff. Everyone was pleased with this new format; it saved time, the meetings were more substantive and candid, and we actually made decisions.

I also found that my schedule was more packed with back-to-back meetings and events than it had been during my first tenure. The typical day's fare shows the amazing variety of the Attorney General's portfolio. It might include: receiving a visiting foreign justice minister; meeting a police group or the families of slain officers; meeting with a senator or congressman; a run over to the White House Situation Room for a meeting on a national security matter; making remarks at an internal DOJ event; several meetings with department divisions or components about significant cases or issues; and a call or meeting with another senior executive branch colleague. We were constantly moving from meeting to meeting, and there was almost no downtime.

Whenever I had an internal meeting on an issue, I tried to keep it focused. Attendance was limited to those who really had to be there, and I liked having the line attorneys present, no matter how junior, if they were the ones who knew most about the matter at hand. I preferred having meetings back in my small personal office rather than in the big ceremonial conference room because I felt it encouraged freer, more relaxed conversation. At some point, Brian Rabbitt, my chief of staff, circulated the message that whoever was leading a discussion should "start with the bottom line and get straight to the point—the AG doesn't like a lot of windup." This was good advice. I hated gabfests and liked meetings that were short, got to the nub of the issue, and resulted in a decision or clear next step.

Rod Rosenstein agreed to stay on as DAG pending Jeff Rosen's confirmation, which occurred in May 2019. I was deeply grateful for that. I did not know Rod well before coming to the department, but after working with him through the Mueller report during my early days, I felt we made a good team. Rod knew the DOJ inside and out. But after more than thirty years of service at the department, he was ready to work in the private sector. Few can appreciate the immense complexities Rod faced during that tumultuous time, and even fewer will know the important contributions he made to the administration and the country.

Rosenstein's right-hand man, Ed O'Callaghan, was outstanding. I also loved his irreverent New York style and big sense of humor. I begged him to stay on to help Rosen once he was confirmed as the new Deputy, and I will always be grateful he agreed to remain for a few months. Ed was indispensable and stayed on well into the fall, far longer than he expected. I will always regret that I failed to get Ed into his dream job—US attorney in the Southern District of New York, where he had been a longtime line prosecutor—before he left the department.

Brian Rabbitt helped assemble a strong, and relatively small, staff in the AG's office. In addition to Will Levi, who was already fortuitously on the staff, I kept on Brian Morrissey, a former clerk to Justice Clarence Thomas, to handle a range of civil matters, and Rachel Bissex, a savvy lawyer and manager who would eventually serve as my deputy chief of staff for administration. I also kept on Gene Hamilton, an immigration law guru who coordinated with the Department of Homeland Security on the many immigration matters that came before the DOJ. We also recruited two of Brian's former colleagues from the White House counsel's office, John Moran and Claire Murray, who'd clerked for Justices Scalia and Alito, respectively, and were former Kirkland & Ellis lawyers. As my criminal counselor, I recruited Seth DuCharme, a career prosecutor with deep experience in national security issues who was serving as the criminal chief in the Brooklyn US Attorney's Office. Seth came highly recommended and did such a good job in my office that, when Ed O'Callaghan left for private practice, Jeff Rosen and I asked Seth to take on that responsibility. To backfill Seth's spot, I recruited Gregg Sofer, the criminal chief for the Western District of Texas, one of the largest and busiest districts in the country. I came to rely on him heavily.

In addition to this newer generation, two old-timers decided to join me again at Justice on my staff. Tim Shea, who had been on my staff back in the early nineties, left private practice to help me handle some of the most difficult management challenges, overseeing the Bureau of Prisons and initially implementing the First Step Act. Jeff Favitta, who had been an FBI agent on my protective detail when I was last Attorney General—and one of several I recruited to Verizon—came back to DOJ to help with outreach to law enforcement groups. The younger members of my staff would jokingly refer to Tim, Jeff, and me as the Space Cowboys—after the Clint Eastwood movie of the same name about geriatric NASA astronauts. My staff all got along tremendously well, and the office had a real esprit de corps that helped us manage through the difficult episodes of my tenure.

At the end of an especially grueling day—around twice a week—I'd have a tray of my single malt scotches and Irish whiskies brought back into my office, where various staff members and I would unwind, joined sometimes by other senior officials.

My interactions with the White House were in some ways comparable to what they had been during my first go-round as AG, but in other ways dramatically different. The Attorney General's main point of contact at the White House is the counsel. Just as I had a good relationship with President Bush's counsel, Boyden Gray, I had a strong partner in my longtime friend Pat Cipollone, President Trump's counsel. Every Monday, I and my chief of staff would join Pat and his deputy, Pat Philbin, for lunch in Pat's West Wing office. The Deputy AG also frequently attended.

The big difference was my contact with the President. When I worked for George H. W. Bush, the vast bulk of my contacts with him were at formal meetings in the Cabinet Room or the Situation Room. During nearly a year and a half, I had perhaps four or five individual meetings with him and perhaps a half dozen phone calls.

With Trump, the calls were virtually daily—sometimes two or three a day—and often came near bedtime. This was especially true during my first year, when our relationship was less tense than it became eventually. Typically, POTUS launched into a long monologue about current events, hopping around discursively among a broad range of topics, only a small fraction of which related to the department. Sometimes he would call just to buck me up when I was being beaten up by the press—which was most of the time. He watched Fox News religiously and would sometimes call to make sure I saw a particular segment. Occasionally he would ask for advice, such as on an appointment or a policy issue, or he would crow about some administration success. But much of the conversation had to do with the unfairness of his opponents and how he was being treated by the media. The President was considerate, however. Although I knew he called other officials after ten o'clock at night, he never called me that late. One day he said he was frequently tempted to do that, but was afraid my wife would be angry.

Most interesting for me, however, was the ad hoc way the President ran his meetings in the Oval Office. In my college fraternity, there was a room—the card room, we called it—where there was a seemingly perpetual card game day and night, kept in session by an ever-shifting cast of characters who came and went. The President's Oval Office reminded me of that. It was a place of unplanned exchanges, with people coming in and out all the time, and one meeting running almost imperceptibly into the next. The President spent a lot of his executive time in the small dining room off the Oval, where he had a large television tuned constantly to Fox News and where impromptu meetings would evolve as officials showed up by happenstance. I would often be meeting with the President only to have another cabinet official or adviser, or a celebrity, pop in to chat with him.

It was easy to get time with President Trump, frequently even on the spur of the moment. Sometimes when he heard I was in the building for another meeting, he'd send word for me to stop by. Or if I was already at the White House and wanted to raise something with him, I'd often just drop in to the Oval Office. His assistants, Madeleine Westerhout and Molly Michael, would usually say, "He is in the back with so-and-so, but go ahead back." I'd wander into the Oval Office and find him with an official—perhaps the Vice President or chief of staff or another cabinet secretary—or a business leader and would get drawn into their conversation for a while before turning to my own subject. It was not unusual to be sitting at an Oval Office group meeting on, say, the opioid crisis, and then be asked to stay on for a meeting on a topic I really was not involved in, like trade.

There were good things about this freewheeling approach. It was easy for cabinet secretaries to communicate quickly with the President, and it helped him stay up with developments in his administration. It also added dynamism: cabinet secretaries could get quick sign-off by the President, and this helped get things done. For those savvy enough to manage the unruliness, there were real advantages to having near-constant access to the boss.

While I found the situation to be a net positive, at least for my agenda, there was also a downside to the unruliness. It allowed officials to short-circuit the internal process designed to ensure collaboration and consultation within the administration. If a cabinet secretary wanted to end-run one of his or her colleagues on an issue, it was occasionally possible to get the President to preempt debate by staking out a position without having heard the other side. This put a major burden on the President's chief of staff trying to run a rational, organized policy process, and it led to a lot of maneuvering and intrigue within the interagency process and among senior advisers.

The downside of the President's free-for-all approach to policy making was not only that presidential decisions were sometimes made preemptively, without vetting them with the responsible departments, but also that finality was sometimes difficult to achieve. Even when President Trump decided an issue after broad and robust interagency debate, it was not uncommon for a disappointed senior official to secretly slip into the Oval and blindside his colleagues by persuading the President to reverse himself. This meant that there was rarely any firm finality until a decision was actually implemented.

I was sandbagged in this way occasionally, including on one of the Justice Department's important national security priorities. Three key provisions of FISA were due to expire in March 2020, and it was important they be reauthorized by Congress before that happened. The provisions at issue were *not* the general wiretapping provisions that were abused by the FBI's Crossfire Hurricane investigation of the President's 2016 campaign. One of the provisions simply allowed the FISA court to authorize "roving surveillance" when a target tried to thwart surveillance—such as by regularly switching out cell phones. The provision allowed the FBI to shift the surveillance from one phone to the next without needing to return to court for a new warrant for each "burner" phone, which was simply not practical.

The second expiring provision was known as the "lone wolf" provision. Normally, surveillance can be conducted under FISA only when the government shows that the target is acting as an agent of a foreign power or international terrorist organization. But this can miss foreign jihadist extremists inside the United States who are inspired to commit terrorist acts by an international terrorist group but are not acting as an "agent" of the group. The lone wolf provision allowed the FBI to surveil a *non-US person* if it could show that he or she was engaged in international terrorism.

And the third expiring provision allowed the FISA court to order third parties—such as banks or transportation companies—to produce business records relevant to a pending national security investigation. This applied only to information not protected by the Fourth Amendment and was the kind of information that can be routinely subpoenaed from third parties in a criminal investigation.

When I arrived on the scene, National Security Adviser John Bolton, Director of National Intelligence Dan Coats, and all the intelligence community, including the FBI, CIA, and NSA, were attempting to get the President to support congressional reauthorization of the three key provisions. By then, President Trump had already flip-flopped once: first supporting it and then reversing himself. Bolton asked me to take the laboring oar at a large Oval Office meeting with all the principals to get the President to flip back to supporting reauthorization. I suspected that both the President and some Republican members of Congress—frustrated by what they saw as past efforts by the FBI and elements of the intelligence community to undercut the President—wanted to use the expiration of these FISA provisions as an opportunity to poke the intelligence agencies in the eye.

I, along with the other principals, were in our usual Oval Office formation: sitting in a semicircle in front of his desk. The President, who does not like spending too much time on the details, cut off conversation after a few minutes, looked toward me, and asked, "What do you want to do, Bill?" I told him I agreed that we had to correct past abuses, but these provisions were not related to those abuses. I said we would have opportunity to deal directly with the problematic aspects of the FISA process, and, in the meantime, these important tools should not be held hostage. The President agreed to my request and approved a letter to the Hill stating the administration's support for reauthorization. The letter was sent out.

Within a couple of weeks, the President had changed his mind, and I was called back to another meeting to hash through the issues still again. I believe several members of Congress had gotten to the President, aided by his then–chief of staff, Mick Mulvaney, who sympathized with them. During my time in office, there were four flip-flops on this single issue. The provisions were not authorized—to the country's detriment, in my view.

Despite allowing the frequent re-litigation of issues, the relaxed, ad hoc meetings in the President's little dining room, though always discursive, could be very productive. President Trump would sit at the head of the table, the TV playing in the background and a huge stack of documents to his left, which he worked his way through methodically—using his big, bold Sharpie to sign photos or annotate news clippings to send to cabinet secretaries. Always the attentive host, he would constantly ensure that everyone had a Diet Coke to drink. If he was feeling especially beneficent, he would open a cigar box and deal out his stash of big Hershey chocolate bars as if dealing cards. I always accepted; you have to play the hand you're dealt. The conversation would meander along, winding through numerous diversions—some prompted by a TV item, some by new arrivals, some by the mysterious workings of the President's stream of consciousness. But we would eventually reach a decision, and it was often fun getting there.

I learned very early on that the President is extremely visual. The best way to present an issue to him was to paint a picture of how something will look on TV. I don't say this critically. In the Reagan White House, Deputy Chief of Staff Mike Deaver had a gift for explaining the visual significance of various proposals. It's an essential part of political decision-making, and any former politico who claims he never cared what something looked like on TV is being less than candid. President Trump was always concerned with physical appearances— how someone or something came across on television. At times, it's true, he took it to unnatural extremes. When he saw a glib talking head on Fox News, he would start throwing around that person's name for a significant executive position in the government, or he would add the person to his list of informal outside advisers. Sometimes this worked. Frequently it didn't.

The President was always prompt in giving me immediate visual feedback when I appeared on TV. "You look great!" "You look strong!" "You look like an Attorney General!"

We had an amusing conversation once about my weight. I made a self-deprecating remark about my jowliness on TV. "No, Bill," he said. "You're fine, you're fine. Yeah, you're big. But you carry it well. Whatever you do, *don't lose too much weight.*" He pointed at me for emphasis. "Because then your face is going to sag. You're lucky because your face, I mean your cheeks—they're filled out. They look smooth and young. But I guarantee you, if you lose a lot of weight, you'll look old and saggy."

I guess I followed his beauty advice. I gained twenty pounds during my two years in the job.

When I started as Attorney General, I walked into the middle of a tempestuous fight between the House Committee on Oversight and Reform and both the Commerce Department and the Justice Department. It ended up with the House taking a shot at me and some jousting between me and the President.

In March 2018, almost a year before I arrived on the scene, Commerce Secretary Wilbur Ross announced that he'd decided to reinstate a question as to citizenship on the census questionnaire. On its face, this was not unreasonable. From 1820 to 1950, that question had been asked of all households, and from 1960 until 2000, the question had been put to at least a portion of the population. In his decision to reinstate the citizenship question for all households, Ross explained that he was responding to a request by the DOJ, which wanted the data to use in enforcing the Voting Rights Act of 1965. Commerce received that request from Justice in a December 2017 letter from the acting head of the Civil Rights Division.

Ross's decision was immediately challenged in federal district court by a number of states and various public interest groups. They believed the administration wanted to reinstate the citizenship question to redraw election maps. Many areas of the country, especially crowded urban areas, have large numbers of undocumented—and therefore nonvoting—residents, and yet these noncitizens are included in census information from which election maps are drawn. Some areas of the country are therefore apportioned more congressional seats than, based on the number of actual voters, should be the case. Democrats were predictably hostile to the effort, since they benefit electorally from the current system. And, just as predictably, the media portrayed the move as an attempt to make the electorate "whiter" and "less diverse"—as usual imputing racist motives in the absence of any rational counterargument.

During that litigation, the government provided documents showing that Ross had been pursuing reinstating the citizenship question since early 2017, well before he got a letter from the Justice Department. The evidence also showed that about three months before the DOJ letter, Ross talked to Attorney General Sessions, raising the idea that the DOJ request the Commerce Department to include the citizenship question. In January 2019 a federal district court in Manhattan found that Ross's decision violated the Administrative Procedure Act because Commerce's declared rationale for asking for the citizenship question was pretextual—that is, it was not the real reason behind the decision. The court enjoined Commerce from adding the question to the census. Arguing that the census forms had to be printed no later than the end of June to be ready for the census, the Justice Department bypassed the court of appeals and persuaded the Supreme Court to hear the case directly.

When I arrived at the department, Ross's decision was being litigated in the Supreme Court, and a ruling was expected before the end of June—the deadline DOJ and Commerce had supplied the court.

At the same time, the House Committee on Oversight and Reform was aggressively trying to obtain thousands of internal Commerce Department and DOJ documents that it believed might relate to the census question issue. Their purpose was to find any document they could sensationalize to influence the court's deliberations. They never found any such thing, and not, as they claimed, because we "stonewalled." During my first few months in office, the department had responded to the committee's subpoenas by producing more than seventeen thousand documents and was preparing to produce thousands more. In addition, the department had made two senior officials available for transcribed interviews.

By early June, things had come to a head. House Democrats were still smarting over the Mueller report's belly flop and were still trying to make headlines to influence the Supreme Court's deliberations. Although DOJ had been bending over backward to respond to their requests, the committee threatened to hold Secretary Ross and me in contempt of Congress unless I agreed to two demands. Both were concessions I could not responsibly make.

The first was that I make available for questioning for a third time the official who had drafted the department's December 2017 request to Commerce. This official had already testified before the committee and had also appeared for a lengthy transcribed interview. This time, however, the committee was demanding that the official appear for a deposition without the presence of department counsel. I could never agree to that. It has long been recognized, by both Republican and Democratic administrations, that, when an executive branch official is testifying about official actions, agency counsel cannot be excluded. That had long been the practice. Under the Obama administration, OLC, while ruling on a different issue, observed that excluding agency counsel would raise "constitutional concerns." I was willing to let the official be questioned a third time, but I would not permit the exclusion of the department's counsel.

The second demand was that we produce a memorandum written by a Commerce Department lawyer to the acting head of the Civil Rights Division and all drafts of DOJ's December 2017 letter to the Commerce Department. But these documents were protected from disclosure by the deliberative process privilege, the attorney-client privilege, and the attorney work product privilege. Indeed, the district court had already ruled that these documents were privileged. Unless the committee could show that it had a compelling need for the documents that outweighed the privilege, I wasn't budging.

The department notified the House committee on June 6—appropriately enough, D-Day—that we could not agree to its specific demands, although we were willing to try to work out some other accommodation. In any event, even if I had been willing to make those concessions—which I was not—the President directed me and Secretary Ross not to accede to the committee's demands. Later, on July 17 the House held Secretary Ross and me in contempt. Because this arose from an interbranch dispute in which the decisions were made by the executive departments and the President, the action had no practical effect. It was a partisan stunt and, I think, seen as such by honest observers.

On June 27 the Supreme Court ruled against the administration. The court found that, while there might well be many good reasons to include the citizenship question, and while an agency can normally have both stated and unstated reasons for its decision, in this case the *sole* reason cited by Secretary Ross for his decision—the request from the Department of Justice relating to voting rights enforcement—was pretextual. In that situation, the court held that the record was not sufficient to support the decision and blocked it, sending the matter back to the Commerce Department.

On the day of the Supreme Court decision, the President tweeted out: "I have asked the lawyers if they can delay the Census." On July 3 he tweeted: "The News Reports about the Department of Commerce dropping its quest to put the Citizenship Question on the Census is incorrect. . . . We are absolutely moving forward, as we must, because of the importance of the answer to this question."

The President was demanding that the Commerce Department make a new decision that would pass judicial muster. *In theory*, it was possible to formulate a new decision that could cure the defect in the original decision-making process. But there was an insuperable problem—a practical one: There was simply not enough time to frame a new decision, which, to have any chance of being upheld, required at least a modicum of deliberation inside the Commerce Department, and then successfully fend off all the court challenges and injunctions that would inevitably ensue. This all had to be completed by June 30, which the Commerce Department had set as the latest date it could get the census forms to the printer and still have them sent out in time to conduct the census. The DOJ's Solicitor General, Noel Francisco, had invoked that deadline with the Supreme Court to convince it to short-circuit the appeals process and take up the matter on an expedited basis. Any appreciable delay beyond that date would not only be inconsistent with our previous representations but also threaten serious disruption of the census itself.

Over the next several days, the President pounded on Ross to come up with a way to include the question in the 2020 census by pushing back the printing date. He was implacable. The lawyers in the Solicitor General's office and the Civil Division were dismayed, and understandably so. Their credibility with the courts would be shot if, after invoking the June 30 deadline, we now tried to embark on a new decision and new set of expedited judicial proceedings that would take us far beyond that date.

Despite the President's public declaration that he was "absolutely moving forward," his goals were just not achievable. I knew also that if we even tried to go down that path, a number of key Justice Department lawyers, both political and career, would likely leave their positions.

This would have been a blow. No administration in history faced the avalanche of court challenges and injunctions that opponents heaped upon the Trump administration to stymie its initiatives. Many dedicated lawyers at the department, both political and career, were working tirelessly and, for the most part, successfully, to vindicate the President's program. They felt the rug was being pulled out from under them.

On July 10 I went over to the Oval Office to tell President Trump that this issue had been taken as far as possible. The meeting promised to be the tensest of any I'd had so far with the President. Pat Cipollone and Mick Mulvaney joined me.

The President, as usual, sitting behind his desk, looked miffed as I walked into the room. He anticipated what was coming. He started performing one of his nervous tics: when he expects controversy, he absentmindedly moves things on his desk to the side, as if to clear a path down the center for the coming fusillade. Repeating the substance of his tweets, he started off blasting the court's decision as ridiculous.

"I agree we should be able to ask the question," I started. "And if people were straightforward from the beginning, it could have gotten done. The trouble is the administration was too cute by half, and Roberts threw the penalty flag."

"Well, I'm hearing from a lot of people that Roberts's opinion is actually inviting us to make another decision and wants us to," the President shot back.

This was the bane of my existence. As I was learning, President

Trump tended to shop around for legal advice until he found someone who told him what he wanted to hear. He had a big stable of outside hangers-on—"legal advisers" who were always ready to do just that. Some of them actually had law degrees.

"No, Mr. President," I said. "Your Solicitor General does not believe that. I don't believe that. And, frankly, no one who understands the Supreme Court believes it. Whoever is telling you this doesn't know what they are talking about."

The President's face reddened with frustration as I continued: "There is just no practical way to get a new decision made and upheld in the courts on time. If we try to go down this path, we will run out of time, jeopardize the census, and succeed only in antagonizing the courts."

To avoid a total loss, I suggested an alternative. Various agencies already had a lot of data on the citizenship of people in the country. Just as important as asking a new question on the questionnaire, I argued, was for the federal government to pull together and integrate all this data. I suggested to the President that he put out an executive order directing all federal agencies to provide the Census Bureau all the data they held concerning citizenship.

President Trump sat quietly for a moment, his frustration gradually giving way. Realizing he had taken the issue as far possible, he reached a place of equanimity. "Okay," he said, "that's what we'll do. It's a good resolution given where we are." The meeting was not that bad after all.

The next day, Ross and I came to the White House to make the announcement with the President. While we were still in the Oval Office, he looked me over and spotted something he didn't like. He took a piece of Scotch tape out of his drawer, walked over to me, and put it on the small end of my tie to hold it in place behind the longer, wider part. "Now, that's better," he said, patting me on the chest.

Then Ross and I accompanied him into the Rose Garden, where he announced he was no longer seeking to reinstate the citizenship question in the 2020 census and that instead he would issue the executive order. In my remarks, I stressed that the Supreme Court's decision made clear there was no legal impediment to including the question.

The reason we couldn't do it now was purely a matter of logistics—we couldn't get it done in time.

The whole census imbroglio was unnecessary. The people involved had little experience handling these kinds of legal matters. The administration tried to buttress its case in a way that made it look like the stated rationale was pretextual. But the question could have been easily justified for any number of reasons. Time ran out before we could fix the mess the administration created for itself.

At the regular Monday lunches that I and Brian Rabbitt had with Pat Cipollone and his deputy, Pat Philbin, typically one of the main orders of business was to inventory the legally problematic ideas floating around the administration. A fair share of them emanated from the President, and Cipollone and I had to decide which of us would have responsibility that week for dealing with the problem. We operated like a tag team, so that neither of us would provoke too much of the President's ire at one time. We referred to this as choosing who would "eat the grenade."

"The President wants to issue the executive order on birthright citizenship by the end of this week," Pat might say.

He was talking about President Trump's idea of ending automatic citizenship for children born in the United States to aliens illegally in the country. This required reinterpreting the Fourteenth Amendment's standard for citizenship and raised a host of legal and practical problems. Even if the Constitution allowed Congress to do this, trying to do this unilaterally by executive order instead of statute was essentially a suicide mission. We were sure to lose in court, given the Supreme Court's composition at that time. Furthermore, a statute could be framed to disallow citizenship only going forward, but an executive order would have to be based on the premise that millions of persons already recognized as citizens over the preceding century were, in fact, not citizens. Issuing an executive order calling into question the citizenship of millions of established citizens did not seem a wise move.

"Come on, Pat," I'd say. "You know OLC feels there are a lot of legal problems there, and those concerns aren't trivial."

"Look," he would say, "I've been taking the heat on this for weeks. You need to explain it personally to the President."

I'd chew on a piece of salmon for a minute.

"Okay, I'll eat the grenade on birthright. *But*," I'd add, "I need your help on this damn census question. I've been trying to explain it to him. After we lost in the Supreme Court, we just don't have the time to make a new decision and litigate it through the courts before the questionnaires have to be distributed."

"Okay," Pat would say. "I can help on that one."

The President sometimes had some brilliant ideas, like using tariffs to get the Mexicans to help us shut down illegal immigration. But he was a hyperactive generator of ideas, many of them bad—the idea of an executive order on birthright citizenship being a prime example. When the problems were legal, it fell to the DOJ and the White House counsel to either fix the legal problems so that the idea could be implemented properly, or, failing that, talk the President out of the idea. Sometimes the back-and-forth with President Trump could be bruising. Hence the desire to spread the joy more equitably.

There were certain issues the President would raise relentlessly no matter how many times the legal problems were explained. Sometimes it seemed the worse the idea, the more fixated on it he became. I referred to these issues as Groundhog Day issues. For non-moviegoing readers, that's a reference to the 1993 comedy in which Bill Murray plays a weatherman who relives the same day, February 2, over and over. Working for Trump could feel like that sometimes. He would raise the same issue again and again at regular intervals. You would think the matter was settled and decided, but then he would bring it up again as though it wasn't. We would discuss it again, and it seemed he was satisfied. Then two weeks later, he'd bring it up again. On some issues, February 3 just wouldn't come.

On the morning of Saturday, August 10, 2019, I was working in my home study when I got a call from Brian Rabbitt. "Boss," he said, "we have a problem."

I had a sinking feeling. "What?"

"Jeffrey Epstein committed suicide in his cell overnight," he said. "Apparently hung himself."

I couldn't believe it. "Shit. You got to be kiddin' me," I said. I sat for a minute, silently thinking through the terrible implications, then said, uselessly, "I thought we had him being closely watched."

"I don't have all the facts, but it looks like a major shitshow," Brian said. "The FBI is jumping on it. Same with the Southern District." Brian gave me the bare-bones facts he had been able to learn so far.

I told him to find out what he could. I would call Inspector General Michael Horowitz and get his people on it. They were deeply familiar with the Bureau of Prisons's processes and could get answers quickly. "I want both the FBI and the IG investigating this," I told Brian. "No one's gonna believe it was a suicide. There'll be conspiracy theories all over the place."

I called the President to tell him. He, too, was shocked that this could happen in a federal facility and worried about the conspiracy theories. I told him we had an aggressive investigation under way, and I would keep him posted. The FBI deputy director, Dave Bowdich, personally monitored developments in the investigation and briefed the Deputy AG several times a day.

I was deeply upset that Epstein had escaped justice, that he had made it harder for us to nail his coconspirators, and that his victims had been denied seeing him stand trial. He'd been arrested on July 6, charged with sex trafficking involving dozens of underage girls, and imprisoned at the Metropolitan Correctional Center in Manhattan to await trial. I considered our sex trafficking case against him one of the most important matters we had under way in the department. It was the centerpiece of our crackdown on human trafficking, which I had designated as a high priority. The prosecution team in the Southern District of New York and the FBI had done great work preparing a case against the wealthy sixty-six-year-old financier.

Over the next couple of days, the facts showed a stunning succession of screwups that, at first blush, were hard to ascribe to mere coincidence. After an initial suicide attempt a little over two weeks earlier, Epstein had been put on suicide watch, which meant he was under continuous observation every minute in a special cell. But, after six days, he had been taken off suicide watch on the recommendation of the prison psychiatric team. He was then placed in the Special Housing Unit, which permits closer scrutiny, and was placed on "special observation status," the next highest level of monitoring below suicide watch. This required that he be housed in the same cell with a trusted inmate and that he be physically checked by correctional staff every thirty minutes. But these safeguards were not carried out. The day before Epstein's death, his cellmate was transferred to another facility, and no new cellmate was assigned. The night of Epstein's death, the correctional officers assigned to the unit failed to conduct any of the required checks and then falsified the records to show they had. The initial reports indicated that cameras that would have shown access to Epstein's cell were not operating that night. I could understand why the public would be suspicious of the circumstances, and I, myself, at that stage, did not rule out foul play.

I was mortified at the breakdown of the process and that the Bureau of Prisons had failed to secure one of the most important prisoners we had in custody—a man facing trial for loathsome crimes. He would be under pressure to incriminate others, perhaps some prominent, powerful people. During my previous tour as Attorney General, the federal prison system was considered one of the most professional and best-managed operations in government. It was always known for its deep bench of talented managers. Since arriving at DOJ for my second tour, it had become clear to me that BOP had lost a step. It was being led by an acting director whose experience was in administrative services rather than operations, and no one leapt out at me as a seasoned manager who could whip the organization into shape.

On Monday I was in New Orleans speaking to the Fraternal Order of Police and started my remarks by saying that I was "appalled" and "angry" at Epstein's death and that we had found "serious irregularities" at the Manhattan Correctional Center. I promised that we would get to the bottom of what happened, and pledged that the sex trafficking case would continue against anybody and everybody who had conspired with Epstein.

That same day, I located the retired management team that had done a superb job running the Bureau of Prisons back in the 1990s. In 1992 I had appointed Kathy Hawk Sawyer as the first woman head of BOP, and she had become highly regarded as an effective, tough but fair manager. Her right-hand man at the time, Tom Kane, was also widely respected as an excellent manager. Both had been retired for many years. I asked them to visit me in DC as soon as they could. I needed more Space Cowboys.

Both Kathy and Tom came to meet me the week of August 12. They had many good personal reasons for not returning to government, but both were willing to come back to help me get BOP in order. They were willing to return as BOP director and deputy director, respectively, for an interim period—hopefully about six months or so—but would be announced as permanent appointees so that they would not be viewed as short-timers. The two of them would assess the management problems at BOP, come up with a plan to address the agency's shortcomings, and help identify both inside and outside talent qualified to replace them permanently. On Monday, August 19, I announced that I was moving the acting director back to his former position and appointing Sawyer and Kane to head BOP. I also reassigned the warden of the Manhattan Correctional Center.

The investigation by the FBI and the Inspector General showed that Epstein's death came after a perfect storm of failures. The prison leadership should not have accepted the recommendation of the psychiatric staff to remove him from suicide watch. The failure to immediately assign a new cellmate to share Epstein's cell was the result of an unintentional oversight. The two correctional officers on duty who were supposed to check on Epstein had spent the night surfing the Internet and apparently sleeping much of the time. They were charged with falsifying the records to conceal their goofing off and eventually pled guilty. There was no evidence of foul play in the malfunctioning of the video camera covering the door to Epstein's cell. Nor has there been any evidence suggesting that correctional personnel intentionally contributed to his death.

By the end of 2019, I was confident that Jeffrey Epstein committed suicide by hanging himself. The New York City medical examiner had conducted an autopsy and ruled that Epstein killed himself by hanging. Other evidence also pointed to suicide, but it was the video evidence that confirmed the medical examiner's finding. In the Special Housing Unit, where Epstein was held, there is a large open common area, where the correctional officers sit at a desk. The desk is at the foot of open stairs leading up to a unit, or "tier," of eight cells in which Epstein's cell was located. There is only *one way* into that tier, and hence to Epstein's cell, and that is to go up the stairs and through a gated entryway immediately at the top of the stairs, which is plainly visible from the desk at the foot of the stairs. Epstein's cell, the first inside the entryway, was only about fifteen feet from the officers' desk. A video camera inside the unit was not functioning that night, but a separate video camera located in the common area had clear coverage of the officers' desk area, the open stairs, and the gated entryway.

I personally reviewed that video footage. It shows conclusively that between the time Epstein was locked in his cell at 7:49 p.m. on the night of August 9 and the time he was discovered the next morning at 6:30 a.m., no one entered his tier.

The fact that so many failures occurred at one time understandably led people to suspect the worst. But thorough investigations have shown once again the wisdom of Hanlon's razor: don't ascribe malice when stupidity is a sufficient explanation. It was inexcusable that the Bureau of Prisons failed to prevent the suicide of one of the most important prisoners in federal custody—someone who had already attempted suicide once and had every motive to avoid trial. The new permanent head of BOP has put in place a rigorous process to ensure these failures do not happen again.

Another factor contributing to the debacle was the shortage of qualified correctional officers in our system, which required the staff to work long and extra shifts. Part of this was self-inflicted by a heavy-handed hiring freeze that was in effect when I arrived. Months before Epstein's suicide, I had seen the issue, ended the freeze, and was pushing BOP to accelerate hiring new officers. The other stubborn problem is that in major metropolitan areas such as New York, it's hard to attract good candidates for correctional positions. The job is stressful, and the pay is not a draw, especially in a full-employment economy. But the management changes I made at the time were good ones, and I think the agency is slowly on its way back.

As for Epstein, it was no consolation to me that an odious criminal was dead. He should have been given a fair trial and, if found guilty, made to answer for his crimes. That he was not is deeply disappointing to me.

Shortly after taking office, I had the opportunity to work closely with Jared Kushner on one of his major projects: the First Step Act. Enacted in December 2018, this rare bipartisan initiative, championed by Kushner, became one of the administration's signature achievements. It was intended to mitigate some of the harsher aspects of the federal system's tough sentencing regime, without undermining the public's safety.

My predecessor, Attorney General Sessions, strongly resisted the legislation. He objected to the provisions tinkering with federal mandatory minimum sentences. Given my long track record favoring incarceration for violent offenders, Jared guessed that I, too, might be unsympathetic to the legislation. During my first week in office, he called me.

"Bill, as you know, I have been deeply involved in the First Step Act," he said. "I recognize that the DOJ has responsibility for implementing it, but I would like to stay involved, along with some of staff who know the issues and key outside interest groups well."

The implementation burden Congress had placed on the department was quite onerous, and I was happy for Jared and his team to help us out. "Absolutely," I responded. I told my staff to go over to meet with his staff and work closely with them.

"I want you to know, Bill, that I know this falls in your domain, and I will respect the department's prerogatives," Jared assured me. "I won't try to go around you. We'll work things out directly with each other."

The fact was that I was not as hostile to the act as AG Sessions had been. I would have preferred that it not have tinkered with some of the federal mandatory minimum sentences, but, all in all, I felt those changes were modest and acceptable. They left in place a sentencing regime for drug traffickers that was still strong and did not appreciably weaken sentencing for those engaged in violent crime.

The main thrust of the act—to reduce recidivism by better preparing inmates for reentry into society—was unobjectionable. Essentially, the act required the department to develop a "risk and needs assessment" tool, so that each inmate could be evaluated as to their risk of recidivism and placed in programs that would best equip them for successful reentry. The department was required to provide an adequate range of programming and training to meet the needs of inmates: education courses, drug treatment, job training. Prisoners who successfully complete the programming could earn "additional time credits," allowing them to be placed in halfway houses or home confinement earlier than they were previously allowed. (Prisoners could not earn additional time credits if they had committed certain violent or other serious crimes.) If we can increase the likelihood that former offenders stay on the straight and narrow after serving their sentences, that would make a major contribution to reducing crime rates and promoting public safety.

Not long after my initial phone call with Jared, I attended a White House meeting on immigration legislation in which he was one of the participants. This was the first time I saw him in action, and I thought his ideas were good and he handled himself well. Once the meeting broke up, we found ourselves walking side by side down the hall.

"I want to thank you," Jared said.

"For what?" I asked.

"For sending your folks over to work with us—the way you're approaching the First Step Act," he said.

I suddenly stopped walking, which caused him to stop also. I stood silently staring at him for a moment. "You mean the First and *Last* Step Act," I said, putting great emphasis on the word *Last*.

Taken aback at first, Jared saw quickly that I was joking and laughed heartily.

Congress had not made implementing the First Step Act easy, and

Jared's support was indeed welcome. Besides imposing unrealistic time-tables, lawmakers failed to appropriate the necessary funds. I scraped together the funds from elsewhere in the department's budget—$75 million for the balance of 2019—and I put one of my counselors, Tim Shea, who had been with me in my first go-round, in charge of driving implementation. Working with Jared's team and the BOP, we were able to set up the requisite advisory board, design an effective assessment tool, proceed on time with the individualized assessment of all federal prisoners, and start getting in place the necessary programming for the inmates to earn credits. It was widely acknowledged on the Hill that the department had diligently carried out the law.

This initial experience with Jared on the First Step Act set the tone of our relationship going forward. I found him a pleasure to work with. Even though he could have easily outflanked me, given his direct relationship with the President, he always dealt with me honestly and directly. He made an effort to understand the issues that were important to me and then tried to reconcile our respective positions. He had a superior staff, bright and collegial. During the remainder of my time in the administration, I found that projects taken on by Jared and his team were handled professionally.

Jared's office was right down the hall from the Oval Office, on the first floor of the West Wing. I'd stop by frequently to chat with him when I saw he was free.

Jared would freely acknowledge that he, and most everyone else who came into the White House during the first two years of the administration, were neophytes. A lot of rookie mistakes were made, and a lot of egos were bruised unnecessarily. But by the time I was dealing with Jared, as well as Ivanka, both had learned from their experiences. I always found them reasonable and down-to-earth. Their offices were oases of rationality and professionalism.

Not infrequently I would seek Jared's advice or try to enlist his help when I was having a disagreement with the President or others on the White House staff. Most of the time, we saw eye to eye, and he would frequently try to help. In a dispute touching on the law, Jared could be counted on to side with DOJ and the White House counsel's office. Both Pat Cipollone and I considered him an important ally.

When Jared disagreed with the President on something, it was always clear that he had genuine affection for his father-in-law and respected his prerogatives. He was also clear eyed about his ability to get the President to change his position on something. "I try to be selective and pick my fights carefully," he told me. "But you got to remember, even when I do weigh in, my batting average is no better than .500."

The role of Attorney General has become more international in scope over the years, as many of DOJ's most challenging missions—drug trafficking, terrorism, organized crime, cybercrime, human trafficking—have required greater collaboration with foreign allies. Every week, I met at the department or communicated with at least one foreign counterpart to discuss our law enforcement cooperation. During my first months in office, I made several foreign trips.

My first trip was to El Salvador in May 2019. This small country is a priority for the Justice Department because, as I will explain in a later chapter, the activities of large Salvadoran transnational criminal organizations, MS-13 and the 18th Street gang, contribute to illegal immigration by Central Americans across our southern border. These violent gangs also have a large presence in the United States. Prior to 2019, El Salvador had a Far Left government and was contemplating allowing China to establish a major naval base. By the time I entered office, a populist, more centrist leader, Nayib Bukele, had won the presidential election. This gave the United States the opportunity to build a stronger relationship with a little nation whose friendship is important.

In mid-June I traveled to Bucharest, Romania, to cochair the EU-US Justice and Home Affairs Ministerial Meeting. This is an annual get-together of the Attorney General and the secretary of homeland security with all our EU counterparts. At this session, we focused on practical steps to increase the sharing of evidence on foreign terrorist fighters collected in Syria and Iraq; fight cybercrime; protect our electoral systems from foreign interference; and bring down "dark markets" on the web used to traffic weapons, drugs, and all forms of criminality. Romania is an important ally, but, like some other Eastern European countries, is plagued by internal corruption. I took time to meet with the Romanian president and other Romanian officials to stress the importance of enforcing anticorruption laws.

The long flight home from Bucharest was broken up with an overnight stop in Dublin. Brian Rabbitt asked if it was possible, while there, to find "an authentic" Irish music session, which he'd never attended. While flying over Europe, I texted an Irish friend in Dublin—one of the top guitarists on the traditional music scene. I asked him where we might find a good session. A few minutes later, he responded, "See you at McNeill's on Capel Street, 9 p.m." It was an excellent pub: obliging staff, good pub food, cluttered décor, and real music instead of deafening technopop. We got in a lot of singing and a lot of Guinness. The owner taught me how to draw a pint. The local clientele could not have been friendlier, and everyone wanted a selfie. My whole staff had worked nonstop on the trip. It was a fitting break.

In late July I traveled to London to meet with our Five Eyes partners to address a critical challenge facing law enforcement and intelligence. The Five Eyes Intelligence Oversight and Review Council (FIORC) started during World War II as essentially an Anglophone intelligence-sharing alliance among the United States, the United Kingdom, Canada, Australia, and New Zealand. While that core function remains, the Five Eyes countries use this partnership to collaborate on a wide range of issues. In London, we discussed a fundamental danger facing all of our law enforcement and intelligence activities: the proliferation of mobile devices and Internet products that allow criminal end users to encrypt data and communications in a way that precludes the government from accessing it, even when the government has obtained a judicial warrant based on probable cause to believe that criminal activity is under way. I couldn't appreciate it at the time, but in just six months, this very problem would severely hamper the FBI's investigation into an Al Qaeda terrorist attack at Pensacola Naval Air Station in Florida.

In London, I and my Five Eyes counterparts hosted a private presentation by advocates for victims of child sexual exploitation, as well as victims and a few tech executives, to discuss the effect of encryption on the ability to detect and catch child predators. All of us agreed to issue a joint statement calling on tech companies to "include mechanisms in the design of their encrypted products and services whereby governments, acting with appropriate legal authority, can obtain access to data in a readable and usable format." We also agreed to work on voluntary principles that companies should adopt to help combat online child sexual exploitation and abuse.

In October 2019 my British and Australian counterparts and I wrote an open letter to Facebook calling on the company not to proceed with its announced end-to-end encryption plan for its messaging service without providing law enforcement court-authorized access to the content of communications.

One of Ivanka Trump's priorities was combating human trafficking and protecting children from online exploitation. I started working closely with her on these issues. We held a number of events together. In March 2020 she hosted a White House session with the Five Eyes, tech company executives, and victims of online child exploitation. At the session, the tech companies unveiled their Voluntary Principles to Counter Online Child Sexual Exploitation and Abuse. These were a positive first step in making it harder for child predators to use online platforms to carry out their grotesque crimes.

I found that Ivanka, like Jared, was a pleasure to work with. She was intelligent, unaffected, capable, and highly dedicated. She also had a very competent staff.

I took a vacation during the last week of August 2019. It turned out to be an exasperating few days. Two events coincided. On August 26 the Department of Justice received a referral from the intelligence community's inspector general, based on an alleged whistle-blower complaint. The allegation was that, during his July call with Volodymyr Zelensky, President Trump tried to pressure the Ukrainians to pursue investigations that could help his reelection bid in 2020. The President, at least according to one interpretation of the call, was asking a foreign entity to perform an action that would hurt his likely foe in an election year.

I was infuriated: having just broken free of Russiagate, the administration was about to get mired in another mess—this one self-inflicted and the result of abject stupidity.

As I was stewing about this, I got an angry call from the President about something completely unrelated: a just-released report from the DOJ Inspector General, Mike Horowitz. He'd been investigating the fact that Jim Comey, after having been fired by the President in 2017, gave his lawyers four of the memos "for the record" he had previously written documenting his interactions with President Trump. Comey claimed he thought the memos contained no classified material. Later, however, the FBI determined that a few words in two of the memos were classified at the "confidential" level—the lowest level of classification. Those who made this determination recognized it as a close call. Horowitz was assessing whether Comey's handling of his memos violated DOJ and FBI policies and Comey's employment agreement. Before issuing his report, the IG referred his factual findings to the department for a decision on whether Comey's conduct involved a prosecutable criminal offense—the principal question being whether Comey could be prosecuted for unauthorized disclosure of classified material.

During the summer, after Horowitz's referral, the matter had been reviewed thoroughly by the US Attorney's Office in Brooklyn, which concluded that, under the department's standards of prosecution, no criminal charges were appropriate. This analysis was reviewed at headquarters by everyone concerned, including me. Everyone agreed that there was not sufficient evidence to show that Comey intended to disclose classified material. Instead, the evidence showed that he had tried to identify classified material and held back any information he thought was classified. The fact that a few words were determined to be classified only after Comey had transmitted the memos and that this classification judgment was a close call made it virtually impossible to show the culpability the department would normally require for prosecution. No one at Justice thought the question was even close. I approved Brooklyn's decision not to bring charges against Comey—a decision that was not to be disclosed publicly until the IG's report was issued later in the summer.

In issuing his final report on August 29, Horowitz was highly critical of Comey's actions, which he found violated a number of DOJ policies. The report also stated that the department was not charging Comey with a crime. This is what prompted the President's call, and he was furious. He made clear he was not suggesting I change the decision—it was obviously too late for that, and he knew I wouldn't change it even if he wanted me to. But he certainly wanted to recriminate.

"How could you do that, Bill?" he kept on repeating. "I read the report—all eighty-plus pages—it was as clear as day. The evidence was all there. Even Horowitz said he should be prosecuted. I'm shocked, Bill. I'm disgusted. I'm not happy about this, Bill."

I told him, as I had said to him when he brought me on, I would apply the same standard for everybody and would not cut corners just to go after a political adversary.

I had to correct him, too. Horowitz's referral *did not* say he thought prosecution was appropriate. He wouldn't have said that even if he thought it. As was his usual practice, he was referring that question to the offices authorized to make the decision. Nobody involved in that case thought it warranted prosecution.

As a matter of principle, I told the President, I could never approve it. And from a practical standpoint, pursuing such a weak case would be obviously vindictive and meet with quick defeat. At a time when we had turned the corner on Russiagate, I said, prosecuting Comey on slender evidence would have undercut our credibility and discredited our far broader efforts to set the record straight.

I had the impression that he wasn't listening to my explanation. When he kept saying, "Everyone says it's a slam dunk," I realized the problem: his usual retinue of outside legal experts were winding him up.

When I asked who "everyone" was, he only said, "Everyone, Bill, everyone." Then the President went into a long monologue about the double standard of justice and how despicable Comey's conduct had been—points on which I could not disagree.

"Look, Mr. President," I said, trying to bring the conversation to a close, "everyone here at Justice agrees this was not a close call. So that's it. The question we were dealing with wasn't about Comey's character or his behavior after the election. The only question we had before us was whether his handling of his memos was a criminal leak of classified information. And it wasn't a 'slam dunk.' It wasn't prosecutable."

The next day, he tweeted:

The fact that James Comey was not prosecuted for the absolutely horrible things he did just shows how fair and reasonable Attorney General Bill Barr is. So many people and experts that I have watched and read would have taken an entirely different course. Comey got Lucky!

President Trump never let me forget how unhappy he was about this decision. He brought it up constantly. "You had the chance to prosecute Comey, and you didn't!" he would say. (I would think, but not say, *You had the chance to fire him when you came into office, but you didn't.*)

Later, it became the first in his oft-repeated litany of grievances about me. But I always remembered that, after we talked about it that day, he still felt the need to call me "fair and reasonable." That told me one thing: he knew I was right.

But this did not matter to Trump. Everyone except family members has a shelf life with him. I was never under any illusion about this. I always saw how Trump treated people. I did not go into government to be popular with Trump, but to ensure the law was applied fairly, and he got his due as President. People are worthwhile to Trump only as means to his ends—as utensils. When they don't help him get what he wants, they are useless. In my case, Trump's disenchantment started—as it was bound to—when he saw I was not willing to bend the law to do his bidding. The next storm would test our relationship further. And that storm was already breaking.

CHAPTER 12

"I BELIEVE YOU'LL BE IMPEACHED"

In late September 2019 I found myself stepping into the Oval Office accompanied by White House Counsel Pat Cipollone and my chief of staff, Brian Rabbitt. It was a typically mild early fall evening in Washington. As the three of us walked into the Oval Office, the strains of "Waltzing Matilda" burst into the room from the Rose Garden outside. The combined choruses from all the armed services were assembled there, singing a beautiful rendition of the Australian ballad. The President, beaming, looked out the French doors to the Rose Garden, where the First Lady was carefully directing a small army of staff. "Isn't that great?" he said with a warm smile. They were rehearsing for the state dinner for the Australians the following night. We all paused to look out the French doors.

Reluctantly, I broke the spell. The reason for my visit was not a happy one, and we needed to talk about it. There was a growing movement in Congress to take "resistance" to another level. "Mr. President," I said, "there is something we need to discuss."

Robert Mueller's testimony before Congress on July 24, 2019, was Russiagate's death rattle. The public seemed to sense, finally, that it was phony. Even Congress and the media—Mueller's relentless cheerleaders for the last two years—were forced to tacitly acknowledge that it was over. At last, it seemed, the burden of a bogus scandal would be lifted from the President's shoulders, and he and his administration could get on with the business of running the country.

It was not to be so. The very next day—July 25, 2019—the President participated in a phone call with the new president of Ukraine.

As a practical matter, of course, President Trump's adversaries had been searching for a reason to remove him from office since the day after he won the 2016 election. By the summer of 2019, it was plain to them that they had been foolish to rely on the collusion fantasy to do the work for them. They would have to do it themselves—and that meant impeachment.

They went to work immediately. On August 12, 2019, an unknown whistle-blower filed a complaint with the Inspector General of the Intelligence Community (ICIG) claiming that, on the July 25 phone call with Volodymyr Zelensky, President Trump had improperly pressured the Ukrainian president to take actions that would benefit Trump's 2020 reelection campaign. The crux of the complaint was that the US President, possibly using the release of foreign aid as leverage, had pressured his Ukrainian counterpart to launch investigations into two matters that Trump and his allies had been promoting since the spring.

One allegation was that the Clinton campaign had colluded with entities in Ukraine to interfere in the 2016 election. The main theory here seemed to be that unnamed Ukrainians were involved in a scheme to make the hacking of the DNC look like it was done by the Russians, and the DNC hid this ruse by withholding its server from the FBI and instead giving it to CrowdStrike, a private cybersecurity firm supposedly controlled by a Ukrainian. The second allegation—entirely unrelated to issues of 2016 election interference—was that in late 2015 Vice President Joe Biden had pressured the Ukrainian government to fire its chief anticorruption prosecutor to prevent him from investigating Burisma, a large Ukrainian oil and gas company at which Biden's son Hunter served as a director.

On August 26 the ICIG forwarded the whistle-blower complaint to his boss, acting Director of National Intelligence (DNI) Admiral Joseph Maguire, claiming that the President's pressure on the

Ukrainians might amount to the solicitation of an illegal campaign contribution. The ICIG also asserted that these allegations about the President were an "urgent concern" that, under applicable law, the DNI had only seven days to review before the law required him to send the material to the congressional intelligence committees. The admiral immediately referred the ICIG's submission to the Justice Department for our evaluation and advice.

Maguire's referral in late August did not catch the department by complete surprise. In mid-August, a senior official in the department's National Security Division had received a vague report from a lawyer in another agency that someone connected with the intelligence community was complaining that the President had engaged in misconduct on a call with Zelensky. This was the first I had heard about the call or any potential problem with it. Because we had no specifics about the substance of the phone conversation or the nature of the alleged impropriety, DOJ lawyers went over to the White House to review a summary transcript, which was the official record of the call.

Shortly after being briefed on the matter—and told that my name had been mentioned during the call—I went to review the transcript myself in Pat Cipollone's White House office. I thought parts of the President's conversation were unseemly and injudicious. But I did not think the transcript showed a criminal offense. I agreed with Cipollone that the best course was to have the President publicly release the transcript as soon as possible.

Still, reading the transcript angered me. What bothered me wasn't just the harebrained gambit of pressing the Ukrainians to investigate Biden, but also that the President, in his usual imprecise and disjointed way, had carelessly lumped me together with his private lawyer, Rudy Giuliani. By doing that, he had created the false impression that I was involved in efforts to get the Ukrainians to open investigations. Nothing could have been further from the truth, but I realized I would have my hands full straightening out the record with a hostile and suspicious press.

More than a month after the call, late in the afternoon on September 19, as hazy news about a whistle-blower began to emerge publicly, I, along with Cipollone, went to visit the President in the Oval Office. Our purpose was to prevail upon him to quickly declassify and release the transcript and also the whistle-blower's complaint. I was still mad at the President's loose talk during the call, but my purpose in going to see him that day was not to criticize but to help deal with the gathering storm. So far the advice Cipollone and I were giving to declassify and release the transcript and complaint was being ignored. These would eventually come out anyway, we argued, and releasing them quickly would help the White House get in front of the controversy and prevent Democrats in Congress and the press from spinning wild theories about what the President said. Time was running out.

As the three of us sat down in front of the Resolute desk, the chorus continued to sing "Waltzing Matilda" in the Rose Garden outside.

"Waltzing Matilda, Waltzing Matilda / You'll come a-waltzing, Matilda, with me."

"Mr. President," I started, "I think you need to get the Zelensky transcript out as soon as possible."

With that, President Trump reached out across his desk and pulled a copy toward him. "This whole thing is ridiculous," he said. "I went over the transcript, and there was nothing wrong with the conversation. It was perfect. A perfect conversation! Look at the transcript!"

"That is exactly the point, Mr. President," I said, "but as long as the content of the conversation is kept secret, people are free to characterize it any way they please, and everyone will think it's being kept secret to hide something."

He resisted. "We just can't make a President's conversations with a foreign leader public," the President said. He argued that other foreign leaders wouldn't speak their minds with him on the phone if they thought the conversation would be made public. That would affect other presidents, too. He was right about that.

"But," I said, "we can deal with that by asking Zelensky's permission to release the transcript. To be frank, Mr. President, on the current course, if we don't release this transcript, I believe you will be impeached."

President Trump was a little taken aback by my emphatic predication. "You think so?" he asked. "I really don't get it—the conversation was perfect!"

"Up jumped the swagman and sprang into the billabong / 'You'll never catch me alive,' said he."

"Mr. President," I responded, "they had a lot riding on Mueller, and they're angry it didn't pan out. I think they are going to move very fast on this—a blitzkrieg. Unless and until you get the transcript out, you won't be able to defend yourself, and people will continue to assume the worst." Cipollone and Rabbitt agreed strongly.

The President shook his head in disgust. "This is crazy. The conversation was perfect."

"Up jumped the swagman and sprang into the billabong / 'You'll never catch me alive,' said he."

"Mr. President," I said, "I remember a story you told me about a friend of yours who was sued for harassing a woman, and he produced a videotape from a surveillance camera showing he wasn't near her and couldn't possibly have done it. He got the suit thrown out." The President smiled and looked up. He remembered the story. "Well, *the transcript is your videotape*," I said. "It's *not* perfect, but it's good enough. It will show people what you really said. You need to get it out, and right away."

He paused and then looked silently at each of us. "I'll think about it," he said at last. The President seemed distracted, focused on other business, and unable to grasp the gravity of the situation. We rose to our feet, and President Trump's attention snapped back to the next day's Australian state visit. He gestured to the French doors. "Go out through the Rose Garden. Melania is out there—she's putting on the finishing touches for the dinner. It's going to be so nice."

I arrived at the White House early the next morning to participate in the arrival ceremony for the Australian delegation. As my chief of staff and I stood on the South Lawn with other senior administration officials, Rudy Giuliani suddenly appeared out of the crowd. Catching my eye, he walked directly toward me. I was reluctant to speak with him or be seen together, but I had nowhere to go. I shook his out-stretched hand. "Good morning, Mr. Mayor, it's good to see you," I lied. Scores of cell phones popped up over the crowd to take photos of us shaking hands. *Terrific*, I thought to myself.

After the Australian state dinner that night—which was a tour de force—the President and much of his senior staff flew up to New York for the United Nations General Assembly meeting. Cipollone and other White House officials continued to press for the transcript's release, but the President had not made a final decision. While they were away in New York, the crisis worsened, with Democrats and the media speculating breathlessly about what, exactly, the President had said and done. I continued making calls, including to Secretaries Pompeo and Mnuchin, who were with the President, arguing for prompt release of the transcript. Once they understood my position, they joined me in urging its release, but it was not until September 24 that the President finally agreed. That delay gave Speaker of the House Nancy Pelosi all the time she needed, and she authorized the impeachment inquiry the same day.

The Democrats had a new line of attack on the President, and off they went. In one sense, the call with Zelensky didn't matter. If it weren't that, it would have been something else. For the Democrats, the call was the nearest club with which to beat on Donald Trump. Even so, we—and the country—would have to deal with that phone call for the next several months.

In retrospect, earlier release of the transcript would probably not have changed the result. At the time, I was not aware of the extent to which Giuliani and others had been actively pressing the Ukrainians to launch investigations. As the case for impeachment took shape, it came to rely more on those activities rather than the President's call with Zelensky. But there is no question that the push for impeachment gained momentum during those early days before the actual content of the President's conversation was known publicly. The vacuum of infor-mation aided that momentum. Yet the transcript did end up helping the President: it was nothing close to the smoking gun of a quid pro quo, as the President's opponents had hoped for, and the President's ability to keep the focus on the transcript helped him blunt the attacks against him.

President Trump's impeachment was a self-inflicted wound. Much of the blame for getting the President impeached, in my view, must be laid at the feet of Rudy Giuliani. The idea that the President's allies could debunk the collusion narrative by digging up evidence hidden in Ukraine—or that they could get the media to report on the Biden family's shameless behavior there—was a fantasy. The idea that goading the Ukrainians into investigating Hunter Biden would help the President's reelection bid was idiotic beyond belief. The whole scheme was bound to backfire. And Giuliani's public grandstanding, and the unsavory figures he got involved with, ended up seriously undermining his credibility—not to mention tainting the President.

Rudy Giuliani saved New York City after 9/11 and should go down as probably the most consequential mayor of a big city in American history. But he will also go down as the man who helped President Trump get himself impeached—not once but, as it turned out, twice.

Predictably, when the transcript was released on September 25, the President's reference to me caused an avalanche of questions from the press about whether I or the department had been involved in pressing the Ukrainians to open investigations. Fortunately, the answer was an emphatic no. From the beginning of my tenure, I'd worried that Giuliani was an unguided missile, and Ukraine, a morass of misinformation. I was determined to steer the department clear of them as best I could and, if we had to deal with them at all, do so with the utmost caution.

As I was launching John Durham's investigation in the spring of 2019, I was aware of the claims that the Ukrainians had interfered in the 2016 election on behalf of Clinton. Because these allegations were relevant to the origins of the Russia collusion narrative, they legitimately fell within the ambit of Durham's inquiry. I put little stock in them and suggested to Durham that he defer any Ukraine-related work, and so these claims weren't being pursued actively at that point. I was dubious of the idea that the Ukrainians, not the Russians, had been responsible for hacking into the DNC. It had the hallmarks of Russian disinformation and seemed contrary to the evidence developed by the intelligence community and by Mueller's investigation. Moreover, contrary to the President's claims, CrowdStrike did not appear to be controlled by Ukrainians and seemed to be a reputable company. I doubted the firm had any reason to fabricate its analysis of the hack. In any event, I wanted Durham to hold back from engaging with Ukraine because I considered it a land of smoke and mirrors, where disinformation was everywhere and reliable evidence extremely difficult to find. There were so many different actors with varying agendas—pro-Western politicians, pro-Russian politicians, countless oligarchs, each with his own aim—that it was hard to determine the provenance and motivations behind any information collected there. Conjuring up criminal conspiracies about political opponents had been honed into a fine art form. I was especially concerned that Ukrainian actors could act as channels for Russian disinformation. I didn't want Durham to get bogged down in that morass.

Consequently, in the spring and early summer of 2019, when John and I discussed the international dimensions of his work, we agreed to engage with the three countries we felt would be most helpful to the investigation: the United Kingdom, Australia, and Italy. I started by making contact with the ambassadors of these countries, and later had discussions with senior officials in each. I traveled to both Italy and the UK to explain Durham's investigation and ask for any assistance or information they could provide. I alerted the President that we would be making these contacts and asked him to mention Durham's investigation to the prime ministers of the three countries, stressing the importance of their help. In contrast, I never talked with the Ukrainians or asked President Trump to talk to the Ukrainians. The President never asked me to talk to the Ukrainians. Nor had I talked with Rudy Giuliani about Ukraine. I was also not aware of anyone at the department requesting the Ukrainians to open up an investigation. As far as I was concerned, if Durham ever found a reason to look into Ukrainian activities, he would do the investigation, not leave it to the Ukrainians.

What really fueled the impeachment drive was the attempt to sic the Ukrainians on allegations about Vice President Biden. It was one thing to argue, as the President's private defense attorneys did, that Ukrainians had interfered with the 2016 election. That would have had a bearing on collusion allegations against the President. It was something else to argue, as the President's defense also did, that Joe Biden's son Hunter had traded on his surname and engaged in unethical deal making in Ukraine. That looked less like defensive work and more like an offensive thrust against President Trump's likely opponent in the 2020 election. Moreover, although the Department of Justice was investigating election interference, DOJ was not investigating Joe Biden, and I didn't think there was a legitimate basis to do so. The conflict-of-interest laws do not apply to the President or Vice President.

The key facts regarding Biden's role in the ouster of the Ukrainian anticorruption prosecutor were largely a matter of public record. In 2014 the Vice President's son Hunter, with virtually no relevant experience, had received a lucrative position on the board of Burisma at a time when the Vice President had the "lead" in the Obama administration's push to get Ukraine to step up anticorruption efforts. In late 2015 Vice President Biden, by his own account, used the threat of withholding loan guarantees to pressure the Ukrainian government to fire Viktor Shokin, the lead Ukrainian anticorruption prosecutor. The public record is fairly clear that there was frustration in US and European policy circles with Shokin's failure to pursue corruption cases aggressively, and his removal was widely favored by key US figures. It also appears he was not actively pursuing Burisma at the time of his dismissal, although he claimed later that he was planning to investigate the company. In my view, while the whole situation was shameful and unethical, the facts did not provide a basis for criminally investigating Vice President Biden.

By the spring of 2019, I had noticed news stories stating that Giuliani was pushing the Ukrainians to investigate Biden's role in Shokin's dismissal. But other than what I glimpsed in the media, I had no knowledge of the former mayor's activities. During the spring, I expressed my concern about Giuliani with the President. As I was leaving an Oval Office meeting on another topic, I paused briefly to raise the matter.

"Mr. President," I said, "I don't think you are being well served by Giuliani at this point. Mueller is over, and Russiagate is dying. Why is Giuliani thrashing about in Ukraine? It is going to blow up—"

"Yeah," the President said, cutting me off. "I told him not to go over there. It was a trap." President Trump gave the impression Giuliani had a degree of independence and was going to pull back. I did not press the point.

Unfortunately, the President's careless statement to Zelensky erroneously implied some connection between me and Giuliani. Early in the conversation, the President asked Zelensky to "get to the bottom" of CrowdStrike and the server allegations, and said he was going to have the Attorney General talk to him about this. If the President had stopped there, I wouldn't have been especially upset, because at least these particular allegations were within Durham's purview, albeit on the back burner. However, later in the conversation, the President asked Zelensky to investigate Biden's role in Shokin's removal and said he should work with the Attorney General and Giuliani. When I read this, I hit the ceiling. When the transcript was released, I had the department put out a categorical statement:

> The President has not spoken with the Attorney General about having Ukraine investigate anything relating to former Vice President Biden or his son. The President has not asked the Attorney General to contact Ukraine—on this or any other matter. The Attorney General has not communicated with Ukraine—on this or any other subject. Nor has the Attorney General discussed this matter, or anything relating to Ukraine, with Rudy Giuliani.

Although this seemed to be largely accepted by journalists covering the department, some commentators still speculated that the President might have been pressing me to have the DOJ investigate Biden's role.

This didn't happen. The President had not asked that the Justice

Department investigate the former Vice President, and it would not have made a difference if he had. As far as I was concerned, the facts about this episode were out in the open and didn't warrant a criminal investigation. Although Hunter Biden's position was obviously a sordid instance of monetizing his father's office, the Vice President did not violate the law because federal conflict-of-interest laws do not apply to Vice Presidents. Moreover, given the evidence that Biden was acting in line with US policy, and the absence of good evidence that Shokin was actively pursuing Burisma and that his removal would inhibit future action against the company, it would be impossible to prove that the Vice President acted with corrupt intent in pressing the Ukrainians to dismiss Shokin. And if there ever were a reason to pursue the matter, we would do it ourselves and certainly not pressure the Ukrainians to do it.

At the same time the transcript was released on September 25, the department also reported publicly on how we had handled the whistle-blower's complaint and the Inspector General of the Intelligence Community's submission after they were referred to us a month earlier by the director of national intelligence. We had to address two issues: one procedural, one substantive. Procedurally, the DNI had asked for the DOJ's opinion on whether the matter qualified as an "urgent concern" under the applicable statutes and thus whether the expedited review procedures had been triggered, as the ICIG was asserting. Substantively, once the DNI referred the ICIG's claim that the President had potentially violated campaign finance laws, we were also required to evaluate that matter. As was normal practice, these matters were handled by the Deputy Attorney General and other senior department officials. I left for an extended Labor Day vacation.

The department answered the DNI's procedural question, in the normal course, by obtaining the opinion of the Office of Legal Counsel, which is the entity that authoritatively interprets statutes within the executive branch. On September 3 OLC advised the DNI that the whistle-blower's complaint did not qualify as an "urgent concern" and was not subject to expedited reporting procedures. Under the relevant statute, an urgent concern includes "[a] serious or flagrant problem, abuse, [or] violation of law . . . relating to the funding, administration, or operation of an intelligence activity within the responsibility and authority of the director of national intelligence involving classified information." OLC concluded that the complaint about the President's diplomatic communication did not qualify as an urgent concern because the alleged misconduct did not arise in connection with "the funding, administration, or operation of an intelligence activity within the responsibility" of the DNI. While I did not participate in this decision, I think OLC's opinion was obviously correct.

Nonetheless, the OLC opinion was hysterically characterized in the media as an attempt by the department to block the intelligence oversight committees from obtaining information about the complaint. Commentators leveling this criticism didn't know what they were talking about. The only question was whether the information was subject to the fixed statutory requirement for reporting within seven days of receipt by the DNI. The fact that a matter does not qualify for expedited reporting does not mean it won't otherwise be reported to the committee in a timely manner. The executive branch has a legitimate interest in having sufficient time to assess incidents before reporting to Congress. When a matter isn't deemed an urgent concern, the timing and manner of reporting are generally worked out between the committees and the White House, as was being done here. DOJ wasn't taking a position on whether, when, or how the complaint should be shared with Congress—just that it didn't have to be done within seven days.

The department's evaluation of the ICIG's claim of a potential campaign finance violation was also done by the book. The department's *Justice Manual* provides that allegations of certain campaign finance violations must be reviewed initially by experts in the Criminal Division's Public Integrity Section before a formal investigation can be opened and further action taken by the FBI. This threshold procedural requirement makes sense, given the highly specialized field of campaign finance law and the tendency of some politicians to weaponize the campaign finance laws against their opponents. Accordingly, the Deputy Attorney General sent the ICIG's complaint down to the

Criminal Division for this review. After confirming that the summary transcript was the best evidence of the actual conversation, the division determined that the July 25 call did not amount to a campaign finance violation. This judgment was made initially by the senior-most career election law prosecutor in the Public Integrity Section and was agreed on by his supervisors up the chain within the division.

While I was not involved in that decision, it was clearly right, in my view. The whole purpose of the campaign finance laws is to place limits on the resources available to campaigns to expend on campaign activity. Something is a contribution if it involves conveying a "thing of value," in the sense that it augments the resources a campaign has available to expend on campaigning. Thus, a thing of value must be a thing that otherwise is purchasable or exchangeable in the market for some ascertainable value. The official act of a foreign government—here starting an investigation—is not a thing of value, in that sense. The mere fact the action is politically beneficial to an American candidate does not make it a thing of value within the meaning of the statute.

As the department was preparing to issue a statement that the Criminal Division had found no campaign finance violation, the President called me. He wanted me to make sure I'd be making clear the DOJ's conclusions on the campaign finance allegations. "We will get our conclusion out, Mr. President," I responded. "We're going to do it in the way we would ordinarily do it for something like this. So I'll figure out the best way." President Trump seemed to accept this and got off the phone.

I directed Kerri Kupec to put out a statement saying that the Criminal Division had reviewed the referral under established procedures and found no campaign finance violation. I was not going to hold a press conference. For one thing, it would have been odd to do so for a statement of this sort and would make it look like I was shilling for the President, which, among other things, would undercut the credibility of the Criminal Division's determination. Also, in a press conference, it might become apparent that the only matter being concluded was the ICIG's referral of a potential campaign violation. We still planned to assess other potential issues that could emerge as the impeachment proceedings unfolded.

Some critics argued that the department should not have limited its decision just to the President's call with Zelensky and the theory that it involved a campaign finance violation. They contend the DOJ should have launched a broader criminal investigation into all the activities potentially involved in pressuring the Ukrainians and should have considered also whether other criminal offenses occurred, such as bribery. This criticism has no validity. Initially, the department had to address the matter specifically raised and referred by the ICIG: whether the phone conversation amounted to a campaign finance violation. That decision did not rule out further assessment of other circumstances as the facts developed. The question was how and when that assessment would be done. At the time the transcript was released, an interbranch political dispute was well under way. The House of Representatives had embarked on the path of impeachment and was starting its own investigation of the relevant circumstances in an effort to impose a constitutional check on a coordinate branch of government. Realistically, we could not start a parallel and competing criminal investigation without disrupting and delaying the impeachment inquiry. And that is precisely what we would have been accused of if we had attempted to do so. The leadership of the department, including the FBI, agreed with me that the appropriate posture for Justice was to continue assessing the matter by monitoring the impeachment proceedings, collecting the facts as they developed during that inquiry, gathering publicly available information, and refraining from taking overt investigative steps for the time being. After the political process was complete and the impeachment proceedings were over, we would assess whether there was anything further to be done by the department.

This approach was plainly right under the unique circumstances we faced. Impeachment inquiries normally would come after criminal investigations. But here the House leadership made the deliberate decision to rush out ahead of the department. It was intent on moving with lightning speed and completing the process around the end of the year. Unquestionably, any attempt to run a parallel criminal investigation, relying on the same witnesses and materials, would have hindered the House's effort and been seen as such. The deeper the impeachment process ran into 2020—the election year—the weaker the case for going through with the process of impeachment, rather than letting the electorate decide. If we interfered with the House's process, we plainly would have been accused of trying to delay the House.

Indeed, House Democrats clearly didn't want the department to reach a conclusion first. From the House leadership's perspective, that is what happened with the Mueller report. Once the department said there had been no obstruction, it became difficult to muster support for impeachment. Advocates of impeachment didn't want that to happen again. From the DOJ's standpoint, there were no factors militating for immediate investigation with overt steps. There was neither a statute of limitation issue nor a risk that evidence would become unavailable. Moreover, we were entering an election year. Under the department's general policy against interfering in an election, any visible investigation of a candidate—here the President—had to be justified by a compelling reason to proceed. The prudent course was to await the outcome of impeachment, while reassessing periodically as circumstances evolved.

The department itself had no role to play in the impeachment proceedings themselves or on advising on them. The President assembled his own team of lawyers to mount his defense. Early on, he asked me about the people he was considering, and I told him I thought they would do an excellent job. I did not consult with the President or his team about the substance of the case.

In January, as the impeachment process headed toward conclusion, Deputy Attorney General Rosen issued a memo to all US attorneys' offices designating Richard Donoghue, the US attorney in the Eastern District of New York, to coordinate Ukraine-related cases. This was done not just for efficiency but also to protect the department from manipulation by foreign interests. As we headed into an election year, we had good reason to worry that Ukraine—a hotbed of political intrigue and conspiracy theories—posed a special concern. It was a channel through which all sides could inject disinformation into our

My parents, Donald and Mary, shown here in 1944, met during World War II. She was teaching English literature at the University of Missouri. My father had been sent there by the army to learn Italian. They married after the war.

The spring of 1959, on the stoop of our apartment building at 445 Riverside Drive in New York City. The boys, from left to right, are Christopher, me, Stephen (in front of me), and Hilary.

Competing in a solo bagpipe contest in 1963 at the Highland Games in New York State. I did fairly well in these events, but stopped participating in competitions after my teacher, Pipe Major John C. MacKenzie, died in 1967 and I started college.

On the Columbia College campus in April 1968 were some Majority Coalition members—students opposed to the occupation of campus buildings by radical protestors. I am to the left of center in a dark windbreaker with my hand up to my chest. We set up a cordon blocking access to the main occupied building and, after protesters tried to break through, a melee ensued, forcing the university to have the police clear the buildings.

I married Christine in June 1973 in the chapel at her college, Mount. St. Vincent. I had just turned twenty-three and Chris was twenty-one. (Unfortunately, sideburns were "in" at the time—one of my rare concessions to a fad.) She has stood by me through thick and thin, living on promises.

In August 1983, I visited President Reagan and Counselor to the President Ed Meese in the Oval Office while serving a stint on the President's Domestic Policy Staff. Watching Reagan taught me much about leadership, and working with Meese much about conservative ideas. Less than two years later, Meese would become the 75th Attorney General, and six years after that I would become the 77th Attorney General.

A typical scene at the Department in 1989, when I was head of Office of Legal Counsel. My deputy Mike Luttig, Attorney General Dick Thornburgh, and I patrol the halls.

Operation Just Cause represented the first time a foreign head of state was captured abroad and taken to the US for trial. Here Panamanian dictator Manuel Noriega is arrested on January 3, 1990, and placed by DEA agents and US Marshals on an Air Force C-130 at Howard AFB in Panama for a flight to Miami to face drug trafficking charges.

In August of 1991, I directed the FBI's Hostage Rescue Team to rescue 9 DOJ employees being held hostage inside our prison in Talladega, Alabama, by 120 Mariel Cuban prisoners who had sworn to kill them if we attempted a rescue. After the successful operation, I posed with the HRT. Deputy FBI Director Floyd Clarke is in a suit on the far left, and the head of FBI's Criminal Division, Bill Baker, is second from the right in the second row.

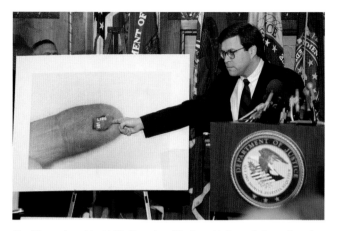

On December 21, 1988, Pan Am Flight 103 bound from London to New York exploded over Lockerbie, Scotland, killing 270 people, including 190 Americans. Here, on November 14, 1991, after a massive investigation, I announced charges against two members of Libyan intelligence. I am pointing to evidence that helped crack the case—a tiny shard of a circuit board amazingly found by the Scots while scouring 849 square miles of the debris field.

On March 26, 1992, I briefed the President on the violent-crime problem in American cities and our initiatives to help the states and local governments deal with it, including Project Triggerlock, cracking down on firearms crimes.

President Bush convened a 5 a.m. meeting on May 1, 1992, to decide how to help end the LA rioting that erupted after a jury acquitted police who had beaten Rodney King. I got the go-ahead on my plan to deploy more than two thousand federal agents, but the President later had to send in regular troops. (*From left to right*: Edie Holliday, cabinet secretary; FBI Director Bill Sessions; me; the Vice President; the President; Don Atwood, Deputy Secretary of Defense; General Colin Powell, Chairman of the Joint Chiefs; and Boyden Gray, counsel to the President.)

My senior team as Attorney General, *from right to left*: Deputy AG George Terwiliger, Associate AG Wayne Budd, and Solicitor General Ken Starr. There has never been a stronger team at DOJ, although I was able to assemble its equal almost thirty years later.

My confirmation hearing was held on January 15, 2019. I was a little rusty but held my own against the aggressive Democrats. Trump thought I was too conciliatory. Behind me are my wife, Christine, my three daughters (Meg, Patricia, and Mary); their husbands; and my oldest grandchild, Liam. To the left on the front row are, *from right to left*: Mike Munn, head of my security detail; Brian Rabbitt, my chief of staff; and Stephen Boyd, head of Legislative Affairs at DOJ.

On February 14, 2019, after I was sworn in as the 85th Attorney General by Chief Justice Roberts in the Oval Office, we posed with the President, my wife, and Judiciary Committee Chairman Senator Lindsey Graham. I couldn't have asked for a better chairman to work with.

On April 18, 2019, I held a news conference to release the Mueller Report, with minimal redactions. The Report found no collusion with Russia. Later evidence continues to show the collusion narrative was phony. On the right is Deputy AG Rod Rosenstein, and on the left is the Principal Associate Deputy, Ed O'Callaghan.

In mid-May 2019, I made a trip to El Salvador to confer with attorneys general from the region to step up efforts against the violent MS-13 and 18th Street gangs operating in Central America and the US. When I visited this prison, gang members sat and turned their backs to show noncooperation. But this 18th Street gang member, who grew up in Los Angeles, was willing to talk with me.

After the Supreme Court barred the Commerce Department from asking a citizenship question on the census, the President held a press conference in the Rose Garden on July 11, 2019, where I explained that we had run out of time to take the fight further.

Blowing out the candle at my sixty-ninth birthday party in the AG's Conference Room. I'd only been AG three months but now felt much older. Looking on, *from left to right:* Kerri Kupec, head of public affairs; the incomparable Theresa Watson, my assistant; James Burnham from Civil Division; and Brian Rabbitt, my chief of staff.

During a visit to the Cherokee Nation in Oklahoma in September 2020, we got a chance to see their buffalo herd. The Cherokee are a wonderful people, and when they learned my staff had nicknamed me the "Buffalo," they insisted I see their herd. *From right to left:* my chief of staff, Will Levi; head of public affairs, Kerri Kupec; me; counselor, Gregg Sofer; and deputy chief of staff, Rachel Bissex.

Chatting with Jeff Rosen and his wife, Kathleen, just after swearing him in as Deputy Attorney General. Looking on are my chief of staff, Brian Rabbitt, and Jeff's chief of staff, Pat Hovakimian. I am not sure why Jeff is smiling.

Chatting at a reception in the AG's conference room with three outstanding lawyers who made my life easier—Solicitor General Noel Francisco *(foreground)*; Assistant AG for OLC Steve Engel *(left)*; and Deputy Solicitor General Jeff Wall, who replaced Noel when he returned to private practice.

In January 2020 I visited the New York Jewish community in Brooklyn to discuss the disturbing rise in hate crimes against Orthodox Jews. Last time as AG, the Orthodox group Agudath Israel named me humanitarian of the year for my vigilance against anti-Semitism. To my left is Richard Donoghue, then U.S. Attorney in Brooklyn. Richard later agreed to come down to Washington to help in the last months of the administration and was indispensable. (To Richard's left is my old friend from my last go-round, Rabbi Zwiebel from Agudath Israel.)

In June 2019, I visited Alaska for three days to see the challenges Alaska Natives face dealing with violent crime in remote villages. Here I join Alaska's senator Lisa Murkowski at the police station in the village of Napaskiak.

On June 11, 2020, in the wake of civil unrest following the killing of George Floyd, I accompanied the President to a church in Dallas, Texas, to discuss race and violence with community leaders. Here talking on Air Force One are Will Levi, my chief of staff, who commandeered the head of the table, and Surgeon General Dr. Jerome Adams.

On December 5, 2019, I met with Mexican president Andrés Manuel López Obrador to discuss stepping up our joint efforts against the drug cartels. While cooperation improved for a while, Covid thwarted our plans.

On September 9, 2019, I joined the President in the East Room, honoring first responders in the mass shootings in El Paso, Texas, and Dayton, Ohio. The Medal of Valor was awarded to six Dayton police officers, and five civilians were given certificates of commendation in connection with the El Paso shootings.

My wife, Christine, and I arrive for the Australian State Dinner in the Rose Garden on September 20, 2019. The First Lady had arranged a memorable evening. We had an enjoyable night sitting with Senator Joe Manchin and his wife, Gayle, and my old colleague Boyden Gray.

On September 9, 2019, President Trump and I walk into the East Room to give awards to heroic police and civilian first responders in the El Paso and Dayton mass shootings that occurred the month before. In our first year together, when I was dealing with the phony Russiagate scandal, we got along very well. In the second year, he became frustrated that more progress wasn't being made investigating the origins of Russiagate.

system. This could be done by feeding spurious "evidence" of supposed criminality to US law enforcement authorities. This vulnerability was compounded in a Justice Department in which any one of ninety-three US attorneys' offices around the country can initiate an investigation based on information it receives. In addition to ensuring information sharing and avoiding conflicts, we wanted to ensure that Ukrainian actors couldn't instigate cases willy-nilly in different jurisdictions around the country. For this reason, we selected one office to take the lead and also serve as a "traffic cop," coordinating existing and any new cases. Rich Donoghue was chosen for this role because he already had related matters pending in his Brooklyn office and was one of the most experienced and respected US attorneys in the department.

With impeachment still pending, Giuliani embarked on yet another round of grandstanding. He went about claiming he had compiled significant evidence relating to the Bidens that he wanted to present to the Justice Department. While anyone is free to present evidence to the DOJ, the fact Giuliani was making such a public display obviously made his motives suspect. It looked to me that Rudy was trying to run the same play against Biden that I thought the Clinton campaign had tried to run against Trump in 2016: giving just enough evidence to law enforcement to have some allegation investigated, then claiming one's adversary was "being investigated." This presented a quandary. On the one hand, I wasn't going to let the department be drawn into Giuliani's game, and I wasn't about to allow the work of other prosecutors on other, potentially related matters be tainted by commingling their evidence with whatever Giuliani had pulled together. On the other hand, the department has an obligation to be open to all comers who believe they possess relevant evidence; we could not merely dismiss his information out of hand without looking at it. Yet merely receiving information does not imply the department believes opening an investigation is warranted. My solution to Giuliani's posturing was to create an intake system for evidence originating in Ukraine—including but not limited to Giuliani's—that dispelled any suggestion that, by accepting the information, the department was signaling it considered the allegations credible.

I set up a screening process whereby an office outside of Washington—in this case, the US Attorney's Office in Pittsburgh—would vet the information provided by Giuliani, working with the FBI and intelligence experts on Ukraine. That office, which was run by a trusted US attorney, Scott Brady, who was well known to me and my staff, would not be responsible for deciding whether to open any investigation, just for assessing the credibility of the information. This would be an intermediary step before any information was forwarded to an office responsible for making any investigative determinations. Employing such a "taint team" is a well-established procedure within the department for screening potentially suspect evidence. These precautions were especially apt in the case of Giuliani, whose political passions and previous associations in Ukraine possibly affected his own critical faculties.

At an unrelated press conference in early February 2020, I made clear I was skeptical of information coming out of Ukraine. "We have to be very careful with respect to any information coming from the Ukraine," I said. "There are a lot of agendas in the Ukraine, a lot of crosscurrents. And we can't take anything we received from Ukraine at face value." My usual critics on the Hill and in the media, as always getting the point exactly backward, screamed that I was giving Giuliani special access to the department. Wrong. It was an exercise in caution and an effort to protect other investigations that the DOJ had going on at the time.

While the effort to push the Ukrainians to investigate Biden was foolish, I do not believe it was criminal. Not all censurable conduct is criminal. The current tendency to conflate the foolish with the legally culpable causes more harm than good. Trying to apply the criminal law to diplomatic give-and-take is especially dangerous. A quid pro quo is inherent in almost all diplomacy, and Presidents frequently ask foreign countries to do things that are politically beneficial to the Presidents. A President might, for example, make a large, secret concession to a foreign country in order to expedite release of a hostage or win some other timely agreement the President expects will yield substantial political benefits prior to an election. The fact that the action sought from the foreign government will yield political benefit should not make the request criminal. It may have been in the national interest. Nor should it be criminal because the concession made by a President seems disproportionate or even reckless. Nor should it make a difference that the President was subjectively motivated by the expectation of political benefit.

The fact is that diplomatic transactions frequently involve "mixed motives." The quo being sought will provide a political benefit *and* will likely satisfy a legitimate policy purpose of the government. In any particular case, the political motive may loom much larger than the governmental purpose, but as long as the latter is present, it would be hazardous to criminalize diplomacy by attempting to assess the balance of subjective motivations. Of course, if the quo being sought objectively has no governmental purpose at all and is purely a private benefit—say, a payment of cash for private use—then we are in the realm of bribery. But so long as the quo arguably advances a public policy objective, then policing the propriety of diplomatic transactions should be left to the political, not the criminal, realm.

To this extent, I viewed Vice President Biden's pushing for Shokin's termination as similar to President Trump's pushing for an investigation of Biden's role. The quo sought by Biden—the firing of Shokin—held a potential political benefit for Biden: avoiding the embarrassment of having his son's company investigated for corruption. It also, ostensibly, had a legitimate public policy purpose: advancing the US anticorruption agenda. Similarly, Trump would benefit politically from an investigation into Shokin's termination, but bringing transparency to that episode would also arguably advance America's anticorruption agenda.

Biden supporters would say that, in his case, his policy purpose was overarching and supervened any possible political agenda. Trump supporters would say the same about *his* aims. My point is that the criminal justice process cannot legitimately be used to investigate politicians' motivations when those politicians are asking for some rational and lawful policy concession. What Biden was demanding in Ukraine, quite apart from whether it would benefit his son, technically had a legitimate governmental purpose. And what Trump was demanding, quite apart from whether it would benefit his reelection, had the same.

Although I had not heard about the President's call with Zelensky until mid-August, I did get an enigmatic call at the beginning of August on my secure line from John Bolton, the White House national security adviser. He started off by asking me whether I knew anything about Giuliani's Ukraine machinations. I told him I did not; I had never talked to Giuliani about Ukraine, had no visibility into what he was doing, and wasn't sure what capacity he was acting in. Bolton seemed relieved, but said he was concerned there could be confusion about the respective roles of the department and Giuliani. I said there was no confusion at DOJ: Giuliani had nothing to do with us, and John Durham's investigation was insulated from whatever Giuliani was doing. Bolton then said he was going to make sure the Ukrainians understood only one person spoke for the administration on legal matters, and that was me. I told him I appreciated that. In retrospect, it is now clear to me that his call was prompted by the President's careless comments during his call with Zelensky. But Bolton did not tell me about the Zelensky call. When I hung up with him, I shared a quizzical look with Brian Rabbitt, who was with me for the call. "What was behind that?" I wondered aloud.

At the end of August, Bolton visited Ukraine and, after returning, pulled me aside at a National Security Council meeting to tell me he had told the Ukrainians that the only lawyer who speaks for the United States government is the Attorney General. As more information came out in the months ahead, I realized that Bolton had an inkling what Giuliani was up to in Ukraine and was doing his best to insulate the department and other parts of the administration from his activities. But I was wary of Giuliani's activities from the outset, and I knew enough to keep myself and the Justice Department away from his Ukraine capers.

In December, during the run-up to impeachment, IG Horowitz finalized his long-awaited final report on the FBI's Crossfire Hurricane investigation and was preparing to make it public. I went over to the

White House residence to brief the President about its contents before it was issued. I met with President Trump, joined by Pat Cipollone, in the Yellow Oval Room. I was accompanied by my counselor, Will Levi, who, like me, had reviewed the report thoroughly and was familiar with all the details. Even though the House was just about to unveil impeachment charges against him, the President was in a remarkably good mood. It was clear he viewed Horowitz's report as a vindication. It was the first time he had met Will, and he was gracious and chatty with him, intrigued by the fact that Will's grandfather had been Attorney General under President Gerald Ford.

We then got down to the details of Horowitz's conclusions, and he wanted to know how "strong" the IG's findings were. I said that, in reality, they were quite strong, but that the media were sure to downplay them. Horowitz made clear that some of the FBI's actions were hard to explain, although he did not uncover direct evidence that bias affected the FBI's decision. The media would portray this falsely as Horowitz affirmatively finding that bias did not affect the FBI's work. But that was not what he was saying. He was not reaching a conclusion one way or the other as to whether the FBI officials acted in good faith. He was simply saying he had no direct evidence on the question. The issue of motivations was now a question for Durham's investigation to explore.

The President was unusually relaxed and talkative and did not seem to want to conclude the meeting. When he saw me leaning forward as if preparing to stand, he said, "Well, I better let you get back to work." Then, studying me, with a twinkle in his eye, he added, "I am going to go and tweet about this."

I glanced up with a look of discomfort. He smiled playfully. "Do you know what the secret is of a really good tweet?" he asked, looking at each of us one by one. We all looked blank. "Just the right amount of crazy," he said.

"Oh, great," I said as I stood up.

The tweeting was always a problem—for nearly everybody in the administration, to one degree or another. Indeed, a single tweet would soon make my job almost impossible.

CHAPTER 13

UPHOLDING FAIRNESS,
EVEN FOR RASCALS

I had always thought there was something strange about the FBI's interview of Michael Flynn at the start of the Trump administration, as well as the charges leveled by Mueller's team against the general for lying to the FBI in that interview. But Flynn had pleaded guilty to those charges, and the Department of Justice ordinarily has a strong interest in keeping guilty pleas from being upset. For that reason, I had planned to let matters play out in the normal course—which meant that I expected Flynn to be sentenced to between zero and six months. I had not discussed the department's handling of the Flynn case with the President or anyone else at the White House.

At the beginning of 2020, however, two developments occurred that required taking a closer look at the charges brought against General Michael Flynn by Mueller's office and the ongoing dispute over Flynn's pending guilty plea.

One of the developments drawing new attention to the Flynn matter was the widening scope of the Durham investigation. Originally, I thought the main focus would be the FBI's activities prior to the 2016 election. But, by the end of 2019, it was clear that the FBI's conduct just after the election potentially raised even more serious questions.

In late December 2016 and January 2017, it appeared that the FBI had doubled down on its counterintelligence investigation of the

Trump campaign—that is, just as Trump was entering office. By then, the collusion narrative was beginning to collapse under the weight of counterevidence, but the bureau's leadership wasn't behaving that way. Instead, it upped the ante by going after Flynn without any apparent basis. Figuring out the FBI's motivations for redoubling its efforts pursuing the discredited collusion narrative required a closer look at its handling of the Flynn affair. Thus, even if Flynn's defense counsel had not challenged the guilty plea, just our own investigative interest in the FBI's actions called for a review of the Flynn case.

The second development requiring an examination of the Flynn case occurred during the fall of 2019 through January 2020, when his new defense counsel, Sidney Powell, filed a raft of motions seeking to withdraw Flynn's guilty plea. The motions claimed prosecutorial misconduct, alleged the withholding of exculpatory evidence by the government, and asserted that the lawyers who advised him to plead guilty to lying to the FBI had a conflict of interest. Flynn's original attorneys, Powell's motions claimed, had advised Flynn, before he returned to government, about his consulting work on behalf of Turkey, which related to the matter that was being dropped as part of the plea.

From early in the Trump administration, Powell, a DOJ alumnus in private practice, had appeared frequently on Fox News shows challenging the Russiagate narrative and the Mueller investigation. Some of her criticisms proved justified, and the President had become a big fan of hers. Before I went into the department, he suggested I consider her for a position there. I took this under advisement but never acted on it. Eventually Powell was to become part of the President's circle of outside informal advisers, and, after the election, she would join Giuliani's team working on alleged election fraud.

Back in the fall, when Flynn hired Sidney Powell as his new lawyer, but before she filed all these motions, she attempted to hand deliver a letter directly to me. The letter, I was told later, previewed the arguments made in her motions. I was down at the FBI Academy, making a speech and visiting the Hostage Rescue Team, when I got word that she had shown up at the Justice Department's visitor center unannounced with a letter for me. I told my chief of staff to make sure the letter was sent right through to the line prosecution team handling the case. I never saw the letter. I did not like the idea of defense lawyers making end runs around the line prosecutors. When I was in private practice, I always kept the line attorneys in the loop whenever I sought to escalate an issue. In any event, her motions raised claims that the department was required to address.

Because these two developments required a new look into the Flynn affair, I thought it sensible to bring in a fresh lawyer to handle the assignment. Durham's team needed additional help to review the matter, and responding to all of Flynn's latest motions also suggested adding a new face, since Flynn's new claims included allegations about the conduct of the lawyers already handling the case. Durham had previously gotten help from the US attorney in Saint Louis, Jeff Jensen, on another aspect of his investigation and was impressed by him, as I had been.

Among other things, Jensen had a great track record as a career employee in the department: ten years as an FBI agent and ten years as a federal prosecutor. He was a thorough, no-nonsense prosecutor. In mid-January I asked him to review the Flynn matter, coordinate with Durham, and advise on responding to Flynn's motions.

While Jensen's review of the Flynn case was under way, on Monday, February 10, 2020, a dispute over the sentencing of Roger Stone was unexpectedly raised with me. The case was prosecuted under me, but otherwise I had no involvement in it, and no interest in getting involved. I had always thought that Stone's indictment and conviction were righteous, and I was content to let matters take their course. I had not discussed the department's handling of the case with the President or anyone else at the White House.

On that Monday, Tim Shea, who had just left my staff to act as interim US attorney for the District of Columbia, had come to my office for an unrelated meeting. Afterward, Tim asked to stay on to discuss a dispute that had just arisen between him and the Stone trial team.

I was surprised to hear that the department's deadline for filing its recommendation on Stone's sentence was that very afternoon. My chief of staff, Brian Rabbitt, was also surprised. Tim explained that the trial team, which included members of Mueller's staff and a lawyer formerly with the Obama White House, was demanding to recommend a sentence of between seven and nine years, which Tim felt was plainly excessive and not in line with the considerations that should guide the department's sentencing recommendations. Tim said the line attorneys were vehement in their demand, and he was worried they were trying to create a political spectacle. He was concerned this was a setup, and they were planning to leak that he overruled them in order to claim "political interference." (And, sure enough, we quickly got word that the *Washington Post* already had the story while the matter was still under discussion in the US Attorney's Office.)

As Tim described the case to me, the sentence of seven to nine years being pushed by the prosecutors was grossly disproportionate and unprecedented. Stone, age sixty-seven, was a first-time, nonviolent offender convicted of obstructing Congress. As Shea informed me, sentences for comparable defendants hovered in the three-year range. Apparently, no one could cite a precedent for a sentence remotely near seven to nine years—more than twice the norm. The prosecutors' proposed range was based on their calculations under the advisory federal sentencing guidelines. In their calculations, the prosecutors applied an "enhancement" for threatening physical injury. This enhancement, typically applied to cases involving violent crime and Mob cases, had the effect of roughly doubling Stone's exposure. In Stone's case, he'd made a late-night call to a witness, a longtime friend, suggesting he was going to fight him and he "should prepare to die," and also saying he would take his friend's dog. The friend wrote the sentencing judge, saying, "I never in any way felt that Stone himself posed a direct physical threat to me or to my dog. I chalked up his bellicose tirades to 'Stone being Stone.' All bark and no bite!" It was questionable whether the enhancement should have been applied to guideline calculations in Stone's case, but even if it applied technically, the resulting calculation did not reflect a fair or reasonable sentence under the circumstances of the case.

I told Shea that I would not allow the department to be bullied by line prosecutors into proposing a sentence that was plainly way out of line. The job of DOJ is to obtain convictions. Determining the right sentence is the judge's responsibility. Some DOJ offices make sentencing recommendations, and others do not. When the Justice Department does make a recommendation, it is required to propose a sentence that meets the statutory requirement of reasonableness—that is, the sentence is "sufficient, but no greater than necessary" to achieve the purposes of justice. Later press reports and comments by former DOJ prosecutors with a partisan axe to grind have asserted that line prosecutors are bound to seek sentences set by the guidelines. This is absolutely false. The guidelines are not dispositive but a factor to be considered, and the department's clear policy is that a guideline sentence should not be recommended unless DOJ believes the sentence satisfies the overarching statutory requirement of reasonableness. As the Supreme Court has noted, a sentencing judge may not presume that a guideline calculation is reasonable; instead, the reasonableness of a sentence must be determined by an individualized assessment of the actual facts in the particular case.

Critics have also claimed that my predecessor, Attorney General Sessions, mandated that prosecutors seek the sentences dictated by the guidelines. This also is absolutely false. AG Sessions issued guidance confirming that line prosecutors should obtain the approval of their supervisors if they plan to depart from the sentencing guidelines. But this approval requirement was meant to provide oversight and in no way relieves prosecutors of their overarching duty to propose sentences that are reasonable as dictated by statute. Indeed, Sessions's memo stated explicitly:

> [P]rosecutors should **in all cases** seek a reasonable sentence under the factors in 18 U.S.C. § 3553. In **most** cases, recommending a sentence within the advisory guideline range will be appropriate. Recommendations for sentencing departures or variances require supervisory approval, and the reasoning must be documented in the file [emphasis added].

The claim that the line prosecutors in this case were constrained to seek the draconian seven-to-nine-year sentence was arrant nonsense.

I told Shea that I did not want the department to affirmatively endorse a sentence so clearly excessive as seven to nine years. I wanted to see Stone sentenced to prison. He deserved it. While he should not be treated any better than others because he was an associate of the President's, he also should not be treated much worse than others. Tim said he thought there could be a solution acceptable to the line prosecutors, whereby, as I understood him, the department's filing would state that the guideline calculations, with the enhancement, resulted in a seven-to-nine-year sentence; point out the relevant considerations in determining whether to apply the enhancement; cite the sentences given in comparable cases; refrain from affirmatively recommending a particular sentence; and leave the sentence to the judge. I and Brian Rabbitt thought this was eminently reasonable, and I instructed Shea to move forward on that basis. Shea said he thought he could accomplish this without a blowup.

That night at home, I saw some news reports saying that the department had filed a recommendation affirmatively seeking a sentence of seven to nine years. At first, I dismissed these as media confusion over the precise terms of our filing. But as I continued to see these reports, I called Brian to see whether he had an explanation. Brian had not been following the Stone case closely other than being present earlier that day when Tim and I agreed on a course of action. He was just as surprised by the news reports as I had been and agreed that, if the filing said what the reports were describing, it was contrary to my instructions. I told Brian that, if Shea's office had affirmatively recommended a seven-to-nine-year sentence, we would have to correct it first thing in the morning. I talked to Shea later that night, and he acknowledged the filing recommended a seven-to-nine-year sentence, but he said he was able to get some language in the filing that identified some countervailing considerations. This was not acceptable. I told Tim I wasn't going to be threatened into endorsing a wildly disproportionate sentence.

Early the next morning, Brian and I met in my office. We were discussing how to approach a supplemental filing that did not endorse a seven-to-nine-year sentence and left sentencing up to the judge. As others started entering the office for our regular morning staff meeting,

Deputy Jeff Rosen walked in and asked, "Did you see the President's tweet?"

"What tweet?" Neither Brian nor I was aware of a tweet.

"After midnight sometime, he tweeted about how outrageous the DOJ's sentencing recommendation was in Stone," Rosen explained.

"Shit . . . Goddamn him," I said. "Now what?" I knew immediately that, if I insisted on doing what was fair and right in the case, people would say we were responding to the President's tweet. I had never discussed Stone's sentencing with President Trump or anyone else at the White House.

The three of us sat quietly for a moment. "Can we let this make a difference?" Brian asked.

"No," I replied. "It is going to be a shitstorm. But no, we can't. It's going to hurt me badly, but we can't let the President's goddamn tweets determine what we do, one way or the other."

We expected the media would be gnawing on the issue all day and beyond, and Brian stressed to everyone in my office that it was imperative there be no communications with anyone at the White House relating to our actions on the Stone case.

Later that day, the department made a supplemental filing, which did not endorse a sentence in the seven-to-nine-year range and deferred to the judge's discretion on the appropriate sentence. Predictably, all hell broke loose, with Democrats and most of the media accusing me of changing our initial position to placate the President. Notably absent from this criticism was any discussion of the decision's merits or any acknowledgment that the original sentence had been unreasonably severe.

I was fed up with the President's tweeting. His need to express an opinion, immediately and in public, on nearly every question in which his administration had an interest, constantly threatened to undermine me and the Department of Justice. When he commented on matters pending in the department, it put me in an impossible position. Even though I was basing decisions on what I thought was right under the law and facts, if my decisions ended up the same as the

President's expressed opinion, it made it easier to attack my actions as politically motivated.

Before I took the job of Attorney General the second time, I could see plainly that the President's adversaries in the media and the Democratic Party were determined to fit me into a prefabricated narrative that went something like this: Trump was a would-be authoritarian, but, so far, his aims to arrogate quasi-dictatorial power had met with one legal roadblock after another. What he wanted, therefore, was an Attorney General who would do his bidding and disregard the rule of law and pursue any policy and break any constitutional norm.

Throughout my tenure, this narrative was constantly peddled on op-ed pages, in denunciatory speeches in Congress, and by ill-informed talking heads on TV. This didn't bother me much. These people weren't acting in good faith. By their logic, I was guilty of kowtowing to Trump anytime I agreed with him. Unless I joined the resistance and was actively attempting to sabotage his administration, I was the tool of a would-be dictator. You can't reason with people who abuse reason and dialogue in this way.

I would have appreciated it, however, if the President could have refrained from contributing to this fiction. That he so often did was a source of growing irritation.

I asked Kerri Kupec to arrange an interview with Pierre Thomas, ABC News's veteran reporter covering the department. Two days later, I sat down with Thomas for an interview in my conference room. Five minutes before the interview, I gave Pat Cipollone at the White House a heads-up but did not tell him what I was going to say. During the interview, I explained my decision on Stone and criticized the President for his constant tweets concerning matters pending at DOJ, which, I said, "make it impossible for me to do my job."

Later, I heard there was a lot of scurrying around at the White House, where people thought I was about to resign. I wasn't. But, as I told my staff that day, I was going to say what needed to be said. If that precipitated my departure, that was fine.

Almost as soon as the interview ended, ABC started sending out excerpts to "tease" the story, including my comments about the President.

As I walked back to my desk after the interview, my cell phone buzzed. It was President Trump.

Well, here it comes, I thought.

"Hello, Mr. President."

"Bill," he said, "I just saw what you said in the interview. Very cool. I thought it was cool. I am good."

I was glad he wasn't in a rage. I took the opportunity to press the point.

"Mr. President, you have got to stop commenting on matters that are in the department," I said.

"But Bill! I have never told you what to do," he countered.

"Yes, but when you go out and say things publicly, it gives the impression that you're telling Justice what to do," I said. "It's bad for me and the department. It makes me look like I'm taking orders. I cannot have it."

"Okay," he said. "See you later."

After he issued a few public comments, making clear he was still the boss, the President curtailed his tweeting about pending cases—at least for a few months.

The sentencing judge in the Stone case ended up agreeing with my position and sentenced Stone to three years and four months in prison. At the sentencing proceeding, the judge stated: "I agree with the defense and with the government's second memorandum, that the eight-level enhancement for threats, while applicable, tends to inflate the guideline level beyond where it fairly reflects the actual conduct involved."

On the day after my TV interview with Pierre Thomas, I had to deal with another high-profile matter. I authorized informing defense lawyers for Andrew McCabe, the former FBI deputy director, that the department was closing its criminal investigation of McCabe for allegedly making false statements during an internal inquiry into leaks about the FBI's investigation into the Clinton Foundation, the nonprofit organization founded by former president Bill Clinton. Almost two years earlier, in April 2018, IG Horowitz had issued a report finding that McCabe had not been forthcoming with former director Comey and with FBI investigators about his role in the unauthorized disclosures during the 2016 campaign. This was referred to the US Attorney's Office in the District of Columbia to determine whether McCabe had committed a criminal violation.

On Twitter, the President had frequently pointed to the failure to prosecute McCabe as an example of the Justice Department's double standard. The DC office had done excellent work on the investigation. After reviewing the case in detail, I determined, for a host of reasons, that the department should not continue to pursue the case. I also concluded that it would not be appropriate for me to disclose beyond the DOJ the various factors that bore on this decision. The department doesn't always notify a target that the matter is being dropped, but in this case, there were related civil matters pending that made it necessary to give McCabe's counsel notice. No sooner had we notified McCabe's defense lawyers than the matter hit the media. I contacted Cipollone and told him that I had decided not to move forward, and that I couldn't go into the reasons.

Over the weekend, I heard that the President was seething about my interview with Pierre Thomas and my decision on McCabe. His initial reaction to my ABC interview—that it was "cool" and he was "good"—came when he thought I was about to resign, and he was trying to defuse the situation. But the McCabe decision made him angry and got him stewing about any and all grievances he had with me, including the shot I had fired across his bow in the TV interview.

Sometime later, he tried to confront me directly about the McCabe decision. After a meeting on another issue in the small dining room off the Oval Office, he started to bring it up. Pat Cipollone was present. I cut off the President peremptorily: "Mr. President, I have told you that there are matters at the department I will not discuss with you, and I cannot get into this matter. Period." President Trump was a little taken aback by my tone, but did not continue.

Pat backed me up. "Just let Bill do his job, Mr. President."

The McCabe matter soon joined my decision not to prosecute Comey in Trump's litany of my failures.

One of the things that made my job a little easier was Cipollone's support. Pat had his own frequent clashes with Trump, but that didn't stop him from helping me when he could. He advised the President on more than one occasion: "You put Barr at Justice, so now let him do his job and trust him to do what is right." Of course, Trump didn't care if my decisions were right so much as whether they helped him. He had trouble distinguishing between the two.

Pat was serving as a reliable guardrail over at the White House, helping keep the President on track. But it came at a price. When Trump felt frustrated by Pat's pushback, he would mercilessly criticize him behind his back. He started doing the same with me.

At the end of April 2020, Jeff Jensen briefed me on his conclusions on the Flynn matter. He recommended that the charges against Flynn be dropped. He concluded that the case against the general did not satisfy the department's standards of prosecution, and he did not think that any US Attorney in the DOJ, aware of all the facts and acting in good faith, would bring the case.

Shortly after the 2016 election, President-elect Trump had offered Flynn the post of national security adviser in his upcoming administration. During the transition period in late December and early January, Flynn had a series of conversations with the Russian ambassador to the United States, Sergey Kislyak. These contacts were typical and legitimate for an incoming national security adviser to have during the transition. In one call, Flynn raised whether Russia would be willing to oppose or delay an upcoming UN resolution condemning Israel. Flynn also talked to Kislyak after President Obama expelled thirty-five suspected Russian intelligence officers from the United States in retaliation for Russia's attempts to influence the 2016 election. In that call, Flynn suggested that Russia keep any response to the expulsions "reciprocal" and not escalate.

On January 24, 2017, Comey and McCabe sent two FBI agents over to the White House to talk to Flynn about his calls with Kislyak. The FBI document memorializing this interview—known as a 302—indicates that Flynn said he did not ask Kislyak to do anything particular on the anti-Israeli resolution. The 302 also states that when the agents asked Flynn whether he recalled encouraging Kislyak to keep the response to the expulsions reciprocal, Flynn responded, "Not really. I don't remember. I wasn't, 'Don't do anything.'"

Ultimately, Mueller's office pursued these statements by Flynn to the FBI as felony false statements, and in December 2017 entered into a plea agreement whereby Flynn pleaded guilty to one count of making false statements to the FBI during the interview. At the same time, Mueller's office had been investigating Flynn for doing consulting work on behalf of Turkey without registering under the Foreign Agents Registration Act (FARA). After Flynn pled to a false-statement charge relating to the Kislyak calls, Mueller's office dropped pursuing a FARA case against him.

Based on his investigation, which turned up previously undisclosed FBI documents, Jensen was deeply troubled by Comey's decision to send the FBI agents to interview Flynn about his conversations with Kislyak. The FBI already knew the precise content of the calls—indeed, it had the transcripts of the relevant calls—and Jensen concluded that the substance of the calls did not create a reasonable basis for the FBI to investigate Flynn about them. Jensen believed that the manner in which the interview was set up and the calculated tactics used were unjustified, and it appeared to him that, instead of having a legitimate investigative purpose, the predominant goal of interviewing Flynn was to cause him to make a statement that could be later characterized as false. In other words, it seemed the purpose was to manufacture a crime—or at least something that could be superficially alleged to be a crime.

Flynn had been one of the original subjects of the Crossfire Hurricane investigation initiated in July and August 2016. The basis for opening that counterintelligence investigation of Flynn in the first place was highly questionable. It rested on nothing more than Papadopoulos's wine bar comment, coupled with the fact that Flynn was someone in the campaign who, due to his former official role as director of the Defense Intelligence Agency (DIA), could have been in a position to talk to Russian officials. After the election, the FBI decided to close its investigation, having found nothing to suggest that Flynn had an inappropriate relationship with the Russians. The closing document stated that the bureau was without "any information on which to predicate further investigative efforts."

The FBI had transcripts of Flynn's conversations with Kislyak and thus knew there was nothing improper about them. Nonetheless, Comey decided to have the incoming national security adviser subjected to an investigative interview about the calls. However, the FBI was not able to specify a sufficient predicate for interviewing Flynn. In other words, it was unable to articulate in writing any reasonable basis for the interview—the minimal requirement before the bureau can investigate American citizens. This presented a quandary for FBI leadership until it discovered that the paperwork closing the earlier Crossfire Hurricane investigation of Flynn had not been finalized. On January 4, the day the closing document was to be filed formally, direction came down from the "seventh floor"—Comey and/or McCabe—to keep the matter open. Internal FBI documents show bureau officials expressing glee that this "serendipitous" circumstance allowed them to characterize the interview of Flynn as a continuation of the old Crossfire Hurricane investigation. This was disingenuous, since the FBI had already concluded that there was no basis to continue the old investigation, and Flynn's calls with Kislyak did not provide any grounds for launching a new counterintelligence investigation of Flynn. This allowed the FBI to bypass the obligation to document that it had a sufficient basis for conducting the interview. Thus, the FBI sidestepped a critical constraint on its investigative powers: the predication threshold for investigating American citizens.

The Deputy Attorney General at the time, Sally Yates, did not approve interviewing Flynn and wanted Comey instead to advise the White House counsel about any concerns over Flynn's calls. She, and other senior DOJ officials at the time, were frustrated that Comey's reasons for wanting to interview Flynn kept changing—"morphed," as they put it. Comey did an end run around Deputy Yates and the

DOJ by precipitously sending the agents over to interview Flynn. Internal FBI documents show that McCabe and others carefully choreographed the interview. The FBI did not follow the normal practice of arranging the interview through White House counsel. McCabe effectively discouraged Flynn from having counsel present or notifying White House counsel. It was decided not to show Flynn the transcripts of his conversations with Kislyak, about which he would be questioned. At the interview, the agents failed to give the common admonition about lying to investigators. These and other decisions led the FBI's head of counterintelligence, Bill Priestap—whom McCabe had gone around to have Peter Strzok run the Crossfire Hurricane investigation—to raise questions about the tactics and motivations for the interview and whether the bureau would be "seen as playing games." He questioned whether the goal of interviewing Flynn was getting at the truth or "to get him to lie, so we can prosecute him or get him fired?"

When McCabe called Flynn to arrange the interview, Flynn—himself the former DIA director—stated that he fully expected that the FBI already knew the content of his conversations with the Russian ambassador, saying, "[Y]ou listen to everything they say." Peter Strzok, one of the two FBI agents who conducted the interview, later reported that he and his fellow agent "had the impression that Flynn was not lying or did not think he was lying."

As I saw it, the Flynn episode boiled down to this: the FBI did not have a legitimate investigative basis for interviewing him about his conversations with Kislyak. The apparent intent of the interview was to try to manufacture a false-statement claim against Flynn. The key parts of the interview consisted of the FBI agents asking Flynn whether he remembered certain things said during his conversations with Kislyak. The agents asking the questions knew exactly what was said, since they had the verbatim transcripts. Flynn, being a former senior intelligence official, would know this and had already said he assumed the FBI had "listen[ed]" to the call. Under these circumstances, it is difficult to understand how the question of whether Flynn did or did not remember certain aspects of his conversation—which the FBI already had the details of—was material to any issue that the bureau could legitimately be investigating. It is also difficult to conclude that Flynn—sitting across from FBI agents whom he assumed had the content of his calls—intentionally lied about whether he recalled saying something. Likewise, it is difficult to understand how Flynn would have thought his responses would be materially false, since he was assuming—correctly—that the FBI knew what he actually said.

Even assuming that Flynn's statements could be material, Jensen doubted the government could prove beyond a reasonable doubt that the general knowingly and willfully made a false statement. Not only had the interviewing agents come away believing that Flynn had not intentionally misled them, but Director Comey—asked whether he thought Flynn lied—answered, "I don't know. I think there is an argument to be made he lied. It is a close one." But the government does not have a case if the question is a "close one." The standard is beyond a reasonable doubt.

Moreover, one of the allegedly false statements attributed to Flynn in the 302 did not appear in the notes of the agents conducting the interview, and it was established that supervisors who were not present at the interview had edited the 302.

Taking all of this—the vagueness of Flynn's answers, the FBI's own preliminary estimation of Flynn's truthfulness, and the inconsistent FBI records as to the actual questions and statements made—I did not think the evidence was sufficient to prove Flynn knowingly and willingly lied to investigators during the interview. For that reason, under the department's principles of federal prosecution, the evidence did not support criminal charges against Flynn for lying to the FBI.

As to Flynn's earlier guilty plea, Jensen noted that Flynn had pleaded without full awareness of the circumstances of the newly discovered, disclosed, or declassified information relating to the FBI's investigation of him and that Flynn had moved to withdraw his plea. Moreover, as Jensen noted, Flynn was also moving to withdraw his plea based in part on a claim that the counsel advising him on the plea had a conflict of interest.

I agreed with Jensen's assessment and recommendation. On May 7, 2020, the Justice Department filed to dismiss the false-statement charges against Flynn. Although the law was clear that the case against him had to be dismissed and could not be maintained once DOJ decided to drop it, various judicial maneuvers succeeded in holding the matter in abeyance past the 2020 election. I had no doubt that the case would have ultimately been dismissed by the courts as the law required, but, after the election, the President decided to pardon Flynn.

Predictably our motion to dismiss the charges led to an election-year media onslaught, flogging the old theme that I was doing this as a favor to Trump. But I concluded that the handling of the Flynn matter by the FBI had been an abuse of power that no responsible AG could let stand. I worried that the decision to bypass the DOJ and "investigate" Flynn's calls with Kislyak was a setup intended to manufacture a false-statement allegation, which could then help breathe new life into the collapsing collusion investigation of the Trump administration.

I also questioned the actions of Mueller's office on the Flynn case. Until Mueller came on the scene, it did not appear anyone was seriously pursuing charges against Flynn for lying to the FBI. In the absence of any real evidence of collusion, pursuing the Flynn matter gave Mueller's efforts the illusion of some substance, and it obviously gave Mueller leverage over a Trump associate. Reaching a plea deal with Flynn based on the Kislyak calls rather than the Turkish FARA matter allowed Mueller to ballyhoo *something* related to Russia. But I have never been satisfied that extracting the plea from Flynn was fair. In the first place, I agreed with Jensen that government was not in a position to prove that Flynn intentionally misled the FBI. Further, given all the facts that were not disclosed to Flynn, including those regarding the FBI's conduct, I did not think Flynn was fairly informed when he agreed to plea.

But as consequential as both the Stone and Flynn cases were, and for all the news media's obsessions with them, neither was typical of the sorts of things that dominated my attention at the Department of

Justice. Even under a tornado of a man like Donald Trump, most of an Attorney General's time is not spent on fights and controversies between the President and his enemies. Indeed, the bulk of my time and energies, as I'll explain, was spent on a far more basic task: trying to protect the American people from crime.

CHAPTER 14

BRINGING JUSTICE TO
VIOLENT PREDATORS

On the night of January 11, 1996, Daniel Lewis Lee and his accomplice, both members of the Aryan People's Resistance, a white supremacist group, broke into the Arkansas home of a gun dealer, where they expected to find a large supply of guns and cash. Their purpose was to rob the gun dealer and use the guns and proceeds to support white supremacist operations in the Pacific Northwest. When the gun dealer, his wife, and eight-year-old daughter returned home, Lee and his accomplice, who had been waiting for them, used a stun gun against each of the three victims, put plastic bags over their heads and sealed them with duct tape, weighted down their bodies with rocks, and dumped them in a bayou.

When I took office, there were sixty-two federal inmates on death row, awaiting execution. One of them was Daniel Lewis Lee.

In general, in the federal system, capital punishment may be imposed for heinous murders subject to federal jurisdiction. It can be imposed only for first-degree murder where a jury decides that there are aggravating factors present that outweigh mitigating factors and justify death. As a first step, in death-eligible cases, senior lawyers at Main Justice and in the US Attorney's Office handling the prosecution make a recommendation to the Attorney General whether or not to seek the death penalty. The Attorney General then personally decides whether to pursue the death penalty in the particular case. If the AG authorizes seeking the death penalty, prosecutors first try the "guilt" phase of the trial before the jury. If the jury finds the defendant guilty of committing the crime, then a further "penalty" phase of the trial is held to determine the suitable penalty. The government presents all the aggravating factors weighing in favor of the death penalty, and the defendant is allowed to present any circumstances weighing against the death penalty. For the death penalty to be imposed, the jury must find unanimously, based on its assessment of the aggravating and mitigating factors, that the death penalty is justified.

President Bill Clinton's Attorney General, Janet Reno, approved seeking the death penalty for Daniel Lewis Lee and his accomplice. The jury found both defendants guilty of triple murder and proceeded to the penalty phase to consider the appropriate sentence. Considering the accomplice first, the jury decided on life imprisonment. At this point, the Arkansas US attorney contacted Eric Holder, Deputy Attorney General at the time, who was standing in for Attorney General Reno while she was out of town.

The US attorney asked Holder for permission to drop the death penalty request for Lee, reasoning that the jury had given the accomplice life imprisonment even though the accomplice seemed to have been more of the leader. Holder denied the US attorney's request and directed that she continue to seek the death penalty against Lee. In May 1999 the jury voted unanimously for the death sentence for three counts of murder in aid of racketeering. After sixteen years of litigation, Lee had exhausted appellate review of his sentence. He was still on death row awaiting execution when I arrived in office in February 2019.

The Constitution permits the death penalty, and there has been a federal death penalty on the books since the very first US Congress enacted one in 1790. During the Clinton administration, in response to new procedural requirements imposed by the Supreme Court, Congress adopted the Federal Death Penalty Act of 1994, prescribing death penalty procedures and applying them to more than forty federal offenses. Since that act, every administration of either party has sought and advocated for the death penalty in appropriate cases. Of those on federal death row when I arrived, the Clinton administration had obtained the death penalty for more than a dozen, George W. Bush's administration for more than two dozen, and Obama's administration for more than a dozen. The Obama administration not only pursued the death penalty in its own cases but also consistently litigated to uphold death sentences handed down during earlier administrations.

The first executions under the 1994 act were carried out by lethal injection using a three-drug cocktail. In March 2011, however, Holder, now the Attorney General, announced that the government no longer had access to one of the three drugs and directed the Bureau of Prisons to explore alternative means of execution. For several years, the BOP studied possible alternatives with a view toward recommending a lethal injection protocol that would readily pass constitutional muster but also could be administered successfully with available drugs. Pending a new lethal injection protocol, Holder declared a moratorium on federal executions. Significantly, during this moratorium, the Obama administration continued to seek death sentences from juries against terrorist Dzhokhar Tsarnaev, a nineteen-year-old originally from Kyrgyzstan who detonated bombs near the finish line of the 2013 Boston Marathon, killing three people and wounding hundreds; and against Dylann Roof, a twenty-one-year-old white supremacist who shot to death nine African Americans attending a prayer meeting at the Emanuel African Methodist Episcopal Church in Charleston, South Carolina in 2015.

When I took office, the Bureau of Prisons was completing its analysis and ready to recommend a protocol using a single drug, pentobarbital. Once the powerful barbiturate was procured and its purity confirmed, the BOP submitted the proposed protocol to me. The use of pentobarbital was clearly constitutional. Its use by multiple states had been upheld by the Supreme Court, and it had been used in more than a hundred executions without incident. In July 2019 I approved the final protocol. This ended the reason for Attorney General Holder's earlier moratorium. I directed that five executions be scheduled for December 2019, the earliest practicable time. All executions were to be carried out at the US Penitentiary at Terre Haute, Indiana.

One of the Attorney General's principal duties is to carry out the sentences imposed by judges and juries. The AG has no power to mitigate those sentences based on his or her personal views. If a criminal is sentenced to a term of incarceration, the Attorney General is duty bound to hold him for the period prescribed by law. For the same reason, once the government has sought the death penalty, a jury approves the sentence, and the courts review and uphold the decision, the Attorney General is duty bound to impose it. He doesn't get to pick and choose. Even if I were personally opposed to the death penalty in principle—which I am not—that would change nothing. It would still be the duty of my office to carry out the sentence. Someone who can't or won't discharge the duties of his office should not hold the office.

I discussed resuming the death penalty only once with the President, and then only briefly. When, during an Oval Office meeting on other matters, I told him that I had approved a new protocol for executions and would be scheduling a number of them, he asked, "So you agree with the death penalty?" When I told him I did, he asked, "Why do you support it?"

He was very interested in understanding my reasoning. It seemed to me that he felt viscerally that it was right but wanted to understand *why* his impulse was reasonable. I explained briefly that I supported the death penalty not because of deterrence but because I believed it was, in the case of heinous murders, the only punishment that fit the crime and was therefore necessary to bring about justice. That seemed to satisfy him.

I eventually scheduled the executions of a total of thirteen inmates convicted of horrible murders. The criteria was based on the vulnerability of their victims. There was no question as to their guilt. The first was Daniel Lewis Lee. Others included Wesley Ira Purkey, who'd violently raped and murdered a sixteen-year-old girl, and then dismembered, burned, and dumped her body in a septic pond. (The state had convicted him previously for bludgeoning to death an eighty-year-old woman with polio.) Dustin Lee Honken killed five people: two men who planned to testify against him, and a single, working mother and her ten-year-old and six-year-old daughters. Keith Dwayne Nelson kidnapped a ten-year-old girl rollerblading in front of her home, then raped her and strangled her to death with a wire. Lezmond Mitchell stabbed to death a sixty-three-year-old grandmother and slit the throat of her nine-year-old granddaughter. Dustin John Higgs kidnapped and murdered three young African American women. Cory Johnson murdered seven people in furtherance of his drug trafficking activities.

Predictably, as I scheduled the executions, intense litigation followed. Most of it had nothing to do with the inmates' guilt or the validity of their sentences. It was almost entirely about ancillary issues and often intended solely to create delay. The inmates initially succeeded in postponing the executions by six months based on a claim—ultimately rejected—that the federal execution protocol had to incorporate all procedural details of state law. After that, they mounted a series of second- and third-choice arguments, each more desperate than the last. Some, for example, claimed that the BOP was required to obtain a doctor's prescription for the pentobarbital. None of these claims withstood appellate review. The Supreme Court alone reversed eight erroneous last-minute orders, and the long-delayed executions proceeded.

Under Justice Department protocol, at the time of each execution—once we verified that no further legal impediment exists, and the inmate was physically in position—I had to give formal verbal approval to the warden to proceed. As I gave approval in each case, I felt the solemnity and pathos of the situation. I took no joy in it. I believed strongly that the punishment fit the crime, and I felt a sense of satisfaction that justice was being fulfilled. Afterward, I was moved by the heartfelt gratitude expressed by the families of the victims. "It is a day we thought would never come," said the family of three victims—two children and their mother, murdered and hidden in some woods twenty-seven years earlier. "[T]his is a step toward the healing of broken hearts and shattered lives." A man whose nine-year-old daughter was bludgeoned to death with rocks after a carjacking said, "I have waited nineteen years to get justice. I will never get [my daughter] back, but I hope that this will bring some closure." The mother of a ten-year-old girl who was raped and murdered after being kidnapped in front of her house said she had accomplished her "number one goal" for the past twenty-one years: to "get her [daughter] justice . . . so that she can rest."

Opponents of the death penalty often mischaracterize the victims' thirst for justice as some kind of debased bloodlust, which it is not. They also claim that retributive justice cannot bring the inner peace yearned for by grieving family members. Of course, if you haven't experienced the pain of learning that your daughter was raped and hacked to death, or that your parents were shot execution style, and the further misery of knowing that the man who did it is now afforded three meals a day at public expense, you probably shouldn't speak too confidently about what will and won't bring relief. I've spoken to survivors, and I believe them when they tell me that justice brought a measure of relief.

Most media coverage of the executions I approved portrayed them as a partisan "execution spree," which they claimed was rushed for purposes of the 2020 election. Few bothered to consider the self-evident falsity of that portrayal: the death sentence in each case was handed down, on average, almost twenty years before execution and was litigated ad nauseam through the courts, so carrying them out over a period of six months in 2020 and 2021 could hardly be called "rushed." And the sentences were obtained and defended across administrations of different political parties—nearly half of them, in fact, during the Clinton administration—so to characterize them as partisan was absurd. And the timing of the executions was dictated by the fact that the reason for the moratorium ended just as I took office. The proximity to the election was the result of delay tactics on the part of the inmates and their attorneys, not the government's schedule.

In truth, most criticism of the executions was a proxy attack on the death penalty itself. Whatever the arguments for and against capital punishment, however, the American people, acting through their elected representatives, have determined that the death penalty is an appropriate punishment for the most egregious federal crimes. In carrying out valid capital sentences imposed long ago, the Department of Justice fulfilled its most basic responsibility to uphold the rule of law.

While the personal feelings of the Attorney General should make no difference, the fact is I agreed with the juries that all thirteen killers whom I scheduled for execution deserved to be put to death. For example, of those thirteen, Keith Dwayne Nelson's crime was far from the most heinous. But in my judgment, his depraved, premeditated, and cold-blooded kidnapping, rape, and murder of ten-year-old Pamela Butler demanded the death penalty.

Nelson did not kill Pamela Butler on impulse. Two weeks before, he had told an acquaintance that he wanted to kidnap, rape, torture, and kill a female. He explained that he was going back to prison for other charges and wanted to go back for "something big." He boasted of killing in the past; talked about future plans to lure women, lock them up, belt them down, rape them, and then kill them; and said he wanted to buy a small plot of land to bury his victims. Days later, he tried to abduct a young lady, but she successfully fought him off. Ten days after that, he told an acquaintance that he had spotted a little girl and wanted to kidnap, rape, torture, and kill her, and the time to do it had come. He drove to the little girl's neighborhood and waited on the street by her house in his van. Pamela, a beautiful, loving, playful, and energetic child, with big dreams, rollerbladed past on the way home from buying a cookie. Nelson pulled her in to his van, where she put up a fight. As her sisters stood on the porch screaming, Nelson gave them the middle finger and drove off with Pamela. Her mother and family, in unspeakable agony, spent three sleepless days and nights making appeals, handing out leaflets, and searching desperately for Pamela. The girl's naked body was found. She had been beaten, raped, and then strangled to death with wire.

After Nelson's capture, an inmate in the next cell said that he would hear Nelson late at night imitating a little girl screaming and crying for "Mommy," and crying, "Help me! Don't hurt me! Don't kill me!"

The man asked Nelson, "How could you do that to that little girl?" Nelson responded, "You wouldn't believe it." There was no doubt whatsoever of Nelson's guilt; the direct evidence was dispositive, and he pleaded guilty. At sentencing, Nelson, showing no remorse for what he had done, blistered the victim's family with a profanity-laden tirade. Thereafter, he never expressed remorse.

When a criminal commits the ultimate crime of willfully and callously snuffing out the life of another human being, extinguishing that person's hopes, loves, and dreams, and hollowing out forever the lives and joys of the victim's loved ones, then the ultimate punishment is called for. For heinous murders, the only punishment that fits the enormity of the crime, adequately expresses society's revulsion, and is sufficient to right the scales of justice is the death penalty. To me, allowing a depraved murderer to live out his days after he has willfully destroyed the lives of his victims is the height of injustice. It mocks the value of the victims' lives and the sanctity of the law.

Frankly, when I read that, in Europe, terrorist mass murderers or genocidal killers are given prison sentences of only two or three decades, I do not think this means Europeans have a heightened moral sensibility; to me, it means their moral code has become degraded.

There is a lot of confusion today about retributive justice. Yet in our legal system, retribution is the basis for all punishment, not just capital punishment. The core idea behind retribution is that, when someone commits a crime, a punishment proportionate to the offense is justified and required solely to redress the transgression and restore society's moral order. That punishment is due regardless of any social utility the punishment may otherwise have in controlling crime in the future. The criminal deserves the punishment for no other reason than he committed the crime. "Justice" is done when the criminal receives his "just deserts."

The effects that punishment may have on future crime levels— through deterrence, incapacitation, or rehabilitation—are simply utilitarian considerations that are byproducts of a punishment. These ancillary considerations cannot justify punishment that is not deserved as retribution, nor can they provide a benchmark for just punishment apart from the proportionality required by retribution. Thus, for example, even though shoplifting is a crisis in San Francisco, a shoplifter cannot be hammered with a harsh penalty just because it would help deterrence, if the penalty is not proportionate to the crime. In other words, retributive justice requires that punishment be deserved based on the nature of the crime, not based on the utilitarian goals of crime control.

Philosophers and legal theorists have offered many rationales for the principle of retributive justice—for example, that it is necessary to restore the moral order that has been upset by the criminal's actions, or to defeat an aggressor's domination of another, thereby upholding the victim's dignity and natural equality. Whatever its philosophical justification, retribution is plainly supported by a powerful, deeply engrained moral intuition. Some demean it as a base urge that civilized people should suppress. But I believe this moral sense—related to the idea of reciprocity—is part of the law "written on our hearts" and is the source and foundation of our noblest concepts of justice and our passion for it. It is not the same as the personal anger felt by the direct victim of an injury. It is the sense of moral indignation that arises when we see someone, even a stranger, treated in a bad way he or she does not deserve. It is what makes us feel that things have to be made right. It encompasses the rational, measured principle of proportionality. A proper sense of justice, like any virtue, can become corrupted by going too far in one direction or the other. Punishment can become unjustly vindictive or unjustly lenient. But the fact that justice can be corrupted does not mean there is not a virtuous sense of justice and proper measure of punishment.

Retribution is not the same as vengeance or revenge, as those terms are currently used. Vengeance is private retaliation carried out by those directly injured by the crime and knows no limit other than the personal pleasure of the avenger. Before government assumed responsibility for preserving the moral order of society, people relied on private retaliation to protect themselves. The ancient principle of the *lex talionis* (an "eye for an eye"), found in the Bible's book of Exodus, was meant to limit the scope of private retaliation. But now private retaliation and the *lex talionis* have been superseded and supplanted by rational systems of retributive justice administered by the state. *Eumenides*, the Greek dramatist Aeschylus's ancient play, dramatizes the Athenians' journey from reliance on private "Fury" to reliance on collective "Reason" to guard society's moral order—a path tread ever since by all Western societies. A justice system, unlike private retaliation, relies on an impartial decision maker to determine the blameworthiness of the suspected offender; it sets the standard for proper punishment as proportionate to the culpability of the guilty party; and it administers justice not to satisfy private passion but to uphold the sanctity of law and society's moral order. Retaliation is ad hoc, whereas retribution is meted out within a system based on general principles mandating punishment in other like cases. Retaliation addresses the private emotions of those hurt, while retribution responds to the collective desire to restore society's moral order. And retaliation can be accomplished in secrecy, while retribution is inherently communicative, expressing society's revulsion at, and censure of, the criminal's behavior.

Opponents cannot dispute that the proportionate penalty for murder is death. But they argue that it is somehow inconsistent to take a life in the name of upholding the value of life. This is a sound-bite argument lacking intellectual coherence. As many have pointed out, it is like saying that locking up a kidnapper for twenty-five years is acting no better than the kidnapper. The highest value is *innocent* life. The malicious murder of an innocent person is simply not on the same moral plane as the execution of the guilty murderer done to uphold the sanctity of the law, the moral order of the community, and the equality of the victim. The book of Genesis's famous verse (9:6) states: "Whoso sheddeth man's blood, by man shall his blood be shed: *for in the image of God made he man*" (emphasis added). The reasoning here is that it is precisely the unique value of human life—made in the image of God—that calls for imposing the ultimate punishment, not a lesser punishment. The value of something is established by what we take in exchange for it. Imposing death on a murderer does not derogate from the unique value of innocent human life, but vindicates and expresses that value.

While I support the death penalty when it is retributively just, I also believe that capital punishment serves as a deterrent. Some suggest that it cannot be proven empirically that the prospect of execution will dissuade someone considering murder from going forward with the act. Even if that were true, these critics misconceive deterrence. One way capital punishment could deter is by dissuading the person who is willing to entertain the idea of murder from following through. But, more fundamentally, the death penalty deters by preventing most people from even being willing to contemplate murder in the first place. As the nineteenth-century British legal scholar James Fitzjames Stephen observed: "Some men, probably, abstain from murder because they fear that if they committed murder they would be hanged. Hundreds of thousands abstain from it because they regard it with horror. One great reason why they regard it with horror is that murderers are hanged with the hearty approbation of all reasonable men."

In other words, when society dramatically communicates that certain acts are so abhorrent that society will execute those who commit them, people generally come to internalize that message and come to regard the act as unthinkable. In this way, capital punishment deters heinous crimes by drawing and reinforcing a psychological boundary that most will not allow themselves to think of crossing.

It is also almost certainly true that the death penalty does deter at least some murders by affecting the calculations of individuals who are considering murder. The fact that this deterrence may not be susceptible to dispositive statistical proof does not mean it does not happen. We know from everyday experience that the higher a penalty, the fewer are those willing to engage in the prohibited behavior. Is it reasonable to think that this principle is somehow inoperative in the context of murder? In any event, as the sociologist Ernest van den Haag pointed out in his famous "best bet" argument, even if there is only a chance that the death penalty will deter, the soundest moral choice is to act on the assumption that it does. If the death penalty would have deterred a further murder, and we failed to use it, then we are responsible for the loss of an innocent life we could have saved. On the other hand, if the death penalty would not have deterred any additional murders, then those executed still deserved their punishment as a matter of retributive justice. And, finally, there are some crimes that can be deterred only by the death penalty. What could deter someone already serving a life sentence from murdering a prison guard or fellow inmate? What could deter someone who has already committed a crime punishable by a life sentence from killing a police officer in order to avoid arrest?

One of the ways I think of deterrence is this: many crimes involve a moment when the criminal is thinking about taking the life of his victim. It is the child rapist, like Nelson, staring down at the rape victim and deciding whether to kill her. It is the armed robber, aiming his gun at the young man working behind the cash register. It is the home invader, deciding what to do with the tied-up residents. In such cases, the criminal's acts up till that point call only for significant prison time. One of the reasons he may want to kill the victim is to eliminate the witness and lower his risks of going to prison. It is at critical moments like these that society owes the helpless victim everything in its power to save his or her life. What are the words that victim needs to have the state whispering in the attacker's ear at this point? The answer is easy: "If you kill this person, you will die." Anything less means the state is not doing its utmost to save the victim's life. The only effective protection the state can give is to stand behind the victim with the credible guarantee that if the aggressor kills the victim, he will forfeit his own life. Maybe it will work, and maybe it won't. But to fail to give this aid is morally bankrupt and a disgraceful abdication of duty.

One of the criticisms directed at me personally for carrying out the death penalty was that I was violating the teachings of my religion, Roman Catholicism. Media coverage has fostered much confusion about the substance of Church doctrine on the death penalty and the extent to which its pronouncements are binding on Catholics.

The Church has always made a distinction between two different kinds of actions: actions that are "intrinsically evil" and can never be justified at any time under any circumstances, such as abortion or rape; and actions that are not *per se* evil but can be moral in particular situations, depending on the circumstances. Determining the morality of an action in this latter category requires making a "prudential judgment" of whether the act is justified by the concrete circumstances in the particular case. In other words, it is a question of applying moral principles to a specific set of facts. An example of this latter category is killing in war, which the Church has always taught is not intrinsically wrong but can be justified when a country is engaged in a "just war." The determination whether a particular war is "just" involves a prudential judgment.

Under Church doctrine, authoritative pronouncements about actions in the first category—in other words, intrinsically evil acts that are never permissible—bind all Catholics. But when Church authorities speak of actions in the second category, they are simply expressing their own prudential judgment that an action is not morally justified under the specific circumstances. While Catholics must give these judgments respectful consideration, they are not strictly bound by them and may end up disagreeing. Thus, for example, in 2003 Pope St. John Paul II said that the United States' invasion of Iraq was an "unjust" war. But American Catholics were not bound by this judgment and could follow their own consciences.

For almost two thousand years, the Church has consistently taught that capital punishment does not fall into the first category—it is *not* intrinsically evil. It has always taught that, in principle, the government has the right to put to death under law those guilty of the most heinous offenses and that society's right to impose the death penalty accords with natural law and is upheld by sacred Scripture. All of the great Fathers and doctors of the church who considered the matter, including Saint Augustine and Saint Thomas Aquinas, and the numerous Popes who addressed the issue, have agreed that capital punishment is not intrinsically wrong.

The Church's teaching that capital punishment is not intrinsically evil has been so categorical, consistent, and universal that it is doubtful that it can be "changed" without gravely upsetting established doctrine on the reliability of the Church's teaching authority. In any event, nothing said to date by recent Popes can be taken as altering long-standing doctrine. Both Popes St. John Paul II and Benedict XVI made pronouncements calling for an end to the death penalty but made clear they were not asserting that capital punishment was intrinsically evil but were expressing their prudential judgment that, under contemporary circumstances, it is rarely justified. Catholics are obliged to give these judgments due consideration but are not bound by them. As Pope Benedict explained to the bishops in 2004, when he was still Cardinal Ratzinger and headed the Congregation for the Doctrine of the Faith:

> Not all moral issues have the same moral weight as abortion and euthanasia. For example, if a Catholic were at odds with the Holy Father on the application of capital punishment or on a decision to wage war, he would not for that reason be considered unworthy to present himself to receive Holy Communion. While the Church exhorts civil authorities to seek peace, not war, and to exercise discretion and mercy in imposing punishment on criminals, it may still be permissible to take up arms to repel an aggressor or to have recourse to capital punishment. There may be a legitimate diversity of opinion even among Catholics about waging war and applying the death penalty, but not, however, with regard to abortion and euthanasia.

Pope Francis's formulation in the Catholic catechism that capital punishment under modern conditions is "inadmissible" must be taken as expressing the same kind of prudential judgment as those expressed by his immediate predecessors. The Church's consistent teaching over the past two thousand years that capital punishment is not intrinsically evil has been explicit and prolific. The term *inadmissible* has no established meaning in moral theology and is certainly too vague and indirect to be read as an attempt to extinguish this vast body of established teaching, even assuming it could be.

Upon taking office, I still believed—as I had my first time around—that the first duty of government is to protect citizens from violent crime. In my conference call to all US attorneys on my first full day in office, I told them their highest priority must be to forge "full speed ahead" with an all-out effort to protect their communities from violent crime.

I was still convinced that most predatory violent crime is committed by a small group of chronic offenders, who continue committing crimes whenever they're out on the streets. The only surefire way of reducing violent crime is to keep these chronic offenders off the streets by making them serve the long prison sentences they deserve. The record of the last thirty years clearly showed the success of this approach. By 1991, the level of violent crime nationwide was at an all-time high, having almost quintupled during the preceding three decades. As I explained earlier, most of this increase occurred in the 1960s and 1970s—a period when liberal policies prevailed, and most state justice systems had become revolving doors. In the 1980s, as the Reagan administration and several populous states adopted tougher policies, the *rate of increase* started to go down, but violent crime levels were still going up. In 1992 violent crime rates suddenly reversed direction and started a steady decline for the next twenty-two years. What finally turned things around was a growing consensus—following the lead of the Reagan and Bush 41 administrations' policies—that the way to reduce violent crime was to target repeat violent criminals and take them off the streets. In my view, three key developments were responsible for driving violent crime down between 1992 and 2014.

First, the federal government, which until 1990 had played only a narrow role in combating violent crime, made it a priority. US agencies started using tough federal laws on guns, gangs, and drug organizations to target the most dangerous offenders for prosecution. Second, following the federal government's lead, states started strengthening their criminal justice systems, adopting reforms providing for effective pretrial detention and substantial prison sentences for violent actors who pose a threat to the community. And third, federal, state, and local law enforcement began expanding the use of joint task forces aimed specifically at identifying and prosecuting chronic violent offenders and making them serve the stiff sentences.

The Left continues to repeat the bromide that instead of putting away violent offenders, we should address the "root causes" of crime. The often unspoken premise here is that poverty breeds crime. A moment's reflection should tell you that that isn't true. Crime rates in all categories were vastly lower in the 1930s and 1940s, for example, than they were in the 1970s, yet Americans of the seventies were far wealthier than those of the Depression and war years.

Even if we accepted that misguided premise, though, the combined intelligence and expertise of American elites for a half century couldn't find a way to eradicate poverty. Since the 1960s, we have spent many trillions of dollars under the Great Society's War on Poverty programs, with no discernable impact on violent crime. In this regard, the War on Poverty failed, except as a way to make white liberals feel better about themselves. Indeed, its programs perversely ended up, as Stanford economist Thomas Sowell has shown, undermining the once-strong Black family structure—all too often taking fathers out of the picture. And if there's a single identifiable root cause of crime, it's the absence of a father in too many families—the one factor the Left refuses to acknowledge as a problem.

But even if we had effective programs to address root causes, they could not be *alternatives* to tough anticrime policies. Addressing root causes, whatever that means, would take decades to have an effect. But there is blood on the streets *today*, and the government has a duty to protect the citizens who are being preyed on *today*. How do we do that? Moreover, social programs to remedy root causes won't have a chance of success if inner-city neighborhoods are overrun by crime. Better schools will not help children if they're dominated by gangs. Businesses won't locate on streets that are shooting galleries. Safe neighborhoods are an essential precondition if social programs are to bear fruit. The Left's "root causes" mantra is really an excuse to do nothing.

Progressives attack the strategy that cut crime in half over the past three decades by denigrating it as a policy of "mass incarceration." The phrase is deceptive. It suggests the strategy involved the wholesale and undifferentiated imprisonment of criminals without regard to the nature of their crimes and the continuing threat they pose to the community. The implication is that this involved warehousing tens of thousands of "low level drug offenders" who posed no threat of violence. Wrong. The strategy I advocated—and it worked—is a precision strategy that identifies and takes off the streets those who pose the greatest danger of violence, especially gun violence. Through community policing programs, police are able to obtain valuable intelligence from law-abiding citizens about the principal violent actors in a community. As I urged when I was previously Attorney General, prison space should be reserved primarily for those who, based on criminally violent behavior, pose a threat of violence.

But after twenty-two years of steady decline, violent crime started to go up again in the last two years of the Obama administration. Large metro areas across the nation—Chicago, Baltimore, Houston, Saint Louis, and many others—were hit with crime waves in 2015 and 2016. Part of the cause was a new "progressive" stance toward violent crime adopted by the White House and by many states.

Another cause was the administration's embrace of the claim promoted by Black Lives Matter activists after the 2014 shooting of eighteen-year-old Michael Brown in Ferguson, Missouri—namely, that systemic racism among the police was the most important source of Black victimization. Even after Obama's Justice Department released a report supporting the officer's account that he reasonably shot Brown in self-defense, Obama suggested disingenuously that the details were too murky to get at the truth. ("We may never know what happened.") Sensing that the administration was waging a "war against police" during its last two years in power, many police agencies in major urban areas pulled back from proactive policing. The vacuum was filled by criminals—the so-called Ferguson effect.

As he made clear during his 2016 campaign, President Trump—as a New Yorker who had witnessed crime decline precipitously under Mayor Giuliani in the 1990s—believed that high crime was not inevitable and that the solution lay in strong enforcement policies. Days after taking office, he issued an executive order making the fight against violent crime one of the top priorities of his administration and directing the DOJ to support local law enforcement nationwide and work with them to restore safety to all communities. Attorney General Jeff Sessions took up the challenge and reinvigorated the programs aimed at getting violent offenders off the streets.

The administration's policies had an immediate effect. While violent crime had increased in 2015 and 2016 under Obama, it started dropping again under Trump in 2017, 2018, and 2019, my first year as Attorney General. While the progress was clear, the battle was hard. By the time I took office, a number of factors were putting upward pressure on crime rates. Many states had relapsed to the revolving-door policies that had led to the high crime rates of the seventies and eighties. In many of the nation's cities, the local criminal justice system was dysfunctional, without the power to detain dangerous criminals before trial or the will to impose meaningful sentences on violent predators.

A goal uppermost in my mind as I took office in February 2019 was to counteract the country's backsliding on violent crime. I spoke out frequently during my first year in office on violent crime issues, starting with the emergence of so-called social justice district attorneys in a number of large US cities. These radical politicos gained office largely as Trojan horses, in cities like Philadelphia, Boston, Los Angeles, San Francisco, Saint Louis, and Chicago.

Typically, with campaign blitzes funded by the likes of billionaire George Soros, they emerged suddenly during the Democratic primaries for district attorney. Voters had no clear understanding of their radical agendas. With their heavy funding, many of them won their primaries, which in heavily Democratic jurisdictions meant they were guaranteed to win general elections. Because only a small fraction of voters participate in local primaries, the swing of a very small number of votes allowed these candidates to win office. Once in power, these self-styled social justice DAs have refused to enforce entire categories of law—including frequently laws against resisting police officers.

Lax enforcement of parole violations, crackdowns on cops rather than criminals, the rejection of bail, the refusal to coordinate with federal immigration authorities, the reluctance to seek jailtime for violent offenders—the policies of these DAs strike at the very root of our law enforcement system. Our system is based on graduated response, in which we impose increasingly severe punishments based on an individual's criminal history. If we're going to protect the community, that means we have to have accurate criminal histories. Even if we are going to treat early and petty offenses leniently, we still need them charged and recorded so that we know who we are dealing with as time goes by. The damage being done by these progressive prosecutors will last for long time and make it hard for future prosecutors to clean up the mess.

The policies of these progressive DAs also sabotage the effectiveness of community and precision policing. To target the most dangerous offenders, officers depend heavily on information from members of the community. When DAs engage in catch-and-release policies, people in the neighborhood who might otherwise provide information are scared to come forward. Why would anybody inform on someone who, even if he's caught, will be back on the street the next day? In 2019 I watched as effective policing that had taken decades of painstaking work to build in many cities was being methodically undermined at every turn by the progressive DAs and their allies. New York City, for example, had one of the best community and precision policing programs in the country. It was crippled in one fell swoop when the New York State Legislature passed a series of "reforms" that, among other things, made it harder to detain dangerous violent criminals before trial or to protect the identity of witnesses and informants.

These DAs may have good intentions, but they are destroying lives. Their policies produce more career criminals. Not always, but often enough, early intervention can help—with young people, in particular. But by allowing young lawbreakers entirely off the hook the first time—and the second time and even the third time—these DAs are helping them along the path of becoming career criminals, committing more and increasingly serious crimes. This puts these troubled and disadvantaged young people in greater peril than they were in already—both on the street from other criminals and from law enforcement when these offenders graduate from petty to more serious offenses.

In the summer of 2019, well before Covid hit, I had lunch with President Trump in his private dining room. As we dug into our three large Italian meatballs in marinara sauce, I told him I was concerned that, even as the violent crime level nationwide continued to fall, it was escalating in some large cities. The President was fixated on the carnage in Chicago. "Violence is totally out of control in that city," he said. "Why can't they get it under control?"

I told him Chicago was a good example of what is happening in many cities—but on a grander scale. Crime levels, I said, were the result of a dismally dysfunctional state criminal justice system, a progressive DA who was soft on crime, and a police force that felt it was not backed by political leadership of the city. The President understood, but he was still aghast at the situation in Chicago.

"But, in Chicago, Bill, the sheer number of shootings!" he exclaimed. "What is that about? You got dozens in just one weekend! It's crazy!" He punctuated his statement by calling on the steward to refresh my Diet Coke.

I told him that street gangs were the main driver of the shootings, adding that the nature of the gang problem had evolved since I had last been Attorney General. In the past, gangs were more hierarchical and structured, frequently with strong national affiliations. They were also focused more on running their illicit businesses. Nowadays, in many cities, gangs are no longer as sharply defined as they once were but rather shifting, ad hoc local alliances among splinter groups. The violence is less "business related" and has more to do with "honor" and responding to "disrespect."

"Well, we got to do something about it," he said.

I told the President I was thinking about "surging" federal resources into a number of the hard-hit cities to show dramatically what could be accomplished with a tougher law enforcement approach. "If we demonstrate in a few places that skyrocketing crime levels are not inevitable—that tough law enforcement policies do work—it will help change the debate."

He liked the idea and started talking about a major effort in Chicago. I told him I did not think Chicago was a good place to launch this. I explained that I wanted to go into cities where we had supportive mayors and strong DAs. I also pointed out that Chicago would soak up a disproportionate amount of our scarce federal resources—for very little return. From the standpoint of federal law enforcement, it would be analogous to getting bogged down in Vietnam.

The President was not convinced and continued to push the idea of a massive effort in Chicago. I told him I would put together a surge plan for multiple cities and get back to him.

Following two mass shootings within a twenty-four-hour period in August 2019 in Dayton, Ohio, and El Paso, Texas, there was an effort to achieve bipartisan legislation on gun violence, which I hoped would include additional resources to enforce federal gun laws. I went up to Capitol Hill to explore whether we could find any common ground on proposals to strengthen the current background check system. Although the President did not take a position publicly, he privately encouraged me to explore options for a deal, but we knew it was a long shot. Whatever chance that legislation had, however, evaporated once it became clear that the House of Representatives was moving toward impeachment. Negotiations over legislation came to a screeching halt.

In late September I told the President that I wanted to move forward with two major initiatives that we could fund out of existing resources. One was a coordinated, nationwide push to use federal gun laws to target the worst violent offenders. Modeled after my old Triggerlock program, the plan was to work jointly with state and local authorities to identify the "trigger pullers" and then get them off the streets with tough prison sentences. This initiative would not only focus on criminals who used guns in crimes or possessed firearms illegally, but would also rachet up enforcement of background checks by charging persons who lied on the federal forms about their eligibility to buy a firearm at the time of purchase. A key aspect of this initiative was to expand use of the Bureau of Alcohol, Tobacco, and Firearms's gun intelligence centers and its amazing NIBIN (National Integrated

Ballistic Information Network) technology, which allows ATF to connect a particular shooting incident to a specific firearm. To address one of the leading causes of homicides against females, we also planned to pursue persons prohibited from possessing a firearm based on prior domestic violence offenses or violations of protective orders.

The President did not like reusing my old Triggerlock moniker; he wanted his own brand. I came up with Project Guardian, which he ultimately approved, having failed to come up with one he liked better. I announced the launch of Project Guardian in November 2019 and could not have imagined how successful the operation would prove to be. The number of federal gun charges brought during the Obama administration had hovered between 6,300 and 8,100 each year. During FY 2020, despite severe constraints and hardships imposed by Covid on the criminal justice system, the department charged more than 14,200 individuals with federal firearms offenses.

The second major initiative I briefed the President on in September was what he—picking up on the term I had initially used with him—referred to as "the surge." This would send additional personnel and funds to seven selected cities to expand the strength of the joint federal-local task forces operated by the FBI, US Marshals, DEA, and ATF. The cities—Albuquerque, Baltimore, Cleveland, Detroit, Kansas City, Memphis, and Milwaukee—all had violent crime levels significantly higher than the national average. The increase in federal agents was to be complemented by a financial commitment in federal grant funding that could be used to hire new local police officers, pay overtime and benefits, finance federally deputized task force officers, and provide equipment and technology. I told the President that I didn't like the term *surge* for public use because, having been used regarding troop levels in Iraq and Afghanistan, it had too much of a military connotation. He finally agreed to the name I proposed for the operation: Relentless Pursuit.

Unfortunately, Relentless Pursuit was forced to relent. I announced it in December 2019. Getting it up and running required mustering the necessary personnel from around the country to deploy on temporary detail to the selected cities. But Covid hit in March 2020, and we could not move agents around as we had planned. The whole effort collapsed. By the end of March, Relentless Pursuit had been aborted.

The year 2020 saw the worst one-year increase in violent crime in US history. The response to Covid certainly played a large role—banning people from productive labor may have worked out fine for the upper middle class and wealthy, but it was a curse on working-class wage earners. Yet I believe a major cause was the wide-scale pullback by police forces after the political Left demonized cops following the killing of George Floyd in late May 2020. I watched with alarm as violent crime, especially murder, skyrocketed during the summer in many cities throughout the country. The violence hit the Black community hardest. By the end of the year, homicides of Black victims jumped from 7,484 to more than 8,600—the biggest one-year increase on record.

By July, it was clear we had to respond to the carnage. Although we were still hampered by Covid, I unveiled a new surge operation intended for eight cities. Starting with Kansas City in early July, the plan was to roll out the operation by early August to Detroit, Cleveland, Saint Louis, Memphis, Albuquerque, Milwaukee, and Indianapolis. The concept was the same as with Relentless Pursuit. We would temporarily increase the number of federal agents assigned to local task forces, which then allowed us to expand the task forces operating in each city. We would also provide substantial federal grants to pay for additional local police and pay overtime for local task force officers.

At the beginning of July, my senior counselor for criminal matters, Gregg Sofer, came into my office to tell me about a four-year-old African American boy in Kansas City who had been shot and killed while he slept. His name was LeGend Taliferro. LeGend had recently recovered from open-heart surgery. That struck me hard. My daughter Mary had gone through open-heart surgery as a small child, and I had a sense of the anguish his parents had endured with the surgery and then the joy of knowing their child would get better. To go through *that* and then to see your child senselessly killed—I couldn't imagine the pain. Gregg showed me a picture of the sweet little boy and suggested naming the surge operation after him. His mother readily gave us permission, and that is what we called our operation: Operation Legend.

When I briefed the President on our plan, he demanded we add Chicago. I argued that Chicago would require far greater resources for fewer results than elsewhere, and we'd see much better progress sooner if we deployed the resources to the cities I picked. But President Trump was adamant. I was less opposed to Chicago than I had been before because the city had brought in a new police superintendent from Dallas, David Brown, whom I regarded very highly. Although the city's mayor, Lori Lightfoot, was difficult, and she and the President were at each other's throats, I felt the hard-pressed Chicago police force and Brown deserved our support. Still, by including Chicago, we significantly depleted the resources we could place elsewhere and reduced the length of time we could maintain an all-out surge across all the cities.

I visited all the Operation Legend cities. I met with both the federal and local law enforcement leadership in those communities and spent time in the police precincts and neighborhoods most affected. The extra federal help was deeply appreciated by local law enforcement and most of the political leadership. The African American police chief of a major city took me aside and said, "I can't say this in public, but God bless what you guys are doing. Our system has collapsed. Without you guys stepping up, things would be completely out of control. Please keep it up." Unfortunately, some politicians and much of the national media attempted to discredit Operation Legend by idiotically mischaracterizing it as an "occupation" by federal forces to suppress peaceful demonstrations. The traditional crime-fighting activities involved in Operation Legend had nothing to do with responding to the rioting touched off by the killing of George Floyd that was continuing in cities like Portland, Oregon. But the mainstream press had a neurotic need to connect every executive policy to Donald Trump and his political travails, and so Operation Legend was portrayed as part of some fascistic putsch.

At any other time, the initiative would have been considered a great success, especially given its short duration and the constraints imposed by Covid. All told, the operation resulted in over 6,000 arrests across the nine cities, including approximately 467 for homicide. Of the total arrested, approximately 1,500 were charged with federal offenses. More than 2,600 firearms were seized, as well as more than 32 kilos of heroin, 17 kilos of fentanyl, 300 kilos of methamphetamine, and 135 kilos of cocaine. But the huge upsurge in violent crime in 2020 nationwide was a powerful tide to swim against, and, while Operation Legend and Project Guardian prevented even worse levels of crime, they could not reverse the overall national increase.

At an Oval Office meeting in the first part of September about civil unrest around the country, the President challenged me on Operation Legend. He was frustrated with the absence of apparent progress on the Durham investigation and my reticence about using the regular army to deal with rioting. But he struck out at Operation Legend. "What the hell are we doing in Chicago? That is a waste of time!" he spat.

"The only reason we are in Chicago, Mr. President, is because you insisted on it. Period!" I hit back.

"No, I did not," he claimed.

The President's senior aide, Stephen Miller, was present and spoke up. "Actually, you did, Mr. President."

This was not an unusual circumstance. More times than I can remember, I saw instances when President Trump pushed a subordinate to adopt a policy or take a position, only to later disclaim responsibility and pull the rug out from under his subordinate. But this particular episode was small potatoes compared with some other examples I'd seen. It was one of the President's less attractive traits.

I observed that Operation Legend was getting a lot of positive attention at the local level, but our ability to break through more in the national media was being hampered by the lack of message discipline at the White House. Every time we had a press conference with good news to report on crime, something provocative came out of the White House that drove everything else out of the news.

"No one gives a shit about Legend," the President said churlishly. "No one has ever heard of it."

Kayleigh McEnany, the White House press secretary, jumped in.

"The Attorney General is right, Mr. President," she said. "There has been a lot of buzz about Legend, and very good coverage at the local level. We do have some opportunities there."

The President showed no interest.

The savage, transnational gangs based in El Salvador, Guatemala, and Honduras—the so-called Northern Triangle countries in Central America—pose a twofold threat. With broad criminal operations in the United States, which they have attempted to expand, these gangs are responsible for extreme violence and heinous crimes around the country. But with tens of thousands of members in Central America, the gangs threaten to overwhelm the law enforcement capacities of the Northern Triangle countries and are destabilizing the region. These countries are now among the most violent in the world. This contributes to the illegal migration to the United States coming out of Central America. Dealing decisively with these violent gangs will make American communities safer. It will also reduce the flow of illegal aliens across our southern border.

A key part of our efforts against violent crime was our campaign to destroy one of the most savage criminal organizations ever to operate in the United States: Mara Salvatrucha, or MS-13. This international gang originated among Salvadorans in Los Angeles who were later deported back to El Salvador after the civil war in that country ended in 1992. It has grown into a major transnational criminal organization with more than ten thousand members in the United States, mostly illegal aliens, and several tens of thousands centered in El Salvador and the rest of Central America, as well as contingents in other countries around the world. MS-13 is the larger of two major rival gangs based largely in Central America, the other being the 18th Street gang, or La 18, which also formed in Los Angeles. Like MS-13, 18th Street is extremely violent and operates in the United States and internationally, although its US activities are not as widespread as MS-13's.

MS-13 is an unusual kind of organization. It has the sheer savagery of a wild street gang but the hierarchical structure of organized crime. Members are not driven by commercial interests so much as a quest for the "honor" of being the most savage, bloodthirsty gangster possible and building up a reputation as a wanton killer. Known for butchering their victims with machetes, MS-13 is really a death cult. It uses the terror whipped up by their savagery to engage in wide-scale extortion. Increasingly, the group has also gotten into narcotics trafficking and human trafficking and prostitution, but these activities are, in a sense, sidelights to its basic objective: terrorizing people with wanton violence.

When I was first briefed on MS-13 in my conference room, I was shown some videos. One showed several men captured by the gang sitting on the ground, their hands tied behind their backs. A number of MS-13 members, brandishing machetes, walked calmly among them. Suddenly the captives were pushed over onto their stomachs, and the gang members started hacking at them with their machetes. It was an orgy of blood, with the MS-13 members dancing on the backs of their victims, hacking away at them. The machete blows made a sickening, dull thud, like chopping a watermelon. The thuds continued well after the screaming stopped. It was bestial.

Each year, MS-13 is responsible for thousands of violent crimes in the United States, including murders, extortion, arms and drug trafficking, assaults, rapes, human trafficking, robberies, and kidnappings. For decades, the gang has exploited weaknesses in the American immigration system to move its members in and out of the United States and to recruit new members from among illegal aliens here. MS-13 has infiltrated both our cities and suburbs, and established "cliques" in California, New York, New Jersey, Maryland, Virginia, Massachusetts, Ohio, North Carolina, Georgia, and Texas.

One of the worst aspects of US immigration policy is the way we admit unaccompanied minors into the country and commit them to the care of relatives or foster families. Instead, we should set up a process of sending them back home. Here in the United States, they have become the principal pool for MS-13 recruiting. Isolated in America, under loose supervision, these children become easy prey of MS-13, lured by the illusion of belonging to a family. We are leading these children like sheep to the slaughter.

At the beginning of the Trump administration, the department established Operation Regional Shield, a coordinated campaign involving El Salvador, Honduras, Guatemala, and the United States to dismantle MS-13 and other gangs in Central America. With US training, advisers, and funding, these Northern Triangle countries started to build an infrastructure of specialized prosecutors, antigang police units, and intelligence capacities targeted against the gangs and their trafficking activities. This program achieved impressive results from the very start, charging more than 3,800 MS-13 and 18th Street members, including 70 in the United States, in September 2017.

In March 2019, the month after I became Attorney General, the President blasted the Northern Triangle countries for failing to stem the flow of illegal aliens from Central America crossing our border. He said he was stopping all foreign aid to those countries until they did more to stop the flow. This would have interrupted the law enforcement progress we were making there. I went to see President Trump to brief him on our joint operations with the Northern Triangle countries and explain that cutting off law enforcement assistance would be cutting off our nose to spite our face. By targeting the gangs and their human trafficking activities, our operations were helping to stabilize the region and directly curtail migration. I told the President that, to underscore our commitment to our joint antigang operations, I planned to make my first foreign trip as Attorney General to El Salvador in May, where I would be meeting with my counterparts from all three Northern Triangle countries. I asked the President to release all the funding for our Central American law enforcement partners and to let me announce that on my trip. Secretary of State Mike Pompeo agreed with me and weighed in on my side.

Trump agreed. In May I traveled to El Salvador, where I had dinner with its newly elected president, Nayib Bukele; met with the three attorneys general of the Northern Triangle countries; and visited DOJ and FBI personnel deployed in the region, as well as the local officials and units working with us. One of the tactics used by MS-13 is the assassination of police and members of their families, and I was deeply impressed by the bravery and commitment of the Salvadoran police officers with whom we were working.

At my press conference in El Salvador, I announced that I had discussed the trip with President Trump, who "supported my coming down here and making clear we remain committed to this effort, and we remain committed to the funding that has been supporting these law enforcement efforts." This was a great shot in the arm for all the Central Americans involved in the fight to rid the region of MS-13 and the 18th Street gang.

In August 2019 I established Joint Task Force Vulcan to attack MS-13's activities in the United States and its connections to gang leaders in El Salvador. Vulcan, led by seasoned Justice Department antigang prosecutors and FBI agents, and involving all DOJ components, as well as elements of the Department of Homeland Security, was directed to use an all-of-government approach to conduct targeted prosecutions of MS-13 elements and leaders who have the greatest impact on the United States. In July 2020 Vulcan coordinated three major indictments. In Virginia, we indicted Melgar Diaz, alleged to be a major MS-13 leader overseeing the twenty cliques in the United States. In New York, we indicted eight members of MS-13 for multiple racketeering offenses in connection with six murders and two attempted murders. In Nevada, thirteen leaders, members, and associates of MS-13 were charged with a violation of the federal "kingpin" statute and multiple drug and firearm offenses. During the Trump administration, the department prosecuted approximately 749 MS-13 gang members. Through international cooperation, hundreds of MS-13 members were arrested abroad, and more than 50 members were extradited for prosecution in the United States.

In January 2021, days before the end of the administration, Vulcan indicted fourteen individuals in El Salvador, charging that they served as the highest-ranking MS-13 leaders—known as the Ranfla Nacional—functioning as the gang's board of directors and masterminding MS-13's violence and criminal activity around the world. MS-13 leaders have established a highly organized, hierarchical command and control structure. Its leaders can issue orders and ensure their enforcement even while they are in prison—a state of affairs with which the Salvadoran prisons cannot cope. From prison, the Ranfla Nacional orders murders and beatings in El Salvador, the United States, and elsewhere, runs military-style training camps for its members, and buys military-grade weapons. Our objective was to extradite these men to the United States for prosecution and incarceration and thus break up the command structure that has run the organization for decades.

At the same time, in the Northern Triangle, Operation Regional Shield continued to press the attack on MS-13 and 18th Street. In November 2020, in a coordinated action, more than 700 gang members were charged in the three countries. All told, during the Trump administration, Operation Regional Shield issued 21,500 arrest warrants against gang members, and successfully convicted almost 17,800 of them.

Under the Trump administration, we got things off to a strong start in confronting the hyper-violent Central American gangs. Major challenges remain. What's essential is that the United States not waver in its commitment to destroy these gangs and double down on the programs that have achieved success so far. MS-13 and 18th Street not only perpetrate atrocious violence but also destabilize the entire region and export their crimes to the US homeland.

Governments of the Northern Triangle brave enough to take on the gangs deserve the full backing of the United States. Without it, they will be sorely tempted, for their own protection, to make peace with the gangs—allowing the gangs to consolidate their power.

As dangerous as they are, the violent sociopaths of MS-13 are not the only lethal export from Latin America bringing carnage to the United States. The drug cartels are pumping ever-increasing volumes of deadly and life-destroying drugs into our country. Yet liberal opinion ignores the human toll and social disorder wrought by the cartels, or seeks feel-good but false panaceas such as treatment or decriminalization that do nothing to stop the spread of this poison. Whatever his faults, Trump saw the problem clearly and was prepared to act on it. It is well past time the American people face up to it.

CHAPTER 15

FIGHTING THE DRUG CARTELS

On December 5, 2019, I entered the National Palace in Mexico City for a meeting with Mexican president Andres Manuel Lopez Obrador. AMLO, as he is known, had been elected one year earlier. The Mexican media, which had been swarming me since my arrival the day before, was abuzz about the meeting, presenting it as a showdown. AMLO's predecessors had used the Mexican military to go after the cartels, but AMLO, a left-of-center populist, had pronounced an end to the drug war and adopted a policy he called "hugs, not bullets." It was my objective to persuade him to step up enforcement efforts against the cartels, explaining that their ability to act with relative impunity in Mexico, while pumping an ever-increasing flow of poison into the United States, was an intolerable situation we could not countenance. The cartels were a mortal danger to the people of Mexico and the United States, and our two countries had to work jointly and aggressively to destroy these organizations.

President Trump had set the stage for my meeting by announcing that he was going to designate the Mexican cartels as foreign terrorist organizations. This would expose any Mexican entity or individual having dealings with the cartel to sanctions such as freezing of assets and travel bans. The move would deal a blow to Mexican national pride. The Mexican media were predicting that Lopez Obrador would educate me on Mexican sovereignty and tell the Yankees to go pound sand.

Despite our frustration with the Mexicans on the drug front, the

President had developed a friendly relationship with AMLO, characterized by candor and apparent mutual respect. President Trump was especially pleased with Mexico's actions on immigration. In May the President had threatened to impose tariffs on Mexican imports unless Mexico helped stop the stream of illegal aliens crossing the US border. AMLO had deployed his military to disrupt the flow. That program required aliens from Central America seeking to claim asylum in the United States to wait in Mexico while their claims were processed. These measures proved decisive in stanching the flow of illegal aliens across our border. I was hoping we could persuade AMLO to take some similarly important steps in combating the cartels.

Mexico's massive National Palace, first built in 1522, and then largely rebuilt after fires in the mid and late 1600s, is a stunning structure of red volcanic stone, taking up the whole east side of Mexico City's central plaza, popularly called the Zocalo. Upon arriving at the palace, we were ushered into a large, richly appointed conference room, where the Mexican president sat at the head of a long table. I sat to AMLO's right. Arrayed along each side of the table were Mexico's national security officials, including Foreign Secretary Marcelo Ebrard and its leading military officers. AMLO, a politician for thirty years, can get fired up on the hustings, but in personal meetings, he has a calm and friendly manner.

Speaking in Spanish, Lopez Obrador started by welcoming me and stressing the value he placed on good relations with the United States. He then mentioned his relationship with President Trump. "Many may not understand, but he and I actually have a lot in common," he said. "We are both disrupters. We came in to bring about much-needed change. We both are trying to bring new approaches. One of the areas where Mexico needs a new approach is in dealing with the drug problem." I knew what was coming, but I had some specific proposals that I felt AMLO should be able to agree to if he had any interest in curtailing the pipeline of drugs into the United States. If he did not agree, then at least we'd know we couldn't count on any help from Mexico on the drug front. In that case, we would have to adjust our strategy.

A lot of planning had gone into preparing for my meeting with the Mexican president, which was occurring almost at the end of my first year in office. The idea for the meeting originated in the late summer of 2019 and was prompted by my view that we had to sharply escalate our efforts against the Mexican cartels. My view on fighting the drug war, going back to my first stint as Attorney General, has long been that the main law enforcement effort to constrain the supply side should be directed outside the United States against the source of the drugs and the foreign cartels involved in production and trafficking. It makes no sense to lock up generation after generation of local street pushers while leaving the cartels unscathed. This doesn't mean we should ignore the local distribution networks on the streets of America, but real progress requires that we confront the cartels on their home turf and eliminate the foreign sanctuaries they need to operate. This is the head of the snake, and federal law enforcement is the only player capable of crushing it—that is where our principal effort should be focused.

The tragedy isn't that the drug war is being lost, it's that the drug war isn't truly being fought—at least not with the force it deserves. In general, any time the United States makes challenging the cartels a priority, the foreign countries hosting them decide they're not willing to help; and when the host countries *are* ready to commit, America's attention has wandered elsewhere. During the short-lived windows when both the United States and the relevant foreign government are in sync, we have made substantial progress—as in Colombia in the 1990s—but these efforts have not been sustained and have left the job half done.

As I took stock during the summer of 2019, I worried about the trajectory of America's drug problem. It seems the country has become inured to the sheer number of lives taken by drugs, but those costs are shocking. I followed the issue closely because my daughter Mary, a longtime narcotics prosecutor, had moved from the field to headquarters to serve as lead opioid coordinator for the department. In 2017 there were more than seventy thousand fatal overdoses in the United States, of which forty-seven thousand were due to opioids. Annual fatal overdoses exceed the total casualties sustained during the *entire* Vietnam War. During the first two years of the Trump administration, drug overdoses declined for the first time in decades. This decline was due mainly to our successful efforts against abuse of prescription drugs.

But as 2019 unfolded, it appeared to me the growing flood of illegal opioids pouring in from Mexico—especially the deadly synthetic opioid fentanyl, which is a hundred times stronger than morphine— would soon undo the progress we had made on prescription drug abuse. The tiniest amount of fentanyl—only 2 milligrams—can kill. The cartels were lacing their other drugs—heroin, cocaine, and methamphetamine—with fentanyl, which meant drug users frequently did not know what they were ingesting. It was tantamount to murder.

While the opioid crisis remained a dire challenge, the country was being hit by a massive surge in Mexican methamphetamine. The cartels were producing meth of unprecedented potency on an industrial scale. To build up new markets, they were inundating areas of the country with this poison at dirt cheap prices. In roughly half of the United States, meth rivaled opioids as the leading drug problem. Meth was increasingly causing overdose deaths, especially when laced with fentanyl. But even when it did not kill immediately, meth use consigned users to a slow, grim death and triggered extreme, violent behavior. This onslaught of Mexican meth was ravaging whole communities wherever it took hold.

This much quickly became clear to me: our drug "supply" problem resides effectively in one place—Mexico. This had changed since I was last Attorney General. In the early 1990s most of the heroin coming into the US was from Asia. Mexican criminal organizations produced marijuana for the US market and transported cocaine on behalf of the Colombians. Over the past twenty-five years, however, Mexican cartels have gained control over the full range of illegal drugs coming into the United States. Now about 95 percent of the heroin seized in the United States is produced in Mexico. Since China cracked down on fentanyl, the cartels have started to produce it themselves, using precursor chemicals from China and India. Cartel laboratories throughout Mexico are saturating the United States with potent, cheap meth.

Although coca plants are grown mostly in remote areas in Colombia and Peru, the overall drug trade is run by the Mexican cartels, who are the buyers and traffickers and, more recently, the refiners. These cartels continue to supply the US market with marijuana, and more recently have turned to human trafficking as a side business that complements their drug trafficking.

The pivotal fact about our supply problem today is that the cartels are essentially able to operate with near impunity inside Mexico. The cartels are close to becoming almost states within the state, operating from safe havens beyond the control of the Mexican government. The two main cartels are the Sinaloa Cartel, formerly run by Joaquin "El Chapo" Guzman Loera, based in the northwest and along Mexico's Pacific coast, and the Jalisco New Generation Cartel, which arose just a decade ago. This latter cartel, referred to as CJNG, appears to be the fastest-growing group, now operating in two-thirds of Mexican states, and is known for extreme violence, including political assassinations. There are numerous other smaller cartels or groups, some substantial, including a number of organizations that operate along the US border and control the smuggling routes. With oceans of cash at their disposal, the cartels have historically been able to buy off Mexican politicians, police, military commanders, and judges. Effective law enforcement efforts have thus long been hampered by significant corruption at both the state and federal levels of the Mexican government. Even when the government resorts to military force, it has difficulty gaining the upper hand. This is partly because sometimes corrupt government officials leak operational information to the cartels in advance. It's also because the cartels have become more paramilitary, with heavily armed, mobile units able to stand their ground against the Mexican military.

In October 2019, as I was working through our Mexican strategy with President Trump, the Mexican government was humiliated in what came to be called the battle of Culiacán. When a large convoy of Mexican troops went into Culiacán, a city in northwestern Mexico, to arrest El Chapo's son, they were surrounded by around seven hundred cartel paramilitary equipped with armored cars, rocket launchers, and heavy machine guns. After the cartel forces took over a housing complex where military families lived, the troops released El Chapo's son.

Even in the best of times, Mexico's criminal justice system has traditionally been ineffectual. Ninety-five percent of all murders and 90 percent of all crimes go unpunished. Yet even the limited ability Mexican law enforcement had to put pressure on the cartels before AMLO's election was put into question once he entered office and indicated he intended to pull back from confronting the cartels. The Mexicans no longer seemed willing to conduct operations to arrest drug kingpins. AMLO's government withdrew navy and marine units from antidrug operations, even though the DEA and other US agencies found them to be the most reliable partners to work with in Mexico. Although Lopez Obrador announced major efforts to deal with corruption, the problem is so entrenched that making real progress will take a long time. He also undertook an ambitious reorganization of the military, law enforcement, and the courts, which—whatever its merit may be over the long run—had the effect of bringing any forward motion to a grinding halt. His proposed hugs-not-bullets approach was to expand social programs to address what he believed were the root causes of crime, principally poverty. Although AMLO had high hopes that his pacific policies would reduce Mexico's soaring homicide rate, that has not happened. According to the Associated Press, the most authoritative figures show homicides in 2019 and 2020 essentially unchanged at 36,661 and 36,579 respectively—a homicide rate roughly five times higher than that in the US.

I believed the existing state of affairs in Mexico held great danger for the United States. The nightmare scenario was the possibility that the cartels had become so strong and entrenched, and the level of violence so overwhelming within Mexico, that a tacit modus vivendi with the cartels would evolve, whereby the Mexican government would, as a practical matter, leave the cartels relatively unhampered to carry on their drug trafficking into the United States, as long as they reduced the level of violence affecting the Mexican population. Of course, under this scenario, there might be the occasional public enforcement action taken—not especially meaningful—to give the false impression of cooperation, while masking the reality of capitulation. This possible state of affairs, if it evolved, would be unacceptable to the United States. It would place on our border a failed narco-state effectively sharing its sovereignty with massive criminal organizations, thereby shielding them to operate freely against the United States, inflicting losses and devastation on our country every year equivalent to those sustained in a major war.

I was also concerned that, even if the Mexican government was willing to work with us against the cartels, these criminal enterprises had become so strong that a joint law enforcement prosecution-by-prosecution approach would not succeed in dismantling them. I wondered, in other words, if the Mexican cartels had become more of a national security threat than just a matter of law enforcement.

After I saw the President use the tariff threat in June to prod the Mexicans to reduce the number of illegal aliens crossing the border, I thought we might use a similar approach to get AMLO to act against the cartels. At around this time, the proposal to designate the cartels as foreign terrorist organizations was gaining traction on Capitol Hill. I had no strong objection to it and generally agreed that we should treat the cartels more like terrorist groups than Mafia crime families. But that designation alone wouldn't allow us to impose severe sanctions. There were other options, especially if we could count on a willing Mexican government. Instead of proceeding with designation, I thought, we should at least try to get the Mexicans to move forward jointly with us on a concrete plan of attack against the cartels.

I set up a skunk works of key players from the department and other agencies to put together a specific plan of action to step up the fight against the Mexican cartels. I picked people who had been operationally involved in the drug war and knew firsthand where the major impediments were, as well as the big opportunities. I referred to each area of activity as a "line of effort," and each had a team identifying the key actions that could be taken to hit the cartels soonest and hardest. There were, for example, lines of effort addressing ocean interdiction, fentanyl precursors, kingpin arrests, meth labs, and a number of others. Two areas that I knew the Mexicans wanted were increased efforts against cartel money laundering and the smuggling of weapons from the United States to Mexico. DHS Secretary Kevin McAleenan, and later his successor, Chad Wolf, helped me cut through the usual bureaucratic obstacles to pull together the plan. Throughout my tenure, I found both McAleenan and Wolf great partners to work with.

As the plan started coming together, I visited with President Trump to get his approval for my course of action. We met in the small dining room off the Oval Office. Dealing with him directly could be a frustrating experience, but this was one of the most satisfying meetings we had. We were very much in sync.

"I came to Washington to actually solve problems, not talk about them and then leave them for somebody else to deal with," he started off. "And I am afraid that is what has been going on in the drug war for decades."

Anticipating my concerns, the President stressed that we could not allow Mexico to become a narco-state on our border, saying, "I've made clear to Mexico that I am willing to do whatever is necessary to help them take down the cartels."

I told President Trump that, assuming Mexico was an active and willing partner, I thought dismantling the cartels would take a huge effort inside Mexico exceeding the scope of anything done before, and it would require significant US involvement in joint actions with the Mexicans. I explained to the President my plan to go down and meet with AMLO and his law enforcement and military officials to explore their willingness to work with us on a range of specific initiatives to press the cartels. If they were willing to work with us, then perhaps we could find a viable way of dealing with the cartels. But if they were not willing to work with us, we would have to come up with a new strategy for addressing the cartels.

"Good," the President said. "You let AMLO know I am willing to do whatever it takes to deal with the cartels."

I wanted to go down to Mexico with a very practical plan already worked out. We had eight separate multiagency teams, each working on a particular line of effort, and each with specific goals that could be achieved within a year. I would invite the Mexicans to propose any additional teams or goals and ask them to designate Mexican members to participate on each team. These would not be planning teams but *action* teams with responsibility for achieving the goals in their areas. The concept was that any disagreements would be escalated quickly to a senior official on both the Mexican and American side. On the American side, that senior official would report to me, and I would ask the Mexicans to designate a cabinet-level official to serve as my counterpart. I was going to propose that I would visit Mexico every other month for a progress review.

Most of the proposal was straightforward. One line of effort, for example, entailed resuming the apprehension, extradition, and US prosecution of significant cartel figures. The United States already had a number of extradition requests pending in Mexico that appeared to be in deep freeze. One of the goals in this area involved the Mexicans following through on the extraditions. Another was for Mexico to allow its marines to work with the US Drug Enforcement Administration in once again apprehending drug kingpins. Still another example of low-hanging fruit was in the area of interdiction. An increasing volume of narcotics was being transported to the United States by way of sea routes along Mexico's Pacific coast and Atlantic coast. We were identifying many more drug vessels than we had the capacity to intercept. We knew with certainty that adding six US ships—three in the Pacific and three in the Gulf of Mexico—would radically increase drug seizures. We would encourage the Mexican navy to step up its efforts as well.

When AMLO talked publicly about resisting the cartels, he focused on the most indirect enforcement activity: stopping the flow of guns being smuggled into Mexico from the United States and disrupting cartel money laundering. He particularly liked talking about the guns because doing so attributed the violence in Mexico to the Americans. I thought the idea of curtailing Mexico's astronomical violent crime rate through gun control was a pipe dream, but I had a number of tangible proposals that could curtail gun smuggling. Simply giving us the serial numbers of seized weapons would help the ATF investigate the networks responsible for sending guns to Mexico.

Before my meeting with AMLO, I had the opportunity to brief

Marcelo Ebrard. Smooth and urbane, the Mexican foreign minister spoke excellent English and seemed to have the lead in working through the terrorist designation issue with the United States. The point he emphasized, in addition to the importance of America respecting Mexican sovereignty, was that Mexico was, in fact, taking steps against the cartels and already had plans for collaborating with us. I stressed that, from our standpoint, things were at a standstill, and we needed to see Mexico take concrete action. I said that President Trump had asked me to come back from Mexico able to answer a specific question: Is there any hope of defeating the cartels through joint law enforcement efforts? For us to answer that question, we would like the Mexican government to work with us over the coming year on a few specific actions. I said this was an important experiment to see whether progress was possible.

I also addressed Mexican sensitivities about sovereignty by making an observation. We fully understand Mexico's concern over her sovereignty, I said, and of course we would honor it. But sovereignty *rights* have corresponding *duties*. A government exercising sovereignty over territory has the duty to ensure that its territory is not used as a launching pad for injurious activities directed against its neighbors. Thus, under international law, if a government knows that lawless groups are using its territory to prey on other countries, it has the duty to eliminate those threats.

As I sat in the National Palace listening to AMLO at his conference table, I was reminded of the debates that raged thirty years ago in the United States about dealing with violent crime. He was speaking eloquently about the impact of violence on Mexican society. "We tried using force against the cartels for many years, and that approach has led to many deaths but not much progress. We must try a new way. We must attack the root causes of violence. We must attack poverty and give people hope."

When it was my turn to speak, I affirmed the importance President Trump placed on our relationship with Mexico, as well as his personal relationship with Lopez Obrador. I assured him that the United States intended to respect Mexico's sovereignty. The problem of the cartels was a joint problem and needed a joint solution. I told the Mexican president that thirty years ago, the US crime rate was double its present level. At the time, many powerful and influential people had been saying for years that the way to control crime was to address its root causes by expanding social programs. Others, like me, thought we needed to return to the policy that had worked in the past: taking violent criminals off the streets. But these two approaches, I said, are not mutually exclusive. They are complementary. I urged him to think of strong enforcement efforts against the cartels and his root-causes social programs as two complementary pillars of an overall approach to bringing peace to Mexico.

AMLO then raised another difficult point: the responsibility of those who use the drugs versus those who supply the drugs. He intimated that the violence in Mexico, as well as the high death toll in the United States, was due to our country's insatiable appetite for drugs and that the real solution for both countries was for America to reduce its demand. My response was that, given the nature of narcotics, both the pusher and the addict shared moral culpability. Neither could fairly make themselves out as the victim of the other. I agreed that the United States had to reduce demand, but—like his attack on the root causes of crime—this was a long-term effort that would take decades.

I then got to the nub of my argument. We cannot wait decades to stop the carnage taking place today. The problem for the United States, I explained, was that the cartels were currently inflicting massive harm on our society. It wasn't just the deaths alone but also the massive social devastation and blighting of whole communities. I then used an example that I thought would have special meaning for him, given his own concern for the indigenous people of Mexico.

"Mr. President," I said, "right now the cartels are flooding areas of the United States with very potent methamphetamine. They are going into areas that have never had a significant meth problem before and almost giving it away to build up a market. One of my personal priorities is the well-being of our Native American people in what we call Indian country. We are now seeing some Native American communities in which two-thirds of the children are in foster homes because their parents are hooked on meth and unable to care for their children."

This figure struck AMLO. I could see it on his face. The bottom line, I said, was that the United States could not sit by passively and watch this devastation and do nothing about the cartels. Both countries had to pursue long-term solutions, but we also had to address the immediate problem, and that required strong joint action against the cartels. I promised we would work with his administration on his priorities of cutting down on guns coming in from the United States and on cartel money laundering, but we would like his support on other components of combating the cartels.

As we concluded the meeting, Mexico's president indicated that designation of the cartels as terrorist organizations would infringe on Mexico's sovereignty and be counterproductive. I said I understood and would be making my recommendation to President Trump as soon as I returned to Washington. I expressed the hope that we could make progress on the set of proposed actions I had discussed with his national security and legal advisers. After the meeting, AMLO put out a statement describing it as a "good" one. In follow-up meetings I held with members of his administration before leaving Mexico City, it appeared they were willing to engage with us on the multiple lines of efforts and most of the specific aims I was proposing. Foreign Secretary Ebrard and I agreed that I would visit again in a month—the end of January—and, in the meantime, we would get our teams working on the first set of action items.

The day after my return to Washington, the President held an Oval Office meeting with the key officials involved in our antidrug effort. I briefed everyone on the results of the trip. The President tweeted: "All necessary work has been completed to declare Mexican Cartels terrorist organizations. Statutorily, we are ready to do so. However, at the request of a man who I like and respect, and has worked so well with us, President Andres Manuel Lopez Obrador—we will temporarily hold off on this designation." Trump said the United States and Mexico would instead "step up our joint efforts to deal decisively with these vicious and ever-growing organizations."

AMLO's response: "I thank Trump for having put off the decision . . . and having chosen understanding and cooperation."

For the first ninety days or so after my first visit to Mexico City, cooperation kicked into high gear. The Mexicans were following up, and we started making progress across all the lines of effort. Nowhere was progress more dramatic than in the area of extraditions. With remarkable speed, the Mexican government started working its way down the list of outstanding US requests. We went from standing still to a total of nearly sixty extraditions within a few months. The Mexican navy informed the US Drug Enforcement Administration that Mexican marines would once again provide it support. More naval resources were committed to interdiction. ATF agents were finally allowed to inspect guns that had been smuggled into Mexico from the United States. Work was proceeding on other goals.

The feeling of progress continued during my next visit to Mexico in January 2020. Foreign Secretary Ebrard told me that, while he would stay involved, my counterpart for operational issues going forward would be Security Minister Alfonso Durazo Montaño.

Sadly, within a couple of months of my January visit, the spirit of cooperation and the apparent progress we were making with the Mexicans all came to a screeching halt. The culprit was Covid. Nearly everything shut down, especially on the Mexican side. All forward motion stopped. Meetings stopped. Operations were canceled.

Even before Covid asserted itself, however, I had begun to see disturbing signs that the Mexicans' efforts were not as robust as we had hoped. On a number of key fronts, such as taking down meth labs, I was concerned the Mexicans might be slow-rolling operations. There were also some disturbing instances in which it appeared the cartels were being tipped off in advance about some important planned actions. This kind of corruption is endemic in Mexico, but these episodes had me questioning the measure to which AMLO had succeeded in purging corruption from his administration. In any event, I always suspected that, when it came to confronting the cartels, the AMLO administration was a reluctant warrior, and without pressure, it would default to passivity. The pandemic gave the Mexicans a good excuse to pull back. Too bad.

On October 15, a couple of weeks before our presidential election, an imbroglio involving Mexican general Salvador Cienfuegos Zepeda clarified the mind-set of AMLO's administration. The Brooklyn US Attorney's Office and the DEA had been investigating General Cienfuegos for allegedly protecting the operations of a cartel when he served as secretary of national defense in the administration of AMLO's predecessor. Hearing that he would be passing through Los Angeles International Airport, DEA seized the opportunity to arrest him. Higher levels of the department had not been notified that the arrest would take place. President Lopez Obrador was furious that he had not been alerted to the investigation or the arrest. Personally, I felt that Cienfuegos's case was not worth scuttling any prospects of broader cooperation with the Mexicans.

On October 26, when Foreign Secretary Ebrard called to object to the arrest, he was dumbfounded by my preemptive concession. I apologized and explained that the arrest had not gone through the normal process, and that neither I nor the head of DEA was aware of it beforehand. I made it clear that I was willing to return Cienfuegos and was taking care of the formalities necessary to do that. I asked that AMLO not proceed with legislation in the Mexican Chamber of Deputies that would effectively neuter the DEA in Mexico. I told him we would be happy to work with his country on protocols to prevent similar events in the future, but that the legislation would make it impossible to work effectively against the cartels. Ebrard took this in. Then he suggested that if we provided Mexico with the evidence against Cienfuegos, Mexican authorities would investigate the matter.

The proposed Mexican legislation required foreign agents operating in Mexico—meaning especially DEA agents—to share with the Mexican government any information they acquired. It also required Mexican officials to obtain prior permission to meet with any foreign agent and to make written reports on the matters discussed. But as the Mexicans knew well, these procedures would make it almost impossible to prevent information shared with the Mexican government from reaching the cartels. The broad information-sharing requirements then under consideration by the Mexican Chamber of Deputies would eviscerate the DEA in Mexico—the most professional, dedicated, and reliable force in that country focused on destroying the cartels.

Unsurprisingly, the driver of events following Cienfuegos's arrest was the US 2020 presidential election. After Trump lost the election, there was no reason for AMLO to continue his cooperation against the cartels. Operations that had been promised were postponed repeatedly. I returned Cienfuegos in mid-November as promised. But after that, there wasn't any semblance of cooperation. The Mexicans went ahead and passed the legislation gravely handicapping the DEA, and they announced exculpation of Cienfuegos.

We are at a critical juncture in fighting against the scourge of illegal narcotics. It's true that the drug war can't be won by a law enforcement approach alone. Reducing demand is critical, and this task requires education and prevention programs to stop people from becoming drug users in the first place. It also requires treatment programs to save those who suffer from addiction and help them lead drug-free lives.

But we also have to address the supply of illegal drugs by going after the criminal enterprises involved in their production, transportation, and distribution. Those who suggest that we can tackle our drug problem by focusing solely on driving down demand are wrong. They don't appreciate, first of all, the degree to which law enforcement contributes to the suppression of demand: the enforcement of drug laws makes it harder for people to get illegal substances, and it makes the use of them less desirable. To put it in plain terms, many people avoid illegal drugs precisely because they're illegal and because an arrest would embarrass them.

Further, many of those receiving treatment do so only because law enforcement requires it. Without law enforcement, far fewer people would be willing to enter into, and stick with, treatment. More fundamentally, with a product such as narcotics—pleasurable, escapist, addictive—a ready supply does, in fact, create demand. That appears to have been the case in the nineteenth century when Britain forced China in the Opium Wars to import India's rapidly increasing opium output. There does seem to have been a correlation between the large influx of new opium supplies and the trajectory of Chinese demand.

But for a more recent example, look no further than the United States in the last three years. Mexican cartels are creating new markets for methamphetamine by shipping quality product at cut-rate prices into regions of the United States where the drug was not used in the past. These huge supplies of inexpensive meth are creating their own demand.

In 2020 I appointed Tim Shea as the interim DEA administrator, and he proved an effective leader. Among other steps, he launched a major enforcement operation—Crystal Shield—targeting the cartels' meth distribution networks within the United States, based in nine major urban hubs. While actions like this can make a difference, the cartels' operations are most vulnerable on their own turf, especially the closer one gets to the source of the drugs. Destroying the meth labs in Mexico would be far more effective in limiting meth supply than chasing after distributors in American cities. Cocaine trade is most vulnerable in the fields where the coca plants are grown. The areas in the world suitable for coca are limited. In the Western Hemisphere, coca is effectively restricted to discrete areas of Colombia, Peru, and Bolivia. Aggressively eradicating these fields would be the most effective way of restricting the supply of cocaine. The most vulnerable part of the fentanyl supply chain are the large container shipments of precursor chemicals coming out of China and India into Mexican ports. Successfully dealing with all these vulnerabilities outside the United States requires a strong will and a more substantial effort than we have been willing to mount so far.

President Trump's instincts were correct on fighting the drug problem. He understood the essence of the crisis, which is more than I can say for a lot of his consensus-oriented critics in government and the media. The melancholy reality is, we must address supply *and* demand. We are already confronting demand, to the extent possible given the realities of our politics. On the supply side, we will have to confront producers *outside the United States* far more aggressively than we have to date—and take whatever steps are necessary to cripple the cartels.

CHAPTER 16

SECURING RELIGIOUS LIBERTY

I f aliens were to arrive from outer space, they would have to think the Little Sisters of the Poor are one of the most dangerous groups on the planet. For over a decade, Democratic administrations and progressive activists have been engaged in an unremitting legal assault against this religious order of nuns whose special vocation is caring for the elderly poor. With three hundred or so nuns in the United States, the order carries out its ministry by staffing and operating twenty-seven homes for the elderly poor around the country.

In August 2011 the Obama administration's Department of Health and Human Services (HHS) issued regulations to implement the Affordable Care Act, aka "Obamacare," which Congress had passed the year before. Those regulations required that employers provide their employees with health care insurance plans covering, at no cost to the employee, all FDA-approved means of contraception, including a number of drugs that cause abortion. Despite the clear issue of conscience raised by this mandate, the regulations allowed only a narrow exemption, which applied only to churches but not to religious non-profits, involving health care, education, and other religious ministries. Because the Little Sisters have employees who assist them in operating their homes, the mandate would have required the nuns to violate their religious conscience by facilitating access to contraception and abortifacients through their health care plans.

Even though the HHS regulations permitted exemptions to commercial firms on secular grounds, such as administrative convenience, and even though the department had granted exemptions to many large commercial companies, it refused to exempt the Little Sisters and threatened to impose heavy fines on the nuns if they failed to comply. Over the next five years, the Little Sisters sought an accommodation of their sincerely held religious beliefs and attempted to win an injunction preventing the mandate from being imposed on them. At first, they were unsuccessful in the lower federal courts. But in May 2016 the Supreme Court overturned the lower court rulings against the Little Sisters and encouraged the government to find a way to provide contraceptive services to those who want them without requiring the complicity of religious nonprofits. Indeed, if the government believes it is sufficiently important to provide free contraception to all comers, there are numerous ways to accomplish this without implicating religious organizations. No one has been able to point to any individual who needs to rely on the Little Sisters to have access to free contraception.

After President Trump won office, he eliminated the issue by having his HHS put out revised regulations in 2017 extending protection to religious nonprofits. But progressives could not stand this. A number of states sued, claiming that the exemption was unconstitutional, discriminatory, and adopted improperly by the administration. A series of lower federal courts enjoined the new exemption. Finally, in July 2020 the Supreme Court upheld the authority of the Trump administration to issue the new rule exempting religious nonprofits. Shortly afterward, presidential candidate Joe Biden declared he was "disappointed" and would, if elected, reinstate the Obama-era policies requiring the Little Sisters to facilitate access to contraception and abortifacients.

The problem today is not that religion is being forced on others. The problem is that secular values are being forced on people of faith. Progressives claim not to like the law being used to force certain moral views on them, but they now want to use the law to force their moral views on others. This reminds me of how some Roman emperors could not leave their loyal Christian subjects in peace but would mandate that they violate their conscience by offering religious sacrifice to the emperor as a god.

President Biden has repeatedly said that transexual rights are "the civil rights issue of our time." I disagree. I believe the civil rights issue of our time is our religious liberty enshrined in the Free Exercise Clause and Establishment Clause of the First Amendment. These are the right to exercise one's religion unburdened by the government, and the right to be free from the impositions that would arise from the government's establishment of a particular religion or, for that matter, from its establishment of irreligion. I say religious liberty is paramount today because, as the Framers understood well, our system of broad personal liberties and limited government presupposes a robust and free religious sphere, and today this foundational freedom is under unprecedented assault.

Whatever the level of President Trump's personal religious devotion— and I don't presume to judge that—he seemed to have a deep intuitive appreciation of the importance of religion to the health of our nation. During his campaign, he promised to protect religious liberty, and, once elected, he actually delivered on those promises. Shortly after his election, on a National Day of Prayer, on May 4, 2017, President Trump signed Executive Order 13798, Presidential Executive Order Promoting Free Speech and Religious Liberty, before a huge audience in the Rose Garden. It was an unusually festive event, with the President in high spirits as he spoke, flanked by the Little Sisters of the Poor, Cardinal Donald Wuerl of Washington, DC, and other heavyweight religious leaders from around the country. I never had a discussion about religion with the President. But I got the sense watching him over two years that his support for religious liberty was genuine.

President Trump's executive order required federal agencies to "vigorously enforce federal law's robust protections for religious freedom . . . to the greatest extent practicable" and "respect and protect the freedom of persons and organizations to engage in religious . . . speech." Before I arrived on the scene, Attorney General Sessions had established the Religious Liberty Task Force in the Justice Department to help implement the President's directive. When I took over as Attorney General, I fully agreed with President Trump's priority and supported the work of the task force. My first major address as Attorney General was delivered on October 11, 2019, at the University of Notre Dame Law School, where I explained my views on the nature of the current threats to religious freedom and why it is so critical to defend against them. The President went out of his way to commend me for it. I am proud of the many successes we had in this arena while I was Attorney General.

The imperative of protecting religious freedom in the Constitution was not just a nod in the direction of piety. It reflects the Framers' belief that a healthy religious sphere is a necessary precondition for a system in which the power of the government can be effectively limited and bound to respect the widest personal freedoms of its citizens. The Framers were practical statesmen who understood that individuals, while having the potential for great good, also had the capacity for great evil. No society can exist without some means for restraining the tendency of individuals to prey on one another. In the Framers' view, there were two separate sources of control capable of restraining men. One came from within each individual: it was the virtue in each person's soul, an internal moral compass enforced by a well-formed conscience. The other source of control was the external coercive power of the state. The Framers believed that the more society had of one, the less it needed of the other. In this, they followed Edmund Burke, who observed: "Men are qualified for civil liberty in exact proportion to their disposition to put moral chains upon their own appetites. . . . Society cannot exist, unless a controlling power upon will and appetite be placed somewhere; and the less of it there is within, the more there must be without." Thus, for the Founders, the idea of self-government was not just about the mechanics of representative democracy, it was primarily about the capacity of each individual to govern himself or herself.

The idea that there are two separate powers over men, corresponding to two separate sets of duties, has a long pedigree in the West. It goes back at least to Christ's injunction to "Render unto Caesar that which is Caesar's, and unto God that which is God's." This duality was enlarged upon by Saint Augustine's conception of two coexisting realms: one transcendent and spiritual ("the City of God") and the other temporal ("the City of Man"). The former is the realm of religion, where each person works toward their eternal destiny by striving for moral perfection through obedience to God's will and the dictates of their moral conscience. The latter is the secular realm, where the state exercises the coercive power necessary to restrain those who cannot restrain themselves from harming their fellow citizens.

This conception eventually led to the idea of separation of church and state. Today this idea of "separation" is regarded by some to connote the ostracism of religion from worldly affairs—the relegation of religion to the cloister. But that is not what separation meant. The idea was a *division of labor* and the autonomy of each authority within its respective sphere. And religion's rightful sphere of labor was not confined to the otherworldly concerns. On the contrary, its function was to make people virtuous *in the world* and more capable of controlling their passions and appetites. As President James Madison observed famously, "If men were angels, no government would be necessary." In simple terms, it is the role of religion—not the state—to make men more like angels. It is the role of the state to deal with the external acts of those who behave more like devils.

In general, in the classical world, before the emergence of Christianity, there was no separation of the realm of religion and moral education from the political or civic sphere. The religious and moral education functions were largely subsumed within the political life of the state, or polis, in ancient Greece. It was the state that instructed men on the purpose of life and what it meant to live a "good" life. The state was thus a positive moral agency: its role was not just restraining the bad but also leading men to be good. Indeed, it was only through participation in the state's political life that men achieved their highest moral purpose.

Christianity forced the bifurcation of authority over men's lives, and this fateful division became the mainspring behind expanding personal freedom. By recognizing that responsibility for moral education and much of the responsibility for maintaining moral discipline was vested in the religious sphere, the separation of church and state eliminated many of the previous social-control functions of the state. The state's role was essentially narrowed to more of a backstop function—restraining the wicked when individual moral discipline failed. A separate and robust religious sphere thus enabled "limited" government and naturally moderated the ambitions of government. Under our system, unlike the Greek polis, it is not the role of government to define the "good" life and lead men to it. It is not the role of government to shape man into its own image. The government has the far more modest purpose of preserving the proper balance of personal freedom and order necessary for a healthy civil society to develop and individual humans to flourish.

In framing our Constitution, the Founders engaged in what they called a great "experiment." Believing the American people to be a virtuous and religious people, they created only a limited government, trusting that "the People" would retain the moral discipline necessary for self-government. In other words, they relied on the continued capacity of the spiritual and religious sphere, not the state, to instill in citizens the moral qualities necessary for self-control. This is what Founding Father John Adams meant when he said that America's limited government was not capable of dealing with a people "unbridled by morality and religion" and that "Our Constitution was made only for a moral and religious people." In short, freedom needs religion—not necessarily in each and every individual, but generally in society.

The crisis in the West today is that, having based our ideas of liberal, limited government on a religious sphere capable of instilling in citizens the capacity for self-control, the religious sphere and its power over people is crumbling. As more people adopt a purely secular outlook, they tend to turn to the government to perform those functions of moral education that have been the domain of religion. Thus, the dynamic today is not that religion is invading the space of the secular state. It is that the secular state is being called on to invade the space of religion.

The ones who ride roughshod over the separation of church and state today are the secular progressives who are attempting to use the power of the government to establish and enforce a comprehensive secular creed as state orthodoxy—a totalizing religion of irreligion—that eclipses the religious sphere altogether and attempts to usurp religion's role in educating men's souls.

Over most of our history, the vast majority of Americans have been religious, or at least sympathetic to the claims of religion. There were certainly sectarian antipathies and even persecution of particular religions. But there was no general hostility toward religion. Consequently, the laws adopted by legislatures usually were compatible with the values of mainstream Protestant Christianity. When laws did implicate the exercise of religion, legislatures and courts tended to be openhanded in trying to accommodate religion.

But things are very different today. Over the past half century, we have seen the growing ascendancy of an especially aggressive form of secularism that has marched through our institutions and is now becoming the dominant orthodoxy among America's elites. This secular movement has been attempting to drive religion from the public square. Initially, this movement concentrated on doing away with legal restrictions on conduct—such as laws against abortion or sodomy—which had long been considered sinful under traditional Judeo-Christian doctrine. Their view was that prohibitions like this were simply the result of religious majorities getting their dogmas enacted into law and imposing them on everyone else. The first wave of secular legal reform therefore involved repealing these strictures.

Most of the rollbacks—such as the legalization of abortion—were accomplished by courts finding previously undeclared rights in the US or state constitutions. A recent watershed development in this process was the Supreme Court's 2015 decision in *Obergefell v. Hodges* that the Constitution guarantees a right to enter into same-sex marriage.

Now, if things had only gone as far as lifting legal restrictions, then a modus vivendi suggested itself. On the gravest matters, such as abortion and euthanasia, religious objectors should be left free to continue to challenge the moral propriety of these practices, and should not be forced to condone them, nor to underwrite or participate in them. As to gay rights, as I said in my confirmation hearing, it would seem the best way forward in a pluralistic society like ours is to adopt a live-and-let-live stance. While allowing gay marriage, we should not force believers, by word or deed, to condone or participate in gay marriages if it violates their religious conscience to do so. While honoring the civil legal validity of the gay marriage, they should not be required to draw back from their *moral* disapproval of same-sex marriage. Similarly, the law should protect gay people from job discrimination generally, but we should not force religious organizations to hire or retain employees when their employment would be incompatible with the organization's religious beliefs and mission.

Unfortunately, such a truce seems unlikely. After winning the first wave of secular legal reform, progressives apparently cannot tolerate a live-and-let-live world. Instead, they are attempting to use the law to compel religious people to subscribe to ideas and participate in practices that are antithetical to their faith. Not content to leave religious people alone to exercise their faith, progressives seem to take delight in compelling people to violate their consciences. It is not enough to legalize abortion—now religious believers must be forced to financially support them and, indeed, perform them. It is not enough that gay people are free to marry—now schoolchildren must be indoctrinated into the worldview that morally validates same-sex marriage.

Religious freedom issues arise most typically when the government enacts a generally applicable law and seeks to apply it to groups or individuals who claim that compliance would violate their sincerely held religious beliefs. This was the case, for example, in the 1972 case of *Wisconsin v. Yoder*, where Amish communities claimed that the right to free exercise of religion required their exemption from a state compulsory education law mandating school attendance until sixteen years old. While the Amish did not object to having their children attend public school through eighth grade, they argued that requiring attendance at high school interfered with their exercise of religion. They claimed mandating more public education at that age exposed their children to values "in marked variance with Amish values and the Amish way of life" and diverted their children from the practical education received by working within the Amish community, which prepared them for future life in the community. The Supreme Court ruled that the Free Exercise Clause required that the Amish be exempted from the compulsory education beyond elementary school. It found that the state did not have a sufficiently compelling reason for insisting on the two additional years of education, especially in light of the alternative practical education Amish children would receive working within the community.

This pre-1990 case was one of several decided in which the Supreme Court seemed to apply a balancing test: when enforcing a generally applicable law that will burden a person's or group's free exercise of religion, the government must refrain from burdening the religious exercise unless it can show that enforcing the requirement is necessary to further a compelling government interest and that no more narrowly tailored requirement will suffice to achieve the government's purpose. Until 1990, the general rule appeared to be that, rather than burdening religion, the government should accommodate it where reasonably feasible to do so.

In 1990, however, the Supreme Court appeared to pull back from a stance requiring accommodation. In *Employment Division v. Smith*, the court held that the state of Oregon could enforce its across-the-board prohibition of peyote use even where it foreclosed the sacramental use of peyote in Native American religions. The court held that accommodation is not required by the Free Exercise Clause as long as the requirement is a generally applicable prohibition and was not intended to target religion. Justice Scalia, who wrote the opinion for the court, distinguished *Yoder* and other cases that had previously applied a "balancing test." He said these were "hybrid cases" that involved the combination of free exercise rights with other constitutional rights, such as free speech rights or, as in *Yoder*, the right of parents to guide the education of their children.

The *Smith* case was controversial. While many agreed with Justice Scalia's analysis, many considered it an unjustified departure from earlier precedents. In any event, there was a strong reaction against it, leading to congressional enactment of the Religious Freedom

Restoration Act (RFRA) in 1993. This act was intended to restore the pre-*Smith* balancing test. Thus, the act provides that, when the government takes a generally applicable action that substantially burdens a person's exercise of religion, it must refrain from such an infringement unless it is necessary to further a compelling government interest and there is no less restrictive way of achieving the government's interest. The accommodation required under RFRA applies only to the federal government. But twenty-two states have adopted their own versions of RFRA applicable to state and local government actions.

The main battleground for disputes over religious liberty continues to be situations where the government seeks to enforce a generally applicable requirement in a way that burdens the free exercise of religion. These generally applicable laws are frequently cast as "antidiscrimination" laws—mandating, for example, that everyone respect same-sex marriage and a transexual's asserted gender. The term *discrimination* in this context is a loaded one. One of its two meanings refers to the *unjust* treatment of different categories of people. This has typically referred to discriminating against persons based on immutable characteristics, such as race, gender, and ethnicity. But *discrimination* also simply means recognizing a difference between one thing and another. Today, where religion is concerned, the kind of differentiation involved is not based on immutable characteristics but on personal conduct—a person's actions. Religion, by its very nature, involves differentiating between various courses of conduct—considering some morally bad and some morally good—and upholding conduct believed good and encouraging people to adhere to that conduct. To compel a religious organization or person to violate their religious scruples by refraining from upholding the difference between what they see as good and bad essentially negates the role of religion in people's lives.

There is reason to question what is really behind some of these antidiscrimination laws. Until relatively recently, there was a long history of accommodating religious entities, even in antidiscrimination laws. Why the sudden need to demand absolute conformity? The ostensible reason in some cases is to ensure that persons whose lifestyles were previously disfavored are provided availability of services and accommodations generally provided the public. This was the rationale for the Colorado Civil Rights Commission's mandate that bakers cannot make wedding cakes unless they serve all weddings, including same-sex weddings. But was this really because same-sex couples were threatened by a lack of availability of wedding cakes? It is hard to escape the conclusion that these statutes are at least in part directed at the viewpoint expression or message inherent in an act of noncompliance or compliance. When a religious person refuses to treat a same-sex marriage as the same as a traditional marriage, he or she is sending a message that there is a moral difference between the two. Conversely, when the state succeeds in getting a religious people or organization to bend the knee, it communicates acceptance of the state's rationale. The object is not really to ensure the availability of services but to stop religious people from acting in ways that convey their views.

The case involving the Colorado baker was decided the year before I joined the Trump administration. In that case, *Masterpiece Cakeshop v. Colorado Civil Rights Commission*, the Trump administration sided with the baker in the Supreme Court. The Justice Department argued that the case was an example of the "hybrid cases" referred to by Justice Scalia. In addition to the baker's religious rights, the state mandate implicated the baker's free speech rights because designing a wedding cake involves creative and expressive activity, and the state cannot compel a person to engage in expression he does not agree with. Although the Supreme Court ultimately ruled for the baker, it did not rule on the position we took. Instead, it found the record showed that the rule Colorado was attempting to apply to the baker was not really a neutral one but was adopted in part based on hostility to religion, which violated the Free Exercise Clause.

After I became Attorney General, I ensured the department followed up on *Masterpiece Cakeshop* and continued to press our arguments in similar contexts. Most significant, we filed a brief in the US Supreme Court arguing that the City of Philadelphia violated the constitutional rights of a faith-based foster care agency when it terminated the agency's contract because of the agency's unwillingness to place children with same-sex couples. That case was decided by the

Supreme Court on June 17, 2021, after I left office. I had been hoping that the court would use the case as an opportunity to cut back on the *Smith* (peyote) case, which had ruled that it was permissible for a state to incidentally burden free exercise of religion as long as the prohibition was neutral and generally applicable. I was hoping the court would adopt a standard closer to the more pro-accommodation approach applied in the *Yoder* (Amish school) case, which required the state to show that the restriction on free exercise was necessary to further a compelling state interest.

In its decision, however, the court did not break any new legal ground. It found that the requirement the city was seeking to enforce against the archdiocese was not really "neutral and generally applicable" because the city's process permitted exceptions to be made at the city's "sole discretion." Thus, the court held that *Smith*'s safe harbor for generally applicable laws did not apply. Instead, where exceptions are permitted, the city had to show a compelling reason for refusing to grant one sought on the grounds of religious hardship. The Philadelphia adoption case will not be the final word on the continued validity of *Smith*'s rule that laws burdening free exercise don't violate the First Amendment as long as they are neutral and generally applicable. From the concurring opinions in that case, it is evident that at least five justices believe that the *Smith* case is on shaky ground and should be reexamined.

In my view, the decisive front in the fight for religious liberty is education. For anyone who has a religious faith, by far the most important part of exercising it is passing the faith on to our children, instilling the faith and its values as a guide to their lives. There is no greater gift we can give our children and no greater expression of love. For the government to interfere in that process is a monstrous invasion of religious liberty, as well as the parents' right to guide the education of their children. Yet this is where the battle for religious liberty has been joined. The fight is being waged on three fronts, all of which involve attempts to constrain or sabotage the ability of families to inculcate religious beliefs in their children.

The first line of attack against religiously affiliated schools involves state measures designed to starve these schools of generally available funds and to encourage students to choose secular education over church-run schools. Among the most offensive policies in this area are reflected in the so-called little Blaine amendments, which more than thirty states added to their constitutions mostly during the latter part of the nineteenth century, a time of rampant anti-Catholic animus in this country. These provisions typically impose an absolute bar on any "sectarian" institutions from receiving any direct or indirect payments from a state's funds. It was my priority to challenge these laws head-on, and we found a perfect vehicle for this in a case coming out of Montana.

Montana had created a program that gave tax credits to those who donated to a scholarship program that underprivileged students could use to attend private school. But when three low-income families who received scholarships tried to use them to attend a Christian school, they were blocked by the Montana courts on the grounds that, under the state's Blaine amendment, the Christian school could not receive the benefits of this state program even when the benefit came indirectly through the parents' choice. The Montana Supreme Court required the state to eliminate the program altogether rather than allow parents to use scholarships for religious schools. We joined with the families in taking this case up to the US Supreme Court, where we argued on the families' side. We contended that, once Montana operated a private-school scholarship program, it could not tell parents they had to stay away from religious schools. In doing so, the state discriminated against religion, which the First Amendment of the US Constitution forbids. The US Supreme Court agreed and ruled for the families. This was a watershed case that, hopefully, will prove to be the death knell of Blaine amendments. When I left office, we had two more challenges to state Blaine amendments working their way through the courts: Vermont and Maine.

The second axis of attack on religious schools are efforts to interfere in the governance of these schools, such as decisions on who teaches. Over the years, there have been attempts to invoke nondiscrimination laws to challenge religious organizations' termination of ministers or

390 ··· WILLIAM P. BARR

employees who otherwise carry out the organization's religious mission. In a 2012 case, *Hosanna-Tabor Evangelical Lutheran Church and School v. EEOC*, the Supreme Court, agreeing with a number of lower federal courts, found that the First Amendment requires a "ministerial exception" to government employment laws. The court held that the Free Exercise Clause precludes the government from contradicting a church's decision on who can act as its ministers. Allowing the government to do so would interfere with the church's internal governance and usurp its control over selection of those chosen to personify its beliefs. The court also ruled that allowing the state to intrude into this kind of ecclesiastical decision would violate the Establishment Clause. The Supreme Court, however, left open who exactly would qualify as a minister under the exception.

After the case, some argued that, under the Supreme Court ruling, the ministerial exception applied only to persons who have theological training and titles such as minister, reflecting some formal, clergy-like status in the church. I did not agree with this crabbed reading, and, while I was Attorney General, a case arose in California that I thought provided an opportunity to ask the court to amplify the scope of the exception. In this new case, two Catholic parochial schoolteachers sued their respective schools, claiming they had been dismissed for discriminatory reasons. The Ninth Circuit Court of Appeals ruled that the ministerial exception did not apply, and the suits could go forward because the teachers had no theological training and no formal recognition as ministers of religion. We sided with the schools in taking the case to the US Supreme Court and argued that the Free Exercise Clause requires the exception be given a broader functional scope. What counts is whether the employee's role involves conveying the religious organization's message and carrying out its religious mission. In July 2020 the Supreme Court agreed with our position, ruling for the schools in *Our Lady of Guadalupe School v. Morrissey-Berru*. The court held that the ministerial exception applied because the teachers performed a religious function—namely, "educating their students in the Catholic faith and guiding their students to live their lives in accordance with that faith."

The third assault on religious liberty in the field of education is the most dangerous. It is the growing effort by state and federal officials to impose certain curricula—initially in public schools but potentially later in religious schools—that effectively indoctrinate students in a secular progressive ideology antithetical to the values and perspectives of a religious viewpoint, including traditional Judeo-Christian teachings.

Throughout Western history, education and religion were regarded as inseparable. Education necessarily included the formation of character. Knowledge, civic and moral virtue, and religion were always understood to be inextricably linked. The educational project was inherently bound up with religion and moral instruction and, for that reason, was viewed as falling within the religious and parental sphere, not the state's.

The 1830s witnessed the movement to make education broadly available to all children at public expense. Enabling universal education was the right idea, but it resulted in a decision to provide this education exclusively through state institutions staffed by public employees. This shift of the educational function from the moral-religious sphere over to the state sphere raised a fundamental question. Would the state schools provide an education that continued to involve a moral dimension? And, if so, what would be the basis for the moral values taught if not religion?

The conundrum for public schools is that they are constitutionally required to be religiously "neutral." But is it possible for an education to be religiously neutral unless it is skinnied down to subjects such as the "three Rs," fact-based courses such as history and science, and purely technical knowledge? Once a school goes beyond this and attempts to espouse or inculcate moral values, theories, or ideologies, two basic problems arise. First, where does the state get the power to mandate indoctrination of children in a moral system or any "ism"? Second, when a school promotes moral values incompatible with traditional religious beliefs of its students and their families—and the only way to avoid teaching these values is to pay for a private school—does this not burden the free exercise of religion in violation of the Constitution?

The fact is that any education seeking to play a role in the moral formation of students will inevitably bump up against religious beliefs. Personal and civic moral systems do not just hover in the ether. They must rest on an explanatory belief system, a metaphysical foundation. When I was little, and my parents told me to do something or to refrain from doing something, I would ask, "Why?" They would respond, "Because we said so!" That might work for children, but it does not work for adults and society at large. It is hard to tell people that they *ought* to behave in a certain way unless you can explain *why*. Any system of morality rests on a set of beliefs that explains why it is necessary to be "good," and why being good requires performing certain duties and refraining from certain conduct. Throughout history, this foundational belief system has largely been religion—in the Mideast, Islam; in much of India, Hinduism. Until recently, the foundation of morality in the West has been provided by religion, the Judeo-Christian tradition. Thus, to the extent education seeks to contribute to a student's moral formation, it inevitably invades the space occupied by religion.

How have America's public schools handled the inherent conflict between the requirement of religious neutrality and the ambition to provide an education involving some degree of moral instruction—a subject that necessarily implicates religion? Essentially, we have gone through three phases.

In the first phase, the problem was ignored. For more than a century, up until the 1960s, the public school system was not religiously neutral and did not pretend to be. When it emerged in the mid-nineteenth century, the public school movement's specific mission was the moral formation of America's youth, and public school advocates, such as educator Horace Mann, agreed explicitly that religion had to be an integral part of education. The strategy was to incorporate Christianity as unobtrusively as possible into the curricula. The religious worldview incorporated into public schools for almost a century was an anodyne version of general American Protestantism composed of the beliefs that Protestant denominations generally agreed on. The Bible was read, and there was Christian prayer. Public schools muddled through with this arrangement because virtually all Americans during this era were attached to Christianity—more than 95 percent self-identified as Christian—and accepted the Judeo-Christian foundation of our moral system. In short, what enabled public education to dodge the issue of neutrality and operate monolithically was that the American people were relatively monolithic in both their religious attachments and beliefs.

This approach began falling apart in the 1960s. The Supreme Court started articulating and enforcing more strictly the requirement of religious neutrality. Just as important, the American people were becoming more diverse in their religious views. While many Americans still adhered to the Judeo-Christian belief system, many others did not. There was less consensus over the content of morals and norms.

The second phase of public education was the initial response to this fracturing of religious belief. It started in the late 1960s and continued roughly to the midpoint of the Obama administration. During this period, the Left embarked on a relentless campaign of secularization intent on driving every vestige of traditional religion from the public square. In a benighted effort to make the schools truly "neutral," the Supreme Court superintended a hyperaggressive campaign to expunge any trace of religion—especially Christianity—from inside public schools. The objective was to totally secularize education by stripping away all traces of religion. It was secularization by *subtraction*. But expunging religion does *not* result in religious neutrality. Instead, the net effect was to elevate the most aggressively secular viewpoints, while suppressing any religious viewpoints.

Yet even as the schools were forcibly secularized, the reformers wanted to retain schools as agencies of moral instruction. But while they wanted to teach morals, they were busily tearing down the Judeo-Christian foundations that had sustained those morals for thousands of years. The rich Judeo-Christian tradition was replaced with mawkish talk of liberal values: be a good person, be caring, and so forth. But there was no underpinning for these values. What passed for morality had no metaphysical foundation. "Values" in public schools became really nothing more than sentimentality, still drawing on the vapor trails of Christianity.

The third phase of public education started during the Obama administration and has grown apace with the ascendance of militant secular progressivism. The objective is no longer secularization by subtraction. Now we see a mounting effort to affirmatively indoctrinate children with the secular progressive belief system—a new official secular ideology. In other words, having created a void by removing the religious foundation upon which moral values once rested, progressives are trying to inculcate an alternative explanatory belief system. But secular values are *not* religiously neutral ones. On the contrary, today's progressive secular ideology is premised on ideas about the nature of man, the universe, man's duties, and the purpose of life that are a substitute for, and subversive of, a religious outlook, especially the traditional Judeo-Christian worldview. As a result, in many parts of the country, the state of our public schools is becoming an absurdity that can scarcely be believed. While an astonishing number of public schools fail to produce students proficient in basic reading and math, they spare no effort or expense in their drive to instill a radical secular ideology that would have been unimaginable to Americans even twenty years ago.

For example, several states have mandated an LGBTQ curriculum in public schools that allows no opting out for parents who disagree with the content of the courses. As of the 2020–21 school year, about one-fifth of Americans live in a state that mandates an LGBTQ curriculum in public schools. In the absence of a statewide mandate, curricula are sometimes adopted in particular school districts. In 2021, for example, an Iowa public school district taught transgenderism and homosexuality to students at all grade levels—including preschool—as part of a Black Lives Matter at School Week of Action. Materials distributed by the school district included a children's coloring book page that teaches: "Everyone gets to choose if they are a girl or a boy or both or neither or someone else, and no one else gets to choose for them." Clearly, the notions that there are more than two genders and that individuals are, in reality, the gender they conceive themselves to be are not established "science." Rather, they are a moral, psychological, and metaphysical dogma of the new progressive orthodoxy—a dogma decidedly at odds with objective reality.

Curricula such as LGBTQ curricula are not just isolated ideas occasionally popping up that are so discrete and fleeting as to do no great harm. What is taking shape is a broader subversion of the religious worldview. For example, while some educators may view each lesson—such as transsexualism—as dealing with a discrete subject, those lessons embody broader ideas that are fundamentally incompatible with the religious viewpoint. Telling schoolchildren that they get to choose their gender—not just male or female, but anything else—and that no one else has anything to say about it does not just contradict particular religious teachings on gender and the authority of parents, but also is a broadside attack on the very idea of natural law, which is integral to the moral doctrines of a number of religious denominations.

The progressive gender and sexuality agenda only begins to scratch the surface of what progressives now seek to introduce into the curricula in government-run schools.

As I discussed earlier, today's radical progressive ideology is a hodgepodge of postmodern thought lumping together elements of Marxism, racial and gender ideologies, radical feminism, transgender ideology, and a host of other isms. But there are at least two overarching ideas that run through this ideology, both of which make it profoundly subversive of religion. First, it is a "united front of negation," in journalist Matt Taibbi's phrase, composed of a mélange of "oppositional ideologies." In other words, its ideas are defined by their *opposition* to—and their program of dismantling—society's traditional conventions and norms, and the metaphysical system that undergirds them, which, in the West, is largely our Judeo-Christian inheritance.

Second, most of the isms in this stew are based on some form of historical materialism, as is the case with so-called critical race theory, for example, which many public schools across the country have rushed to embrace. CRT is, at bottom, essentially the materialist philosophy of Marxism, substituting racial antagonism for class antagonism. It posits the same ideas as traditional Marxism: that there are meta-historical forces at work; that society's pathologies are due to societal conventions and power structures that have to be destroyed; that conflict between the oppressed and the oppressors provides the dynamic and progressive movement of history; and that individual morality is determined by where one fits in with the impersonal movement of these historical forces. This philosophy posits a view of man and his relation to society and fellow human beings that is incompatible with Christianity.

Putting aside its impact on religious freedom, what is the state's authority in the first place to compel people to submit to indoctrination on transgenderism, CRT, Socialism, or any other ism? The state has a legitimate interest in requiring people to take courses in the three Rs, civics, science, languages, history, safety, hygiene, and a host of other subjects. But I doubt the state has untrammeled power to compel people to submit to indoctrination into particular ideologies—whether it be transgenderism, CRT, or Socialism. Today, as part of CRT indoctrination, students are being compelled to publicly confess their "white privilege" and identify themselves as "oppressors." No state has the power to compel this. States do not have the authority to make people think the way it wants them to think.

In any event, the kind of indoctrination that is occurring these days in public schools plainly implicates the Free Exercise Clause of the Constitution. When the state gets into the business of indoctrinating students into secular belief systems that are contrary to the religious beliefs of them and their families, it is clearly burdening the free exercise of religion, as well as the rights of parents to guide the religious upbringing of their children. The state has no compelling interest in demanding submission to its preferred, secular beliefs rather than the beliefs that are religiously grounded. Thus, a state that proposes to teach a child that he gets to choose his gender, and no one else has anything to say about it, is teaching an ideological dogma that is patently contrary to traditional Judeo-Christian beliefs. That violates the Constitution.

While the free exercise violations resulting from indoctrination are clear enough, I think things have also reached a point where states may be running afoul of the Establishment Clause. When we are no longer talking about simply stripping religion out of school curriculum, but now talking about indoctrination into an affirmative value system—a new credo—resting on materialist metaphysics and taking the place of religion, then this raises the question whether this indoctrination involves establishment of a religion.

Early in my legal career, I noticed there was a constitutional double standard when it came to secular ersatz religions such as secular humanism. They were given the *protection* of the Free Exercise Clause but were generally not subject to the *prohibitions* of the Establishment Clause. When it suits the secularist cause, secular humanism and other "nontheistic" religions are treated as religions. When atheists sought conscientious-objector status during World War II, the courts construed the phrase "religious training or belief" to include beliefs that are "the equivalent of what has always been thought a religious impulse." The Supreme Court followed suit in a similar case during the Vietnam War. Instead of "belief in a Supreme Being," as the relevant statute required, the Supreme Court held that an objector to military service need demonstrate only a "belief that is sincere and meaningful [and] occupies a place in the life of its possessor parallel to that filled by [traditional religion]."

But if God-less materialist philosophies are treated as "religions" for free exercise purposes, why shouldn't official efforts to teach them in lieu of religious beliefs be deemed an establishment of religion? Official sponsorship of a nontheistic ideology that takes the place of religion has the same effect on nonadherents as endorsing a particular theistic religion. Indeed, the Supreme Court foresaw the potential for secularism itself becoming established as a state religion. In one of the first cases abolishing school prayer, the Supreme Court acknowledged that "the State *may not* establish a 'religion of secularism' in the sense of affirmatively opposing or showing hostility to religion, thus 'preferring those who believe in no religion over those who do believe.'" We have to consider whether our public schools, as currently constituted, are doing exactly that.

In my view, the increasing diversity of attitudes and beliefs among

Americans in the past few decades makes the states' continued insistence on a monopoly over publicly funded education constitutionally untenable. This arrangement can no longer finesse the challenge of neutrality, as it did when the religious attitudes of Americans were more monolithic. Nor is it capable of producing genuine religious neutrality. It has deformed and impoverished the very nature of the educational enterprise either by purging it of any moral dimension or by trying to substitute for religion a secular value system that is at war with religion. It is reducing public schools to cockpits for a vicious, winner-take-all culture war over the moral formation of our children. The point is not that we should mandate Christianity in the state's one-size-fits-all educational monopoly. It is that the diversity of religious belief should lead us to jettison the monopoly.

The rise of militant secularism in the United States forces upon us a fundamental question about the way our society is now providing public education. One of the main purposes of public education is to provide for public funding of basic education for all citizens up to a certain level of schooling. But public funding does not require that the education be provided by means of government schools. The alternative is to have public funds travel with each student, allowing the student and parents to choose the school—private, public, nonsectarian, or sectarian—that best meets their needs. In other words, the purchasing power needed for a quality education would be put in the hands of each family by giving every student an educational voucher to be spent at a school of choice. The state's interest in ensuring that a certain level of basic skills is taught can be met by accreditation standards, but the government's ability to dictate the content of curriculum beyond this would be severely curtailed. While there will likely still be occasional conflicts over the accreditation standards, instances of government overreach would be far more transparent. This would not only be the most efficient way of providing publicly funded education, but also I believe we may well have reached the point that it is the only way it can be provided today without trenching on the religious liberties of families.

Looking around today, especially at the effectively segregated and failing inner-city schools, I do not think we can say that the public school system has any unique virtue in facilitating America's melting pot. Indeed, parochial schools are an example of a nonexclusive school system that has been extremely successful integrating wave after wave of new immigrants into American society. More than that, the record of these schools in promoting patriotism and economic success compares favorably to any similarly situated public school system. There is no reason to think that vouchers, and the diversity of educational choices that will come with them, will in any way undermine our national cohesion.

On the contrary, it is now the public school monopoly that is undermining national cohesion. One of the main justifications for the public schools was that they would be institutions to promote our common identity and a solidarity based on being an American. But now the public schools are adopting curricula designed for the opposite mission of separating us, of teaching unbridgeable differences, of dividing us into many different identities destined to be antagonistic. It is all the more alarming and bizarre that the new state-sanctioned ideology challenges the very legitimacy of the nation itself—to the point of explicitly attacking its founding documents, principles, and symbols. If the state-operated schools are now waging war on the nation's moral, historical, philosophical, and religious foundations, then they would seem to have forfeited their legitimacy as the proper vehicle to carry out the mission with which the American people have charged them.

I have always thought it ironic that the first settlers came to America from England in pursuit of religious liberty, and yet, despite all our pretensions, there is, in fundamental respects, more religious liberty in England today than in the United States—even though England has a national church. In England, the government directly funds "faith schools" and "faith academies"—religiously affiliated schools. There are almost 7,000 state-funded religiously affiliated schools in England—roughly 37 percent of state-funded elementary schools and almost 20 percent of secondary schools. Of these schools, about

4,500 are Church of England schools, and 2,000 are Roman Catholic. There are much smaller numbers of Muslim, Sikh, and Hindu schools. Interestingly, students from faith schools perform better on average on national examinations. In England, the funding goes to the school, whereas a voucher program in the United States would put the spending power into the hands of parents to use at any accredited school of their choice. Of course, secularists criticize the English system, but the fact is that England accommodates religion and allows parents to raise their children within their religious tradition without having to pay a massive penalty for the privilege. The students emerge well educated and good citizens. What more could society want?

Vouchers will also help us address a great injustice in our society today. The place where there is "systemic racism" in our country is in the public school system in our inner cities. For decades, in far too many of our inner cities, children have been trapped in failing public schools, essentially being warehoused, while their dreams and future potential are being destroyed. Periodic bursts of spending or "reform" have made no difference. Sometimes it seems that the whole purpose of the system is to keep these children disadvantaged. When President Obama took office, there was a publicly funded scholarship program in Washington, DC, that allowed disadvantaged students to attend the school of their choice—public, private, or parochial. It was wildly successful, with significantly higher graduation rates, and parents loved it. But, as one of his early acts as President, as a favor to the teachers' union, Obama curtailed the program. At the very same time, he enrolled his daughters in one of the most exclusive private schools in the city. This was a perfect example of the attitude of smug elites and their disregard of the aspirations of ordinary Americans. Inner-city parents, like all parents, are desperate for their children to have a chance. But elitists like Obama, as long as they and their children get to live exclusive lives, could not care less about the opportunities available to Americans lower down on the economic scale. "Pull the ladder up, I'm aboard," is their motto. It is time to stop destroying the future of these inner-city children and start giving them the opportunity to attend schools of their choice.

The argument I've mapped out here is, in the final analysis, a simple matter of acknowledging reality—the reality that we are a religious and pluralistic society that no totalizing secularist ideology can govern. It's not a matter of arguing *for* such a society; we already *are* one. The question is how we can arrange ourselves most peaceably.

CHAPTER 17

PROTECTING NATIONAL SECURITY

Early in the 2000's, Hao Zhang and Wei Pang, from the People's Republic of China (PRC), enrolled in the University of Southern California's graduate electrical engineering program. They joined the hundreds of thousands of other PRC students who, at any given time, are studying at American universities. Awarded their PhDs in 2006, the two went to work for American companies—Zhang for Skyworks Solutions, an innovator of high-performance semiconductors in Massachusetts; and Pang for Avago Technologies in California, a leading developer of optoelectronics components.

These two companies held valuable trade secrets relating to radio frequency filters, especially a type of filter, known as Film Bulk Acoustic Resonators, or FBARs, used primarily for wireless devices to reduce interference. With the number of wireless signals growing exponentially, filtering out unwanted signals has become important. Advances in FBAR technology allow for smaller, more efficient wireless devices for both consumer and military uses.

In 2015, the DOJ indicted Zhang and Pang, alleging that they had conspired with four other Chinese nationals, including individuals in China, in an elaborate scheme to steal trade secrets relating to FBARs from Avago and Skyworks and appropriate them for use by Chinese entities. When the charges were handed down, all the alleged conspirators were in China. But, because the indictment was initially kept sealed, the FBI was able to arrest Zhang when he unwittingly returned to the US for a conference.

In June 2020 Zhang was tried and convicted of economic espionage, theft of trade secrets, and conspiracy. The evidence at trial showed that Zhang conspired with Pang and others, including officials at the state-run Tianjin University, in a scheme to steal filter technology from the two US companies, disguise the sources of the stolen technology, and have it used by Chinese entities to develop civilian and military products.

Cases like this are becoming more common and reflect a massive Chinese program to leapfrog America by pilfering our technology.

By far the greatest challenge facing the United States in the national security arena today is the rapid rise of Communist China as an aggressive adversary. Most Americans are broadly aware that China poses a threat to the United States, but they don't understand how that threat is taking shape. A brief explanation may give a sense of what's happening.

On August 12, 2021, the commander of US Strategic Command, Admiral Charles Richard, speaking at the Space & Missile Defense Symposium in Huntsville, Alabama, warned, "We are witnessing a strategic breakout by China. . . . The explosive growth in their nuclear and conventional forces can only be what I described as breathtaking." He referred to China as a "peer" nuclear competitor and noted that we now face two nuclear peer competitors: China and Russia. China's nuclear buildup has been matched by its extraordinary and sustained modernization of conventional forces—with an already formidable navy and a potent air force.

In dealing with China, the Department of Justice's principal area of responsibility is counterespionage—protecting our country from China's attempts to steal our diplomatic, military, industrial, and technological secrets. When I left office in 1993, the Soviet Union had collapsed, the United States stood as the world's sole superpower, and we were scaling back our counterespionage program in the expectation of a "peace dividend." When I arrived in office again almost thirty years later, I found that Communist China, in its drive to supplant the United States as the world's leading technological power, was waging an aggressive campaign—unprecedented in scope, intensity, and sophistication—to steal our advanced technology. Even at the height of the Cold War, the United States has faced no comparable espionage challenge.

Since the end of the nineteenth century, America has been the world's leader in technological innovation. Our prowess has made us prosperous and secure. Perhaps because today's Americans have known nothing else, we take our technological dominance, and all that comes with it, for granted. When the United States leads the way with a new technology, we benefit exponentially from all the economic value it generates. By giving birth to the Internet, America has spawned countless related industries and added trillions in value to our economy. America's standard of living, economic opportunities for our young people and future generations, and our national security all depend on our continued technological leadership. When the Chinese steal our technology, they are stealing the future of our children and grandchildren.

When the United States opened up to the People's Republic of China in 1972, our hope was that integrating the sleeping giant of Asia into the international economic system would encourage its leaders to liberalize its economy, and that a free market and economic growth would gradually lead to greater political freedom for its citizens. That turned out to be a false hope. The PRC remains an authoritarian, one-party state in which the Chinese Communist Party wields absolute power and represses any real or perceived challenge to its rule harshly.

While individuals have been permitted a modicum of economic freedom in their private sphere, the party remains in firm control of an economy whose principal features are central planning, state-owned enterprises, and government subsidies. Although China participates in the global economy, it has not played by the rules of free and fair competition. To tilt the playing field to its advantage, its Communist government has perfected a wide array of predatory and often unlawful tactics: currency manipulation, tariffs, quotas, state-led strategic investment and acquisitions, theft and forced transfer of intellectual property, state subsidies, dumping, cyberattacks, and industrial espionage.

Chinese leader Deng Xiaoping, who succeeded Mao Tse-tung in

1978, and whose economic reform launched China's remarkable rise, had a motto: "Hide your strength and bide your time." That is precisely what Beijing has done. Its economy has grown quietly from about 2 percent of the world's gross domestic product (GDP) in 1980, to nearly 20 percent today. And by some estimates based on purchasing parity, the Chinese economy is already larger than ours. Xi Jinping, president of the People's Republic of China since 2013, has centralized power to a degree not seen since Mao's twenty-seven-year dictatorship. Xi makes clear that the PRC is no longer biding its time—the time to overtake the United States has arrived.

China is now engaged in an economic blitzkrieg—an aggressive, orchestrated, whole-of-government (indeed, whole-of-society) campaign to seize the commanding heights of the global economy and to surpass the United States as the world's preeminent technological power. The centerpiece of this effort is the Chinese Communist Party's Made in China 2025 initiative, a plan for China to dominate the technology of the future in ten key economic sectors: renewable energy, robotics, aviation, advanced rail equipment, electric generation, new materials, maritime engineering, biotechnology, information technology, and agriculture. Backed by hundreds of billions of dollars in subsidies, this initiative poses a profound threat to US technological leadership.

China's strategy for achieving technological superiority has been simple. Assistant Attorney General John Demers, who headed the Justice Department's National Security Division when I led the DOJ, has put it aptly and succinctly: China's strategy is to "rob, replicate, and replace." China first jump-starts a competitive business by robbing a US company of its intellectual property—either by theft or forced transfer. Then a Chinese company replicates the technology, thus supplanting the American company in China's domestic market, using an array of unfair tactics. After that, exploiting the advantages of its now large market share, the Chinese company, relying on state subsidies and other unfair practices, muscles aside the US company in the global market.

No one should underestimate the ingenuity and industriousness of the Chinese people. But no one should doubt that America has made China's meteoric rise possible. In 2019 *Newsweek* magazine ran a cover story titled "How America's Biggest Companies Made China Great Again." The article details how China's Communist leaders lured US business with the promise of market access, and then, having profited from American investment and know-how, turned increasingly hostile. The PRC used tariffs and quotas to pressure American firms into giving up their technology and forming joint ventures with Chinese companies. Chinese regulators then discriminated against American businesses, using tactics such as holding up permits. After the US companies unwittingly served their purpose as "host bodies" for the new, emerging Chinese companies, the American companies were discarded.

The increasingly short-term perspective of many US business executives makes America vulnerable to these tactics. Many want a short-term payoff and don't have the time or attention to build a business with long-term staying power. Too many are managing their companies to achieve a transient uptick in the stock price so that they can cash in their options and retire to a comfortable life in a gated luxury golf resort. They don't seem to realize—or don't seem to care— that China's goal isn't to *trade* with the United States. It is to *raid* the United States.

Another way the Chinese have tried to pilfer US technology is by investing in American companies and then using their ownership position to acquire confidential technological information. As Attorney General, I sat on the Committee on Foreign Investment in the United States, chaired by the secretary of the Treasury. CFIUS investigates foreign investments in the United States and can recommend to the President that he prohibit certain transactions based on the risk to national security.

Just as American companies have become dependent on the Chinese market, the United States as a whole now relies on the PRC for many vital goods and services. The Covid-19 pandemic has revealed our dependency on China for personal protective equipment such as face masks and medical gowns. But there are numerous other areas where the United States depends on Chinese supply chains in vital sectors such as medical devices and pharmaceuticals.

A crucial area of concern—and one related to recent events in Afghanistan—is the supply of rare earth metals and minerals. Part of China's drive for supremacy is its plan to monopolize rare earth materials, which play a vital role in industries such as consumer electronics, electric vehicles, medical devices, and military hardware. According to the Congressional Research Service, from the 1960s to the 1980s, the United States led the world in rare earth production. Since then, production has shifted almost entirely to China, which now supplies roughly 85 percent of rare earth materials to world markets. Our country is now dangerously dependent on the PRC for these materials. And the risks of dependence are real. In 2010, for example, Beijing cut exports of rare earth materials to Japan after an incident involving disputed islands in the East China Sea. The PRC could do the same to us and disrupt our entire economy.

The critical importance of rare earth materials makes President Joe Biden's catastrophic withdrawal from Afghanistan in 2021 all the more inexplicable. Afghanistan has one of the world's richest deposits of minerals, including rare earth minerals and, especially, lithium, an essential component for rechargeable batteries, which will become indispensable as we reduce our use of fossil fuels. China is now poised to ally with the Taliban and to develop Afghanistan's mineral resources, gaining even further control over materials essential to numerous advanced technologies. Other than the Taliban, China is the major beneficiary of Biden's precipitous withdrawal.

In its drive to achieve technological supremacy, Beijing's most insidious tactic—and the one that falls squarely within the Justice Department's area of responsibility—is its intense program to steal US technology outright. In recent years, about 80 percent of all federal economic espionage prosecutions have alleged conduct that would benefit the Chinese state, and about 60 percent of all trade secret theft cases have been connected to China. Chinese industrial espionage against America is conducted only in part by traditional intelligence service activity. Inside the United States, China also relies on a host of nontraditional intelligence collectors—including graduate students, businessmen, and co-opted company employees—all ultimately working for the benefit of China.

The PRC uses a multipronged approach to stealing American technology: engaging in cyber intrusions to steal information by hacking; using its intelligence services to recruit company employees or university professors engaged in research; sponsoring graduate students participating in university research projects; fraudulently using American fronts to avoid export controls; and acquiring control over, or investing in, US companies to gain access to their technologies. Academic and other research institutions—due to their culture of openness and collaboration—are particularly vulnerable to Chinese espionage. To encourage theft of US intellectual property, China uses so-called talent programs, such as the Thousand Talents Plan, to provide financial incentives to individuals engaged in research in the United States to transmit the knowledge and research they gain back to China in exchange for salaries, research funding, lab space, and other enticements. Through these talent programs, the PRC recruits not only Chinese nationals in the United States, but also US citizens.

When I was first briefed by the FBI on the Chinese industrial espionage threat, I was stunned by its sheer breadth. While aggressively targeting technologies in the ten sectors it plans to dominate under its Made in China 2025 initiative, Chinese technology theft does not stop with these sectors. It is omnivorous and ubiquitous—seeking to steal any useful technology or know-how across a wide span of business and industrial activity. On my travels around America, I was shocked to find that, even in smaller communities off the beaten path, if there is technological work going on, the Chinese are there—if only in the guise of graduate students doing research.

Why must China rely so heavily on theft? The ability of totalitarian countries to engage in central economic planning can, at times, appear to be an advantage, especially when mobilizing the kind of broad and rapid technological offensive we see China engaged in today. What Western admirers of totalitarian societies overlook is that central planning suppresses technological innovation. Breakthrough ideas arise in free societies like ours, which have long led the way in cutting-edge technological development. The Chinese are trying to have it both ways: they'll impose totalitarian controls on Chinese society, and they'll steal the West's innovations. Or to put it another way: they are attempting to capture the benefits of our free society by outright stealing our technology.

Theft of technology isn't a sideshow. It's the main event. It undergirds the entire Chinese Communist project.

Prior to the Trump administration, the United States did not have a coordinated response to counter the threat posed by China's systematic pillaging of our technology. In November 2018, days before he resigned, Attorney General Jeff Sessions established the China Initiative within the Department of Justice to confront China's malign behavior and protect US technology. This initiative was led by the department's National Security Division, under John Demers's leadership. The FBI was its main engine, bringing the bureau's broad capabilities to bear across numerous disciplines. NSD prosecutors, as well as prosecutors in our US attorneys' offices around the country, supported the investigations and conducted the prosecutions.

The China Initiative has had impressive results: the Justice Department has arrested and prosecuted scores of individuals accused of working on behalf of China. But the more we've uncovered, the more sobering the threat has become. We have found numerous academic and other research institutions where China is using talent programs to obtain intellectual property. Just one example among many: Shannon You, an American citizen, was working as a PhD chemist for the Coca-Cola Company in Atlanta and the Eastman Chemical Company in Kingsport, Tennessee. She gained access to formulations for safer internal coatings for the inside of beverage cans and other food containers—valuable trade secrets that cost $120 million to develop. In 2019 the fifty-seven-year-old woman was indicted, and later convicted, for stealing trade secrets to set up a new coating company in China. Evidence at trial showed that You and her Chinese corporate partner received millions of dollars in Chinese government grants, including awards from the Thousand Talents Plan, to support the new company.

China also uses computer hacking to steal technology. In December 2018 the DOJ indicted a group of hackers called APT 10. The group was conducting a global campaign, associated with the Chinese Ministry of State Security, that targeted intellectual property and confidential business and technology information belonging to hundreds of clients of managed service providers worldwide. In February 2020 the department indicted four members of the Chinese People's Liberation Army, charging them with hacking into the computer systems of the credit reporting agency Equifax and stealing Americans' personal data and other valuable trade secrets. In July 2020, the department indicted two Chinese hackers working with the Ministry of State Security on charges of running a global computer intrusion campaign targeting intellectual property and confidential business information, including Covid-19 research. In August 2019 and August 2020, the department indicted five computer hackers, all Chinese residents, with computer intrusions affecting more than a hundred unsuspecting companies in the United States and abroad, including software development firms, computer hardware manufacturers, telecommunications providers, social media companies, video game companies, nonprofit organizations, universities, and think tanks.

China also uses people in the United States, acting on its behalf, to evade export restrictions on technology. For example, in June 2019 a sixty-four-year-old electrical engineer named Yi-Chi Shih, a part-time Los Angeles resident, was found guilty of multiple criminal charges—including a scheme to illegally obtain integrated circuits with military applications that were later exported to China without the required export license—earning him five years in federal prison. In September 2020 a woman named Yang Yang, from Jacksonville, Florida, pleaded guilty to conspiring to submit false export information to fraudulently export to China maritime raiding craft and engines.

The scope and intensity of Chinese technology theft is such that the US government cannot deal with it effectively without the vigilance and help of the private sector, including academic research institutions. For that reason, the FBI has vastly expanded its outreach and educational efforts to inform academia and the private sector of the threat and to help them put in place adequate safeguards.

As a dictatorship, China can marshal an all-of-nation approach, with the government, private companies, and academia acting together as one. We are not able to compel that. When we've faced similar challenges in the past—such as during World War II and Russia's Cold War technological challenge—we rallied together. We were able to form a close partnership among government, the private sector, and academia. Through that cooperation, America prevailed. But the cooperative bonds and consolidated sense of purpose we were able to muster in the past are not available to us today. The causes of our fracturing are many and complex—liberal self-hatred and anti-Americanism, the valorization of individual autonomy, the balkanization and alienation brought about by the Internet, and so on. I don't propose to solve these problems here. But I will say this with a high level of confidence: if the United States has any hope of maintaining its technological leadership, preserving past levels of economic growth and prosperity, and securing itself from external threats, Americans are going to have to figure out a way to work together as one nation. Otherwise, perhaps only two or three decades from now, we will find ourselves in a world in which there is only one military and economic superpower: the expansionist totalitarian dictatorship the People's Republic of China.

As China has gained ground on America—and while the United States has been distracted by its own internal divisions—it has been alarming to me how belligerent and bullying the Chinese government has become. Beijing has threatened both Japan and Australia with missile attacks if they side with the United States in opposing Chinese efforts to take over the island of Taiwan. After the disastrous fall of Kabul, Afghanistan, to the Taliban in 2021, Hu Xijin, editor in chief of the *Global Times*, China's state media, taunted the Taiwanese: "[T]he Taiwan authorities must be trembling. Don't look forward to the US to protect them. Taipei officials need to quietly mail-order a Five-Star Red Flag from the Chinese mainland. It will be useful one day when they surrender to the [People's Liberation Army]." If the Chinese are this bellicose at this stage, how aggressive will they be when they think they have the advantage in the western Pacific?

As Attorney General, I was not involved much in the Trump administration's internal discussions over US geopolitical strategy. But I worried that one of the most dangerous effects of the bogus Russiagate scandal was to artificially constrain our strategic options for addressing China's grave challenge. Let me put it briefly. Managing the single threat from China will be hard enough, but dealing simultaneously with a hostile Russia is a challenge we should seek to avoid. A sensible foreign policy at this stage would be to engage with Russia to explore whether there is a feasible framework for a more constructive relationship. Unfortunately, with the media ready to pounce on President Trump as a Russian stooge—if not a Manchurian candidate—at the slightest sign of détente, the President's hands were severely tied, especially during an election year.

Throughout most of my life—really up until the rise of Trump— the Democrats were always eager to engage diplomatically with the Russians. Trump's victory sent Democrats on a treasure hunt to find an explanation for their loss, and what they came up with, thanks in part to James Comey's conduct, was a preposterous theory about Russian collusion and an illegitimate election. Suddenly it was the *Democrats* who wanted full-scale Cold War with the Russians.

This is not the way grown-ups should think. The threat posed by Russia has changed dramatically since the fall of the Soviet Union. The Russian Federation of today has roughly half the population the old Soviet Union had and less than half the US population. The larger Warsaw Pact countries—Poland and the former East Germany— are now part of the North Atlantic Treaty Organization (NATO). The combined defense budgets of the three big Western European countries—Britain, France, and Germany—are comparable to Russia's. While Russia still has a potent nuclear arsenal, the prospect of Russian tanks rolling to the English Channel—a realistic scenario during the Cold War—is just not plausible now. Further, while some Russian foreign policy goals are in tension with our own, Russia's leaders no longer promote a revolutionary ideology that foreordains general antagonism with the West. For them, foreign policy is now more purely a matter of Realpolitik.

I am afraid that, with a wavering, intermittently alert Joe Biden in the Oval Office, Vladimir Putin will pursue Russian strategic goals more assertively and feel little need to find agreed-upon frameworks with the United States. Given Biden's manifest weakness, Putin is likely to feel he's better off making no concessions at all. Demonizing Putin is not a foreign policy. If the world is still in one piece after Biden's term, the United States needs to explore the feasibility of putting our relations with Russia on a more positive footing.

Other than frustrating Chinese espionage and malign influence, a second major national security responsibility of the Department of Justice is counteracting foreign terrorist activities. The Trump administration as a whole had some major successes combating terrorism—including the defeat of ISIS in Syria, and the killing of terrorist leaders such as Abu Bakr al-Baghdadi, the leader of ISIS, and General Qasem Soleimani, commander of Iran's Quds Force—which I will not address here. Within the DOJ's bailiwick, however, several significant foreign terrorism cases arose during my tenure.

In recent decades, no terrorist group has acted with greater barbarity than ISIS during its brutal campaign from 2014 to 2019 to establish a caliphate in Syria and Iraq. Few Americans will forget the sickening succession of videos released in 2014 showing an ISIS executioner, boasting in a British accent, his face concealed behind a black balaclava, brandishing a large knife with which he proceeded to behead Western hostages as they knelt at his feet in orange jumpsuits. The ISIS terrorist cell believed responsible for jailing, torturing, and executing hostages was a group of four individuals who spoke in British accents and were dubbed by their captives "the Beatles" (and, individually, Jihadi John, Paul, George, and Ringo). Surviving kidnap victims reported that the Beatles were especially cruel and took pleasure in torturing their victims. Among the hostages killed were American journalists James Foley and Steven Sotloff; US aid worker Peter

Kassig; and two British citizens, aid worker David Haines and humanitarian volunteer Alan Henning. The Beatles also were alleged to have been involved in the captivity of Kayla Mueller, a young American aid worker who was tortured and raped by al-Baghdadi before she was executed in 2015.

In November 2015 the Beatle who seems to have performed most of the beheadings, Jihadi John (real name Mohammed Emwazi), was killed by an American drone strike in Syria. Also in 2015 a second alleged member of the Beatles, Aine Davis (Jihadi Paul), was arrested and convicted on terrorism charges in Turkey. And in January 2018 El Shafee Elsheikh and Alexanda Kotey, both raised in Britain, were captured in Syria by US-backed Kurdish forces. They were thought to be Jihadi George and Jihadi Ringo, respectively. The two men were stripped of their British citizenship in July 2018.

Before I arrived at the department, the British government and Attorney General Jeff Sessions had agreed that the best way to secure justice was to charge Kotey and Elsheikh under US law and have them stand trial in the United States. The British, however, had evidence that America considered important to presenting the strongest case. The British home secretary at the time, Sajid Javid, agreed to transfer the evidence without requiring the United States to forsake seeking the death penalty. We were very grateful for Javid's strong stand, but his move was blocked when Elsheikh's mother filed a lawsuit in the United Kingdom challenging the decision. That litigation dragged on for almost two years. When I entered office, the litigation was still grinding along, and Kotey and Elsheikh remained in the custody of allied Kurdish forces in Syria. When Home Secretary Javid moved on to become chancellor of the exchequer, I started working with the new home secretary, Priti Patel, who remained very supportive and worked hard to prevail in the litigation.

In October 2019 a sudden crisis erupted. The Turkish military pushed down into northeastern Syria, threatening positions held by our Kurdish allies, including prison camps holding thousands of ISIS prisoners. The Beatles and certain other high-value prisoners were in those camps. There was high risk that, as the Kurdish forces pulled back, prisoners would be let loose or escape. I called over to the Defense Department and requested that nearby US troops secure custody of the high-value ISIS prisoners, including the Beatles, but I was informed that the situation on the ground was too fluid and dangerous to carry out that mission.

There were times when the President's bias for action got him in trouble. But there were also times when his willingness to cut through bureaucratic inertia was a great strength. This was such a time. Rebuffed by the DOD, I jumped in my car and raced to the White House to catch President Trump. I didn't tell him I was coming. As usual he was in and available. As it happened, national security officials, including two from Defense, were with the President, discussing the situation in Syria.

"What's up, Bill?" he asked. As soon as I explained, he looked over at the Defense officials and said: "Get 'em right now." The President turned back to me and asked, "Anyone else you want?"

"Yes, but let me start with them," I responded. Hours later, I got word the Beatles were secured by our Special Forces and in military custody in Iraq.

Up until July 2020, the DOJ's strong preference was to bring Kotey and Elsheikh back to the United States for trial to face the death penalty, even though this required waiting to win the litigation pending in the United Kingdom. There had been legal setbacks, but Prime Minister Boris Johnson's government was still committed to the case, and I thought there was a reasonable chance of success—although I realized it could take time. Also, although some of the victims' families wanted to abandon the litigation and give up the death penalty to expedite delivery of the Beatles, not all the families agreed. For the family of Kayla Mueller in particular, the Beatles seemed to be their last best hope of learning about the circumstances of the young woman's murder and the whereabouts of her remains. The Muellers felt that, given Kotey's and Elsheikh's contemptuous attitude in the past, keeping the death penalty on the table would be the only way of extracting this information and thus giving the Muellers a chance at justice.

But then the Muellers told me they had changed their minds and were willing to forego the death penalty if it meant bringing the Beatles to justice without further delay. In late July, all the American families made a joint request that I do whatever it took to bring the four men back to the United States for trial as quickly as possible, even if it meant giving up the death penalty. One of their concerns—one that I shared—was that changing circumstances in the Mideast, including the withdrawal of US forces in Iraq, might risk our ability to get custody of the Beatles if things dragged on too long.

After discussions with Secretary of State Pompeo, Secretary of Defense Mark Esper, and National Security Adviser Robert O'Brien, and consultations with UK home secretary Patel, I moved to force a full resolution of the matter. On August 18 I wrote to Patel, giving her the assurance that, if the United Kingdom provided us the necessary evidence, the United States would not seek the death penalty against Kotey and Elsheikh. However, just as important, I gave an ultimatum—not to Her Majesty's government, which was working hard to assist us, but to anyone who might be tempted to engage in further legal machinations to delay the United Kingdom from providing the evidence. Advising the home secretary that "[f]urther delay is no longer possible," I stated: "It should be clearly understood that the United States will move forward with plans to transfer Kotey and Elsheikh to Iraq for prosecution in the Iraqi justice system, unless by October 15, 2020, all litigation in the United Kingdom seeking to prevent use of [the] evidence . . . has been fully and finally resolved, and the United Kingdom has transferred the requested evidence to us."

This was not a bluff. I had already satisfied myself that transferring the Beatles to face Iraqi justice was a viable alternative. Thus, the duo's choice was simple: be tried in an American court, without the prospect of the death penalty, or face the Iraqis.

Eight days later, the UK Supreme Court removed all impediments to the British government's cooperation, ruling that there were no further grounds to block the transfer of evidence. On the same day as the court's opinion, the British government shared the evidence with the DOJ and committed to assisting in our prosecution. On October 7 I had Kotey and Elsheikh transferred from military custody in Iraq to Department of Justice custody in Alexandria, Virginia, the federal district in which they were indicted and would face trial. On September 2, 2021, one of the defendants, Kotey, pleaded guilty to eight charges that ensure he will spend the rest of his life in prison.

A second significant terrorist case that required my attention occurred one year into my tenure. The Royal Saudi Air Force, which flies American-made aircraft, is an important military partner and has long trained many of its pilots at Pensacola Naval Air Station in Florida. On December 6, 2019, a trainee, Second Lieutenant Mohammed Saeed Alshamrani, a member of the Saudi Air Force, entered a building on the grounds of Pensacola and killed three US sailors and severely wounded eight other Americans. After a protracted gunfight with federal and local responders in the corridors of the building, Alshamrani was killed.

It was clear to me that the local US attorney needed an experienced national security prosecutor to help, and I rushed a seasoned career prosecutor named Mike Sherwin down to Pensacola to help handle the matter. Mike had been a naval intelligence officer and was currently serving as Deputy Rosen's national security adviser. David Bowdich, the FBI's deputy director, personally jumped on the case, driving forward a broadscale investigation. Within a few days, the FBI had combed through Alshamrani's background and conducted hundreds of interviews of Saudi cadets stationed around the country. A few days later, Sherwin briefed me on the case. He put his laptop on my desk and ran a video taken from the various surveillance cameras from inside the building where the shootings occurred. It showed Alshamrani walking calmly through the building, casing it. It then showed him pulling out a handgun and walking methodically around, gunning down sailors in the hallways and offices. At one point, a nineteen-year-old African American sailor—Mohammed Haitham from Saint Petersburg, Florida—walked into the building and, seeing Alshamrani with a gun, raised his hands and backed up against the wall. Alshamrani calmly gunned him down in cold blood as he walked by. Wounded victims tried to crawl away, leaving trails of blood across the hallway floors. As I watched, I was shaken and could hardly speak.

There was also moving heroism that day. Naval airman Ryan Blackwell saved many lives. Alshamrani shot Blackwell five times, yet the twenty-seven-year-old still managed to jump on top of a fellow sailor to keep her from being shot, and he helped other students escape, all while taking additional fire from the shooter. I also watched the gallant acts of two US Marines: Gunnery Sergeant Ryan Maisel and Staff Sergeant Samuel Mullins. They were outside the building when they heard gunfire and, although unarmed, ran inside to confront the shooter. Their only weapon was a fire extinguisher they had pulled off the wall as they dashed toward the gunfire. Although they were unable to engage Alshamrani, they performed CPR and other medical aid on the victims. Who but the marines?

By January 13, 2020, we were able to give our initial assessment of the attack. It was an act of foreign terrorism. The evidence showed that Alshamrani was motivated by jihadist ideology. On September 11, 2019—three months before his attack—he posted a message on a social media account: "the countdown has begun." Over Thanksgiving weekend, he visited the 9/11 Memorial in New York City. He also posted other anti-American, anti-Israeli, and jihadist messages on social media, and did so two hours before his attack at the naval base. There was no evidence of assistance or prior knowledge of the attack by other members of the Saudi military (or any other foreign nationals) who were training with him in the United States.

But there was a critical gap in the evidence. Alshamrani had two Apple iPhones. During the gunfight with first responders, the gunman disengaged long enough to place one of the phones on the floor and shoot a single round into the device. It also appears he damaged the other phone. Experts at the FBI crime lab were able to fix both damaged phones so they were operational. However, both phones are engineered to make it virtually impossible to unlock them without the password. It was critical to know with whom, and about what, the shooter was communicating before he died. We asked Apple for assistance in unlocking the phones, but Apple did not provide help unlocking the phones. The company had designed them so that only the user—in this case, a terrorist—could gain access to their contents.

That impasse signified an emerging crisis for law enforcement and intelligence agencies—one I had been talking about since arriving at the department. Tech companies are designing their products with encryption codes that prevent anyone but the end user from accessing the products' data. That makes sense in ordinary circumstances. But in the twenty-first century, most evidence in criminal cases is digital—putting tech companies in charge of who gets to see it. So even when the public safety is at stake and the government has a court order based on probable cause, a company like Apple can simply say "no."

Even before Pensacola, both Christopher Wray and I had been calling on Apple and other tech companies to help us find a solution that allowed the government to gain lawful access to critical evidence. Encryption, in our view, shouldn't be warrant proof. I had been holding off discussing this matter with President Trump and wasn't sure where he would come down on the issue. It turned out I didn't need to talk to him. As soon as it was reported that Apple was not helping us obtain access to the Alshamrani data, he tweeted:

We are helping Apple all of the time on TRADE and so many other issues, and yet they refuse to unlock phones used by killers, drug dealers and other violent criminal elements. They will have to step up to the plate and help our great Country, NOW! MAKE AMERICA GREAT AGAIN.

Now, *that's* the kind of tweet I liked.

Four months after my initial announcement about the Pensacola shooting, the FBI succeeded in unlocking Alshamrani's iPhones. As expected, they did contain critical evidence that established definitively the shooter's deep ties to AQAP—Al Qaeda in the Arabian Peninsula—not only before the attack but also before he even arrived in the United States. We were able to trace Alshamrani's associations and activities for months and years leading up to his attack. On May 18, 2020, Wray and I held a press conference to announce these further findings. As I said at that time, the evidence derived from Alshamrani's unlocked phones proved useful in protecting the American people. In particular, prior to the press conference, a counterterrorism operation targeting AQAP operative Abdullah al-Maliki, one of Alshamrani's overseas associates, was conducted in Yemen.

A third terrorism case had special meaning for me. Two days before my leaving the department—on December 21, 2020—I announced charges in a case that I had personally pushed for and felt deeply about. We charged Abu Agila Muhammad Mas'ud Kheir Al-Marimi, a Libyan, as the bombmaker and the "third conspirator" in the 1988 terrorist bombing of Pan Am 103. That attack, which occurred over Lockerbie, killed 270 people, and it gave me great satisfaction to announce the charges exactly thirty-two years, to the day, after the attack.

The Lockerbie bombing case held special significance for me because, when I first served as Attorney General, I had announced the original charges in 1991 against two Libyan intelligence officers—Abdel Baset Ali al-Megrahi and Lamen Khalifa Fhimah—alleging they had conspired and participated in placing the bomb on Pan Am 103. In those days, I became deeply committed to the case as I witnessed firsthand the agony of the victims' families and watched FBI agents and their Scottish counterparts work tirelessly to crack one of the most complex cases in history. At the time, we believed that, besides al-Megrahi and Fhimah, there was at least one other conspirator involved in the operation but initially were not able to identify him. Even after the trial of Fhimah and al-Megrahi, the joint Scottish-American investigation into Pan Am 103 continued.

The breakthrough came when the FBI learned in 2017 that, after the collapse of the Gadhafi regime, Libyan law enforcement had arrested and interviewed Mas'ud. Based on information from that interview, combined with evidence from the first case and other evidence, the Justice Department was able to bring terrorism charges against Mas'ud for his role in the bombing. According to the criminal complaint affidavit, he built the bomb that destroyed Pan Am Flight 103 and worked with al-Megrahi and Fhimah to carry out the plot. The affidavit also alleges that the operation had been ordered by the leadership of Libyan intelligence and that, after the bombing, Gadhafi had personally thanked Mas'ud for the successful attack on the United States. In addition to his involvement in the Lockerbie bombing, Mas'ud was also involved in the 1986 bombing of the LaBelle Discotheque in West Berlin, which killed two American service members and a Turkish woman.

When we announced the charges, Mas'ud was still in Libyan custody. I had taken appropriate preliminary soundings, however, and felt reasonably confident that Libyan authorities, if pressed, would turn Mas'ud over to the United States for trial. I am hopeful that the Biden administration gives this matter the priority it deserves. Mas'ud and his accomplices murdered 270 people, including 190 Americans.

These cases are important, but the fact that our country hasn't yet brought those responsible for the 9/11 attacks to justice is a national scandal. More than eighteen years ago, we captured Khalid Shaikh Mohammed, whom we've accused of masterminding the attacks, along with four of his coconspirators. Over a dozen years ago, during the administration of President George W. Bush, we charged these men with murder and other terrorism offenses, to be tried before military commissions at the Guantanamo Bay US Naval Base in Cuba. We sought the death penalty. The fact that these individuals haven't even been tried yet, much less executed, is a disgrace. It suggests that, as a nation, we have lost the will to survive.

The proper forum for trying foreign persons who engage in war crimes or terrorism during a conflict with the United States is a military tribunal, not our civilian domestic courts. Most ordinary Americans understand that without having to be told—it makes no sense for a country to afford its foreign enemies the rights of US citizens. Unfortunately, an assemblage of misguided but influential Americans—some in the US court system, others in the Obama administration, still others in the military justice system itself—have tied the military commissions in knots. The whole situation would be a comedy if it wasn't so tragic. Under the rules put in place during the Obama administration, the military judges in charge of trials simply are not given the necessary authority to make definitive rulings and move the proceedings forward. When a judge rules on some argument raised by the defense lawyers, the matter is immediately taken up on appeal to a military authority, who typically proceeds to issue an impractical decision that undermines the judge's ruling. The case has had seven different judges. The commissions spend months hand-wringing over defense ploys that an experienced federal district court trial judge would be able to deal with definitively in a day. Although the trial of the five accused 9/11 conspirators was most recently scheduled for January 2021, it was then postponed indefinitely. The military can't seem to get out of its own way and complete the trial. Even if it does move ahead, I doubt military commissions, as currently set up, are capable of reaching sensible outcomes. In addition to the interminable legal jousting, too many of the military personnel involved with these proceedings have adopted a hyper-ACLU mind-set ready to indulge every silly technical maneuver to let defendants off the hook and avoid dealing with the merits of the charges.

Although foreign terrorists should typically be tried in military tribunals, the United States always has the option, if we deem it in the national interest, to try foreign terrorists such as Khalid Shaikh Mohammed and his coconspirators in our domestic federal criminal courts. Normally I wouldn't consider the idea, but I did in the summer of 2019. Ed O'Callaghan, Principal Associate Deputy Attorney General and one of the department's most experienced terrorism prosecutors, suggested we should at least explore the possibility of prosecuting KSM and his codefendants in federal district court in New York. After a preliminary review of the evidence, we concluded that, if we shifted the case to federal district court, we would likely succeed in obtaining a conviction.

I realized that Eric Holder, Attorney General under President Obama, had proposed prosecuting these defendants in New York in 2009. But he did it because he was opposed to military tribunals in principle and wanted to close Guantanamo. At that time, congressional Republicans acted quickly to stop the move. They believed— correctly, in my view—that this would be a first step toward closing the Guantanamo facility. In 2011 Congress passed a law as part of the

National Defense Authorization Act that prohibited the movement of Guantanamo prisoners into the United States.

The reason I thought it might be worth revisiting the domestic trial option was that more than a decade had passed, and the military tribunals had become a hopeless mess. I thought we might have more success in the courts than we would with the tribunals. I knew, too, that President Trump had no intention of closing Guantanamo. On the contrary, he had made clear he wanted to put more terrorists in that facility. I strongly favored keeping Guantanamo open and wanted to use it for especially dangerous ISIS fighters then held by the Kurds in Syria.

Before I proposed a domestic trial, I needed to talk to the President to see what he thought of getting an amendment to the Defense Authorization Act that would give me discretion to bring the five defendants to the United States. I also wanted the trial team to conduct a fresh review of the case to see how likely it was that we'd get convictions. Without making a decision, the President authorized me to see if Jim Inhofe, then the chairman of the Senate Armed Services Committee, was willing to push through the amendment I would need. But the Republican senator from Oklahoma was against the move. Inhofe also doubted that he could get the legislative fix without the Democrats loading up the bill with objectionable provisions on Guantanamo. That was the end of the idea.

Fault for our inability to bring to justice foreign terrorists must be laid partly at the feet of the Supreme Court. Until recently, both as a matter of constitutional law and historical practice, no serious person disputed that the core of executive power is the exclusive authority to direct military operations against foreign enemies. This includes plenary discretion over the taking and holding of foreign forces engaged in armed hostilities against the United States. It includes the President's total discretion, as commander in chief, to impose punishment on foreign forces he determines have engaged in war crimes. He has the power to use military commissions to assist him in determining guilt. The decision to constitute commissions and set their rules and procedures is, furthermore, purely within the President's discretion. Although commissions outwardly have judicial attributes, they are, in fact, executive instruments. The President's power over commissions is identical to the authority he exercises over military units on the battlefield.

But in 2008's *Boumediene v. Bush* and other cases decided in the wake of 9/11, the Supreme Court, without legal precedent and contrary to hundreds of years of British and American practice, effectively held that foreign military prisoners captured during an armed conflict had a constitutional right to seek the writ of habeas corpus in federal courts. This ends up giving our federal domestic courts supervisory authority over the executive's capture, holding, and punishment of foreign combatants, including irregular and guerrilla forces. Supreme Court rulings have also had the practical effect of extending rights applicable to domestic defendants in our criminal justice system to foreign combatants taken prisoner in an armed conflict. This has created a deplorable mess. The US military now avoids capturing prisoners rather than getting embroiled in endless legal jousting with self-appointed "human rights" lawyers claiming to represent enemy combatants. It has throttled the capacity of military commissions to carry out the functions assigned them by the President, as he deems them consistent with the country's defense needs. Restoring sanity to this area—the military functions of taking prisoners and punishing enemy war crimes—will require the Supreme Court to overrule *Boumediene* and other decisions that usurped the President's authority over military operations. This should be a top priority of the next Republican administration.

During the Trump administration, one of the most important counterterrorism missions was ensuring that the Taliban did not take power in Afghanistan and turn that country back into a training base and launching pad for terrorism against America. In 2001, following 9/11, the United States had succeeded in driving out the Taliban with a shoestring, CIA-led operation, relying on anti-Taliban warlords of the Northern Alliance and American airpower. Over the next few years, we had some modest success improving the political stability of the country. But the Taliban regrouped in Pakistan and added to its numbers. Eventually it reentered Afghanistan in force. This prompted stepping up American military operations, as well as efforts to win the hearts and minds of that country's people.

One of the mistakes that we made was pursuing the ambitious goal of re-creating Afghanistan into a unified, democratic nation—sort of a mini United States. But no matter how much time and money we spent on the project, we found we could not impose our institutional structure on an inveterately tribal country. Among other things, we took the fighters away from the warlords and attempted to meld them together into a unitary national army, essentially modeled on the US military.

I have often wondered over the years whether there was an alternative "lower intensity" approach building on the CIA's original success—*using* the tribal system rather than trying to supersede it. The Taliban derives its support from among Pashtun tribes. A possible strategy would have been to maintain an alliance of non-Pashtun warlords, such as the Northern Alliance, as well as any willing Pashtun tribes opposed to the Taliban. Just as the CIA did originally, we would have relied on warlord militias and limited our military presence largely to Bagram Air Base, from which we would provide air support to allied militias, fly our drones, and strike at any significant Taliban foothold sufficient to project terrorism outside of the country. We would effectively be serving as the biggest warlord—one with airpower—allied with other warlords, keeping the Taliban at bay and depriving them of the ability to use Afghanistan as a secure base for terrorism. Efforts at political stabilization and economic development could have been pursued in a more phased and decentralized fashion.

In any event, President Trump's goal was to "end the war" in Afghanistan, which for him meant withdrawing American forces. I believe Trump's distrust of the intelligence and military communities prevented him from considering alternatives to complete withdrawal. I had only one conversation with him about Afghanistan. In 2019 I was with him when he took a call from the Defense Department about force drawdowns in Afghanistan. After hanging up, he asked me what I thought. I told him I felt we should explore options that involved the lowest level of commitment consistent with propping up the anti-Taliban side and giving them a fighting chance to hold the Taliban at bay, but we should not just pull the plug and wash our hands of the whole matter. Before the 2020 election, I think Trump was conflicted. He had the impulse to sweep everything off the table. But he also did not like the idea of an obvious surrender.

According to news reports, in mid-November 2020, after losing the election, the President, consulting only with his thirty-year-old personnel director, John McEntee, cut an order directing the DOD to withdraw from Afghanistan by January 15, 2021. The same news reports say he was eventually persuaded by senior advisers to abandon that directive. I had no involvement in these matters and cannot say what happened. But it appeared to me that, when Trump left office, he had made no decision on the end game. The question whether to withdraw completely—and, if so, when and how—were all matters left open.

I don't know what would have ultimately happened in Afghanistan if Trump had won the election. But this I am sure of: even if he had decided on a complete military withdrawal, he would not have carried it out in the reckless and moronic way it was done by President Biden.

President Biden has consistently pointed to Trump's 2020 Doha Agreement for Bringing Peace to Afghanistan as locking him in to complete withdrawal. This is untrue. In the Doha Agreement, Trump held out the prospect of withdrawing as early as May 2021 on the condition that the Taliban fulfilled a number of preconditions, including negotiating with the Afghan government to achieve a "permanent and comprehensive cease-fire" and to agree upon a "political road map" for Afghanistan's future. Thus, any withdrawal was *conditional* on Taliban behavior. If the Taliban failed to carry out the political terms and resorted to force to take control of the country, the President would, as he said, "bomb the shit" out of them.

Biden, by sharp contrast, made clear that he would withdraw completely regardless of Taliban conduct. He declared unilaterally that American air support for the Afghan military would cease. Correctly sensing Biden's weakness, the Taliban escalated its military offensive.

Later, of course, Biden would outrageously blame the Afghan military for not fighting, but it was he who abandoned them and encouraged their enemies.

One can only hope that the Biden administration, and the administrations that follow, will learn from its mistakes and begin again to treat America's enemies—the Taliban, the Iranian regime, and especially Beijing—as what they are.

At home, meanwhile, a broad consensus has emerged about an internal menace resulting from the power of certain of our largest corporations. They are not enemies, in the sense I've outlined in this chapter, but, taken together, their behavior poses a threat to individual liberty and democratic self-determination. Administrations over the next decade, Democrat and Republican, have an opportunity to meet that threat head-on.

CHAPTER 18

TAKING ON BIG TECH

For all our disagreements, Americans on the Right and the Left agree on one thing: Big Tech has too much power.

During my tenure as AG, this was an issue that President Trump raised frequently. When he originally interviewed me for the job, he asked me what I thought about the power of Big Tech and said he thought this was an area crying out for scrutiny.

"Mr. President, I think this is a monumental issue," I told him. "It's not just the problem of economic power and the impact it has on competition, but of the effects that concentrated power has on our society and culture. One of my top priorities would be looking at the large online platforms from an antitrust perspective."

"What do you think of the antitrust people over there—that guy Makan seems okay, right?" he asked, referring to the head of the Antitrust Division, Makan Delrahim.

"I've known Makan forever," I said, "and he's fine. But I have dealt with the division for decades. They move like molasses and are behind the times. They need to be pushed. Remember, these online companies grew into behemoths right under the regulators' noses—even with their help."

Most conservatives are focused on censorship by Big Tech, I acknowledged, but that is not an area in which the DOJ has direct regulatory authority. I pointed out that the power to censor is the result of their economic power, and *that* power is an antitrust issue the department *does* have authority over.

"I know Congress is looking at this, and some of the state attorneys general are also," the President observed. "I don't want us to be on the sideline."

The President was happy I viewed the issue of Big Tech as a priority. He never suggested any particular outcome he wanted to see. But, throughout my two years in office, he consistently reminded me of the need to examine Big Tech's economic power.

I've already mentioned the President's routine during his executive time in his private dining room of reviewing newspapers and annotating them with his big, bold Sharpie, sending out his comments to the relevant subordinate. He sent me a number of articles about Big Tech that reported on members of Congress making legislative proposals or state attorneys general initiating investigations. On the clipping was usually a Sharpie annotation, saying something like, "*We Must Lead!*"

The President, it's fair to say, won office by circumventing the mainstream press and speaking directly to the American people via Twitter. But he understood instinctively that what the tech giants want is power—power to dominate the American economy, culture, and national discourse.

Liberals and progressives worry about the spread of misinformation and disinformation on Facebook and other platforms, and the poisoning of our political discourse. The Left's anxieties about the largest tech companies' control over our collective life are not unreasonable. It's true that pernicious lies are spread on social media, and it's true, too, that sites like Twitter and Facebook reward and amplify vitriol and unreason. Foreign entities, moreover, do use tech platforms to spread chaos in the political sphere, and criminal gangs do use them to facilitate fraud and human trafficking.

Conservatives, meanwhile, worry most about the tech companies' ability to censor, downgrade, or eliminate political speech they don't like. In the past year, Amazon delisted a thoughtful book by an accomplished scholar on gender dysphoria. YouTube scrubbed videos that included Stanford University professors offering nuanced views that departed from public health orthodoxy on pandemic lockdowns. Google announced that it would prohibit web ads that contradict "well-established scientific consensus around the existence and causes of climate change." Twitter banned a former US President from its platform but still allows leaders of the Taliban to tweet as much as they like. And both Facebook and Twitter limited the sharing of a *New York Post* report about Hunter Biden's e-mails—a story later corroborated as factual.

But it's not simply a Right-Left issue. Ordinary Americans are no longer as comfortable as they were a decade ago with tech companies' collecting their personal information. There is something bizarre and creepy, for example, about using the words "snow boots" in a casual conversation and, that same day, finding ads on your smartphone's browser for snow boots. There must be very few middle-class Americans who haven't lost a friend or felt alienated from a neighbor as a consequence of aggressive posting on social media—activity the tech platforms encourage actively. The revelation that high-level employees at Facebook are fully aware of the psychological devastation wrought on teenage girls by Instagram, but deliberately keep that awareness under wraps, is unnerving to many parents—especially since there's nothing anybody can do to shake Facebook-Instagram's dominance.

Or is there?

Over the past twenty years, vital areas of our lives have been drawn into the digital world. At a stunning pace, our interactions with other people and the world around us—our shopping, entertainment, social relations, learning, gathering and sharing information, and public conversation—are conducted more and more through streams of bits over digital platforms. A small number of titanic companies—Google, Facebook, Amazon—have gained dominance over key digital markets. Their powerful position allows these online platforms to operate as gateways to a vast array of markets, with growing control over what we see, hear, and read, what we buy, and even now what we can say. Having collected voluminous personal information about their users, and using artificial intelligence, or AI, to analyze it, these companies use algorithms that enmesh users, subtly shepherding them through the digital world, increasingly capable of manipulating their decisions, beliefs, and behavior. The dominance of these companies gives them both massive economic power and overweening political and social control. They have the capacity to throttle free markets and warp our collective life.

President Trump—he stressed this to me from my first meeting with him—wanted to ensure that the power and practices of Big Tech companies were scrutinized carefully under antitrust laws.

I had watched these companies operate from my position at Verizon, and I agreed with him fully. I was pleasantly surprised, during my confirmation process, to see the degree of bipartisan consensus that has emerged about the need to address the power of these platforms. Virtually every senator I met with on either side of the aisle raised these platforms as a main area of concern. It is true that the Democrats have been aroused by the concentration of economic power, whereas many Republican eyes have been opened by the arrogant censorship practices of these companies—practices that are, in the end, a manifestation of their economic power. It's also true that many elected officials on the progressive Left no longer believe in free speech and rail against tech companies for not policing "misinformation" with sufficient vigor—*misinformation* meaning conservative opinion. But, again, wildly misguided as I believe these progressives are, they are responding to the same reality: namely, that the tech companies, by virtue of their economic might, hold enormous power over what can be written and said in American public life. However our political leaders have come to the realization, their basic complaint is sound: Big Tech has too much power.

The irony, of course, is that these massive aggregations of power grew up right under the noses of antitrust enforcers and regulators, and of Congress itself, despite constant warnings over the years from informed voices in the industry. It wasn't just inaction. During the formative stages of these markets, the government adopted policies that *facilitated* these companies' march to dominance. Sometimes the companies were afforded favorable treatment because they had the right political alignment; just as often, they were given a free pass because regulators are prone to inertia, befuddlement, and a strong tendency to fight the last war.

When I arrived at the Justice Department, there was no formal investigation under way into Google or other major online platforms. I encouraged the Antitrust Division to start a review of Google's market power in the Internet search and search advertising markets, and asked that they extend this over time to all dominant online platforms. I was frustrated by the slow pace of things. A big part of the problem was that investigations of this magnitude require a lot of lawyers dedicated to it, and the tech team was understaffed. I added more lawyers and brought on an excellent career lawyer in the division, Lauren Willard, to help me ramrod the process. In July 2019 I established a broad review of all the major online platforms, focusing initially on Google. Working with my Deputy, Jeffrey Rosen, I recruited from private practice an accomplished antitrust lawyer, Ryan Shores, to drive the effort—assigning him first to the Deputy's staff and, later, to head the project in the division. (The head of Antitrust, Makan Delrahim, had done work involving Google when he was in the private sector and therefore recused himself from handling Google matters.) I also encouraged collaboration with the state attorneys general—all of whom, with the exception of California's, were investigating Google and Facebook through joint bipartisan working groups.

Each of the dominant platforms is distinctive, but each poses the same three dangers. First, as an economic matter, the largest tech companies hold monopoly or near-monopoly power in vital digital market sectors. They are in a position, given the attributes of those markets, to strangle any competitive challenge to their supremacy. The unique characteristics of these markets allow their dominance to snowball, enabling them to play the role of the digital world's gatekeepers.

Second, the ability of these companies to collect vast quantities of personal data makes them a danger. The more personal information a company has about its users, the stronger it will be as a competitor—and no company can remotely compare to the data possessed by the top tech giants of Silicon Valley. These companies have vacuumed up such unfathomable stockpiles of personal data that they are effectively impregnable. That in turn raises grave concerns over privacy and power: if only a few tech giants own massive troves of information about American citizens, those few companies can, without any transparency, manipulate the decisions and behaviors of their users.

Third, because the markets controlled by these companies essentially compose the "marketplace of ideas"—the arena in which people get and impart information, voice their views, and debate social and political questions—these companies can, in essence, control the public discourse. They can amplify, suppress, or censor particular information and opinions and control and distort what's said and written by journalists, politicians, and voters. This power is antithetical to the kind of untrammeled marketplace of ideas and public debate necessary for a free people to govern themselves.

To understand how these platforms achieved dominance, it is critical to grasp the phenomenon of "network effects." The idea is that a user will derive greater value from a good or service as more people use it. The effect is most powerful where the service involves connecting the user to other users. Take, for example, an unregulated market of 5,000 households with no existing phone service and no requirement for competing phone companies to interconnect with one another. Suppose several companies are simultaneously building separate networks to provide competing phone service. One company quickly gets 2,500 households on its network; a second gets 500; a third gets 100. Which network would have the most value for a prospective customer? The larger one, obviously, because it allows a user to reach more households. Customers of the smaller networks will flock to the larger one in order to connect to more people.

That's a physical network. In the world of the Internet, everyone is already physically interconnected, and so the networks that enjoy network effects are the "virtual" ones of users. For example, in the personal social networking market, Facebook has the largest share of users; among general online marketplaces, Amazon has the widest range of sellers. The network effects of these online platforms have proven at least as powerful as those arising in the past from physical networks.

Digital markets are typically characterized by high capital costs, low marginal costs, and powerful network effects. This dramatically favors the first mover, which rapidly acquires a large share on its virtual network. The market soon reaches a point at which it becomes all but impossible for the smaller network to catch up and compete. In the absence of regulatory intervention, the market becomes winner-take-all—which, of course, isn't a "market" at all. The stock market knows this, which is why it gives astronomical valuations to companies with an early lead in network-effect businesses even while the companies are losing money hand over fist—traders know the payoff is eventual market domination. These companies can then use their extravagant stock prices to attract and retain the best and brightest employees and to purchase smaller companies—effectively co-opting and buying out potential competition. Real competition in these markets will usually arise, if at all, not from a mirror-image competitor but from a new entrant that builds a new network around an innovative product. But the Big Tech platforms have followed a pattern of buying these emerging players before they can build up a competing business.

It is important to recognize that, where strong network effects operate, as they do in many digital markets, market hegemony isn't the normal form of market dominance. In a less network-dependent market, a company may achieve premier status based on the fact that it produces a superior product or offers a superior service. That company may use its power to protect itself from competition, but its lead position doesn't itself make competition impossible. In the case of dominant online platforms, however, it's not obvious that the products *are* superior. But even if a technically superior platform enters the market and attempts to attract new users, the scale of the incumbent precludes success.

The regulators, always ten years behind the times, facilitated the tech companies' control of digital markets by allowing them to avoid paying the costs of transporting all the data traffic associated with their businesses. To prevent big, bad phone companies from using their imaginary power to "discriminate" against the likes of Google and Facebook, regulators adopted the policy known as network, or net, neutrality. This rule required the data transport companies, like the phone and cable companies, to treat all Internet content equally with regard to price and bandwidth speeds. This sounds like apple pie, but the rule's real and intended effect was to prevent data transport companies from charging the online platforms—Google, Facebook, Amazon, and others—for the costs of carrying their traffic with the speed and reliability necessary for the platforms to offer their services. Instead, the regulators required the phone and cable companies to recover these data transport costs through the prices they charged consumer end users to connect to the Internet. Thus, while the large online platforms were generating most of the Internet traffic, the costs of handling this high volume were shifted to Grandma and Grandpa. They might send out a few e-mails each month—but they have paid a higher price for their Internet service to cover the transport costs attributable to the Big Tech platforms.

Allowing these tech companies to avoid the costs of data transport helped to turbocharge their growth. Government regulators were, in effect, subsidizing them, and customers were picking up the tab. That in turn enabled the online platforms to make the crucial exchange that's at the heart of their business model: offering their service to customers "for free." The customers need only agree to let the platforms have their personal information.

Of course, none of it is "free." The use of search engines, e-mail services, map sites, social networking apps—users pay for these things by letting the tech platforms know everything about them. Once users click that alluring "terms of service" button, they surrender their personal data to the platforms: what posts they "like" on social media, what sites they browse, what links they're likely to click on, what they buy, whom they interact with, where they get news. The large tech platforms apply artificial intelligence and machine learning to analyze all this data, and that enables them to develop more effective algorithms, more accurately targeted advertising, and more attractive recommendations tailored to each user.

Big Tech's capture of so much of our personal information raises two important concerns. The first is its economic effect: the mushrooming data advantage of the major platforms further helps stifle competition and decisively reinforces their economic market power. Once a company has a lot of information about a user, he or she becomes more locked into the service. More important, user data collection has its own network effects that fortify the incumbent's grip on the market. Data advantages quickly accelerate: the more data a company has, the more adept its offerings; the more adept its offerings, the more it is able to hold existing customers and attract more customers, which allows it to collect even more data. The volume of data amassed by the dominant platforms gives them overwhelming competitive advantages that no other would-be competitor could hope to match. The failure of the government to provide any effective regulation of the collection and use of personal data has given a major boost to the platforms' rapid growth and reinforced their ascendancy.

The second concern is the effect of this data collection on personal privacy. The kinds of data these companies are collecting on users are granular and intimate, including information about users' whereabouts, purchases, reading and watching habits, browsing, likes, associates, current interests and tastes, health matters, and so forth. Many users, it's safe to say, did not fully understand what they were agreeing to let online platforms gather about them. Even if they did understand, many felt they had little choice because of the commanding position these companies have as gatekeepers to the digital market.

But leave aside the issue of consent. There is the basic question of whether American society should allow a few behemoth companies to collect vast stores of private information about individuals as the price of entry into the digital world. An entity with this much information about a person holds substantial potential power over him or her, and it may be able to exercise that power alone or in tandem with the government.

The most pernicious danger, however, is that by allowing the companies to amass and use this data, we are giving them the wherewithal to subtly guide and influence individual choices and behaviors—and to do so without any transparency. In the aftermath of the 2016 election, a chorus of media personalities, politicos, and academics purported to be outraged and terrified that Russian actors influenced the election simply by *using* Facebook to target certain audiences with false and malign messages. What's genuinely chilling—what they ought to be outraged and terrified by—is the power of the platforms themselves. They can limit and curate the content available to the user without the user even knowing it; they can choose the time and place that content becomes available, depending on the behavior deemed most desirable by those controlling the algorithms; and they can do this not only for commercial products but also for social and political content. This is infinitely more consequential and dangerous than anything carried out by Russian trolls in an effort to sow chaos.

There is another concern related to the dominant platforms' use of AI and machine learning to analyze their mountainous collections of users' personal information. Use of these tools, and the algorithms generated through their use, has the effect of pouring gasoline on the fire in two respects. First, these tools have their own network effects and therefore further reinforce the platform's dominant position. The more voluminous the data fed into the AI and machine learning maw, the smarter these tools become and the better the algorithms they help generate. Thus, there is a snowball effect: the more user data a company has, the better its AI and machine learning become, and this improvement leads to attracting even more data for the company to use to feed its AI and machine learning tools, and so on.

Second, there is reason for concern that the way AI is used and the algorithms generated by these profit-motivated companies will have a bias toward disseminating "click bait"—more incendiary content representing the extremes. There is legitimate worry that platform algorithms give more prominence to the more extreme and coarse content, further distorting a civilized and responsible marketplace of ideas. The tech companies have every incentive to get users stimulated and riled up with ever more incendiary click bait. For the tech giants, it is a positive good for Americans to move to the poles of Left and Right.

The unique challenge posed by the dominance of Big Tech arises from the critical nature of the markets it controls. If the market for vacuum cleaners was to become a monopoly, there would undoubtedly be some diminution in consumer welfare—prices of vacuum cleaners would be higher, and their quality lower. In the general scheme of things, however, monopolization of the vacuum cleaner market would not be of earth-shattering significance. What the tech companies control, however, is the marketplace of *ideas*. They are privatizing the village green—the space where people receive and disseminate information, express their views, and engage in public discourse—and turning it into a virtual forum controlled by a few large companies. These companies have unprecedented power over what information and viewpoints people see and hear. They can silence some voices and give others a megaphone. They can limit the dissemination of information they deem harmful or dangerous: a talk that questions public health orthodoxy by a Stanford medical doctor, for example, or a legitimate and newsworthy report about the laptop of a presidential candidate's son. Or they can magnify information they deem healthy or praiseworthy: a story about a celebrity's gender reassignment surgery, an ill-advised remark by a disfavored politician. Never before has control over the flow of information and ideas in our society become so concentrated in so few hands.

The gatekeepers can use their power to shape the flow of information to advantage themselves economically or to boost their own favored political outcomes. They can also use "smart" processes to skew the flow of information—algorithms to determine which posts or news stories appear on an individual's social media feed—that are opaque to outside observers and thus nearly impossible to detect and monitor.

The greatest danger lies in the political realm. In a democracy, a free people make collective decisions by initially trying to forge some consensus through public debate and deliberation, and then, if necessary, having an informed citizenry vote. A free and robust marketplace of ideas in which public discourse is unconstrained is indispensable to a democratic society. In the early days of the Internet, Americans were led to believe that the web would be that open marketplace. Things may have tended in that direction for a short time, but, in our day, the opposite has happened. The bulk of our marketplace, such as it is, is stewarded by a few secretive and powerful companies capable of distorting, choking off, or skewing the flow of information of which, for any reason or no reason, they disapprove. This state of affairs is antithetical to the workings of a healthy democracy.

How should we respond to Big Tech's dominance over digital markets? The starting point must be vigorous enforcement of antitrust laws. I don't believe antitrust enforcement by itself will be sufficient to address the problems posed by the invincible online platforms, but it must be part of any solution. Antitrust law focuses on the *economic* dimensions of market power and the promotion of competition. It is meant to address anticompetitive misconduct: unreasonable restraints on competition and anticompetitive practices used to gain and maintain market power. Although the interrelated problems posed by the dominance of online platforms aren't just economic but also social and political, the latter flow largely from the former—that is, Big Tech's economic hegemony generates social and political problems. Curtailing these companies' economic power therefore should, over the long term, alleviate some of the cultural pathologies exacerbated by their omnipresence.

After a lot of hard work by the DOJ Antitrust Division, in October 2020 the department—joined by eleven state attorneys general—filed an antitrust lawsuit to stop Google from unlawfully maintaining monopolies over multiple markets. Twenty years ago, Google was an upstart. Today it is a monopoly gatekeeper for the Internet, and one of the wealthiest companies on the planet, with a market value of $1 trillion and annual revenue exceeding $160 billion. Our lawsuit claimed that Google has for many years used a series of anticompetitive tactics to maintain, reinforce, and extend its monopolies in the markets for general search services, search advertising, and general search text advertising—the cornerstones of its empire.

The case of Google captures nicely the anticompetitive tactics online platforms use to establish supremacy. General search engines are distributed primarily on mobile devices (smartphones and tablets) and computers (desktops and laptops). By far, the most effective way to distribute these search engines is to set them as the default on the computers and devices. Users rarely change the default setting, so presetting a search engine as the default gives it de facto exclusivity. For many years, Google has used a series of exclusionary agreements that collectively lock up these distribution channels and block rivals by requiring that Google be preset as the default general search engine on billions of mobile devices and computers worldwide. In many cases, these agreements forbid preinstallation of any competing search service, require preinstallation of Google's search applications in prime locations on mobile devices, and make them undeletable, regardless of consumer preference.

The DOJ lawsuit is pretty simple to explain. Google, largely as a result of its anticompetitive conduct, has in recent years accounted for nearly 90 percent of all general search engine queries in the United States, and almost 95 percent of queries on mobile devices. Google has monetized this monopoly by leveraging its power over the search advertising markets, too. Then, having extracted monopoly advertising revenues, Google has "shared" these profits with distributors in return for further commitments to favor Google's search engine. In this way, the company creates a continuous, self-reinforcing cycle of monopolization over multiple markets.

I hope the Biden administration will steadfastly pursue the case. The Trump administration asked the court to enjoin Google's anticompetitive practices and to award "structural remedies" needed to cure the harm done, including potentially breaking up Google.

On a parallel track, as we worked on the case challenging Google's search monopoly, the Antitrust Division was also exploring a possible challenge to Google's 2007 acquisition of the company DoubleClick and its market power in the Internet advertising market. It was not ready to file by the time I left the department, but news reports indicate the Biden Antitrust Division is considering that suit.

In December 2020 the US Federal Trade Commission brought an antitrust suit against Facebook. Antitrust cases like these may well signal renewed bipartisan appreciation of antitrust enforcement as a means of protecting competition. Many of the practices used by the largest online platforms cry out for antitrust scrutiny. These cases are, I hope, just the start. The DOJ and FTC, as well as private litigants, will continue to use antitrust law to challenge anticompetitive tactics and foster more competition in these markets.

Still, antitrust law can't remedy everything awry in American tech and data markets. Unlike regulatory power—which allows proactive supervision of, and setting rules for, an entire market—antitrust addresses only wrongdoing by particular actors. And, like all complex litigation, the process is numbingly slow and cumbersome. The best law firms in the country will be marshaled against the government enforcers in a scorched-earth legal battle destined to drag out for years. Even if the government wins on the merits, implementing remedies will take years more.

Some argue that antitrust law needs updating to address these limitations, especially given the specific characteristics of digital markets. They suggest that the "consumer welfare" standard—the principle that courts should assess antitrust cases on whether consumers are actually harmed by monopolies—needs to be broadened beyond purely economic considerations of price, output, quality, and innovation. These critics contend that we should widen the scope of antitrust law to include the kind of multifaceted problems we confront in the digital marketplace—the ability, for example, to consider noneconomic harms.

I remain skeptical of those arguments. Antitrust is a *general* tool applicable to all markets. Tailoring it to specific markets may well end up causing more mischief than good. Further, the problem isn't with the consumer welfare standard itself—which, if applied properly, is sufficiently capacious to address competitive harms in whichever market they arise. The problem, rather, is that Republicans and free-market conservatives, among whom I count myself, have in recent years tended to give the consumer welfare standard a crabbed application. We have basically allowed rarefied, speculative economic analysis to supplant the facts on the ground.

This point about the overreliance on speculative economic analysis in antitrust enforcement has been well articulated by Rachel Bovard, formerly with the Heritage Foundation and now with the Conservative Partnership Institute in DC. Instead of heeding the advice of Judge Robert Bork—one of the chief advocates of the consumer welfare standard—courts today have come to allow an "economic extravaganza," to use Bork's phrase, to distract us from what's actually happening in the market. Bovard argues that economic analysis was once applied to inform and supplement antitrust enforcement, whereas today economic analysis controls it:

> Antitrust enforcement has been steered away from its broad congressional mandate to police concentrated power in the market and toward the exclusive terrain of complicated, theoretical economic models, and the esoteric ruminations of economists, often with no direct experience in the business world. In a sense, this has subjected antitrust law to the cult of the well-compensated expert, and well-heeled legal and economic practitioners.

As general counsel for Verizon, I had a lot of exposure to antitrust battles: I oversaw three of the country's largest telecom mergers, and actively opposed several major mergers in the United States and Europe. From my experience, Bovard's description is dead-on.

As with so many fields of expertise, the job of antitrust economists is now to tell people that the reality manifest before their eyes is not really there. This was the case, for example, when Google acquired the Internet ad company DoubleClick. It was obvious to everyone in the industry that this combination would allow Google to achieve dominance in the digital ad space. Yet the FTC, bamboozled by economic mumbo jumbo, approved the acquisition. And now, fourteen years later, the DOJ is thinking about how to address Google's lock on the ad market. The enforcers are coming late to the party. It is much harder to use antitrust laws to undo entrenched and concentrated power than it is to stop ongoing and future anticompetitive conduct.

One of the reasons people are talking about "updating" the antitrust laws is because, at bottom, they see a need for market intervention in a form more like that provided by regulation. My reaction to that is that we should frankly acknowledge the need for some regulation in these markets, rather than trying to convert antitrust into a regulatory tool. I think it is both possible and desirable at this stage for Congress to grant tightly defined regulatory authority—limited in both scope and duration—to the FTC, or some other existing entity, that could significantly help address some of the complex issues caused by the monopolistic online platforms.

There are at least two considerations that militate strongly for a statutory regime that authorizes an expert body to take certain *defined* actions. The first consideration is that the markets at issue here are subject to powerful network effects and thus prone to monopolization, and the networks involved provide services important to modern life. In these circumstances, society's ultimate choice boils down to either (1) accepting establishment of a legal monopoly and regulating it as such to ensure fair and reasonable access to services by end users, or (2) intervening in the market with regulations designed to limit the operation of network effects and promote a degree of competition. For these reasons, we have historically subjected these kinds of markets— for instance, transportation, media, and telephone—to regulation, of one type or the other, by agencies specialized in the relevant industry, such as the Interstate Commerce Commission (railroads), the Civil Aeronautics Board (airlines), and the Federal Communications Commission (telephone, cable, broadcast). This reflects recognition that in some markets, market dominance can have bad effects that must be addressed, even if the dominance was not the result of previous wrongdoing. While over the long run, technology or other modalities may emerge that eliminate the previous constraints on competition in certain markets and thus permit deregulation, the reality is that natural monopoly conditions can persist for many decades—after all, the local telephone business remained a natural monopoly for almost a hundred years—and often market-opening regulation is a necessary precursor for deregulation.

The second consideration suggesting the need for regulation is the composite nature of the issues in this sector. As I've suggested, Big Tech's dominance over digital markets poses three closely interrelated challenges: the degree of economic power and its impact on competition; the collection and use of personal data and their privacy implications; and the constraints and distortions imposed over the free flow of information and public discourse. Any coherent approach requires that, in adopting remedial measures, all three aspects must be kept in view simultaneously. For example, a privacy rule that may in isolation enhance privacy may also help consolidate the market power of the big players.

For these reasons, relying solely on ad hoc, judge-imposed remedies against individual players for specific misconduct on a case-by-case basis will not result in a rational, coherent approach to the multifaceted problems caused by the unchallenged supremacy of a few tech giants. I have natural reservations about imposing a regulatory framework on market activities, as most conservatives do, but the reality is that some markets, or market conditions, require a degree of regulatory intervention. In the case of Big Tech's major platforms, it is hard to see how the challenges they pose to competition, privacy, and the free flow of information can be addressed in the absence of a regulatory framework. But I believe there is a way to go about this with prudent, incremental steps—subject to close congressional supervision—that does not punt difficult issues to some unaccountable agency.

One possible approach would be for Congress to empower the Federal Trade Commission or some other regulatory agency to carry out three specific tasks, only one of which would involve direct regulatory authority. First, the agency could order platforms to divest certain previously acquired firms, with the aim of reducing the platforms' market dominance and promoting competition. The statute would not direct specific divestitures by name but would define the particular characteristics requiring divestiture. This could lead, for example, to companies such as Amazon being required to divest businesses like Zappos and Whole Foods; and Google, to divest businesses such as YouTube, Waze, and Nest; and Facebook, businesses such as Instagram and WhatsApp. The statute could also grant the regulatory entity authority to direct that dominant platforms conduct certain businesses through structurally separate affiliates.

Second, the regulatory agency, after study, could propose a specific regime governing the collection, use, and analysis of personal information. The agency would not have the power to mandate this regime, only propose it for enactment by Congress. An area requiring exploration is the feasibility of allowing users to control as much information as possible. It may be possible to allow users to determine what, how, and when to provide information to the websites and platforms they use.

Third, the agency could prepare a public report addressing the feasibility of imposing—by law—"essential facility" obligations on the largest platforms. That's a common approach in dealing with natural monopolies. In essence, the monopolist would be obliged to provide competitors access to key components of its platform, which would enable them to compete on a more equal footing. The FCC took this approach in the 1990s when it required local phone companies to open up their networks to competitors. That exercise turned out to be a dead end because it happened just as Internet technology and wireless ended the phone companies' natural monopoly. But it doesn't follow that any similar technology will end the dominance of Facebook, Amazon, Google, and the rest. A report from Stanford's Program on Democracy and the Internet, for example, proposes allowing a new competitive layer of companies to attach themselves to the top platforms and offer "middleware" products: software and services that would give users the ability to shape their own algorithms, determine their own feed, and hold on to their personal information if they wish.

The most serious harm caused by Big Tech dominance is their mounting control over the flow of information and public discourse. Our system of free self-government depends on—and the First Amendment was meant to secure, as the Supreme Court has said—"the widest possible dissemination of information from diverse and antagonistic sources." For that reason, as the Supreme Court has also said, "[a]ssuring that the public has access to a multiplicity of information sources is a governmental purpose of the highest order." The power of hegemonic online platforms to constrain what people hear, see, and say is incompatible with our system of government. The First Amendment prohibits only governmental abridgement of speech, but censorship by private companies that control essential channels of information can distort and vitiate public life as effectively as government suppression of speech.

When overconcentration threatens a media or information market, the United States has not hesitated to use its regulatory power to promote greater diversity of content. Any government regulation of this sort must be "viewpoint neutral": the government may promote wider access to constrained communication channels, but it may not promote content with particular viewpoints. The FCC's cross-ownership rules, for example, limit the number of radio stations, TV stations, and newspapers that one entity can own in a single market. Similarly, FCC rules used to prohibit any person from reaching, through owned or controlled cable systems, more than 30 percent of all homes passed nationwide by cable. Another roughly analogous situation existed when, as a result of constraints on available spectrum, three large TV networks dominated the broadcast media market. In 1969 the Supreme Court upheld the Federal Communications Commission's adoption, twenty years before, of the Fairness Doctrine, which regulated the kinds of speech that the networks could carry. The Fairness Doctrine, a ham-handed regulation in many ways, outlived whatever utility it may have had, and the Reagan administration was right to kill it in 1987, but in its original manifestation, it was not an irrational or unconstitutional response to an intolerable level of market concentration.

Regulation of this type may not be required at this stage, especially if effective steps are taken to reduce platform market power. But the government has a legitimate interest in promoting multiple sources of news and information, and there is no reason to think that interest doesn't apply to today's digital markets.

The solution is not to jawbone Big Tech, pressing its CEOs to become more "responsible" in exercising their control. American society should not have to plead with private interests not to abuse hegemonic power. That does not fix the problem; it exacerbates it. Moreover, the government's role in encouraging private companies to use their power in particular ways might make it possible to characterize the actions taken as, in effect, governmental actions.

Addressing censorship by major online platforms requires revisiting Section 230 of the Communications Decency Act of 1996, which gave online platforms legal immunity when they remove third-party content from their sites. That statute was intended to protect interactive online services from lawsuits arising from user-generated content. The idea was that websites operating as bulletin boards or open forums could not realistically monitor and edit every post to ensure it did not run afoul of defamation or other laws. So, for instance, if a user defames a restaurant on the website Yelp, the restaurant may not sue Yelp for defamation.

Before Section 230, courts had maintained that an online company that removes or curates content on its platform may be held liable as a publisher or speaker for all other content. Platforms thus faced a dilemma. If they tried to moderate third-party content, they risked being held liable as a "publisher" for any and all content posted by a third party. But if they didn't moderate content, they risked having the platform overrun with obscene or defamatory content. Section 230 was meant to solve this problem by allowing companies to remove content if they act in "good faith," believing the content inconsistent with their terms of service or to be "obscene, lewd, lascivious, filthy, excessively violent, harassing, or otherwise objectionable."

But Congress's purpose in granting immunity was not to give the platforms a blank check to censor any content they wanted. Rather, Congress's goal was to encourage platforms to offer a "forum for a true diversity of political discourse, unique opportunities for cultural development, and myriad avenues for intellectual activity." Unfortunately, the term *objectionable* has become a gaping loophole. It should have been construed as limited to material similar to the categories listed immediately before the term. Instead, some courts have interpreted it so broadly as to allow immunity for platforms that censor any content they want.

In September 2020 the Department of Justice proposed amendments to Section 230 intended to stop its use as an open-ended license to censor. Under the amendments, we proposed that, to retain immunity, the platform must show it acted in good faith in removing content, believing either that the content was inconsistent with the platform's terms of service or that it fell into one of the specifically named categories of excludable material (obscene, excessively violent, and so on) or was "unlawful." Substituting the term *unlawful* for *objectionable* would substantially limit a platform's latitude in removing content that otherwise satisfied its terms of service. Moreover, DOJ's proposed amendments would have required platforms that remove content based on terms-of-service violations to explain much more clearly how the content broke the rules. Finally, our amendments required that any decision to remove content be *objectively* reasonable.

Taken together, these amendments would significantly curtail the ability of platforms to simultaneously assert immunity while engaging in discretionary censorship.

President Trump made a number of public comments—particularly after we sent our proposed amendments up to the Hill—calling for the complete repeal of Section 230 immunity. I was skeptical of this approach because I believe that many platforms have reasonably limited their content to certain subject matters—for example, travel or restaurant reviews. As long as their decisions are taken in good faith and are objectively reasonable, those platforms should be able to remove nongermane third-party material. Further, platforms are still faced with the dilemma of how to deal with user-generated content that they believe in good faith is obscene or otherwise unlawful. A platform's inability to retain immunity while removing this content could result in the platform being overrun by vile or unlawful content. At the time I left the department, no action had been taken on our proposals.

The experience of Section 230 illustrates one of the more noxious features of the rise of the online platforms: a bait and switch. When some of these platforms first came on the scene, they presented themselves as essentially open forums of free-flowing discourse. It was this feature that initially attracted so many users and gave them the early momentum to capture the benefits of network effects, which ultimately led to market dominance. But once they achieved supremacy, they began wantonly censoring content based on cryptic criteria. It was clear, for anybody with eyes to see, that their decisions had to do with the political and social views of company leaders and managers. Would these companies have grown as they did if, from the beginning, they had presented themselves as the censors they have become? Doubtful.

The issue of Big Tech's economic dominance and choke hold on Americans' free speech rights was a constant worry during my second time as Attorney General. Every day, it seemed, some tech-giant executive offered obsequious testimony before a congressional committee, or someone on Capitol Hill sought our guidance on legislation to curb tech companies' power, or a social media company perpetrated some new outrage. Big Tech occupied the attention of the Justice Department every day.

Until early 2020, that is. Then something Justice hadn't thought about much at all came crashing into American life.

CHAPTER 19

FACING THE COVID PANDEMIC

In the first part of April 2020, I stopped by the Oval Office for an impromptu visit with the President. No one fully understood at the time what we were facing with Covid-19. Many, including me, were hoping that it would behave much like the flu and abate somewhat during the summer months. One model had just lowered its estimate for total US deaths by August from about a hundred thousand to sixty thousand, suggesting that the President's guidelines for social distancing "to flatten the curve" might be having some success.

I was visiting to add my two cents. I was concerned that we not allow ourselves to drift from a policy of protecting the vulnerable and slowing the spread into one of shutting down the country in a misbegotten attempt to stop the disease altogether. I was also worried about the extent to which the White House had Dr. Anthony Fauci out in front and the degree of control he seemed to be exercising over our whole pandemic response. I didn't know Fauci personally but had watched him over the years, including his lackluster response to AIDs in the 1980s and 1990s. At almost eighty years of age and with thirty-six years in the same government job, he struck me as a consummate bureaucrat—one with a huge ego and penchant for self-promotion. I thought his bureaucratic mind-set—typical of many in the government's public health establishment—would lead to intolerance of opposing views, the overcentralization of medical decision-making, and myopia when it came to weighing costs and benefits. Because of all the uncertainties inherent in this pandemic, it was important that the President get advice from a wide array of doctors and public health experts in the private sector and not get locked into the views of a narrow set of government officials.

As I walked in, it appeared a Covid meeting had already broken up. Mark Meadows and Pat Cipollone were hanging back, chatting with the President, and Fauci's name was mentioned.

"Don't get between him and a camera," I said. "He is everywhere. Are we encouraging that?"

"You know what Fauci said?" President Trump asked. "He said he likes to predict the worst outcomes. That way you'll end up looking good when the worst case doesn't happen. You'll get credit for preventing it."

"Doesn't surprise me," I said.

"I can't do that as President," he continued. "I have to be optimistic—keep the country's spirit up. Make people feel we will get through this soon."

"I think you guys are giving him too much prominence," I said. "You're making him the lead player. Think about broadening the circle and bringing in an outsider to take the point."

The President went on to grouse about the inconsistent advice he was getting from Fauci and other public health officials. "You can't get a straight answer," he said, visibly exasperated.

"You remember the pandemic of 1957, Mr. President—the Asian flu?" I asked. "We were kids, but I remember it distinctly."

The President nodded.

"Well, I went back to look at it," I said. "US deaths from the Asian flu are now estimated to have been about a hundred sixteen thousand. Today that would be the equivalent of about a quarter million deaths."

I was offering this as a reassuring thought. Based on the models, perhaps Covid fatalities might not be dramatically different. The President seemed a bit surprised the Asian flu's death toll had been that high.

"The point is, Mr. President, we did not shut down the whole country in 1957," I continued. "It was the vaccine that ultimately saved us."

"We're going to get the vaccine," the President said firmly. "But, Bill, don't make the mistake of underestimating this disease. I am telling you, people who think this is just a bad flu are wrong. This is a really nasty disease." He then described some friends of his who had contracted the virus, a number of whom had died.

"This is serious business," he said. "Nothing to play around with. We have never seen anything like this."

Over the ensuing weeks, I was to hear him repeatedly make this same point, calling the disease "nasty" and reciting a litany of all the people he knew who had succumbed to it.

On January 21, 2020, US authorities confirmed what was then the first known case of Covid in the country. Ten days later, the President restricted travel from China. On February 29, authorities reported the first known death from Covid. On March 16 the President issued social distancing guidelines for the country intended to flatten the curve—that is, slow the rate of spread. Originally planned for just two weeks, the guidelines were later extended.

The Department of Justice did not have a central role in addressing the Covid pandemic. We were not represented on the Vice President's task force, and I was not involved in the administration's internal deliberations about the crisis. But the President was preoccupied with it, and, in my regular discussions with him and others at the White House, I learned something of the issues they were grappling with.

In the fall and winter, the economy had been roaring. The President's policies were letting American businesses do what they knew how to do: create wealth and opportunity. Strong economic growth; record-high employment levels for every racial, ethnic, and socioeconomic group; and rising wages across the board—the success was formidable. The President was confident in his reelection, and so were many of us in the administration. Many political professionals, too, agreed that Trump would be hard to beat in November. All this despite his enemies' round-the-clock obsession with destroying him by impeachment, leaks, defamation, or whatever tool they could find.

The President's State of the Union address in February was the high-water mark of this optimism. I thought it was the best speech of his administration. His demeanor was restrained yet confident. He was in command of a vast range of issues. He laid out a clear and cogent agenda to ensure broad economic prosperity and social comity. Best of all, he omitted the pettiness and recrimination that often punctuated his speeches at public rallies. That night, Trump looked like a statesman, and his enemies looked like idiots: some turning their backs to him; Nancy Pelosi ripping up his speech like a spoiled child.

Then Covid struck. It was Trump's downfall.

The pandemic required steady, principled leadership. It would no longer be possible for the President to run mainly on his achievements to date. He would be judged on the basis of his leadership in a national crisis. That presented two problems for him. The first was that his enemies in the political sphere and in the media would use the pandemic to accuse him of every conceivable misdeed at every opportunity. They wouldn't care about truth or real-world outcomes, and they would pretend to know vastly more than they did about the virus for the sole purpose of portraying the President as culpably mishandling the situation. Every new infection was his fault, every death a result of his inability. That was his enemies' attitude, sometimes expressed subtly and sometimes baldly. And there was nothing he could do to change it.

The second problem was within his power to change, however. That was his own tendency to respond to every unreasonable and irresponsible accusation. He failed to control himself. Trump saw his enemies' unreasoning hatred and lack of principle for what they were, but he couldn't stop himself from reacting to every one of their charges— often in harsh, unbecoming ways. They in turn exploited his weakness, with the result that Trump made the pandemic crisis all about himself—precisely what Americans did not want to see in their leader at such a time.

The President made mistakes on policy, as any president would in those novel circumstances. But his substantive decisions were largely sound and defensible. His prompt action shutting down foreign travel into the United States—initially not supported by Fauci—was timely and probably saved hundreds of thousands of lives. Otherwise, he mostly followed the recommendations of his public health advisers. His decision in March to adopt short-term lockdowns to flatten the curve was reasonable, given our uncertainty about the nature of the disease and its rapid spread. After the disastrous failure of the Obama administration's policy of relying on the public health agencies to perform testing, President Trump moved decisively to mobilize the private sector to supply necessary testing kits. When stockpiles of personal protective equipment left by the previous administration proved woefully inadequate, the President quickly invoked the Defense Production Act to escalate production of ample supplies. He also orchestrated an upsurge in production of ventilators and mobilized federal resources to help hard-hit states such as New York.

Most important, he was primarily responsible for the single best decision made at the governmental level during the crisis: simultaneously fast-tracking the development of multiple vaccine candidates and promoting their mass production.

But public dissatisfaction with the President's handling of the pandemic wasn't so much about the substance of his policies as the attitude he projected, and the tenor and consistency of his public communications. Many people got the sense that he wasn't taking the pandemic seriously enough. From what I saw, this was not true. His consistent sobering statements to me about the seriousness of Covid, and how it should not be equated with the flu, showed me early on he understood the danger of the virus.

Just as early on, most of the news media decided Trump wasn't taking the virus seriously. That was their narrative, and no sum of contrary evidence would shake them from it. On the other hand, he was partly to blame for the ease with which his critics portrayed him as nonchalant. He wouldn't wear a mask, then he would. His off-the-cuff remarks seemingly minimizing the risks and offering unduly optimistic forecasts, though intended to keep people from panicking, lent themselves to the allegation that he wasn't treating the situation with the gravity it deserved.

The President felt his job was to keep people's spirits up. That was understandable and laudable. But he also had a deep need to project himself as a strongman. In this instance, that meant adopting a defiant bravado to show he was not going to be pushed around by a mere virus. Whatever his thinking, his conduct was sometimes strangely out of whack with the government's otherwise more somber messaging. The disconnect made the administration's response appear incoherent. If the President had just made a minor adjustment in his behavior and spent more time stressing the imperative for disciplined adherence to social distancing requirements, that alone would likely have given him a narrow victory in November.

Even before Covid, I thought, along with a number of others in the administration, that the President's general behavior—his frequent pettiness and overly contentious style—was turning off a lot of voters who were otherwise generally sympathetic to his policies. His tonal problems on Covid were part and parcel of the broader problem of his off-putting style generally. But Covid put the President's leadership qualities under a microscope as nothing else could. It called the question: Was Donald Trump capable of rising to the occasion and showing the statesmanship needed to lead the country through the crisis?

Covid was a staggering blow to the President's political fortunes because, instead of serving as an opportunity to demonstrate his leadership qualities, it proved to be a stage on which he displayed some of the more alienating aspects of his behavior. In short, the pandemic threw into bold relief Trump's deficiencies as leader—showcasing his failings, not his strengths.

What proved the most damaging to Trump was his stubborn insistence on giving daily rambling ad hoc commentary on the pandemic, starting with his interminable and cringe-inducing press conferences in March and April. His first outings were relatively well received, but as they continued, and assembled journalists became more aggressive in their questions, the whole thing became a ridiculous spectacle of petty arguments. The polling and other feedback made it clear that these televised appearances had become a liability. People were appalled. The President seemed incapable of maintaining a consistent message. He undermined his credibility by making imprecise and exaggerated statements. Policies seemed to drift and morph without coherent explanation. He indulged his penchant for casting blame on others and in all directions, and was drawn into small-minded wrangling with governors or other politicians with whom he disagreed. Internal administration squabbles broke out into the open, further conveying a sense of dysfunction. The President allowed journalists to get under his skin, and the press conferences became marked by stupid exchanges that reflected poorly on the media but, more important, diminished the President.

The more he talked, the lower his approval ratings on Covid sank. All his advisers urged the President to curtail his daily appearances. He pressed ahead. Whenever he did take a break, his approval ratings started heading back up. But then he resumed his gabfests, and his ratings would head back down again. I sometimes thought of the advice given to Howard Baker, the highly respected longtime Republican senator from Tennessee, by his father-in-law, Senator Everett Dirksen of Illinois, after Baker delivered his windy maiden speech in the Senate in 1967: "Perhaps you should occasionally allow yourself the luxury of an unexpressed thought."

After a few weeks of the President's daily appearances, including one I was required to attend, I caught President Trump after an Oval Office meeting to raise concerns. Mark Meadows was also in the room. "Mr. President," I said. "I think you're getting massively overexposed. By campaign season, people will be sick of seeing you."

"Have you seen the ratings?" he answered combatively. "We are getting huge audiences. There has never been anything like it."

"That shows people are worried, but it doesn't mean they like what they're seeing," I said. "I think you need to stop these daily briefings and be a lot more selective."

He looked at me blankly. He couldn't fathom the idea that people would ever tire of him.

Meadows walked out of the Oval with me. "I'm working on it, Bill," he confided with a smile.

"Mark, he is just blowing it," I said. "The more he runs off at the mouth, the more erratic and out of control he seems."

Meadows seemed to share my frustration. "I got it, Bill. We're working on it."

As I headed down the hall on my way out of the West Wing, I decided to pile on a little. As I came to Jared Kushner's office, I stuck my head in. "Do you have a second, Jared?" I said, gesturing toward the interior of his office.

"Sure, c'mon in." He closed the door behind me, and we stood chatting.

"I just told the President I thought he needs to stop his daily press conferences. They are counterproductive."

"You and everybody else. Everyone here is working on it," he said with a hint of frustration. "You know him. He has his own views but—believe me—we're all trying."

Having talked with the President, Meadows, and now Jared, I felt I had done what I could. I was encouraged there was unanimity among the White House staff, and they were pushing the President.

One factor that made it especially challenging to respond to Covid with a coherent policy and public messaging was the need to deal with it within the framework of our decentralized, Federalist structure of government. Unlike a foreign policy crisis, in which every lever of power is at the President's command, a domestic crisis on a national scale requires the federal government to work jointly with the states. The idea that the pandemic could have been managed by experts from Washington by centralized diktat was a fantasy. And, given how wrong the experts were about a range of questions, we are fortunate this was not attempted. Under our system, the states have their own sovereign responsibility for the well-being of their citizens and are afforded wide latitude in determining how to protect the public's welfare. Efforts to ride roughshod over the states would have engendered more acrimony—and ultimately more dysfunctionality—than attempting to work collaboratively with them, as difficult and untidy as that can often be. But Federalism has its advantages, too: conditions in circumstances such as these vary dramatically around the country, and those closest to the scene and directly accountable to the local citizenry are almost always in the best position to make wise judgments.

The President's desire to honor our federal structure and accommodate the states' sovereign role was both sensible and, ultimately, unavoidable. It allowed the federal government to provide broad guidance, while relying on the states to apply and adapt it to their local circumstances. But this collaborative approach required a statesman capable of herding cats—one with boundless patience and diplomatic skills, especially in an election year when his adversaries were at their worst in scoring cheap shots against him. It required a statesman with the ability to explain complex matters and regional variations to the public with precision and clarity. Trump was not that statesman. He was a disrupter—he liked to move forward by confusing and rattling his opponents. After March 2020, that was basically the opposite of what his job called for.

Making matters even more difficult for him was the emergence of two competing strategies for dealing with the pandemic. They are drearily familiar now, but in the spring of 2020 they were still nascent and evolving. The first, implemented in March, emphasized the need to slow the virus's spread. The idea was not to eliminate it, or to stop it completely, but to acknowledge that some spread was inevitable. This approach would focus on protecting the elderly and vulnerable, while relying on reasonable social distancing measures and canceling large indoor events to slow the spread. This would allow the health care system to absorb a more modest rise in hospitalizations without canceling or shifting resources away from other services. It would allow the economy to continue functioning, schools to remain in session, and individuals to make responsible decisions for themselves and their families.

The other strategy was to "stop" or "defeat" the virus. Draconian stay-at-home orders, business lockdowns, school closures—the idea was to bring civil society to a near-complete standstill and hope the virus would stop spreading. But this approach imposed massive economic, social, and psychological costs on society, and yet had as much chance of success as King Canute had when he commanded the incoming tide to halt.

The competition between the two rival strategies became highly politicized, with the Right favoring an approach that acknowledged the inevitability of spread, and the Left favoring sweeping dictates to close schools and businesses for indefinite periods. One of the most annoying aspects of this debate was the tiresome cant that decision-making on the virus ought to just "follow the science"—"science" as defined by public health officials like Fauci. This was absurd. "Science" in a situation like this is rarely fixed, but uncertain and shifting. The reality is that the decisions that have to be made are not scientific by nature. Rather, they involve managing uncertainties—including uncertainties surrounding "the science"—by making trade-offs and striking balances among a broad array of competing values and risks. "Science" doesn't tell us whether the benefits derived from lockdowns outweigh the full range of costs imposed on various populations over the long term. Public health officials have neither the competence nor the statutory authority nor the moral authority to make these decisions. We do not cease to be a democracy when some public authority says so. These are political decisions to be made by those who represent and are accountable to the people for their decisions.

Negotiating the tensions between these two strategies required *nuance*. One thing Trump is incapable of is nuance. His rhetorical skills, while potent within a very narrow range, are hopelessly ineffective on questions requiring subtle distinctions. His main tools are hyperbole and ridicule. These aren't suitable when the task is to steer a sensible course between two opposing poles, tacking to move closer to one than the other. When he wanted to criticize lockdown orthodoxy, he sounded as though he wanted a let-'er-rip approach involving no guidelines of any kind. His opponents found it easy to caricature him.

It's not clear to me that some other leader would have made better decisions. The acute divisions in our political life, together with the resilience of the virus and the inherent messiness of a democratic society, would have tested any leader to the breaking point. All countries have eventually found themselves muddling through. Many countries initially extolled for their early apparent success later met with grievous setbacks and responded with incompetence and overreach. And vice versa. As for the United States, Americans are accustomed by long tradition to going where they please, when they please. They are not easily regimented. Public health authorities were better advised to work with that reality than to pretend they could abolish it. In any case, despite all the sniping at the President, he did end up following the key recommendation of the medical experts. The broad lockdown approach that the Left favored is essentially what most of the country got from their governors. There is much we still don't know about the effectiveness of mitigation efforts, and it will be a long time before anybody can render definitive judgments about which authorities handled the virus well or poorly.

The Department of Justice was not involved in deliberations over the public health aspects of Covid, but we did make a concerted effort to push back against state restrictions that placed unreasonable burdens on constitutional liberties. I had to remind governors that the Constitution does not take a holiday during crises, and that it required them to ensure that their emergency measures didn't infringe on personal rights any more than what was truly necessary to protect the public's health.

In wars, natural disasters, and outbreaks of deadly diseases, societies need the capacity to act with decisive speed, frequently in the face of uncertainty. By its very nature, the executive power—the President in the federal government, governors in the states—is the organ of government empowered to respond in extreme, fast-moving emergencies to protect society. In my speech to the Federalist Society in November 2019, I explained that one vital part of executive power "is the power to address exigent circumstances that demand quick action to protect the well-being of the nation but on which the law is either silent or inadequate—such as dealing with a plague or natural disaster." There is no question in my mind that, in the case of a fast-spreading, moderately dangerous virus like Covid, the President and state governors had authority to impose emergency measures, even onerous ones. When the community as a whole faces an impending, sudden, and grave harm of this magnitude, and where the measures are tailored to meeting the imminent danger, the Constitution does allow some temporary restrictions that would be rightly repudiated in normal circumstances.

At the same time, except for the institution of slavery—which involved oppression of an entirely different order—the lockdown measures adopted by many governors were the most sweeping and onerous denial of civil liberties ever imposed in the United States. They involved far greater restrictions than those imposed during World War II. Many communities were subject to comprehensive stay-at-home orders—in essence, house arrest for extended periods. People were prohibited from working, thus depriving them of their livelihood and the satisfactions of work and industry. Businesses, many of which had taken families generations to build up, were declared "nonessential" and destroyed. In many places, these burdensome rules were being put in place by local officials rather than by state constitutional officers.

One of the ironies of the Covid crisis was the political Left's gross hypocrisy on the scope of executive power. Usually—and especially under Republican administrations—the Left can be counted on to rant about unilateral executive action and demand immediate accountability through judicial review. I believe the executive must be afforded the widest latitude in directing foreign affairs, foreign intelligence, and armed conflict against foreign enemies—contexts in which those affected primarily are foreign persons, not American citizens. Thus, the Left has frequently castigated me as an advocate of "unfettered" executive power. And yet, with Covid, liberal and progressive officials and the Left's commentariat appeared perfectly content to allow the federal and state executive agencies to exercise sweeping, unilateral powers over an extended period of time that deprived American citizens of their most fundamental liberties.

When there is no statutory basis for executive action, the executive's claim of emergency domestic power rests on the immediacy and gravity of the danger. It also rests on the fact that the legislative branch is not suited to carry out the kind of action needed—action requiring exceptional speed, adaptability to rapidly changing and uncertain circumstances, and maintaining unity of purpose in executing a plan.

The question of how far the executive can go in facing a domestic exigency like a deadly pandemic has no easy answer in the law. Where the country faces an imminent catastrophe, it seems to me that there must be an initial period of time during which the executive should be given the broadest latitude. During this time, second-guessing by either the courts or legislature will defeat the distinctive advantages of executive power.

When the crisis is domestic in nature, the longer it persists, and the deeper the infringements on civil liberties, the more we should expect some form of legislative oversight and endorsement of the executive's actions. If it has not already done so, the legislature should put in place statutory authorization for continuing executive exercises of emergency powers. If the legislature has had ample time to study and react to the executive's action, and has not endorsed it, less deference is due unilateral executive action that significantly burdens civil liberties. In the case of the novel coronavirus of 2020, some states' legislatures had not provided a statutory basis for emergency executive action, or the statutory authority had expired. Some unilateral gubernatorial directives had become extremely ambitious, imposing heavy regulatory burdens on the lives of Americans that appeared inconsistent and unreasonable.

Given the Attorney General's duty to uphold the Constitution, I felt there was the need to challenge clear instances of state overreach. While the law was gray in this area, I thought the best way to encourage reasonable rules was to let the state and local governments know their orders were subject to scrutiny by the Department of Justice. In a memorandum to all US attorneys, dated April 27, 2020, I directed they be "on the lookout for state and local directives that could be violating the constitutional rights and civil liberties of individual citizens." I designated the head of the Civil Rights Division, Assistant Attorney General Eric Dreiband, and the US attorney in Detroit, Matt Schneider, to coordinate the department's efforts around the country.

The principal area in which state and local measures had clearly crossed the line involved the imposition of discriminatory burdens on religious worship. On April 17 I issued a public statement stressing that citizens should rigorously observe social distancing and follow the directions of their state and local authorities. But, I went on,

> even in times of emergency, when reasonable and temporary restrictions are placed on rights, the First Amendment and federal statutory law prohibit discrimination against religious institutions and religious believers. Thus, government may not impose special restrictions on religious activity that do not also apply to similar nonreligious activity. For example, if a government allows movie theaters, restaurants, concert halls, and other comparable places of assembly to remain open and unrestricted, it may not order houses of worship to close, limit their congregation size, or otherwise impede religious gatherings. Religious institutions must not be singled out for special burdens.

The first case in which we supported a religious body involved a church in Greenville, Mississippi. The church sought to hold parking lot worship services in which congregants listened to their pastor preach over their car radios, while sitting in their cars in the church parking lot with their windows rolled up. The City of Greenville fined congregants $500 per person for attending these parking lot services—while permitting citizens to attend nearby drive-in restaurants, even with their windows open. Under the city's rules, only churches were totally banned from providing services even when they were complying with the state's social distancing rules. The church brought a lawsuit, and within days of the department's filing in support of the church, the city withdrew its objectionable rules.

Similarly, we successfully challenged a Colorado rule limiting religious worship gatherings to ten or fewer persons, while allowing restaurants to operate with up to fifty customers. After losing in lower courts, the Supreme Court ruled in our favor. In Washington, DC, we filed in support of Capitol Hill Baptist Church, challenging the mayor's Covid rules limiting outdoor religious services to a hundred people, while placing no such limit on outdoor protests and rallies. The federal district court agreed with us and ruled for the church. I was gratified when, following the election, in *Roman Catholic Diocese of Brooklyn v. Cuomo*, the Supreme Court struck down certain of Governor Andrew Cuomo's Covid restrictions on religious services on the grounds that they treated religious facilities more restrictively than nonreligious facilities.

When the department had concerns over state and local Covid rules, we generally preferred to jawbone the relevant governments privately into adjusting their regulations. We had success behind the scenes working with state and local governments to craft more reasonable rules. If this did not work, we resorted to public statements or letters to prod the relevant local officials to make changes. In September 2020, for example, we sent a letter to San Francisco's mayor, London Breed, explaining that the city's policy of allowing only a single congregant in places of worship regardless of their size, while allowing multiple patrons in other indoor settings, including gyms, tattoo parlors, hair salons, massage studios, and day care centers, was discriminatory and violated the First Amendment. Days later, the mayor withdrew the objectionable regulation. Similarly, we wrote Mayor Bill de Blasio of New York to express concerns that, while permitting large gatherings for political protest, he was not permitting in-person religious gatherings, and urged him to adopt a more evenhanded approach in framing his phase 2 reopening plans. A few days later, the mayor issued reopening plans providing relief for religious services.

Most of our challenges related to potential discrimination against religious activity, but in a few cases, we objected to arbitrary, unreasonable, and oppressive business regulations. In May 2020, for example, the DOJ filed in support of several Michigan businesses challenging the restrictions imposed by Governor Gretchen Whitmer in response to the pandemic. Over a two-month period, the governor had issued more than a hundred executive orders that, taken together, erected a mind-numbingly intricate regulatory regime, imposing frequently arbitrary limitations on nearly all aspects of life for citizens of Michigan. On June 1 the governor rescinded some of her earlier more restrictive business and stay-at-home orders. As controversy continued over Whitmer's authority to issue broad regulatory orders, the department wrote to her in June urging her to cooperate with the Michigan State Legislature in framing her response to the Covid crisis. In October the Supreme Court of Michigan ruled that Governor Whitmer did not have authority to issue many of her emergency orders, and the court invited the governor and the legislature to work together to address the challenges of the pandemic.

The department also moved aggressively to tackle a wave of Covid-related fraud schemes preying on the public's fears. By mid-March, we were seeing an explosion of scams: fake cures, immunizations, and test kits; phishing e-mails from entities posing as health organizations; malware embedded in phony Covid tracking apps; and so on. I asked the Deputy to draw up a plan to attack these scams, harnessing all our field offices, as well as our headquarters resources. Later, after Congress passed the $2.2 trillion economic relief bill known as the CARES Act, providing emergency financial assistance, we expanded our efforts to investigate and prosecute people and groups trying to rip off these programs—especially those filing false claims under the CARES Act's Paycheck Protection Program. I am proud of the department's efforts against Covid-related fraud. A year after I launched it, my successor, Attorney General Merrick Garland, praised the DOJ's work as a "historic enforcement initiative."

The pandemic—or, more precisely, the governmental and cultural response to the pandemic—put the country's political institutions to a severe test. That test is still going on, and the effects of it will remain when Covid-19 has disappeared from the headlines. The melancholy fact is that no administration could have handled this pandemic in a way that avoided the intense acrimony and contention we saw beginning in the spring of 2020. These arise from cultural pathologies that public policies are powerless to cure.

Unfortunately, Covid was not the only upheaval in 2020. In late May the harrowing video of George Floyd's death at the hands of Minneapolis police officers shocked the nation and touched off civil unrest and senseless destruction on an unprecedented scale around the country. The frustrations of living under Covid contributed to the intensity of the violence over the summer. But, unlike Covid, the issues of police, race, and civil unrest fell squarely in the Justice Department's area of responsibility.

CHAPTER 20

COPS, RACE, AND THE BIG LIE

The first time I discussed the issue of policing and race with President Trump was in July 2019. I visited the Oval Office to advise him that the Department of Justice had decided not to pursue criminal charges against New York police officer Daniel Pantaleo for the death of Eric Garner, a forty-three-year-old African American man.

In an incident five years earlier, caught on video, Garner died after Pantaleo put him in what appeared to be a choke hold to wrestle him to the ground while arresting him for selling untaxed cigarettes. As he was held down by multiple officers, Garner repeatedly said the words, "I can't breathe." Garner's death, along with the shooting death of Michael Brown in Ferguson, Missouri, the following month, propelled the Black Lives Matter movement to prominence. The phrase "I can't breathe" became one of its rallying cries.

At the time of the incident, the state grand jury declined to indict Pantaleo. Federal prosecutors in the Brooklyn US Attorney's Office—then under Loretta Lynch, who later became Obama's Attorney General—also recommended against bringing charges. Lawyers in the Civil Rights Division back in Washington favored prosecution. The case languished in the department for almost five years, with no one willing to make a decision. I felt it would be wrong for the department to allow the statute of limitations to expire without a decision, so I resolved the matter, siding with the Brooklyn US Attorney's Office.

The President and I were alone together. If all you knew about Donald Trump was the caricature of him in the news media, you might assume he would automatically side with the police and callously disregard the possibility of excessive force. That wasn't his reaction. "*Really?*" he said, showing genuine surprise, almost shock, when I told him we weren't going to charge the police officer. "I saw the tape several times on TV," he said, shaking his head and looking perplexed. "It looked pretty bad to me."

I started to explain my decision, when the President cut me off. "I grew up in Queens. I know some cops can be bullies. You're from New York—you know. Were those cops looking for a fight with this guy just for selling cigarettes? Were they picking on him?"

This was the first time I saw in Trump a trait I would see many times in the months to come. He hated the idea of a bully pushing people around. That may seem odd to people who think of Trump as a bully. Some of the media and other elites who take that view don't appreciate the fact that they themselves are bullies. They have been lording it over working-class Americans for years. What such people don't understand about Trump, though, is that he got the most satisfaction when he felt he was using his power to rectify an injustice on behalf of an underdog. He felt many of his supporters were underdogs—"forgotten" Americans—and he was standing up for them.

The President continued to ask questions as he pressed me to justify my decision. I had personally gone painstakingly over the evidence, including a second-by-second breakdown of the video. I explained that this had not been a discretionary decision by the officers; rather they had been sent out with specific orders to deal with Garner. When Garner physically resisted being taken into custody, the officers were permitted to use reasonable force to subdue him. Officer Pantaleo initially used two NYPD-approved tactics: an "arm bar" and a "rear takedown." While executing the takedown, Pantaleo initially had his arms in the appropriate position: his right arm under Garner's armpit, and his left over his upper chest. Garner, who at six foot two and close to four hundred pounds was much larger than Pantaleo, struggled forcefully, trying to buck the officer off his back and slamming Pantaleo against a store window with such force that the window buckled.

In response to that collision, and to keep his hold on Garner, Pantaleo's left arm slid up around Garner's neck in what was, in effect, a choke hold, which he maintained as both men fell to the ground, after which point Pantaleo pulled away his arm. Pantaleo's arm was around Garner's neck for approximately seven seconds. After Pantaleo released his grip, as officers were holding Garner down, Garner said he could not breathe. I explained to the President's satisfaction that, given these facts, we could not prove beyond a reasonable doubt that Pantaleo acted "willfully"—which is the applicable standard under the federal civil rights statute. Nor could we show, given conflicting medical evidence, that the seven-second choke hold caused Eric Garner's death.

President Trump showed the same concern when similar tragic situations occurred. In early May 2020 I got a call from an agitated President, upset by the fatal shooting of Ahmaud Arbery near Brunswick, Georgia, by two white men—not police—who pursued the unarmed twenty-five-year-old Black jogger believing that he was involved in local burglaries. The killing actually had occurred in February, but a video of the shooting had only just surfaced. This was one of the rare times where the President called me to ensure we were aggressively following up on a publicized case. He had seen the video and told me, "It's very ugly! It's just unbelievable they shot this fellow down. He seemed to be a good guy. And some people are saying there might've been some cover-up at the beginning. I want to make sure you're all over this." I told President Trump we were on top of it and would be looking into the possibility of a cover-up. For the next few months, the President continued to raise Arbery's case with me.

A few weeks later, when videos went public showing George Floyd's death while being held down by Minneapolis police officers, I got an angry call from the President. "What the hell were those cops thinking?" he snapped. "I couldn't watch the whole thing. It was terrible." He wanted to make sure we were aggressively investigating the matter and wanted our US attorney to address it publicly as soon as possible. He later tweeted, "At my request, the FBI and the Department of Justice are already well into an investigation as to the very sad and tragic death in Minnesota of George Floyd. . . . I have asked for this investigation to be expedited." This was true.

I was pleased that the President, while strongly supporting police generally, was willing to examine incidents fairly and honestly and to call out use of excessive force when it was there. The fact is that, as a general rule, police in this country are highly professional. Instances of improper use of deadly force are rare and becoming rarer. In many of the cases sensationalized by the media, the police action was ultimately justified. Officers sometimes have to make shoot/no-shoot decisions in less than a second, with their own lives at stake. But political and law enforcement leaders can't credibly support officers in the vast majority of cases when they act properly if they aren't willing to acknowledge abuses and hold officers accountable in the rare cases of abuse.

The harrowing circumstances of George Floyd's death understandably jarred the whole country and forced the nation to reflect on long-standing issues concerning the relationship between law enforcement and the African American community. It is understandable how the image of a white police officer with his knee on the neck of a Black man pleading for his life would be so evocative to Black Americans in particular. It captured something central to the experience of African Americans for most of their history on this continent. Even after more than 250 years of slavery, for almost an additional 100 years—until just the last 50 years or so—the nation's laws and many institutions discriminated against Black citizens. It wasn't until the 1960s that the civil rights movement finally succeeded in tearing down Jim Crow in the South and discriminatory practices elsewhere in the country. Our laws finally came to require, at least in form, equality. But de facto discrimination continued, and since the 1960s the work of securing civil rights has rightly focused on reforming our institutions to ensure they conform better to the noble ideals of the founding.

Still, it's understandable that Black Americans should remain unsure. Their ambivalence about law enforcement, so long the instrument of injustice and abuse, has the weight of history behind it.

At the same time, in my conversations with African American community leaders in the days following Floyd's death, I found that, while there was still deep concern that Black Americans were frequently not treated evenhandedly by the police, there was also definite acknowledgment that police departments had made real progress. These leaders recognized that most police officers were well-intentioned, decent people who were performing risky jobs, and that the overarching danger to the Black community was not the police, but the victimization of Black people and the blighting of their neighborhoods by violent crime. They wanted more police, not fewer, and they wanted to build stronger bonds between the police force and the community. This was the message I got, for example, while I was touring some of the most dangerous neighborhoods in Detroit after Floyd's death. Citizens told me that they felt safe outside only if the police were in sight or if they were near a "green light" camera—a system of video cameras located in the neighborhood, linked to the police and marked by a distinctive green light. Citizens in Milwaukee, Charleston, Dallas, Kansas City, and other cities stressed similarly how critical a strong police presence was to them.

Any honest appraisal of the relationship between police and the Black community must start with the stark reality that violent crime rates within the Black community are devastatingly high. African Americans are disproportionately both the offenders and victims of serious violent crime. Whereas only 13 percent of the population is Black, Black offenders commit roughly 37 percent of the serious violent crime and about half of homicides and robberies. While there are likely a number of factors contributing to this, including past discrimination, as well as family breakdown caused by social programs, it has been a stubborn reality for some time.

The victims who suffer from this violent crime are African American. Black Americans are more likely to be victims of violent crime than whites are. Before the upsurge in violent crime in the last half of 2020 and 2021, there were typically more than 7,500 Black homicide victims every year—about half of all homicides—the vast majority shot to death by Black offenders. If there is an epidemic of shooting deaths, this is it. For Black males between eighteen and thirty years old, the leading cause of death is homicide. For white people of the same age group, the leading cause of death is unintentional injury, followed by suicide.

But the toll taken by violent crime in the inner cities goes beyond these hideous numbers. The prevalence of violent crime strangles opportunity in these communities. Schools cannot educate children when the schools are dominated by violent gangs. Businesses cannot thrive where streets are shooting galleries. The lives of Black victims of violent crime matter. That is why police officers risk their lives policing high-crime inner-city neighborhoods: to protect those Black lives. These communities are entitled to the same peace and security as any predominantly white neighborhood in the suburbs. The police are in these communities and are inevitably drawn into risky encounters precisely because they are trying to bring that peace and security.

At a time when racial justice activists are demonizing all police, proclaiming "All Cops Are Bastards," two truths should dominate our thinking. First, even in the best of times, there is no more challenging profession than serving as a police officer. It requires commitment, courage, and the patience of Job. Those attracted to this tough profession are, by and large, civic-minded men and woman with a strong desire to serve and protect their fellow citizens. The constant stress imposes huge wear and tear on the officer and family life. Suicide rates among police officers are increasing sharply. Police are being called on to pick up the pieces where others have failed. Homelessness, drug addiction, domestic violence, and mental illness—the grim harvest of decades of "progressive" policies—are not their making, but they are called on to deal with these pathologies because others couldn't or wouldn't. Even before the recent abuse hurled against the police, it was becoming harder to attract and retain officers. But the scapegoating police suffer today will make it near impossible to continue to recruit and keep officers of the high caliber society needs.

The second reality is that our country has made vast progress in reforming and professionalizing our police departments. Just as our military—once a bastion of segregation—has now become an exemplar of racial equality and advancement, so, too, we have steadily improved our police forces over the past several decades. Today we are fortunate to have the most effective, professional, and well-led police departments in the world—and they are more diverse, with more Black police chiefs and more Black officers in the ranks than ever before. There is more work to be done, as there always will be in an establishment of almost a million officers in roughly eighteen thousand separate police agencies. But in my experience, no one is more committed to the further professionalization of policing than police leaders themselves.

Two different kinds of people say they want better relationships between the police and the people they serve. The first: people of goodwill who are protesting legitimate grievances and are genuinely interested in improving policing and bringing about safer neighborhoods. The second: people who seize on singular and tragic incidents and use them to demonize all police and to advance a broader, radical political agenda. In my view, the organization known as Black Lives Matter, or BLM, belongs to the latter group. The phrase "Black lives matter" states a truism—no one disagrees with it. But the organization BLM is based on a lie.

BLM's approach has become familiar since 2014. When an unarmed Black person is killed during a police encounter, the group and its media supporters portray it as part of an epidemic of unjustified killings by police. BLM's rallying cry is that this rash of unjustified killings is the result of the inherent institutional racism of police and their wanton disregard for Black life. At protests, this incendiary narrative is often accompanied by even more inflammatory rhetoric, dehumanizing and demonizing police and thus inspiring further violence against police. Usually, the violence, when it arises, involves "protesters" throwing bricks and stones and bottles of urine at police. Sometimes it has been graver, as in July 2016, when eight officers were assassinated and twelve wounded during a ten-day period in the wake of BLM protests. BLM embraces a Marxist ideology in which the "powerful" are overthrown by force, and American society—the family, the private sector, representative institutions—is reduced to rubble. The "cops are racists" lie is only the tool by which it pursues its radical aims.

The grueling scene of forty-six-year-old George Floyd being killed understandably ignited street demonstrations, starting in Minneapolis and Saint Paul, and spreading rapidly around the country. Initially, the violence was limited, and the demonstrations appeared to be spontaneous protests against the perceived police brutality against African Americans. After three days, however, the character of the demonstrations in many of the larger cities changed dramatically. The voices of peaceful and legitimate protests were hijacked by Far Left and anarchistic elements and outside agitators who whipped up mob violence, orchestrating violent attacks on police and the senseless destruction of property. In the first week of rioting, more than seven hundred police officers were injured across the country. By the end of July, that number topped two thousand.

BLM's narrative—that racist cops routinely and gratuitously gun down unarmed Black men—is false. The truth is that, over the past several years, in cases in which African Americans have been fatally shot by police, only a handful each year involve shootings that were not reasonably justified. In the overwhelming majority of cases, the suspect was armed. In the few cases in which the suspect was unarmed, the person shot was, in most cases, assaulting the officer or taking other actions the officer perceived reasonably as life endangering. Cases in which there was no apparent justification for lethal force are very rare. Importantly, in the few instances in which no justification is found, the officers responsible are prosecuted.

According to the *Washington Post* database, the total number of persons fatally shot by police—white and Black—has been remarkably stable since 2015, at about a thousand per year. While every death is regrettable, considering the levels of violent crime in this country, the sheer volume of arrests, and other police-civilian interactions, and the shocking frequency with which violent attacks are carried out against police officers, the total of a thousand fatally shot by police each year is not surprising. Police report about 1.3 million violent crimes annually, while the Bureau of Justice Statistics, based on its victims' survey, estimates that 3.8 million violent crime incidents occur each year. In 2018, 65 million Americans reported at least one interaction with police, which means total interactions are likely near 100 million a year. The police make more than 10 million arrests every year. Reports from jurisdictions covering two-thirds of police officers show there are about 56,000 assaults on police every year. This comes to one assault on a police officer every ten minutes. Thirty percent of these assaults result in injury to the officer, and almost 21 percent of the assaults—more than 11,600—are made with firearms, knives, or other dangerous weapons, which means police officers are attacked with dangerous weapons more than thirty-two times a day. Extrapolating from the reporting jurisdictions to the other one-third of the country would suggest there could be as many as forty-eight assaults with dangerous weapons against police officers per day. If men were angels, the police would never have to resort to deadly force, but, given the sheer volume of their risky encounters and the violence faced by police, the fact that 1,000 people are fatally shot each year does not suggest that cops are trigger-happy.

The claim that Black people are disproportionately killed by police rests on a fallacious statistical comparison. Among the 1,000 fatally shot, the number of African Americans has also been stable at about 25 percent of the total every year—249 in 2019 and 241 in 2020, for example. The white percentage of those killed has consistently hovered around 45 percent. The claim that these numbers show racism is that, while the white percentage of those killed (45 percent) is lower than the white percentage of overall population (60 percent), the Black percentage of those killed (25 percent) is higher than the Black percentage of population (13 percent). The argument is that, since white people are underrepresented among those killed relative to their share of population, Black people should likewise be underrepresented among those killed relative to their share of population. This analysis is the source of the oft-repeated claim that Black people are two and a half times more likely to be fatally shot by police than whites. But the premise for this is that we should expect the racial composition of the 1,000 fatally shot by police each year to correlate directly to each racial group's share of overall population. Put another way, the proposition is that the 1,000 people who get into fatal shooting encounters with police each year are just a cross section of average Americans. This is obviously absurd.

The idea that the race of those killed by police should mirror the racial makeup of society as a whole could be true only if, among other things, crime rates were evenly spread throughout all population groups—which they are not—and only if police interactions with citizens were entirely random. However, the 1,000 shooting episodes do not arise from random interactions with the general population, but from interactions related to pursuing potential criminal activity. By and large, they occur while executing warrants, attempting arrests or lawful stops, responding to crime victims' calls, or otherwise intervening in crimes that are in progress. As a result, the racial composition of the 1,000 fatalities will tend to be skewed toward racial groups with higher crime rates who live in higher-crime, more heavily patrolled neighborhoods. If a group is overrepresented among criminal offenders, it will tend to be overrepresented among those who get into deadly encounters with police. If it is underrepresented, the group will likely be underrepresented among those fatally shot by police. And this is what the numbers reflect.

White people commit roughly 45 percent of serious violent crimes and are roughly 45 percent of those fatally shot by police. Black people commit roughly 37 percent of serious violent crimes, and more than half of homicides and robberies, but are roughly 25 percent of those shot by police. This does not suggest racism. On the contrary, to the extent that existing data show anything, it undercuts the case for racism. Harvard economist Roland Fryer, an African American, performed a comprehensive study of officer-involved shootings, expecting to find evidence of racial bias. He studied 1,332 shootings between 2000 and 2015 in ten major police departments. Unlike others, he included cases where lethal force could have been used but wasn't. He called his findings "the most surprising result of my career." He found no racial bias in police-involved shootings. Black suspects were *not* more likely to be fired upon during tense confrontations. They were, if anything, *less* likely to be fired upon. Fryer's more recent studies in this area have continued to support these findings.

Other studies have reached similar conclusions. A March 2015 Justice Department study of the Philadelphia police found that Black officers were more likely than white officers to shoot Black suspects based on "threat misperception"—that is, the mistaken perception that the suspect is armed. A 2015 study by a University of Pennsylvania criminologist found that, at a crime scene where gunfire is involved, Black officers in the New York City Police Department were 3.3 times more likely to discharge their weapons than other officers at the scene. A 2016 study at Washington State found that officers were three times less likely to shoot unarmed Black suspects than unarmed white suspects. A 2019 study published in the journal *Proceedings of the National Academy of Sciences* found "no evidence of anti-Black or anti-Hispanic disparities across shootings, and white officers are not more likely to shoot minority civilians than nonwhite officers." While standing by the accuracy of their study, the authors later retracted it because they felt it was being misinterpreted as addressing the relative probability of Black or white people being shot by police. Rather, the authors explained, the study addressed whether there was a correlation between the race of the officer and the race of the civilian shot, and found no correlation.

Moving away from statistical comparisons and taking a deeper look at the facts surrounding each of the 1,000 shooting cases shows that, in all but a small number, the shootings were justified. In 95 percent of the fatal shooting cases over the past six years, the subject was armed with a dangerous weapon when shot. In only 5 percent of the cases was the subject unarmed. According to the *Washington Post* database, fatal shootings by police of unarmed Black subjects amounted to twelve in 2019 and eighteen in 2020. But in most of these cases, the unarmed subject was physically fighting the officer, charging at the officer, or defying orders to "show hands" and leading the officer to believe the suspect was going for a weapon. There are only a half dozen or so cases each year in which there appear to be no reasonable grounds for the shooting of an unarmed Black subject.

Yet we have reached a point at which, nearly any time an African American is shot by police for any reason, the news media can be counted on to present the interaction as evidence of racism. The coverage ignores or downplays evidence tending to exonerate the officer and ballyhoos any detail that, taken by itself, might cast the officer in a poor light. No matter how justified the shooting may have been, BLM and local activists move swiftly to advance their narrative by often giving misleading, inflammatory accounts and calling for the officer to be charged with murder. All this fosters broad public misconceptions about the risks faced by police officers in fraught confrontations and about the circumstances justifying lethal force even when a subject is unarmed.

A prime example of distorted coverage was the shooting of Jacob Blake on August 23, 2020. The media's and BLM's response to the shooting sparked riots and arson in Kenosha, Wisconsin. Evidence justifying the shooting was easily available to the media from the outset. The mother of Blake's children had called for the police, reporting that he was about to take her car. The officers confirmed that Blake had an outstanding felony arrest warrant for sexual assault, which meant the officers were required to arrest him. When they arrived, Blake had put the three children in the car. Blake physically resisted arrest and overpowered the officers. Three attempts to taser Blake were ineffective. A witness told the Associated Press that the police yelled, "Drop the knife! Drop the knife!" as Blake headed toward the driver's side of the car. The media knew that video showed an indistinct object in Blake's hand. The Wisconsin Attorney General stated that Blake admitted being "in possession" of a knife and that a knife was found on the car floor where Blake fell. On August 29 the police union confirmed Blake had a knife in his hand when he broke away from the officers. Yet media coverage largely ignored the possibility of the knife or minimized it, saying it wasn't clear what role it might have played.

Instead, news reports hammered away on the theme that the officer had shot a Black father in the back seven times at point-blank range, paralyzing him.

I learned quickly after the incident that Blake had a knife in his hand when shot. Police are taught that someone with a knife as close as Blake was to them is a lethal danger and can strike a mortal blow before the officer has a chance to react. The officers here showed restraint by not shooting when he refused to drop the knife. But once Blake opened the driver's side door, the officers were in an impossible situation: they could not let him leave; Blake had already overpowered them physically; nonlethal means had failed; they could not allow him to get in the car with the children (whom he could harm, or use as hostages); they could not allow him to leave with the children, which would have required a chase, endangering the children and the community; and, finally, they could not physically stop Blake, armed with a knife, without putting themselves in even greater danger. The fact that Blake had his back to the officer made the situation more dangerous because the officer could not tell what he was doing with the knife. When the officer saw Blake start twisting his body—indicating to a rational person that he was preparing to turn and lunge—the officer shot Blake until the threat was neutralized.

Noble Wray, an African American reform-minded former police chief and use-of-force expert, was brought in to advise on the case. His conclusion: "Any officer worth their salt, they're not going to let someone leave under these circumstances."

The most insidious aspect of contemporary public discourse about police shooting incidents is the failure to address the most important factor involved: resistance to police. Indeed, the common denominator in almost all fatal police shootings of armed and unarmed subjects alike is that, when shot, the subjects were resisting the police. The media, BLM activists, and radical "community leaders" studiously avoid talking about resistance. It used to be widely understood that, regardless of circumstance, physical resistance is the one thing you can't engage in. Given police officers' responsibilities, it leads inexorably to escalation and violence. Virtually all jurisdictions have for that reason made resistance a serious crime in its own right.

There is no question that most of those fatally shot would be alive today had they complied with police directions instead of putting up a fight. If we wish to reduce the number of Black lives lost to police shootings, the most important step we can take is to reestablish the principle that there is no valid justification for physically resisting a police officer.

Officers aren't looking for opportunities to shoot people or engage in wrestling matches with violent suspects. Unlike the rest of us, however, officers don't have the luxury of avoiding dangerous confrontations. When someone resists arrest or refuses to submit to a lawful stop, police officers can't walk away. If they can't safely talk a subject into submission, they have to use force—not only to protect themselves from assault, but also to overcome resistance and compel compliance. And they must do this even when—as is often the case—they have to take on men who are bigger and stronger than they are. In almost any physical contest, the officer is at a disadvantage because he has to worry about his firearm being taken and used against him.

That's an underappreciated point. When things get physical, the fact the officer is carrying a firearm presents a potentially mortal risk—to the officer. Once a suspect starts physical resistance, it isn't quite right to think of him as completely "unarmed." There is always a gun within reach: the officer's own gun. If, just for an instant, the officer loses full control, he risks losing his weapon and thus his life. From the officer's standpoint, every struggle is literally a fight for his life. Those who are so quick to second-guess a cop in these situations should reflect upon how they would feel if a gun was strapped on their hip, and they were sent into a wrestling match against a stronger criminal suspect disposed to use whatever force is necessary to avoid arrest. Would they not feel in mortal danger? How long would they risk being overpowered before drawing their weapon and ending the fight while they still could?

A common situation in which unarmed subjects are shot occurs when there is a "misperception of threat"—the officer mistakenly believes the subject is about to use a weapon even though the subject doesn't have one. As long as the officer thinks a weapon could be in easy reach, the encounter might go either way. A suspect can produce and use a weapon in a split second before an officer has a chance to react. The only way the officer can "de-escalate" the situation is to command the subject to take specific action showing there is no weapon present. "Show me your hands." "Take your hand slowly out of your pocket." "Keep your hands up." "Don't reach for anything." If a subject ignores these directions, the officer is entitled to assume a threat and react accordingly.

When I was Attorney General the first time, I took firearms instruction on the so-called FATS machine, or Firearms Training Simulator, at Quantico. The student is confronted with various scenarios on a large video screen and—with a specially equipped gun on his hip—must decide when to draw and when to shoot. Like most students, I was resolved to make perfect use-of-force decisions.

I told myself to be cautious and restrained. The result: I was late shooting and got killed in almost every scenario. Then I erred in the other direction and ended up shooting many people when I shouldn't have. I went on a FATS machine again after I returned as Attorney General. Although the simulator was much improved, I wasn't. Before anyone feels he can Monday-morning-quarterback these decisions, he should be required to go on the FATS machine and see just how difficult it is.

If we're going to send our police officers into complicated, volatile, and potentially fatal situations, we need to be fair and realistic when we're judging their actions. Their reasonableness must be judged in light of all the circumstances confronting them at the time, not with the benefit of hindsight and from a position of comfort and safety.

Demonizing police ends up hurting Black communities most of all. The Ferguson effect is real. When the media sensationalize officer-involved shootings, when politicos and celebrities and other publicity hunters denounce cops as racists and talk stupidly about systemic racism, cops pull back from proactively policing the most difficult neighborhoods of our large cities. Cops watch television, too. They see what the famous and the powerful say about them, and they're affected by it. A 2017 study found that because of the fallout from high-profile incidents, 72 percent of police across the nation are now more reluctant to stop and question people who seem suspicious. When police come to feel their acts of self-defense won't be judged fairly and that they'll be scapegoated the moment anything goes wrong, they back off discretionary enforcement. Who can blame them? Violent crime increases, especially in inner-city neighborhoods already suffering from high crime rates. The rioting during the summer of 2020 prompted a similar upsurge in violent crime, especially homicides, in many cities around the country. While Covid contributed to the increase, police pullbacks played a major role. The grim result is more Black victims of violent crime and more Black deaths.

More Black men killed? Do the radical talking heads on CNN, the Hollywood heavyweights intoning about systemic racism, the opportunists on Capitol Hill, the prattling editorialists actually give a damn about Black communities? It is hard to conclude they do when they appear so fixated on an obviously fraudulent narrative that they ignore the plain interests of the Black families they claim to care about.

The only tangible steps taken after George Floyd's death to reduce incidents involving police use of excessive force were taken by the President in signing his Executive Order 13929, Safe Policing for Safe Communities, on June 16, 2020. It required that, in order to receive federal funds, police and sheriffs' departments must be certified by an independent certification organization as having use-of-force policies that prohibit choke holds, except in situations where the use of deadly force is allowed by law. In addition, their use-of-force policies must be certified as complying with all federal, state, and local laws. While the Attorney General can add more requirements over time, the certifying agencies are initially encouraged to assess use-of-force training, de-escalation training, and other policies designed to promote public and officer safety.

The President's executive order also set up a national database of officers determined to have used unreasonable force and requires police and sheriffs' departments to report necessary data. This permits departments, as part of their hiring process, to check whether a job applicant has previously used excessive force. Finally, the order directed that the Attorney General and the secretary of HHS coordinate grant money to assist police departments in developing "co-responder programs," whereby mental health professionals are available to accompany police officers responding to certain kinds of incidents. On October 28, 2020, I finalized and announced the certification standards, the implementation of the database, and the fact that more than three thousand police departments would be certified over the next ninety days. These were important steps forward in addressing police use of excessive force and were supported by the International Association of Chiefs of Police and the Fraternal Order of Police.

The lies and half-truths about law enforcement officers perpetuated by the media and organizations such as BLM produced their repugnant fruit in the summer of 2020. Americans in large metropolitan areas had been locked down for weeks. Many, including lawless troublemakers and gullible victims of the BLM lie, were looking for a reason to protest and riot in the streets. The death of George Floyd gave them all the reason they needed. The national conflagration quickly became my top concern.

CHAPTER 21

PROTEST AND MAYHEM

In the days following George Floyd's death, protests broke out all over the country. While most of these protest events were peaceful, in scores of cities they became violent. The demonstrations started in Minneapolis on May 26, and over three nights—May 27 through May 29—rioting and violence steadily increased. Looting and arson spread. Numerous businesses were torched or otherwise destroyed. In both Minneapolis and Saint Paul violence sharply escalated on Thursday, May 28, when a police precinct was burned, and the violence continued out of control well into Saturday. The rioting in Minneapolis became the most costly and destructive in any American city since the 1992 LA riots. On May 30 the leftist mayor of Minneapolis announced: "What started as largely peaceful protests for George Floyd have turned to outright looting and domestic terrorism in our region." Fortunately, Governor Walz had accelerated mobilization of the National Guard and, by late Saturday, they were at full strength on the Twin Cities' streets. With the strong presence of the National Guard, violence quickly subsided and peace returned to the streets.

Just as rioting had erupted in Minneapolis, demonstrations turned violent in many other cities around the country, like Los Angeles, New York, Memphis, and Miami. On Saturday morning, May 30, I asked the US attorney in the Eastern District of Virginia, Zach Terwilliger, to come over to the District of Columbia and set up a unit in the Justice Command Center on the seventh floor of Main Justice to gather information from all the US attorneys' offices around the country. The reports we were getting from US attorneys and also from local police departments suggested that the character of protests in many of the major cities was changing. May 29 seemed to be a turning point. Organized violence erupted in scores of cities. Cadres of hard-core actors, many reportedly coming from outside the area, were joining the protests and instigating violent attacks on police and destruction of property and arson.

These agitators were largely from Far Left or anarchistic groups such as antifa and similar extremist groups. They arrived prepared for street battle and engaged in orchestrated violence that showed planning and coordination. There were reports of bulk purchases, delivery and pre-positioning of projectiles, bats, lasers, the makings for incendiary devices, and other weapons. Actors would arrive with umbrellas, knapsacks full of projectiles, leaf blowers (to disperse tear gas), and other paraphernalia needed for preplanned activities. Encrypted radio communications were being used to coordinate the movement of cadres of violent actors at the protests. At the same time, the focus of demonstrations started morphing from the particular issue of police excessive force into a broader condemnation of American institutions and calls for "revolutionary" transformation of the country.

On Saturday, May 30, I issued a statement on the violence:

Unfortunately, with the rioting that is occurring in many of our cities around the country, the voices of peaceful protest are being hijacked by violent radical elements.

Groups of outside radicals and agitators are exploiting the situation to pursue their own separate and violent agenda. In many places, it appears the violence is planned, organized, and driven by anarchistic and Far Left extremists, using Antifa-like tactics, many of whom travel from out of state to promote the violence.

During this first weekend of widespread and escalating violence, a number of police chiefs and local political leaders started using the same term—*hijacking*—to characterize the violence they were facing on their cities' streets.

I had long been concerned by the gradual acceptance of violence in our nation's political process. Toward the end of the Obama administration, the use of black bloc tactics was becoming more frequent at demonstrations. These are tactics where "protesters" wearing black outfits, with masks and helmets, and often carrying shields and clubs, engage in coordinated violent actions. During the 2016 election campaign, reporters for mainstream news outlets, unable to let go of the idea that Trump supporters were "Fascists," seized on a couple of episodes in which low-level scuffles broke out at Trump rallies between hecklers and supporters. When Trump himself used hyperbolic tough-guy language about the people who disrupted his rallies ("I'd like to punch him in the face"), CNN and the *New York Times* could be counted on to report that Trump was "instigating violence."

In fact, however—as these and other news outlets would have known if they cared about documentable facts rather than narrative—Trump supporters weren't generating the rise in political violence. It came from the Left. There were, in fact, a number of instances in which Trump supporters were the victims of violence. In June 2016, for example, antifa activists attacked Trump supporters leaving a rally in San Jose, California, punching them and throwing eggs. A left-wing publication referred to it as a "righteous beating." Documents obtained by Politico show that by April 2016—during the Obama administration—a joint DHS and FBI intelligence assessment pointed to "anarchist extremists" as the primary instigators of violent attacks on the police, government, and political institutions. Occasionally liberal writers acknowledged the increase in political violence on the Left. Peter Beinart's piece "The Rise of the Violent Left," published in the September 2017 issue of the *Atlantic*, was a notably honest assessment.

During my first days in office in February 2019, I had discussed with FBI director Chris Wray the emergence of political violence. We agreed on the need for the bureau, which already had a robust program keeping tabs on Far Right actors, to ensure it was staying abreast of extremist threats across the ideological spectrum. Going back to my first stint as Attorney General, I was familiar with the bureau's potent capacity to surveil and develop intelligence on Far Right extremists. But it is fair to say the FBI had not been as forward leaning in monitoring Far Left extremists. The bureau has been so successful at collecting information on the Far Right that the flow of intelligence on domestic threats has skewed in that direction. This intelligence gap is not all the bureau's fault. Going back to the 1960s, whenever the bureau has gotten into serious trouble with the political establishment, it has been for surveillance of left-wing organizations, and so there is institutional reluctance to move in this area. Another reason for the gap is that the Far Left groups today have a decentralized, cell-like structure and more sophisticated ways of operating that make it harder to get a handle on. By insinuating themselves into protests and interweaving their violence with legitimate protest activity, these groups are able to deftly exploit the seam between rioting and legitimate First Amendment protest.

From the summer of 2020 until today, various commentators and political actors have engaged in a largely fruitless debate over which side of the political spectrum is more responsible for political violence. But arguing at this stage over which set of extremists is more dangerous is largely a waste of time and diverts us from a far more important task. Instead of jockeying for political advantage on the issue, both parties have a solemn obligation to take a clear and unequivocal stand against all political violence. At a time when the country is deeply divided, it is imperative that we have zero tolerance for political violence. We cannot end up like the Weimar Republic with armed political thugs from Left and Right battling it out on the streets. Our Constitution binds us to peaceful means of resolving differences. As long as it stands, we must rally around the clear message that mob violence, from whichever side of the political spectrum, is never justified, and the government must respond vigorously to suppress violent mobs and punish those involved.

The rioting I had dealt with in 1992 relating to Rodney King was mostly concentrated in Los Angeles. Now we were confronting riots in large and midsized cities from coast to coast, flaring up all at once, and through the use of encrypted communications and social media, the mobs were able to quickly adapt tactics, change routes, and reconstitute much quicker than those in 1992.

As the violence intensified during the first weekend, I already had in mind a framework for dealing with it. In my view, the states and localities must shoulder primary responsibility for handling such riots, and we had to encourage them to discharge that responsibility. Many cities had simultaneous outbreaks, but the numbers of rioters in any one city usually didn't rise to more than a few thousand. The situation was dangerous but, in general, state and local authorities have sufficient resources to deal with civil unrest at that scale. Local police forces can be augmented, if necessary, by other police agencies, including state police and officers from nearby jurisdictions. Most police departments have "mutual assistance" agreements with other jurisdictions to provide this kind of reinforcement. If more manpower is needed, the governor can deploy the state's National Guard under state authority.

The state governments also have plenary "police power" to maintain law and order. As a result, states usually have the broadest panoply of laws for addressing mob violence, including laws that permit police to declare "unlawful assemblies" and arrest those who fail to disperse without having to show that each individual is committing violence. In my experience, as long as the authorities have the will—the mayor, the governor, the district attorney, and the chief of police—most localities are fully capable of stopping mob violence without significant federal intervention.

The federal government, by contrast, has limited capacity to confront widescale rioting, unless it uses military forces. The number of deputy US marshals the DOJ can readily deploy around the country to deal with civil disturbances is only about two hundred. After that, the department can muster a "pick up" force of approximately two thousand to three thousand FBI, USMS, DEA, ATF, and other personnel to deploy to a hotspot, but these are mainly tactical units, like SWAT teams, that don't have optimal training or equipment to deal with rioters. By diverting personnel from their border protection and immigration responsibilities, the Department of Homeland Security can assemble several thousand more personnel, but not all would be fully trained and equipped for civil disturbances. Further, the federal statutes applicable to rioting are not as broad as state law, and they are usually insufficient to allow the federal government to address the full array of illegal conduct involved in rioting, unless the state is operating jointly with federal law enforcement. The bottom line is that, if the federal government relies only on its own civilian agencies, and if it's acting without the full support of the state, it has the wherewithal to deal with only a couple of large-scale riots in the country at any one time—and even that would be a stretch.

The federal government does have one very powerful tool at its disposal, however. Ordinarily, federal troops cannot be used within the United States to enforce domestic law. But under the Insurrection Act, first adopted in 1807, the President may use troops to suppress "unlawful obstructions, combinations, or assemblages, or rebellion against the authority of the United States" which he believes "make[s] it impracticable to enforce th[ose] laws . . . by the ordinary course of judicial proceedings." The act also authorizes the President to use any means he considers necessary, including the use of troops, to suppress "any insurrection, domestic violence, unlawful combination, or conspiracy" that interferes with the execution of federal law; or that hinders the execution of any state or federal law so as to deprive people of their Constitutional rights. In addition to authorizing the use of federal troops, the act essentially gives the President the equivalent of states' power to declare an "unlawful assembly."

The Insurrection Act has been invoked many times in our history to deal with civil disturbances. I was involved in using it in the last two situations in which it was invoked—restoring order in Saint Croix after Hurricane Hugo in 1989, and suppressing the 1992 Los Angeles riots. Now facing the spreading violence in the last days of May 2020, I would not have hesitated to recommend use of the act if I thought it was needed to protect life and property. But, under the circumstances, I thought we shouldn't federalize the effort too readily. I believed the states and localities were able to address the riots and, if the federal government was too precipitous in jumping in, we would be taking the pressure off of them—essentially letting them off the hook. I was also concerned that the prospect of direct confrontation with federal forces would encourage radical groups to carry out more rioting around the country. We could potentially end up overcommitted in multiple cities, requiring large commitments of military forces, as we rushed troops around the country playing "whack a mole" with rioters. Nothing would have made the radical groups and the President's opponents happier than this scenario.

My priority was to push the states to deploy whatever manpower was needed to get control of the streets, including their own National Guard where necessary. We could support state efforts in several ways. Where needed, we would send relatively small contingents of federal tactical personnel from DOJ and DHS to protect federal buildings, thus freeing up local police for antiriot assignments. We would also help logistically by rapidly resupplying the states with essential anti-riot equipment. And, through the Defense Department, we would work with governors to keep on standby a continuous reserve of National Guard military police units in various states around the country that could rapidly deploy to any state that needed to use them. Guard military police are the best units to use for civil disturbances, but only a few states have large numbers of them. If a state called on these out-of-state units, they would still be operating under state—not federal—authority, but the federal government could shoulder the costs of keeping them at the ready and deploying them, which was a big help to the states.

This did not mean the federal government would stand idly by. While local authorities took the lead in securing the streets, we were mobilizing a nationwide effort to identify, arrest, and prosecute the extremist ringleaders instigating the violence. Director Wray and I agreed to use the FBI's Joint Terrorism Task Forces (JTTF) for this purpose. This was the existing network of fifty-six regional task forces, designed to deal with domestic and homegrown terrorists, as well as foreign terrorists. Each task force, led by the FBI and including all the relevant federal, state, and local law enforcement entities in the region, is charged with investigating and identifying threats; gathering, sharing, and fusing intelligence and evidence; and making arrests. We were now expanding the scope of these task forces to reach not just domestic terrorists who set off bombs but also extremist agitators who were orchestrating mob violence.

My statement on Saturday, May 30, stated the key elements of our strategy:

> We must have law and order on our streets and in our communities, and it is the responsibility of the local and state leadership, in the first instance, to halt this violence. The Department of Justice (including the FBI, Marshals, ATF, and DEA), and all of our ninety-three US attorneys across the country, will support these local efforts and take all action necessary to enforce federal law.
>
> In that regard, it is a federal crime to cross state lines or to use interstate facilities to incite or participate in violent rioting. We will enforce these laws.

In some cities around the country, notably Newark and Detroit, a combination of good policing and strong community leadership kept demonstrations largely peaceful. Elsewhere, however, the police were having difficulty getting the upper hand, and violence continued to spread.

From the reports I was receiving, it appeared two basic tactical problems had emerged. First, in many places the police were using approaches designed to manage peaceful demonstrations rather than planned, purposeful mob violence. Police lines were frequently thinly manned, intentionally keeping a "low profile" so as not to provoke the "demonstrators." There were too few police on the streets to handle the violent mobs. When violence erupted, the police were forced to hang back and watch the destruction, hoping the violence would "burn itself out." When mobs were dispersed, they were allowed to rampage through neighborhoods, wreaking havoc unchallenged.

The second problem was that the radical ringleaders instigating the violence used tactics that made it hard to identify, reach, and arrest them. Typically, these agitators—often white radicals who did not live in the city—arrived with knapsacks of projectiles and rioting gear, and used crowds of demonstrators as a kind of host body. Masked and dressed alike, moving quickly about in small clusters usually to the rear of the frontline demonstrators, these actors used the crowds to conceal their violent attacks on police and property. While many protesters were disgusted with these tactics and left the demonstrations when they turned violent, agitators were sometimes successful in inciting some demonstrators to join in their violence—throwing bricks at police and torching cars and buildings. The police, hard-pressed in holding their line, were often unable to keep an eye on the bad actors and penetrate back into the crowds to arrest them. When the police did make a foray to arrest a ringleader, they were typically met by "de-arrest" tactics—swarmed and blocked by activists as the culprit got away.

I felt it was critical that the states put larger forces out on the streets capable of controlling events, rather than being controlled by them. When a mob is bent on violence, having too small a police presence is more dangerous for everybody involved. It can lead to uncontrolled street melees with increased risk of injury to all sides. Adequate force levels are also essential to target and arrest the violent ringleaders.

On Sunday, May 31, I issued a statement calling on state leaders to be more proactive and confirming the department would be using our joint task forces to identify and arrest ringleaders:

> It is time to stop watching the violence and to confront and stop it. The continued violence and destruction of property endangers the lives and livelihoods of others, and interferes with the rights of peaceful protestors, as well as all other citizens. It is the responsibility of state and local leaders to ensure that adequate law enforcement resources, including the National Guard where necessary, are deployed on the streets to reestablish law and order. We saw this finally happen in Minneapolis last night, and it worked.
>
> Federal law enforcement actions will be directed at apprehending and charging the violent radical agitators who have hijacked peaceful

protest and are engaged in violations of federal law. To identify criminal organizers and instigators, and to coordinate federal resources with our state and local partners, federal law enforcement is using our existing network of 56 regional FBI Joint Terrorism Task Forces (JTTF).

The President had scheduled a video conference call with state governors for Monday, June 1, and asked me, Defense Secretary Mark Esper, and Chairman of the Joint Chiefs General Mark Milley to participate. The President and those participating from his administration sat together in the White House Situation Room. The governors, piped in by video links, appeared on a big screen. The meeting was supposed to be nonpartisan and was meant to encourage the governors to move decisively to deal with violence and to promise we'd work collaboratively with them.

Unfortunately, the conference came right after a pre-meeting in the Oval Office that focused mainly on the rioting in the capital over the weekend. There, as I will discuss shortly, the President had gotten very worked up over rioting near the White House and especially news reports that he had been taken down to a bunker for his safety. As a result, the President walked into the Situation Room with a chip on his shoulder and adopted a belligerent tone with the governors from the outset that was, I thought, counterproductive. Even though the President had just come from a meeting where it was explicitly decided that the military would *not* be in charge of dealing with the riots, he started off by introducing General Milley: "General Milley is here. He's head of the Joint Chiefs of Staff, a fighter, a war hero, a lot of victories and no losses and he hates to see the way it's being handled in the various states and I just put him in charge."

This reflected the President's instinct—a bad one I thought—to federalize and militarize the response to rioting, and I could see Milley and Esper, off camera, subtly cringe at this description.

The President's basic message was that the governors had to get tougher, "dominate" the streets, and prosecute more people for illegal rioting. I agreed with the message, but it was delivered in an accusatory way—essentially blaming the governors for being weak. The President

also picked the wrong forum to debate the point that the violent agitators were mostly leftists. This unnecessarily introduced a tinge of
partisanship into the discussion. For purposes of this meeting, it didn't
matter who was committing the violence; our message should have
been that violence was unacceptable regardless of who was involved.
One of our basic objectives was to encourage the governors to use
their National Guard where necessary to stop the rioting. Here the
President was a little more conciliatory, citing with approval Governor
Walz's actions in Minnesota calling out the National Guard, and encouraging other governors to follow his example.

In my remarks, I noted that most demonstrators were not violent,
but urged governors to confront the violent actors and looters. Like
the President, I stressed the need to put adequate manpower on the
streets—which could be National Guard (as in Minnesota) or more
police (as in New Jersey). I explained that having enough of a presence on the streets allowed them to better control events, avoided wild
melees, and made it safer for everyone. The President was criticized by
the media and others for his bellicosity on the call. Yet many states responded to the President: more of them called up the National Guard
or otherwise increased their manpower available to deal with the riots.

As riots worsened around the country for three successive nights—
from Friday, May 29, through Sunday, May 31—violence also erupted
in Washington, DC. Riots in the nation's capital city required particular attention. I asked the FBI to bring tactical units into the city,
posted temporarily in their headquarters building, to be available to
protect that building and the Main Justice Building across the street. I
also brought in two BOP antiriot units, stationing them in the Main
Justice Building to secure our headquarters. During the Rodney King
riots in 1992, after organizers announced they were going to "shut
down" the Justice Department, the DC government told us it could
not protect our building. If that experience repeated itself, I wanted to
make sure I had the personnel necessary to secure Main Justice.

The violence in Washington centered on Lafayette Park, directly
across the street from the White House. Throughout all three nights,

rioters made repeated violent assaults on US Park Police and uniformed Secret Service officers who were attempting to hold a line behind temporary bike rack fencing. Officers were pummeled by projectiles, including bricks, rocks, caustic liquids, water bottles, lit flares, fireworks, and sections of wooden two-by-fours. Rioters directly assaulted officers, seizing and wielding sections of the fencing itself as weapons. They used crowbars to pry up pavers from the park and throw them at the officers. On Friday the rioters breached the adjacent Treasury Department complex, alarming the Secret Service enough to rush the President down to the White House bunker, which was designed for use in emergencies like terrorist attacks.

Violence sharply escalated on Sunday night. The chief of police described Sunday to me as the most violent night he had seen in Washington in thirty years. As the rioters continued attacking the police line, they burned down the old lodge house in the park; set fire to the historic St. John's Church, known as the "Church of Presidents" attended by every President since Madison; torched cars and set a bonfire on H Street along the park; and started a fire in the lobby of the AFL-CIO building, as well as a sandwich shop, immediately to the north of the park. To clear the way for the fire department, police had to use tear gas to disperse the rioters.

These weren't "protesters," though—they were rioters who came to destroy. Once they were dispersed, groups of them marauded through several neighborhoods, bashing out the windows of shops and office buildings. Near the park, groups systematically went down the street smashing out car windshields with metal baseball bats. National monuments were defaced around the city. Looting broke out in several neighborhoods, stretching northward to Maryland suburbs.

During these three days of riots, more than one hundred Park Police and Secret Service officers were injured at Lafayette Park. Twenty-two had to be taken to the hospital. Among these were numerous head injuries, including concussions. Because their ranks had become so depleted, the Park Police requested police from Northern Virginia police departments to be made available for Monday. The District's police force was also hard-pressed during Sunday night. The mayor had called in some National Guard support for the police but it took time to deploy and, in the meantime, DOJ personnel responded to police calls for assistance. As violence continued through the weekend, I asked DOJ components—FBI, DEA, USMS, and BOP—to station additional personnel in the capital to be on hand if needed.

As I later learned, earlier that weekend, on Saturday night, the Park Police and Secret Service conceived of a plan to relieve the pressure on Lafayette Park and create a buffer. The plan was finalized and initially set in motion late on Sunday night and the early morning hours of Monday. It called for clearing H Street, which runs along the northern side of the park, and pushing the perimeter up toward I Street, which would allow construction of a ten-foot-high, non-scalable fence across the northern end of the park. The plan was to make this movement when sufficient police units were in place to carry it out. The order for fencing was placed from the vendor for delivery as soon as possible on Monday, and the Park Police started making arrangements for the necessary police units to be in place Monday afternoon.

On Monday morning I was called over to a ten thirty meeting with the President in the Oval Office. Originally scheduled as a short "prep" session for the President's eleven o'clock telephone conference with governors, the meeting had shifted to a more general discussion on dealing with the rioting. After three days of escalating violence, no one knew what to expect going forward. I arrived late and the Oval Office was already packed with White House staff and officials from the various departments, some standing along the walls. The President, sitting behind the Resolute desk as usual, interrupted his angry denunciation of the rioting and waved me to a seat in front of his desk, where I sat next to Secretary Esper, General Milley, and DHS acting secretary Chad Wolf. The President resumed expressing frustration over continuing scenes of violence around the White House and around the country.

Outraged by the violence and especially the news reports that he was taken to the bunker, the President lost his composure. Glaring around the semicircle of officials in front of his desk, he swept his index finger around the semicircle, pointing at all of us. "You're all losers!" he yelled, his face reddening. He felt we were responsible for the violence around the country, especially around the White House. "You're losers!" he yelled, again, tiny flecks of spit arcing to his desktop. "Fucking losers!" It was a tantrum. Although the brunt of his outburst was probably directed at the Defense Department team, I was taken aback and indignant. I could tell General Milley, clenching his jaw, was angry, too.

Taking a moment to calm down, the President pointed toward Lafayette Park, and asked, "Can you imagine the impact these scenes have around the world? Fires and rioting directly across the street from the White House? This is an invitation for our enemies to take advantage of us. We can't have this continue."

I thought to myself: That is exactly the reason the Founding Fathers insisted on a separate federal zone for the national capital. In 1783, during a mutiny of a few hundred Pennsylvania militia, the Congress of the Confederation had been forced to flee Philadelphia, the capital, because the state and local authorities refused to defend the government. The Framers never wanted to see that kind of humiliation again, where the federal government was at the mercy of local authorities for protection. That is why they wanted the federal authority to have control over the District of Columbia. But over the years, more and more control has been ceded to the city government.

White House staff told the President that a plan was already under way to move the perimeter out north of Lafayette Park and add fencing and that virtually the entire DC National Guard—about 1,200 military police—were being brought in to help the DC police around the city and support the Park Police and Secret Service. That was the first I had heard of the plan to move north of Lafayette. The President asked me what I thought, and I told him I agreed with both these measures and added that, between DOJ and DHS, we would have more than 2,000 additional officers in a position to help with any contingency. He referred to a provision in DC law that allows the President to take control of the DC police force and said he would like to invoke that authority. I told him I would take a look at it.

The President then raised the role of the military. He appeared to want the military to play the lead role in reacting to the rioting. The

President told General Milley that he wanted to put him in charge of dealing with the unrest and asked whether he should invoke the Insurrection Act, which would permit the use of regular troops. Understandably, Secretary Esper and General Milley recoiled at this idea, expressing the view that regular military forces should not be used except as a last resort and that, absent a real insurrection, the military should not be in charge but should provide support to civilian agencies. I agreed, as did acting DHS secretary Wolf. All the principals present agreed that it would be prudent to have regular military police units standing by if needed, but that we likely had enough resources to deal with the situation without them. I told the President that I would not hesitate to recommend invoking the Insurrection Act if it were really needed, but it just was not necessary right now.

Esper and Milley summarized for the President the regular army units—mostly military police—that were being placed on standby or pre-positioned to be available at a moment's notice. These would remain outside the District unless needed. They also explained to the President that several hundred National Guard military police from other states were being brought in to augment the DC National Guard. Because of the unique status of DC, this could be carried out by the US secretary of the Army without invoking the Insurrection Act. He reiterated to the President that DOD should not be the lead agency but rather be providing support to a civilian agency. I absolutely agreed with their position. At that point, the President pointed at Milley and said, "Okay, okay: you provide support to the Attorney General." The President then pointed at me: "And, Bill, you take the lead. Coordinate with DOD. You tell Milley what you need."

After the President's eleven o'clock governors' call, I had a brief meeting with Esper and Milley in the Situation Room to ensure everyone was on the same page concerning the National Guard and military support, which we were. I left the White House and spent the rest of the day rushing among three different command centers—the DOJ's national command center at Main Justice, linking the US attorneys throughout the country; the FBI's Strategic Information and Operations Center (SIOC) at bureau headquarters, coordinating federal law enforcement's response nationwide; and the ad hoc command center set up in the FBI's Washington Field Office to coordinate the federal response to rioting in the capital.

A meeting was held at SIOC at two o'clock to coordinate activities between the National Guard leadership and the relevant law enforcement agency officials. Just beforehand, Chief Peter Newsham, chief of DC's Metropolitan Police Department, took me aside to express concern over the President's plan to take over temporary command of the police department. He felt relations between the mayor and the President were becoming increasingly contentious, which was threatening the kind of cooperation necessary to deal effectively with the rioting. He warned that taking over the police force would become an explosive issue in the District. He also made a good practical point—at least half of the police force was out on patrol doing their normal neighborhood policing. He assumed we did not want to take command of those officers, and we'd have to do some rejiggering of chain of command to arrange everything properly. I told Newsham that, as long as we were cooperating closely, and I could count on him being responsive to federal needs, I would not recommend the President take over the police at this point. We had our hands full without that. I called Mark Meadows, the President's chief of staff, who agreed. Even though the mayor and the President continued to fight publicly, behind the scenes Meadows was able to keep relations with the mayor on a professional and constructive basis, which helped immeasurably on the operational level. From June 1 forward, we did not have any major problems working with the DC police.

At the SIOC meeting, Chief Newsham reviewed his operational plans for the day, and National Guard commanders discussed how their troops would be allocated to protect key monuments, support the Park Police at Lafayette Park, and support the DC police around the city. I confirmed my understanding that the movement of the perimeter toward I Street would be taking place later in the day. Chief Newsham confirmed his plans to make sure that any protestors moving away from the White House were closely escorted by police to avoid the kind of rampaging that had occurred the previous night.

During the afternoon, I caught glimpses of video coverage of the Lafayette Park area and wondered why the perimeter movement hadn't yet been carried out. I was frustrated by this because the number of demonstrators along H Street, only a few hundred in the early afternoon, was gradually growing as the day went on. I wanted the movement to occur as early as possible before the crowd got too big. The sooner the movement occurred the easier it would be. I was told that the units were taking longer to assemble than expected but that the operation would proceed as soon as they were in place. Late in the afternoon, General Milley and I left the Washington Field Office and headed over to the White House to brief the President. I had heard the movement at Lafayette was imminent and thought it might be done by the time I arrived. But when I pulled into the White House complex, I saw the operation hadn't started. A large crowd of protestors was still on H Street. General Milley and I walked up to Lafayette Park to check on things and greet some of the participating units.

After we initially greeted some of the units, a law enforcement commander on the scene told me that I was within range of projectiles the protestors had been throwing and suggested I move back. I saw projectiles being thrown and took his suggestion. I asked one of the commanders when they planned to move forward. He said the last units they had been waiting on were getting into place, and a series of three formal warnings was just about to be given to the crowd. I had been told before leaving WFO for the White House that the President might "go for a walk outside" that evening. I did not know the details. I asked the police commander when the President was coming out. He seemed surprised. Chief of Staff Meadows's deputy, Tony Ornato, was standing next to me and pulled me aside. He whispered, "We are not telling people the President is coming out." General Milley and I left the park to go to the Oval Office. Before leaving, I heard the first announcement being given over the loudspeaker.

When General Milley and I arrived at the Oval Office, we learned the President was about to make remarks in the Rose Garden and that he wanted us to wait to accompany him for a walk across Lafayette Park to St. John's Church. His staff was packed in the Oval as the

President put the finishing touches on his remarks. This was the first I heard that he was giving remarks in the Rose Garden and would then go to St. John's Church. Esper, Milley, and I were told that we should wait in the outer office and then accompany the President on his walk to the church. I watched the Park Police clear H Street on the TV screens outside the Oval Office. I could tell neither Esper nor Milley were keen on the idea of walking over to the church with the President. Nor was I thrilled about it. Nevertheless, we were assembled with the party that would be going with the President and told to walk fifteen feet or so behind the President.

That night, after the clearing of H Street, the Park Police successfully erected the non-scalable fencing along the north side of Lafayette Park. After this, violence subsided around the White House and injuries among federal police officers in the area were almost eliminated. General Milley and I drove around parts of the city and were impressed to find the Metropolitan Police, supported by National Guardsmen, in complete control. Wherever a knot of protesters had gathered, there was a strong force of police, immediately adjacent, closely monitoring them. Any outbreak of lawlessness was met immediately by the police. Peace steadily returned to the capital.

The media, of course, went crazy over the clearing of H Street. They perpetrated two false claims—in a word, lies. One was that I "ordered" an attack on "peaceful demonstrators" after I showed up in Lafayette Park. But the clearing of H Street had been preplanned over the weekend, and execution of the plan was already under way on Monday morning. I agreed with the plan at the Oval Office meeting in the morning, and thus no further decision had to be made—it was going to be done as soon as necessary units were in place. Tactical responsibility for carrying out the movement rested with the normal law enforcement command structure for operations relating to Lafayette Park—the Park Police as lead agency, acting in conjunction with the Secret Service. Furthermore, as I understood it, clearing H Street had nothing to do with the tenor of the demonstrators at that moment. It was not a reaction to the temperament of the crowd. The purpose for the operation was to clear the area so that fencing could be erected before another night of violence. Even if the crowd had been entirely peaceful, they still would have been directed—and, if necessary, compelled—to move. Although law enforcement officials on the scene did not consider the crowd to be peaceable, their volatility had no bearing on whether they would be moved.

The second lie was that H Street was cleared in order to give the President a "photo op," as the media obsessively called it, at St. John's Church. That the clearing of H Street allowed the photo op to happen does not mean the clearing took place for that purpose. The idea of moving the perimeter to permit erection of a fence originated within the Park Police over the weekend as a reaction to intensifying violence and mounting officer casualties. It plainly was not prompted by the idea of a photo op. It is not unusual in our society that completion of a mission becomes the occasion for a photograph memorializing the event. It does not follow that the mission's purpose was to make the photograph possible. Clearing H Street was a mundane law enforcement movement that does not equate to a feat of arms. Still, saying it was done for a photo op is like saying our amphibious invasion of the Philippines in 1945 was carried out so that General MacArthur could have a photo op walking onto the beach. It is ridiculous.

That is not to say that I thought the timing and manner of the St. John's Church photo was wise. Late in the afternoon I initially heard only that the President might go outside that evening. I did not know when, where, or how this would be done, but imagined he might go over to Lafayette Park well after the police activity. I could understand that, after three days of rioting, and his descent to the bunker, the President might want to signal that he was not holed up like a prisoner in the White House. But later, when I got to the Oval Office, I learned that he planned to go right away over to St. John's and brandish a Bible. I felt this was being done too quickly, and the stage-managing felt very awkward.

The President walked slowly, solemnly alone out in front, a scowl on his face, followed about fifteen feet behind by me, Esper, Milley, and others. Instead of showing solicitude for the church, which had been set afire, the procession had the feel of spiking the football and overdramatizing a relatively ordinary law enforcement action as a significant presidential "victory" over the demonstrators. This feeling was reinforced when the President returned to the White House and was greeted by an honor guard at the gate with a pathway through opposing ranks of uniformed Secret Service officers holding up their riot shields. I did not want to walk through. It was too much.

Mob violence ended in the District of Columbia after Monday, June 1. It started dissipating around the country later that week, too, with the notable exceptions of Portland and Seattle. Although there continued to be sporadic violent flare-ups through the summer—there were confrontations in Richmond, Virginia, and Austin, Texas, for example—these incidents were limited in both scope and duration. State and local governments had the will and the means to deal with them. There was also a wave of attacks on public monuments and statues, which abated after President Trump issued an executive order on June 26 prioritizing federal prosecution for damaging federal monuments and directing DHS to set up task forces to protect these sites.

Violence diminished for a number of reasons. In many places, community leaders, though supportive of peaceful protests, firmly rejected the agitators. State and local leaders were also showing greater willingness to marshal sufficient manpower—police and National Guard—and to use more effective tactics like enforcing curfews and arresting rioters. It also became clear to the ringleaders of the violence that the federal government was intensifying its scrutiny and targeting them for arrest and prosecution. It also likely helped that Democratic politicians largely concluded that sustained violence could end up hurting their party's chances in November. To the extent they had any influence over the activists, they started using it to discourage violence.

The main focal point for continuing violence was the Pacific Northwest. Portland, a hive of antifa activism for many years, was an intractable problem. The political culture of Portland has long run along radical leftist lines. Violent protests had become a way of life in the city. After George Floyd's death, rioters launched orchestrated attacks on the federal courthouse every night for more than a hundred succes-

sive nights. The local government was essentially aligned with the rioters, refusing to acknowledge the violence or do anything about it. The
police department got no backing from the political establishment,
was hamstrung by restrictions on the tactics officers could use to deal
with rioters, was largely confined to the defense of its own precinct
stations, and was prohibited from helping or coordinating with federal
law enforcement.

The primary mission of federal law enforcement in Portland was
therefore defensive—protecting the federal buildings under attack.
The DOJ's responsibility was to protect the main target of attacks: the
federal courthouse, where we had stationed a small group of deputies
from the US Marshals Service, the agency charged by statute with
defending courthouses. DHS, while augmenting the deputy marshals
with some of their personnel, had primary responsibility for protecting
their own Immigration and Customs Enforcement building, which
was being periodically attacked, as well as three other federal buildings
nearby the federal courthouse.

Every night for months, a mob of hundreds of rioters laid siege
to the federal courthouse. What unfolded nightly around the courthouse could not reasonably be called a protest; it was, by any objective measure, an assault on the United States government. The rioters
arrived equipped for a fight, armed with powerful slingshots, lasers,
sledgehammers, saws, knives, rifles, and explosive devices. Early on,
the rioters breached the courthouse and started a fire in the building's
atrium. After this, as deputies hunkered down inside the building, they
repeatedly tried to set the courthouse on fire. During their assaults,
rioters would barricade the front door so deputies couldn't get out and
then use crowbars to pry plywood off the windows and throw flammable liquids and commercial-grade fireworks into the building. The
rioters would also start fires up against the building and then attack
federal officers who attempted to put them out—by pelting them with
rocks, frozen water bottles, cans of food, and balloons filled with urine
and fecal matter, and physically assaulting them with hand weapons,
like hammers and two-by-fours.

I wondered at the time what kind of sick hatred it must take to fill balloons with human excrement and throw them at people who've done no harm to you or anyone else. No verbiage about "systemic racism" and "rage against oppression" can explain or excuse that kind of vile behavior.

Federal officers erected non-scalable fencing around the courthouse, but rioters came with power saws to cut it away. The defense of the courthouse fell into a pattern. Every night, thinly manned shifts of federal officers would stand behind the fencing outside trying to protect it and under steady attack, while the next shift of officers tried to rest inside awaiting their turn outside on the line.

The major news outlets—the national networks, CNN, MSNBC, the *New York Times*, the *Washington Post*—virtually ignored the whole sordid mess. These organizations, whose job it is to tell Americans what notable things are happening in the country, gave almost no attention to the sustained attack on the courthouse. When they did, they portrayed rioters and arsonists as concerned citizens trying to defend themselves from the federal government's "militarized" thugs.

A report in the *Times* on July 23 began this way: "Shields were made of pool noodles, umbrellas and sleds. The body armor was pieced together with bicycle helmets and football pads. The weapons included water bottles and cigarette lighters. Facing federal forces who came to Portland to subdue them, many of the city's protesters have taken to the streets this week with items scrounged from home." Somehow the reporters forgot to mention that several hard-core antifa groups in the Pacific Northwest were conducting the nightly attacks on the courthouse; that the "water bottles" hurled by these pool-noodle-clad citizens were usually frozen, intended to break the bones of their targets; or that at other times the bottles were full of gasoline, and the cigarette lighters intended to light the rag fuse at the opening. No mention, either, of the thrown bricks and chunks of concrete, slingshots shooting large steel ball bearings, commercial-grade fireworks shot at federal marshals, hundreds of lasers pointed at the eyes of federal agents to blind them, not to mention knives, baseball bats, and shit-balloons.

I wonder how the coverage might have been different if the rioters were Far Right activists. In that case, news organizations would have done their jobs. We would have known about every brick and every Molotov cocktail. Every injury to a federal officer would have been rightly lamented. The *Washington Post* editorial board and MSNBC hosts would have demanded the arrest and prosecution of the perpetrators. There would have been no weepy reports about pool noodles.

The mayor and the city council began making the absurd claim that federal agents were aggressors who had come to "occupy" the city, and these same news organizations simply repeated the claim as though it were valid. As I said at the time, it was a hell of a way to invade and occupy a city—keeping a few dozen officers hunkered down behind a tight fence line around a single courthouse. Why were the rioters fighting so fiercely every night to breach the courthouse? To file papers?

On July 28, at a hearing before the House Judiciary Committee— the one at which the Democrats prevented me from answering questions—I asked the Democratic members whether it would be acceptable if a mob attacked the federal courthouse down the street from the Capitol, broke the windows, threw flammable liquids and commercial-grade fireworks inside to burn it down. I found it amazing that not a single Democrat on that committee was willing to condemn attacking a federal courthouse.

There were a few brave exceptions to the media's corruption. In late July AP reporter Mike Balsamo went to spend the weekend with the deputy marshals protecting the courthouse and sent out stories and tweets describing the violent onslaught they faced. Several of his tweets from July 27 give the flavor of what he saw:

I spent the weekend inside the Portland federal courthouse w/ the US Marshals. Mortars were being fired off repeatedly, fireworks & flares shot into the lobby, frozen bottles, concrete, cans . . . regularly whizzed over the fence at high speeds.

I watched as injured officers were hauled inside. In one case, the commercial firework came over so fast the officer didn't have time to respond. It burned through his sleeves & he had bloody gashes on both forearms. Another had a concussion from being hit in the head w/ a mortar

The lights inside the courthouse have to be turned off for safety & the light from high-powered lasers bounced across the lobby almost all night. The fear is palpable. Three officers were struck in the last few weeks & still haven't regained their vision.

When we were out inside the fence line, someone fired off a mortar. It exploded inches away from us, but no one was hurt. A large bonfire had been started in the street & people were aiming fireworks through the fire at officers behind the fence.

Also in late July, Oregon governor Kate Brown, who refused to use the National Guard in Portland, reached an agreement with Vice President Pence to interpose a contingent of Oregon State Police outside the fence line around the courthouse if our officers took a lower profile. We welcomed this. But, after two weeks, the state police left in frustration with the local district attorney's decision not to prosecute people arrested by the police. Oregon State Police captain Timothy Fox put it devastatingly: "At this time, we are inclined to move [our] resources back to counties where prosecution of criminal conduct is still a priority."

The situation in Portland festered through the summer of the election year. The department was able to defend the courthouse, but relatively small-scale rioting kept going at a slow burn, occasionally flaring up. This was to become a continuing source of tension between me and the President.

Like Portland, the Seattle political establishment did not support its police force, although they were lucky to have an excellent police chief in Carmen Best. While the rioters in Seattle were not engaged in sustained violence against federal buildings and officers, in early June they "occupied" a six-block neighborhood on the city's Capitol Hill, declaring it a "cop free" autonomous zone—initially referred to as CHAZ (Capitol Hill Autonomous Zone) and later as CHOP (Capitol Hill Occupied Protest). Local residents and businesses were subjected to the rule of armed protesters who appointed themselves as "security guards." The mayor described the zone as a "block party," but local business owners trapped by these block-partiers described harrowing scenes of armed and masked gunmen harassing customers and demanding business owners get their permission before entering their shops.

This spectacle of armed thugs in Seattle lording it over citizens made the President deeply angry, as it should have. He called me over for a meeting in the Oval. Mark Meadows forewarned me that the President wanted to do something immediately to eliminate CHAZ. Before heading over I got briefed by the FBI.

As I sat down, along with Meadows, in front of the President's desk, the President launched directly into a tirade—a justified one—over the events in Seattle.

"Can you believe this crap!" he growled, holding up some news articles. "An autonomous zone in the United States! We can't have this bullshit! Bill, you have to do something about this immediately."

"Look, I agree," I said. "It is outrageous and we cannot allow it to stand, but—"

"But what?" The President cut me off. "You should be able to bust this up in seconds."

"You are right, Mr. President, we could take this down quickly and easily," I assured him. "But the rioting is dying down around the country, and we have to think about the best way of dealing with Seattle without reigniting broader violence around the country—which then will require a wider response by us."

"We look weak by not acting," the President pressed.

"Mr. President, I have the same impulse and know how you feel," I assured him, "but let me deal with it." I explained that the FBI was on top of the situation, and we had good information coming out of CHAZ. I told the President that I was confident the local police would act soon to dismantle CHAZ and, if they did not, we would deal with it.

"Don't let it drag out. You look weak," the President said, begrudgingly giving me some time.

On June 11, after my meeting with the President, he publicly threatened to take back the "autonomous zone" if the mayor or governor failed to act.

Over the next month, the President grew more exasperated by the delay. But I knew that Seattle chief of police Carmen Best was pushing to put an end to CHAZ, and I was getting almost daily reports from the FBI and all the DOJ law enforcement leaders in Seattle who had insight into the local dynamics. These gave me good reasons to believe that the zone would either soon implode or the mayor would soon be politically forced to let Chief Best clean it out. Either of these results would be preferable, I thought, to mounting a federal operation, and so I advised the President to wait a little while longer. I thought it was important to support Chief Best and the Seattle police, by helping them do the job.

On June 20 gunfire around the zone killed a young Black male and wounded another. The next day, a teenager was wounded by gunfire in the zone. Two days after that, another victim was wounded by gunfire near the zone. Chief Best made clear she could not stand by and countenance the "shootings, a rape, assault, burglary, arson, and property destruction." On June 29 a sixteen-year-old Black male was killed, and a fourteen-year-old Black male was critically wounded by gunfire near the zone. Chief Best announced, "Enough is enough. We need to be able to get back into the area." I told the President, who was infuriated by the spate of shootings, that liberation of the zone was imminent. Early on the morning of July 1, with FBI support, Seattle's police department moved in, cleared the zone, and took back their East Precinct station, from which they had been ousted weeks before. About seventy arrests were made.

It should have been a moment of, if not celebration, at least gratitude to law enforcement. But on August 11 Seattle's city council, as a first step in "reimagining" the police—*defunding* is the more accurate term—cut 100 positions from the force's 1,400 officers and cut salaries of police commanders. Carmen Best, a twenty-eight-year veteran of the force and its first African American chief, resigned. "It really is," she said, "about the overarching lack of respect for the officers."

The last significant outbreak of civil unrest arose on August 23 in Kenosha, Wisconsin, after Jacob Blake was shot by police. The shooting was plainly justified, as I've explained, but in the summer of 2020 the media had to interpret any interaction between a white cop and a Black suspect as prima facie evidence of racial injustice. News coverage only encouraged mob violence, which began the very next day. Robberies, arson, gunfire, and looting engulfed Kenosha on August 24.

That night, I talked to the FBI deputy director, Dave Bowdich, and he prepared to deploy forty FBI SWAT team agents, principally from Chicago, to Kenosha. I also asked the US Marshals and the ATF to assemble teams that could be sent to Kenosha. The next morning, I called the US attorney in Chicago, John Lausch, a strong leader with broad experience and good judgment. I told him to get up to Kenosha and take charge of the federal law enforcement elements that were on their way. General Milley and I had weeks before agreed on a plan to keep several companies of National Guard military police in various states on a "short string" so they could be rapidly deployed to help anywhere in the country.

On Monday, August 24, the day after the Blake shooting, there appeared to be a disconnect between Wisconsin governor Tony Evers and local law enforcement leaders in Kenosha. The local authorities made clear that they needed more resources and would welcome federal law enforcement help. They were concerned that the governor initially only planned to send around 125 guardsmen to Kenosha. We agreed this was woefully inadequate. As for federal law enforcement, we did not need to be asked, or given permission, to send our agents anywhere we deemed them needed. They were already arriving in Kenosha and by late Wednesday we had more than two hundred in place, with more on their way.

The problem was getting the National Guard deployed. The President was willing to federalize National Guard units and send them if the governor failed to use his authority. Mark Meadows and I felt the governor could be persuaded to move, and we wouldn't need to federalize them and invoke the Insurrection Act. I talked to General Milley, who had the general in charge of DOD's National Guard Bureau start working with the Wisconsin National Guard to ensure that the state had adequate numbers of guardsmen to help in Kenosha. Because Wisconsin did not have many military police, we wanted them to know multiple military police companies were standing by in several other states. The President publicly and privately urged the governor to get more National Guard to Kenosha. It wasn't until late on August 25—a full forty-eight hours after violence began—that the governor said he would send five hundred Wisconsin guardsmen to Kenosha. The next day, he followed through on our suggestion to use units standing by in other states, which added seven hundred military police from Alabama, Michigan, and Arizona. Eventually he called in another seven hundred Wisconsin guardsmen, for a total of about two thousand National Guard on the ground in Kenosha. It took longer than it should have.

Kenosha illustrates one of the reasons it is so important for state authorities to move quickly and decisively to handle mob violence. If government authorities deal with mob violence in a lethargic way, the private citizens affected by the violence will deal with it in their own way. To put it another way: If we allow lawlessness on the streets, we'll see armed groups come in to oppose the violence in the name of protecting property and the community. That happened in Kenosha, with tragic results.

In an ordered republic such as ours, armed groups of citizens can't be allowed to fight each other. In the United States, we decide matters by legislatures and courts, not by looting and street melees. A class of emotionally infantile journalists may think it romantic that street fighters want "justice," but grown-ups understand that mobs beget chaos. Vigilante justice—whether to combat systemic racism or leftist insurrectionism—is not the rational and humane arrangement bequeathed to us by our ancestors.

CHAPTER 22

TRUMP VS. TRUMP

In the spring of 2020, I had a sense of déjà vu. Twenty-eight years earlier, when George H. W. Bush was running for a second term, I thought he was headed for defeat. My friend Jack Kemp, then the housing secretary, thought the same. In March 1992 we raised our concerns directly with the President, urging more focus on a range of domestic issues.

I now had the sinking feeling that, on his current course, President Trump would lose in the fall. I was frustrated because, even with Covid, it was Trump's election to lose. But he was frittering away the opportunity. The outcome would be determined, in my view, by a narrow segment of Republican and independent suburban voters in critical states. Those voters normally voted Republican, but many were turned off by the President's excessively petulant behavior and exasperated by the constant sense of drama, chaos, and rancor surrounding him. I thought there was time for the President to repair the damage, but he had to act soon.

In his first election, in 2016, the Trump campaign came very close to destruction the month before the election. The *Washington Post* revealed a recording from 2005 in which Trump, speaking to host Billy Bush before filming an episode of *Access Hollywood*, spoke in crude terms about seducing a married woman and the freedom a "star" had to "grab" women by the "pussy." For a day or two, it looked as if his candidacy was over—some of his advisers thought he should withdraw from the race, but he stayed in. That near-death experience, if I could put it that way, had the salutary effect of chastening candidate Trump. He started listening to advisers and tempering his conduct. He spoke in measured tones and stayed more or less on script. And he was rewarded for it. During the campaign's final month, undecided voters broke substantially in his favor.

I thought, in the spring of 2020, he needed to do the same. He couldn't wait till October to make the change. He was no longer an unknown; he was the most recognizable and talked-about person in the world. The voters knew him. A lot of them were willing to give him another chance, but not if he kept behaving like a hyperactive maniac. I won't say I was hoping for another *Access Hollywood* moment, but Trump needed badly to settle down, listen to his advisers, and fix his mind on the goal.

I was not involved in any election campaign discussions. But I gathered there were roughly two schools of thought. One group held the election was all about firing up the base. The other thought that the base was already motivated and more attention had to be paid to reconnecting Trump to the segment of suburban voters who might either stay home or defect because they found Trump's behavior offensive. I agreed with the latter view, and most of my fellow cabinet officers seemed to be of the same mind. The purely "base" strategy might have made sense before the pandemic, when the President could go to the American people with a substantial list of successes. But once Covid hit, it was clear the election would be decided by a razor-thin margin. It made no sense to ignore a significant block of suburban voters whose main reservations centered on the President's conduct.

I realized that the President's combative, frontal style had many pluses. But too often, especially during the worst of the Covid crisis, he yielded to his impulse for pettiness and pointless nastiness. He would get into idiotic name-calling spats with every minor celebrity who called him a name, and in his press conferences he would make every controversy about himself. If he could manage just a little reticence, he could make himself a little less odious to voters put off by the Left's insanity but equally repelled by Trump's erratic egotism.

Even his most committed supporters often expressed a wish for him to stay out of pointless disputes. When I traveled around the country, both before and during the pandemic, I spoke with countless Trump supporters. It was always the same. They would start by saying, "We love the President, and we love you." After taking the obligatory selfie, their parting comment was, invariably, "Would you please tell the President to dial it back a little," or "Please tell the President to cut back on the tweeting." I cannot remember an encounter in which this sentiment was not expressed one way or another. While there are certainly many Trump supporters who adored every aspect of his personality, I believe the overwhelming majority of the President's base supported him *despite* his excesses, not *because* of them.

If he could manage to follow this simple counsel, many of us in the administration felt, he would win.

Not that the President was solely responsible for the rancor. He was under a constant barrage of heinously unfair attacks from his Democratic opponents and their allies in the media. But the Trumpian imperative of automatically responding to any provocation with massive retaliation added to the bedlam, got him distracted, and gave his adversaries an easy way to portray him as a bully.

They had his number. It was too easy to provoke him into overreaction.

In the summer of 2019, after an Oval Office meeting on another topic, I mentioned this to the President. "Mr. President, you are like a bull in a bullring," I said. "Your enemies know exactly how to provoke you. They are controlling you. They wave a red flag, and you go charging full tilt at them. Then someone waves another red flag, and you go charging off in that direction. Pretty soon you'll be standing in the middle of the ring, sweating and exhausted, and the matador will walk over and put a sword through you."

The President did not think much of the analogy and waved me out.

In the weeks following the President's acquittal in his first impeachment trial, Trump showed no sign of tempering his tone or adopting the self-discipline necessary for a campaign. He seemed to give freer vent to his most petty instincts. That angered me. Many people had been working hard for his success. They had sacrificed a lot to help dig him out from under an avalanche of false and dirty attacks. He was facing an incredibly weak candidate, and the election was winnable. But Trump showed no sign that he understood the situation's gravity. He kept indulging his worst instincts, kept getting himself into stupid disputes.

By April I had become so distraught at the President's self-destructive behavior that I felt I had to talk to him directly about it. Before doing that, I went over to see Jared Kushner in his West Wing office. The more I had gotten to know Jared, the more I was impressed with his calm rationality and common sense. I had the feeling he would share my concern. Jared's office, though near to the Oval Office, was small. Most of the space was taken up with a large conference table. Other than that, there was just a stand-up desk. He welcomed me warmly, and we sat at the conference table.

"I am really worried that the President is going to boot this election," I said. "I think the main danger is that a lot of voters, who otherwise might be up for grabs, are just exhausted by the 24/7 drama around the President. If they conclude that the Democrats are responsible for the turmoil, they will support the President. But if they think the President is to blame, they will vote to get rid of the President. They are just tired of the constant chaos and contention."

Jared, who puts a lot of stock in data, responded by initially reviewing the most recent polling and analysis. "The bottom line is that I have the same concerns. I think what you say is essentially right," he said. "As they say, there is only one man who can beat Donald Trump, and his name is Donald Trump."

"I am worried that so far Trump is doing a good job at beating Trump," I said. "I think he is running out of time to clean up his act. I'd like to go in and talk to him about it."

"Well, you are not alone in your thinking," Jared said. "I think he has to be at the top of his game by May. A couple of other cabinet secretaries and some key people here and on the outside are planning to deliver the same message. It should all come around the same time, so I will let you know when it's time for you to go in."

Jared alerted me the right time had arrived at the end of April. I went to visit the President, meeting one-on-one in his small dining area adjoining the Oval Office. I told him that I felt it was important for him to hear me out. He nodded and went into rare listening mode. I said I was not speaking to him as Attorney General but as a friend who wanted him and his administration to succeed. I said I believed he was headed for defeat. A substantial number of voters in the suburbs had given up on him, I said, because they'd concluded—I was explicit—that he was an "asshole."

I urged him to temper his tone. I told him he did two things as well as anyone I'd ever seen. First, he was a fighter—and that was what we needed in 2016 to bring working-class voters firmly into the Republican camp. Second, he charmed people, lured them to his message. He didn't charm the media or the Democrats, but he made ordinary people feel as though someone in high office understood them.

This time around, I said, he needed to win a lot of people back. Some middle-class suburban voters had left the camp. But he could speak to them again. He could remind them that, for all his pugnacity and unpredictability, he still understood them in ways the dominant political class didn't.

"My base needs me to fight. I need my base," he said.

"Mr. President, you already have your base," I assured him. I told him his base wasn't going anywhere. He didn't need to ratchet up the aggression to keep them. Cooling things down wouldn't jeopardize his status in the eyes of his base. It would broaden his base, I said. I told him I had talked to literally hundreds of supporters around the country, and I hadn't met one who didn't ask me to tell him to dial it back. "I'm delivering *their* message," I told him. "Have you noticed that whenever you're quiet for a few days, your poll numbers go up?"

He wasn't convinced. "These people are vicious," he said, speaking of his adversaries. "I need to fight back." The President told me he'd think about what I'd said and thanked me for my advice. I didn't think my advice by itself would have any impact. But I knew several others in the administration, and on the outside, were delivering the same message at the same time. I hoped the collective advice would move him.

He didn't listen. That was soon obvious. As the summer wore on, it was clear that Trump was beating Trump pretty badly. The Republican convention was masterfully done—positive, optimistic, balanced; vastly superior to the dull and grievance-laden Democratic convention. I give Jared Kushner a lot of credit for the GOP convention's success. But it should have resulted in significant momentum for the President. The fact that it didn't signaled serious trouble.

On September 29 I had stopped in Tulsa to visit the Cherokee Nation. At the hotel that evening, my staff and I assembled in the lobby lounge to watch the first presidential debate. The initially cheerful atmosphere quickly gave way to stunned silence. After the first twenty minutes or so, I was disgusted and had to leave. It was a catastrophe. The President displayed all the traits undecided voters found obnoxious: the constant, ill-tempered interruptions, the name-calling, the bizarre fondness for making every controversy about Donald J. Trump. It was as if he had considered the advice of everyone around him and then did the opposite. I wondered who was in charge of debate preparation.

I was stunned the following week when the President effectively canceled the second debate by refusing to do it remotely. This would at least have been a chance to do some damage control. As it was, by the time of the last debate, eleven days before the election, 65 percent of the electorate had already voted. The President's performance in the final debate was an improvement, but the contest was a draw. And it was too little, too late.

In the months after the President's first impeachment acquittal, just as I was becoming more discouraged by the President's lack of self-control, he was becoming more dissatisfied with me. Our relationship gradually deteriorated. There were several points of friction, but the main one had to do with the Durham investigation: there were unlikely to be any developments in that probe before the election.

The President always made clear the importance he placed on Durham's investigation. He never asked me about the substance of the investigation but instead repeatedly stressed its priority and called it "the most important thing" the department was working on. From time to time, he or Meadows would ask generally whether Durham was making progress and when I thought he might be done. In response, I would assure the President that Durham and his team were working hard and making progress, but I could not predict with any confidence how long the investigation would take. Nor could I predict how it would come out. I kept stressing that the outcome and timing of investigations like this are dictated by the evidence as it is developed and are largely beyond anyone's control. I used the same mantra several times with the President: The department isn't a pizzeria where you can order whatever you want and have it delivered whenever you want.

As the summer approached, the President started complaining about how long the Durham investigation was taking. I tried to tell him that, in fact, Durham had only been able to focus on the meat of the case for the past few months. As long as the Inspector General, Michael Horowitz, was still scrutinizing Crossfire Hurricane—the FBI's highly irregular investigation into the Trump campaign—Durham had to wait to get into that key area of the investigation. Originally, Horowitz said he expected to be done in June 2019, around the time Durham was up and running. This was successively moved out until the end of 2019. The Inspector General submitted his report in December 2019—less than a year before the election. Only then could Durham's investigation of the FBI's conduct begin in earnest. Soon after that, however, the response to Covid shut down the court system—including grand juries. As a practical matter, that meant that witnesses could refuse to make themselves available for interviews voluntarily: even if Durham had wanted to use a grand jury to compel their testimony, none was available.

Aside from the delay, I tried to temper the President's expectations—as I had from the beginning. I thought Durham would uncover most of the facts, and I told him so, but I stressed, in general terms, the difficulty of proving that government officials had committed a crime. Durham would need to prove beyond reasonable doubt that officials acted with criminal intent. As I repeatedly explained to the President, the very same legal principles governing my review of volume two of Mueller's report and making it hard to show that the President had the necessary criminal intent to obstruct Mueller's investigation, also made it hard to show that the officials handling Crossfire Hurricane acted with criminal intent. Unless an official commits an inherently wrongful act—like altering a document—it's a tall order to prove criminal intent—as opposed to carelessness or poor judgment. Usually proving criminal intent requires finding a smoking-gun document or having one of those involved turn on his colleagues.

On Mother's Day Weekend, May 9–10, 2020—days after the department moved to drop the Flynn case—the President went on a wild tweetstorm of 126 tweets and retweets. The main theme of his outburst was that President Obama and Vice President Biden were directly involved in a conspiracy to use the bogus Russiagate claims, and the FBI's investigation of them, to cripple Trump's administration at its inception. He also claimed, or endorsed the claim through retweets, that part of this conspiracy involved targeting General Michael Flynn with ginned-up charges. In his tweets, the President unveiled the term *Obamagate* to refer to this conspiracy, which he called, with his usual penchant for superlatives, the "greatest political crime in history." The clear implication of the President's tweets, and his subsequent comments, was that Obama and Biden were behind the Russiagate "hoax," had "been caught" in this "crime," and were the ultimate quarry in Durham's investigation. He touted the disclosures made in connection with the dropping of charges against Flynn, implying that they supported his claims about Obama and Biden.

The President's tweets angered me. He had gone right back to commenting on cases pending before the department, and this case was one of the most sensitive. In the first place, his allegations about President Obama and Vice President Biden were far afield from the evidence developed to date in Durham's investigation. The President was trying to draw Durham's investigation into the political fray, make it about Biden, and harness it into the service of his campaign. This was anathema to me and unfair to Durham, who was running a careful and professional investigation. The President's suggestion that the dropping of the Flynn case somehow incriminated Obama and Biden was not only unsupported but distinctly unhelpful. I had taken the decision to drop the charges against General Flynn based on the merits and the recommendation of the US attorney who had reviewed the case. The President's comments made the decision look political—as if I had done it to help his campaign.

I could not permit the President to undermine Durham's investigation and had to nip in the bud the idea that it was directed at, or closing in on, Obama and Biden. I took the earliest opportunity. On May 18 I held a press conference to announce important developments in the case involving the killing of US servicemen at the Pensacola Naval Air Station by an Al Qaeda–inspired Saudi cadet. NBC's Pete Williams asked about the President's comments, as I thought he might, and I stated my position. I intended my answer to be a comprehensive statement on how I would proceed between then and the election. I intended it as a message for all sides—including the President.

I started by reiterating my often-stated criticism "that over the past few decades there have been increasing attempts to use the criminal justice system as a political weapon." I promised that "[a]s long as I am Attorney General, the system will not be used for partisan political ends [and] this is especially true for the upcoming elections in November." I continued:

> We live in a very divided country right now and I think it is critical that we have an election where the American people are allowed to make a decision, a choice, between President Trump and Vice President Biden based on a robust debate of policy issues. We cannot allow this process to be hijacked by efforts to drum up criminal investigations of either candidate. I am committed that this election will be conducted without this kind of interference.

I acknowledged that what had happened to President Trump in 2016 was abhorrent and should not happen again. I said that the Durham investigation was trying to get to the bottom of what happened but "cannot be, and it will not be, a tit-for-tat exercise." I pledged that

Durham would adhere to the department's standards and would not lower them just to get results. I then added a point, meant to temper any expectation that the investigation would necessarily produce any further indictments:

> [W]e have to bear in mind [what] the Supreme Court recently reminded [us] in the "Bridgegate" case—there is a difference between an abuse of power and a federal crime. Not every abuse of power, no matter how outrageous, is necessarily a federal crime.

Most important, I made clear that neither President Obama nor Vice President Biden were in Durham's crosshairs. "Whatever their involvement," I said, "based on the information I have today, I don't expect Mr. Durham's work will lead to a criminal investigation of either man."

Asked later that day about my comments, the President expressed surprise and disagreement.

"I think Obama and Biden knew about it. They were participants, but, so I'm a little surprised by that statement," the President said. Had he done what Obama and Biden had done, he said, people would be going after him, so "I think it's just a continuation of a double standard. I'm surprised by it." He said he would now "stay out" of the matter and leave it to his "honorable Attorney General."

As I have said, there were certain issues the President would raise throughout my tenure that I referred to as Groundhog Day issues. He would raise these issues again and again at regular intervals. One of those issues was his desire to replace Chris Wray.

The President started raising removing Wray early in my tenure. He felt Wray had not been aggressive enough in getting rid of "Comey's people" and those responsible for ginning up the phony Russiagate scandal. Despite my assurances to the contrary, Trump thought Wray wasn't fully cooperating with the Durham investigation and that the FBI was concealing relevant information. He thought Wray wasn't forceful enough in his public appearances. The President's ire was especially triggered when he thought Wray was too mealy mouthed in backing up something I had said publicly. He felt, for example, that Wray avoided using my term, *spying*, in describing the Crossfire Hurricane team's abuse of FISA, and that he was not explicit enough about the role antifa was playing in the rioting over the summer. Initially, I resisted making a change because I had never worked with Wray before and had not yet assessed his effectiveness. I saw no good reason to replace him, and having three FBI directors within two years would have been unduly disruptive—especially at a time when the administration was dealing with the Mueller investigation and impeachment. The subject was also a waste of time, I felt, since Trump didn't have in mind a markedly superior and confirmable candidate. I was, in fact, not aware of such a candidate.

The more I worked with Wray, the more I thought he should stay. He and I developed a good working relationship. Our communications were direct, open, and honest. He moved methodically, but without fanfare, to bring in a new leadership team at the bureau, which I judged a strong group. I thought his low-key, businesslike style—he called himself a "workhorse, not a show horse"—was refreshing after Comey's insufferable exhibitionism. I repeatedly explained to the President that I was not upset by Wray's measured statements when asked to comment on something I had said. His tenor reflected the nonpartisan nature of an FBI director, who—unlike a cabinet secretary—is expected to serve for a term regardless of the party in power. Like most of his idées fixes, the President's attitude toward Wray was fueled, I sensed, by a coterie of outside kibitzers who constantly sniped at the FBI director.

I still don't know why Trump stepped up the pressure to replace Wray after his first impeachment acquittal. He said it was our "last opportunity to make a change." I told him, more than once, that attempting to replace Wray would create a lot of discombobulation in an election year, with no obvious benefit. I was content with Wray, and I thought the chances of finding and enlisting a candidate clearly superior to Wray, and then successfully getting that candidate confirmed during an election campaign, were remote. No quality candidate would be willing to put himself forward under those circumstances. In any event, all really hinged on his winning the election. If he won, he could consider what he wanted to do at the FBI. But if he lost, then any change he made now would simply open the way for Biden to put his choice in as FBI director.

The President then started advancing the idea of appointing Kash Patel as deputy FBI director. Patel, who was completing a stint as deputy to Acting Director of National Intelligence Ric Grenell, had been a staffer to Congressman Devin Nunes, and had served briefly on the NSC staff at the White House under Trump. I categorically opposed making Patel deputy FBI director. I told Mark Meadows it would happen "over my dead body." In the first place, all leadership positions in the bureau, except the director, have always been FBI agents. They've all gone through the same agent training and have had broad experience in the field and at headquarters. Someone with no background as an agent would never be able to command the respect necessary to run the day-to-day operations of the bureau. Furthermore, Patel had virtually no experience that would qualify him to serve at the highest level of the world's preeminent law enforcement agency. The bureau already had an exceptionally able deputy, Dave Bowdich, in whom I had total confidence. He was a strong leader with high integrity. He was indispensable as far as I was concerned. The very idea of moving Patel into a role like this showed a shocking detachment from reality.

Trump wouldn't give up. In April I was supposed to attend a meeting in Mark Meadows's West Wing office. I arrived with my chief of staff, Will Levi. We were told Meadows was still in a meeting but that we should go to the Roosevelt Room down the hall, where others would be gathering. When we got to the Roosevelt Room, it was empty. We stood around for several minutes waiting. John McEntee, the young head of presidential personnel, drifted in, his faced buried in his cell phone. Kash Patel made an entrance. I asked, "What is this meeting about?" No one answered. McEntee said they were waiting on others. There was an awkward silence. Suddenly a man in his fifties walked in and introduced himself as Bill Evanina, an FBI agent currently serving in a senior position in the Office of the Director of National Intelligence. Everyone continued to stand around the conference table in awkward silence. I surmised quickly the purpose of the meeting. I didn't know who was supposed to show up to lead it, but I wasn't going to wait around to find out. "Bye," I said and walked out. Returning to Meadows's office, I complained this was obviously a setup to try to get me to agree to take Evanina as FBI director, along with Patel as deputy. "What the hell is going on?" I asked.

Meadows shook his head. "I didn't know they were going to pull that," he said. "Don't worry about it."

I learned later from Meadows and Cipollone that the President had approved the meeting to get me to agree to replacing FBI leadership with Evanina and Patel. Trump brought up the idea of changing FBI leadership a time or two again. But eventually the subject died.

As the summer unfolded, the President's complaints about the pace of Durham's investigation became more barbed, as it became clearer there was little chance of any major development until after the election. When I tried to explain the stubborn realities governing the pace of the investigation, the President bristled. I understood the impatience of the President and his supporters, but I knew how hard Durham's office was working, and appreciated both the complexities of the case and the difficulties of the evidentiary and witness issues they were dealing with. I was generally aware of the various avenues Durham was exploring, and at times my hopes, as well as his, were raised that there might be at least some modest sign of progress before the end of summer, but these prospects did not play out. I had come to respect Durham immensely—he was very much his own man. I was not going to second-guess his judgment on what was to be done and when it was to be done. I felt if there was a legitimate case to be made, he would get there. He wouldn't cut corners to meet some arbitrary timetable.

I had not yet appointed Durham "Special Counsel" under the department's regulations used in Mueller's case. Technically, that meant I could still give him directions on handling the case. But I had selected Durham because he was a thoroughgoing professional, with a reputation for calling things straight. My intent was to allow him the independence to handle the case as he thought appropriate. As it became clearer that would likely go on for quite awhile, Durham and I began discussing his appointment as Special Counsel under the same regulations used for Mueller. This designation would give Durham more formal independence and also make him more difficult to remove. My aim was to ensure that Durham's investigation would continue in the event Trump lost the election.

On August 13, in an interview with the Fox Business Network's Maria Bartiromo, the President made remarks widely understood as "throwing down the gauntlet" on me. Speaking of the spying on his campaign, Trump asserted, "Obama knew everything. Vice President Biden, as dumb as he may be, knew everything, and everybody else knew." He said he hoped Durham's team was "not going to be politically correct" and say "[l]et's just get a couple of the lower guys," warning that, depending on what Durham did, "Bill Barr can go down as the greatest Attorney General in the history of our country, or he can go down as an average guy." Doubling down on Obama and Biden's involvement, he asserted, "It goes all to Obama, and it goes right to Biden." He claimed that Comey, Brennan, and Clapper engaged in "treason" and were involved in "the single biggest political crime in the history of our country." Concluding, Trump repeated, "Bill Barr is great most of the time, but if he wants to be politically correct, he'll be just another guy."

Even accounting for the President's habitual hyperbole and imprecision, these comments were grossly improper for a President. I myself had referred to Russiagate as perhaps "the biggest *political injustice*" in our history, but there had been no determination of criminality as described by the President. His labeling of individuals, including President Obama and Vice President Biden, as criminals far outstripped the existing evidence and, as chief executive, the President had no business prejudging a pending investigation and calling for scalps.

The President's comments suggested one of two things. Either (a) he was convinced we had sufficient evidence to indict senior individuals but I was afraid to pull the trigger because of political correctness, or (b) he wanted me, whatever the evidence, to deliver the results he wanted before the election. Probably both attitudes were present to a degree, but I think the former—that we already had sufficient evidence—was the dominant idea. As I've said, Trump has a strong penchant for treating as true the representations of people who tell him what he wants to hear. This is especially so in the legal sphere, in which he tends to shop around until he finds a lawyer willing to give him the advice he wants. In the case of Russiagate, there were plenty of lawyers outside the administration—some on the Hill, some in the private sphere—who were all too glad to hype the strength of the case against Obama and FBI officials. Many of these lawyers, I have no doubt, told him that if they were in charge, they would have already gotten indictments.

I also thought it was telling at this time that the President railed more than usual against my decision more than a year before not to prosecute Comey for providing to his lawyers the memos he had written for the record about his meetings with Trump. Claiming to have personally studied the IG's eighty-page report on the matter, he insisted that there was a mountain of evidence to support criminal charges against Comey but that, for whatever reason, I recoiled at approving an indictment. His renewed harping on this suggested to me that he had concluded that the impediment to getting results was likely not a deficit in evidence—but my lack of will.

Emblematic of the fraying relationship between the President and me was a sharp exchange at the end of the summer in the Oval Office. To give the President credit, he never asked about the substance of the investigation but just asked pointedly when there might be some sign of progress. On this occasion, we had met on something else, but at the end he complained that the investigation had been dragging on a long time. I explained that Durham did not get the Horowitz report until the end of 2019, and up till then had been looking at questions, like any possible CIA role, that had to be run down but did not pan out.

"What do you mean, they didn't pan out?" the President snapped.

"As far as we can tell, the CIA stayed in its lane in the run-up to the election," I said.

The President bristled. "You buy that bullshit, Bill?" he snarled. "Everyone knows Brennan was right in the middle of this."

I lost it and answered in a sarcastic tone. "Well, if you know what happened, Mr. President, I am all ears. Maybe we are wasting time doing an investigation. Maybe all the armchair quarterbacks telling you they have all the evidence can come in and enlighten us."

Afterward, I regretted my tone. Although he didn't seem offended at the time, it was not appropriate to address the President that way. But I resented the President's comments on Bartiromo's show and the attitude among some of his supporters that, just because they suspect something, it must be true and easily provable. This is one of the pathologies of our age. People have come to think that, simply because circumstances suggest wrongdoing, some set of people should go to prison for a crime. Some on the Left and the Right seem always ready to "lock 'em up" without worrying about pesky things like sufficient evidence. But our system is deliberately designed to make it hard to convict someone of a crime. It's frustrating at times, but over the long run it serves as a safeguard against government abuse.

Early in the summer, I decided to buttress the senior leadership ranks at Main Justice for what would be a difficult fall. One of the US attorneys who most impressed me was Richard Donoghue in Brooklyn. He was an incisive lawyer and a strong, seasoned leader with a spine. I asked him to consider coming down to Washington later that summer. Serendipitously, Seth DuCharme, then serving as Principal Associate Deputy to Jeff Rosen, was thinking about returning to Brooklyn after almost a year and a half of commuting to Washington. Richard and Seth were interested in shifting positions. I agreed. In midsummer, Seth moved up to serve as acting US attorney in Brooklyn, and Richard made arrangements to join Deputy AG Rosen as Principal Associate Deputy.

Over the summer, as tension grew between the President and me, our contacts dwindled. For the first year of my tenure, I would have contact with the President almost every day, often multiple times. Other than scheduled meetings at the White House, he would typically phone me just to touch base. These calls took a lot of time, though very little effort. Generally, the President delivered a monologue, and my role was just to listen and grunt occasionally to let him know the phone line was still live. During the spring and summer, the number of his calls steadily dropped. By September the President had stopped calling me altogether. When he wanted to convey something, it usually came through Pat Cipollone or Mark Meadows. I was happy with this development and, for my part, tried to limit my visits to the White House. Despite the pandemic, I spent a lot of time traveling out of town, visiting cities where we were conducting Operation Legend.

Another source of conflict between the President and me emerged over the summer—how to respond to riots across the country, and especially in Portland. From the very beginning of the rioting at the end of May, the President expressed a strong inclination to make visible use of the military in suppressing it. Initially, he tried to showcase General Mark Milley as the man to deal with the urban mayhem. In the June 1 Oval Office meeting to discuss the riots, the President raised the military option and the Insurrection Act. He introduced Milley in that vein to state governors during a conference call later that morning. And in his early comments about the riots, he talked frequently about using the military to deal with riots if local authorities failed to control them.

Throughout the summer, using the military was one of the President's fixations that had to be batted down on a regular basis. That mission frequently fell to me. I had no problem using the military to restore law and order, but I felt it should be a last resort. I argued instead that state and local governments had the wherewithal to deal with the rioting and we should press them to act and, where necessary, call up their own National Guard to provide whatever additional manpower was needed. Outside the Pacific Northwest, the rioting was dying away, and the state and local governments were becoming more effective in dealing with it.

The situation in Portland raised an important question. Some state and municipal governments simply refused to deal with the rioters. Did that mean the federal government could, or should, unilaterally intervene to confront the violence and restore law and order? The President would become exercised watching the wanton thuggery happening in Portland, with hardly a hint of pushback from law enforcement. He wanted to intervene decisively. For a time, almost on a weekly basis, he would give me ultimatums—he said he was ready to invoke the Insurrection Act and deploy the military in twenty-four hours unless I came forward with an alternative plan. He was talking to advisers on the outside who were telling him that he looked "weak" by failing to pacify Portland. I understood his frustration. I felt it keenly myself. Many times, as I watched scenes on TV showing packs of white punks dressed in black throwing bricks and pointing lasers at law enforcement officers, I felt like jumping through the TV screens and personally throttling the little bastards. But, upon cool reflection, I still knew that using federal troops would not make matters better and risked making them much worse.

As detestable as the rioting was in Portland, it had dwindled to a few hundred rioters each night. We could protect the courthouse with the resources we had. We didn't need federal troops to do that. What would the mission of the troops be? If we gave them the mission of imposing order throughout the city, there is no question that the arrival of the troops would itself massively swell the number of rioters and the scale of the unrest—not just in Portland, but across the nation. And if we tasked the regular army with pacifying Portland, what powers would they use to accomplish it? If state and federal judges in Portland did not sympathize with our invocation of the Insurrection Act—and I was confident they would not—they would not support the arrest and detention of rioters. Other than occupying space, the troops would have no teeth, unless we were willing to resort to extraordinary military detention powers. Without a more urgent threat of insurrection or violence on a wider scale—and without local political leaders who wanted our help—I doubted the American public would react well to having the military detaining citizens who would inevitably be portrayed by the media as "peaceful protesters."

We had no good end game. If we sent in troops, they would have to stand around having things thrown at them, which would send another and grander message of helplessness and cowardice. We could guarantee that the news media would portray the introduction of troops as an act of fascistic aggression, thus triggering far larger riots around the country, just at a time when the violence appeared to diminish. Earlier, just sending in a few additional Federal Protective Service police to help guard federal buildings in Portland had triggered "sympathy" rioting in several cities which, before that, had quieted down. These were not normal times—Covid was affecting people's temper. Given the nation's volatility at that moment, it was my judgment that sending the Eighty-Second Airborne into Portland would end up touching off serious violent rioting throughout the nation. How would we respond to that? On top of this, it was almost a sure thing that the volatile mixture of armed troops and aggressive, hardened radicals would lead to civilian casualties. While I understood the President's impulses, following through on them would have risked taking a manageable situation and sending it spinning completely out of control—and just months away from a national election. I urged patience and caution as strenuously as I could.

The President continued to press me. Things came to a head at a small meeting in the Oval Office in August. Mark Meadows had warned me the President was on the warpath and I had better have some good options. The President spoke passionately about the need to restore law and order, and that our failure to do so in Portland made us look weak. I made my case against using the federal troops at this stage, pointing out that, outside of Portland, violence was ebbing and was being handled effectively by local law enforcement. I assured him that I would support using military forces if there was any significant metastasis of the violence to other cities. I had already sent Dave Bowdich, the FBI deputy director, and Rich Donoghue, slated to be the new PADAG, out to Portland. They had been out on the streets during the unrest and were reporting back to me. I outlined for the President our plan in Portland, which was low profile but would be more proactive in identifying the ringleaders and making federal arrests, and we had already added the law enforcement resources to carry out the plan. The President slammed his hand on the desk and shouted, "No one supports me!" He stood up. "No one gives me any fucking support!" Then

530 ... WILLIAM P. BARR

he walked out toward his private dining area. I glanced over at Mark Meadows, who was flushed and had an I-told-you-so look on his face.

"Well," I said, "that went well."

As the election picked up, the President soon got back to his main frustration—my failure to deliver scalps in time for the election. On September 1, I joined the President on Air Force One for a visit to Kenosha, Wisconsin, after local authorities, with strong support from federal law enforcement agencies, and National Guard units—many deployed from other states—succeeded in putting an end to the rioting after the shooting of Jacob Blake. The President was happy with the results in Kenosha and took some credit for it, and so he was in a good mood on the trip. He spent most of his time in his large conference room chatting pleasantly with members of Congress, senior aides, DHS acting secretary Chad Wolf, and me. There was no obvious friction between us.

He called me forward to his private office to get my views on some correspondence he'd received. As I was leaving, he couldn't help himself. He looked up and, echoing his remarks on Bartiromo's show a couple of weeks earlier, said pointedly, "You know you could be a hero, right?"

I gave him a deadpan look, said "Huh, huh," and walked out.

Things worsened between us in October. On October 6 and 7 the President went on a twenty-four-hour tweetstorm about why the Durham investigation wouldn't lead to any arrests before the election. He retweeted somebody's image of me, sitting placidly, with Chris Farley yelling in my face, "For the love of God, *arrest somebody*!"

He later tweeted,

DO SOMETHING ABOUT THIS, THE BIGGEST OF ALL PO-LITICAL SCANDALS (IN HISTORY)!!! BIDEN, OBAMA AND CROOKED HILLARY LED THIS TREASONOUS PLOT!!! BIDEN SHOULDN'T BE ALLOWED TO RUN - GOT CAUGHT!!!

On October 8 Trump went on Bartiromo's show again to claim that President Obama and Vice President Biden had been involved in crimes against him. I cringed when I heard him say, "Unless Bill Barr indicts these people for crimes—the greatest political crime in the history of our country—then we're going to get little satisfaction, unless I win. . . . But these people should be indicted, this was the greatest political crime in the history of our country and that includes Obama and it includes Biden."

The following week, in an interview on Newsmax, the President said he was "not happy" with me.

In mid-October I received a call from the President, which was the last time I spoke to him prior to the election. It was a very short conversation. The call came soon after Rudy Giuliani succeeded in making public information about Hunter Biden's laptop. I had walked over to my desk to take the call. These calls had become rare, so Will Levi stood nearby waiting expectantly to see what it was about. After brief pleasantry about his being out on the campaign trail, the President said, "You know this stuff from Hunter Biden's laptop?"

I cut the President off sharply. "Mr. President, I can't talk about that, and I am not going to."

President Trump hesitated, then continued in a plaintive tone, "You know, if that was one of my kids—"

I cut him off again, raising my voice, "Dammit, Mr. President, I am not going to talk to you about Hunter Biden. Period!"

He was silent for a moment, then quickly got off the line.

I looked up at Will, whose eyes were as big as saucers. "You yelled at the President?" he asked, confirming the obvious. I nodded. He shook his head in disbelief.

A month after the election, the *Washington Post* reported that there was already an investigation of Hunter Biden under way when I started as Attorney General and that this fact was never leaked. The President never confronted me about that report directly, but I had heard he was angry that I didn't say anything after the presidential debate in which Biden falsely suggested the relevant e-mails on his son Hunter's laptop may have been placed there by the Russians. Biden's bogus statement relied on a letter published a few days before by a coterie of retired intelligence officials who had lost their professional bearings and lent their names to partisan hackery. Their claim was exposed a few days later when the FBI, together with John Ratcliffe, the director of national intelligence, made clear there were no grounds to think the laptop's damning content reflected foreign disinformation. But, of course, the media, having heralded the letter's fictitious claims, stayed mostly quiet about its debunking. The damage was done. Biden got away with deception. And Trump thought I was to blame.

CHAPTER 23

ELECTION AND AFTERMATH

More than a year before the 2020 election, commentators from all points on the political spectrum were predicting the country might end up with a contested election, making the chaos of Bush vs. Gore in 2000 look like child's play. Even before Covid hit, the parties in a number of states were skirmishing over proposed election law changes, some of which loosened safeguards designed to prevent fraud. The prospect of a contested election worried me. The stability of our country has long rested on our capacity to ensure the peaceful transfer of power. But recently the country had become so intensely divided that I feared a disputed election could lead to a serious constitutional crisis.

There is only one way to avoid the kind of hostility and resentment that might rend the nation over an election—and that is to *ensure* the election's integrity. There is no room, in a hotly contested race like that of 2020's presidential election, for mischief of any kind. It was therefore the time to tighten measures protecting election integrity, not loosen them.

The pivotal fact about election fraud is that it is extremely hard to detect and rectify after the voting. The only effective way to protect election integrity is to have adequate antifraud measures in place before votes are cast.

Under our system, the states are primarily responsible for setting the rules for elections, including elections for the President and other federal officials. In 2020 some states used the pandemic to justify substantial, last-minute changes to voting rules. Some of the changes reasonably addressed the special challenges of Covid-19. Others relaxed antifraud measures and had nothing to do with public health. I started expressing concern about some of the changes, especially universal mail-in voting, as soon as I heard about them. The massive volume of mail-in ballots, the dilution of integrity assurance protocols, the unaccustomed burdens placed on county election personnel, the haphazardly extended voting periods—it all seemed calculated to throw the entire election into confusion. That was precisely what we should have avoided in an election that was guaranteed to be both close and extremely acrimonious. The losing side should have been given more reason to accept the result; instead, it had less.

Contrary to media claims, I was not just parroting President Trump. The worries I expressed were my own, and I had not discussed them with the President. Indeed, in the spring of 2020 I had asked the office of the Deputy to pull together the literature on voting fraud and some of the changes being proposed. The concerns I was raising had been widely shared long before Trump arrived on the scene. Journalistic and academic commentary frankly acknowledged that practices like universal mail-in voting increased risks of fraud. The 2005 bipartisan commission on election reform, headed by former president Jimmy Carter and former secretary of state James Baker, recommended against broadscale mail-in voting, as well as the practice of ballot "harvesting" whereby voters fill out their ballots away from polling places and then have them picked up by party workers. This latter practice effectively eliminates the secret ballot and makes voters susceptible to undue influence, intimidation, or inducements.

Once Trump was elected, however, the media did a complete about-face on the subject of election fraud. Suddenly to suggest there ought to be tight rules governing elections was a form of paranoia or dishonest Republican partisanship. The media heaped scorn on any suggestion that the changes to election laws effected in the summer and fall of 2020 posed a danger to election integrity.

Part of the media's about-face had to do with Trump, it's true. Before and after the 2016 election, he talked stupidly about "millions" of illegal immigrants voting and throwing elections for the Democrats. That was irresponsible, to be sure, but the nation's elite journalists ought to be able to assess these questions with some level of objectivity. The fact that Trump falsely said election fraud is everywhere doesn't mean it's nowhere.

I had no objection to absentee voting by mail, in which the voter files an application confirming his or her identity and requesting an absentee ballot. What I objected to was universal mail-in voting, in which ballots were automatically sent out indiscriminately to every voter listed on the voting rolls. Voting rolls are always inaccurate—state election commissions don't have up-to-date lists of people who've died or moved away. Sending out ballots to all and sundry guaranteed that a large proportion of them were sent to "voters" who no longer existed, or who now existed in some other place. Having such a large volume of ballots sloshing around the system greatly expanded the opportunities for fraud, especially in states that didn't have effective measures in place to verify the voter's identity and current qualification.

I also objected to allowing voting over an extended period of time, as long as almost two months, and frequently over a month. Inherent in the idea of an election is a reasonably contemporaneous collective choice in which everyone is working off the same set of facts. It's hardly a common decision when people base their votes on different sets of circumstance. That is why juries vote all together after all the evidence is in. Allowing voters to cast ballots over a two-month period is like allowing each juror to vote at any time during a trial. Circumstances can change radically overnight—as when Ruth Bader Ginsburg died a few weeks before the 2020 election.

The rule changes adopted by many states put them at higher risk of fraud, and finding that fraud would be extremely challenging. As it turned out, the spread between the candidates was sufficiently large that fraud was very unlikely to change the outcome; in any case no evidence of fraud on that scale has been found. But this fortuity does not invalidate the legitimate criticisms of voting procedures plainly prone to abuse. That a drunk driver manages to get home safely does not make his conduct advisable or something that should be repeated. A large segment of the electorate doubts the integrity of the 2020 election, and these doubts are due in large measure to the accurate perception that safeguards against fraud were deficient in many states. The idea that the lack of public confidence arose from the *criticisms* of these deficient procedures rather than from their *use* is self-serving hogwash.

Post-2016 media orthodoxy notwithstanding, election fraud happens. Concerns about fraud are well founded and remain valid. Detecting fraud after the fact, however, is difficult; and so it is imperative that the country, Republicans and Democrats alike, resolve to ensure the integrity of our elections by having antifraud measures in place before the voting begins. That is the only way we will avoid crises of confidence of the kind we witnessed in 2020–21.

One of the misimpressions created during the 2020 election concerned the Department of Justice's role in ensuring the integrity of elections. That role is necessarily a limited one. Following an election, there is only a narrow window in which to demonstrate that fraud or other irregularities affected the outcome—in the case of a presidential election, just five or six weeks before state electors vote. As a practical matter, it's nearly impossible to prove that irregularities affected the outcome unless the relevant state officials perform audit-type reviews of ballots, voter rolls, and mail-in envelopes to validate votes and voters in the key precincts. The campaign contesting an election's outcome has the burden of pursuing these remedies with state officials and, ultimately, through the court system. The Department of Justice has neither the authority nor the tools to perform this broad quality-assurance function for state-run elections. The department's role is to investigate specific and credible allegations of fraud. As with all criminal investigations, these inquiries are conducted in secret and generally take time to complete. Indictments for fraud committed during the 2018 election, for example, were just being handed down by the time of the 2020 election. Clearly then, as a general matter, the department's criminal fraud investigations are singularly ill-suited to the task of mounting challenges to disputed elections.

When the department does receive specific and credible allegations of voter fraud, its normal practice, reflected in its *Justice Manual*, is to permit US attorneys latitude to conduct preliminary investigations, but to require them to consult with the Public Integrity Section in the Criminal Division before embarking on a full-fledged investigation. A longtime career employee in the Public Integrity Section had taken the view—never adopted by the department—that investigation of election fraud should be deferred until after an election has been certified. The rationale for this counterintuitive position was that any investigation into election fraud might itself affect the outcome of the election. While this might be true in some scenarios, it is obviously not true in every case, especially when the investigation takes place after the election. I concluded that the Public Integrity Section's practice of deferring voting fraud investigations should not be treated as a categorical rule. It was adopted to make things easy for the department, not to protect the public interest. Given the unique circumstances of the 2020 election—including the extended voting period and widespread use of mail-in voting—I concluded that the timing of an investigation should be considered on a case-by-case basis. There clearly might be circumstances before the election, for example, in which incipient irregularities could be dealt with before they could affect the election.

In the weeks before the election, the department received only a handful of allegations relating to potentially significant election fraud. In a few cases, I authorized the US attorneys to investigate the allegations where I thought there was little risk of interfering in the election itself and where there was a prospect that the alleged fraud or other irregularities could be prevented before influencing the election. None of these preelection cases proved to be significant.

In 2016 I woke up on Election Day feeling in my gut that Trump was going to win. Now in 2020 my gut told me he was going to lose. I didn't believe the flood of polls showing the President losing decisively. I gave a lot more credence to a handful of polls, such as Trafalgar, which showed razor-thin margins in the key swing states. But even these showed the race was within 2 percentage points or so in swing states like Pennsylvania and Michigan, and some showed the race too close for comfort in must-win red states like North Carolina and Georgia. The President had to run the table of the close races in order to win. I watched his amazing display of will and stamina rallying his base during the last week of the campaign—it was admirable. But I still felt he made no effort to recapture the white, college-educated suburbanites put off by his crass behavior.

My wife and I went to the White House for the election night "watch party." Initially, I did not want to attend—I wasn't expecting a good result and I felt the strain in my relationship with the President might make it awkward. But I felt I owed it to the President and cabinet colleagues to be there. There were several hundred guests from the administration, Congress, and the President's closest supporters congregating on the first floor of the mansion between the State Dining Room and the East Room. Most were optimistic. They saw the rapidly narrowing polls and the enormous crowds gathered at Trump rallies.

While most guests circulated, Rudy Giuliani and his crew were ostentatiously manning a table in the middle of the Red Room, as if they were Election Central, fixated on their laptop screens. My wife and I left early, around ten thirty. The President had not yet made an appearance. He did not come down from the residence until the early morning hours, when he made a statement to the effect that he had won the election and that a "major fraud" was under way.

The spectacular crowds at his rallies and the polls showing he had closed the gap in key states seem to have convinced the President he was going to win. He ran up huge margins early in the evening in several of the battleground states, only to see those leads evaporate suddenly in the early morning hours as large blocks of mail-in votes—mostly for Biden—were added to the totals.

I was relying on the US attorneys in the various states to assess any credible claims of voting fraud. These US attorneys were first-rate and each knew their state well. I had asked them to remain vigilant for signs of significant fraud, while also avoiding taking any action that could influence the voting itself. In the days following the election, Deputy Rosen and his staff, as well as my office, stayed in contact with our US attorneys. While there were isolated instances of alleged fraud, we did not receive credible evidence of widescale fraud that could change the outcome in any state.

In the days that followed, Giuliani seemed to take over leadership of the President's legal team contesting election results. A gap soon developed between what Giuliani and his team were saying in public and what they were telling courts. In public, they aired sweeping but unsubstantiated assertions of voter fraud. But in their court papers—as Giuliani frankly acknowledged—they were not claiming fraud. Instead, the complaints concerned failures by state officials to follow their own election rules. While some of those failures—such as giving absentee ballots to voters who had not filled out applications—increased *opportunities* for fraud, they were not evidence of *actual* fraud. The President's campaign lawyers were free to pursue these claims with the states and through the courts, which indeed they did. But these were not subjects for the Department of Justice.

Prior to the election, the last time I had been with the President was September 23, when I attended his meeting with state attorneys general in the Cabinet Room. The last time I talked with him was the mid-October phone call that I had peremptorily cut off when he tried to raise the subject of Hunter Biden. After the election, I didn't try to see him. I had no direct contact with him until I went to see him on November 23, almost three weeks after the election. We communicated through Mark Meadows and Pat Cipollone. I told both these men that the department would assess specific and credible allegations of major fraud that could have affected the election's outcome and that we had yet to see any evidence of fraud on that scale.

One of the earliest specific fraud claims the department received came from the Nevada Republican Party within two days of the election. It claimed that more than three thousand out-of-state voters had illegally cast votes in Nevada. Soon the claimed number grew to nine thousand. I asked the US attorney, Nick Trutanich, to let me know what he thought about it. Sampling by the state secretary, a Republican, indicated that, except for a tiny few, the vast majority of the identified voters cast their ballots legally and were only temporarily out of the state for legitimate reasons—for example, serving in the military.

The US attorney continued to investigate various other claims of irregularities in Nevada, but none turned out to be consequential.

I approached the claims of pervasive fraud with some skepticism. In the first place, I thought the chances of reversing the election's overall outcome were almost nil. The President had fallen short in several crucial states, and the gaps in those states were substantial. Deficits of this magnitude had never been surmounted before. I did not begrudge the President his day in court through the normal process of court challenges. But I doubted that the overall outcome was attributable to voting fraud. That would have required fraud on a huge scale in multiple states, and we had seen no evidence of that so far. I had no doubt that some level of fraud occurred—but not nearly on the scale necessary to steal a presidential election. I suspected that, especially in some Democratic strongholds, restrictions on ballot harvesting had not been strictly observed. Yet we had not seen evidence that a large number of votes were cast by nonexistent or ineligible voters.

The hard numbers simply did not point to a stolen election. The President did an amazing job wringing every possible vote out of the heavily Republican rural counties. In the major Democratic cities, however, there did not appear to have been an unexplained surge in urban votes against Trump. In these cities, the President's losing margins were comparable to—and in some cases better than—those in 2016. As I read the numbers, his decisive shortfall occurred in swing-state suburbs. That is where Trump's margins were generally lower than they had been in 2016, even in the heavily red exurbs he won.

It seemed to me that the President lost the election because he lost a segment of Republican and independent suburban voters turned off by his behavior. The fact that Trump generally performed worse in the battleground states than down-ballot Republican candidates powerfully supports this interpretation. It suggests that a critical group of voters who otherwise cast their ballots for Republicans withheld their votes from Trump. This should not have surprised the President. This is what many of his advisers had been warning him about for months.

I doubted the President could ever admit to himself that he lost the election. In his cosmos, a "loser" was the lowest form of life. Shortly after the election he was already persuading himself, and his followers, that the election had been stolen. The Internet was awash with unsupported conspiracy theories and outright falsehoods, which the President was all too ready to repeat. His ever-hovering circle of outside advisers—experts in telling him what he wanted to hear—were feeding him a steady diet of sensational fraud allegations. These were presented to the President, and publicly, in such detail and with such certitude as to sound—at first—very convincing and troubling. I got calls from senators and members of the House asking me what I thought about all the claims of fraud. On this trajectory, the peaceful transition of power was not an obviously attainable goal.

I educated myself quickly on the key fraud claims then in circulation. I felt I had to, so that I could discuss them intelligently with the President and congressional leaders. My position was simple. The people alleging massive fraud needed to put up or shut up. If there was real evidence of major fraud, we needed to see it. Without that evidence, the American people had spoken, and Joe Biden was President-elect. I authorized the US attorneys to evaluate specific and credible allegations of voting and vote tabulation irregularities that, if true, would make a difference in the outcome of an election in an individual state. On November 9 I issued a formal memorandum confirming this guidance.

Not every allegation called for a full-scale investigation. I instructed the US attorneys to take a preliminary look at claims and determine whether any fuller investigation was warranted. In some cases, allegations could be disposed of just by checking public information or talking to knowledgeable officials. Others might call for a deeper assessment. Fuller investigation might be justified when, after a preliminary assessment, a specific allegation of major fraud appeared credible.

During the time I remained in office, the claims of widescale fraud—although constantly morphing—came to center on a cluster of roughly a half dozen major assertions—that the Dominion counting machines used in a number of states had been rigged; that thousands of votes in Nevada had been cast by nonresidents; that video footage from Fulton

County, Georgia, showed a box of bogus ballots being insinuated into the vote count while poll watchers were absent; that massive numbers of Biden ballots had been inexplicably dumped in the early morning hours in Detroit and Milwaukee; that more absentee ballots than had been requested were cast in Pennsylvania; and that a truck driver had delivered many thousands of filled-out ballots from Bethpage, Long Island, to Pennsylvania. I relied on the US attorneys, working with the FBI, to check out these and a few lesser claims. Several didn't require too much work to resolve. But a few would require FBI help.

I called Director Wray and explained why I felt it was important for me to get my arms around these key allegations. He understood this was a good-faith effort to get to the truth and assured me the necessary help would be provided—and it was. Wray also stayed personally informed on the critical items. On the Dominion claims, he organized two sets of comprehensive briefings by DHS and FBI computer experts, which both he and I attended.

Throughout the rest of November and into December, the relevant US attorneys' offices, with the FBI's assistance, worked diligently to assess the major fraud claims. In Atlanta, our able US attorney B. J. Pak—coordinating with the Georgia Bureau of Investigation, which was conducting its own investigation—assessed the claim that illegal votes had been insinuated into the vote count in the absence of poll watchers. All the video evidence was reviewed, and numerous interviews were conducted. He, along with all the others investigating the matter, found no evidence of fraud. Contrary to allegations, the evidence showed that the ballots counted during the relevant period were legal ballots and were not double counted, as had been alleged.

In Philadelphia, our US attorney investigated, with the help of the FBI and Postal Inspectors, the allegation that thousands of filled-in absentee ballots were trucked into Pennsylvania from Bethpage, Long Island. While the details must remain confidential, suffice it to say that the investigation showed dispositively that the allegations were baseless. I told Mark Meadows and Pat Cipollone that this claim and others we'd been looking at had no merit.

The claims that most offended me were the grossly irresponsible allegations regarding the Dominion voting machines. These were presented with such assurance, and sounded so sinister, that they undoubtedly shook the confidence of many Americans in the election. But, as far as we could tell, the claims were absolute nonsense. Neither the DHS nor FBI experts saw any basis for the assertions that the machines had been rigged in some way. In any event, all the dark speculation about how the machines *might* be susceptible to manipulation was irrelevant. The core question was whether the machines accurately counted the paper ballots that were fed into them—and that fact was readily discoverable. By law, the paper ballots had been saved, and so it's easy to establish the accuracy of the count by comparing the paper ballots with the totals reported by the machines. In other words, if the machine reported a thousand votes, with five hundred for Biden and five hundred for Trump, one simply has to check this against the stack of ballots that were fed into the machine on election night. If those ballots total a thousand and show the same vote breakdown, then all the talk about algorithms and hacking was meaningless twaddle. As far as I was aware, whenever this comparison was done, the machine counts were validated. No material discrepancy came to my attention.

The absence of evidence didn't deter the President. His legal team had a difficult case to make, and they made it as badly and unprofessionally as I could have imagined—starting with Giuliani's bizarre press conference in front of the Four Seasons Total Landscaping company in Philadelphia on November 7, through the November 19 press event in which mascara appeared to drip from the former mayor's sideburns. It was all a grotesque embarrassment. I knew of several accomplished lawyers with exceptional national reputations standing by to help once the polls closed, but they quickly lost interest when Trump put Giuliani in charge, with Sidney Powell and Jenna Ellis as sidekicks.

After many weeks of silence between me and Trump, Cipollone persuaded me it was time to pay the President a visit. On November 23 I met with the President in the Oval Office, along with Meadows and Cipollone. Our relationship was badly strained by that point, but he was remarkably calm and civil. He asked me if I wanted a Diet Coke. Without waiting for an answer, he signaled the steward to bring me one.

I started by expressing my admiration for his Homeric performance for the last days of the campaign. I suggested it would probably never be equaled. I also said I was disappointed the election ended as it did. He went into a long soliloquy, saying he had won the election—"by a lot." There had been "major fraud." Once the facts were out, he said, the election results would be reversed. This went on for some time.

Then he said—I knew it was coming—he'd heard the Justice Department wasn't looking into the fraud, and that I apparently didn't think that was my role.

I told him I *did* think it was my role to look into credible allegations of fraud, and that we *had* looked into them. "The claims just aren't panning out," I said.

I also explained to him that the main allegations his legal team were raising weren't about fraud. They had to do with state officials failing to follow their own election rules. The Trump campaign's attorneys would have to address those claims with state officials or in court. The only way to show the requisite levels of fraud, I said, was to get states to conduct audits of the results in key precincts. The department didn't have the statutory authority or the capacity to do that.

"Mr. President," I said, "the Justice Department can't take sides in an election. It's only there to enforce existing law. It's not an extension of your legal team."

He then grumbled that he'd heard I'd been away shooting in South Dakota, as if to suggest this was some inexcusable diversion of attention away from the tasks at hand. I said yes, I had gone for one day of shooting pheasant in South Dakota. I assured him it didn't detract from the department's work.

Then came the hard part. I told him that Rudy Giuliani and his sidekicks were doubtless telling him that the problem lay with DOJ refusing to investigate fraud claims. The reason they were telling him that, I said, was that they'd been promising evidence of widespread fraud but hadn't come up with any, and they needed an explanation for their failure. So far, I had not seen the evidence. But instead of acknowledging that fact and regrouping, they were telling him it was the fault of DOJ's reticence.

I told him specifically that whoever was feeding him this business about Dominion voting machines was doing him a terrible disservice. His legal team had a limited amount of time, I said, and they were wasting it on an idiotic theory that had no basis in reality.

The President then pulled out two sheets of paper with graphs showing the vote counts in Wisconsin and Michigan at various times during the evening. "Have you seen these?" he asked. They showed how the election results in both states shifted sharply in the early morning hours when huge tranches of votes heavily favoring Biden were "dropped" into the count. "This is statistically impossible," he said. I thought I knew the reason for this: the big urban areas in these states—principally Milwaukee and Detroit—typically report their vote totals toward the end of the state's vote counting process. Because those cities are heavily Democratic, the vote totals arriving in the later stages of vote counting normally skew heavily toward the Democrats. This standard pattern was intensified in 2020 because these states were required to wait to count the large volumes of mail-in ballots until the election, and those mail-in vote totals were added to the totals reported at the end of the counting. While in-person voters leaned Republican, mail-in votes were heavily Democrat. I thought the late "drops" of predominantly Democratic votes probably reflected these urban and absentee ballots.

I was right. But at the time I took the graphs and told the President I would look into it.

I then moved to my final point—one I thought critical. "Mr. President, the single most important thing you could do to vindicate yourself and preserve your legacy is to go all in helping the Republicans win the Georgia Senate elections."

The President stared at me sullenly, with a trace of defiance. After a long silence, he said, "Well, our Republican senators haven't done much for me. Now they need me."

"I disagree, Mr. President," I said. "The Republican senators have fought for you. They have fought for you on impeachment, on Russiagate, on your whole program."

"I really don't know these Georgia senators too well," the President said offhandedly as he fidgeted with papers on his desk.

"These are great senators, Mr. President," I assured him. "I know Perdue the best, and he's superb. But that is not the main point. If the Democrats get control of the House, Senate, and the presidency, they will dismantle all you accomplished and be able to pursue a Far Left agenda completely unchecked. The people who will suffer the most are your base."

The President seemed to be deliberately acting disinterested to convey his pique to me. "I will have a rally down there," he said perfunctorily.

I was discouraged. I could see from the President's tepid reaction he was not going to do much to help in Georgia.

As I stood to leave, I made one last pitch. "My advice, Mr. President, is that you start talking about your record of achievement and help deliver a big victory in Georgia. That is the best end game. It vindicates you and sets the stage for the future."

As I walked out through the outer office, I ran into Jared Kushner, who was chatting with Dan Scavino. Dan handled the President's social media presence, and we had become friendly. I found him a sensible, levelheaded influence in the White House. "I am worried about how far the President is taking this stolen election thing," I said to Jared and Dan.

By this time, Meadows, also leaving the Oval, had caught up to me. "Look," he said, "I think he is becoming more realistic and knows there is a limit on how far he can take things." Jared and Dan both nodded agreement.

"We are working on it," Jared assured me.

As I left the White House that day, this conversation gave me some hope that the President recognized that he might be taking things too far. I came away with the impression that he might soon start laying the groundwork for a transition and graceful exit. Later that day, he authorized his administration to engage in transition activities with the Biden team—a good sign.

By this time, I was talking with several Republican senators, including Senate Majority Leader Mitch McConnell, as well as a few members of Congress. Everyone I talked to on the Hill was worried about how far the President was going with the idea that he had won the election. They were concerned the country would get mired in a constitutional crisis. After my visit with the President, I conveyed to McConnell my impression that Trump might be starting to understand that he couldn't take things too much further.

"Bill," McConnell said to me, "when I look around, it seems to me that you are the best person to inject some reality into the situation. I hope you consider speaking up."

"I've been planning to," I responded, "but I need to find the right time and pin down some crucial facts before I do."

Things did not get better. My inquiries, as I told Meadows and Cipollone, led me to discount unsubstantiated claims of widespread fraud. The President's lawsuits moved from one defeat to another. Key states certified their election results. Yet the President and his legal team were doubling down on their fraud claims, voicing them ever more categorically and hysterically. Take Giuliani's preposterous assertion that over a half million more absentee votes were cast in Pennsylvania than the number of absentee ballots requested by voters. I had asked the US attorney to check this out for me, and it did not take an investigation to debunk the claim. Giuliani had mistakenly taken the number of absentee ballot requests made in the *primary* election and compared it to the number of absentee votes cast in the *general* election. Once this was corrected, there was no discrepancy. The number of absentee ballots requested in the general election significantly *exceeded* the number of absentee votes cast. But the claim continued to be repeated publicly.

I called over to my friend, Eric Herschmann, at the White House. Eric was an experienced former prosecutor from New York who had later been partner at the Kasowitz firm, but had achieved independent success in the natural gas business. I worked to get Herschmann over at the White House for the last year of the administration. The President seemed impressed with him. Herschmann didn't pull his punches and, because he was financially independent, I felt he would not hesitate to tell the President what he needed to hear—the truth. For that reason, I thought he'd be an ally for "the lawyers"—Cipollone and me—and ultimately a good influence on Trump. This proved prescient, as Herschmann was to play an important positive role in the weeks to come.

"Jesus, Eric," I started. "We are just not seeing the evidence of widespread fraud, and I am worried how far the President is taking this stolen election stuff."

"Here is the problem, Bill. There's a group of outsiders, like Giuliani and his crew—but also others—who are hammering away on him nonstop about all the evidence of fraud," he explained. "They are telling him what he wants to hear, and they are so categorical about the facts that he is disposed to believe them."

"The so-called evidence of fraud they've come up with so far is nonsense," I said.

"I am pushing back," Herschmann assured me, "and I've told them the deck was stacked against Trump by rule changes and so forth, and there may well have been some cheating on vote harvesting, like in nursing homes in Pennsylvania. But evidence that the election was stolen in the sense they're saying hasn't been produced."

Soon it was clear the President didn't appreciate the reality of his position at all. He started meeting with state legislators—seemingly in an effort to move the fight out of the courts and into the legislatures. I had no problem with the President pressing the states to investigate the integrity of their elections, but this was pretty evidently aimed at disrupting the Electoral College and could lead to a paralyzing constitutional crisis. It would be one thing if there was evidence of major fraud, but Giuliani hadn't produced any, and I heard from numerous sources that he was loudly blaming the department for his failure.

On November 29 the President, appearing on Maria Bartiromo's Fox Sunday show, claimed the election was stolen and attacked the Department of Justice as "missing in action." That's when I concluded it was time to inject reality into the situation. On December 1 I had lunch with Mike Balsamo, the AP reporter, and told him, "To date, we have not seen fraud on a scale that could have effected a different outcome in the election."

I could have said more, but I knew this would be plenty. I also released the news at midday that, prior to the election, I had confidentially appointed Durham as Special Counsel to provide greater assurance that he would be permitted to complete his investigation.

After lunch with Balsamo, I headed to the White House for a prescheduled meeting at three o'clock with Meadows and Cipollone. Mark, though courteous as always, was obviously upset, and told me that the President was extremely angry. What surprised me was that Meadows seemed to be more concerned at my appointment of Durham than my comments on the lack of evidence of election fraud. At first, I didn't understand why—the appointment protected Durham and made it more likely he'd be able to complete his investigation after Trump left office.

Then it hit me. The President didn't want to wait to have Durham's findings out after January 20. I thought his aim might be to push aside Durham and then have his own legal team—a farcical collection akin to his election team, I guessed—rifle through Durham's materials and publish right away whatever documents helped Trump. It wasn't clear to me whether he wanted to get this stuff out to support his efforts to stay in office, or whether he simply did not trust that it would get out after he left office.

I put the question to Meadows. "Why would the President want to blow up the Durham investigation? People have sacrificed a lot to get to the bottom of things. It's been making good progress since Covid let up."

"Sorry, Bill. I don't know what the President will do, but he might decide not to wait any longer," Meadows responded.

"Well," I said, "under the department's regulations, he can only be removed by me. And I won't do it."

I regretted having to spar with Meadows. Mark truly had the hardest job in the administration and he worked hard to serve the President, while at the same time laboring mightily to cure or head off the President's frequent bad ideas or his impulsive mistakes. There were occasions when Mark took heat for helping me and Pat Cipollone protect the Department of Justice. Before the election, Mark's job was like a high-wire act; after Trump's defeat, he was like a lion tamer without a whip and chair.

After leaving Meadows's office, I went upstairs to Cipollone's office to chat. Like me, Pat could not accept the direction the President was taking since losing the election. He was struggling hard to keep crazy things from happening and understood I had to speak up when I did. He was just sad that things were ending this way. The President, having heard I was with Pat, sent word he wanted to see me.

That's when we met in the President's private dining room and, after a tense discussion of the impasse, he responded to my offer to resign with a shouted "Accepted!" and then reversed himself.

I headed off to meet Mike Pompeo for dinner at a small neighborhood Italian restaurant in an Arlington strip mall. When Mike and I and our wives ate out together, this had become our regular place. Despite my exciting exit from the White House that evening, I got to the restaurant on time. As I walked in, I spotted Mike at our usual table. A beaming smile broke over his face as I approached.

Mike did not know about my meeting with the President, but he had read about my statement to Balsamo. "I can only imagine how your day has been," he said, shaking his head and chuckling.

"I just had a pleasant meeting with the President," I told him.

"Well, you still seem to have your job," Mike said, studying me for confirmation.

I nodded and then called the waiter over to order some wine.

"You know," Mike continued, "given all you've had to deal with, what is really surprising is you lasted this long. You were always in the crosshairs, but the nature of my work meant I wasn't a target as much as you were."

"You had another surefire strategy for deflecting him, too," I reminded him, winking. Mike knew what I was referring to, and we both laughed. Mike had told me—and it had become a running joke between us—that, on occasions when the President got to raking him over the coals on an issue, all he would have to do is muse aloud, saying something like, "I really hope the FBI brass responsible for Russiagate are held accountable." That would inexorably spark a half hour monologue by the President about the Russiagate hoax. By the time the President was done, he had forgotten any gripe he had with Pompeo.

I told Mike I was inclined to resign and get out as soon as I could, hopefully no later than Christmas. I also told him that, once the states' electors voted on December 14 and the states certified those votes and sent them to Congress, the election was over as a practical matter, and I did not want to hang around.

Mike and I toasted to our time together and the good things we were able to accomplish. We were both disappointed at how things were ending up. I said I felt Trump had taken a dangerous turn since the election. It had always been difficult to keep him on track—you had to put up with endless bitching and exercise a superhuman level of patience, but it could be done. After the election, though, he was beyond restraint. He would only listen to a few sycophants who told him what he wanted to hear. Reasoning with him was hopeless.

Mike expressed concern about the situation at the Defense Department. He asked if I was aware that, after Mark Esper left, the President had moved Chris Miller, a special operations expert, into the job of acting secretary of defense, and sent Kash Patel over to be his chief of staff. Mike was concerned there wasn't much gray hair in senior civilian positions at Defense, and worried that, during this period of confusion, our foreign adversaries might take advantage of the situation. Mike said he was monitoring things as closely as he could and was having regular calls with General Milley, CIA chief Gina Haspel, and Mark Meadows. I was glad to hear Mike was doing that. If anyone could keep things under control during this unsteady time, it was Mike. I also knew that National Security Adviser Robert O'Brien would help prevent anything crazy.

After dinner, I went home and unwound in my library, savoring a single malt and reflecting on the present state of affairs. I felt things had come full circle. The role I was playing on the election fraud narrative was the same as I had played at the start of my tenure on the Russiagate narrative. We live in a time when people, especially the country's most educated and influential people, are more attached to self-serving narratives than to factual truth. After Trump won the election in 2016, his political opponents, including most of the media, sought to overturn the election by cultivating a factually false but politically gratifying narrative that Trump had colluded with the Russians and thus forfeited all respect. That the narrative was false made no difference—it was the story his cultured despisers needed to tell themselves. But it is the Department of Justice's role to uphold the truth, and I saw that as my duty in dealing with the false claims of Russiagate.

It was the same in the case of Trump's sweeping, fact-free claims of fraud. The President and his legal team were peddling the narrative of widespread fraud and a stolen election. The available facts did not substantiate those claims, but the peddlers didn't feel bound to any objective reality; what counted, to them, was whatever Trump wanted to hear. I felt I had the duty to state the truth as I understood it at that time.

The next morning, I got a call from Mark Meadows. He said, "I think we have a way through this. We don't want to be surprised by you leaving without warning between now and January twentieth. Are you willing to stay until January twentieth?"

I told Meadows that I would not surprise the President by leaving without warning. Otherwise, I said, "I'm willing to stay as long as I'm needed." I wasn't sure why the President wanted to keep me around at that stage. I suspected he was trying to buy time—ensuring against an acrimonious departure while he figured out what to do.

I had told my staff right after the election that I wanted to leave office before Christmas. In the days following my conversation with Meadows, I decided to stick with that plan and tell the President I thought it best if we had a dignified parting of the ways. I had lived through the last days of another lame-duck administration and saw nothing to be gained by hanging around beyond Christmas. I had completed the positive things I wanted to do at the department. Going forward, I saw no chance I could have a positive influence on the President's thinking. He seemed impervious to my advice and entirely in the grip of a group of outside minions. I did not agree with his stolen election mantra and, since I was given no say in the matter, I was not going along for that ride. I believed that the election was effectively over on December 14, when the states certified results and electors cast their votes. I felt I had protected the department by publicly separating it from the President's unsupported claims of a stolen election. I knew that, when I left, the President would have no choice but to stick with my Deputy, Jeff Rosen, as my replacement, and Rosen's Principal Deputy, Rich Donoghue, as the acting Deputy. I also knew that our stalwart head of the Office of Legal Counsel, Steve Engel, planned to stay on to help Rosen and Donoghue when I left. I had total confidence that these three individuals would continue to protect the department from getting drawn into the President's machinations and, together with Pat Cipollone, would not let the President get away with anything improper.

On December 14 I went over to tell the President that I would like to leave before Christmas. I had prepared my resignation letter over the weekend. Meadows was initially in the Oval Office with the President and me. Before I could tell the President why I was there, he launched into a monologue. He said he now had definitive evidence that there had been major election fraud using the Dominion voting machines. He lifted up a study done by a group called Allied Security Operations Group, which described itself as a cybersecurity firm in Texas, and said, "This is absolute proof that the Dominion machines were rigged. This report means I won the election and will have a second term." He handed a copy to me across the desk. It was a little over twenty pages. I took it and leafed through it as he continued to talk. "This is a very reputable company," he asserted, "and they caught the Dominion machines cheating red-handed."

I saw the report was focused exclusively on an error that occurred in Antrim County, Michigan, a heavily Republican county. I had already received a detailed briefing on the incident from the DHS and FBI experts. What had happened in Antrim was well understood. A longtime Republican election clerk had properly updated data storage devices used in certain precincts where the ballots had to be changed to reflect the addition of new local candidates. She failed to update the devices for the rest of Antrim County's precincts. This resulted in an inaccurate preliminary tabulation. The problem had been quickly found and corrected. Trump handily won the county. The initial mis-tabulation was unquestionably due to human error by a county official and had nothing to do with the reliability of the Dominion machines. Moreover, the problem was restricted to Trump-friendly Antrim County, where there is no urban Democratic machine exploiting the rules for its own benefit, and did not appear in any other Michigan county.

As the President continued to extol the definitive nature of the report, I skimmed portions of it. It was signed by a businessman who had unsuccessfully run for Congress in Texas. The report did not indicate the identity or credentials of those involved in its preparation. As a senior executive at Verizon, I had reviewed many consultant reports on cybersecurity matters. This one looked amateurish to me. Portions of it revealed a lack of understanding of how the machines operated, as well as the election procedures used in Antrim County. The report made the sensational claim that the Dominion machines were "intentionally and purposefully designed with inherent errors to create systemic fraud and influence election results." But, as far as I could tell, this conclusion was stated as an ipse dixit, a bald claim without even the pretense of supporting evidence.

As the President talked assuredly about a second term, I was saddened. If he actually believed this stuff he had become significantly detached from reality.

"I'd like you to look into this and tell me what you think," the President said.

"I will, Mr. President. But there are a couple of things," I responded. "My understanding is that our experts have looked at the Antrim situation and are sure it was a human error that did not occur anywhere else. And, in any event, Antrim is doing a hand recount of the paper ballots, so we should know in a couple of days whether there is any real problem with the machines."

I then moved quickly to my reason for being there. I told the President I'd like to talk to him privately, and Mark Meadows withdrew.

I told him I'd worked hard to ensure his administration's success, but that it was clear he was dissatisfied with me. I said I would like us to part while we still could in a dignified way.

I gave him my resignation letter. He read it carefully and said, "Whew, that's the best summary of our accomplishments I've seen." I thought to myself, *Maybe if you had talked about these things, instead of your grievances, things would have worked out differently.*

He asked when I wanted to leave, and I said by December 23. The President said I was very honorable, and he, too, would like to part amicably. He asked me whom I would recommend to replace me. I said I would recommend my Deputy, Jeff Rosen, as Acting Attorney General, and Rich Donoghue as acting Deputy Attorney General. The President called Meadows back into the Oval Office and explained what we had decided. He said he would tweet something out shortly. We shook hands, and that was the last I spoke with him.

Within the hour, the President tweeted:

> Just had a very nice meeting with Attorney General Bill Barr at the White House. Our relationship has been a very good one, he has done an outstanding job! As per letter, Bill will be leaving just before Christmas to spend the holidays with his family.

Back at my office, I felt a great sense of relief and liberation. My staff and a number of senior officials held the usual impromptu unwinding session that evening—it was bittersweet. The next day, I met with Jeff Rosen and Rich Donoghue, who appeared already a little shell-shocked by their initial encounter with Trump. But they were steadfast in their determination to protect the department from improper political machinations. We all agreed that Trump was in for a rude awakening if he thought there was any daylight between us or that he could push Rosen or Donoghue around.

I got back to Meadows and Cipollone on the "Allied Security Operations Group" report. I'd known it was nonsense from the moment I looked at it in the Oval Office. I told them that the report had over a dozen major mistakes and gave them a few examples. One of its major claims was that vote "adjudication" data files were missing. When there is a ballot that is not marked clearly, an adjudication is made. A jurisdiction has the option of having human beings make this judgment by examining the ballots, in which case the paper ballots themselves are available after the election to verify the adjudication process. Alternatively, the Dominion machines have an option that permits them to make the adjudication electronically, in which case the pertinent data is sent into the machine's adjudication files. The reason Antrim County's machines did not preserve adjudication files is that Antrim Country did not use machine adjudication—it used real people to do it. Another major miss: The report was based on a newer generation of equipment. But some of the features the report criticized weren't even present in the older machines used by Antrim.

On December 21 I held my last press conference to announce the terrorism charges against the Libyan we were accusing of making the bomb used to bring down Pan Am 103 in 1988. There was, for me, a deeply strange feeling about it all. The Pan Am bombing had loomed large in my first term as AG almost thirty years before, and I was disappointed then that we had not delivered to the victims' families the justice they were due. But now, concluding my second stint in the post, I was determined to do all I could to complete this mission.

Naturally, the press also wanted to talk about the election. Somebody asked if I still maintained there was no evidence of widespread fraud in the 2020 election. I said I stood by my previous statement that we still had not found any so far that would have affected the outcome of the election. I was also asked if I thought a Special Counsel should be appointed to investigate election fraud. Apparently, there had been talk of naming Sidney Powell as a Special Counsel at the White House. I answered that, if I thought a Special Counsel was needed, I would appoint one, and I wasn't planning to do so.

I was asked, finally, whether I would consider appointing a Special Counsel to handle the reported investigation of Hunter Biden. To the extent there was any pending investigation, I said, I was confident that it was being handled responsibly by the department's lawyers, and I saw no reason to appoint a Special Counsel.

I did not hear about the great brouhaha on January 3 involving an effort by the President to replace Rosen with Jeffrey Clark, acting head of the Civil Division, who was far more sympathetic to claims of nationwide fraud than either Rosen or I had been. As I later heard it, Rosen, Donoghue, and Steve Engel stood their ground admirably, as did Pat Cipollone and Eric Herschmann, and persuaded the President to abandon the plan. They did the country a great service.

I was saddened and disgusted to witness, as an outsider, the President's despicable treatment of Vice President Pence. The Vice President had the highest integrity and always took care to act well within the bounds of legality and propriety. No one could have been more loyal or worked harder for the President than the Vice President. Yet Trump seized on a harebrained legal theory holding that instead of counting electoral votes as cast by the states, as the Constitution required, the Vice President could unilaterally send electoral votes back to state legislatures for further proceedings. He demanded that the Vice President do this when the electoral votes were counted in front of the House and Senate on January 6. After obtaining legal advice from a range of constitutional scholars—including my friend and colleague from the George H. W. Bush administration, Judge Mike Luttig—Vice President Pence rightly concluded that his constitutional responsibility was faithfully to count the Electoral College votes as they had been cast. The President nonetheless scapegoated the Vice President and castigated him for supposed disloyalty. After January 6, I told Pence how much I respected him for what he had done. He is a patriot, loyal to the Constitution, and he did his duty regardless of any political cost to himself.

On January 6 I was working in my library at home when I got a call from Kerri Kupec asking me if I was watching what was happening on Capitol Hill. I quickly turned on the TV and was disgusted by the spectacle of thugs marauding through the Capitol. I could not understand the lack of law enforcement response and asked her to put out a statement right away from me—old habits die hard. The statement said: "The violence at the Capitol Building is outrageous and despicable. Federal agencies should move immediately to disperse it." I was shocked that my statement went out before anyone in the administration said anything.

The next day, angry at what had happened, I put out another statement: "Orchestrating a mob to pressure Congress is inexcusable. The President's conduct yesterday was a betrayal of his office and supporters." I did not think, from what I heard, that Trump "incited" violence in the legal sense. Incitement has a legal definition, and Trump's statements would not fit that definition in any American court. But it is wrong, all the same, for one branch of government in any way to encourage a mob to pressure another branch of government while it performs its constitutional duties, and here the Vice President was acting in his capacity as President of the Senate.

As I watched the Trump administration's demise, I felt a complex mixture of emotions. As I had said in my resignation letter, I appreciated the many successes the President delivered for the American people. Among other things, his administration's tax reform and deregulatory efforts generated the strongest and most resilient economy in American history—one that brought unprecedented progress to many marginalized Americans. He had begun to restore US military strength. He correctly identified the economic, technological, and military threats to the United States posed by China's aggressive policies and moved to address them. By brokering historic peace deals in the Mideast, he achieved what most thought impossible. He had the courage to pull us out of ill-advised and detrimental agreements with Iran and Russia, and he fulfilled the US government's promise to move its Israeli embassy to Jerusalem. He curbed illegal immigration and enhanced the security of our nation's borders. And he kept his promise of advancing the rule of law by appointing a record number of judges committed to constitutional principles. And I was proud of the Department of Justice's contributions to the administration's achievements.

I also admired the fact that the President forged forward with this positive agenda in the face of bitter, implacable attacks. Yes, he contributed to some of the venom—he was sometimes his own worst enemy.

But most of the attacks against him were grossly unfair. Few leaders could have weathered the battering he took and kept pushing forward.

There was something else I credited Trump for. In the past, a dismaying number of Republicans would stick to their stated principles and support their colleagues—except when doing so put them in disfavor with the mainstream press and the chattering class. They were conservatives except when the political and media elite judged their position outré—whereupon they would abandon it. Trump exposed the media and cultural elites as the outright partisans they have long been—mere extensions of the Democratic Party. Instead of seeking their approval and kowtowing to them, Trump showed Republicans they must stick to their guns and ignore them. Their hackneyed attacks are just background noise.

Despite all that—and also because of it—I felt mostly frustration, sadness, and anger. Trump, through his self-indulgence and lack of self-control, had blown the election. It was the most important election in my lifetime—so much was riding on it—and it was eminently winnable. Yes, the media, Big Tech, and the coastal elites did all they could to help the Democrats. That was unfair and wrong, but Trump had it within his power to surmount these forces. I found it impossible to believe, thinking back to the singularly unimpressive roster of Democrats who had run for the nomination, that any one of them could have beaten Trump. Only Trump could have beaten Trump, and he did. Even with confusion and unease brought about by the pandemic, if President Trump had just exercised a modicum of self-restraint, moderating even a little of his pettiness, he would have won.

The election was not "stolen." Trump lost it. He was repeatedly warned by his advisers—and the data showed it clearly—that a significant segment of voters who supported him in 2016 had grown tired of him. They liked his policies, they liked the results of his policies, but they hated his obnoxious behavior. He did not have to win back all these defectors, just a few. He could have done this without diminishing the enthusiasm of his base, but he made no effort—none. His conduct in the first presidential debate was abysmal and mortifying for the people who supported and worked for him. It crystalized the overall tone of his campaign: Don't win back doubters. Don't highlight accomplishments. Just offend everybody.

During his stand-up-comic routine at rallies, the President referred to the advice he was getting to act "more presidential." He claimed that "acting presidential" was easy and, if he did it, he would be the most presidential of any President. But, he said, standing up and doing what he was doing at his rallies was much harder. That, of course, was nonsense. It is not hard to get up in front of an adoring crowd of convinced supporters and say whatever thrills them. What is challenging—and requires sustained attention and work—is persuading skeptics that, despite their misgivings, they should support you; or at least not vote for your opponent.

He took the easy path, and he lost. The fact that his margin of defeat was so slim underscores just how small was the adjustment he needed to make. He wouldn't make it.

I was also frustrated over the President's reckless claims of fraud and the ugly way he brought his presidency to a close. It was a disservice to the nation, and a disservice to the people who had labored and sacrificed to make his administration a success.

Voter fraud has a specific meaning. It involves knowingly nullifying legal votes; or knowingly casting or counting the votes of persons who are ineligible, nonexistent, or whose votes were procured by improper inducements. The President repeatedly claimed he had "won by a lot" and that the election was "stolen" through "major fraud," but he never substantiated this claim.

Our country would descend into chaos if an incumbent administration could ignore election results based solely on bald assertions of fraud. To justify setting aside an election, you have to produce solid evidence. No such evidence has emerged.

I was angered, too, by the President's spiteful conduct concerning the Georgia Senate runoff elections, which was inexcusable and a sellout of his supporters and their interests. He actively sabotaged Republican chances by provoking a civil war inside the state party and encouraging his supporters not to vote. He gave control of the Senate—you could almost say he *deliberately* gave control of the Senate—to the Democrats. A Republican Senate would have decisively limited the damage the Biden administration could do with its radical agenda. But for Trump, an irremediable personal grievance was more important.

The best that can be said for him on that score is that he acted in pique, motivated by the same self-pitying egotism that led Achilles in the *Iliad* to pout in his tent while the Trojans slaughtered his comrades, including his best friend. Any idea that Trump could rise above his self-indulgence was shattered. In the final months of his administration, Trump cared only about one thing: himself. Country and principle took second place.

My frustration deepened after the election when I saw that Trump would continue his egoistic and fratricidal tactics going forward. He made clear that he planned to purge the Republican Party of those he considers insufficiently orthodox or lacking in "loyalty," and he has since embarked on this effort. That Trump, of all people, should consider himself an arbiter of ideological purity—a man whose political allegiances oscillated randomly over the decades—is comical. In reality, he has no concern with ideology or political principle. His motive is revenge, and is entirely personal. His objective is to purge those who did not actively support his attempts to overturn the 2020 election, and to seed the party with more compliant members personally loyal to him.

Purges are a form of suicide for political parties. Winning elections requires building up a broad-based coalition. While a successful party must be based on agreement over fundamental principles and key policies—and thus stand for *something*—it must also tolerate some diversity of opinion over subsidiary matters if it is to remain broad-based enough to command a majority. For this reason, successful parties will inevitably have internal squabbles. Great political leaders, however, don't fan discord within their party or indulge petty personal grievances. Rather, they exercise discipline and patience with the aim of holding the party together and keeping it focused on the defeat of its political adversaries.

As I watched the sad end of Trump's administration, the prospect that he'd seek the presidency again was dismaying to me. Although Trump's unattractive qualities did not doom his candidacy in 2016—

and in some ways helped—his behavior has worn thin. I believe his candidacy would make it more difficult for the Republican Party to achieve the historic opportunity that it has had since 2016—revival of something like the old Reagan coalition: the combination of more affluent professionals and suburbanites, on the one hand, and culturally conservative working-class voters, on the other.

The problem with Trump is that his over-the-top pandering to rally his working-class base needlessly alienates a large group of white-collar suburbanites, especially women, who would otherwise vote Republican. In concrete terms, when Trump is the issue, Republicans start the campaign in many swing states by writing off 10 percent of the electorate who otherwise lean Republican. The question then becomes whether Trump will make up for this loss by bringing in more voters from his base than he has driven away. The answer starting with the 2018 midterm elections has been no. But why should this trade-off be necessary? Why should gaining more middle- and working-class voters require driving away suburban voters? It doesn't. As Glenn Youngkin showed in winning the 2021 governor's race in Virginia, winning back the suburban defectors and keeping the rural voters who are Trump's strongest supporters are not mutually exclusive objectives. It's only Trump's incorrigible behavior that make them so.

What especially infuriated me—and still does—is that the low-road pandering that cost Trump the election serves no useful purpose. How does it help Trump or the conservative cause to say and tweet insulting things about John McCain or Colin Powell on the occasion of their deaths? Or to repeatedly insult women based on their physical appearance? Is this kind of classless behavior really necessary to win, keep, or energize the support of his base? I think the answer is no. Trump voters aren't won over to him by this low and puerile behavior; they're willing to overlook it because they dislike the alternative more.

A great deal of ego is involved in Trump's pooh-poohing the idea of "acting presidential" and his disdain for the dignity and decorum Americans generally, and *rightly*, expect of their Presidents. The American presidency is a unique office. Most countries separate the highest government leadership post—a partisan political position, like prime minister—from the office serving as head of state. This latter function—performed in some countries by a constitutional monarch, in others by a figurehead president—is primarily a representative office, standing for the sovereignty of the state, and symbolizing the unity and singular identity of the country at home and abroad. Because we do not separate these functions, the American presidency is a hybrid office that symbolizes the country. Indeed, the Framers conceived of the President—the only officer selected by the entire nation—as representing the interests of the country as a whole. This is why Americans want their Presidents to act with a certain dignity, and this dimension of the presidency gives the office extra cachet and indeed strengthens the President's hand in his other capacity of political leader.

This does not mean that Presidents must always forego tough partisan fights. But it does mean that Americans don't want their Presidents constantly brawling, rolling around in the mud. Again, Reagan mastered this dichotomy. He could remain a bit above the fray, allowing able surrogates to carry the fight, unless and until his personal intervention was needed, and then he could weigh in with devastating effect. I appreciate Trump's tenacious battling when it's necessary. The trouble is that it's often *not* necessary. His constant bellicosity diminishes him and the office.

In a similar way, Trump's divisive style undercuts a central goal of the populism he claims to represent. Conservative populism is not just about fighting against the Left's efforts to break America apart. It's also about offering a unifying vision that brings Americans together. Ideologies based on racial and ethnic identity, like those advanced by progressives, fracture nations and lead only to their destruction. Pluralistic countries like ours need a strong bond that surmounts racial and ethnic differences and pulls people together so that they see themselves as, for all their differences, one people. From the beginning, the American creed held that our nation is transformative—from many disparate groups, it would create one people. Hence our national motto: *E pluribus unum.*

But what is it that melds many into one? It is necessarily a form of nationalism—not one based on racial or ethnic background, but on *citizenship* in our great republic. There is no other tie that can bind us together as one people. The aphorism that America is simply "an idea" is misleading. She is more than that. America is a *nation* founded on ideals. Our Founders set themselves apart from other peoples by establishing a distinct "People" in a "Union" with a government, borders, and foundational law. It is allegiance to this nation and its founding ideals—and the fellowship that flows from a common commitment to this national community—that binds us together. True enough, for much of our history, we have not always lived up to our ideals— nonwhite Americans were denied their full rights. But our national story is one of striving to achieve the promise of those ideals. If we still fall short, the answer is not to abandon the idea of unity and oneness, and degenerate into warring racial and ethnic camps.

This unifying vision of "One Nation" was integral to Ronald Reagan's brand of Republican populism, and it remains a core component of Republican rhetoric and policy making at their best. One Nation conservatism denies the idea that the nation consists merely of competing interest groups and ethnicities. It acknowledges the obligations we have toward each other, and emphasizes the privileges of citizenship and equality under the law. Martin Luther King Jr. was no conservative, but the idea of One Nation was part of his vision.

I am under no illusion about who is responsible for dividing the country, embittering our politics, and weakening and demoralizing our nation. It is the progressive Left and their increasingly totalitarian ideals. But to truly Make America Great Again, we must do more than battle the Left's aggressions. Conservatives also must affirmatively lead America back to a greater sense of unity. We need leaders not only capable of fighting and "punching," but also persuading and attracting—leaders who can frame, and advocate for, an uplifting vision of what it means to share in American citizenship.

Donald Trump has shown he has neither the temperament nor persuasive powers to provide the kind of positive leadership that is needed. He deserves enormous credit for sparing the nation a Hillary Clinton presidency; exposing the hypocrisy and hackery of a supposedly professional mainstream news media; and pursuing sound, conservative policies. But Trump's political persona is too negative for the task ahead. Rarely has the public been more eager for capable and principled Republican leadership—and less interested in petty quarrels and erratic personal behavior. The Republicans have an impressive array of younger candidates fully capable of driving forward with MAGA's positive agenda and cultivating greater national unity, while also tenaciously opposing destructive progressive policies. It is time to look forward.

ACKNOWLEDGMENTS

This is a memoir of my life, and I thank most of all my parents, Donald and Mary Barr, who gave me life, love, and everything of true value that any son could hope for in this world. I also thank my family—the center of my life—my wife, Christine, to whom I have dedicated this book, and our three daughters, Mary, Patricia, and Margaret, and their families. Being husband, father, and grandfather is my greatest honor. Christine and all three of my daughters have taken a strong interest in this book and have improved it with their suggestions.

Any value this memoir has arises primarily from the positions I have held. But those have come to me as the result of the tutelage, support, and efforts of others. While I have been able to mention some of these individuals in this book, I could not name them all. I owe a great debt to all of those teachers, mentors, and colleagues, from the government and the private sector, upon whom I have depended and who have enriched my life in so many ways.

I am especially grateful to the astute Barton Swaim, who devoted many hours to carefully reviewing my drafts and talking through ideas. His edits and suggestions immeasurably enhanced this book. I thank Keith Urbahn and Matt Latimer for helping me through the process of writing a book and having it published.

As a first-time author, I owe a special debt of gratitude to Mauro DiPreta and his team at HarperCollins whose encouragement, advice, and editorial acuity helped ease the path and greatly improve the final product.

And finally I want to thank all the men and women of the Department of Justice I've had the honor to serve with for their dedication and their tireless work on behalf of the American people.

PHOTO CREDITS

p. 10, top: Department of Justice

p. 10, bottom: Kerri Kupec

p. 11, both: Department of Justice

p. 12, both: Kerri Kupec

p. 13, top: Official White House Photo

p. 13, bottom: AP/Shutterstock

p. 14: Official White House Photo

p. 15: Paul Morigi/Stringer/Getty Images

p. 16: Nicholas Kamm/AFP via Getty Images

INDEX